Managing Internetworks with SNMP

Second Edition

The Definitive Guide to The Simple Network Management Protocol, SNMPv2, RMON, and RMON2

THE NETWORK TROUBLESHOOTING LIBRARY

Managing Internetworks with SNMP

Second Edition

The Definitive Guide to The Simple Network Management
Protocol, SNMPv2, RMON, and RMON2

Mark A. Miller, P.E.

M&T BOOKS

M&T Books
A Division of MIS:Press, Inc.
A Subsidiary of Henry Holt and Company, Inc.
115 West 18th Street
New York, New York 10011
http://www.mandt.com

Copyright © 1997 by Mark A. Miller

Printed in the United States of America

Limits of Liability and Disclaimer of Warranty

Library of Congress Cataloging-in-Publication Data

Miller, Mark, 1955-
    Managing internetworks with SNMP / by Mark Miller. — 2nd ed.
        p. cm.
    Includes bibliographical references.
    ISBN 1-55851-561-5
    1. Simple Network Management Protocol (Computer network protocol) 2. Computer networks — Managment. 3. Internet (Computer network) I. Title.
    TK5105.55.M55   1997   97-20495
    005.7'1--dc21   CIP

96   95   94   93   4   3   2   1

Trademarks

All products, names and services are trademarks or registered trademarks of their respective companies. See *Trademarks* section beginning on page 687.

Permissions

This book contains material that is reproduced with permission from American National Standards ANSI X3.139-1987, copyright 1987 by the American National Standards Institute. Copies of this standard may be purchased from the American National Standards Institute at 11 West 42nd Street, New York, NY 10036.

The information contained herein in italics is copyrighted information of the IEEE, extracted from IEEE Std 802.1B-1992, IEEE Network Magazine, March 1988 and July 1990, copyright 1988, 1990, and 1992 by the Institute of Electrical and Electronics Engineers, Inc. This information was written within the context of IEEE Std 802.1B-1992. The IEEE takes no responsibility or liability for and will assume no liability for the damages resulting from the reader's misinterpretation of said information resulting from the placement and context in this publication. Information is reproduced with the permission of IEEE.

Associate Publisher: *Paul Farrell*

Editor: *Debra Williams Cauley*   **Technical Editor:** *John Thompson*
Managing Editor: *Shari Chapell*   **Production Editor:** *Kitty May*
Copy Edit Manager: *Karen Tongish*   **Copy Editor:** *Annette Devlin*

To Holly,
for her steadfast support

Table of Contents

Table of Illustrations

Preface to the Second Edition

The network management industry in general, and the SNMP protocol in particular, have matured since the first edition of this book was published in 1993. New architectures supporting Web-based network management paradigms are emerging, and vendors are enhancing their products to embrace these new technologies. In addition, significant revisions to SNMP version 2, plus enhancements to the Remote Monitoring MIB, known as RMON2, have occurred in the last few years. All of these changes made the updating of this, the sixth volume of the *Network Troubleshooting Library*, a necessary project.

As is always the case, many individuals contributed to the book you are reading.

A number of vendors, whose network management consoles are profiled in Chapter 1, provided invaluable information on their architectures and products. In alphabetical order, they are: Dennis Drogseth, William Leong, Min Tung, and Andy Vanagunas.

Several SNMP experts assisted with the development of new case studies for this edition. Special thanks go to Rob Finlay, John Hardin, and John Rezabek.

My support team at M&T Books, including Paul Farrell, Debra Williams Cauley, Janice Borzendowski, Annette Sroka Devlin, Kitty May, and Maya Riddick, provided editorial support. The network management experience of my technical editor, Dr. John Thompson, was particularly valuable. Donna Mullen did much of the research for the appendices and figures, and David Hertzke of Integrated Graphic Communication assisted with the production of many of the figures.

Most importantly, Holly, Nathan, and Nicholas added their support and encouragement at all of the right times. It's nice to have so many good friends.

mark@diginet.com
May 1997

xvii

Preface to the First Edition

When I embarked on the writing of this, the sixth volume of the *Network Troubleshooting Library*, network management appeared to me to be a technical utopia that we strive for but never quite achieve. After studying the subject for about a year, I am convinced that this is true. (If you doubt this premise, spend a few days reading the messages on the Internet's SNMP mailing list, and you will become a believer as well!)

This being the case, it's nice to have a few friends, whom I also consider experts in network management, along for the journey to this utopia. The following individuals added their expertise by reviewing individual sections of the text. In alphabetical order, they are: Dan Callahan, Paul Franchois, Robert Graham, Dan Hansen, David Perkins, Carl Shinn, Jr., Rodney Thayer, and Steve Wong.

My editors, Brenda McLaughlin, John Thompson, and Cheryl Goldberg, did an excellent job of balancing the technical with the literary, thus creating *technical literature*. Merideth Ittner and Laura Moorehead provided the much-needed production support which kept the project on schedule. Carol Goodwin did much of the research for the appendices, Krystal Valdez provided word processing support, and David Hertzke turned my rough sketches into legible figures. Thanks to all of you for the excellent support.

Several members of the vendor community assisted with information on their network management architectures. These individuals were: Jack Dwyer, Susan Kaufman, Stan Kimer, Jim McQuaid, Jeff Thiemann, and Sally Swift.

All of the case studies shown in this book were captured using a Network General Sniffer protocol analyzer. Bob Berger of Network General Corporation is to be thanked for this contribution. I also appreciate the generous time given by the following network managers who provided their networks for this research:

Eural Authement, John Case, John Cornell, Paul Franchois, Jude George, John Hardin, James Davidson, David Heck, Mark Ryding, and Rodney Thayer.

As always, I owe a great deal to my family. Holly, Nathan, and Nicholas provide a support system that accommodates the long hours and teaching trips. Boomer and Brutus take responsibility for household security in my absence. I am indeed grateful for this companionship on the journey!

mark@diginet.com
June 1993

Introduction

Since it was developed in 1988, the Simple Network Management Protocol (SNMP) has become the de facto standard for internetwork management. SNMP has a number of advantages that contribute to its popularity. Because it is a simple solution, requiring relatively little code to implement, vendors can easily build SNMP agents into their products. SNMP is extensible, allowing vendors to easily add network management functions. And SNMP separates the management architecture from the architecture of the hardware devices, which broadens the base of multivendor support. Perhaps most importantly, unlike other so-called standards, SNMP is not a mere paper specification, but is an implementation that is widely available today.

This book, the sixth volume in the *Network Troubleshooting Library*, discusses network management in general, and SNMP in particular.

In a nutshell, a network management system contains two primary elements: a manager and agents. The manager is the console through which the (human) network administrator performs network management functions. Agents are the entities that interface to the actual devices being managed. Bridges, routers, switches, or network servers are examples of managed devices that contain managed objects. These managed objects might be hardware, configuration parameters, performance statistics, and so on, that directly relate to the current operation of the device in question. These objects are arranged in what is known as a virtual information database, called a management information base (MIB). SNMP allows managers and agents to communicate for the purpose of accessing these objects.

In order to fully understand the depth of network management, let's discuss these concepts one chapter at a time.

Chapter 1 provides an overview of the concepts of network management. Individual sections discuss the OSI, IEEE, and Internet network management standards. Other sections consider architectures from key vendors that support these standards: Asanté Technologies, Cabletron Systems, Hewlett-Packard, Novell, Sun Microsystems, and Tivoli Systems.

SNMP is only part of what is known as the Internet Network Management Framework. Chapters 2, 3, and 4 discuss individual sections of that framework. In order, these topics are the structure of management information (SMI), management information bases (MIBs), and SNMP itself.

The SMI provides a mechanism for describing and naming the objects being managed. This structure allows the values of these objects to be retrieved and manipulated, that is, managed. It accomplishes this by using a message description language, defined by ISO 8824, known as the Abstract Syntax Notation One (ASN.1). ASN.1 is used to define the syntax, or form, of a management message. Once this syntax has been specified with ASN.1, the Basic Encoding Rules (BER)—from ISO 8825—encode that message into a format that can be transmitted on a LAN or WAN.

The MIBs more precisely delineate the managed objects and organize these objects for ease of use. Different types of MIBs are available, including the Internet-standard MIB, defined in Request for Comments (RFC) documents 1212 and 1213; the remote monitoring MIBs, defined in RFCs 1513, 1757, and 2021; and numerous private enterprise MIBs that vendors define specifically for their products.

SNMP completes the story by providing a mechanism for the manager to communicate with the agents. This communication involves reading the values of the objects within a MIB and altering the values as appropriate—in other words, managing the objects.

Enhancements, known as SNMP version 2 (SNMPv2), extend the capabilities of this popular protocol. Chapter 5 provides an overview of the management and security improvements found in SNMPv2.

Since SNMP is an Application Layer protocol, it must rely on other protocols at the lower OSI layers for other communication functions. Chapter 6 studies these protocols. For example, the User Datagram Protocol (UDP) transports the SNMP message through the internetwork. The Internet Protocol (IP) provides Network Layer functions, such as addressing, for the datagram. A third protocol, such as Ethernet or token ring, then delivers the information to the local network.

Once we have studied the protocols, we can look at examples of their use. Chapter 7 offers twelve case studies that detail the use of SNMP in managing actual networks.

With this information, you'll have a full understanding of the real-world, practical applications of this popular network management standard.

Why This Book is for You

Managing Internetworks with SNMP, the sixth volume in The Network Troubleshooting Library, is a comprehensive guide and reference for network managers and administrators responsible for maintaining a complex internetwork. This book will give you a clear understanding of SNMP and SNMP version 2, the protocols developed by the Internet community to simplify the management of internetworks. It is packed with illustrations, case studies, and helpful examples that give you the techniques and know-how you'll need to maintain a productive LAN or WAN using the SNMP.

Some of the topics covered in *Managing Internetworks with SNMP* are network-management concepts and standards from ISO, IEEE, and the Internet. There is also an analysis of network management architectures from Asanté Technologies, Cabletron Systems, Hewlett-Packard, Novell, Sun Microsystems, and Tivoli Systems. Additionally, the book provides you with a tutorial on the Structure of Management Information (SMI), including ASN.1 encoding examples. Management Information Bases (MIBs), including MIB-I and MIB-II, the Remote Monitoring MIBs, RMON, and RMON2, plus private enterprise MIBs defined by vendors, are also covered in detail.

Find out about SNMP version 2 and the enhancements it provides in areas of bulk data retrieval and multiprotocol-transport support. Other areas discussed are SNMP operation, including the Protocol Data Unit (PDU) formats and application examples, and lower-layer protocol support for SNMP, including UDP, IP, ICMP, ARP, and RARP. Real-world experience is provided in case studies taken from live internetworks demonstrating SNMP in use. Use the appendices, which are packed with vendor information and Internet network-management parameters, as a handy reference.

If you are responsible for a complex internetwork, put this book next to your network management console.

Network Management Architectures

This chapter gives an overview of the currently available network management technologies and explains how the subject of this book, the Simple Network Management Protocol (SNMP), fits into the big picture.

1.1 Three Decades of Network Evolution

The 1970s was the decade of the centralized network. In a decade dominated by mainframe processing, data communication allowed terminals to talk to the mainframe (see Figure 1-1). Low speed, asynchronous transmission was the norm. Mainframe providers such as IBM and communication circuit providers such as AT&T or the local telephone company managed the network for those systems.

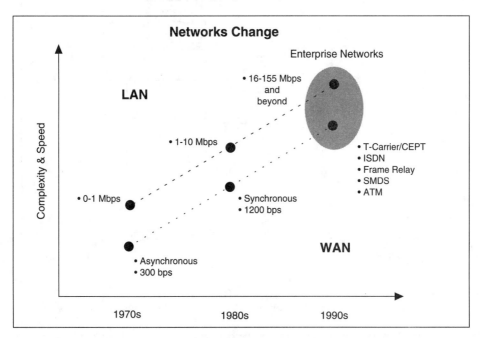

Figure 1-1. Evolution in networking complexity and speed (Courtesy Wandel & Goltermann)

The 1980s saw three significant changes in data communications. Microprocessors came onto the scene, offering significant price and performance advantages over mainframes. The number of microcomputer-based LANs increased. And high-speed wide area transmission facilities, such as T-carrier circuits, emerged to connect microcomputer-based LANs. The proliferation of LANs gave rise to distributed processing and moved applications off the mainframe and onto the desktop. And as data communication shifted to distributed networks, network management became distributed as well (see Figure 1-2). Further shifts are coming from the use of World Wide Web–based technologies, which utilize widely available Web browsers to access network management information.

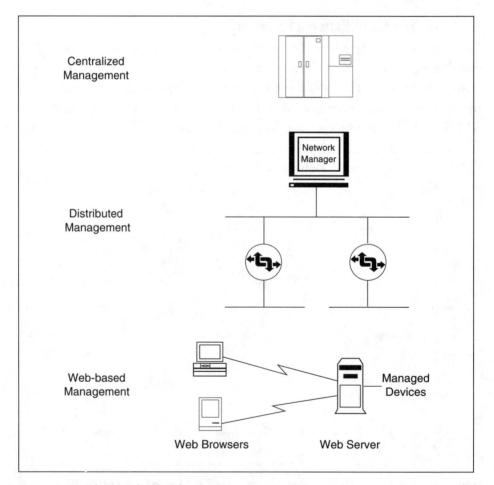

Figure 1-2. Evolution in distributed systems

Today, LANs and distributed computing have matured. Wide area network (WAN) technologies such as Asynchronous Transfer Mode (ATM), Switched Multimegabit Data Service (SMDS), and Frame Relay are meeting the needs of high-speed applications. Network management capabilities have matured as well.

1.2 The Challenge of Distributed Network Management

Sometimes people forget that network management has two parts: the network and the management. To manage a network properly, all of the people involved must agree on the meaning of network management and on its objectives.

Network management can mean different things to the different individuals in an organization, such as the chief executive officer (CEO), the chief information officer (CIO), and the end users. The CEO tends to view the network (and its manager) as a line item on the expense budget. CEOs consider computing and data communications as a way to manage orders, inventory, accounting information, and so on. As long as overall corporate revenues hit their target, these budget items are likely to remain intact. Therefore, the CEO would define network management as the financial management of the corporate communications network.

The CIO must look at network management from the theoretical perspective of the CEO and the corporate budget as well as from the practical perspective of the end users. The goal is to keep the corporate network running 99.99 percent of the time and to schedule periods of downtime on weekends and holidays when few are around to notice. The CIO would, therefore, define network management as the ability to balance increasing end-user requirements with decreasing resources—that is, the ability to provide more service with less money.

End users spend their days in the network trenches, designing airplanes, writing dissertations, and attending boring meetings. Their jobs depend on the network remaining operational. Thus, end users would define network management as something that keeps the data communication infrastructure on which they depend working at all times. A network failure could threaten their livelihood.

From the standpoint of the financial health of the corporation, its customers, and its employees, an all-encompassing definition of network management would be something like this: the communications network is the vital link between customers and products. Our objective is to keep that link operating at all times, because when it fails our financial health suffers.

1.3 The System Being Managed

Now, let's shift to a systems-engineering perspective on network management. Figure 1-3 shows the big picture. On the left side of the diagram are centralized applications such as an inventory control system or the corporate financial database. The right side illustrates distributed applications, such as those that run on client-server LANs. In the middle is the glue that connects the different types of systems—the wide area transport. This transport may consist of public and private networks and software defined networks (SDN).

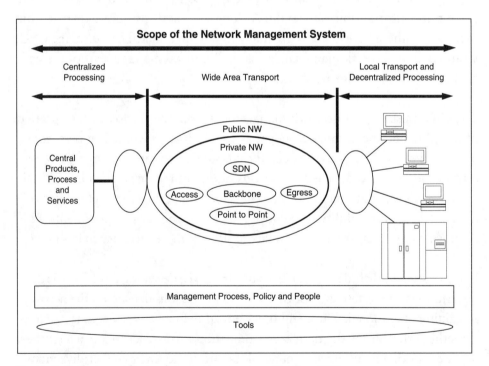

Figure 1-3. The scope of network management systems (Courtesy EDS)

1.4 Elements of a Network Management Architecture

How does a network manager know what he or she is responsible for and then manage such a network? To answer these questions, you need to understand the architecture of a network management system and how it accomplishes its tasks.

The network management system, called the *manager/agent model*, consists of a manager, a managed system, a database of management information, and the network protocol (see Figure 1-4).

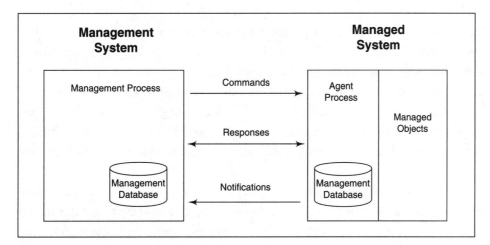

Figure 1-4. Network manager/agent relationships

The manager provides the interface between the human network manager and the devices being managed. It also provides the network management process. The management process performs tasks such as measuring traffic on a remote LAN segment or recording the transmission speed and physical address of a router's LAN interface. The manager also includes some type of output, usually graphical, to display management data, historical statistics, and so on. A common example of a graphical display is a map of the inter-network topology showing the locations of the LAN segments; selecting a particular segment might display its current operational status.

As Figure 1-4 shows, the managed system consists of the agent process and the managed objects. The agent process performs network management operations such as setting configuration parameters and current operational statistics for a router on a given segment. The managed objects include workstations, servers, wiring hubs, communication circuits, and so on. Associated with the managed objects are attributes, which may be statically defined (such as the speed of the interface), dynamic (such as entries in a routing table), or require ongoing measurement (such as the number of packets transmitted without errors in a given time period).

A database of network management information, called the *management information base* (MIB), is associated with both the manager and the managed system. Just as a numerical database has a structure for storing and retrieving data, a MIB has a defined organization. This logical organization is called the *structure of management information* (SMI). The SMI is organized in a tree structure, beginning at the root, with branches that organize the managed objects by logical categories. The MIB represents the managed objects as leaves on the branches.

The network management protocol provides a way for the manager, the managed objects, and their agents to communicate. To structure the communication process, the protocol defines specific messages, referred to as commands, responses, and notifications. The manager uses these messages to request specific management information, and the agent uses them to respond. The building blocks of the messages are called *protocol data units* (PDUs). For example, a manager sends a GetRequest PDU to retrieve information, and the agent responds with a GetResponse PDU.

How does the manager/agent model relate to the network you need to manage? As you can see in Figure 1-5, a console, such as a SPARC station from Sun Microsystems, Inc., typically performs the network manager functions. The devices on the internetwork, such as routers and host computers, contain network management agents. MIBs are associated with both the manager and agents, but the router's MIB and the host's MIB are unlikely to be the same for two reasons. First, these devices usually come from different manufacturers who have implemented network management functions in different, but complementary, ways. Second, routers and hosts perform different internetworking functions and may not need to store the same information. For example, the host may not require routing tables, and thus won't need to store routing table–related parameters such as the next hop to a particular destination in its MIB. Conversely, a router's MIB wouldn't contain a statistic such as CPU utilization that may be significant to a host.

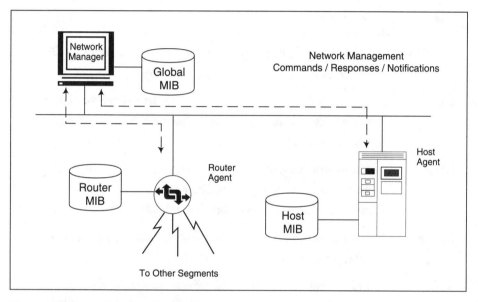

Figure 1-5. Network manager/agent realization

A protocol such as SNMP allows the manager and the agents to communicate. This protocol provides the structure for commands from the manager, notifies the manager of significant events from the agent, and responds to either the manager or the agent.

Before examining systems from specific vendors, it is useful to look at the various network management implementations. These include the network management system for the International Standards Organization's (ISO) Open Systems Interconnection (OSI) model (examined in Section 1.5), the IEEE network management architecture (Section 1.6), the Internet Network Management Framework (Section 1.7), SNMP (Section 1.8), and Web-based management (Section 1.10).

1.5 The OSI Network Management Architecture

The ISO/OSI model [1-1] has been a benchmark for computer networking since it was first published in 1978. Figure 1-6 shows the familiar seven-layer structure. Following is a summary of the seven layers:

Layer	Description
Physical	Provides the physical transmission medium for carrying the raw data, such as electrical or optical impulses, from one network node to the next.
Data Link	Provides reliable communications on the link; that is, it creates the channel between adjacent nodes on a LAN, MAN, or WAN. Functions include addressing, framing, and error control on the link.
Network	Provides communications functions for an internetwork. These include tasks such as the global addressing, routing, and switching that take data from its source to its destination via an internetwork of LANs, MANs, and WANs.
Transport	Assures the reliable end-to-end delivery of data. Its functions include error control and sequence control.
Session	Establishes the logical connection between end-user applications. These functions include mechanisms that synchronize the data transfer once a connection is established.
Presentation	Represents the application data so that it can be properly interpreted at the distant location. Examples of these functions include data compression/decompression, encryption, or ASCII to EBCDIC code conversion.
Application	Includes the functions responsible for end-user applications, such as file transfer, electronic mail, or remote terminal access. SNMP is an Application layer protocol.

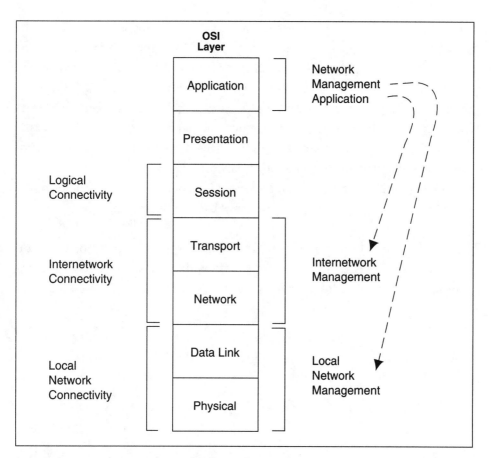

Figure 1-6. Network management within the OSI framework

While the entire OSI model has yet to be widely implemented, elements of its architecture are finding their way into multivendor systems such as electronic mail, directory services, and network management applications. History may prove, however, that the real value of the OSI model is in the organizational structure it provides for multivendor networks rather than in specific protocol implementations.

Reviewing Figure 1-6, note that the network management application manages internetwork and local network functions.

What do these seven layers have to do with managing a real network? Consider the network shown in Figure 1-7. Suppose that a network management console (called the manager) needs to retrieve entries from a routing table. To do so, the manager generates a request message and passes it down through the layers of the protocol stack. The Data Link layer inserts the message (or fragments of a long message) into a frame for transmission on the local network. (Figure 1-7 shows an Ethernet LAN, so an Ethernet frame would contain the request message.) The Data Link layer would then convert the frame into a bit stream and transmit it over the physical network to the intended receiver. At the distant end, the network management command would trigger another network management process (the agent) to perform the requested function, and build a response message. The response would follow a similar, but opposite, journey back to the console.

The ISO/OSI model extends beyond the seven layers, however, for the management of open systems. OSI standards include a model of network management and a network management protocol.

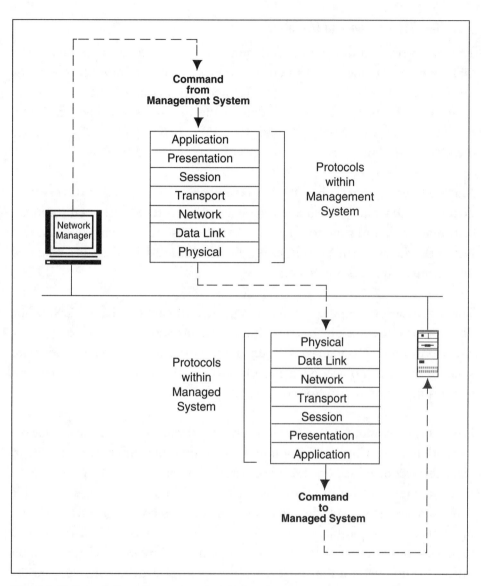

Figure 1-7. Network Management protocol stack operation

1.5.1 The OSI Management Model

The manager/agent model includes a number of interactive components. The OSI network management framework defines the roles of those components. ISO/IEC 7498-4 [1-2] defines the OSI network management framework. ISO/IEC 9595, or CCITT X.710, defines the Common Management Information Service, or CMIS [1-3]; ISO/IEC 9596-1, or CCITT X.711, defines the Common Management Information Protocol, or CMIP [1-4].

Mark Klerer's paper "The OSI Management Architecture: An Overview" divides the OSI management environment into several models: organizational, informational, and functional [1-5]. Another resource, Yemini's "The OSI Network Management Model" [1-6], discusses the relationships between OSI management systems and agents.

The organizational model uses a management domain (see Figure 1-8a). The domain may contain one or more management systems, managed systems, and subdomains. The managed system may, in turn, contain one or more managed objects. Each object is a network resource that one of the management systems may monitor and/or control.

From this example, we can make several observations. First, the manager's network management application must be compatible with that of the agent. Since this example used an OSI-based network management scheme, the Common Management Information Protocol (CMIP) could provide compatible communication. Second, the other layers of the two computing architectures must also be compatible. If the Network layer of the console uses the ISO Connectionless Network Protocol (CLNP), defined by ISO 8473, the router must also understand that protocol. (For example, if the console used the CLNP network addressing scheme to insert the 20-octet CLNP address in its Network layer process, the router's Network layer process would have to recognize that address in order to respond.) Finally, the same physical path must connect the manager and agent, although that path doesn't have to be on the same LAN or even in the same country.

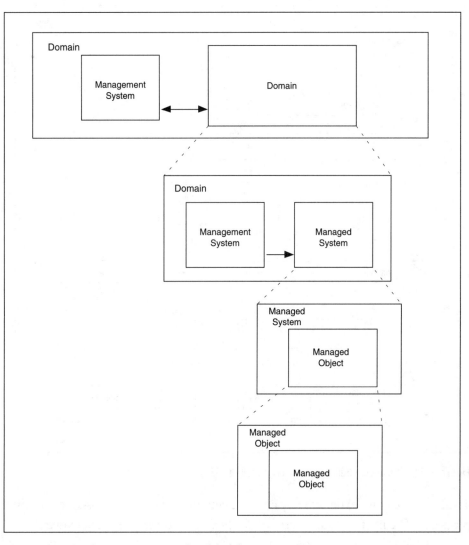

Figure 1-8a. An abstract organizational model of the management environment (©1988, IEEE)

An information model associated with the organizational model defines the structure of the management information and the management information base (MIB). As you can see in Figure 1-8b, a tree structure groups objects sharing similar characteristics into classes. These objects are represented as an entry in the management information tree; each entry has defined attributes and values.

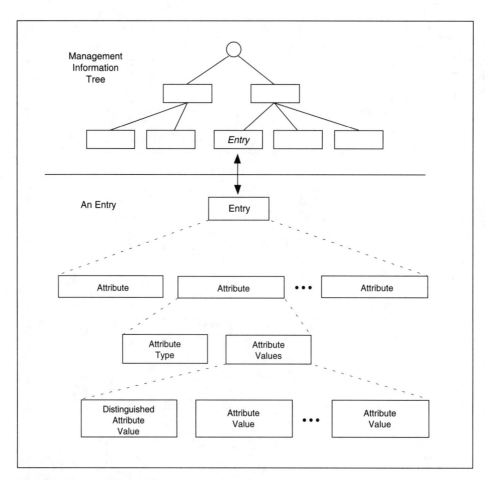

Figure 1-8b. Management information tree (©1988, IEEE)

The functional model defines five areas of network management used for specific purposes. The next section (Section 1.5.2) explores these five areas in detail.

Figure 1-8c demonstrates how the various elements work together. This model relates the system management application process (SMAP) to the management information base (MIB) and the seven layers of the network management system. It defines interfaces for system management (the system management interface, or SMI) and layer management (the layer management interface, or LMI). The layer management functions are specific to a particular OSI layer entity. Examples of these functions would include layer specific parameters, tests, or services which would reside in a layer management entity (LME). The model also specifies a protocol for manager/agent communication, known as the Common Management Information Protocol, or CMIP.

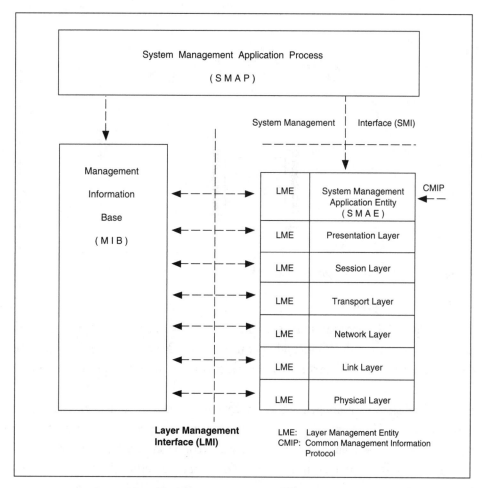

Figure 1-8c. Architectural model of OSI management (©1988, IEEE)

1.5.2 OSI Specific Management Functional Areas (SMFAs)

The OSI management environment includes five areas of network management, which are called the OSI specific management functional areas (SMFAs) (see Figure 1-9). These are fault management, accounting management, configuration management, performance management, and security management.

ISO 7498-4 discusses these functional areas using academic—and often incomprehensible—language, so I'll explain how these functional areas relate to the management of real networks.

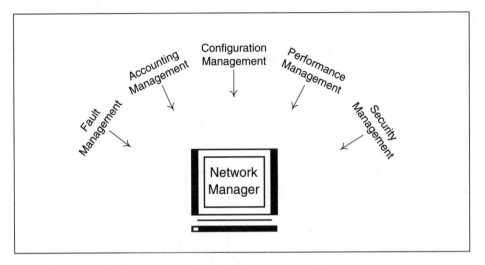

Figure 1-9. OSI network management functional areas

1.5.2.1 Fault Management

The standard says that fault management "encompasses fault detection, isolation, and the correction of the abnormal operation of the OSI environment." The standard goes on to consider error logs, fault identification, and diagnostic testing.

In plain English, fault management means that you need to first identify, then repair, network faults. There are two ways to manage faults: reactively or proactively. A reactive manager waits for a problem and then troubleshoots it. A proactive manager examines the manager and agents to determine whether they are exceeding critical operational thresholds, such as network utilization. If excesses occur, the proactive administrator determines their source and reduces them accordingly.

1.5.2.2 Accounting Management

The standard says that accounting management "enables charges to be established for the use of resources in the OSI environment, and for cost to be identified for the use of those resources." Other considerations include informing the users of the costs and resources consumed, setting accounting limits, and incorporating tariff information into the overall accounting process.

In the real world, accounting means dealing with real people using real network resources with real operating expenses. Examples of these costs include disk usage and data archiving, telecommunication expenses for access to remote data, and charges for sending electronic mail messages. You can also use accounting management to determine whether network resource utilization is increasing because of growth, which might indicate the need for additions or rearrangements in the near future.

1.5.2.3 Configuration Management

The standard says that configuration management "identifies, exercises control over, collects data from and provides data to open systems for the purpose of preparing for, initializing, starting, providing for the continuous operation of, and terminating interconnection services." These services might include the collection of information regarding the system, alerts regarding system changes, and changes to the configuration of the system.

In the real world, the acronym MAC, which stands for moves, adds, and changes, typifies the management work. Networks are dynamic systems, and network administrators need to move personnel and rearrange their processing needs. This aspect of network management may be as simple as rearranging modular connectors at a wiring hub, or as complex as installing a LAN and its associated servers, communication circuits, and so on, at a remote location. Therefore, a significant aspect of the network management function involves keeping track of all these changes by using some type of database.

1.5.2.4 Performance Management

In the standard, performance management "enables the behavior of resources in the OSI environment and the effectiveness of communication activities to be evaluated." These functions include gathering statistical and historical information and evaluating the system's performance under a variety of real and hypothetical conditions.

Practically, performance management assures that the administrator satisfies the end users' needs at all times. To do this, the administrator must select hardware and software systems according to the needs of the internetwork, then exercise these systems to their maximum potential. Performance and fault management are closely related, since you need to eliminate, or at least minimize, faults to obtain optimum performance. Many tools are available to measure performance. These include protocol analyzers, network monitoring software, and various utilities that come with the console programs of network operating systems.

1.5.2.5 Security Management

Academically, "the purpose of security management is to support the application of security policies by means of functions which include the creation, deletion, and control of security services and mechanisms; the distribution of security-relevant information; and the reporting of security related events."

In other words, security protects the network. It defends against viruses, assures that remote and local users are authenticated, and installs encryption systems on any communication circuits that connect to a remote site.

1.6 The IEEE Network Management Architecture

The Institute of Electrical and Electronics Engineers (IEEE) is perhaps best known for developing the 802 series of LAN standards. These include specifications for Carrier Sense Multiple Access with Collision Detection (CSMA/CD) LANs such as 802.3 10BASE-T and 802.5 token-ring LANs. But the IEEE 802.1B LAN/MAN management standards are another key element of the IEEE work.

The IEEE Project 802 addresses the Physical and Data Link layers and extends into the higher layers of the architecture where appropriate. The IEEE LAN/MAN management standard uses ISO's CMIP, which was discussed in Section 1.5, to extend into the higher layer. This architecture includes three elements (see Figure 1-10a): the LAN/MAN Management Service (LMMS), the LAN/MAN Management Protocol Entity (LMMPE), and the Convergence Protocol Entity (CPE). The LMMS defines the management service available to the LAN/MAN Management User (LMMU). The LMMPE communicates management information via protocol exchanges. LMMS and LMMPE use the ISO CMIS and CMIP standards and enable two LMMUs to exchange management information. The CPE allows LAN/MAN environments to provide LMMS. The CPE adds functions of reliable and sequential data delivery on top of the unacknowledged connectionless service provided by the IEEE 802.2 Logical Link Control (LLC) layer. The unacknowledged connectionless service is known as LLC Type 1.

Figure 1-10b illustrates the interaction between these network management operations. Several cooperative processes make up the request from a manager (an LMMU) to an agent (another LMMU). The manager's LMMS communicates a request (REQ) using the LAN/MAN Management Protocol (LMMP). The agent receives this request as an indication (IND). The agent performs operations on the managed objects and then returns the results as a response (RSP). Finally, the LMMPE conveys the confirmation (CONF) to the manager.

A managed object performs a similar series of steps to notify the manager of events (see Figure 1-10c). The managed object sends a notification to the agent, generating a request (REQ) at the LMMS. The LMMPE communicates that request across the LAN, yielding an indicate (IND) to the manager. Finally, the manager issues a response (RSP), which the agent receives as a Confirmation (CONF).

Figure 1-10d compares the IEEE architecture with the OSI model. The complexity of the two protocol stacks varies significantly. While CMIP uses all seven layers of the ISO model, the IEEE model runs CMIP and the CPE directly over the LLC layer—hence the acronym CMOL, which stands for CMIP over LLC. Because LLC provides connectionless service to the management application, some of the Association Control Service Element (ACSE) functions in the full CMIP stack are unnecessary. The CPE fills in and performs some, but not all, of the Network through Presentation layer functions. As Mary Jander's article "Can CMOL Challenge SNMP" [1-8] notes, the benefit of the reduced CMOL stack is that it minimizes the memory requirements for agents. The disadvantage is that you cannot route CMOL across internetworks because it lacks Network layer functionality. This is not surprising, since CMOL was designed from a LAN and not an internetwork perspective.

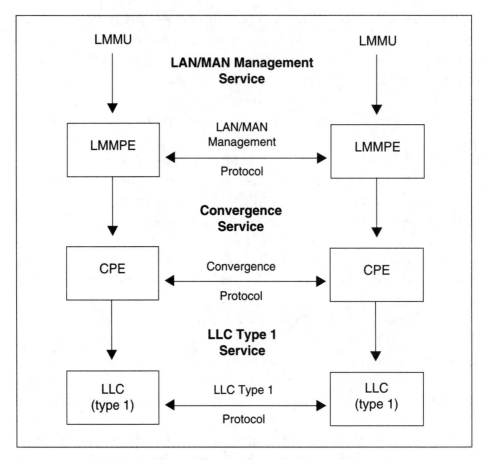

Figure 1-10a. LAN/MAN management communication architecture (©1992, IEEE)

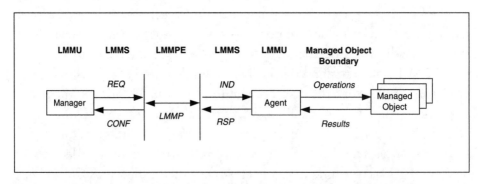

Figure 1-10b. LAN/MAN management information exchanges: operations (©1992, IEEE)

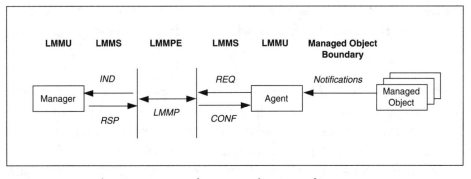

Figure 1-10c. LAN/MAN management information exchanges: notifications (©1992, IEEE)

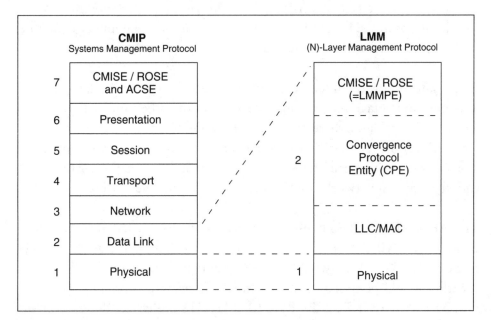

Figure 1-10d. Comparing CMIP and LMMP protocol stacks (©1992, IEEE)

1.7 The Internet Network Management Framework

The three network management architectures discussed so far have one common denominator: their design was a formal process involving participants worldwide. More importantly, the network management architecture was put in place first, and vendors were then encouraged to implement it.

The Internet, however, was an operational worldwide internetwork, so its administrators couldn't study network management for years before coming up with an implementation.

The Internet was derived from U.S. Government research that began in 1969. The objective was to develop communication technologies and protocols so that government organizations, defense contractors, and academic researchers using dissimilar computer systems could collaborate on projects. The result of the government's research project was the Advanced Research Projects Agency network (ARPANET), which used packet switching technology to connect dissimilar systems. ARPANET came on-line in 1969 with nodes in four locations in the United States. From that humble beginning, the Internet now connects more than one million host computers worldwide.

By the late 1980s, the Internet Activities Board (IAB) realized that it needed a method to manage the growing Internet and the other attached networks. The board considered three proposals: the high-level entity management system (HEMS) [1-9]; an OSI-based system, utilizing CMIS and CMIP; and extensions to the existing Simple Gateway Monitoring Protocol (SGMP) [1-10] that the regional networks that made up the Internet were using.

The IAB decided to take a two-step approach to Internet management. Enhancements to the SGMP, which became known as the Simple Network Management Protocol (SNMP), would provide a short-term solution. The long-term solution would be based on the CMIS/CMIP architecture, and was called CMOT (CMIP over TCP/IP). RFC 1052 [1-11] summarizes these directives.

(Documentation for the Internet and its protocols is based on the Request for Comments (RFC) documents. Upon publication, these documents are given a number, such as 1052, that is used for identification. This text will make numerous references to RFCs. Appendix D gives complete details on how to obtain the RFCs and other pertinent Internet documentation.)

The long-term CMOT solution, however, has never received the widespread acceptance of SNMP, though it is still discussed with some network management architectures. CMOT is currently designated "historic," meaning that more recent standards have superseded it or it is considered obsolete for some other reason. Nevertheless, Section 1.7.2 will discuss CMOT briefly.

1.7.1 SNMP, the Simple Network Management Protocol

SNMP is based on the manager/agent model (see Figure 1-4). SNMP is referred to as "simple" because the agent requires minimal software. Most of the processing power and data storage resides on the management system, while a complementary subset of those functions resides on the managed system.

To achieve its goal of being simple, SNMP includes a limited set of management commands and responses (see Figure 1-11a). The management system issues Get, GetNext, and Set messages to retrieve single or multiple object variables or to establish the value of a single variable. The managed system sends a Response message to complete the Get, GetNext, or Set. The managed system sends an event notification, called a trap, to the management system to identify the occurrence of conditions such as a threshold that exceeds a predetermined value.

SNMP assumes that the communication path is a connectionless communication subnetwork. In other words, no prearranged communication path is established prior to the transmission of data. As a result, SNMP makes no guarantees about the reliable delivery of the data; however, in practice most messages get through, and those that don't can be retransmitted. Reviewing Figure 1-11a, the primary protocols that SNMP implements are the User Datagram Protocol (UDP) and the Internet Protocol (IP). SNMP also requires Data Link layer protocols, such as Ethernet or token ring, to implement the communication channel from the management to the managed system.

SNMP's simplicity and connectionless communication also produce a degree of robustness. Neither the manager nor the agent relies on the other for its operation. Thus, a manager may continue to function even if a remote agent fails. When the agent resumes functioning, it can send a trap to the manager, notifying it of its change in operational status.

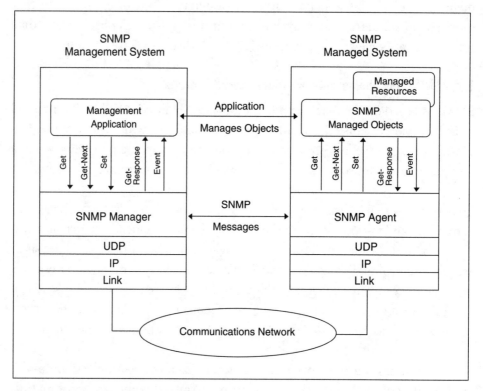

Figure 1-11a. SNMP architecture (©1990, IEEE)

SNMP is defined in RFC 1157 [1-12]. For more information, refer to references [1-13] and [1-14].

1.7.2 CMIP over TCP/IP (CMOT)

As a result of its study of various Internetwork management strategies, in 1990 the IAB developed a strategy to implement CMOT [1-15]. Although the Internet Engineering Task Force (IETF, the standards setting body of the Internet) has designated this work as "historic," a number of vendors have included CMOT in their architecture plans. Therefore, a brief discussion is in order.

Architecturally, CMOT fits the manager/agent paradigm (see Figure 1-11b). Unlike SNMP, which provides connectionless service using UDP/IP, however, CMOT uses an association-oriented communication mechanism and the TCP/IP protocol to assure reliable transport of data. To guarantee reliable transport, CMOT systems establish Application layer connections prior to transmitting management information. CMOT's Application layer services are built on three OSI services: the Common Management Information Service Element (CMISE), the Remote Operation Service Element (ROSE), and the Association Control Service Element (ACSE). A Lightweight Presentation Protocol (LPP) provides Presentation layer services.

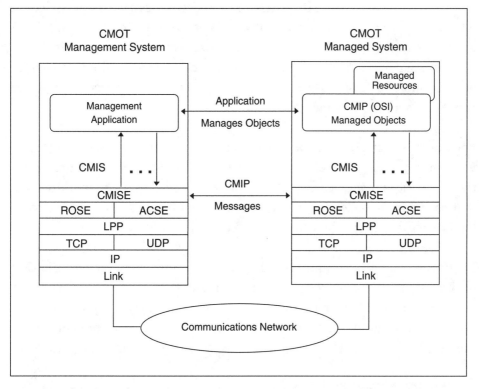

Figure 1-11b. CMOT architecture (©1990, IEEE)

The CMOT model is also more rigorous than SNMP. Ben-Artzi's paper [1-14] notes that the CMIP object definitions are more comprehensive and include attributes, events emitted, and imperative actions. As we will discuss, SNMP primarily defines objects by functional groups.

Nonetheless, SNMP is here today, and many vendors of both agent and management systems implement SNMP. As testimony to its widespread use, SNMP continues to be enhanced. In April 1993, RFCs 1443 to 1452 defined SNMP version 2. These RFCs were subsequently revised in January 1996, and published as RFCs 1901 to 1910. Chapter 5 will study the details of these enhancements.

1.8 Supporting SNMP: Agents

The use of SNMP agents within internetworking devices has increased dramatically in the last few years. There are five general categories of devices in which you'll find agents: wiring hubs; network servers and their associated operating systems; network interface cards and the associated hosts; internetworking devices, such as bridges and routers; and test equipment, such as network monitors and analyzers. Other devices, such as uninterruptible power supplies, have also become SNMP compatible.

Each of these categories makes a significant contribution to the overall network management scheme. Thus, network administrators who practice proactive network management should seriously consider using network devices that have these imbedded agents. References [1-16] and [1-17] list recent journal articles that detail the widespread acceptance of SNMP.

In conclusion, you can find SNMP agents in almost every internetworking device. Some vendor implementations are better than others. As a result—as the case studies in Chapter 7 demonstrate—not all of these agents are interoperable. You should therefore become as knowledgeable as possible about the details of SNMP. The rest of this book will help with that assignment.

1.9 Desktop Management Task Force

The Desktop Management Task Force (DMTF) was founded in 1992 by Digital Equipment, Hewlett-Packard, IBM, Intel, Microsoft, Novell, SunSoft, and SynOptics Communications (now Bay Networks). The purpose of the DMTF is to develop a standard set of application programming interfaces (APIs) that access and manage desktop systems, components, and related peripherals. At the present time, over 300 organizations are members of the DMTF.

The Desktop Management Interface (DMI) technology is the management architecture developed by the DMTF (see Figure 1-12). The focus of the DMI is on desktop and LAN management, independent of the system, operating system, or network operating system. DMI is designed to be integrated with all network management protocols and consoles, such as SNMP or CMIP.

The DMI architecture is divided into three layers: the Management Applications Layer, which interfaces with various agents; the Service Layer, which includes the Management Information File (MIF) database; and the Hardware/Software Components Layer, which interfaces with the actual components being managed. Further information on DMTF can be found in references [1-18] and [1-19].

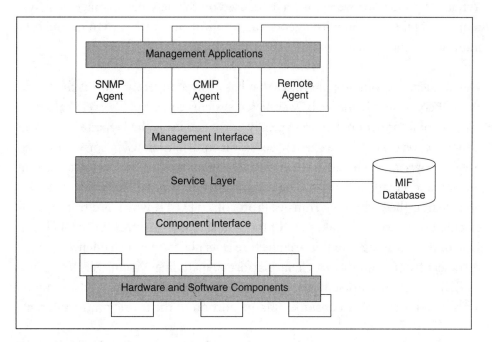

Figure 1-12. Desktop Management Interface

1.10 Web-based Network Management

Network management platforms have evolved in the last few years as client systems have become more distributed and complex. For example, management systems in the late 1980s, often called device managers, were focused on a single device or system, such as a multiplexer or high speed modem network. The first evolutionary progression occurred in the early 1990s as network management platforms attempted to integrate multiple device managers into a cohesive, communicating environment. Further integration became possible when the industry began using SNMP as the communication standard between agents and managers, thus assuring multivendor interoperability between components. Other moves toward integration involved the sharing of database information between various applications so that, for example, an agent's alarm could automatically trigger a page to the network manager and log an entry in the trouble ticket reporting application.

Yet, all of these improvements have focused on the network management system and its interaction with agents and applications, rather than on the user interface to the network management information.

One of the most common interfaces that has evolved in recent years is the World Wide Web, or simply the Web. Web-based systems consist of a server that stores "pages" of information that are typically formatted using the Hypertext Markup Language, or HTML. The client accesses the information using software called a Web browser, which may have integrated capabilities for printing, file retrieval and storage, email, and so on. The communication protocol between the server and client is the Hypertext Transfer Protocol, or HTTP, which is a transaction-oriented protocol that makes use of the Transmission Control Protocol (TCP). One of the advantages of this architecture is its platform independence, as Web browsers from a number of client platforms, including Macintosh, Windows, UNIX, and other workstations, can access the Web server in a similar manner. Web-based traffic now consumes a large portion of the traffic on the Internet.

The popularity of these Web-based systems has created another application for this technology—storing network management information on a Web server so that it can be accessed and disseminated to distributed users in a platform-independent fashion. Web-based network management can take on one of several forms (see Figure 1-13):

➤ Web-enabled agents that can be managed through a browser using the HyperText Transfer Protocol (HTTP) for communication.

➤ Web-enabled managers, which may include a Web server front end to an existing platform, or a stand-alone manager running on a Web server, either of which may use HTTP for communication.

In addition, there are two standardization efforts underway in this area:

➤ The Web-based Enterprise Management (WBEM) proposal, from a consortium of vendors which include Microsoft, Compaq Computer, Cisco Systems, and many others.

➤ The Java Management Application Programming Interface (JMAPI) proposal from SunSoft.

In any event, however, SNMP still enters into the equation, either from the perspective of communication with existing (legacy) SNMP agents and/or managers, or the need to provide technical functionality that other solutions do not adequately cover. For example, the HyperText Markup Language (HTML) that is used to define the format of Web pages and is then transmitted with the HyperText Transfer Protocol (HTTP) is not well-suited for manager/agent polling because a requirement exists for the "local human" to push a button to initiate the communication sequence. Manager/agent communication using existing SNMP communication methods are likely to be prevalent until other proposals, such as JMAPI and WEBM, reach maturity. References [1-20] through [1-25] discuss the advantages of Web-based network management.

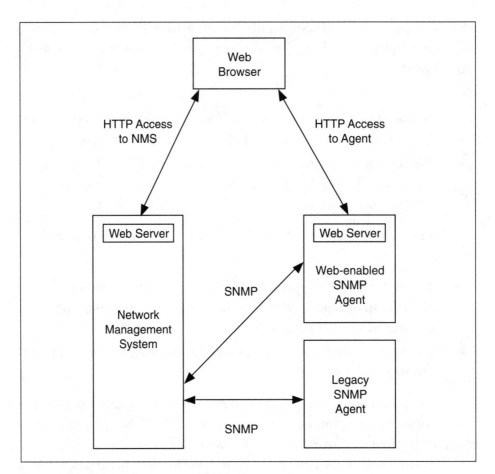

Figure 1-13. Web-based management architecture

1.10.1 Web-based Enterprise Management

The Web-Based Enterprise Management (WBEM) initiative was launched by vendors BMC Software, Cisco Systems, Compaq Computer, Intel, and Microsoft to address the challenge of distributed networks using emerging Web-based technologies. Other goals included the integration of network, systems, and application management; platform and management environment independence; scalability to grow as networks expand; plus leveraging the low cost of Web-enabled clients.

The WBEM proposal consists of several elements (see Figure 1-14):

➤ Hypermedia Management Schema (HMMS), an extensible data model which can be used to describe the managed objects. The DMTF was chartered with further defining of the HMMS.

➤ HyperMedia Management Protocol (HMMP), which is a communication protocol that embodies HMMS and runs over the HyperText Transport Protocol (HTTP), with interfaces to SNMP and DMI in the future. The HMMP allows the aggregated data to be queried across the network and shared among top-level applications. The IETF was chartered with further refinement of the HMMP.

➤ HyperMedia Managed Object (HMMO) is a managed entity, containing at least one URL, that contains data that can be managed by a client browser, either directly or through some type of management schema.

➤ HyperMedia Object Manager (HMOM) is a generic definition for management applications that combines information from multiple sources and uses a communication protocol to present that information to the client (browser) using the HyperText Markup Language (HTML). It is anticipated that the HMOM could be implemented using a number of development platforms, such as Java, Active X, Common Gateway Interface (CGI), the Common Object Request Broker Architecture (CORBA), and others.

References [1-26] and [1-27] provide details on WBEM.

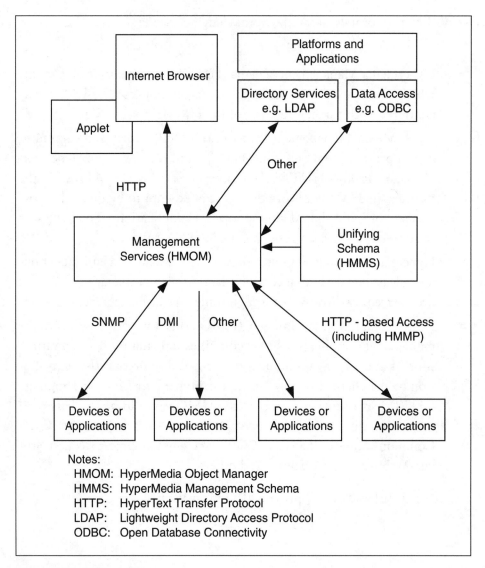

Figure 1-14. WBEM architecture

1.10.2 Java Management API

SunSoft's Java is a simple yet robust object-oriented programming language that has been implemented across a wide variety of platforms and operating systems. The Java Management API (JMAPI) is a set of objects and development tools for creating network management solutions that can be utilized

by a wide variety of heterogeneous networks. Thus, the JMAPI leverages the platform-independence of the Java computing environment, extending Java's "write once, run everywhere" capabilities to the traditionally proprietary architectures of network management systems and consoles. In addition, the JMAPI allows for the integration of SNMP agent information into the Java environment, thus leveraging classic network management solutions with the emerging technology of Web-based network management.

The JMAPI consists of three functional components: a Browser User Interface, an Admin Runtime Module, and Appliances (see Figure 1-15).

The Browser User Interface (BUI) is the means by which the network administrator issues the management queries and commands. The BUI requires a Java-enabled Web browser that has the capabilities to run Java applets. *Applets* are Java programs that can be included in a HyperText Markup Language (HTML) page, in much the same way that graphics, such as .GIF files, may be included in a page. When a Java-compatible browser views a page containing an applet, the applet code is transferred to, and executed on, the browser. The BUI uses the HyperText Transfer Protocol (HTTP) for communication with an HTTP server within the Admin Runtime Module, which loads the initial Java applet and JMAPI objects. Other communication across machine boundaries uses the Remote Method Invocation (RMI). The JMAPI applet consists of the Administrative View Module (AVM), which provides a set of building blocks for user interface and application-level functionality. The Managed Object Interfaces perform remote management functions.

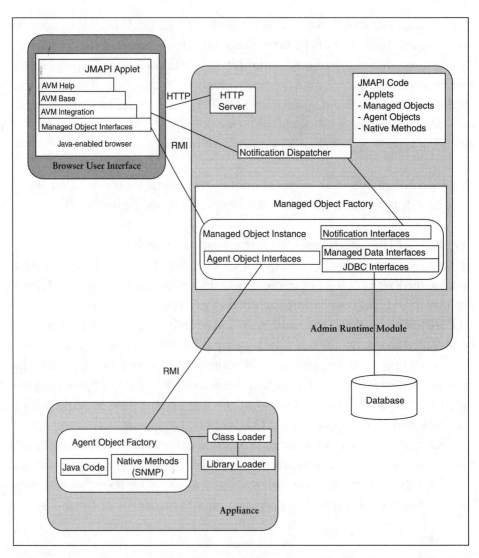

Figure 1-15. Java Management API architecture components (Copyright 1996, Sun Microsystems, Inc.)

The Admin Runtime Module (ARM) is the focus of the administration efforts; it consists of several elements. The HTTP Server provides bootstrap services for the Java elements. After the Java applets take control, the Managed Objects Interfaces in the BUI provide the communication link to the ARM. The Managed Object Factory implements the management operations and interacts with the

Agent Object Interfaces and the Managed Data Interfaces. The Managed Data Interfaces access a relational database through the Java Database Connectivity (JDBC) Interface, which provides the repository of management information.

The Appliances are the devices being managed by the Admin Runtime Module. An Appliance contains an Agent Object Factory which creates and maintains instances of agent objects. When the objects are invoked, they may download Java code to implement the management operations. Integration with SNMP agents, which implements the protocol and handles traps, has also been designed into the system.

Thus, the Java Management API provides the tools for developing network and service management systems that can operate across a diversity of systems and platforms. References [1-28] and [1-29] provide further details on JMAPI.

1.11 Supporting SNMP: Managers

Now that we have considered the elements of a network management system, we can describe management architectures from prominent vendors that support SNMP-based network management. This section discusses, in alphabetical order, offerings from Asante Technologies, Inc., Hewlett-Packard Company, Novell, SunSoft, Inc., and Tivoli Systems. References [1-30] through [1-32] provide general information and product evaluations.

1.11.1 Asante Technologies' IntraSpection

Asante Technologies Inc.'s IntraSpection is the first SNMP management product based entirely on Intranet technology, a technology that is being widely and rapidly adopted. IntraSpection is an open, standards-based SNMP management platform that runs on a Windows NT Web server and delivers standard SNMP data graphically to any Java-enabled Web browser. Thus, IntraSpection provides network management capabilities for your entire network anytime, anywhere you have access to the World Wide Web (see Figure 1-16).

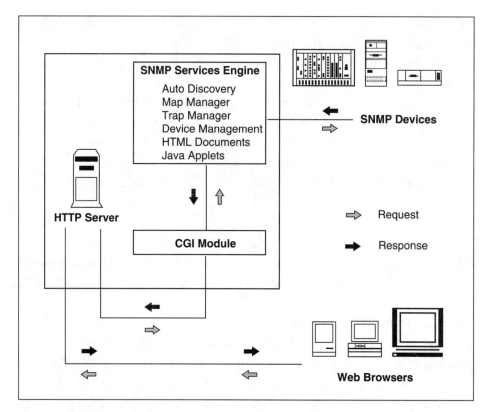

Figure 1-16. Asante Technologies' IntraSpection architecture (Courtesy of Asante Technologies, Inc.)

IntraSpection includes true multiple platform support, as network managers can now manage the entire network with one Java-enabled client browser using a Macintosh, Windows NT, or UNIX workstation. IntraSpection provides the same GUI, operating procedure, and functionality across all platforms. Java technologies enable IntraSpection to deliver real-time network status monitoring, statistic graphs, network discoveries, and problem reports. All of this information is constantly updated and delivered to the client browser automatically.

In addition, the product speeds up problem identification, isolation, and resolution. Network managers have the flexibility to identify, isolate, resolve, and monitor the entire network from anywhere there's access to the Web. There's no need to rush back to the management station—you can resolve the issue and monitor the progress when the problem occurs from wherever you are. IntraSpection also simplifies the implementation of the Simple Network Management Protocol by providing multivendor hardware support in a single unified platform. Both Asante and third-party hardware devices may be managed down to the port level.

IntraSpection is compliant with the following SNMP-based management standards:

- ➤ MIB II (RFC 1213)
- ➤ Standard Repeater MIB (RFC 1516)
- ➤ Ethernet-Like MIB (RFC 1643)
- ➤ Standard Bridge MIB (RFC 1493)

IntraSpection is comprised of five software modules. The Map Manager builds a topology diagram of the network. The Device Manager graphically represents each network element. The Trap Manager gathers device statistics and stores that information on a third-party database that is running on the same server. A HyperText Transfer Protocol (HTTP) module can be used to turn the IntraSpection server into a Web server. Finally, the Common Gateway Interface (CGI) module translates the HyperText Markup Language (HTML) to/from SNMP commands/responses.

IntraSpection also provides a powerful development platform. Unlike the traditional network management software platform which requires special programming, IntraSpection gives users the ability to develop a complete device management system with one HTML page. It is completely modifiable and can be customized to meet your specific needs.

Reference [1-33] provides further information on IntraSpection.

1.11.2 Cabletron Systems' SPECTRUM

Cabletron Systems' SPECTRUM Enterprise Manager is designed as an open system to be implemented in multivendor environments. The architecture is based on a client/server paradigm, with various interfaces to other systems. SPECTRUM consists of two principal elements. A graphical user interface (GUI), called Spec-troGRAPH, provides a Motif-based interface for the end user. The management server, called SpectroSERVER, consists of two sections. The Virtual Network Machine (VNM) creates models of the various network entities, such as cables or network devices. The Device Communication Manager (DCM) is a multi-protocol communications engine with protocol support for SNMP, IEEE 802.1, and ICMP/PING commands, and with future support planned for CMIP as well as extensions (via a tool kit) for any proprietary protocol (see Figure 1-17).

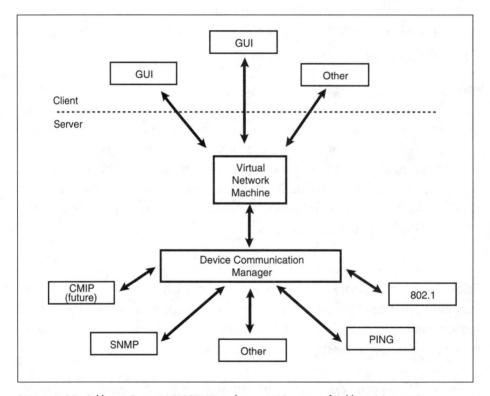

Figure 1-17. Cabletron Systems' SPECTRUM architecture (Courtesy of Cabletron Systems)

In a typical implementation, the SpectroGRAPH and SpectroSERVER run on different hosts on the network. The two systems are typically connected via a BSD UNIX socket. SPECTRUM's client/server architecture has allowed it to achieve high levels of scalability, including environments with hundreds and even thousands of SpectroSERVERS working in parallel.

SPECTRUM Enterprise Manager can support both UNIX and NT workstations with complete fluidity. For instance, an NT-based SpectroGRAPH can fully interoperate with a UNIX-based SpectroSERVER. It is even possible for a UNIX-based SpectroGRAPH to interoperate with an NT-based SpectroSERVER. SPECTRUM on NT has all the features, functions, and most of the applications currently available on UNIX.

SPECTRUM utilizes two databases. The Distributed Database Manager (DDM) contains an archive of network events and statistics. The Inductive Modeling Technology (IMT) database models network relationships from a variety of perspectives, such as topology, alarms, hierarchies, and even organizations. Both databases are resident with the SpectroSERVER but can provide integrated, enterprise-wide reports, alarm views, automated application notification, and other enterprise-wide features.

Many of SPECTRUM's advanced applications exploit its IMT to build higher levels of automation. For instance, SPECTRUM Resolution Expert provides customers with automated fault resolution using an artificial intelligence technology called Case-based reasoning. This technology helps to diagnose network and systems problems using the same paradigm that lawyers use when they attempt to prove a point drawing on past case history.

Reference [1-34] provides further information on SPECTRUM.

1.11.3 Hewlett-Packard OpenView

The Hewlett-Packard OpenView family provides an integrated network and systems management solution for end-to-end service management of the complete information technology environment. Solutions consist of a broad portfolio of management products from HP and OpenView Solutions Partners, and a complete set of services that help customers improve service and reduce operations cost (see Figure 1-18). The solutions include:

➤ Network Node Manager—meeting the requirements for a powerful network management solution that provides an unconstrained view of the network to monitor and control the entire computing environment.

➤ IT/Operations—an advanced operations and problem management solution which allows the network manager to keep a distributed, multivendor computing environment up and running.

➤ IT/Administration—an effective solution for inventory, software, and user management which will improve security, provide better control of managed devices, and support industry standards for software distribution.

➤ PerfView/MeasureWare and NetMetrix—resource and performance management solutions which provide the foundation for service level management, including objectives for response time measurement, WAN/LAN link latency, and continuous monitoring of computing resource availability.

➤ OmniBack II and OmniStorage—for data and storage management, they provide reliable high performance backup to protect the data of the enterprise.

In addition, the OpenView Forum, an association of users and developers, provides conferences, newsletters, and valuable contact information for network management professionals. The OpenView Forum may be contacted at (415) 512-0865, or http://www.ovforum.org.

Reference [1-35] provides further information on OpenView.

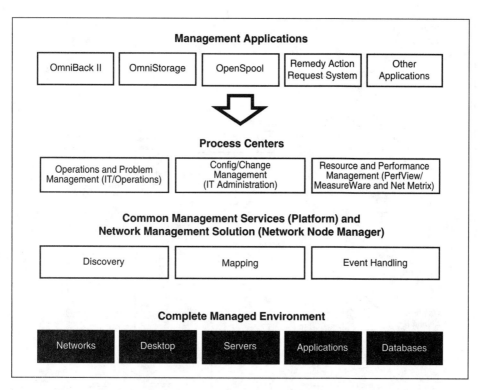

Figure 1-18. Hewlett-Packard OpenView solution framework (Courtesy of Hewlett-Packard)

1.11.4 Novell's ManageWise

Novell's ManageWise is a comprehensive, integrated management solution that lets you successfully manage and optimize a heterogeneous network. It reduces the cost of owning and managing a network and enhances business operations by increasing network reliability and user productivity (see Figure 1-19).

ManageWise lets you proactively manage an entire network through NetWare and Windows NT server management, desktop management, network traffic analysis, automated network inventory, remote control, virus protection, and software management:

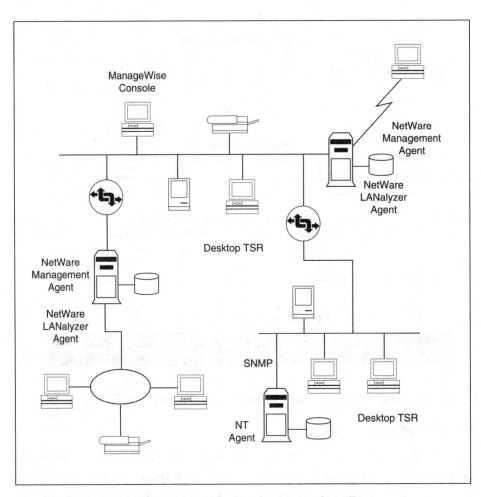

Figure 1-19. Novell's ManageWise solution framework (Courtesy of Novell, Inc.)

➤ Server management: ManageWise builds on Novell's IntraNet-Ware/NetWare expertise to provide comprehensive server management. It automatically detects thousands of problems on both IntraNet-Ware/NetWare and NT servers and lets the user set thresholds for notification when tolerance levels have been exceeded. ManageWise Agent for Windows NT Server is an add-on product that integrates with ManageWise for seamless management of mixed IntraNet-Ware/NetWare and NT environments from a single user interface.

➤ Virus Protection: ManageWise continuously monitors viruses across the entire network and desktops, notifies of detection, and quarantines the viruses until they can be eliminated.

➤ Desktop Management: ManageWise remote controls Windows 95, 3.1, 3.11, OS/2 2.1, OS/2 Warp, and DOS desktops. These desktop management capabilities include configuration management, user administration, and desktop access.

In addition, ManageWise continuously works in the background to monitor network activity and trend performance. As a result, you can easily plan for future network changes and growth, predict future bottlenecks, and plan for resegmentation of the network before problems occur:

➤ Network Planning: ManageWise allows the user to collect real-time and long-term performance trends to understand changing environments or unusual conditions.

➤ Network Analysis: ManageWise monitors network traffic analysis trends on Ethernet and token ring networks so network traffic paths can be optimized.

➤ Software Management: ManageWise Application Manager delivers applications down to the desktop by utilizing Novell Directory Services, which increases the network administrator's leverage and span of control while reducing the complexity and repetitiveness of administrative tasks.

➤ Asset Management: ManageWise simplifies the task of tracking network assets through autodiscovery capabilities that build topology maps and discover hardware. The process automatically inventories networking devices, including NetWare servers, hubs routers, and desktops, as well as hardware and software.

Reference [1-36] provides further information on ManageWise.

1.11.5 Sun Microsystems' Solstice Domain Manager

Sun Microsystems' network management product family includes Solstice Site Manager (SM), Solstice Domain Manager (DM), and Solstice Enterprise Manager (EM) (see Figure 1-20).

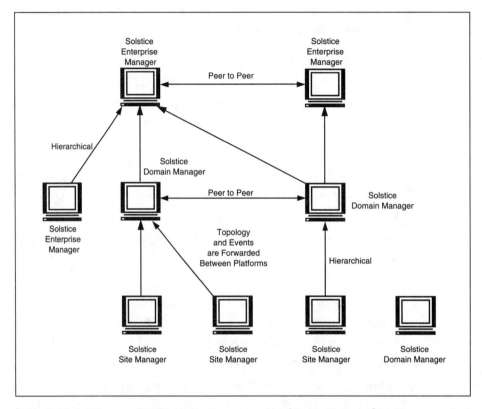

Figure 1-20. Sun Microsystems' Solstice Enterprise management architecture (Courtesy of Sun Microsystems, Inc.)

Sun's Solstice SunNet Manager (SNM), one of the most widely accepted network management platforms, plus Solstice Cooperative Consoles (CC), became the basis for Solstice Site Manager and Solstice Domain Manager.

Solstice Site Manager is designed to meet the requirements of smaller sites managing up to 100 nodes. Solstice Site Manager includes Solstice SNM 2.3, plus the sender portion of Solstice CC, which allows management data, including topological information, events, and traps, to be forwarded to the Solstice Domain Manager. Solstice Site Manager can also access Novell's NetWare Management System, an agent residing on a Novell Server, and import topological information from Novell's ManageWise network management console.

Solstice Domain Manager is designed to meet the requirements of larger or multisite environments. This product includes Solstice SNM 2.3, the sender and receiver portions of Solstice CC, and an advanced Layout Tool. Solstice Domain Manager may be used in one of three configurations: as a stand-alone platform for large sites, as a central manager connecting multiple Site Managers/Domain Managers, or in a cooperative (peer-to-peer) environment with other Domain Managers to manage an enterprise.

Key features of the Domain Manager include: event management, including event-based actions, scheduled requests, and alarm reports; and user tools, including the console, topological map, link management, as well as discover, layout, browser, and grapher tools.

Distributed network management is the foundation for the Solstice Site and Domain Managers. Multiple Site Managers can be deployed and can be connected to a Domain Manager. Multiple Domain Managers are also possible. In addition, the management of larger networks can be simplified by spreading the management load across two different types of agents: device-based agents and proxy agents that act as middle managers. The middle managers localize network management polling to minimize network management traffic.

Both the Site and Domain Managers include a number of integrated SNMP features, including: the Proxy Agent, Trap Daemon to translate and forward traps, the mib2schema utility for MIB translation, and support for the protocol operations enhancements for SNMPv2.

Solstice Enterprise Manager is the next generation network management platform from Sun. It is based on a distributed, object-oriented, client/server architecture that allows it to scale to manage large, distributed, or mission-critical networks. The client/server architecture provides true multiuser support. Security is based on defined users and groups. Access controls can be specified on a platform (all applications), on selected applications, or on an application-feature basis. For example, the SNMP Browser can allow GETs but not SETs. Multiple management servers, called Management Information Servers (MIS), can be deployed for scalability. Management Information Servers can communicate with each other to present a consistent view to the network operator.

Reference [1-37] provides further information on the Solstice family of management products.

1.11.6 Tivoli Systems' TME 10 NetView

TME 10 NetView breaks down the traditional barriers between network management and systems management by providing tight integration with Tivoli's complimentary TME 10 management applications. Combined with its ability to easily effect changes on many devices, a global support infrastructure, and the backing of hundreds of third-party vendors, Tivoli's TME 10 NetView is a widely implemented management platform (Figure 1-21). Further, TME 10 NetView not only enables you to manage your network, it also positions you for planned and future growth with a complete systems management solution.

TME 10 NetView enables users to discover TCP/IP networks, display network topologies, correlate and manage events and SNMP traps, monitor network health, and gather performance data. TME 10 NetView meets the needs of small network managers and can grow with you to manage even the largest networks. By using the TME 10 NetView Mid-Level Manager (MLM) throughout your enterprise, you can scale TME 10 NetView in a truly distributed fashion, providing an effective means to reduce your total cost of ownership and keep network management traffic close to the source.

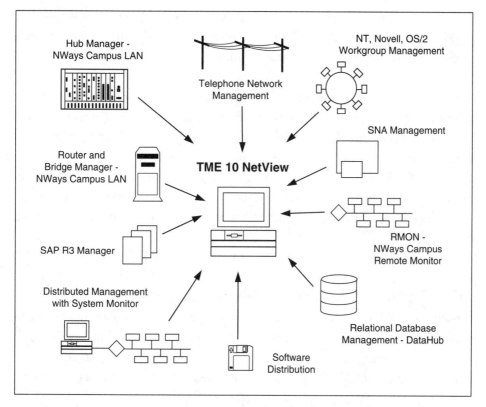

Figure 1-21. Tivoli and IBM application integration (Courtesy of Tivoli Systems)

TME 10 NetView is rich in powerful features that provide you with pertinent, up-to-the-minute information. For example, TME 10 NetView Object Collections enable you to dynamically group resources by common characteristics such as resource type or location. Using Object Collections, you can monitor groups of devices without manually searching for them. Object Collections enable you to dynamically group network objects according to any logical scheme. You can view, for example, all down routers (exception reporting), all routers from a specified manufacturer (all Brand X routers), or all routers in a specified subnet. Unlike some collection facilities, TME 10 NetView Object Collections are dynamically updated in real time, eliminating human error and outdated information.

In a single action, you can centrally set and enforce policy to multiple network devices using the Agent Policy Manager. Changes to hundreds or thousands of remote devices take place in minutes instead of hours or days.

A sophisticated rules-based event correlation engine allows you to graphically build rules that define how you want to implement business policies. Events can be handled locally, centrally, or passed to other Tivoli applications for further correlation. In essence, the ability to implement business policies in the form of rules enables you to quickly diagnose root problems rather than report only symptomatic events. Further, exception reporting declares serious problems with specific network devices when defined thresholds are violated.

Reference [1-38] provides further information on TME 10 NetView.

1.12 Fitting SNMP into the Role of Network Management

This chapter covered a lot of ground, from defining network management to exploring network management concepts, ranging from the familiar ISO/OSI model to examining the architecture of popular network management systems. So where does SNMP fit into the big picture of network management?

SNMP is a protocol that communicates network management information. Therefore, SNMP fits into the Application layer of the OSI model. But if you only look at SNMP in this context, you're ignoring the structure that supports it—and that fills out the remaining layers of the OSI model. In order to study SNMP in detail, you need to thoroughly understand the supporting structures.

This book takes several chapters to explain these structures. Chapter 2 discusses the structure of management information (or the SMI), which provides the organization and communication structures for the management information. Chapter 3 discusses management information bases (MIBs) that formally define the managed objects and their attributes. Chapter 4 examines the SNMP protocol in detail. Chapter 5 examines the second-generation protocol, SNMP Version 2. Chapter 6 discusses the underlying protocols, including the User Datagram Protocol (UDP), the Internet Protocol (IP), and the local network protocols, such as Ethernet or token ring, upon which SNMP operates. Chapter 7 provides case studies of live networks that demonstrate these protocols in action.

So put that network management console in monitor mode, get yourself a strong cup of coffee, and fasten your seat belt. The work for the real network manager is about to begin!

1.13 References

[1-1]   International Organization for Standardization, Information Processing Systems: Open Systems Interconnection, Basic Reference Model, ISO 7498-1984.

[1-2]   International Organization for Standardization, Information Processing Systems: Open Systems Interconnection, Basic Reference Model, Part 4: Management Framework, ISO 7498-4-1989.

[1-3]   International Organization for Standardization, Information Processing Systems: Open Systems Interconnection, Common management information service definition, ISO/ICE 9595, ITU-T Recommendation X.710, April 1991.

[1-4]   International Organization for Standardization, Information Processing Systems: Open Systems Interconnection, Common management information protocol specification, ISO/IEC 9596-1, CCITT Recommendation X.711, June 1991.

[1-5]   Klerer, S. Mark. "The OSI Management Architecture: An Overview." *IEEE Network* (March 1988): 20–29.

[1-6]   Yemini, Yechiam. "The OSI Network Management Model." *IEEE Communications Magazine* (May 1993): 20–29.

[1-7]   Institute of Electrical and Electronics Engineers. LAN/MAN Management. ANSI/IEEE Std 802.1B, 1995.

[1-8] Jander, Mary. "Can CMOL Challenge SNMP?" *Data Communications* (May 21, 1992): 53–57.

[1-9] Partridge, Craig, and Glenn Trewitt. "The High-Level Entity Management System (HEMS)." *IEEE Network* (March 1988): 37–42.

[1-10] Case, Jeffrey D., et al. "Introduction to the Simple Gateway Monitoring Protocol." *IEEE Network* (March 1988): 43–49.

[1-11] Cerf, V. "IAB Recommendations for the Development of Internet Network Management Standards." *RFC 1052*, April 1988.

[1-12] Case, J.D., M. Fedor, M.L. Schoffstall, and C. Davin. "Simple Network Management Protocol (SNMP)." *RFC 1157*, May 1990.

[1-13] Rose, Marshall T. "A Brief History of Network Management of TCP/IP Internets." *ConneXions, the Interoperability Report* (August 1990): 18–27.

[1-14] Ben-Artzi, Amatzia, et al. "Network Management of TCP/IP Networks: Present and Future." *IEEE Network* (July 1990): 35–43.

[1-15] Warrier, U.S., et al. "Common Management Information Services and Protocols for the Internet (CMOT and CMIP)." *RFC 1189*, October 1990.

[1-16] Jander, Mary. "Extending SNMP to the Desktop." *Data Communications* (November 21, 1992): 49–52.

[1-17] "Product Guide: SNMP Management Applications." *LAN Magazine* (September 1995): 129–140.

[1-18] Hudgins-Bonafield, Christine. "The Desktop Management Discontinuity." *Network Computing* (January 15, 1995): 78–86.

[1-19] The Desktop Management Task Force may be contacted at telephone (503) 264-9300, or at http://www.dmtf.org.

[1-20]   Mullaney, Patrick. "Overview of a Web-based Agent." *The Simple Times, The Quarterly Newsletter of SNMP Technology, Comment and Events.* (July 1996): 12–18. Available electronically from http://www.simple-times.org.

[1-21]   Wellens, Chris, and Karl Auerbach. "Towards Useful Management." *ConneXions, The Interoperability Report* (September 1996): 2–9. Available electronically from http://www.interop.com.

[1-22]   Paone, Joe. "The Management Console of the Future." *Internetwork* (September 1996): 25–49.

[1-23]   Jander, Mary. "Welcome to the Revolution." *Data Communications* (November 21, 1996): 39–53.

[1-24]   Horwitt, Elisabeth. "Getting to the Point." *Intranet* (December 1996): 35–38.

[1-25]   Huntington-Lee, Jill. "Be Ready to Manage a Move to the Web." *Internetwork* (January 1997): 15.

[1-26]   BMC Software, Inc., Cisco Systems, Inc., et al. "Enterprise Management Using Web-Based Technology." Available electronically from: http://wbem.freerange.com/wbem.

[1-27]   *Web–Based Enterprise Management Initiative.* Available electronically from: http://wbem.freerange.com.

[1-28]   SunSoft, Inc. *Java Management API Architecture.* Document 805-0084-01, September 1996.

[1-29]   SunSoft, Inc. "Java Management API Overview." Available electronically from http://www.javasoft.com.

[1-30]   Boardman, Bruce. "Global Network Management." *Network Computing* (August 15, 1996): 63–78.

[1-31]   Snell, Monica. "Intranets Dictate Platform Directions." *LAN Times* (January 6, 1997): 29.

[1-32]   Snell, Monica. "Apps to Stand Alone." *LAN Times* (February 3, 1997): 51–52.

[1-33]   Further information on Asante Technologies' IntraSpection is available from: http://www.intraspection.com.

[1-34]   Further information on Cabletron Systems' SPECTRUM is available from: http://www.cabletron.com/spectrum.

[1-35]   Further information on Hewlett-Packard's OpenView is available from: http://www.hp.com/go/openview/.

[1-36]   Further information on Novell's ManageWise is available from: http://www.novell.com.

[1-37]   Further information on Sun Microsystems' Solstice Enterprise Manager is available from: http://www.sun.com.

[1-38]   Further information on Tivoli Systems' TME 10 NetView is available from: http://www.tivoli.com.

# The Structure of Management Information

This and the next three chapters explore the theory of network management and the components of version 1 of the Internet Network Management Framework. In this chapter, you'll learn about the structure of management information (SMI), which defines the rules for identifying managed objects. SMI is described in RFC 1155 [2-1] and refined in RFC 1212 and RFC 1215. Chapter 3 discusses the management information bases (MIBs), examined in RFC 1213 [2-2], that describe the managed objects themselves. Chapter 4 discusses SNMP, which defines the mechanism by which managers and agents communicate, and is described in RFC 1157 [2-3].

We will revisit the SMI, MIB, and SNMP in Chapter 5 to compare and contrast SNMP with its intended successor, SNMP version 2, which is part of version 2 of the Internet Network Management Framework. Since this entire framework has been enhanced, there are changes to all elements of that framework: the SMI, the MIB, and the protocols. The migration from version 1 to version 2 has been a rather slow process, however, so it is very likely that SNMP version 1-based devices will be in service for some time. Therefore, if you are primarily interested in SNMP version 1, study Chapters 2, 3, and 4. To learn more about the enhancements with SNMP version 2, study Chapter 5. It is recommended that the section on SNMP version 1 be studied before moving to the section on version 2, because many of the underlying principles of version 2 assume a working knowledge of version 1.

For clarity, we will use the term *SNMP* to refer to SNMP version 1, and the term *SNMPv2* to refer to SNMP version 2.

Chapter 6 studies the underlying communication protocols, such as the User Datagram Protocol (UDP) and the Internet Protocol (IP), that transport SNMP messages between the manager and agents. Chapter 7 puts the entire architecture together by presenting case studies that demonstrate real-world use of SNMP.

2.1 Managing Management Information

In the manager/agent paradigm for network management, managed network objects must be physically and logically accessible. The term *physically accessible* means that some entity must physically check the address, count the packets, or otherwise quantify the network management information. Logical accessibility means that management information must be stored somewhere and, therefore, that the information must be retrievable and modifiable. (SNMP actually performs the retrieval and modification.) The structure of management information (SMI) (RFC 1155 [2-1]) organizes, names, and describes information so that logical access can occur.

The SMI states that each managed object must have a name, a syntax, and an encoding. The *name,* an object identifier (OID), uniquely identifies the object. The *syntax* defines the data type, such as an integer or a string of octets. The *encoding* describes how the information associated with the managed objects is serialized for transmission between machines.

This chapter discusses how the SMI applies to SNMP. It begins by looking at the syntax (the Abstract Syntax Notation One, ASN.1, in Sections 2.3 and 2.4), the encoding (the Basic Encoding Rules, examined in Section 2.5), and finally the names (the object identifier, discussed in Section 2.6). In this way, the discussion moves from the abstract to the practical. Chapter 3 discusses how the MIBs use these names.

2.2 Presenting Management Information

In terms of the ISO/OSI model [2-4], the ASN.1 syntax is a Presentation-layer (layer 6) function. Recall that the Presentation layer defines the format of the data stored within a host computer system.

In order for managers and agents to exchange data, both must understand it, regardless of the way either machine represents data internally. For this to occur, two items must be standardized: the abstract syntax and the transfer syntax. The *abstract syntax* defines specifications for data notation. The *transfer syntax* defines (transmittable) encodings for the elements in the abstract syntax.

The Internet SMI specifies that ASN.1 define the abstract syntax for messages; that is, ASN.1 defines the basic language elements and provides rules for combining elements into messages. The Basic Encoding Rules (BER) provide the transfer syntax. The BER are associated with the abstract syntax and provide bit-level communication between machines. Thus the SMI and SNMP use the ASN.1 formalizations (ISO 8824-1 [2-5]) and BER (ISO 8825-1 [2-6]) to define various aspects of the Internet network management framework. The specifics of ASN.1 are discussed in the next section.

2.3 ASN.1 Elements

Network administrators often criticize ASN.1 for its complexity. Some of their criticisms are fair: it is quite difficult to interpret the standard. However, ASN.1 has a straightforward objective. It is designed to define structured information (messages) in a machine-independent (or host-independent) fashion. To do this, ASN.1 defines basic data types, such as integers and strings, and new data types that are based on combinations of the basic ones. The BER then define the way the data is serialized for transmission.

ASN.1 defines *data* as a pattern of bits in computer memory, just as any high-level computer programming language defines data that the language manipulates as *variables*. The BER define a standard way to convert ASN.1 definitions into bit patterns for transmission, and then they actually transfer the data between computers. The BER are necessary because the ASN.1 description is "human-readable" and must be translated differently for each type of computer. The BER representation, however, is always the same for any ASN.1 description, regardless of the computers that send or receive that information. This assures communication between machines, regardless of their internal architecture.

The objective here is to describe ASN.1 to the level of detail necessary to apply it to network management and SNMP. (SNMP uses a subset of ASN.1 for the sake of simplicity.) For additional information, refer to Douglas Steedman's *Abstract Syntax Notation One (ASN.1), the Tutorial and Reference* [2-7] or Motteler and Sidhu's "Components of OSI: Abstract Syntax Notation One (ASN.1)" [2-8].

ASN.1 uses some unique terms to define its procedures, including type definitions, value assignments, macro definitions and evocations, and module definitions. You need to understand these terms before the discussion can proceed. Moreover, ASN.1 specifies some words as keywords, or reserved character sequences. Keywords, such as INTEGER, OBJECT, and NULL, have special meanings and appear in uppercase letters.

2.3.1 Types and Values

A *type* is a class of data. It defines the data structure that the machine needs in order to understand and process information. The SMI defines three types: Primitive, Constructor, and Defined. ASN.1 defines several *Primitive types* (also known as Simple types), including INTEGER, OCTET STRING, OBJECT IDENTIFIER, and NULL. By convention, types begin with an uppercase letter. (ASN.1 also defines the four types listed here as reserved character sequences, and therefore represents them entirely in uppercase.) *Constructor types* (also known as Aggregate types) generate lists and tables. *Defined types* are alternate names for either simple or complex ASN.1 types and are usually more descriptive. Examples of SNMP-defined types include IpAddress, which represents a 32-bit Internet address, and TimeTicks, which is a time-stamp.

The *value* quantifies the type. In other words, once you know the type, such as INTEGER or OCTET STRING, the value provides a specific instance for that type. For example, a value could be an entry in a routing table. By convention, values begin with lowercase letters.

Some applications allow only a subset of the possible type values. A subtype specification indicates such a constraint. The subtype specification appears after the type and shows the permissible value or values, called the *subtype values*, in parentheses. For example, if an application uses an INTEGER type and the permissible values must fit within an 8-bit field, the possible range of values must be between 0 and 255. You would express this as:

INTEGER (0..255)

The two periods (..) are the range separator and indicate the validity of any integer value between 0 and 255.

2.3.2 Macros

Annex J of ISO 8824-1 defines a macro notation that allows you to extend the ASN.1 language. By convention, a macro reference (or macro name) appears entirely in uppercase letters.

For example, MIB definitions make extensive use of the ASN.1 macro, OBJECT-TYPE (originally defined in RFC 1155 and now replaced by the definition in RFC 1212 [2-9]). The first object in MIB-II is a system description (sysDescr). RFC 1213 uses the OBJECT-TYPE macro to define sysDescr, as follows:

```
sysDescr OBJECT-TYPE
    SYNTAX  DisplayString (SIZE (0..255))
    ACCESS  read-only
    STATUS  mandatory
    DESCRIPTION
"A textual description of the entity. This value should include the full name and
version identification of the system's hardware type, software operating-system, and
networking software. This must contain only printable ASCII characters."
    ::= { system 1 }
```

Thus, one concise package defines the object sysDescr. Section 2.4.1 explores the details of the OBJECT-TYPE macro (SYNTAX, ACCESS, and so on). Note that the range notation (0..255) specifies the permissible size of the DisplayString type, which in this case is between 0 and 255.

2.3.3 Modules

ASN.1 also collects descriptions into convenient groups, called *modules*. For example, the remote monitoring (RMON) MIB is a discrete unit that is also part of MIB-II.

The module starts with a module name, such as RMON-MIB. Module names must begin with an uppercase letter. The BEGIN and END statements enclose the body of the module. The body may contain IMPORTS, which are the names of types, values, and macros, and the modules in which they are declared. In the following example, the first line after IMPORTS specifies that the Counter type, which will be used in this MIB module, is from another MIB module, RFC1155-SMI.

Following is the header section of the RMON MIB (from RFC 1757), which represents a MIB module. Comment lines within ASN.1 syntax begin with a double hyphen (--):

```
RMON-MIB DEFINITIONS ::= BEGIN
     IMPORTS
            Counter              FROM RFC1155-SMI
            DisplayString        FROM RFC1158-MIB
            mib-2                FROM RFC1213-MIB
            OBJECT-TYPE          FROM RFC-1212
            TRAP-TYPE            FROM RFC-1215;
--   Remote Network Monitoring MIB
     rmon     OBJECT IDENTIFIER ::= { mib-2 16 }

     -- textual conventions
            .

            .

            .


     END
```

In the preceding example, you can see the OBJECT IDENTIFIER value notation for RMON. Section 2.6 discusses this notation in detail, but for now simply note that the value of RMON is the sixteenth defined object under the mib-2 object tree. The curly brackets ({}) indicate the beginning and end of a list—in this case a list of the OBJECT IDENTIFIER values defining RMON.

2.3.4 Summary of ASN.1 conventions

In summary, ASN.1 makes distinctions between uppercase and lowercase letters, as follows:

Item	Convention
Types	Initial uppercase letter
Values	Initial lowercase letter
Macros	All uppercase letters
Modules	Initial uppercase letter
ASN.1 keywords	All uppercase letters

The ASN.1 keywords that are frequently used within SNMP are BEGIN, CHOICE, DEFINED, DEFINITIONS, END, EXPORTS, IDENTIFIER, IMPORTS, INTEGER, NULL, OBJECT, OCTET, OF, SEQUENCE, and STRING.

ASN.1 also gives special meanings to certain characters:

Item	Name
-	Signed number
--	Comment
::=	Assignment (defined as)
		Alternation (options of a list)

{}	Starts and ends a list
[ ]	Starts and ends a tag
( )	Starts and ends a subtype expression
..	Indicates a range

The sections that follow emphasize some of these special characters. Philip Gaudett's paper, "A Tutorial on ASN.1" [2-10], provides a good summary of this notation.

2.4 Details of ASN.1—Objects and Types

The previous discussion provided an overview of ASN.1. This section focuses on the ASN.1 objects and data types used within the Internet Network Management framework. Where possible, I will provide examples derived from the SMI (RFC 1155), the Concise MIB Definitions (RFC 1212), and MIB-II (RFC 1213) documents.

2.4.1 Defining Objects in the MIBs

A MIB contains the objects to be managed. The OBJECT-TYPE macro defines these objects in a standard format that is consistent across various public and private MIBs. (Chapter 3 will discuss MIBs in greater detail.) The MIB-II ASN.1 definitions (RFC 1213, page 48) appear as follows:

```
tcpInSegs OBJECT-TYPE
        SYNTAX  Counter
        ACCESS  read-only
        STATUS  mandatory
        ::= { tcp 10 }
```

In English, this ASN.1 definition means: This defines an object named tcpIn-Segs that contains Counter information. The Counter type is a nonnegative number that increases monotonically. (Section 2.4.4 discusses counters, which is a defined type.) This object is read-only and is mandatory for all managed devices that support its parent, mib-2.tcp. When a management protocol accesses this object, it uses the name { tcp 10 }, which identifies the tenth defined object within the tcp group. (Section 2.6 provides more detail on how the SMI names manage objects.)

2.4.2 Primitive (Simple) Types

To maintain SNMP's simplicity, the Internet SMI uses a subset of the ASN.1 data types. These are divided into two categories, the Primitive types and Constructor types (see Section 2.4.3). Primitive data types (also called Simple types) include INTEGER, OCTET STRING, OBJECT IDENTIFIER, and NULL. The following examples come from MIB-II (RFC 1213). You may also want to refer to Section 2.7, "The Concise SMI Definition," and locate the Primitive types under the SimpleSyntax definition.

INTEGER is a Primitive type with distinguished (or unique) values that are positive and negative whole numbers, including zero. The INTEGER type has two special cases. The first is the *enumerated integer type*, in which the objects have a specific, nonzero number such as 1, 2, or 3. The second, the *integer-bitstring type*, is used for short bit strings such as (0..127) and displays the value in hexidecimal. An example of INTEGER would be:

```
ipDefaultTTL    OBJECT-TYPE
        SYNTAX   INTEGER
        ACCESS   read-write
        STATUS   mandatory
        DESCRIPTION
                "The default value inserted into the Time-To-Live field of the IP header
                of datagrams originating at this entity, whenever a TTL value is not
                supplied by the transport layer protocol."
        ::= { ip 2 }
```

The OCTET STRING is a Primitive type whose distinguished values are an ordered sequence of zero, one, or more octets. SNMP uses three special cases of the OCTET STRING type: the DisplayString, the octetBitstring, and the PhysAddress. In the

DisplayString, all of the octets are printable ASCII characters. The octetBitstring is used for bit strings that exceed 32 bits in length. (TCP/IP frequently includes 32-bit fields. This quantity is a typical value for the internal word width of various processors—hosts and routers—within the Internet.) MIB-II defines the PhysAddress and uses it to represent media (or Physical layer) addresses.

An example of the use of a DisplayString would be:

```
sysContact      OBJECT-TYPE
        SYNTAX  DisplayString (SIZE (0..255))
        ACCESS  read-write
        STATUS  mandatory
        DESCRIPTION
                "The textual identification of the contact person for this managed
                node, and information on how to contact this person."
        ::= { system 4 }
```

Note that the subtype indicates that the permissible size of the DisplayString is between 0 and 255 octets.

The OBJECT IDENTIFIER is a type whose distinguishing values are the set of all object identifiers allocated according to the rules of ISO 8824-1. The ObjectName type, a special case that SNMP uses, is restricted to the object identifiers of the objects and subtrees within the MIB, as for example:

```
ipRouteInfo     OBJECT-TYPE
        SYNTAX  OBJECT IDENTIFIER
        ACCESS  read-only
        STATUS  mandatory
        DESCRIPTION
                "A reference to MIB definitions specific to the particular routing
                protocol responsible for this route, as determined by the value
                specified in the route's ipRouteProto value. If this information is not
                present, its value should be set to the OBJECT IDENTIFIER { 0 0 }, which
```

is a syntactically valid object identifier, and any conforming implementation of ASN.1 and BER must be able to generate and recognize this value."

::= { ipRouteEntry 13 }

NULL is a type with a single value, also called *null*. The null serves as a place-holder, but is not currently used for SNMP objects. (You can see NULL used as a placeholder in the variable bindings field of the SNMP GetRequest PDU. The NULL is assigned to be the value of the unknown variable, that is, the value the GetRequest PDU seeks. For more information see Section 4.3.)

Section 2.5.3 discusses the Primitive types and their encodings in more detail.

2.4.3 Constructor (Structured) Types

The Constructor types, SEQUENCE and SEQUENCE OF, define tables and rows (entries) within those tables. By convention, names for table objects end with the suffix *Table*, and names for rows end with the suffix *Entry*. The following discussion defines the Constructor types. The example comes from MIB-II.

SEQUENCE is a Constructor type defined by referencing a fixed, ordered, list of types. Some of the types may be optional, and all may be different ASN.1 types. Each value of the new type consists of an ordered list of values, one from each component type. The SEQUENCE as a whole defines a row within a table. Each entry in the SEQUENCE specifies a column within the row.

SEQUENCE OF is a Constructor type that is defined by referencing a single existing type; each value in the new type is an ordered list of zero, one, or more values of that existing type. Like SEQUENCE, SEQUENCE OF defines the rows in a table; unlike SEQUENCE, SEQUENCE OF only uses elements of the same ASN.1 type.

The TCP connection table that follows illustrates both the SEQUENCE and SEQUENCE OF:

```
tcpConnTable   OBJECT-TYPE
      SYNTAX   SEQUENCE OF TcpConnEntry
      ACCESS   not-accessible
      STATUS   mandatory
      DESCRIPTION
              "A table containing TCP connection-specific information."
      ::= { tcp 13 }
tcpConnEntry   OBJECT-TYPE
      SYNTAX   TcpConnEntry
      ACCESS   not-accessible
      STATUS   mandatory
      DESCRIPTION
              "Information about a particular current TCP connection. An object
              of this type is transient; it ceases to exist when (or soon after) the
              connection makes the transition to the CLOSED state."
      INDEX   { tcpConnLocalAddress,
            tcpConnLocalPort,
            tcpConnRemAddress,
            tcpConnRemPort }
      ::= { tcpConnTable 1 }
      TcpConnEntry ::=
      SEQUENCE {
      tcpConnState
          INTEGER,
      tcpConnLocalAddress
          IpAddress,
      tcpConnLocalPort
          INTEGER (0..65535),
      tcpConnRemAddress
          IpAddress,
      tcpConnRemPort
          INTEGER (0..65535)
      }
```

This example expands your ASN.1 grammar. The table name, tcpConnTable, ends with the suffix *Table*. The row name, tcpConnEntry, ends with the suffix *Entry*. The sequence name, TcpConnEntry, is the same as the row name, except that it begins with an uppercase letter. The INDEX clause defines the construction and order of the columns that make up the rows. Dave Perkins' excellent article, "How to Read and Use an SNMP MIB" [2-11] explores table and row objects in greater detail.

2.4.4 Defined Types

The Internet Network Management Framework uses the Defined (or application-wide) types (described in RFC 1155). The Defined types include NetworkAddress, IpAddress, Counter, Gauge, TimeTicks, and Opaque. The examples that follow come from RFC 1213. For more information, refer to Section 2.7 and locate the defined types under the ApplicationSyntax definition section.

The NetworkAddress type was designed to represent an address from one of several protocol families. A CHOICE is a primitive type that provides alternatives between other types, and is found in several sections of the SMI definition given in Section 2.7. Currently, however, only one protocol family, the Internet family (called internet IpAddress in the SMI definition), has been defined for this CHOICE. Here is an example:

```
atNetAddress OBJECT-TYPE
    SYNTAX    NetworkAddress
    ACCESS    read-write
    STATUS    deprecated
    DESCRIPTION
            "The NetworkAddress (e.g., the IP address) corresponding to the
            media-dependent 'physical' address."
    ::= { atEntry 3 }
```

Because it supports only IP addresses (hence the default "choice"), use of this type is discouraged.

IpAddress is an application-wide type that represents a 32-bit Internet address. It is represented as an OCTET STRING of length 4 (octets) in network byte-order (the order bytes are transmitted over the network):

```
tcpConnRemAddress  OBJECT-TYPE
        SYNTAX      IpAddress
        ACCESS      read-only
        STATUS      mandatory
        DESCRIPTION
                    "The remote IP address for this TCP connection."
        ::= {tcpConnEntry 4 }
```

The Counter is an application-wide type that represents a nonnegative integer that increases monotonically until it reaches a maximum value, then wraps around and increases again from zero. The maximum counter value is $2^{32}-1$, or 4,294,967,295 decimal. In other words, the Counter is an unsigned 32-bit number. An INTEGER is a signed 32-bit value. By convention, you write the name of a Counter object as a plural; it ends in a lowercase s. Here is an example:

```
icmpInDestUnreachs  OBJECT-TYPE
        SYNTAX      Counter
        ACCESS      read-only
        STATUS      mandatory
        DESCRIPTION
                    "The number of ICMP Destination Unreachable messages
                    received."
        ::= { icmp 3 }
```

A Gauge is an application-wide type that represents a nonnegative integer. It may increase or decrease, but it latches at a maximum value. The maximum counter value is $2^{32}-1$ (4,294,967,295 decimal). Here is an example:

```
ifSpeed      OBJECT-TYPE
        SYNTAX   Gauge
```

```
ACCESS      read-only
STATUS      mandatory
DESCRIPTION
            "An estimate of the interface's current bandwidth in bits per
            second. For interfaces that do not vary in bandwidth or for
            those where no accurate estimation can be made, this object
            should contain the nominal bandwidth."
::= { ifEntry 5 }
```

TimeTicks is an application-wide type that represents a nonnegative integer that counts the time in hundredths of a second since some epoch, or point in time. When the MIB defines object types that use this ASN.1 type, the description of the object type identifies the reference epoch. Here is an example:

```
sysUpTime   OBJECT-TYPE
      SYNTAX  TimeTicks
      ACCESS  read-only
      STATUS  mandatory
      DESCRIPTION
            "The time (in hundredths of a second) since the network
            management portion of the system was last re-initialized."
      ::= { system 3 }
```

Opaque is an application-wide type that permits the passing of arbitrary ASN.1 syntax. The ASN.1 basic rules encode a value into a string of octets. This string, in turn, is encoded as an OCTET STRING, in effect "double-wrapping" the original ASN.1 value. SNMP does not currently use Opaque, although it may be found in some private MIBs.

2.4.5 Tagged Types

Tags distinguish between defined objects unequivocally. While a human reader might be able to distinguish defined objects through their names in ASN.1 notation, a machine can't without additional information. Therefore, the tagged types use a previously defined type as a base, and then add unique information. ASN.1 defines four classes of tags: universal, application, context specific, and private. ASN.1 (ISO 8824-1) defines universal tags. Other standards, such as the Internet standards, assign application class tags. The SNMP definition (RFC 1157) interprets context-specific class tags according to their context. Enterprise-specific applications use private class tags.

A number within square brackets ([ ]) identifies tagged types. For example, the concise SMI definition (Section 2.7) shows that

```
TimeTicks ::=
    [APPLICATION 3]
        IMPLICIT INTEGER (0..4294967295)
```

Therefore, the TimeTicks type is a tagged type, designated APPLICATION 3. It is of the application class, and the tag number is 3. It may take on the range of values between 0 and 4294967295. The IMPLICIT keyword indicates that the tag associated with the INTEGER type is not transmitted, but the tag associated with TimeTicks is. This reduces the amount of data that must be encoded and transmitted.

2.5 Encoding Rules

Section 2.4 discusses the abstract syntax that represents management information. This section discusses the encoding rules that allow that information to be transmitted on a network. The Basic Encoding Rules (BER) define this transfer syntax, and ISO 8825-1 specifies it [2-6].

2.5.1 Encoding Management Information

Recall that each machine in the management system can have its own internal representation of the management information. The ASN.1 syntax describes that information in a standard form. The transfer syntax performs the bit-level communication (the external representation) between machines. For example, assume that the host needs management information from another device. The management application would generate an SNMP request, which the BER would encode and transmit on the network media. The destination machine would receive the information from the network, decode it using the BER rules, and interpret it as an SNMP command. The SNMP response would return in a similar, but reverse, manner. The encoding structure used for the external representation is called *Type-Length-Value encoding* (see Figure 2-1).

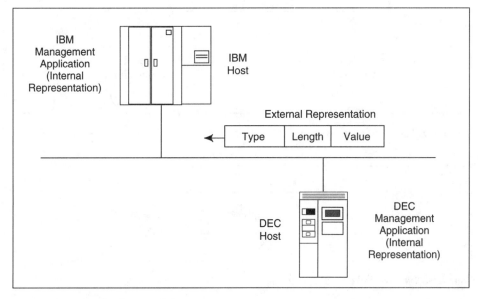

Figure 2-1. Internal and external data representations

2.5.2 Type-Length-Value Encoding

To define the external data representation, the BER first specify the position of each bit within the octets being transmitted. Each octet transmits the *most significant bit* (MSB) first and defines it as bit 8 on the left-hand side of the octet. The octet defines the *least significant bit* (LSB) as bit 1 on the right-hand side (see Figure 2-2).

The data encoding structure itself has three components: the Type, Length, and Value (TLV). Note that in the literature you will run across other names for Type-Length-Value, including Tag-Length-Value and Identifier-Length-Contents (from ISO 8825-1). The structure of a TLV encoding used with SNMP is shown in Figure 2-3.

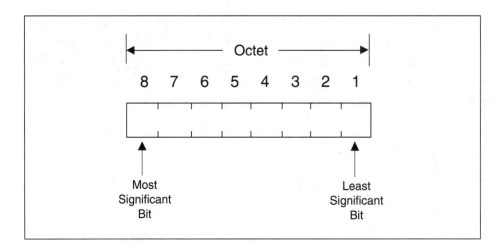

Figure 2-2 BER bit ordering, as defined in ISO 8825-1

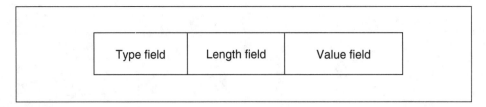

Figure 2-3 Type-Length-Value (TLV) encoding

By defining the order and structure of the bits, the BER guarantee that both ends of the communication channel interpret the bit stream consistently. The following sections examine the structure of each TLV field individually.

2.5.2.1 Type Field

The Type field comes first and alerts the destination to the structure that follows. Thus, the Type field contains an identification for the encoding structure; it encodes the ASN.1 tag (both the class and number) for the type of data contained in the Value field. A subfield within the Type field contains a bit designated as P/C that indicates whether the coding is Primitive (P/C = 0) or Constructed (P/C = 1), as shown in Figure 2-4.

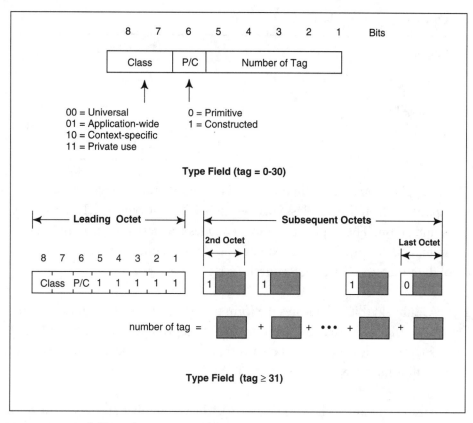

Figure 2-4 Type field encoding *(Source: ISO 8825-1)*

There are two types of Type fields; and their use depends on the magnitude of the tag number. When the tag number is between 0 and 30, the Tag field contains a single octet (see Figure 2-4). When the tag number is 31 or greater, the Type field contains multiple octets. In either case, the first octet contains three subfields: the Class, P/C bit, and tag number. The Class subfield encodes the class of tag in use:

Class	Bit 8	Bit 7
Universal	0	0
Application	0	1
Context-specific	1	0
Private	1	1

SNMP applications use the first three classes: universal, application, and context specific. The universal class encodes the INTEGER type, OCTET STRING type, and so on. The application class encodes the defined types (IpAddress, Counter, and so on). The context-specific class encodes the five SNMP protocol data units (PDUs), GetRequest, GetResponse, and so on.

The P/C subfield (bit 6) indicates the form of the data element. Primitive encoding (P/C = 0) means that the contents octets represent the value directly. A Constructor encoding (P/C = 1) means that the contents octets encode one or more additional data values, such as a SEQUENCE.

SNMP uses tag numbers between 0 and 30. The tag number appears in the third subfield and is represented in binary. Bit 5 is the tag's MSB; bit 1 is its LSB.

ISO 8824-1 contains tag numbers for the universal class (for example, UNIVERSAL 2 represents the INTEGER type). The SMI specification, RFC 1155, contains tag numbers for the application class (for example, IpAddress is a primitive type with tag [0]). The SNMP specification, RFC 1157, contains tag numbers for the context-specific class (for example, GetRequest PDU is a constructed type with tag [0]).

The following list summarizes the three classes of Type fields used with SNMP and the encodings for those fields: class, P/C, and tag number. These encodings appear in both binary and hexadecimal notation, where the *H* represents hexadecimal notation:

Universal Class	Type Field Value
INTEGER	00000010 = 02H
OCTET STRING	00000100 = 04H
NULL	00000101 = 05H
OBJECT IDENTIFIER	00000110 = 06H
SEQUENCE	00110000 = 30H
SEQUENCE-OF	00110000 = 30H

Application Class	Type Field Value
IpAddress	01000000 = 40H
Counter	01000001 = 41H
Gauge	01000010 = 42H
TimeTicks	01000011 = 43H
Opaque	01000100 = 44H

Context-Specific Class	Type Field Value
GetRequest	10100000 = A0H
GetNextRequest	10100001 = A1H
GetResponse	10100010 = A2H
SetRequest	10100011 = A3H
Trap	10100100 = A4H

Although the BER also provide tag numbers of 31 or greater, SNMP does not use these (see the lower portion of Figure 2-4). For tag numbers larger than 31, the Type field uses a different format. The tag number in the first octet is set to binary 11111, and subsequent octets are added to carry the tag number. Bit 8 = 1 of an octet indicates that more octets will follow; Bit 8 = 0 of an octet specifies the last octet. Bits 7 through 1 of each subsequent octet carry the unsigned binary integer of the tag number. Bit 7 of the first subsequent octet indicates the MSB of the tag number.

2.5.2.2 Length Field

The Length field follows the Type field and determines the number of octets the Value field will contain. The Length field may take either the short definite or the long definite form, as shown in Figure 2-5. (Another form, called "indefinite," is not used with SNMP.) The *Definite* indicates that the length of the encoding is known prior to transmission; the *indefinite* indicates otherwise.

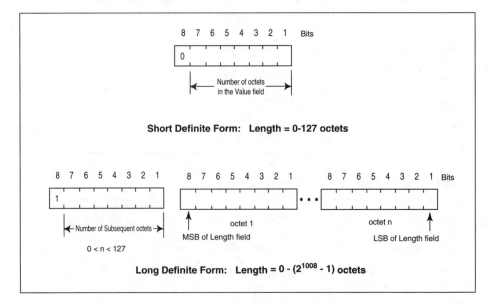

Figure 2-5 Length field encoding

The short definite form indicates a length of between 0 and 127 octets in the Contents field; the long definite form indicates 128 or more octets in the Contents field, although it can indicate shorter lengths.

The long form uses multiple octets to represent the total length. In the long form, the first octet of the Length field has Bit 8 = 1, followed by a binary number indicating the number of octets to follow. This number must be between 1 and 126; 127 is reserved for future extensions. Bit 8 of the second octet is considered the MSB of the Length field, and the following octets make up the rest of the length. Thus, the long definite form may represent a length up to 2^{1008}-1 octets. (The 1008 is derived from the product of 126 and 8 — 126 subsequent octets times 8 bits per octet.)

2.5.2.3 Value Field

The Value field contains zero or more contents octets, which convey the data values. Examples include an integer, ASCII character, or OBJECT IDENTIFIER, such as { 1.3.6.1.2. }.

2.5.3 Encoding Examples

Section 2.4.2 mentioned that the Internet SMI defines a subset of the ASN.1 types. This subset includes the following universal Primitive types: INTEGER, OCTET STRING, OBJECT IDENTIFIER, and NULL. The universal Constructor types are SEQUENCE And SEQUENCE OF. The application Primitive types are IpAddress, Counter, Gauge, and TimeTicks. SNMP-related applications use only these ten types. I will use this information in the case studies presented in the following chapters. For illustrations of the other types, consult ISO 8825-1.

2.5.3.1 INTEGER Type Encoding

The INTEGER type is a Simple type that has values of zero, positive, or negative whole numbers. It is a Primitive type encoded with a Value field containing one or more Contents octets. The Contents octets are "two's-complement" binary number equal to the integer value, and they can use as many octets as necessary. For example, Boomer, my Labrador, weighs 75 pounds. The value of his weight would be encoded as: Type field = 02H, Length field = 01H, and Value field = 4BH (see Figure 2-6). Note that the value appears in quotes (Value = "75") to indicate that it represents a quantity, which can be numerical, ASCII characters, an IP address, and so on.

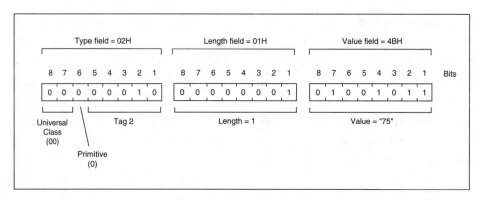

Figure 2-6 Encoding for the INTEGER type, Value = "75"

2.5.3.2 OCTET STRING Type Encoding

The OCTET STRING is a Simple type whose distinguished values are an ordered sequence of zero, one, or more octets, each of which must be a multiple of 8 bits. Encoding for OCTET STRING values is primitive, with the Type field = 04H. The Length field and Value field depend on the encoded information.

Let's again use Boomer as an example to show the OCTET STRING type encoding. Figure 2-7 shows how I encoded the value for Boomer's initials (BBM, for Boomerang Buddy Miller). The Type field contains 04H, indicating a Primitive type, OCTET STRING (tag number 4). The Length field indicates 3 octets in the Value field. The Value field encodings come from the ASCII chart.

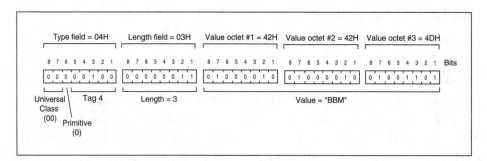

Figure 2-7 Encoding for the OCTET STRING type, Value = "BBM"

2.5.3.3 OBJECT IDENTIFIER Type Encoding

The OBJECT IDENTIFIER names (or identifies) items. (In SNMP, these identify managed objects.) Its Value field contains an ordered list of subidentifiers. To save encoding and transmission effort, you can take advantage of the fact that the first subidentifier is a small number, such as 0, 1, or 2, and combine it mathematically with the second subidentifier, which may be larger. The total number of subidentifiers is, therefore, less than the number of object identifier components in the OID value being encoded. This reduced number (one less) results from a mathematical expression that uses the first two OID components to produce another expression:

Given X is the value of the first OID, and Y is the second:
First subidentifier = (X * 40) + Y

The values for these subidentifiers are encoded and placed within the Value field. Bit 8 of each octet indicates whether or not that octet is the last in the series of octets required to fully describe the value. If Bit 8 = 1, at least one octet follows; Bit 8 = 0 indicates the last (or only) octet. Bits 7 through1 of each octet encode subidentifiers. Using an example from the MIB-II object tree, the System group, assume that an OBJECT IDENTIFIER has a value of

{ iso org(3) dod(6) internet(1) mgmt(2) mib-2 (1) 1 }

From the object tree (also discussed below), this is represented by

{ 1 3 6 1 2 1 1 }

Using the values of X = 1 and Y = 3, and the expression above for the first subidentifier value,

(1 * 40) + 3 = 43

This results in the first subidentifier value of 43, the second subidentifier value of 6, the third subidentifier value of 1, and so on. The first value (43) needs 6 bits, or one octet, for encoding (00101011). The second value (6) needs 3 bits for encoding (110), and requires only one octet. Subsequent values also require one octet. As you can see in Figure 2-8, the encoding becomes: Type field = 06H (OBJECT IDENTIFIER, tag = 6); Length field = 06H, and Value field = 2B 06 01 02 01 01 H.

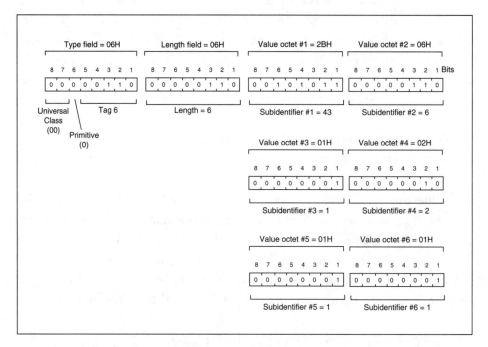

Figure 2-8 Encoding for OBJECT IDENTIFIER type, Value = { 1 3 6 1 2 1 1 }

2.5.3.4 NULL Type Encoding

The NULL type is a placeholder that communicates the absence of information. For example, when a manager requests the value of a variable, it uses the NULL type as a placeholder in the position where the agent will fill in the response.

Encoding for the NULL type is a primitive. The Type field = 05H, and the Length field = 00H. The Value field is empty (no value octets), as shown in Figure 2-9.

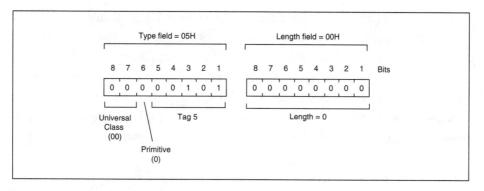

Figure 2-9 Encoding for the NULL type, Value = NULL

2.5.3.5 SEQUENCE Type Encoding

Recall from the discussion in Section 2.4.3 that the SEQUENCE type is a list of ASN.1 types. A SEQUENCE value is always encoded in Constructed form. The variable bindings used within the SNMP messages provide a good example of SEQUENCE. The variable bindings (or VarBind) pair an object name with its value, which is transmitted inside the Value field, as shown in Figure 2-3. SNMP (RFC 1157, page 32) defines the VarBind:

```
VarBind ::=
     SEQUENCE {
         name
             ObjectName

         value
             ObjectSyntax
     }


VarBindList ::=
     SEQUENCE OF
         VarBind
```

As this syntax shows, the VarBind is a SEQUENCE (pairing) of a name and a value, and the VarBindList is a list of names and values.

Although this is getting ahead of the sequence of our SMI, MIB, and SNMP story, I'll provide an example. Suppose you need the system description for a particular object whose name is sysDescr. To obtain the system description, the manager transmits an SNMP GetRequest to the agent asking for the value of object sysDescr. The agent responds with an SNMP GetResponse message containing the value, such as "Retix Local Ethernet Bridge Model 2265M." The VarBind associates the object (sysDescr) and its value ("Retix ..."), as shown in Figure 2-10.

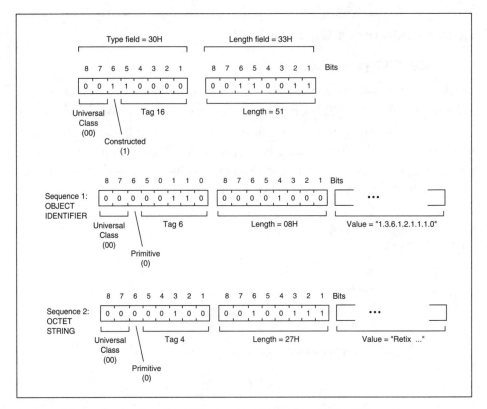

Figure 2-10 Encoding for the SEQUENCE type, a Variable Binding (VarBind)

The first Type field (30H) indicates a Constructed type, with Tag = 16 (SEQUENCE). The first Length field contains 33H, indicating that 51 Value octets follow. The BER are then applied for every type in the SEQUENCE. The first sequence identifies a Primitive type with Tag = 6 (OBJECT IDENTIFIER) and Length = 08H. The Value field contains the numeric representation of the sysDescr object {1.3.6.1.2.1.1.1.0}. The second sequence identifies a Primitive type with Tag = 4 (OCTET STRING), and Length = 27H (39 decimal). The second Value field represents the value of the object sysDescr ("Retix Local Bridge ..."). If you've got a calculator, look at the total length of the encoding. Sequence #1 contains 10 octets (1 from the type field + 1 from the length + 8 from the value). Sequence #2 contains 41 octets (1 + 1 + 39). Sequence #1 plus Sequence #2 (10 + 41) equals the value of the first Length field (51 octets).

2.5.3.6 SEQUENCE-OF Type Encoding

The SEQUENCE-OF type value is encoded in Constructed form in the same way as the SEQUENCE type.

2.5.3.7 IpAddress Type Encoding

The discussion now moves to the application class of encodings. You can find these in Section 2.7, "The Concise SMI Definition," as tagged types. Since they are all application Class (01), Primitive (P/C = 0) encodings, with tag numbers between 0 and 4, the Type fields will range from 40 to 44H (see Figures 2-11 through 2-14).

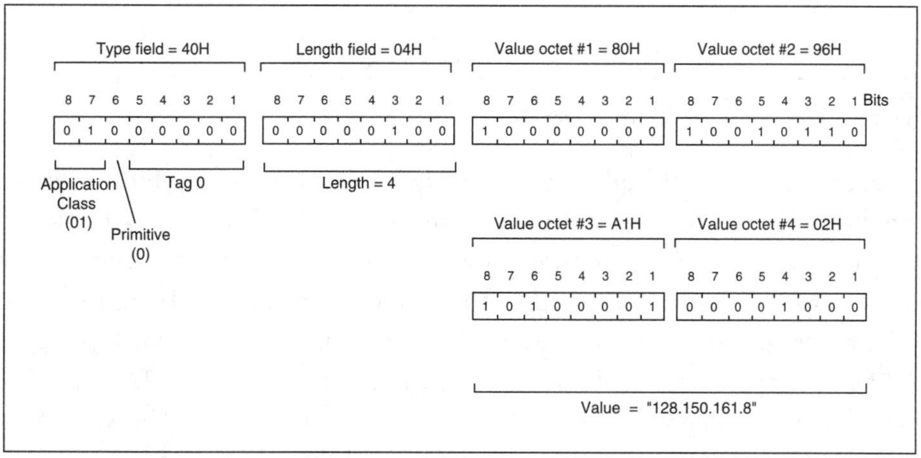

Figure 2-11 Encoding for the IpAddress type, Value = "128.150.161.8"

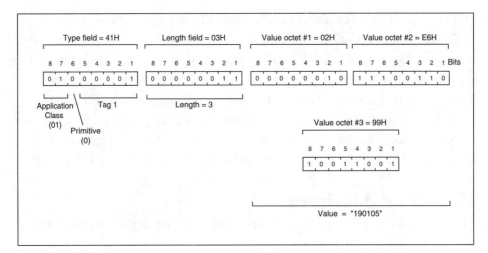

Figure 2-12 Encoding for the Counter type, Value = "190105"

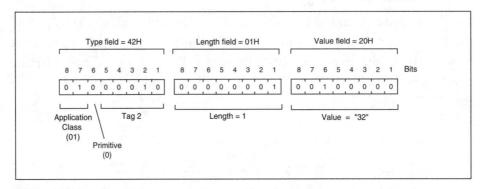

Figure 2-13 Encoding for the Gauge type, Value = "32"

The SMI defines the IpAddress type. The IpAddress carries a 32-bit IP address, which is represented in four octets. Jumping to the discussion of MIBs in Chapter 3, the IP group contains objects that relate to the IP process on a router or host. An object called IpAdEntAddr identifies the IP address that subsequent information is related to. To encode the IpAdEntAddr (see Figure 2-11), the Type field is set to 40H (application class, Primitive, Tag = 0). The Length field = 4, representing the four octets in the IP address. The Value field contains four contents octets, which convey the IP address in dotted decimal notation. For the address shown in the example [128.150.161.8], the first octet in the Value field contains the binary equivalent of 128 (10000000), the second the binary equivalent of 150, and so on.

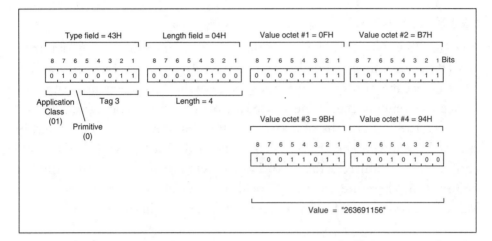

Figure 2-14 Encoding for the TimeTicks type, Value = "263691156"

2.5.3.8 Counter Type Encoding

A Counter type (also defined in the SMI) represents a nonnegative integer that increases monitonically to a maximum of 4,294,967,295, and then wraps around to zero. The ICMP Group uses many counters to record message statistics. One object, icmpInMsgs, records the number of messages that the ICMP process on a router or host has received. A sample encoding (see Figure 2-12) would have a Type field = 41H, representing application class, primitive encoding, and Tag = 1. The Value (190,105) requires three octets. The Length field is, therefore, 03H, and the Value field contains 02 E6 99H, representing the 190,105 messages.

2.5.3.9 Gauge Type Encoding

A Gauge type (also defined in the SMI) is a nonnegative integer that may increase or decrease, but latches at a maximum value of 4,294,967,295. The Gauge is not used frequently. MIB-II defines it for the ifSpeed, ifOutQLen, and tcpCurrEstab objects only. For example, Figure 2-13 assumes that the maximum output queue length of a particular interface is 32 packets. To encode this Gauge value, the Type field is set to 42H (application class, Primitive, Tag = 2). One octet encodes decimal 32; therefore, the Length field = 01H and the Value field contains 20H, the desired value of 32 decimal.

2.5.3.10 TimeTicks Type Encoding

The TimeTicks type (also defined in the SMI) contains a time-stamp that measures the elapsed time (in hundredths of a second) since some event. The sysUpTime object measures the time since the network management entity on a device was reinitialized. If the sysUpTime value for a particular device was 263,691,156 hundredths of a second (about 30 days), its value would be encoded as shown in Figure 2-14. The Type field would be set to 43H (application class, Primitive, Tag = 3). Four octets represent a Value equal to 263691156. Therefore, the Length field contains 04H. The four octets in the Value field contain the binary representation of the TimeTicks value.

2.5.3.11 Context-Specific Encodings for SNMP

The final class of encodings discussed in this chapter are the context-specific encodings, which are used within the context of SNMP. Five protocol data units (PDUs), which Chapter 4 discusses in greater detail, convey SNMP information. The PDUs are GetRequest, GetNextRequest, GetResponse, SetRequest, and Trap. These PDUs have tag numbers of 0 to 4, respectively. These encodings are all context-specific class (10) and constructed (P/C = 1). The Type fields thus have values ranging from A0 to A4H (see Figure 2-15). The Length and Value fields depend on the information conveyed.

2.6 Object Names

Each object, whether it's a device or a characteristic of a device, must have a name by which it can be uniquely identified. That name is the object identifier. It is written as a sequence of integers separated by periods. For example, the sequence {1.3.6.1.2.1.1.1.0} specifies the system description, within the system group, of the mgmt subtree.

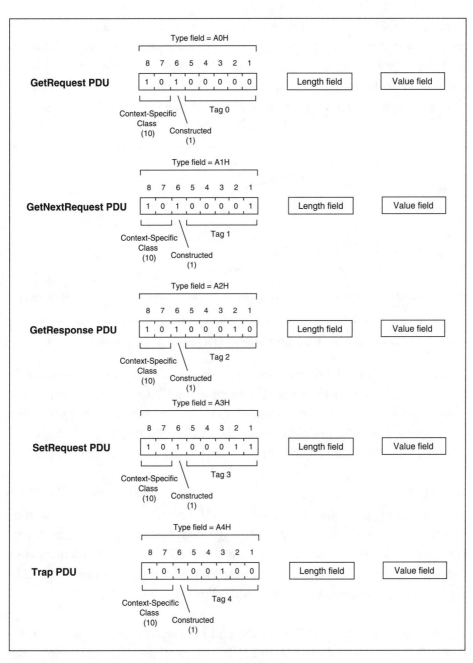

Figure 2-15 Encoding for the context-specific types used with SNMP

Annexes B, C, D and E of ISO 8824-1 define the numerical sequences; they resemble a tree with a root and several directly attached branches, referred to as *children* (see Figure 2-16). These branches connect to other branches. You can use the structure of root, branches, subbranches, and leaves to diagram all of the objects within a particular MIB and their relationships.

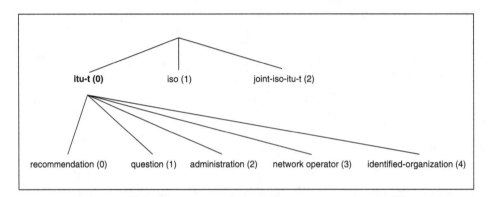

Figure 2-16 The root node and ITU-T-assigned OBJECT IDENTIFIER component values

The root does not need a designation, but a specific numeric value designates the three connected arcs, or branches. The International Telecommunications Union - Telecommunications Standards Sector (ITU-T) administers the branch labeled 0, the International Organization for Standardization (ISO) administers the branch labeled 1, and ISO and ITU-T jointly administer the third branch, labeled 2.

The ITU-T branch has five children: recommendation (0) identifies ITU-T recommendations; question (1) is used for ITU-T study groups; administration (2) identifies the values of the X.121 DCCs (Data Country Codes); network-operator (3) identifies the values of the X.121 Data Network Identification codes (DNICs); and identified-organization (4) identifies values assigned by the ITU Telecommunication Standardization Bureau (TSB).

The ISO branch (Figure 2-17) has three children: standard (0) designates international standards; member-body (2) is a three-digit numeric country code that ISO 3166 assigns to each member of ISO/IEC; and identified-organizations (3) have values of an international code designator (ICD), defined in

ISO 6523. (Branch (1) was previously assigned to registration -authority (1), but it is no longer in use, per ISO 8834-1.)

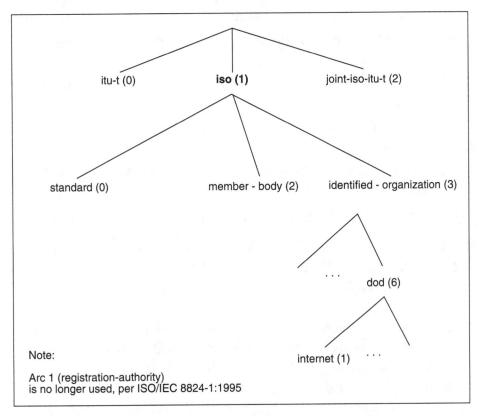

Figure 2-17 The root node and ISO assigned OBJECT IDENTIFIER component values

The U.S. Department of Defense is assigned to one of the children under 1.3, and is designated as 6. On this tree, the Internet community has designation 1.

To identify a particular position on the tree, you list the numeric values in a string, separated by periods. For example, to identify the position of the Internet sub-tree, you start at the root and move down until you reach position {1.3.6.1}.

At the Internet level (Figure 2-18), you begin to see details germane to network management and SNMP. The Internet subtree has seven branches:

➤ The directory (1) subtree, {internet 1} or {1.3.6.1.1}, is reserved for future use by the OSI directory within the Internet.

➤ The mgmt (2) subtree, {internet 2} or {1.3.6.1.2}, is managed by the Internet Assigned Numbers Authority, and includes the standard MIBs.

➤ The experimental (3) subtree, {internet 3} or {1.3.6.1.3}, is used for Internet experiments.

➤ The private (4) subtree, {internet 4} or {1.3.6.1.4}, allows vendors to register objects.

➤ The security (5) subtree, {internet 5} or {1.3.6.1.5} for security-related objects.

➤ The snmpV2 (6) subtree, {internet 6} or {1.3.6.1.6}, for SNMP version 2 objects.

➤ The mail (7) subtree, {internet 7} or {1.3.6.1.7}, for mail objects.

The Internet Assigned Numbers Authority (IANA) administers these subtrees and publishes them in the current Assigned Numbers document (currently RFC 1700). Appendix F excerpts RFC 1700 for your reference.

Chapter 3 discusses various MIBs in detail. This chapter now looks at the structure of trees applicable to the Internet Standard Network Management Framework. The Internet Standard MIB is defined by {mgmt 1} or {1.3.6.1.2.1}. Under this tree are objects defined by MIB-II (RFC 1213), such as the remote network monitoring (RMON) MIB, (RFC 1757), and many others.

Let's now return to the example given at the beginning of this section. Now that you know the identities of the individual tree structures, we can construct the following sequence:

```
internet OBJECT IDENTIFIER ::= {iso org(3) dod(6) 1 }
mgmt OBJECT IDENTIFIER ::= { internet 2 }
mib OBJECT IDENTIFIER ::= { mgmt 1 }
system OBJECT IDENTIFIER ::= { mib-2 1 }
sysDescr OBJECT IDENTIFIER ::= { system 1 }
```

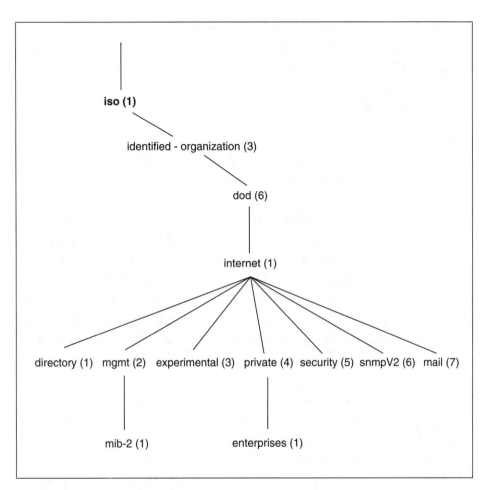

Figure 2-18 Internet assigned OBJECT IDENTIFIER component values

When these tree structures are combined, the result becomes:

sysDescr OBJECT IDENTIFIER ::= { 1.3.6.1.2.1.1.1 }

To the OID we need to add one last element—a suffix that identifies whether a particular variable occurs just once (a *scalar*) or whether the variable occurs multiple times (as in *columnar* entries).

Since sysDescr is a scalar, not columnar, object, there is only one instance of it. (In other words, you can have only one description of the system being managed.) Therefore, a .0 is added to the end of the OID:

{1.3.6.1.2.1.1.1.0.}

If the object was a columnar entry, which could have multiple instances, an index plus a nonzero suffix (.1, .2, an IP address, and so on) would identify the object within the table. Chapter 3 discusses tables in greater detail.

Experimental codes, with prefix {1.3.6.1.3}, have been assigned for many LAN and WAN objects and MIBs, such as ISO CLNS (Connectionless Network Service), the Synchronous Optical Network (SONET) objects, and Asynchronous Transfer Mode (ATM) objects, while the technologies and their MIBs were in the testing phase of development. Thus as the Internet Engineering Task Force (IETF) working groups develop MIBs, they define them under a branch in the experimental tree. Once these MIBs are published and put on the standards track, they move to a branch on the Internet subtree.

Vendor-specific MIBs use private enterprise codes with prefix {1.3.6.1.4.1}. This is an area of rapid growth, because numerous vendors are developing structures to support their Internetworking devices, servers, and so on. Examples include 3Com Corporation (Santa Clara, CA) with code {1.3.6.1.4.1.43}; FTP Software Inc. (North Andover, MA) with code {1.3.6.1.4.1.121}; and US West Advanced Technologies (Denver, CO) with code {1.3.6.1.4.1.312}. Appendix F includes a complete listing of the currently assigned private enterprise codes. Readers with Internet access may obtain this information from:

ftp://venera.isi.edu/mib/snmp-vendor-contacts

2.7 The Concise SMI Definition

Perhaps the best way to summarize this chapter is to include a module entitled RFC1155-SMI from RFC 1155, shown in Definition 2-1. This module defines all of the constructs discussed in this chapter and puts them in a form that will be useful in Chapters 3, 4, and 5. Note that a revision in RFC 1212

[2-9] makes the OBJECT-TYPE macro originally given in RFC 1155 obsolete. In the interest of timeliness, the SMI definition includes the new OBJECT-TYPE macro. Comment lines enclosed within angle brackets (<...>) indicate the beginning and end of the revised section from RFC 1212.

Definition 2-1. Concise SMI Definition

```
RFC1155-SMI DEFINITIONS ::= BEGIN
    EXPORTS -- EVERYTHING
    internet, directory, mgmt,
    experimental, private, enterprises,
    OBJECT-TYPE, ObjectName, ObjectSyntax,SimpleSyntax,
    ApplicationSyntax, NetworkAddress, IpAddress,
    Counter, Gauge, TimeTicks, Opaque;
    -- the path to the root (from RFC 1155)
    internet  OBJECT IDENTIFIER ::= { iso org(3) dod(6) 1 }
    directory  OBJECT IDENTIFIER ::= { internet 1 }
    mgmt  OBJECT IDENTIFIER ::= { internet 2 }
    experimental  OBJECT IDENTIFIER ::= { internet 3 }
    private      OBJECT IDENTIFIER ::= { internet 4 }
    enterprises  OBJECT IDENTIFIER ::= { private 1 }


  < definition of object types (taken from RFC 1212) >

OBJECT-TYPE MACRO ::=
    BEGIN
      TYPE NOTATION ::=
              -- must conform to
              -- RFC1155's ObjectSyntax
              "SYNTAX" type(ObjectSyntax)
              "ACCESS" Access
              "STATUS" Status
              DescrPart
              ReferPart
              IndexPart
```

```
            DefValPart
VALUE NOTATION ::= value (VALUE ObjectName)
Access ::= "read-only"
         | "read-write"
         | "write-only"
         | "not-accessible"
Status ::= "mandatory"
         | "optional"
         | "obsolete"
         | "deprecated"
DescrPart ::=
    "DESCRIPTION" value (description DisplayString)
         | empty
ReferPart ::=
    "REFERENCE" value (reference DisplayString)
         | empty
IndexPart ::=
    "INDEX" "{" IndexTypes "}"
         | empty
  IndexTypes ::=
         IndexType | IndexTypes "," IndexType
  IndexType ::=
              -- if indexobject, use the SYNTAX
              -- value of the correspondent
              -- OBJECT-TYPE invocation
         value (indexobject ObjectName)
              -- otherwise use named SMI type
              -- must conform to IndexSyntax below
         | type (indextype)
DefValPart ::=
    "DEFVAL" "{" value (defvalue ObjectSyntax) "}"
         | empty
END
IndexSyntax ::=
```

```
        CHOICE {
          number
             INTEGER (0..MAX),
          string
             OCTET STRING,
          object
             OBJECT IDENTIFIER,
          address
             NetworkAddress,
          ipAddress
             IpAddress
        }
< names of objects in the MIB (taken from RFC 1155) >
ObjectName ::= OBJECT IDENTIFIER
-- syntax of objects in the MIB
   ObjectSyntax ::=
       CHOICE {
           simple
                 SimpleSyntax,
-- note that simple SEQUENCEs are not directly
-- mentioned here to keep things simple (i.e.,
-- prevent mis-use). However, application-wide
-- types which are IMPLICITly encoded simple
-- SEQUENCEs may appear in the following CHOICE
           application-wide
                 ApplicationSyntax
       }
SimpleSyntax ::=
     CHOICE {
        number
             INTEGER,
        string
             OCTET STRING,
        object
```

```
                    OBJECT IDENTIFIER,
                empty
                    NULL
            }
    ApplicationSyntax ::=
            CHOICE {
                address
                    NetworkAddress,
                counter
                    Counter,
                gauge
                    Gauge,
                ticks
                    TimeTicks,
                arbitrary
                    Opaque
    -- other application-wide types, as they are
    -- defined, will be added here
            }
    -- application-wide types
    NetworkAddress ::=
            CHOICE {
                internet
                    IpAddress
            }
    IpAddress ::=
     [APPLICATION 0]        -- in network-byte order
        IMPLICIT OCTET STRING (SIZE (4))
    Counter ::=
     [APPLICATION 1]
        IMPLICIT INTEGER (0..4294967295)
    Gauge ::=
     [APPLICATION 2]
        IMPLICIT INTEGER (0..4294967295)
```

```
TimeTicks ::=
 [APPLICATION 3]
     IMPLICIT INTEGER (0..4294967295)
Opaque ::=
 [APPLICATION 4]      -- arbitrary ASN.1 value,
     IMPLICIT OCTET STRING  --  "double-wrapped"
END
```

This concludes the discussion of the SMI for SNMP version 1. Chapter 3 will study Management Information Bases (MIBs).

2.8 References

[2-1]   Rose, M.T., and K. McCloghrie. "Structure and Identification of Management Information for TCP/IP-based Internets." *RFC 1155*, May 1990.

[2-2]   McCloghrie, K., and M.T. Rose, editors. "Management Information Base for Network Management of TCP/IP-based Internets: MIB-II." *RFC 1213*, March 1991.

[2-3]   J.D. Case, M. Fedor, M.L. Schoffstall, and C. Davin. "Simple Network Management Protocol (SNMP)." *RFC 1157*, May 1990.

[2-4]   International Organization for Standardization, Information Processing Systems: Open Systems Interconnection, Basic Reference Model-Part 4: Management framework, ISO 7498-4: 1989.

[2-5]   International Organization for Standardization, Information Technology: Abstract Syntax Notation One (ASN.1): Specification of Basic Notation, ISO/IEC 8824-1: 1995.

[2-6]   International Organization for Standardization, Information Technology: ASN.1 Encoding Rules: Specification of Basic Encoding Rules (BER), Canonical Encoding Rules (CER) and Distinguished Encoding Rules (DER), ISO/IEC 8825-1: 1995.

[2-7]   Steedman, Douglas. *Abstract Syntax Notation One (ASN.1), the Tutorial and Reference.* Isleworth, Middlesex, UK: Technology Appraisals, Ltd. ISBN 1-871802-06-7, 1990.

[2-8]   Motteler, Howard, and Deepinder Sidhu. "Components of OSI: Abstract Syntax Notation One (ASN.1)." *ConneXions, the Interoperability Report* (January 1992): 2–19.

[2-9]   Rose, M., and K. McCloghrie. "Concise MIB Definitions." *RFC 1212*, March 1991.

[2-10]   Gaudett, Philip. "A Tutorial on ASN.1." NIST *Technical Report NCSL/SNA-89/12* (May 1989).

[2-11]   Perkins, Dave. "How to Read and Use an SNMP MIB." *3TECH, the 3Com Technical Journal* (Spring 1991): 31–55.

3 Management Information Bases

This chapter is the second of three to discuss Internet network management standards. Chapter 2 discussed the SMI, which defines the syntax that retrieves and communicates information, the ways information is placed into logical groups, and the naming mechanisms, known as the object identifiers, that identify each managed object.

This chapter extends the discussion of naming mechanisms to include *management information bases* (MIBs), which store management information. Chapter 4 considers the protocol mechanisms, including SNMP, the User Datagram Protocol (UDP), the Internet Protocol (IP), and the Internet Control Message Protocol (ICMP), that communicate management information.

You can think of a MIB as a virtual information warehouse. Like a physical warehouse with specific floors, aisles, and bins, the MIB must implement an inventory control scheme. SMI defines the scheme for the MIBs. Just as a large company can have several warehouses, there are several different types of MIBs. Some, such as Internet standards, are for public use; specific organizations have developed others for private use for their products.

Network managers must understand the concepts underlying the SMI and learn to apply them to the available MIBs.

3.1 MIBs within the Internet Object Identifier Subtree

Section 2.6 discussed the Internet network management naming structure. A tree represents the management structure, with branches and leaves representing the managed objects (Figure 3-1). This discussion focuses on the Internet subtree, designated {1.3.6.1}. In the figure, you can see seven subtrees under Internet: directory (1), mgmt (2), experimental (3), private (4), security (5), snmpV2 (6), and mail (7).

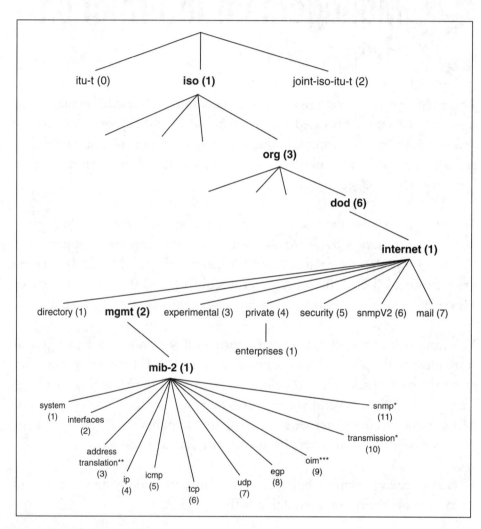

Figure 3-1. The Internet OID tree

The directory (1) subtree is reserved for future use of the OSI directory within the Internet. The mgmt (2) subtree handles Internet-approved documents, such as the Internet standard MIBs, which are MIB-I (see RFC 1156) and

MIB-II (see RFC 1213). An object identifier (OID) with a prefix of {1.3.6.1.2.1} denotes managed objects within MIB-I and MIB-II.

Internet experiments use the experimental subtree (3). The Internet Assigned Numbers Authority (IANA) at the USC-Information Sciences Institute (e-mail iana@isi.edu) administers this subtree.

The private subtree (4) allows vendors to register a MIB for their equipment. The enterprise subtree, whose branches are private organizations, falls under the private subtree. The IANA assigns "enterprise codes" to branches representing private organizations and publishes them in the current assigned numbers RFC (currently RFC 1700). Enterprise OIDs begin with the prefix {1.3.6.1.4.1}. Appendix F lists the currently assigned enterprise codes.

This chapter focuses primarily on the mgmt MIBs. MIB-I was the first version of the mgmt MIBs and was defined in RFC 1156 ([reference 3-1]). MIB-II (RFC 1213) {3.2} replaced the earlier version. This chapter also discusses the *remote network monitoring* (RMON) MIBs for Ethernet and token ring networks, which are also under the mgmt subtree. Other subtrees contain objects for security, SNMP version 2 (which will be discussed in Chapter 5), and mail.

3.2. MIB Development

As noted previously, MIBs address the need for a standard network management platform by the Internet as a whole and by private enterprises. These MIBs require a consistent objective and format to realize this objective. Let's begin by discussing the history of various MIBs so you can see the basis of these developments.

3.2.1 MIB-I—RFC 1156

The first MIB, MIB-I (RFC 1156), was published in May 1990. MIB-I divided managed objects into eight groups in order to simplify OID assignment and implementation (that is, the SMI "structure"). Those groups were System, Interfaces, Address Translation, IP, ICMP, TCP, UDP, and EGP. Elements from RFC 1212, The Concise MIB Definitions, and RFC 1213, known as MIB-II and published in March 1991, have replaced MIB-I.

3.2.2 Concise MIB Definitions—RFC 1212

With different private enterprises developing MIBs, it's necessary to develop a consistent format for MIB modules. RFC 1212, entitled "Concise MIB Definitions," addresses this issue [3-3]. Prior to the publication of RFC 1212, there were two ways to define objects: a textual definition and the ASN.1 OBJECT-TYPE macro, which is discussed in Section 2.4.1. RFC 1212 embedded the textual definition within the OBJECT-TYPE macro, reducing the amount of documentation. The Concise SMI Definition includes this macro (review Section 2.7).

3.2.3 Elements of the OBJECT-TYPE macro

Since the OBJECT-TYPE macro seems cryptic to most people, a few words of explanation are in order. Each object has a number of attributes: SYNTAX, ACCESS, STATUS, DESCRIPTION, REFERENCE, INDEX, and DEFVAL. (David Perkins' and Evan McGinnis' book *Understanding SNMP MIBs* [3-4] provides all the details.)

SYNTAX defines the object's data structure. Simple data types such as INTEGER, OCTET STRING, or NULL are examples of these data structures. SYNTAX also defines special cases of the simple objects, including an enumerated integer that defines an integer value, and a DisplayString restricted to printable ASCII characters. Table objects use the SEQUENCE OF syntax.

ACCESS defines the minimum level of access to (or support of) an object. ACCESS may have values of read-only, read-write, not-accessible, or write-only. SNMP does not permit the write-only value. Table or row objects define ACCESS to be not-accessible.

STATUS defines the implementation support for the object, which may be mandatory, optional, deprecated (discouraged), or obsolete. When STATUS defines a level of support for a particular group, that level applies to all objects within the group. Objects that have been replaced by backwards-compatible objects are "deprecated." Objects that are no longer supported are "obsolete."

DESCRIPTION, which is not always present, provides a textual definition of an object type. REFERENCE, also not necessarily present, is a textual cross-reference to an object defined by another MIB module.

INDEX works only with row objects. It indexes the order in which objects appear in a row, that is, the column order.

Agents use DEFVAL, also optional, to populate values of columnar objects. For example, when an SNMP agent creates a new row, the DEFVAL clause assigns a default value to the objects within the row. For example, an OCTET STRING object may have a DEFVAL clause of 'FFFFFFFFFFFF'H.

3.2.4 Defining Table Structures in MIBs

To put all of the information discussed in the previous sections in perspective, Definition 3-1 (taken from RFC 1213) dissects the elements of a table. The italicized text after each section is my explanation. Double hyphens (--) indicate a comment line within the table structure. The comment defines the purpose of the table.

Definition 3-1. Defining the UDP Listener table from RFC 1213

```
-- the UDP Listener table
-- The UDP listener table contains information about this
-- entity's UDP end-points on which a local application is
-- currently accepting datagrams.

udpTable      OBJECT-TYPE
      SYNTAX   SEQUENCE OF UdpEntry
      ACCESS   not-accessible
      STATUS   mandatory
      DESCRIPTION
            "A table containing UDP listener information."
      ::= { udp 5 }
```

The object name (or table name) udpTable identifies a table object. Note that this name begins with a lowercase letter. The SYNTAX defines a SEQUENCE OF UdpEntry. This refers to a type definition (listed below) that defines the objects that make up each row of the table.

```
udpEntry        OBJECT-TYPE
      SYNTAX   UdpEntry
      ACCESS   not-accessible
      STATUS   mandatory
      DESCRIPTION
              "Information about a particular current UDP listener."
      INDEX  { udpLocalAddress, udpLocalPort }
      ::= { udpTable 1 }
```

The object name (or row name) udpEntry defines each row of the table. The INDEX clause specifies instances for columnar objects in the table. The instance values determine the order in which the objects are retrieved.

```
UdpEntry ::=
    SEQUENCE {
        udpLocalAddress IpAddress,
        udpLocalPort INTEGER (0..65535)
    }
```

The type definition UdpEntry identifies the objects that make up the row. Note that the type definition, often called a sequence name, is the same as the row name except that it begins with an uppercase letter. Each row has two columns, the udpLocalAddress (an IpAddress type) and the udpLocalPort (an INTEGER type).

```
udpLocalAddress  OBJECT-TYPE
      SYNTAX      IpAddress
      ACCESS      read-only
      STATUS      mandatory
      DESCRIPTION
```

"The local IP address for this UDP listener. A UDP listener willing to accept
datagrams for any IP interface associated with the node, uses the value 0.0.0.0."
::= { udpEntry 1 }

*The notation { udpEntry 1 } indicates the first column in the table. The SYNTAX is a
defined type, IpAddress. The description provides the address {0.0.0.0}.*

udpLocalPort   OBJECT-TYPE
        SYNTAX   INTEGER (0..65535)
        ACCESS   read-only
        STATUS   mandatory
        DESCRIPTION
                "The local port number for this UDP listener."
::= { udpEntry 2 }

*The notation { udpEntry 2 } indicates the second column in the table. The SYNTAX is
an INTEGER type, with values ranging from 0 to 65,535.*

An example of this table would be:

Local Address	Local Port
0.0.0.0	69 (TFTP)
0.0.0.0	161 (SNMP)
0.0.0.0	520 (Router)

In this example, the table contains three rows and two columns. All local
addresses are [0.0.0.0], which indicates that the table is willing to accept IP
datagrams from any address on this port.

Definition 3-2 is a second example of a table, the Ethernet Statistics table,
which comes from the RMON MIB, RFC 1757.

Definition 3-2. The Ethernet Statistics table from RFC 1757

```
-- The Ethernet Statistics Group
--
-- Implementation of the Ethernet Statistics group is
-- optional.
--
-- The Ethernet Statistics group contains statistics
-- measured by the probe for each monitored interface on
-- this device. These statistics take the form of free
-- running counters that start from zero when a valid entry
-- is created.
--
-- This group currently has statistics defined only for
-- Ethernet interfaces. Each etherStatsEntry contains
-- statistics for one Ethernet interface. The probe must
-- create one etherStats entry for each monitored Ethernet
-- interface on the device.

        etherStatsTable OBJECT-TYPE
                SYNTAX SEQUENCE OF EtherStatsEntry
                ACCESS not-accessible
                STATUS mandatory
                DESCRIPTION
                  "A list of Ethernet statistics entries."
                ::= { statistics 1 }
```

The object name (or table name) etherStatsTable begins with a lowercase letter, indicating a Value (see Section 2.3.4). The associated syntax definition is a sequence of the EtherStatsEntry, which begins with an uppercase letter to indicate a Type. This object is nonaccessible because it is a table. The status is mandatory, meaning all implementations must support this object. A description of the object is "A list of Ethernet statistics entries." The { statistics 1 } designation indicates that this table is the first subtree under the statistics group.

etherStatsEntry OBJECT-TYPE
       SYNTAX   EtherStatsEntry
       ACCESS   not-accessible
       STATUS   mandatory
       DESCRIPTION
               "A collection of statistics kept for a particular
               Ethernet interface. As an example, an instance of the
               etherStatsPkts object might be named etherStatsPkts.1"
       INDEX { etherStatsIndex }
       ::= { etherStatsTable 1 }

The object value (etherStatsEntry) ends with "Entry." This identifies a table row
object. The index clause specifies the columns within each row that form the table.
This object is the first object under the etherStatsTable subtree.

    EtherStatsEntry ::= SEQUENCE {
    etherStatsIndex   INTEGER (1..65535),
    etherStatsDataSource   OBJECT IDENTIFIER,
    etherStatsDropEvents   Counter,
    etherStatsOctets   Counter,
    etherStatsPkts   Counter,
    etherStatsBroadcastPkts   Counter,
    etherStatsMulticastPkts   Counter,
    etherStatsCRCAlignErrors   Counter,
    etherStatsUndersizePkts   Counter,
    etherStatsOversizePkts   Counter,
    etherStatsFragments   Counter,
    etherStatsJabbers   Counter,
    etherStatsCollisions   Counter,
    etherStatsPkts64Octets   Counter,
    etherStatsPkts65to127Octets   Counter,
    etherStatsPkts128to255Octets   Counter,
    etherStatsPkts256to511Octets   Counter,
    etherStatsPkts512to1023Octets   Counter,
    etherStatsPkts1024to1518Octets   Counter,

```
        etherStatsOwner              OwnerString,
        etherStatsStatus             EntryStatus
        }
```

The syntax of the etherStatsTable is a sequence of EtherStatsEntry. The sequence contains 21 objects that will make up the columns of each row.

```
etherStatsIndex    OBJECT-TYPE
        SYNTAX       INTEGER (1..65535)
        ACCESS       read-only
        STATUS       mandatory
        DESCRIPTION
                    "The value of this object uniquely identifies this
                    etherStats entry."
        ::= { etherStatsEntry 1 }
```

The etherStatsIndex object may take on a value between 1 and 65,545. This index determines how the various objects will be retrieved.

3.3 MIB I and MIB II Groups

Managed objects are arranged into groups for two reasons. First, a logical grouping facilitates the use of the object identifiers and tree structure discussed in Section 3.1. Second, it makes the SNMP agent design more straightforward because the implementation of a group implies the implementation of all objects within the group. Thus, both the software developer and the end user can clearly understand a statement of support for, say, the TCP Group.

The next sections discuss the Internet standard MIB-I (RFC 1156) and MIB-II (RFC 1213) managed objects. MIB-I contained 114 objects. MIB-II, which is backward-compatible with MIB-I, contains these 114 objects plus 57 more, for a total of 171 objects. Chris VandenBerg's article [3-5] discusses the MIB-II enhancements. Appendix G details the various objects.

3.3.1 The System Group

The System group provides a textual description of the entity in printable ASCII characters. This text includes a system description, OID, the length of time since the reinitialization of its network management entity, and other administrative details. Implementation of the System group is mandatory. The OID tree for the System group is designated {1.3.6.1.2.1.1}, as shown in Figure 3-2.

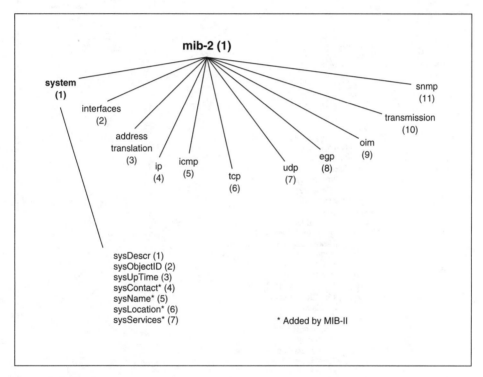

Figure 3-2. The System group

3.3.2 The Interfaces Group

The Interfaces group {1.3.6.1.2.1.2} provides information about the hardware interfaces on a managed device, as shown in Figure 3-3. This information is presented in a table. The first object (ifNumber) indicates the number of interfaces on the device. For each interface, a row entry is made into the table,

107

with 22 column entries per row. The column entries provide information about the interfaces, such as the interface speed, physical (hardware) address, current operational state, and packet statistics.

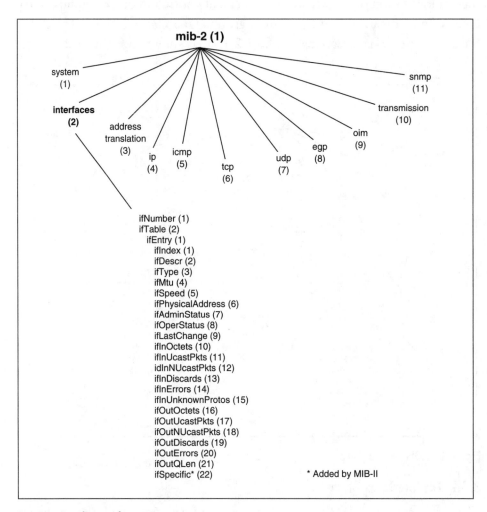

Figure 3-3. The Interfaces group

3.3.3 The Address Translation Group

MIB-I included the Address Translation group, shown in Figure 3-4, but it was deprecated in MIB-II. The "deprecated" status means that MIB-II includes the Address Translation group for compatibility with MIB-I, but will probably exclude it from future MIB releases. The Address Translation group provided a table that translated between IP addresses and physical (hardware) addresses. In MIB-II and future releases, each protocol group will contain its own translation tables. The Address Translation group is designated {1.3.6.1.2.1.3}. It contains one table with three columns per row.

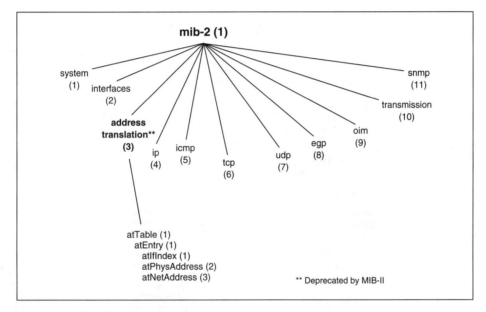

Figure 3-4. The Address Translation group

3.3.4 The IP Group

The Internet Protocol (IP) group, shown in Figure 3-5, is mandatory for all managed nodes and provides information on host and router use of the IP. This group includes a number of scalar objects that provide IP-related datagram statistics and the following three tables: an address table (ipAddrTable); an IP to physical address translation table (ipNetToMediaTable); and an IP forwarding table (ipForwardTable). Note that RFC 1354 defined the ipForwardTable, which replaces and obsoletes the ipRoutingTable in MIB-II. The IP subtree is designated {1.3.6.1.2.1.4}.

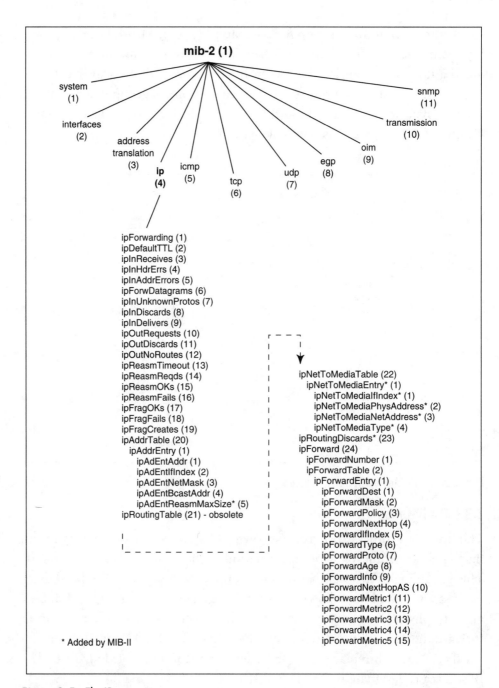

Figure 3-5. The IP group

3.3.5 The ICMP Group

The Internet Control Message Protocol (ICMP) group, shown in Figure 3-6, is a mandatory component of IP and is defined in RFC 792. The ICMP group provides intranetwork control messages and represents various ICMP operations within the managed entity. The ICMP group contains 26 scalar objects that maintain statistics for various ICMP messages, such as the number of ICMP Echo Request messages received or ICMP Redirect messages sent. This group is designated {1.3.6.1.2.1.5} on the OID tree.

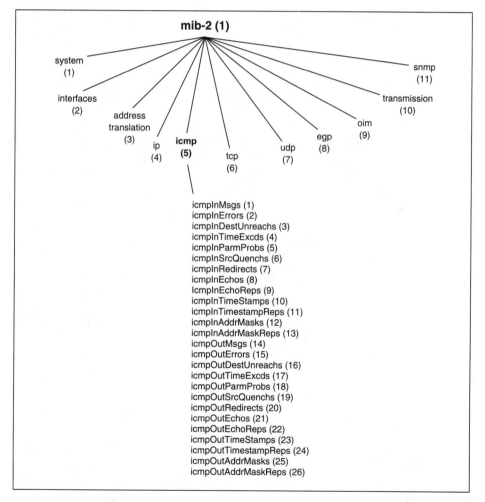

Figure 3-6. The ICMP group

3.3.6 The TCP Group

The Transmission Control Protocol (TCP) group, shown in Figure 3-7, is mandatory and provides information regarding TCP operation and connections. This group contains 14 scalar objects and one table. The scalar objects record various TCP parameters and statistics, such as the number of TCP connections that the device supports, or the total number of TCP segments transmitted. The table, tcpConnTable, contains information concerning a particular TCP connection. The OID for this group is {1.3.6.1.2.1.6}.

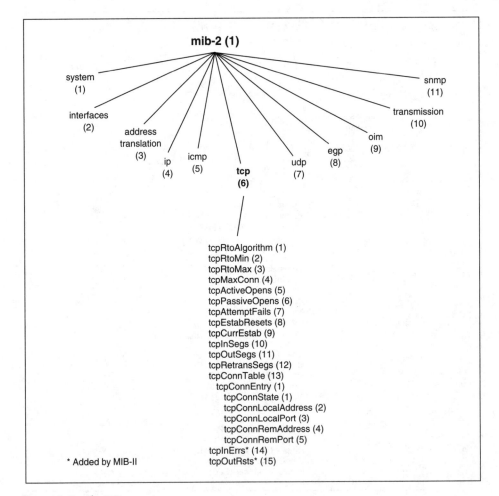

Figure 3-7. The TCP group

3.3.7 The UDP Group

The User Datagram Protocol (UDP) group, shown in Figure 3-8, is mandatory and provides information regarding UDP operation. Because UDP is connectionless, this group is much smaller than the connection-oriented TCP group. It does not have to compile information on connection attempts, establishment, reset, and so on. The UDP group contains four scalars and one table. The scalar objects maintain UDP-related datagram statistics, such as the number of datagrams sent from this entity. The table, udpTable, contains address and port information. The OID for this group is {1.3.6.1.2.1.7}.

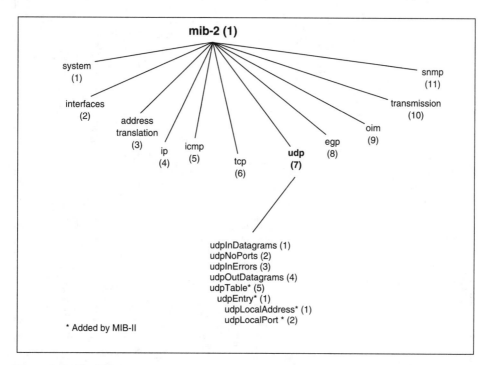

Figure 3-8. The UDP group

3.3.8 The EGP Group

The Exterior Gateway Protocol (EGP) group, shown in Figure 3-9, is mandatory for all systems that implement the EGP. The EGP communicates between autonomous (self-contained) systems, and RFC 904 describes it in detail. The

EGP group includes 5 scalar objects and one table. The scalars maintain EGP-related message statistics. The table, egpNeighTable, contains EGP neighbor information. The OID for this group is {1.3.6.1.2.1.8}.

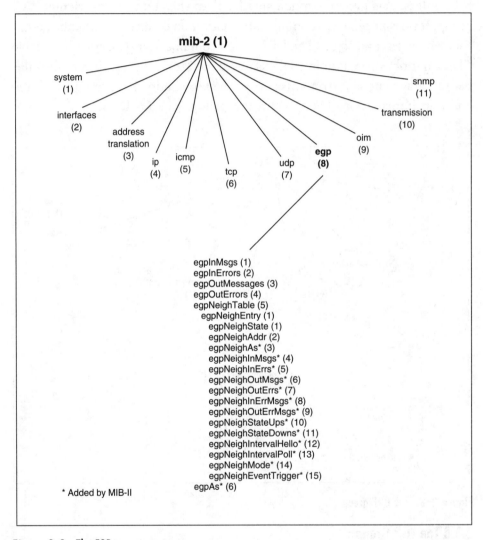

Figure 3-9. The EGP group

3.3.9 The CMOT (OIM) Group

At one time, during the development of the Internet Network Management Framework, there was an effort to use SNMP as an interim step in the push for a network management standard, and to make the Common Management Information Protocol (CMIP) over TCP/IP (CMOT) the long-term, OSI-compliant solution. As a result, the CMOT group was placed within MIB-II. Experience has shown, however, that SNMP is not an interim solution, and that the OSI-related network management protocol requires unique MIBs. Therefore, it's unlikely that you'll encounter the OIM group within any commercially available SNMP managers or agents.

Nonetheless, the CMOT group was given a placeholder of {1.3.6.1.2.1.9 } in MIB-II (review Figure 3-1). RFC 1214 details that subtree, which specifies the OSI Internet Management (OIM) MIB [3-6]. At this time, RFC 1214 is classified as a "historic" protocol.

3.3.10 The Transmission Group

The Transmission group, shown in Figure 3-10 and designated {1.3.6.1.2.1.10}, contains objects that relate to the transmission of the data. RFC 1213 defines none of these objects explicitly. However, the document does say that these transmission objects will reside in the experimental subtree {1.3.6.1.3} until they are "proven."

The "Assigned Numbers" document (currently RFC 1700 [3-7]) lists the following objects under the Transmission group:

➤   X25 – X.25 Packet layer objects

➤   IEEE802.3—CSMA/CD-like objects

➤   IEEE802.4—Token Bus-like objects

➤   dot5—Token Ring-like objects

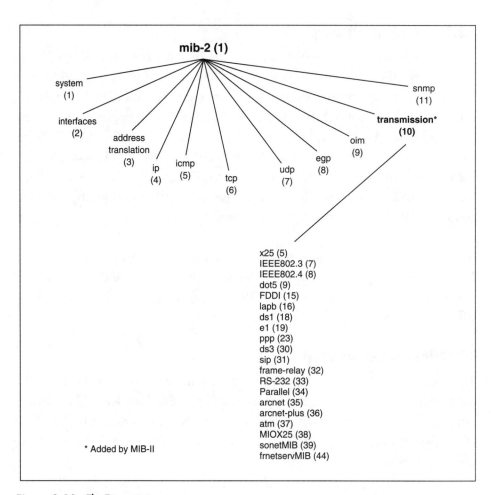

Figure 3-10. The Transmission group

➤ FDDI—FDDI objects

➤ LAPB—X.25 LAPB objects

➤ DS1—T1 carrier objects

➤ E1—E1 carrier objects

➤ PPP—Point-to-Point Protocol objects

➤ DS3/E3—DS3/E3 Interface objects

➤ SIP—SMDS interface objects

➤ FRAME-RELAY—Frame Relay objects

➤ RS-232—RS-232 objects

➤ Parallel—Parallel printer objects

➤ ARCNET—ARC network objects

➤ ARCNET-PLUS—ARC network plus objects

➤ ATM—ATM objects

➤ MIOX25 —Multiprotocol interconnect over X.25 objects

➤ SONET—SONET objects

➤ FRNETSERV—Frame Relay service MIB for DCE objects

RFC 1700 also lists other RFC references that provide details on these transmission types. By way of example, the sections below describe some of the transmission media MIBs that have been defined for broadband networks.

3.3.10.1 The DS1/E1 MIB

DS1 and E1 objects are designated by {transmission 18}, with OID {1.3.6.2.1.10.18}, as shown in Figure 3-11. This MIB module consists of three groups: the DS1 Near End group, the DS1 Far End group, and the Fractional Table. The DS1 Near End group consists of four tables that contain configuration information and statistics about the DS1 interface at the near end of the communications link. This group contains four tables: the DS1 Configuration Table, which specifies the line coding, circuit identifier, line status, and other configuration details; the DS1 Current Table, which contains statistics collected over the current 15-minute interval; the DS1 Interval Table, which contains statistics collected over the previous 24 hours, broken into 96 complete 15-minute intervals; and the DS1 Far End Total Table, which contains the cumulative sum of various statistics for the 24 hours preceding the current interval.

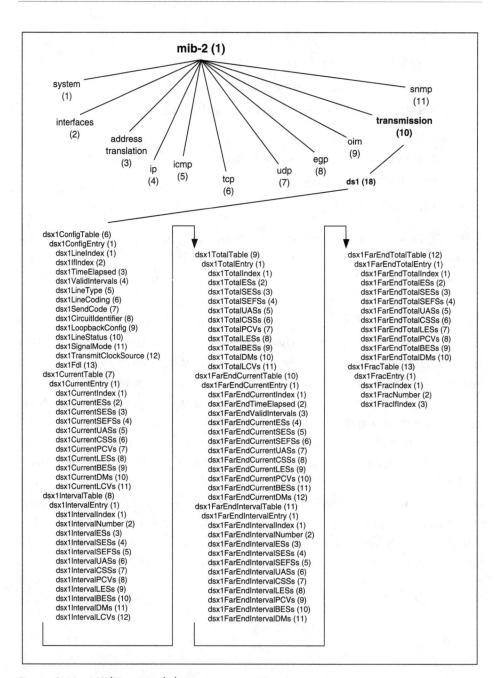

Figure 3-11. DS1/E1 managed objects

The Fractional Table contains information regarding channels derived from subdividing DS1, such as a 64 Kbps channel used for voice traffic, or a 384 Kbps channel used for data traffic.

RFC 1406 [3-8] discusses details of the DS1/E1 MIB, as well as DS1 error events, performance defects, performance parameters, and failure states.

3.3.10.2 The DS3/E3 MIB

DS3 and E3 objects are designated by {transmission 30}, with OID {1.3.6.1.2.1.10.30}, as shown in Figure 3-12. This MIB module is similar in structure to the DS1 module discussed in the section above. It places DS3 objects in three groups: the DS3/E3 Near End Group, the DS3 Far End Group, or the DS3 Fractional Group. The tables and objects within those groups are similar to those for DS1/E1.

RFC 1407 [3-9] discusses details of the DS3/E3 MIBas well as explanation of the DS3 error events, performance parameters, and perfomance defects.

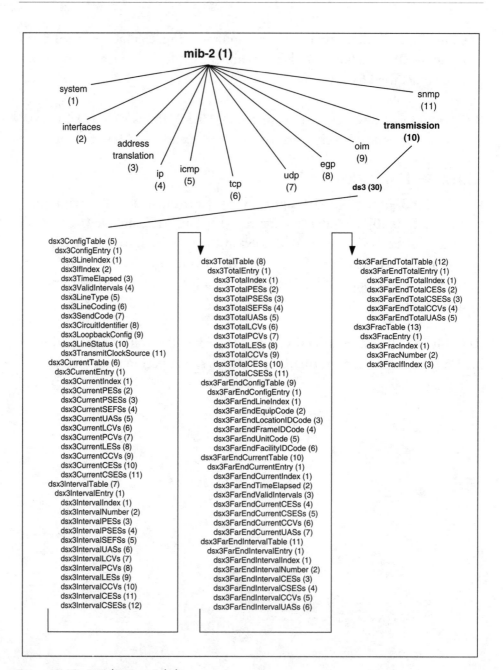

Figure 3-12. DS3/E3 Managed objects

3.3.10.3 The SONET/SDH MIB

The SONET and SDH objects are designated by {transmission 39}, with OID {1.3.6.1.2.10.39}, as shown in Figure 3-13. This MIB module contains eight groups.

The SONET/SDH Medium Group contains configuration information for optical and electrical SONET/SDH interfaces. The SONET/SDH Section group contains two tables that pertain to the SONET/SDH Section Layer: the SONET Section Current Table, with current statistics collected over a 15-minute interval; and the SONET/SDH Section Interval Table, with statistics collected over the previous 24 hours. The SONET/SDH Line group contains interval and current tables that pertain to the SONET/SDH Line layer. The SONET/SDH Far End Line group is implemented for systems that provide for FEBE information at the SONET/SDH Line layer; it contains both current and interval tables. The SONET/SDH Path and SONET/SDH Far End Path groups contain current interval information regarding the SONET/SDH Path layer. Finally, the SONET/SDH Virtual Tributary (VT) and SONET/SDH Far End VT groups contain current and interval information regarding the SONET/SDH VT Layer.

Details of the SONET/SDH are discussed in RFC 1595 [3-10], which is considered a companion document to the DS1/E1 and DS3/E3 MIBs. The SONET/SDH MIB also includes a listing of applicable terms and error conditions.

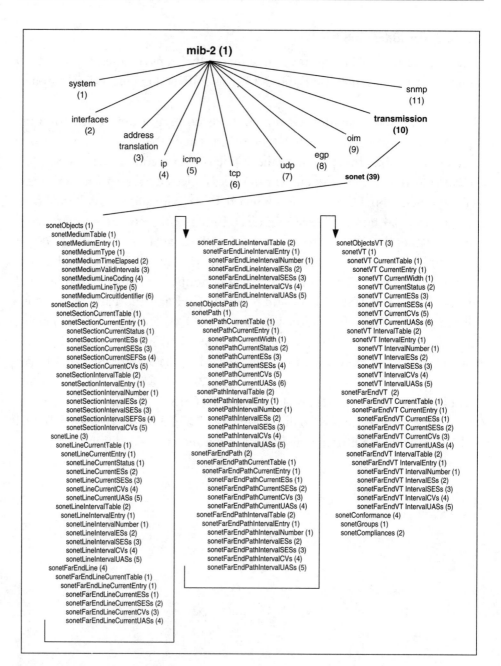

Figure 3-13. SONET managed objects

3.3.10.4 The Frame Relay DTE MIB

Frame relay DTE objects are designated by {transmission 32}, with OID {1.3.6.1.2.1.10.32}, as shown in Figure 3-14. This module contains three principle groups: the Data Link Connection Management Interface (DLCMI) group, the Circuits group, and the Errors group.

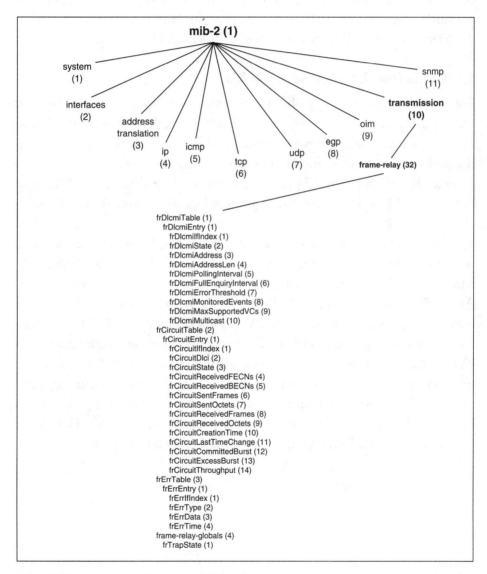

Figure 3-14. Frame relay DTE managed objects

The DLCMI group contains variables that configure the DLCMI, such as the Address field length, the interval between T1.617 Annex D STATUS ENQUIRY messages, the maximum number of virtual circuits on this interface, and so on. The Circuit group contains one table with information regarding specific DLCIs and their corresponding virtual circuits. The Error group contains one table that describes errors that have occurred on that frame relay interface. A fourth group, Frame-Relay-Globals, contains trap information. Details of the Frame Relay DTE MIB are discussed in RFC 1315 [3-11].

3.3.10.5 The Frame Relay Network Service MIB

Frame relay network service objects are designated by {transmission 44}, with OID {1.3.6.1.2.1.10.44} (as shown in Figure 3-15). This MIB is intended for CNM of a frame relay network service and lets customers obtain details of the performance, faults, and configuration about their frame relay network service. The network's SNMP proxy agent obtains those details. A PVC between that agent and the customer constitutes the logical transmission path.

This MIB module consists of seven groups. The Frame Relay Logical Port group is an addendum to the ifTable found in MIB-II (RFC 1213). The Frame Relay Management VC Signaling group contains objects that relate to the T1.617 Annex D signaling channel. The PVC End-Point group identifies traffic parameters and provides statistics for a PVC segment end-point. The Frame Relay PVC Connection group models PVC information flows and connections. The PVC Connection Table contains connection information. The PVC Accounting on a Frame Relay Logical Port basis group contains additional accounting information. Two additional groups define traps and conformance information. Details of the Frame Relay Service MIB are discussed in RFC 1604 [3-12]. This MIB also includes a listing of applicable frame relay terms and parameters.

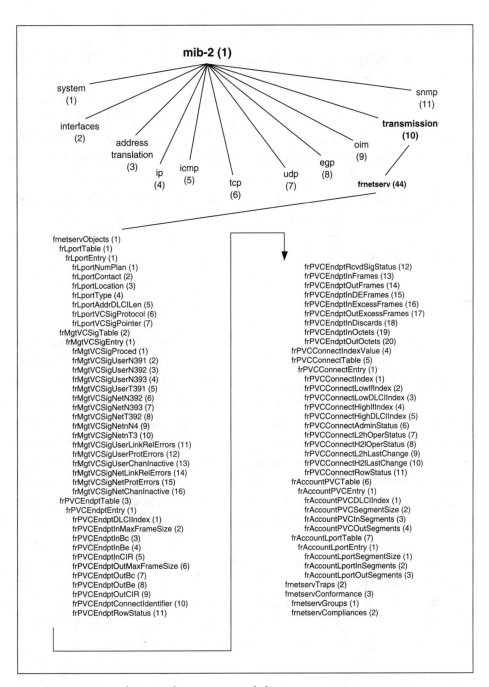

Figure 3-15. Frame relay network service managed objects

3.3.10.6 The SIP Interface MIB

SIP objects are designated by {transmission 31} with OID {1.3.6.1.2.1.10.31}, as shown in Figure 3-16. This MIB module consists of six groups. The SIP Level 3 group contains SIP L3 parameters and state variables. The SIP Level 2 group contains SIP L2 parameters and state variables. The SIP PLCP group contains tables with both DS1 and DS3 PLCP parameters and state variables. The SMDS Applications group is used with IP over SMDS (from RFC 1209). The SMDS Carrier Selection group is a place holder for carrier-selection objects. The SIP Error Log group is a table that contains SIP L3 PDU errors. RFC 1694 [3-13] provides details of the SIP Interface MIB.

3.3.10.7 The ATM MIB

ATM objects have OID {1.3.6.1.2.1.37}, as shown in Figure 3-17. This MIB module consists of nine groups.

The ATM Interface Configuration Parameters group contains configuration information associated with an ATM interface, which supplements the information provided in MIB-II. The ATM Interface DS3 PLCP group contains configuration and state parameters for DS3-based ATM interfaces. The ATM Interface TC Sublayer group contains Transmission Convergence configuration information and state parameters. The ATM Traffic Descriptor Parameter group contains traffic parameters such as the QoS class. The ATM Interface Virtual Path Link (VPL) group contains configuration and state information of a bidirectional VPL. The ATM Interfaces Virtual Channel Link (VCL) group contains configuration and state information of a bidirectional VCL. The ATM Virtual Path (VP) Cross Connect group contains configuration and state information of all point-to-point, point-to-multipoint, or multipoint-to-multipoint VP cross connects. The ATM Virtual Channel (VC) Cross Connect group contains configuration and state information of a bidirectional VC cross connect. The AAL5 Virtual Channel Connection (VCC) Performance Statistics group contains AAL5 VCC performance parameters.

RFC 1695 [3-14] defines the ATM MIB.

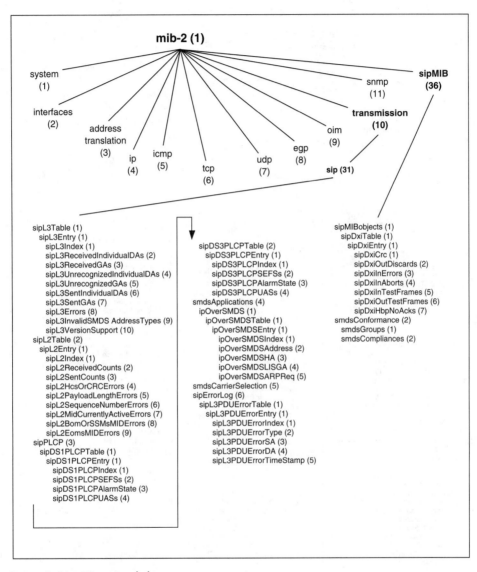

Figure 3-16. SIP managed objects

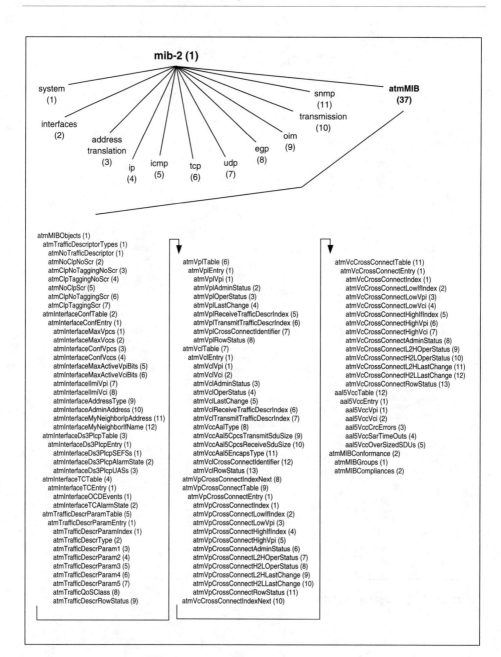

Figure 3-17. ATM managed objects

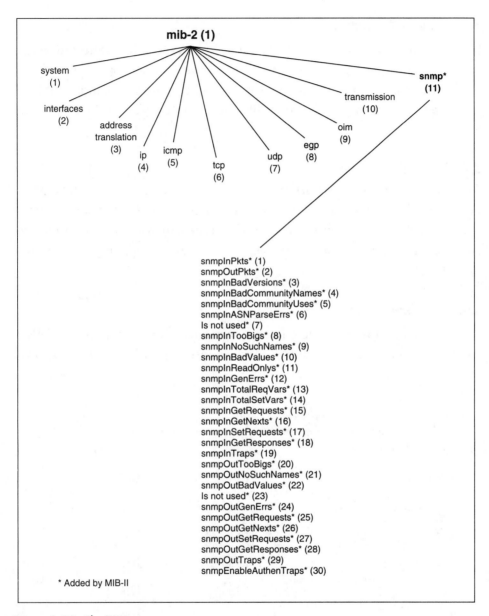

Figure 3-18. The SNMP group

3.3.11 The SNMP Group

Since this book is about SNMP, you should be especially interested in the SNMP group, which provides information about SNMP objects (see Figure 3-18). There are a total of 30 scalar objects in this group, including SNMP message statistics, the number of MIB objects retrieved, and the number of SNMP traps sent. This group is designated {1.3.6.1.2.1.11}.

3.4. Other MIBs

The growing need for network management in general, along with SNMP's popularity, has led to the definition of a number of MIBs that support specific network architectures or platforms. Included are MIBs to support a specific architecture, protocol, or interface, and those that support specific transmission media types.

3.4.1 Specific-use MIBs

The following table lists the currently approved Internet-standard MIBs included under the MIB-II subtree that support a specific architecture, protocol, or interface:

MIB	OID	RFC
Generic Interface Extensions	1.3.6.1.2.1.12	1229, 1239
Appletalk Protocols	1.3.6.1.2.1.13	1742
Open Shortest Path First (OSPF)	1.3.6.1.2.1.14	1253
Border Gateway Protocol (BGP)	1.3.6.1.2.1.15	1657
Remote Monitoring (RMON)	1.3.6.1.2.1.16	1757
Bridges	1.3.6.1.2.1.17	1286
DECnet Phase 4	1.3.6.1.2.1.18	1559
Character Streams	1.3.6.1.2.1.19	1658
SNMP Parties (Historic, see SNMPv2)	1.3.6.1.2.1.20	1353

SNMP Secrets (Historic, see SNMPv2)	1.3.6.1.2.1.21	1353
IEEE 802.3 Repeaters	1.3.6.1.2.1.22	1516
Routing Information Protocol	1.3.6.1.2.1.23	1389
Identification Protocol	1.3.6.1.2.1.24	1414
Host Resources	1.3.6.1.2.1.25	1514
IEEE 802.3 Medium Attachment Units	1.3.6.1.2.1.26	1515
Network Services Monitoring	1.3.6.1.2.1.27	1565
Mail Monitoring	1.3.6.1.2.1.28	1566
X.500 Directory Monitoring	1.3.6.1.2.1.29	1567
Interface Types	1.3.6.1.2.1.30	1573
Interface Types	1.3.6.1.2.1.31	1573
Domain Name System	1.3.6.1.2.1.32	1611
Uninterruptible Power Supplies	1.3.6.1.2.1.33	1628
SNA NAU	1.3.6.1.2.1.34	1666
Ethernet-like generic objects	1.3.6.1.2.1.35	1650
SMDS interface objects	1.3.6.1.2.1.36	1694
ATM objects	1.3.6.1.2.1.37	1695
Dial-up modem objects	1.3.6.1.2.1.38	1696
Relational database objects	1.3.6.1.2.1.39	1697
Traffic flow objects	1.3.6.1.2.1.40	2064
SNA SDLC	1.3.6.1.2.1.41	1747
Token Ring Station Source Route	1.3.6.1.2.1.42	1748
Printer	1.3.6.1.2.1.43	1759
Mobile IP	1.3.6.1.2.1.44	2006
IEEE 802.12	1.3.6.1.2.1.45	2020

Data Link Switch	1.3.6.1.2.1.46	2024
Entity	1.3.6.1.2.1.47	2037
Internet Protocol MIB Module	1.3.6.1.2.1.48	2011
TCP MIB Module	1.3.6.1.2.1.49	2012
UDP MIB Module	1.3.6.1.2.1.50	2013

3.4.2 Transmission Media MIBs

Other Internet-standard MIBs have been approved for specific transmission media, and are listed under the transmission subtree, {1.3.6.1.2.1.10}. As defined in RFC 1700, these include:

MIB	OID	RFC
X.25 Packet Layer objects	1.3.6.1.2.1.10.5	1382
CSMA/CD-like objects	1.3.6.1.2.1.10.7	1650
Token Bus-like objects	1.3.6.1.2.1.10.8	1230, 1239
Token Ring-like objects	1.3.6.1.2.1.10.9	1748
FDDI objects	1.3.6.1.2.1.10.15	1285, 1512
X.25 LAPB objects	1.3.6.1.2.1.10.16	1381
DS1 Interface objects	1.3.6.1.2.1.10.18	1406
E1 Interface objects	1.3.6.1.2.1.10.19	1406
PPP objects	1.3.6.1.2.1.10.23	1471
DS3/E3 Interface objects	1.3.6.1.2.1.10.30	1407
SMDS Interface objects	1.3.6.1.2.1.10.31	1694
Frame Relay objects	1.3.6.1.2.1.10.32	1315
RS-232 objects	1.3.6.1.2.1.10.33	1659

Parallel Printer objects	1.3.6.1.2.1.10.34	1660
ARCNET objects	1.3.6.1.2.1.10.35	N/A
ARCNETPLUS objects	1.3.6.1.2.1.10.36	N/A
ATM objects	1.3.6.1.2.1.10.37	1695
Multiprotocol Interconnect over X.25 (miox)	1.3.6.1.2.1.10.38	1461
SONET objects	1.3.6.1.2.1.10.39	1595
Frame relay network service objects	1.3.6.1.2.1.10.44	1695

For more up-to-date information, see the network management section of the "Assigned Numbers" document (currently RFC 1700), or the on-line version of the file (ftp://ftp.isi.edu/in-notes/iana/assignments/network-management-numbers).

3.5. The Ethernet RMON MIB

As networks have become increasingly distributed, geographically and logically, network management has become more challenging. One solution is to place remote management devices, sometimes called probes, on remote segments. The probes act as the eyes and ears of the network management system, providing managers with statistical information. The remote network monitoring (RMON) MIB standardizes the management information sent to and from these probes; it is presented in RFC 1757 [3-15]. A vendor-specific RMON implementation is the focus of "Continuous Monitoring of Remote Networks: The RMON MIB," in the April 1993 issue of *Hewlett-Packard Journal* [3-16]. References 3–17 through 3–23 discuss various applications of the RMON architecture.

The RMON MIB is assigned OID {1.3.6.1.2.1.16} and contains 9 groups. All of these groups are optional (not mandatory), but the implementation of some groups requires other groups. For example, the Filter group requires the Packet Capture group. The following is a summary of the nine Ethernet groups shown in Figure 3-19:

Group	Description
statistics (1)	Provides probe-measured statistics, such as the number and sizes of packets, broadcasts, collisions, and so on.
history (2)	Records periodic statistical samples over time that you can use to analyze trends.
alarm (3)	Compares statistical samples with preset thresholds, generating alarms when a particular threshold is crossed.
host (4)	Maintains statistics of the hosts on the network, including the MAC addresses of the active hosts.
hostTopN (5)	Provides reports sorted by host table statistics, indicating which hosts are at the top of the list in a particular category.
matrix (6)	Stores statistics in a traffic matrix that tracks conversations between pairs of hosts.
filter (7)	Allows packets to be matched according to a filter equation.
capture (8)	Allows packets to be captured after they pass through a logical channel.
event (9)	Controls the generation and notification of events, which may include SNMP trap messages.

The current standard, RFC 1757, addresses only Ethernet network monitoring. The next section will discuss the draft for the token ring extensions.

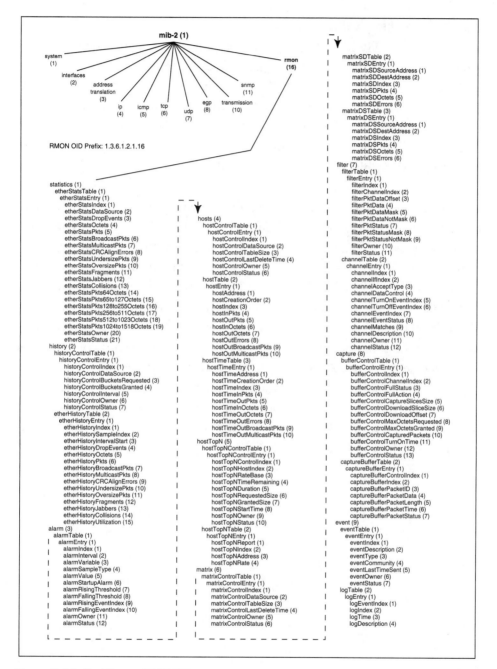

Figure 3-19. The Ethernet RMON MIB

3.6 The Token Ring RMON MIB

The token ring RMON MIB is under development as an extension to the Ethernet RMON MIB discussed in the previous section. Because of the popularity of token ring networks, this MIB has received a great deal of attention [3-24]. Recall that the Ethernet RMON MIB defines nine groups, Statistics through Events. The token ring RMON MIB extends two of these groups, Statistics and History, and adds one unique group. This new group is called tokenRing, with object identifier { rmon 10 }.

The statistics extensions allow an RMON-compatible device to collect token ring MAC-Layer errors and promiscuous errors. The MAC-Layer errors, such as token errors and frame-copied errors, are specific to the token ring protocol; the promiscuous errors, such as counting number of broadcast packages or data packets between 512 and 1023 octets in length, are more general. Similarly, the history information (discussed in Appendix G) is divided into MAC-Layer and promiscuous details. The token ring group contains four sub groups: ring station, which monitors station- and ring-specific events; ring station order, which tracks the network topology; ring station configuration, which controls the removal and/or configuration of stations on the ring; and source routing, which details source routing bridging information. Figure 3-20 illustrates these token ring additions; it also shows the major Ethernet groups for clarification. Reference [3-25] discusses test results of token ring RMON probes and managers.

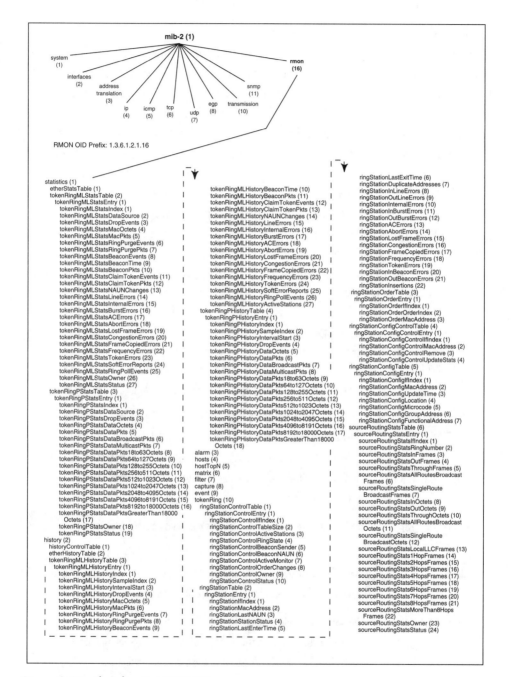

Figure 3-20. The token ring RMON MIB

3.7 RMON2

The original RMON MIBs for Ethernet and token ring networks are primarily concerned with the operation and management of the Physical and Data Link Layers of a remote network. As such, they can compile statistics and historical information regarding Ethernet collisions, token ring frame copied errors, and so on, but they cannot look into the operation of the OSI Network through Application layers of that remote network.

RMON2, defined in RFC 2021 [3-26], extends the RMON capabilities to those higher layers by adding 10 new groups, designated {rmon 11} through {rmon 20}. Figure 3-21 illustrates the OID branches for both RMON and RMON2. Thus, the higher layer protocols, such as TCP/IP or SPX/IPX, can be monitored for greater management visibility within the internetwork. The ten groups within RMON2 are:

Group	Description
protocolDir (11)	Protocol Directory: lists, in a table, the inventory of protocols that the probe has the capability of monitoring. Each protocol is described by an entry in the table.
ProtocolDist (12)	Protocol Distribution: collects the relative amounts of octets and packets for the different protocols that are detected on a network segment. Each protocol is described by an entry in a table, and the network management station can easily determine the bandwidth consumed per protocol by accessing the information in that table.
addressMap (13)	Address Map: correlates Network Layer addresses and MAC Layer addresses, and stores the information in tables.
nlHost (14)	Network Layer Host: counts the amount of traffic sent from and to each Network Layer address discovered by the probe, and stores the information in tables.
nlMatrix (15)	Network Layer Matrix: counts the amount of traffic sent between each pair of network addresses discovered by the probe, and stores the information in tables from both source to destination and destination to source.

alHost (16)	Application Layer Host: counts the amount of traffic, by protocol and by host, that is sent from and to each network address discovered by the probe.
alMatrix (17)	Application Layer Matrix: counts the amount of traffic, by protocol, sent between each pair of network addresses discovered by the probe, and stores this information in tables. This group is similar to the nlMatrix group, but the focus is on the protocol in operation.
usrHistory (18)	Combines mechanisms seen in the alarm (3) and history (2) groups to provide user-specified history collection, and storing that information in tables.
probeConfig (19)	Controls the configuration of various operational parameters by the probe, such as the Ethernet and token ring RMON groups that are supported by the probe, software and hardware revision numbers of the probe, a trap destination table, and so on.
rmonConformance (20)	Describes the requirements for conformance to the RMON2 MIB.

Figures 3-22a, 3-22b, and 3-22c show the various RMON2 groups and objects. Reference [3-27] provides a good overview of the technology.

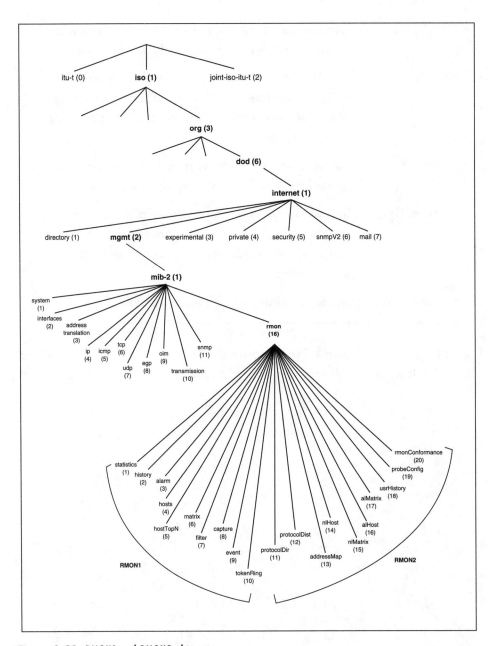

Figure 3-21. RMON1 and RMON2 object trees.

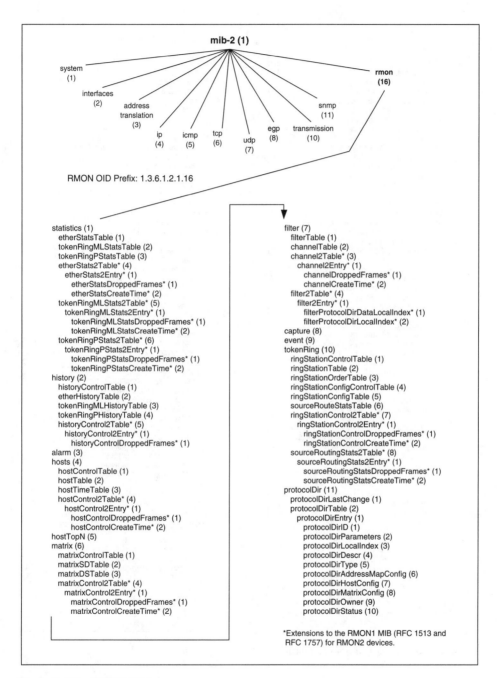

Figure 3-22a. RMON2 OID tree

protocolDist (12)
  protocolDistControlTable (1)
    protocolDistControlEntry (1)
      protocolDistControlIndex (1)
      protocolDistControlDataSource (2)
      protocolDistControlDroppedFrames (3)
      protocolDistControlCreateTime (4)
      protocolDistControlOwner (5)
      protocolDistControlStatus (6)
  protocolDistStatsTable (2)
    protocolDistStatsEntry (1)
      protocolDistStatsPkts (1)
      protocolDistStatsOctets (2)
addressMap (13)
  addressMapInserts (1)
  addressMapDeletes (2)
  addressMapMaxDesiredEntries (3)
  addressMapControlTable (4)
    addressMapControlEntry (1)
      addressMapControlIndex (1)
      addressMapControlDataSource (2)
      addressMapControlDroppedFrames (3)
      addressMapControlOwner (4)
      addressMapControlStatus (5)
  addressMapTable (5)
    addressMapEntry (1)
      addressMapTimeMark (1)
      addressMapNetworkAddress (2)
      addressMapSource (3)
      addressMapPhysicalAddress (4)
      addressMapLastChange (5)
nlhost (14)
  hlHostControlTable (1)
    hlHostControlEntry (1)
      hlHostControlIndex (1)
      hlHostControlDataSource (2)
      hlHostControlNlDroppedFrames (3)
      hlHostControlNlInserts (4)
      hlHostControlNlDeletes (5)
      hlHostControlNlMaxDesiredEntries (6)
      hlHostControlAlDroppedFrames (7)
      hlHostControlAlInserts (8)
      hlHostControlAlDeletes (9)
      hlHostControlAlMaxDesiredEntries (10)
      hlHostControlOwner (11)
      hlHostControlStatus (12)
  nlHostTable (2)
    nlHostEntry (1)
      nlHostTimeMark (1)
      nlHostAddress (2)
      nlHostInPkts (3)
      nlHostOutPkts (4)
      nlHostInOctets (5)
      nlHostOutOctets (6)
      nlHostOutMacNonUnicastPkts (7)
      nlHostCreateTime (8)

nlMatrix (15)
  hlMatrixControlTable (1)
    hlMatrixControlEntry (1)
      hlMatrixControlIndex (1)
      hlMatrixControlDataSource (2)
      hlMatrixControlNlDroppedFrames (3)
      hlMatrixControlNlInserts (4)
      hlMatrixControlNlDeletes (5)
      hlMatrixControlNlMaxDesiredEntries (6)
      hlMatrixControlAlDroppedFrames (7)
      hlMatrixControlAlInserts (8)
      hlMatrixControlAlDeletes (9)
      hlMatrixControlAlMaxDesiredEntries (10)
      hlMatrixControlOwner (11)
      hlMatrixControlStatus (12)
  nlMatrixSDTable (2)
    nlMatrixSDEntry (1)
      nlMatrixSDTimeMark (1)
      nlMatrixSDSourceAddress (2)
      nlMatrixSDDestAddress (3)
      nlMatrixSDPkts (4)
      nlMatrixSDOctets (5)
      nlMatrixSDCreateTime (6)
  nlMatrixDSTabl (3)
    nlMatrixDSEntry (1)
      nlMatrixDSTimeMark (1)
      nlMatrixDSSourceAddress (2)
      nlMatrixDSDestAddress (3)
      nlMatrixDSPkts (4)
      nlMatrixDSOctets (5)
      nlMatrixDSCreateTime (6)
  nlMatrixTopNControlTable (4)
    nlMatrixTopNControlEntry (1)
      nlMatrixTopNControlIndex (1)
      nlMatrixTopNControlMatrixIndex (2)
      nlMatrixTopNControlRateBase (3)
      nlMatrixTopNControlTimeRemaining (4)
      nlMatrixTopNControlGeneratedReports (5)
      nlMatrixTopNControlDuration (6)
      nlMatrixTopNControlRequestedSize (7)
      nlMatrixTopNControlGrantedSize (8)
      nlMatrixTopNControlStartTime (9)
      nlMatrixTopNControlOwner (10)
      nlMatrixTopNControlStatus (11)
  nlMatrixTopNTable (5)
    nlMatrixTopNEntry (1)
      nlMatrixTopNIndex (1)
      nlMatrixTopNProtocolDirLocalIndex (2)
      nlMatrixTopNSourceAddress (3)
      nlMatrixTopNDestAddress (4)
      nlMatrixTopNPktRate (5)
      nlMatrixTopNReversePktRate (6)
      nlMatrixTopNOctetRate (7)
      nlMatrixTopNReverseOctetRate (8)

Figure 3-22b. RMON2 OID tree, continued

alHost (16)
  alHostTable (1)
    alHostEntry (1)
      alHostTimeMark (1)
      alHostInPkts (2)
      alHostOutPkts (3)
      alHostInOctets (4)
      alHostOutOctets (5)
      alHostCreateTime (6)
alMatrix (17)
  alMatrixSDTable (1)
    alMatrixSDEntry (1)
      alMatrixSDTimeMark (1)
      alMatrixSDPkts (2)
      aMatrixSDOctets (3)
      alMatrixSDCreateTime (4)
  alMatrixDSTable (2)
    alMatrixDSEntry (1)
      alMatrixDSTimeMark (1)
      alMatrixDSPkts (2)
      alMatrixDSOctets (3)
      alMatrixDSCreateTime (4)
  alMatrixTopNControlTable (3)
    alMatrixTopNControlEntry (1)
      alMatrixTopNControlIndex (1)
      alMatrixTopNControlMatrixIndex (2)
      alMatrixTopNControlRateBase (3)
      alMatrixTopNControlTimeRemaining (4)
      alMatrixTopNControlGeneratedReports (5)
      alMatrixTopNControlDuration (6)
      alMatrixTopNControlRequestedSize (7)
      alMatrixTopNControlGrantedSize (8)
      alMatrixTopNControlStartTime (9)
      alMatrixTopNControlOwner (10)
      alMatrixTopNControlStatus (11)
  alMatrixTopNTable (5)
    alMatrixTopNEntry (1)
      alMatrixTopNIndex (1)
      alMatrixTopNProtocolDirLocalIndex (2)
      alMatrixTopNSourceAddress (3)
      alMatrixTopNDestAddress (4)
      alMatrixTopNAppProtocolDirLocalIndex (5)
      alMatrixTopNPktRate (6)
      alMatrixTopNReversePktRate (7)
      alMatrixTopNOctetRate (8)
      alMatrixTopNReverseOctetRate (9)
usrHistory (18)
  usrHistoryControlTable (1)
    usrHistoryControlEntry (1)
      usrHistoryControlIndex (1)
      usrHistoryControlObjects (2)
      usrHistoryControlBucketsRequested (3)
      usrHistoryControlBucketsGranted (4)
      usrHistoryControlInterval (5)
      usrHistoryControlOwner (6)
      usrHistoryControlStatus (7)
  usrHistoryObjectTable (2)
    usrHistoryObjectEntry (1)
      usrHistoryObjectIndex (1)
      usrHistoryObjectVariable (2)
      usrHistoryObjectSampleType (3)
  usrHistoryTable (3)
    usrHistoryEntry (1)
      usrHistorySampleIndex (1)
      usrHistoryIntervalStart (2)
      usrHistoryIntervalEnd (3)

      usrHistoryAbsValue (4)
      usrHistoryValStatus (5)
probeConfig (19)
  probeCapabilities (1)
  probeSoftwareRev (2)
  probeHardwareRev (3)
  probeDateTime (4)
  probeResetControl (5)
  probeDownloadFile (6)
  probeDownloadTFTPServer (7)
  probeDownloadAction (8)
  probeDownloadStatus (9)
  serialConfigTable (10)
    serialConfigEntry (1)
      serialMode (1)
      serialProtocol (2)
      serialTimeout (3)
      serialModeminitString (4)
      serialModemHangUpString (5)
      serialModemConnectResp (6)
      serialModemNoConnectResp (7)
      serialDialoutTimeout (8)
      serialStatus (9)
  netConfigTable (11)
    netConfigEntry (1)
      netConfigIPAddress (1)
      netConfigSubnetMask (2)
      netConfigStatus (3)
  netDefaultGateway (12)
  trapDestTable (13)
    trapDestEntry (1)
      trapDestIndex (1)
      trapDestCommunity (2)
      trapDestProtocol (3)
      trapDestAddress (4)
      trapDestOwner (5)
      trapDestStatus (6)
  serialConnectionTable (14)
    serialConnectionEntry (1)
      serialConnectIndex (1)
      serialConnectDestIpAddress (2)
      serialConnectType (3)
      serialConnectDialString (4)
      serialConnectSwitchConnectSeq (5)
      serialConnectSwitchDisconnectSeq (6)
      serialConnectSwitchResetSeq (7)
      serialConnectOwner (8)
      serialConnectStatus (9)
rmonConformance (20)
  rmon2MIBCompliances (1)
    rmon2MIBCompliance (1)
    rmon2MIBApplicationLayerCompliance (2)
  rmon2MIBGroups (2)
    protocolDirectoryGroup (1)
    protocolDistributionGroup (2)
    addressMapGroup (3)
    nlHostGroup (4)
    nlMatrixGroup (5)
    alHostGroup (6)
    alMatrixGroup (7)
    usrHistoryGroup (8)
    probeInformationGroup (9)
    probeConfigurationGroup (10)
    rmon1EnhancementGroup (11)
    rmon1EthernetEnhancementGroup (12)
    rmon1TokenRingEnhancementGroup (13)

Figure 3-22c. RMON2 OID tree, continued

3.8 Private MIBs

Many vendors have developed private MIBs that support hubs, terminal servers, and other networking systems. You can find these MIBs under the enterprises subtree, {1.3.6.1.4.1.A}. The A indicates a private enterprise code, defined in the "Assigned Numbers" RFC (currently RFC 1700) in the network management section. (Appendix F lists these enterprise numbers.)

Information on these private MIBs is available via anonymous FTP from host venera.isi.edu, directory /mib. One interesting file is snmp-vendors-contacts, which lists the currently assigned private enterprise codes. Many vendors also place their private MIBs in this subdirectory. Because of these private MIBs are vendor-specific, interoperability is not always possible.

3.9. Accessing a MIB

This section gives an example of an SNMP management console retrieving values for MIB objects from a remote SNMP agent. In this case, the manager is a Sun Microsystems' SunNet Manager, and the agent is located in a Proteon's p4100+ router. Both devices connect to an Ethernet backbone. A Network General Corp. Sniffer protocol analyzer captured the data shown in Trace 3.9.

Readers unfamiliar with the Sniffer Analyzer will find a short explanation of the functions of a protocol analyzer helpful. A protocol analyzer captures, then decodes, frames of data as they are transmitted on the LAN or WAN. These frames are numbered sequentially and stored in the same order. The analyzer can display these frames several ways; it can show all of the protocol layers, or just one. The example in this section shows only the highest layer, SNMP. The analyzer also lets you choose the amount of detail included. The minimum detail is a single summary line, and the maximum is the hexadecimal representation of the bits received on the wire. This example uses an English-language detail of the SNMP constructs. A second detail shows the ASN.1 constructs and the hexadecimal decode of the actual data. With that background, I'll summarize what we have been studying.

This exchange between the manager and the agent (see Trace 3.9a) involves two frames of information. Frame 109 contains an SNMP GetRequest PDU (protocol data unit, the core of the SNMP message) and Frame 110 contains a GetResponse PDU. (Chapter 4 examines the PDUs in depth.)

The manager sends the GetRequest to the agent asking for the values of the objects within the system subtree, OID {1.3.6.1.2.1.1}. The PDU requests information about all seven of the objects: sysDescr, sysObjectID, sysUpTime, sysContact, SysName, sysLocation, and sysServices. On the trace, you can see two coding elements for each of these objects. First, the manager requests the sysUpTime object to determine whether the agent within the router has restarted (warm or cold boot). Second, the manager asks for the values of each individual object in order (review Figure 3-2). This trace also illustrates the use of the SEQUENCE type encoding of VarBinds discussed in Section 2.5.3.5. Each object is encoded with an OBJECT IDENTIFIER type, for example {1.3.6.1.2.1.1.2.0}. The Object Value field is encoded with a NULL type because the manager does not know this information.

Frame 110 gives the agent's GetResponse. The response returns each object and its associated value in the order that Frame 109 requested. The sysDescr provides a textual description of the device (Portable I80386 C Gateway ...). The sysObjectID has a value of {1.3.6.1.4.1.1.1.1.41}. From the prefix {1.3.6.1.4.1}, you know that this is a private enterprise subtree. The next digit (.1) is the enterprise code for Proteon, Inc. (see RFC 1700, page 134, or Appendix F).

The sysUpTime object has a value of 263,621,778 hundredths of a second, which translates to roughly 30 days because the router's network management system was restarted. Two of the objects, sysContact {system 4} and sysLocation {system 6} appear not to have a value. In reality, they have a value of a zero-length string, but the network manager entered no values for those objects in the router's configuration file. The sysName is the domain name of the node (boulder.org). Finally, the sysServices {system 7} is a calculated sum that indicates the services this node performs. In this case, the value is 72, indicating a host offering application services (see RFC 1213, page 15).

See Trace 3.9b for a quick review of the ASN.1-encoding discussed in Chapter 2. This data shows the details of Frame 110, but with the Sniffer's ASN.1 decoding option activated. You can trace each ASN.1 element, identifying the Type-Length-Value encodings as well as the hexadecimal display of those values. As a reference point, the first SNMP encoding (SEQUENCE [of], Length=235) appears in bold type with the characters 30 81 EB. Reviewing Chapter 2, we know that the Type field = 30H (the SEQUENCE OF type, see Figure 2-10). The Length field is the Long Definite form, with one subsequent octet (see Figure 2-5) having a value of 81 EBH. (Hexadecimal values of X are dummy characters to maintain the confidentiality of the trace.)

Trace 3.9a. Browsing the system subtree (SNMP protocol decode)

```
Sniffer Network Analyzer data 10-Nov at 10:42:04 file ASAN_SYS.ENC Pg 1
---------------------------------------- Frame 109 ----------------------------------------
SNMP: ----- Simple Network Management Protocol -----
SNMP:
SNMP: Version = 0
SNMP: Community = boulder
SNMP: Command = Get request
SNMP: Request ID = 0
SNMP: Error status = 0 (No error)
SNMP: Error index = 0
SNMP:
SNMP: Object = {1.3.6.1.2.1.1.3.0} (sysUpTime.0)
SNMP: Value = NULL
SNMP:
SNMP: Object = {1.3.6.1.2.1.1.1.0} (sysDescr.0)
SNMP: Value = NULL
SNMP:
SNMP: Object = {1.3.6.1.2.1.1.2.0} (sysObjectID.0)
SNMP: Value = NULL
SNMP:
SNMP: Object = {1.3.6.1.2.1.1.3.0} (sysUpTime.0)
```

SNMP: Value = NULL
SNMP:
SNMP: Object = {1.3.6.1.2.1.1.4.0} (system.4.0)
SNMP: Value = NULL
SNMP:
SNMP: Object = {1.3.6.1.2.1.1.5.0} (system.5.0)
SNMP: Value = NULL
SNMP:
SNMP: Object = {1.3.6.1.2.1.1.6.0} (system 6.0)
SNMP: Value = NULL
SNMP:
SNMP: Object = {1.3.6.1.2.1.1.7.0} (system 7.0)
SNMP: Value = NULL
SNMP:
-- Frame 110 --
SNMP: ----- Simple Network Management Protocol -----
SNMP:
SNMP: Version = 0
SNMP: Community = boulder
SNMP: Command = Get response
SNMP: Request ID = 0
SNMP: Error status = 0 (No error)
SNMP: Error index = 0
SNMP:
SNMP: Object = {1.3.6.1.2.1.1.3.0] (sysUpTime.0)
SNMP: Value = 263621778 hundredths of a second
SNMP:
SNMP: Object = {1.3.6.1.2.1.1.1.0} (sysDescr.0)
SNMP: Value = Portable I80386 C Gateway BOULDER.ORG S/N XXX V12.0
SNMP:
SNMP: Object = {1.3.6.1.2.1.1.2.0} (sysObjectID.0)
SNMP: Value = {1.3.6.1.4.1.1.1.1.41}
SNMP:
SNMP: Object = {1.3.6.1.2.1.1.3.0} (sysUpTime.0)

SNMP: Value = 263621778 hundredths of a second
SNMP:
SNMP: Object = {1.3.6.1.2.1.1.4.0} (system.4.0)
SNMP: Value =
SNMP:
SNMP: Object = {1.3.6.1.2.1.1.5.0} (system.5.0)
SNMP: Value = BOULDER.ORG
SNMP:
SNMP: Object = {1.3.6.1.2.1.1.6.0} (system.6.0)
SNMP: Value =
SNMP:
SNMP: Object = {1.3.6.1.2.1.1.7.0} (system.7.0)
SNMP: Value = 72
SNMP:

Trace 3.9b. Browsing the system subtree (ASN.1 and Hexadecimal decode)

Sniffer Network Analyzer data 10-Nov at 10:42:04 file ASAN_SYS.ENC Pg 1
--- Frame 110 ---
SNMP: 1.1 SEQUENCE [of], Length=235
SNMP: 2.1 INTEGER, Length=1, Value = "0"
SNMP: 2.2 OCTET STRING, Length=7, Value = "boulder"
SNMP: 2.3 Context-Specific Constructed [2], Length=220
SNMP: 3.1 INTEGER, Length=1, Value = "0"
SNMP: 3.2 INTEGER, Length=1, Value = "0"
SNMP: 3.3 INTEGER, Length=1, Value = "0"
SNMP: 3.4 SEQUENCE [of], Length=208
SNMP: 4.1 SEQUENCE [of], Length=16
SNMP: 5.1 OBJECT IDENTIFIER, Length=8, Value = "{1.3.6.1.2.1.1.3.0}"
SNMP: 5.2 Application Primitive [3], Length=4, Data = "<0FB68C92>"
SNMP: 4.2 SEQUENCE [of], Length=74
SNMP: 5.1 OBJECT IDENTIFIER, Length=8, Value = "{1.3.6.1.2.1.1.1.0}"
SNMP: 5.2 OCTET STRING, Length=62, Value = "Portable I80386 C Gateway
                        XXX.XXX.XXXX.XXX ..."

SNMP: 4.3   SEQUENCE [of], Length=21
SNMP: 5.1   OBJECT IDENTIFIER, Length=8,Value="{1.3.6.1.2.1.1.2.0}"
SNMP: 5.2   OBJECT IDENTIFIER, Length=9,Value="{1.3.6.1.4.1.1.1.1.41}"
SNMP: 4.4   SEQUENCE [of], Length=16
SNMP: 5.1   OBJECT IDENTIFIER, Length=8,Value="{1.3.6.1.2.1.1.3.0}"
SNMP: 5.2   Application Primitive [3], Length=4, Data = "<0FB68C92>"
SNMP: 4.5   SEQUENCE [of], Length=12
SNMP: 5.1   OBJECT IDENTIFIER, Length=8, Value="{1.3.6.1.2.1.1.4.0}"
SNMP: 5.2   OCTET STRING, Length=0, Value = ""
SNMP: 4.6   SEQUENCE [of], Length=28
SNMP: 5.1   OBJECT IDENTIFIER, Length=8, Value="{1.3.6.1.2.1.1.5.0}"
SNMP: 5.2   OCTET STRING, Length=16, Value="XXX.XXX.XXXX.XXX"
SNMP: 4.7   SEQUENCE [of], Length=12
SNMP: 5.1   OBJECT IDENTIFIER, Length=8, Value="{1.3.6.1.2.1.1.6.0}"
SNMP: 5.2   OCTET STRING, Length=0, Value = ""
SNMP: 4.8   SEQUENCE [of], Length=13
SNMP: 5.1   OBJECT IDENTIFIER, Length=8, Value = "{1.3.6.1.2.1.1.7.0}"
SNMP: 5.2   INTEGER, Length=1, Value = "72"
SNMP:

```
ADDR  HEX                                              ASCII
0000  08 00 20 09 00 C8 AA 00 04 00 44 86 08 00 45 00  .. .......D...E.
0010  01 0A 81 20 00 00 3B 11 73 77 84 A3 01 01 84 A3  ... ..;.sw......
0020  80 04 00 A1 0D 20 00 F6 C6 62 30 81 EB 02 01 00  ..... ...b0.....
0030  04 07 XX XX XX XX XX XX XX A2 81 DC 02 01 00 02  ..XXXXXXX.......
0040  01 00 02 01 00 30 81 D0 30 10 06 08 2B 06 01 02  .....0..0...+...
0050  01 01 03 00 43 04 0F B6 8C 92 30 4A 06 08 2B 06  ....C.....0J..+.
0060  01 02 01 01 01 00 04 3E 50 6F 72 74 61 62 6C 65  .......>Portable
0070  20 49 38 30 33 38 36 20 43 20 47 61 74 65 77 61   I80386 C Gatewa
0080  79 20 XX XX XX XX XX XX XX XX XX XX XX XX XX XX  y XXX.XXX.XXXX.X
0090  XX XX 20 53 2F 4E 20 33 33 33 20 56 31 32 2E 30  XX S/N 333 V12.0
00A0  20 20 5B 20 20 5D 30 15 06 08 2B 06 01 02 01 01   [ ]0...+.....
00B0  02 00 06 09 2B 06 01 04 01 01 01 01 29 30 10 06  ....+........)0..
00C0  08 2B 06 01 02 01 01 03 00 43 04 0F B6 8C 92 30  .+.......C.....0
00D0  0C 06 08 2B 06 01 02 01 01 04 00 04 00 30 1C 06  ...+.........0..
```

```
00E0   08  2B 06 01 02 01 01 05 00 04 10 XX XX XX XX XX  .+.........XXX.X
00F0   XX  XX XX XX XX XX XX XX XX XX XX XX 30 0C 06 08 2B  XX.XXXX.XXX0...+
0100   06  01 02 01 01 06 00 04 00 30 0D 06 08 2B 06 01  .........0...+..
0110   02  01 01 07 00 02 01 48                          .......H
```

We have now tackled two of the three technical subjects in our tour of the Internet network management framework: the SMI and the MIBs. The next chapter studies SNMP, which provides the communication mechanism for network management functions.

3.10 References

[3-1]   McCloghrie, K., and M.T. Rose. "Management Information Base for Network Management of TCP/IP-based Internets." *RFC 1156*, May 1990.

[3-2]   McCloghrie, K., and M.T. Rose. "Management Information Base for Network Management of TCP/IP-based Internets: MIB-II." *RFC 1213*, March 1991.

[3-3]   Rose, M., and K. McCloghrie. "Concise MIB Definitions." *RFC 1212*, March 1991.

[3-4]   Perkins, Dave, and Evan McGinnis. *Understanding SNMP MIBs.* New York, NY: Prentice-Hall PTR, 1997.

[3-5]   VandenBerg, Chris. "MIB II Extends SNMP Interoperability." *Data Communications* (October 1990): 119–124.

[3-6]   LaBarre, L. "OSI Internet Management: Management Information Base." *RFC 1214*, April 1991.

[3-7]   Reynolds, J., and J. Postel. "Assigned Numbers." *RFC 1700*, October 1994.

[3-8]   Baker, F., and J. Watt, editors. "Definitions of Managed Objects for the DS1 and E1 Interface Types." *RFC 1406*, January 1993.

[3-9]   Cox, T., and Tesink, K., editors. "Definitions of Managed Objects for the DS3/E3 Interface Type." *RFC 1407*, January 1993.

[3-10]   Brown, T., and K. Tesink, editors. "Definitions of Managed Objects for the SONET/SDH Interface Type." *RFC 1595*, March 1994.

[3-11]   Brown, C., et al. "Management Information Base for Frame Relay DTEs." *RFC 1315*, April 1992.

[3-12]   Brown, T., editor. "Definitions of Managed Objects for Frame Relay Service." *RFC 1604*, March 1994.

[3-13]   Cox, T., and K. Tesink, editors. "Definitions of Managed Objects for SMDS Interfaces Using SMIv2." *RFC 1694*, August 1994.

[3-14]   Ahmed, M., and K. Tesink, editors. "Definitions of Managed Objects for ATM Management Version 8.0 using SMIv2." *RFC 1695*, August 1994.

[3-15]   Waldbusser, S. "Remote Network Monitoring Management Information Base." *RFC 1757*, February 1995.

[3-16]   Burdick, Matthew J. "Continuous Monitoring of Remote Networks: The RMON MIB," *Hewlett-Packard Journal* (April 1993): 82-89.

[3-17]   de Bruyn, Mark. "RMON MIB Tutorial." *3TECH, the 3Com Technical Journal* (April 1994): 22-25.

[3-18]   Tolly, Kevin, and David Newman. "A for RMON." *Data Communications* (December 1994): 52-68.

[3-19]   Boardman, Bruce, and Peter Morrissey. "Probing the Depths of RMON (Amen for Extensions)." *Network Computing* (February 1, 1995).

[3-20]   Thomas, Richard. "Interoperable RMON? Plug and Pray." *Data Communications* (May 1995): 79-88.

[3-21]   Steinke, Steve. "A Diamond in the Rough." *LAN Magazine* (October 1995): 81-86.

[3-22]   Rosenbach, Bibi, and Jeremy Soref. "RMON—The Enterprise Management Standard." *Data Communications* (March 21, 1996): 69-72.

[3-23]   Boardman, Bruce. "RMON—Unfinished Business. Get the Picture?" *Network Computing* (May 16, 1996): 66-83.

[3-24]   Waldbusser, S. "Token Ring Extensions to the Remote Network Monitoring MIB." *RFC 1513*, September 1993.

[3-25]   Tolly, Kevin. "RMON: A Ray of Hope for Token Ring Managers." *Data Communications* (October 1995): 72-80.

[3-26]   Waldbusser, S. "Remote Network Monitoring Management Information Base Version 2 using SMIv2." *RFC 2021*, January 1997.

[3-27]   Stallings, William. "RMON2—The Next Generation of Remote Network Monitoring." *ConneXions, the Interoperability Report* (May 1996): 34-40.

# 4 The Simple Network Management Protocol

So far, this book has discussed the structure of management information (SMI) and management information bases (MIBs). This chapter completes the discussion of the Internet Network Management Framework by looking at SNMP, the protocol that communicates management information. This chapter will discuss SNMP version 1, and the next chapter will consider SNMP version 2. Note that we will adopt the convention of referring to SNMP version 1 as SNMP, and SNMP version 2 as SNMPv2.

4.1 SNMP Objectives and Architecture

RFC 1157 states that "SNMP explicitly minimizes the number and complexity of management functions realized by the management agent itself" [4-1]. In other words, SNMP is designed to be simple. SNMP does this in three ways. By reducing the development cost of the agent software, SNMP has decreased the burden on vendors who wish to support the protocol, thereby increasing the protocol's acceptance. Second, SNMP is extensible, allowing vendors to add network management functions. Third, it separates the management architecture from the architecture of hardware devices, such as hosts and routers, widening the base of multivendor support. "Network Management and the Design of SNMP" discusses additional architectural issues relating to SNMP [4-2].

SNMP has a very straightforward architecture. Figure 4-1a compares the SNMP architecture to the ISO/OSI model and the Advanced Research Projects Agency (ARPA) model, around which the Internet protocols and TCP/IP were developed. Note that the four layers of the ARPA model do not map evenly to the seven layers of the OSI model.

OSI Layer	SNMP - Related Function	ARPA Layer
Application	Management Application (SNMP PDU)	Process / Application
Presentation	Structure of Management Information (ASN.1 & BER Encoding)	
Session	Authentication (SNMP Header)	
Transport	User Datagram Protocol (UDP)	Host-to-Host
Network	Internet Protocol (IP)	Internet
Data Link	LAN or WAN Interface Protocol	Network Interface
Physical		

Figure 4-1a. Comparing the SNMP architecture with the OSI and ARPA models

Let's use an example to see how the processes within the SNMP architecture interact. Suppose a management console requests information about one of the managed nodes. The SNMP processes in both the manager and the agent respond to the console. The ASN.1 encoding at the Application layer provides the proper syntax for the SNMP message. The remaining functions authenticate the data (attach the SNMP header) and communicate the information request.

Because most management information does not demand the reliable delivery that connection-oriented systems provide, the communication channel between the SNMP manager and the agent is connectionless. When you compare the SNMP model to the ISO/OSI model, SNMP's connectionless communication mechanism removes some of the need for a Session layer and reduces the responsibilities of the lower four layers. For most implementations, the User Datagram Protocol (UDP) performs the Transport layer functions, the Internet Protocol (IP) provides the Network layer functions, and LANs such as Ethernet or token ring or WANs such as a leased line or a frame relay connection provide the Data Link and Physical layer functions. (There are some exceptions to this rule. RFCs 1418, 1419, and 1420 describe implementations that use other transport mechanisms, such as OSI Apple Computer's AppleTalk, or Novell Inc.'s IPX protocols. However, RFC 1270, called "SNMP Communication Services" [4-3], states that UDP/IP are the protocols of choice for most circumstances.)

If you compare SNMP to the Internet (or ARPA) architectural model (see Figure 4-1b), you'll notice that the ARPA model uses four layers to describe the entire communication function. In the ARPA model, SNMP would reside at the Process/Application layer. However, while the ARPA Host-to-Host layer provides end-to-end communication reliability, SNMP's use of UDP assures only proper port addressing and a checksum; it does not provide octet-by-octet error control. IP provides the Internet layer functions, such as addressing and fragmentation, that are necessary to deliver an SNMP message from the source to the destination. Finally, the Network Interface layer deals with the LAN or WAN hardware, such as an interface to an FDDI or Frame Relay network connection. Notice that Figure 4-1b also shows the relative complexities of the host and router functions. Hosts implement all four layers of the ARPA model, whereas routers implement only the lower two.

Comparing the SNMP architecture to the ISO/OSI and ARPA architectural models provides a theoretical basis for this discussion. But from a practical perspective, the SNMP model works as shown in Figure 4-2. This model contains several elements discussed in Chapter 1. It includes a management system that uses the SNMP manager, an SNMP agent, and managed resources, and the SNMP messages communicate management information via five SNMP protocol data units (PDUs). The management application issues the Get, GetNext, or Set PDUs. The managed system returns a GetResponse PDU. The agent may initiate a Trap (sometimes called an Event) PDU when predefined conditions are met. Section 4.3 discusses these five PDUs in detail.

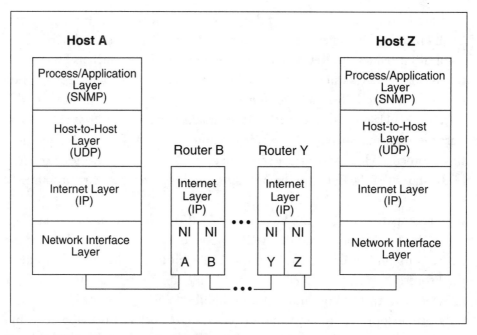

Figure 4-1b. Application-to-application connection

4.2 SNMP Operation

The SNMP processes described in the previous sections must occur in physical devices. For example, a router must have a physical processor that implements the software acting as an SNMP agent. Two sets of logical processes occur within those physical elements: the relationships that are specified between various network management entities, and the way network management information is communicated.

4.2.1 Network Management Relationships

The SNMP standard, RFC 1157, and the "SNMP Administrative Model," RFC 1351 [4-4], define a number of terms. Many of these definitions describe relationships between management entities:

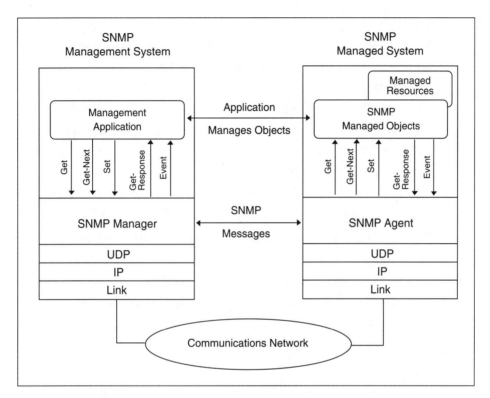

Figure 4-2. SNMP architecture (c 1990, IEEE)

> ➤ *Network management stations* are devices that execute the management applications that control and monitor the network elements.

> ➤ *Network elements* are devices such as hosts, bridges, routers, and hubs that contain an agent and perform the network management functions that the network management stations request.

> ➤ The *SNMP* allows network management stations and the agents in the network elements to communicate.

> ➤ *SNMP application entities* reside at either a management station or a managed node, and use SNMP as a communication mechanism.

> ➤ *Protocol entities* are peer processes that implement SNMP, thus supporting the SNMP application entities.

➤ The *SNMP community* pairs an SNMP agent with an arbitrary set of SNMP application entities. The network administrator assigns the community a name (called the *community name*) which is essentially a password with associated rights and privileges. A management application with multiple community names may belong to multiple communities.

➤ *Authentic SNMP messages* are SNMP messages sent from an application entity to a specific SNMP community. The message contains the community name of interest.

➤ The *authentication scheme* is the method by which an SNMP message is identified as belonging to a specific SNMP community.

➤ The *MIB View* is the subset of MIB objects, which may be contained within several subtrees, that pertain to a network element.

➤ The SNMP *access mode* determines the level of access to objects that a particular application entity is allowed. The choices are read-only and read-write.

➤ The *community profile* pairs the SNMP access mode with the SNMP MIB View. The community profile represents specific access privileges for the variables in a MIB view.

➤ The SNMP *access policy* pairs an SNMP community with a SNMP community profile. The access policy represents the specific community profile that an agent permits the other members of the community to have.

➤ The SNMP *proxy agent* provides management functions on behalf of network elements that would otherwise be inaccessible.

Figure 4-3 illustrates some of the definitions described above.

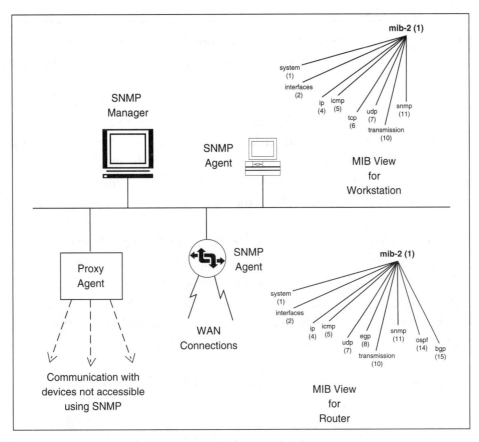

Figure 4-3. Network management relationships

4.2.2 Identifying and Communicating Object Instances

SMI managed object types have an object identifier (OID) that uniquely names them and locates their place on the object tree. An instance of an object type is an occurrence of that object type and has an assigned value. For example, the object sysDescr {1.3.6.1.2.1.1.1.0} might have a value of "Retix Remote Bridge Model 2265M."

Suppose a network management station wishes to retrieve an instance of a specific object. The management station must use SNMP to communicate its question to the agent.

Now, suppose multiple instances (or occurrences) of that object are possible. For example, say a router's routing table contains a number of entries. How would the network management station retrieve just the value of the third entry in the table?

RFC 1157, pages 12-15 specifies these tasks. For these SNMP operations, a *variable name* uniquely identifies each instance of an object type. This name consists of two parts of the form $x.y$. The x portion is the object type defined in the MIB, and the y portion is an OID fragment that identifies the desired instance. The following examples should clarify this.

Consider a scalar object that has one instance. The objects contained in the System group are all scalar objects. For example, the sysServices object has an OID of {1.3.6.1.2.1.1.7} and occurs once. The x portion of the variable name is the OID, and the y portion has been assigned to 0. You can derive this by following the OID tree down to the object sysServices and adding the appropriate instance suffix (with the suffix, or y portion, shown in boldface type):

iso	org	dod	internet	mgmt	mib-2	system	sysServices	Instance
1	3	6	1	2	1	1	7	**0**

Thus, the variable name for sysServices is {1.3.6.1.2.1.1.7.0}.

The variable name for a columnar object is more complicated because it must identify the location of an object within a two-dimensional data structure, such as a table having both rows and columns. (Within the RMON MIB, three-dimensional data structures are added, making the identification even more complex.) Using the familiar speadsheet as an example, the identification of a particular cell requires two coordinates, X and Y, which describe the horizontal and vertical positions, respectively. With columnar objects, an indexing scheme, specified in the INDEX clause in the ASN.1 definition for that object, provides a means for identifying the specific instance. The INDEX clause then further identifies the syntax to be used. And as one might expect, some of the indexing schemes are more complicated than others. RFC 1212, pages 8-10 lists many of the INDEX clauses that are found within the MIB-2. Let's look at some examples for further clarification.

Consider the IP Address Table object, ipAdEntBcastAddr, which specifies the value of the least significant bit (LSB) of the IP broadcast address (see Figures 4-4a and 4-4b). To begin, follow the OID tree down to ipAdEntBcastAddr:

iso	org	dod	internet	mgmt	mib-2	ip	ipAddrTable	ipAddrEntry	ipAdEntBcastAddr
1	3	6	1	2	1	4	20	1	4

The OID is {1.3.6.1.2.1.4.20.1.4}, consisting of the IP Group {1.3.6.1.2.1.4}, the IP Address Table (20), the ipAddrEntry (1), and the object ipAdEntBcastAddr (4), shown in Figure 4-4a.

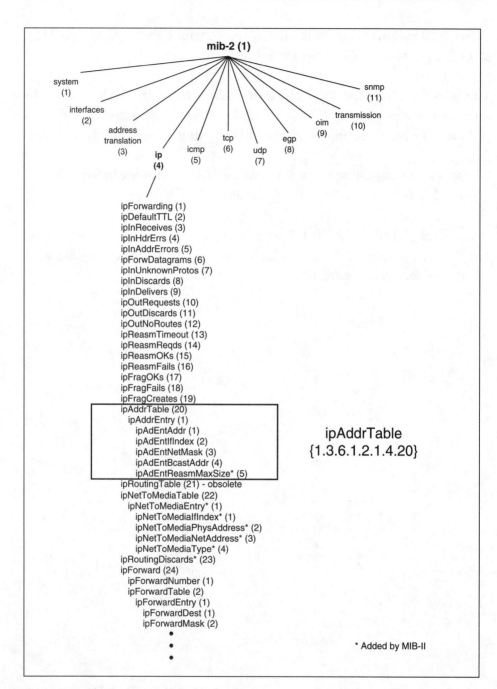

Figure 4-4a. The IP address table within the OID tree

Consulting MIB-2, RFC 1157 page 31, the ASN.1 definition for the object ipAd-drEntry includes an INDEX clause that specifies the object ipAdEntAddr. Moving a few lines down in RFC 1157, we see that the object ipAdEntAddr has a SYNTAX of IpAddress. Thus, we would expect the index for this object to be defined by an IP address and shown in dotted decimal notation: a.b.c.d. (More on IP addresses and dotted decimal notation can be found in Section 6.3.)

Returning to our example, to complete the variable name, the suffix (or y portion) is added, which consists of an IP address: a.b.c.d. The variable name for ipAdEntBcastAddr associated with IP Address a.b.c.d would therefore be {1.3.6.1.2.1.4.20.1.4.a.b.c.d}.

Figure 4-4b is a completed IP Address Table, built by retrieving all the IP Address Table variables. The column headings show the five objects, ipAdEntAddr through ipAdEntReasmMaxSize. Each row contains the values of the five variables: ipAdEntAddr [XXX.YYY.150.2], ipAdEntIfIndex (1), and so on. A different index (2) identifies the second row, and it contains different values. Additional row entries are made, as necessary, until the table is completed.

ipAddrTable {1.3.6.1.2.1.4.20}				
ipAdEntAddr {1.3.6.1.2.1.4.20.1.1}	ipAdEntIfIndex {1.3.6.1.2.1.4.20.1.2}	ipAdEntNetMask {1.3.6.1.2.1.4.20.1.3}	ipAdEntBcastAddr {1.3.6.1.2.1.4.20.1.4}	ipAdEntReasmMaxSize {1.3.6.1.2.1.4.20.1.5}
Row 1 XXX.YYY.150.2	1	255.255.255.0	0	12000
Row 2 XXX.YYY.1.1	2	255.255.0.0	1	12000
Row n				

Figure 4-4b. Object instance in the IP address tables

A final example (derived from RFC 1157, section 3.2.6.3) is from the TCP Connection Table, tcpConnTable. Suppose you wish to retrieve the state of the connection between port 575 on local address {a.b.c.d} and port 441 on remote address {w.x.y.z}. The OID for tcpConnState is {1.3.6.1.2.1.6.13.1.1}. The INDEX clause consists of four parts: tcpConnLocalAddress, tcp-ConnLocalPort, tcpConnRemAddress, and tcpConnRemPort. The y suffix would therefore be expressed as {a.b.c.d.575.w.x.y.z.441}. Therefore, the complete variable name would be:

{1.3.6.1.2.1.6.13.1.1.a.b.c.d.575.w.x.y.z.441}

The following examples show specific variable names for both scalar and columnar object types:

➤ The description of this system's services:
sysServices ::=
{1.3.6.1.2.1.1.7.0}

➤ The speed of interface 3:
ifSpeed.3 ::=
{1.3.6.1.2.1.2.2.1.5.3}

➤ The physical address associated with interface 2 and IP address {a.b.c.d} (Note that the first component is a .1, which indicates an IP address [see RFC 1157, page 13]):
atPhysAddress.2.1.a.b.c.d ::=
{1.3.6.1.2.1.3.1.1.2.2.1.a.b.c.d}

➤ The maximum IP datagram reassembly size associated with IP address {a.b.c.d}:
ipAdEntReasmMaxSize.a.b.c.d ::=
{1.3.6.1.2.1.4.20.1.5.a.b.c.d}

➤ The number of ICMP Echo (request) messages received at this device:
icmpInEchos ::=

{1.3.6.1.2.1.5.8.0}

➤ The state of a TCP connection between local port e, local address {a.b.c.d}, and remote port j, remote address {f.g.h.i}:

tcpConnState.a.b.c.d.e.f.g.h.i.j ::=
{1.3.6.1.2.1.6.13.1.1.a.b.c.d.e.f.g.h.i.j}

➤ Verification that a UDP listener is operational on port e of local IP address a.b.c.d:

udpLocalAddress.a.b.c.d.e ::=
{1.3.6.1.2.1.7.5.1.1.a.b.c.d.e}

➤ The neighbor state for the IP address a.b.c.d:

egpNeighState.a.b.c.d ::=
{1.3.6.1.2.1.8.5.1.1.a.b.c.d}

➤ The number of SNMP messages delivered to this device with unknown community names (a scalar):

snmpInBadCommNames ::=
{1.3.6.1.2.1.11.4.0}

RFC 1157, pages 12-15, and RFC 1212, pages 8-10 provide other examples that are worth further study.

With this background into the methods of identifying object instances, let's now discuss the SNMP protocol data units (PDUs) that carry the requests and responses for this information between manager and agent devices. The PDUs use the object instance examples shown here to identify the specific network management information that the manager is seeking.

4.3 SNMP Protocol Data Units (PDUs)

We will begin the discussion of PDUs by describing the position of the SNMP message within a transmitted frame. The frame is the unit of information transmitted between network nodes. For example, an IEEE 802.5 frame format defines the transmission between token ring nodes, and an ANSI T1.617 format defines the transmission between Frame Relay nodes. Chapter 6 explores the various frame formats and the supporting protocols, such as IP, UDP, and ICMP, that may also require analysis.

The local network header and trailers defined by the LAN or WAN protocol delimit the frame (see Figure 4-5). The transmitted data is called an *Internet Protocol (IP) datagram*. The IP datagram is a self-contained unit of information sent from the source host to its intended destination via the internetwork. Inside the datagram is a destination IP address that steers the datagram to the intended recipient. Next, the User Datagram Protocol (UDP) header identifies the higher-layer protocol process (SNMP) that will process the datagram, and provides error control using a checksum. The SNMP message is the innermost part of the frame, carrying the actual data from the manager to and from the agent.

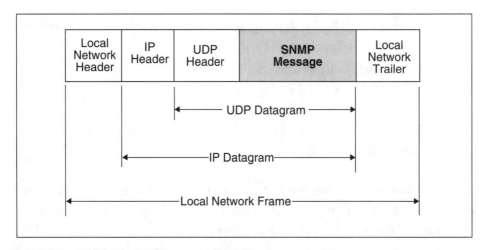

Figure 4-5. SNMP message within a transmission frame

When the IP is too long to fit inside one frame, it may be divided (or fragmented) into several frames for transmission on the LAN. For example, a datagram containing 2500 octets would require two Ethernet frames, each of which may contain a maximum of 1500 octets of higher-layer data. The general structure of each frame, as shown in Figure 4-5, would remain the same.

The SNMP message itself is divided into two sections: a version identifier plus community name, and a PDU. The version identifier and community name are sometimes referred to as the SNMP authentication header. There are five different PDU types: GetRequest, GetNextRequest, GetResponse, SetRequest, and Trap. The Get, Set, and Response PDUs have a common format (see Figure 4-6), while the Trap PDU format is unique (Figure 4-10 later in this chapter illustrates the Trap PDU format).

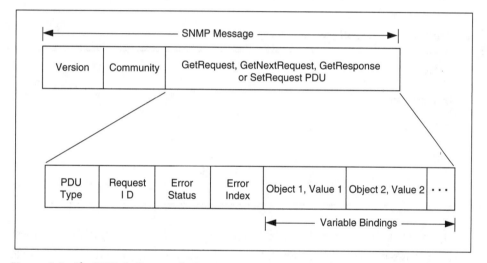

Figure 4-6. The SNMP GetRequest, GetNextRequest, GetResponse, and SetRequest PDU structures

The version number (an INTEGER type) assures that both manager and agent are using the same version of the SNMP protocol. Messages between manager and agent containing different version numbers are discarded without further processing. The community name (an OCTET STRING type) authenticates the manager before allowing access to the agent. The community name, along with the manager's IP address, is stored in the agent's community profile. If there's a difference between the manager and agent values for the community name, the agent will send an authentication failure trap message to the manager. If both the version number and community name from the manager match the ones stored in the agent, the SNMP PDU begins processing.

In the following sections, we'll discuss the fields of the two PDU formats and the operation of the five PDUs. If you feel comfortable with ASN.1 notation, you may wish to refer to the SNMP definition in Section 4.5.

4.3.1 Get, Set, and Response PDU Formats

The GetRequest, GetNextRequest, SetRequest, and GetResponse PDUs share a common format (see Figure 4-6). The first field, PDU Type, specifies the type of PDU the message contains:

PDU	PDU Type Field Value
GetRequest	0
GetNextRequest	1
GetResponse	2
SetRequest	3
Trap	4

The Request ID field is an INTEGER type that correlates the manager's request to the agent's response. The Error Status field is an enumerated INTEGER type that indicates normal operation (noError) or one of five error conditions. The possible values are:

Error	Value	Meaning
noError	0	Proper manager/agent operation.
TooBig	1	The size of the required GetResponse PDU exceeds a local limitation.
noSuchName	2	The requested object name did not match the names available in the relevant MIB View.

badValue	3	A SetRequest contained an inconsistent type, length, and value for the variable.
readOnly	4	Not defined in RFC 1157. (Historical footnote: this error is listed, but the description of the SetRequest PDU processing does not describe how this error is generated. The standard interpretation is that this error should not be generated, although some vendor's agents nevertheless do.)
genErr	5	Other errors, not explicitly defined, have occurred.

When an error occurs, the Error Index field identifies the entry within the variable bindings list that caused the error. For example, if a readOnly error occurred, it would return an Error Index = 4.

A Variable Binding (VarBind) pairs a variable name with its value. A VarBindList is a list of such pairings. Note that within the Variable Bindings fields of the SNMP PDUs (see Figures 4-6 through 4-11), the word Object identifies the variable name (OID encoding of object type plus the instance) for which a value is being communicated. Also note that GetRequest or GetNextRequest PDUs use a value of NULL, which is a special ASN.1 data type.

4.3.2 Using the GetRequest PDU

The manager uses the GetRequest PDU to retrieve the value of one or more object(s) from an agent. In most cases, these are scalar, not columnar, objects. To generate the GetRequest PDU, the manager assigns PDU Type = 0, specifies a locally defined Request ID, and sets both the ErrorStatus and ErrorIndex to 0. A VarBindList, containing the requested variables and corresponding NULL (placeholder) values, completes the PDU. Under error-free conditions, the agent generates a GetResponse PDU, which is assigned PDU Type = 2, the same value of Request ID, Error Status = noError, and Error Index = 0. The Variable Bindings now contain the values associated with each of the variables noted in the GetRequest PDU (see Figure 4-7). Recall that the term variable refers to an instance of a managed object.

Four error conditions are possible:

➤ If a variable in the Variable Bindings field does not exactly match an available object, the agent returns a GetResponse PDU with Error Status = noSuchName, and with the Error Index indicating the index of the variable in question.

➤ If a variable is an aggregate type, such as a row object, the agent returns a GetResponse PDU with Error Status = noSuchName, and with the Error Index indicating the index of the variable in question.

➤ If the size of the appropriate GetResponse PDU would exceed a local limitation, then the agent returns a GetResponse PDU of identical form, with Error Status = tooBig, and Error Index = 0.

➤ If the value of a requested variable cannot be retrieved for any other reason, then the agent returns a GetResponse PDU with Error Status = genErr, and the Error Index indicating the index of the variable in question.

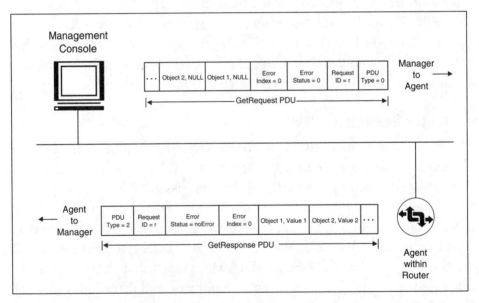

Figure 4-7. GetRequest/GetResponse PDU transmission (with no errors) *(Courtesy 3Com Corp.)*

4.3.3 Using the GetNextRequest PDU

The manager uses the GetNextRequest PDU to retrieve one or more objects and their values from an agent. In most cases, these multiple objects will reside within a table. As you can see in Figure 4-8, to generate the GetNextRequest

PDU the manager assigns PDU Type = 1, specifies a locally defined Request ID, and sets both the ErrorStatus and the ErrorIndex to 0. A VarBindList, containing the OIDs and corresponding NULL (placeholder) values, completes the PDU. These OIDs can be any OID (which may be a variable) that immediately precedes the variable and value returned. Under error-free conditions, the agent generates a GetResponse PDU, which is assigned PDU Type = 2, the same value of Request ID, Error Status = noError, and Error Index = 0. The Variable Bindings contain the name and value associated with the lexicographical successor of each of the OIDs noted in the GetNextRequest PDU.

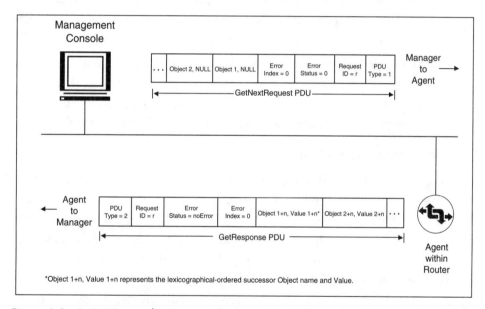

Figure 4-8. GetNextRequest/GetResponse PDU transmission (with no errors) *(Courtesy 3Com Corp.)*

The key difference between the GetRequest and the GetNextRequest PDUs is the word *lexicographical*. That means that the GetNextRequest retrieves the value of the next object within the agent's MIB View. Section 4.4.2 provides an example.

Three error conditions are possible:

> If a variable in the Variable Bindings field does not lexicographically precede the name of an object that may be retrieved (that is, an object available for Get operations and within the relevant MIB View), the agent returns a GetResponse PDU with Error Status = noSuchName, and with the Error Index indicating the index of the variable in question. This condition is called "running off the end of the MIB View."

> If the size of the appropriate GetResponse PDU exceeds a local limitation, the agent returns a GetResponse PDU of identical form, with Error Status = tooBig and Error Index = 0.

> If the value of the lexicographical successor to a requested variable in the Variable Bindings field cannot be retrieved for any other reason, the agent returns a GetResponse PDU, with Error Status = genErr, and the Error Index indicating the index of the variable in question.

4.3.4 Using the SetRequest PDU

The manager uses the SetRequest PDU to assign a value to an object residing in the agent. As you can see in Figure 4-9, to generate that PDU the manager assigns PDU Type = 3, specifies a locally defined Request ID, and sets both the ErrorStatus and ErrorIndex to 0. A VarBindList, containing the specified variables and their corresponding values, completes the PDU. When the agent receives the SetRequest PDU, it alters the values of the named objects to the values in the variable binding. Under error-free conditions, the agent generates a GetResponse PDU of identical form, except that the assigned PDU Type = 2, Error Status = noError, and Error Index = 0

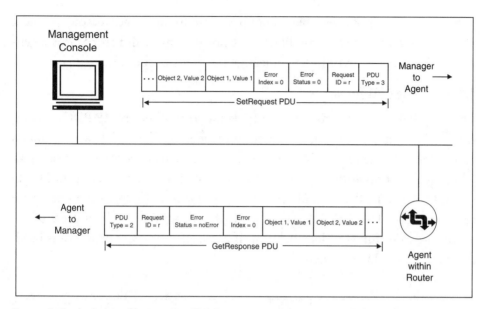

Figure 4-9. SetRequest/GetResponse PDU transmission (with no errors) *(Courtesy 3Com Corp.)*

Four error conditions are possible:

➤   If a variable in the Variable Bindings field is not available for Set operations within the relevant MIB View, the agent returns a GetResponse PDU of identical form, with Error Status = noSuchName, and with the Error Index indicating the index of the object name in question. (Historical note: Some agent implementations return Error Status = readOnly if the object exists, but Access = read-only for that variable.)

➤   If the value of a variable named in the Variable Bindings field does not conform to the ASN.1 Type, Length, and Value required, the agent returns a GetResponse PDU of identical form, with Error Status = badValue and the Error Index indicating the index of the variable in question.

➤   If the size of the appropriate GetResponse PDU exceeds a local limitation, the agent returns a GetResponse PDU of identical form, with Error Status = tooBig, and Error Index = 0.

➤   If the value of a variable cannot be altered for any other reason, the agent returns a GetResponse PDU of identical form, with Error Status = genErr and the Error Index indicating the index of the variable in question.

4.3.5 The Trap PDU Format

The Trap PDU has a format distinct from the four other SNMP PDUs, as you can see in Figure 4-10. The first field indicates the Trap PDU and contains PDU Type = 4. The Enterprise field identifies the management enterprise under whose registration authority the trap was defined. For example, the OID prefix {1.3.6.1.4.1.110} would identify Network General Corp. as the Enterprise sending a trap. The Agent Address field, which contains the IP address of the agent, provides further identification. If a non-IP transport protocol is used, the value 0.0.0.0 is returned.

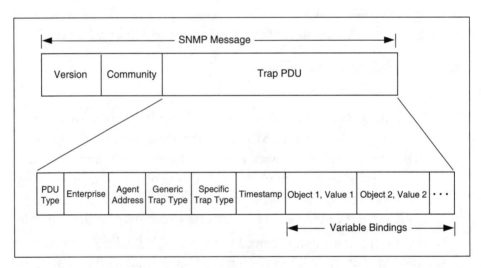

Figure 4-10. SNMP Trap PDU structure

The Generic Trap type provides more specific information on the event being reported. There are seven defined values (enumerated INTEGER types) for this field:

Trap	Value	Meaning
coldStart	0	The sending protocol entity (higher-layer network management) has reinitialized, indicating that the agent's configuration or entity implementation may be altered.
warmStart	1	The sending protocol has reinitialized, but neither the agent's configuration nor the protocol entity implementation has been altered.
linkDown	2	A communication link has failed. The affected interface is identified as the first element within the Variable Bindings field: name and value of the *ifIndex* instance.
linkUp	3	A communication link has come up. The affected interface is identified as the first element within the Variable Bindings field: name and value of the *ifIndex* instance.
authenticationFailure	4	The agent has received an improperly authenticated SNMP message from the manager; that is, the community name was incorrect.
egpNeighborLoss	5	An EGP peer neighbor is down.
enterpriseSpecific	6	A nongeneric trap has occurred, which is further identified by the Specific Trap Type field and Enterprise field.

Two additional fields complete the Trap PDU. The Timestamp field contains the value of the sysUpTime object, representing the amount of time elapsed between the last (re-)initialization of the agent and the generation of that Trap. The last field contains the Variable Bindings.

4.3.6 Using the Trap PDU

The agent uses the Trap PDU to alert the manager that a predefined event has occurred. To generate the Trap PDU, the agent assigns PDU Type = 4 and fills in the Enterprise, Agent Address, Generic Trap, Specific Trap Type, and Timestamp fields, as well as the Variable Bindings list.

By definition (and convention), Traps are application specific. Therefore, it would be difficult to cover the range of uses for this PDU. RFC 1215, "A Convention for Defining Traps for Use with the SNMP," offers some guidelines for their use [4-5]. Figure 4-11 illustrates how an agent in a router could use a Trap to communicate a significant event to the manager. Section 4.4.4 provides an example of a real-world application.

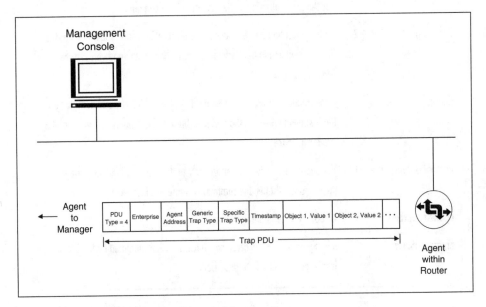

Figure 4-11. Trap PDU operation *(Courtesy 3Com Corp.)*

4.3.7 SNMP PDU Encoding

Recall from our discussion in Chapter 2 that the SNMP PDUs are encoded using the context-specific class, with a tag that identifies the PDU (review Figure 2-15). The Length and Value fields are then constructed to convey a particular structure and quantity of information. Now that we have discussed the structure of the SNMP PDUs, we can revisit these encodings in more detail.

Figure 4-12 shows an example of a TLV encoding of an SNMP PDU. Note that the entire encoding begins with a SEQUENCE OF type. The version is an INTEGER type, and the community name is an OCTET STRING type. A context-specific type then indicates the specific PDU and its length. Three

INTEGER types provide the Request ID, Error Status, and Error Index. The VarBind list, consisting of multiple SEQUENCE OF encodings, completes the PDU. The following examples illustrate the details of this encoding structure.

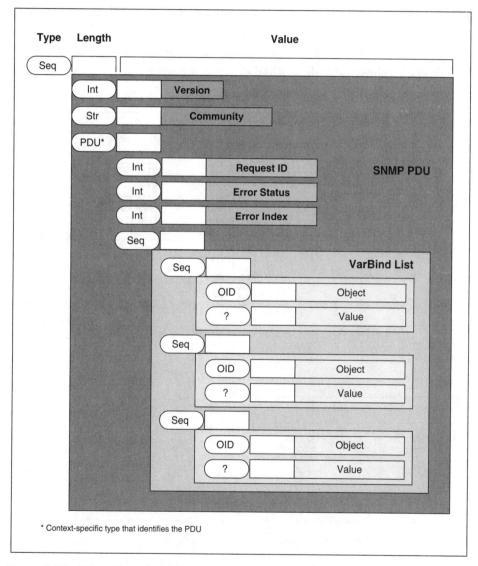

Figure 4-12. TLV encoding of an SNMP PDU *(Courtesy Network General Corp.)*

4.4 Application Examples

To illustrate the SNMP PDUs discussed in this chapter, this section presents four examples of the protocol in use. The network analyzer captured each sample from an Ethernet backbone, which contained several other Ethernet segments connected by bridges and routers (see Figure 4-13). For these cases, the SNMP manager was a Sun workstation running SunNet Manager, and a Proteon router contained the SNMP agent. In all of these examples, the traces are filtered to show only the SNMP protocol interaction.

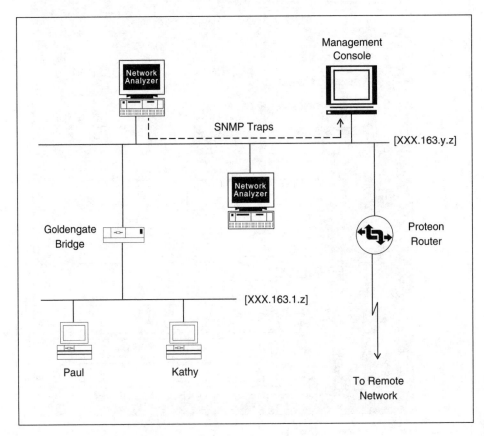

Figure 4-13. SNMP traps from a network analyzer

4.4.1 SNMP GetRequest Example

Recall from our earlier discussion that the GetRequest PDU retrieves one or more objects. Trace 4.4.1 illustrates how the UDP group (review Figure 3-8) does this.

Trace 4.4.1. Retrieving scalar data using the GetRequest PDU: The UDP Group

Sniffer Network Analyzer data 10-Nov at 11:03:08, file UDP.ENC, Pg 1

```
----------------------------------------- Frame 61 -----------------------------------------
SNMP: ----- Simple Network Management Protocol -----
SNMP:
SNMP: Version = 0
SNMP: Community = Brutus
SNMP: Command = Get request
SNMP: Request ID = 0
SNMP: Error status = 0 (No error)
SNMP: Error index = 0
SNMP:
SNMP: Object = {1.3.6.1.2.1.1.3.0} (sysUpTime.0)
SNMP: Value  = NULL
SNMP:
SNMP: Object = {1.3.6.1.2.1.7.1.0} (udpInDatagrams.0)
SNMP: Value  = NULL
SNMP:
SNMP: Object = {1.3.6.1.2.1.7.2.0} (udpNoPorts.0)
SNMP: Value  = NULL
SNMP:
SNMP: Object = {1.3.6.1.2.1.7.3.0} (udpInErrors.0)
SNMP: Value  = NULL
SNMP:
SNMP: Object = {1.3.6.1.2.1.7.4.0} (udpOutDatagrams.0)
SNMP: Value  = NULL
SNMP:
```

```
----------------------------------------- Frame 62 -----------------------------------------
SNMP: ----- Simple Network Management Protocol -----
SNMP:
SNMP: Version = 0
SNMP: Community = Brutus
SNMP: Command = Get response
SNMP: Request ID = 0
SNMP: Error status = 0 (No error)
SNMP: Error index = 0
SNMP:
SNMP: Object = {1.3.6.1.2.1.1.3.0} (sysUpTime.0)
SNMP: Value  = 263748621 hundredths of a second
SNMP:
SNMP: Object = {1.3.6.1.2.1.7.1.0} (udpInDatagrams.0)
SNMP: Value  = 573894 datagrams
SNMP:
SNMP: Object = {1.3.6.1.2.1.7.2.0} (udpNoPorts.0)
SNMP: Value  = 419103 datagrams
SNMP:
SNMP: Object = {1.3.6.1.2.1.7.3.0} (udpInErrors.0)
SNMP: Value  = 0 datagrams
SNMP:
SNMP: Object = {1.3.6.1.2.1.7.4.0} (udpOutDatagrams.0)
SNMP: Value  = 288892 datagrams
SNMP:
```

Trace 4.4.1 consists of two SNMP PDUs: the GetRequest (Frame 61) and the GetResponse (Frame 62). Both frames illustrate their respective PDU structures (as described in Figures 4-6 and 4-7): Version = 0, Community = Brutus, Command (PDU Type 0 or 2), Request ID = 0, Error Status = 0, and Error Index = 0.

Next, the VarBindList indicates the variables and associated values being requested or supplied. You can observe two things here. First, the SunNet

Manager always asks for the sysUpTime before requesting other objects. (Other management consoles may construct the VarBindList in another fashion.) The sysUpTime provides a time-stamp update for the Sun console, and is an input to the Sun graphical display of the network management statistics. Second, the values associated with the objects in the GetRequest have a Value = NULL. Recall that NULL is the ASN.1 type used as a placeholder in the data stream. When you look at the GetResponse in Frame 62, you'll see that each NULL value has been replaced with a measured value. For example, the number of UDP datagrams that have been delivered to UDP users, udpInDatagrams {1.3.6.1.2.1.7.1.0}, has a value of 573,894 datagrams. You can interpret the rest of the VarBindList in Frame 62 in a similar manner.

4.4.2 SNMP GetNextRequest Example

The GetNextRequest PDU retrieves the lexicographical successor (or next) object, and is often used to retrieve objects from a table. Reviewing Figure 3-8, consider the UDP table, {1.3.6.1.2.7.5}. This table contains two columns, udpLocalAddress and udpLocalPort. Together, these two entries associate a local IP address with a local port number, as follows:

udpTable

udpLocalAddress	udpLocalPort
0.0.0.0	1
a.b.c.d	2
.	.
.	.
.	.

Note that the address [0.0.0.0] indicates that a UDP listener is willing to accept datagrams for any interface on this node.

In Trace 4.4.2, the SunNet Manager wishes to retrieve all the values in the UDP Table. To do so, it issues the first GetNextRequest to specify OIDs that are lexicographically immediately before any udpLocalAddress objects and before udpLocalPort objects (see Frame 33). Frame 34 returns the contents of the first row, indicating a udpLocalAddress [0.0.0.0], udpLocalPort 69, the Trivial File Transfer Protocol (TFTP) port, and object {1.3.6.1.2.1.7.5.1.1.0.0.0.0.69}. [Reviewing Section 4.2.2, note that this table is indexed by the IP address (e.g. 0.0.0.0) and the local port (e.g. 69).]

The GetNextRequest in Frame 35 is identical to the one in Frame 33, except that it requests the object returned in Frame 34, that is, the next value after {1.3.6.1.2.1.7.5.1.1.0.0.0.0.69}. Frame 36 returns the response, which is the value of the second row: {1.3.6.1.2.1.7.5.1.1.0.0.0.0.161}, which identifies the SNMP port. Frames 37 continues the pattern, with the value of the third row identifying port 520 (a local routing port).

Note that Frame 38 reaches the end of the table, indicated by the GetResponse given in Frame 40, which moves to a different group within the OID tree. This final value is the lexicographical next item in the router's MIB, object snmpInPkts, the first object of the SNMP group. This means that the router did not have any item in the Transmission group {mib-2 10} in its MIB View. (These groups were in the router's MIB, however, so access to those groups using the same community name was not possible.)

The UDP table constructed from the data in Trace 4.4.2 is as follows:

udpTable

udpLocalAddress	udpLocalPort
0.0.0.0	69 (TFTP)
0.0.0.0	161 (SNMP)
0.0.0.0	520 (Router)

Trace 4.4.2. Retrieving tabular data with the GetNextRequest PDU: The udpTable

Sniffer Network Analyzer data 10-Nov at 11:03:58, file UDT.ENC, Pg 1

--- Frame 33 ---
SNMP: ----- Simple Network Management Protocol -----
SNMP:
SNMP: Version = 0
SNMP: Community = Brutus
SNMP: Command = Get next request
SNMP: Request ID = 0
SNMP: Error status = 0 (No error)
SNMP: Error index = 0
SNMP:
SNMP: Object = {1.3.6.1.2.1.1.3} (sysUpTime)
SNMP: Value = NULL
SNMP:
SNMP: Object = {1.3.6.1.2.1.7.5.1.1} (udpLocalAddress)
SNMP: Value = NULL
SNMP:
SNMP: Object = {1.3.6.1.2.1.7.5.1.2} (udpLocalPort)
SNMP: Value = NULL
SNMP:

--- Frame 34 ---
SNMP: ----- Simple Network Management Protocol -----
SNMP:
SNMP: Version = 0
SNMP: Community = Brutus
SNMP: Command = Get response
SNMP: Request ID = 0
SNMP: Error status = 0 (No error)
SNMP: Error index = 0
SNMP:

SNMP: Object = {1.3.6.1.2.1.1.3.0} (sysUpTime.0)
SNMP: Value = 263753458 hundredths of a second
SNMP:
SNMP: Object = {1.3.6.1.2.1.7.5.1.1.0.0.0.0.69} (udpLocalAddress.0.0.0.0.69)
SNMP: Value = [0.0.0.0]
SNMP:
SNMP: Object = {1.3.6.1.2.1.7.5.1.2.0.0.0.0.69} (udpLocalPort.0.0.0.0.69)
SNMP: Value = 69
SNMP:

--- Frame 35 ---
SNMP: ----- Simple Network Management Protocol -----
SNMP:
SNMP: Version = 0
SNMP: Community = Brutus
SNMP: Command = Get next request
SNMP: Request ID = 0
SNMP: Error status = 0 (No error)
SNMP: Error index = 0
SNMP:
SNMP: Object = {1.3.6.1.2.1.1.3} (sysUpTime)
SNMP: Value = NULL
SNMP:
SNMP: Object = {1.3.6.1.2.1.7.5.1.1.0.0.0.0.69} (udpLocalAddress.0.0.0.0.69)
SNMP: Value = NULL
SNMP:
SNMP: Object = {1.3.6.1.2.1.7.5.1.2.0.0.0.0.69} (udpLocalPort.0.0.0.0.69)
SNMP: Value = NULL
SNMP:

--- Frame 36 ---
SNMP: ----- Simple Network Management Protocol -----
SNMP:
SNMP: Version = 0
SNMP: Community = Brutus

SNMP: Command = Get response
SNMP: Request ID = 0
SNMP: Error status = 0 (No error)
SNMP: Error index = 0
SNMP:
SNMP: Object = {1.3.6.1.2.1.1.3.0} (sysUpTime.0)
SNMP: Value = 263753461 hundredths of a second
SNMP:
SNMP: Object = {1.3.6.1.2.1.7.5.1.1.0.0.0.0.161} (udpLocalAddress.0.0.0.0.161)
SNMP: Value = [0.0.0.0]
SNMP:
SNMP: Object = {1.3.6.1.2.1.7.5.1.2.0.0.0.0.161} (udpLocalPort.0.0.0.0.161)
SNMP: Value = 161
SNMP:

-- Frame 37 --
SNMP: ----- Simple Network Management Protocol -----
SNMP:
SNMP: Version = 0
SNMP: Community = Brutus
SNMP: Command = Get next request
SNMP: Request ID = 0
SNMP: Error status = 0 (No error)
SNMP: Error index = 0
SNMP:
SNMP: Object = {1.3.6.1.2.1.1.3} (sysUpTime)
SNMP: Value = NULL
SNMP:
SNMP: Object = {1.3.6.1.2.1.7.5.1.1.0.0.0.0.161} (udpLocalAddress.0.0.0.0.161)
SNMP: Value = NULL
SNMP:
SNMP: Object = {1.3.6.1.2.1.7.5.1.2.0.0.0.0.161} (udpLocalPort.0.0.0.0.161)
SNMP: Value = NULL
SNMP:

```
--------------------------------------- Frame 38 ---------------------------------------
SNMP: ----- Simple Network Management Protocol -----
SNMP:
SNMP: Version = 0
SNMP: Community = Brutus
SNMP: Command = Get response
SNMP: Request ID = 0
SNMP: Error status = 0 (No error)
SNMP: Error index = 0
SNMP:
SNMP: Object = {1.3.6.1.2.1.1.3.0} (sysUpTime.0)
SNMP: Value  = 263753463 hundredths of a second
SNMP:
SNMP: Object = {1.3.6.1.2.1.7.5.1.1.0.0.0.0.520} (udpLocalAddress.0.0.0.0.520)
SNMP: Value  = [0.0.0.0]
SNMP:
SNMP: Object = {1.3.6.1.2.1.7.5.1.2.0.0.0.0.520} (udpLocalPort.0.0.0.0.520)
SNMP: Value  = 520
SNMP:


--------------------------------------- Frame 39 ---------------------------------------
SNMP: ----- Simple Network Management Protocol -----
SNMP:
SNMP: Version = 0
SNMP: Community = Brutus
SNMP: Command = Get next request
SNMP: Request ID = 0
SNMP: Error status = 0 (No error)
SNMP: Error index = 0
SNMP:
SNMP: Object = {1.3.6.1.2.1.1.3} (sysUpTime)
SNMP: Value  = NULL
SNMP:
SNMP: Object = {1.3.6.1.2.1.7.5.1.1.0.0.0.0.520} (udpLocalAddress.0.0.0.0.520)
```

```
SNMP: Value  = NULL
SNMP:
SNMP: Object = {1.3.6.1.2.1.7.5.1.2.0.0.0.0.520} (udpLocalPort.0.0.0.0.520)
SNMP: Value  = NULL
SNMP:


----------------------------------- Frame 40 -----------------------------------
SNMP: ----- Simple Network Management Protocol -----
SNMP:
SNMP: Version = 0
SNMP: Community = Brutus
SNMP: Command = Get response
SNMP: Request ID = 0
SNMP: Error status = 0 (No error)
SNMP: Error index = 0
SNMP:
SNMP: Object = {1.3.6.1.2.1.1.3.0} (sysUpTime.0)
SNMP: Value  = 263753466 hundredths of a second
SNMP:
SNMP: Object = {1.3.6.1.2.1.7.5.1.2.0.0.0.0.69} (udpLocalPort.0.0.0.0.69)
SNMP: Value  = 69
SNMP:
SNMP: Object = {1.3.6.1.2.1.11.1.0} (snmpInPkts.0)
SNMP: Value  = 116744 (counter)
SNMP:
```

4.4.3 SNMP SetRequest Example

This example issues a SetRequest PDU for an object on the Proteon router, then issues a GetRequest for the same object (see Trace 4.4.3) to verify that the action was properly completed. Frames 1 and 2 retrieve the current value of ipDefaultTTL; Frames 3 and 4 set a new value for that object; Frames 5 and 6 verify the new value; Frames 7 and 8 set the value back to the original; and finally, Frames 9 and 10 verify the previous operation.

Looking at the details, notice that in Frame 1 the Value = NULL as in the previous example. The GetResponse PDU (Frame 2) contains the requested value (60) of ipDefaultTTL (the default value of the Time-to-Live field within the IP header). Frame 3 contains a SetRequest PDU, assigning Value = 64 to ipDefaultTTL. The router sends a confirming GetResponse PDU in Frame 4. Frame 5 issues a GetRequest PDU to verify that the SetRequest changed the value of ipDefaultTTL to 64 (Frame 6). Frame 7 issues a second SetRequest, this time with Value = 60, which is acknowledged in Frame 8. Frames 9 and 10 confirm that the operation was successful.

Trace 4.4.3. SNNP Set ipDefaultTTL details

Sniffer Network Analyzer data 11-Dec at 15:16:52 file SETIPTTL.ENC Pg 1

```
----------------------------------------- Frame 1 -----------------------------------------
SNMP: ----- Simple Network Management Protocol -----
SNMP:
SNMP: Version = 0
SNMP: Community = Brutus
SNMP: Command = Get request
SNMP: Request ID = 0
SNMP: Error status = 0 (No error)
SNMP: Error index = 0
SNMP:
SNMP: Object = {1.3.6.1.2.1.1.3.0} (sysUpTime.0)
SNMP: Value  = NULL
SNMP:
SNMP: Object = {1.3.6.1.2.1.4.1.0} (ipForwarding.0)
SNMP: Value  = NULL
SNMP:
SNMP: Object = {1.3.6.1.2.1.4.2.0} (ipDefaultTTL.0)
SNMP: Value  = NULL
SNMP:
```

```
------------------------------------- Frame 2 -------------------------------------
SNMP: ----- Simple Network Management Protocol -----
SNMP:
SNMP: Version = 0
SNMP: Community = Brutus
SNMP: Command = Get response
SNMP: Request ID = 0
SNMP: Error status = 0 (No error)
SNMP: Error index = 0
SNMP:
SNMP: Object = {1.3.6.1.2.1.1.3.0} (sysUpTime.0)
SNMP: Value  = 16862273 hundredths of a second
SNMP:
SNMP: Object = {1.3.6.1.2.1.4.1.0} (ipForwarding.0)
SNMP: Value  = 1 (gateway)
SNMP:
SNMP: Object = {1.3.6.1.2.1.4.2.0} (ipDefaultTTL.0)
SNMP: Value  = 60
SNMP:


------------------------------------- Frame 3 -------------------------------------
SNMP: ----- Simple Network Management Protocol -----
SNMP:
SNMP: Version = 0
SNMP: Community = Brutus
SNMP: Command = Set request
SNMP: Request ID = 0
SNMP: Error status = 0 (No error)
SNMP: Error index = 0
SNMP:
SNMP: Object = {1.3.6.1.2.1.4.2.0} (ipDefaultTTL.0)
SNMP: Value  = 64
SNMP:
```

```
---------------------------------------- Frame 4 ----------------------------------------
SNMP: ----- Simple Network Management Protocol -----
SNMP:
SNMP: Version = 0
SNMP: Community = Brutus
SNMP: Command = Get response
SNMP: Request ID = 0
SNMP: Error status = 0 (No error)
SNMP: Error index = 0
SNMP:
SNMP: Object = {1.3.6.1.2.1.4.2.0} (ipDefaultTTL.0)
SNMP: Value  = 64
SNMP:


---------------------------------------- Frame 5 ----------------------------------------
SNMP: ----- Simple Network Management Protocol -----
SNMP:
SNMP: Version = 0
SNMP: Community = Brutus
SNMP: Command = Get request
SNMP: Request ID = 0
SNMP: Error status = 0 (No error)
SNMP: Error index = 0
SNMP:
SNMP: Object = {1.3.6.1.2.1.1.3.0} (sysUpTime.0)
SNMP: Value  = NULL
SNMP:
SNMP: Object = {1.3.6.1.2.1.4.1.0} (ipForwarding.0)
SNMP: Value  = NULL
SNMP:
SNMP: Object = {1.3.6.1.2.1.4.2.0} (ipDefaultTTL.0)
SNMP: Value  = NULL
SNMP:
```

```
------------------------------------ Frame 6 ------------------------------------
SNMP: ----- Simple Network Management Protocol -----
SNMP:
SNMP: Version = 0
SNMP: Community = Brutus
SNMP: Command = Get response
SNMP: Request ID = 0
SNMP: Error status = 0 (No error)
SNMP: Error index = 0
SNMP:
SNMP: Object = {1.3.6.1.2.1.1.3.0} (sysUpTime.0)
SNMP: Value  = 16863228 hundredths of a second
SNMP:
SNMP: Object = {1.3.6.1.2.1.4.1.0} (ipForwarding.0)
SNMP: Value  = 1 (gateway)
SNMP:
SNMP: Object = {1.3.6.1.2.1.4.2.0} (ipDefaultTTL.0)
SNMP: Value  = 64
SNMP:


------------------------------------ Frame 7 ------------------------------------
SNMP: ----- Simple Network Management Protocol -----
SNMP:
SNMP: Version = 0
SNMP: Community = Brutus
SNMP: Command = Set request
SNMP: Request ID = 0
SNMP: Error status = 0 (No error)
SNMP: Error index = 0
SNMP:
SNMP: Object = {1.3.6.1.2.1.4.2.0} (ipDefaultTTL.0)
SNMP: Value  = 60
SNMP:
```

```
---------------------------------------- Frame 8 ----------------------------------------
SNMP: ----- Simple Network Management Protocol -----
SNMP:
SNMP: Version = 0
SNMP: Community = Brutus
SNMP: Command = Get response
SNMP: Request ID = 0
SNMP: Error status = 0 (No error)
SNMP: Error index = 0
SNMP:
SNMP: Object = {1.3.6.1.2.1.4.2.0} (ipDefaultTTL.0)
SNMP: Value  = 60
SNMP:


---------------------------------------- Frame 9 ----------------------------------------
SNMP: ----- Simple Network Management Protocol -----
SNMP:
SNMP: Version = 0
SNMP: Community = Brutus
SNMP: Command = Get request
SNMP: Request ID = 0
SNMP: Error status = 0 (No error)
SNMP: Error index = 0
SNMP:
SNMP: Object = {1.3.6.1.2.1.1.3.0} (sysUpTime.0)
SNMP: Value  = NULL
SNMP:
SNMP: Object = {1.3.6.1.2.1.4.1.0} (ipForwarding.0)
SNMP: Value  = NULL
SNMP:
SNMP: Object = {1.3.6.1.2.1.4.2.0} (ipDefaultTTL.0)
SNMP: Value  = NULL
SNMP:
```

```
-------------------------------------- Frame 10 --------------------------------------
SNMP: ----- Simple Network Management Protocol -----
SNMP:
SNMP: Version = 0
SNMP: Community = Brutus
SNMP: Command = Get response
SNMP: Request ID = 0
SNMP: Error status = 0 (No error)
SNMP: Error index = 0
SNMP:
SNMP: Object = {1.3.6.1.2.1.1.3.0} (sysUpTime.0)
SNMP: Value  = 16863846 hundredths of a second
SNMP:
SNMP: Object = {1.3.6.1.2.1.4.1.0} (ipForwarding.0)
SNMP: Value  = 1 (gateway)
SNMP:
SNMP: Object = {1.3.6.1.2.1.4.2.0} (ipDefaultTTL.0)
SNMP: Value  = 60
SNMP:
```

4.4.4 SNMP Trap Example

The final example shows how a Trap PDU indicates an alarm condition to the network manager. In this case, the agent generating the trap is a Network General Sniffer protocol analyzer (see Figure 4-13).

One set of network statistics is network utilization. Network utilization is a ratio between the total number of bits transmitted in a period of time (in this case five seconds) divided by the total number of bits that could theoretically be transmitted during the same period. A typical network would have a network utilization in the 5 to 20 percent range. For this example, I set the threshold to the unrealistically low value of 1 percent over a five second period. When the network reaches that threshold, the Sniffer generates a Trap PDU and sends it to the SunNet Manager. Another Sniffer analyzer captured the results.

This transmission follows the Trap PDU structure shown in Figure 4-10. The SNMP authentication header contains the version number and community string, and the PDU Type specifies a Trap (PDU Type = 4). The Enterprise field gives the OID for the authority that defined the trap. The prefix {1.3.6.1.4.1} identifies the Private Enterprises subtree, and the 110 identifies Network General Corporation (see RFC 1700, or Appendix F). The Generic Trap field indicates an enterprise-specific trap (Trap = 6). This means that the value of the Enterprise field indicates the authority (Network General) that defined this trap.

The Specific Trap field has Type = 7, which Network General defined. The variable bindings also contain variables and values that Network General defined. The third object's value (Abs usage exceeded 1 percent) indicates the threshold set in the protocol analyzer.

Trace 4.4.4. An enterprise-specific trap: Network utilization exceeded 1 percent during a five second period.

```
Sniffer Network Analyzer data 11-Dec at 16:13:26 file SNIFTRAP.ENC Pg 1

---------------------------------------- Frame 1 ----------------------------------------
SNMP: ----- Simple Network Management Protocol -----
SNMP:
SNMP: Version = 0
SNMP: Community = public
SNMP: Command = Trap
SNMP: Enterprise = {1.3.6.1.4.1.110.1.1.1.0}
SNMP: Network address = [132.163.128.102]
SNMP: Generic trap = 6 (Enterprise specific)
SNMP: Specific trap = 7
SNMP: Time ticks = 244894900
SNMP:
SNMP: Object = {1.3.6.1.4.1.110.1.1.1.1.1.1.1.1}
                (Network General Corp.1.1.1.1.1.1.1.1)
SNMP: Value  = 53 (counter)
SNMP:
```

```
SNMP: Object = {1.3.6.1.4.1.110.1.1.1.1.1.1.2.1}
              (Network General Corp.1.1.1.1.1.1.2.1)
SNMP: Value  = 1
SNMP:
SNMP: Object = {1.3.6.1.4.1.110.1.1.1.1.1.1.3.1}
              (Network General Corp.1.1.1.1.1.1.3.1)
SNMP: Value  = Abs usage exceeded 1%
SNMP:
SNMP: Object = {1.3.6.1.4.1.110.1.1.1.1.1.1.4.1
              (Network General Corp.1.1.1.1.1.1.4.1)
SNMP: Value  = 5
SNMP:
SNMP: Object = {1.3.6.1.4.1.110.1.1.1.1.1.1.5.1}
              (Network General Corp.1.1.1.1.1.1.5.1)
SNMP: Value  = 0
SNMP:
SNMP: Object = {1.3.6.1.4.1.110.1.1.1.1.1.1.6.1}
              (Network General Corp.1.1.1.1.1.1.6.1)
SNMP: Value  = 7
SNMP:
SNMP: Object = {1.3.6.1.4.1.110.1.1.1.1.1.1.7.1}
              (Network General Corp.1.1.1.1.1.1.7.1)
SNMP: Value  = 724119640 (counter)
SNMP:
SNMP: Object = {1.3.6.1.4.1.110.1.1.1.1.1.1.8.1}
              (Network General Corp .1.1.1.1.1.1.8.1)
SNMP: Value  = Global Network
SNMP:
```

4.5 The ASN.1 SNMP Definition

To conclude the discussion of SNMP protocol operation, Definition 4-1 is the ASN.1 definition of SNMP (from RFC 1157). Of special interest are the constructs of the various SNMP PDUs. Those constructs summarize the variables used within the PDUs, plus the values that those variables may assume.

Definition 4-1. The ASN.1 definition of SNMP

```
RFC1157-SNMP DEFINITIONS ::= BEGIN
IMPORTS
    ObjectName, ObjectSyntax, NetworkAddress, IpAddress, TimeTicks
        FROM RFC1155-SMI;


-- top-level message

    Message ::=
        SEQUENCE {
            version                 -- version-1 for this RFC
                INTEGER {
                    version-1(0)
                },
            community               -- community name
                OCTET STRING,
            data                    -- e.g., PDUs if trivial
                ANY                 -- authentication is being used
        }
    -- protocol data units

    PDUs ::=
        CHOICE {
                get-request
                    GetRequest-PDU,

                get-next-request
                    GetNextRequest-PDU,

                get-response
                    GetResponse-PDU,

                set-request
                    SetRequest-PDU,
```

```
        trap
           Trap-PDU
          }

-- PDUs
GetRequest-PDU ::=
   [0]
       IMPLICIT PDU
GetNextRequest-PDU ::=
   [1]
       IMPLICIT PDU
GetResponse-PDU ::=
   [2]
       IMPLICIT PDU
SetRequest-PDU ::=
   [3]
       IMPLICIT PDU
PDU ::=
       SEQUENCE {
          request-id
             INTEGER,
          error-status          -- sometimes ignored
             INTEGER {
                 noError(0),
                 tooBig(1),
                 noSuchName(2),
                 badValue(3),
                 readOnly(4),
                 genErr(5)
             },
          error-index          -- sometimes ignored
             INTEGER,
          variable-bindings    -- values are sometimes ignored
             VarBindList
```

```
            }
Trap-PDU ::=
    [4]
    IMPLICIT SEQUENCE {
        enterprise                  -- type of object generating
                                    -- trap, see sysObjectID in [5]

        OBJECT IDENTIFIER,
        agent-addr                  -- address of object generating
            NetworkAddress,          -- trap
        generic-trap                -- generic trap type
            INTEGER {
                coldStart(0),
                warmStart(1),
                linkDown(2),
                linkUp(3),
                authenticationFailure(4),
                egpNeighborLoss(5),
                enterpriseSpecific(6)
            },
        specific-trap               -- specific code, present even
            INTEGER,                 -- if generic-trap is not
                                    -- enterpriseSpecific
        time-stamp                  -- time elapsed between the last
            TimeTicks,               -- (re-)initialization of the
                                    --    network
                                    -- entity and the generation of
                                    --    the trap
        variable-bindings           -- "interesting" information
            VarBindList
    }

-- variable bindings
```

```
VarBind ::=
    SEQUENCE {
        name
            ObjectName,
        value
            ObjectSyntax
    }
VarBindList ::=
    SEQUENCE OF
        VarBind
END
```

This chapter has explored the structure of the SNMP messages and looked at some examples of various SNMP PDUs. The Internet Engineering Task Force (IETF) has enhanced SNMP by adding support for new PDUs, security and other features. These enhancements are part of SNMP version 2, which will be discussed in the next chapter.

4.6 References

[4-1]   Case, J.D., M. Fedor, M.L. Schoffstall, and C. Davin. "Simple Network Management Protocol (SNMP)." *RFC 1157*, May 1990.

[4-2]   Case, Jeffrey D., et al. "Network Management and the Design of SNMP." *ConneXions* (March 1989): 22-26.

[4-3]   Kastenholz, F., ed. "SNMP Communication Services." *RFC 1270*, October 1991.

[4-4]   Davin, J., J. Galvin, and K. Mcloghrie. "SNMP Administrative Model." *RFC 1351*, July 1992.

[4-5]   Rose, M.T. ed. "A Convention for Defining Traps for Use with the SNMP." *RFC 1215*, March 1991.

5 SNMP Version 2

The original version of SNMP (SNMPv1) was derived from the Simple Gateway Monitoring Protocol (SGMP) and published as an RFC in 1988. At that time, the industry agreed that SNMP would be an interim solution until OSI-based network management using CMIS/CMIP became more mature. Since then, however, SNMP has become more popular while the OSI solution has been less widely adopted than was anticipated originally. As a result, it became appropriate to revise and improve SNMPv1. This chapter will discuss the development of SNMPv2 and the resulting enhancements to SNMPv1.

5.1 The Development of SNMPv2

In March of 1992, the IETF solicited proposals to enhance SNMPv1. A team consisting of Jeffrey Case, Keith McCloghrie, Marshall Rose, and Steven Waldbusser prepared a proposal called the Simple Management Protocol (SMP). At about the same time, the IETF initiated another effort aimed at enhancing SNMP security. These two research efforts merged and became known as version 2 of the Internet-standard Network Management Framework, or simply the SNMPv2 framework. The new documentation comprised more than 400 pages in twelve documents (RFCs 1441 to 1452). The first document, "An Introduction to SNMPv2" [5-1], provided an overview of the remaining documents.

Unfortunately, the first SNMPv2 design (which is now referred to as Party-based SNMPv2) was not widely accepted in the marketplace. Frequently cited reasons were the complexities of the security enhancements and the administrative framework. The SNMPv2 Working Group reconvened in late 1994 and several simplified approaches for the administrative framework were considered; however, no consensus was reached. As a result, three actions occurred:

➤ Documents which had the consensus of the SNMPv2 Working Group were published in January 1996 as RFCs 1902–1908.

➤ Minor modifications to the SNMPv2 Security and Administrative model, called *Community-based SNMPv2* (or SNMPv2C), were published in January 1996 as RFC 1901 [5-2].

➤ Work continues on the unfinished elements: security, administrative framework, a remote configuration MIB, and Manager-to-Manager communication.

The documentation for the April 1993 and January 1996 publications of SNMPv2 can be compared as follows (Obsolete RFCs are noted with an "O" and Historic RFCs are noted with an "H"):

Previous RFC	Subject	Current RFC
1441	Introduction to SNMPv2 Introduction to Community-based SNMPv2	1901
1442-O	Structure of Management Information for version 2 of the Simple Network Management Protocol (SNMPv2)	1902
1443-O	Textual Conventions for version 2 of the Simple Network Management Protocol (SNMPv2)	1903
1444-O	Conformance Statements for version 2 of the Simple Network Management Protocol (SNMPv2)	1904
1445-H	Administrative Model for version 2 of the Simple Network Management Protocol (SNMPv2)	
1446-H	Security Protocols for version 2 of the Simple Network Management Protocol (SNMPv2)	
1447-H	Party MIB for version 2 of the Simple Network Management Protocol (SNMPv2)	
1448-O	Protocol Operations for version 2 of the Simple Network Management Protocol (SNMPv2)	1905

1449-0	Transport Mappings for version 2 of the Simple Network Management Protocol (SNMPv2)	1906
1450-0	Management Information Base for version 2 of the Simple Network Management Protocol (SNMPv2)	1907
1451-H	Manager-to-Manager Management Information Base	
1452-0	Coexistence between version 1 and version 2 of the Internet-standard Network Management Framework	1908

The major enhancements included in SNMPv2 include: new data types, new macros, textual conventions, protocol operations that facilitate bulk data transfers, richer error codes, and multiprotocol transport support. This chapter will discuss these key enhancements in the SNMPv2C framework and will refer you to the appropriate sources for further details.

5.2 The SNMPv2 Structure of Management Information

As Chapter 2 discussed, MIB modules provide a mechanism for grouping similar objects. The SMI for SNMPv2 [5-3] defines the subset of the ASN.1 language that describes various MIB modules. SNMPv2 has two documents that support the SMI: the Conformance Statements and the Textual Conventions. The Textual Conventions define the data types used within these MIB modules and make it easier to read the modules [5-4]. The conformance statements provide an implementation baseline and include, for example, a lower bound on what agents must support [5-5].

The SMI also defines two new branches of the Internet OID tree: security {1.3.6.1.5} and snmpV2 {1.3.6.1.6}. Under snmpV2 are the Transport domains (snmpDomains); Transport proxies (snmpProxys); and Module identities (snmp-Modules). Defined under the snmpModules are the SNMPv2 MIB (snmpMIB); the Manager to Manager MIB, (snmpM2M); and the Party MIB (partyMIB). Note that at the time of this writing, the snmpM2M and partyMIB branches are not populated with any objects, pending the outcome of the SNMPv2 security research. (For that matter, it is also possible that entirely new MIBs, having new OIDs, will be developed as replacements for snmpM2M and partyMIB. Make sure to consult the final RFC documents when these issues are settled. Figure 5-1 illustrates the positions of these new elements of the OID tree.

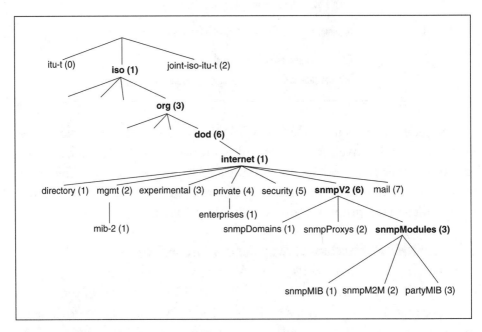

Figure 5-1. SNMPv2 elements within the OID tree

According to RFC 1901, the SMI is divided into three parts:

➤ Module definitions which are used to describe information modules, such MIB modules, compliance statements for MIB modules and capability statements for agent implementations

➤ Object Definitions, which are used to describe managed objects

➤ Notification definitions, which are used to describe unsolicited transmissions of management information, such as traps.

The next three sections discuss these three elements of the SMI.

5.2.1 SNMPv2 SMI Module Definitions

As documented in RFC 1902 [5-3], module definitions are used when describing information modules. An ASN.1 macro, called MODULE-IDENTITY, is used to convey the semantics of an information module. More specifically, it conveys the contact and revision history for each information module, using the following clauses: LAST-UPDATED, ORGANIZATION, CONTACT-INFO, DESCRIPTION, and REVISION. The SMI definition in RFC 1902 explicitly defines the MODULE-IDENTITY macro. Other module definitions will be discussed in the following sections on textual conventions and conformance statements.

5.2.2 SNMPv2 Object Definitions

The object definitions in SNMPv2 are enhanced from SNMPv1 through the use of the new OBJECT-IDENTITY module, some new data types that were not used in SNMPv1, and a revised OBJECT-TYPE module. The OBJECT-IDENTITY module is used to define information about an OBJECT IDENTIFIER assignment. This module includes the following clauses: STATUS, DESCRIPTION, and REFERENCE.

The SNMPv2 SMI has added support for ASN.1 data types that SNMPv1 did not use, and it has also defined new data types. ASN.1 data types that remain unchanged from RFC 1155 include INTEGER, OCTET STRING, and OBJECT IDENTIFIER. Application-wide data types from RFC 1155 that have not changed are IpAddress, TimeTicks, and Opaque. New SNMPv2 data types include:

Data Type	Description
Integer32	A defined type that represents integer-valued information between -2^{31} and 2^{31}-1 inclusive (-2147483648 and 2147483647 decimal). (Note: This type is indistinguishable from the INTEGER type, although the INTEGER type may have different numerical constraints.)
Counter32	A defined type that represents a non-negative integer that monotonically increases until it reaches a maximum value of 2^{32}-1 (4294967295 decimal) then wraps around and starts increasing again from zero.

Counter64	A defined type that represents a nonnegative integer that monotonically increases until it reaches a maximum value of 2^{64}-1 (18446744073709551615 decimal), then wraps around and starts increasing again from zero. Counter64 is used for objects for which the 32-bit counter (Counter32) is too small, or which would wrap around too quickly. RFC 1902 states that the Counter64 type may be used only if the information being modeled would wrap in less than one hour using the Counter32 type.
Unsigned32	A defined type that represents integer-valued information between 0 and 232-1 (4294967295 decimal), inclusive.
Gauge32	A defined type that represents a nonnegative integer which may increase or decrease, but which never exceeds a maximum value (2^{32}-1, as above).
BITS	A construct which represents an enumeration of named bits.

It should be noted that three data types—BIT STRING, NsapAddress, and UInteger32—were defined in the original version of the SNMPv2 SMI (RFC 1442), but were removed from the current version of the SNMPv2 SMI (RFC 1902).

The SNMPv2 SMI extends the OBJECT-TYPE macro (discussed in Section 3.2.3), which conveys the syntax and semantics of a managed object. Because of the OBJECT-TYPE macro's global significance, this section describes it in detail. The OBJECT-TYPE macro from RFC 1902 is as follows:

```
OBJECT-TYPE MACRO ::=
BEGIN
   TYPE NOTATION ::=
               "SYNTAX" Syntax
               UnitsPart
               "MAX-ACCESS" Access
               "STATUS" Status
               "DESCRIPTION" Text
               ReferPart
               IndexPart
               DefValPart
```

```
VALUE NOTATION ::=
            value(VALUE ObjectName)
Syntax ::=
            type(ObjectSyntax)
            | "BITS" "{" Kibbles "}"
Kibbles ::=
            Kibble
            | Kibbles "," Kibble
Kibble ::=
            identifier "(" nonNegativeNumber ")"
UnitsPart ::=
            "UNITS" Text
            | empty
Access ::=
            "not-accessible"
            | "accessible-for-notify"
            | "read-only"
            | "read-write"
            | "read-create"
Status ::=
            "current"
            | "deprecated"
            | "obsolete"
ReferPart ::=
            "REFERENCE" Text
            | empty
IndexPart ::=
            "INDEX"    "{" IndexTypes "}"
            | "AUGMENTS" "{" Entry     "}"
            | empty
IndexTypes ::=
            IndexType
            | IndexTypes "," IndexType
IndexType ::=
```

```
                  "IMPLIED" Index
                 | Index
          Index ::=
                  -- use the SYNTAX value of the
                  -- correspondent OBJECT-TYPE invocation
                  value(Indexobject ObjectName)
          Entry ::=
                  -- use the INDEX value of the
                  -- correspondent OBJECT-TYPE invocation
                  value(Entryobject ObjectName)
        DefValPart ::=
    "DEFVAL" "{" value(Defval Syntax) "}"
             | empty
        -- uses the NVT ASCII character set
        Text ::= """" string """"
    END
```

Note that the OBJECT-TYPE macro has been enhanced from versions defined
in RFC 1155 and RFC 1212. In the TYPE NOTATION, a new UNITS clause
contains a textual definition of the units associated with that object. Examples
include "packets," "messages," or "seconds." The MAX-ACCESS clause defines
the maximum level of access for an object. In other words, this clause determines whether it makes sense within the proper operation of the protocol to
read, write, and/or create an instance of an object. The values are ordered from
least to greatest accessibility: not-accessible, accessible-for-notify, read-only,
read-write, and read-create (where read-create is a superset of read-write).

The revised STATUS clause of the OBJECT-TYPE macro eliminates the
"optional" value in earlier versions of the macro. The DESCRIPTION clause
is now mandatory, and the REFERENCE clause can provide a textual cross
reference to another module. The INDEX clause, which identifies instances
of columnar objects within a table, can now be replaced with the AUGMENTS
clause if the object corresponds to a conceptual row. The AUGMENTS clause

thus augments (or extends) a conceptual row within a table. Finally, the DEF-VAL clause defines a default value for the object.

5.2.3 SNMPv2 SMI Notification Definitions

The SNMPv2 SMI's new NOTIFICATION-TYPE macro defines the information contained within the unsolicited transmission of management information. This includes an SNMPv2-Trap-PDU or an Inform-Request-PDU. The SNMP Protocol Operations document (RFC 1905) contains details on using the NOTIFICATION-TYPE macro.

SMIv2 also references three other new ASN.1 macros: MODULE-COMPLI-ANCE, OBJECT-GROUP, and AGENT-CAPABILITIES, which are described in detail in RFC 1904 and discussed in Section 5.4.

5.3 The SNMPv2 Textual Conventions

The SMI defines a number of data types, such as INTEGER and OCTET STRING, that are used in defining managed objects. In some cases, it is useful to define new types, which are similar in syntax (form) but with a more precise semantics (meaning), than those types defined in the SMI. These newly defined types are called *textual conventions,* and they are specified in RFC 1903 [5-4]. The key advantage of these textual conventions is that they enable the human reader of a MIB module to more easily read and understand that module's intent.

The textual convention consists of a data type with a specific name and associated syntax and semantics. An ASN.1 macro, TEXTUAL-CONVENTION, also found in RFC 1903, is used to convey that syntax and semantics. For example, the textual convention MacAddress represents an IEEE 802 MAC address, which is an OCTET STRING of size 6. In other words, the MacAddress type is based on the existing OCTET STRING type, but with the restrictions that it is limited to six octets in length and is defined to represent an IEEE 802 MAC address.

Within the TEXTUAL-CONVENTION macro, the DISPLAY-HINT clause is particularly useful because it describes how the value of the object will be displayed. It uses abbreviations such as **x** (hexadecimal), **d** (decimal), **o** (octal), and **b** (binary), and **a** (ASCII) to more fully define the display format.

Here is the TEXTUAL-CONVENTION macro from RFC 1903:

```
SNMPv2-TC DEFINITIONS ::= BEGIN
IMPORTS
        ObjectSyntax, TimeTicks
            FROM SNMPv2-SMI;
-- definition of textual conventions
TEXTUAL-CONVENTION MACRO ::=
BEGId             "SYNTAX" (Syntax)
    VALUE NOTATION ::=
                        value(VALUE Syntax)
        DisplayPart ::=
                        "DISPLAY-HINT" Text
                        | empty
        Status ::=
                        "current"
                        | "deprecated"
                        | "obsolete"
        ReferPart ::=
                        d | empty
-- uses the NVT ASCII character set
Text ::= """" string """"
Syntax ::=
                        type (ObjectSyntax)
                        | "BITS" "{" Kibbles "}"
        Kibbles ::=
                        Kibble
                        | Kibbles "," Kibble
        Kibble ::=
                        identifier "(" nonNegativeNudmber ")"


END
```

The following textual conventions have been defined for use with SNMPv2 [5-4]:

Convention	Description
DisplayString	Represents textual information taken from the NVT ASCII character set (see RFC 854).
PhysAddress	Represents Media- or Physical-level addresses. (Originally from RFC 1213).
MacAddress	An 802 MAC address represented in the "canonical" order defined by IEEE 802.1a; that is, it is represented as if it were transmitted least significant bit first, even though 802.5 requires MAC addresses to be transmitted most significant bit first. (Originally from RFCs 1230 and 1231.)
TruthValue	Represents a boolean value, true or false. (Originally from RFC 1253.)
TestAndIncr	Represents integer-valued information for atomic operations. Atomic operations are self-contained but are performed in a specific order or sequence. The TestAndIncr assures that these required sequences are maintained.
AutonomousType	Represents an independently extensible type identification value. It may, for example, indicate a particular subtree with further MIB definitions, or define a particular type of protocol or hardware. (Originally from RFC 1316.)
InstancePointer	A pointer to a row of a MIB table in the managed device. By convention, it is the name of the first columnar object in the conceptual row. Note that the term "conceptual row" defines all of the objects having the same instance value in a MIB table. The terms *conceptual row* and *row* are generally used interchangeably. (Originally from RFC 1316, but obsoleted in RFC 1903.)
VariablePointer	A pointer to a specific object instance (from the obsoleted InstancePointer).
RowPointer	A pointer to a conceptual row.
RowStatus	Creates and deletes conceptual rows, and is used as the value of the SYNTAX clause for the status column of a conceptual row. (See the SMI document for further details; originally from RFC 1271, the first version of the RMON MIB.)
TimeStamp	The value of the sysUpTime object at which a specific occurrence happened.
TimeInterval	A period of time, measured in hundredths of a second, between two events.
DateAndTime	A date-time specification, which can indicate the year, month, day, time, etc.

StorageType	Describes the memory realization of a conceptual row, such as volatile, nonvolatile, read only, etc. (Originally from RFC 1447.)
TDomain	Denotes a kind of transport service, such as those specified in the Transport Mappings document, RFC 1906.
TAddress	Denotes a transport service address, such as those specified in the Transport Mappings document, RFC 1906.

5.4 SNMPv2 Conformance Statements

The Conformance Statements are used to define acceptable lower bounds of implementation, along with the actual level of implementation for SNMPv2 that is achieved by the device. The Conformance Statements document, RFC 1904 [5-5], defines the notations, along with ASN.1 macros, that are used for these purposes. Two kinds of notations are used:

> *Compliance statements,* which describe requirements for agents with respect to object definitions. The MODULE-COMPLIANCE macro is used to convey a minimum set of requirements with respect to implementation of one or more MIB modules. In other words, the MODULE-COMPLIANCE macro conveys a minimum conformance specification, including objects and groups required, which may come from different MIB modules.

> *Capability statements,* which describe the capabilities of agents with respect to object definitions. The AGENT-CAPABILITIES macro describes the capabilities of an SNMPv2 agent. It defines the MIB modules, objects, and values implemented within the agent. A description of the precise level of support that an agent claims is bound to the instance of the sysORID object. (See the SNMPv2 MIB, RFC 1907, for a complete definition of the sysORID object and other objects that convey object resource information.)

The Conformance Statements also define two other ASN.1 macros. The OBJECT-GROUP macro defines collections of related, managed objects. Similarly, collections of notifications may be grouped using the NOTIFICATION-GROUP macro.

5.5 SNMPv2 Protocol Operations

When it comes to processing protocol messages, an SNMPv2 entity may act as an agent, a manager, or both. The entity acts as an agent when it responds to protocol messages (other than the Inform notification, which is reserved for managers) or when it sends Trap notifications. The entity acts as a manager when it initiates protocol messages or responds to Trap or Inform notifications. The entity may also act as a proxy agent.

SNMPv2 provides three types of access to network management information: these types are determined by the network management entity's role and relate to the Manager-to-Manager capabilities. The first type of interaction, called request-response, is where an SNMPv2 manager sends a request to an SNMPv2 agent, which responds. The second type of interaction is a request-response where both entities are SNMPv2 managers. The third type is an unconfirmed interaction, where an SNMPv2 agent sends an unsolicited message, or trap, to the manager and no response is returned.

SNMPv2 has significantly enhanced the PDUs that convey this management information (see Figure 5-2). SNMPv2 offers new PDUs and adds error codes and exception responses. The latter allows a management application to easily determine why a management operation failed.

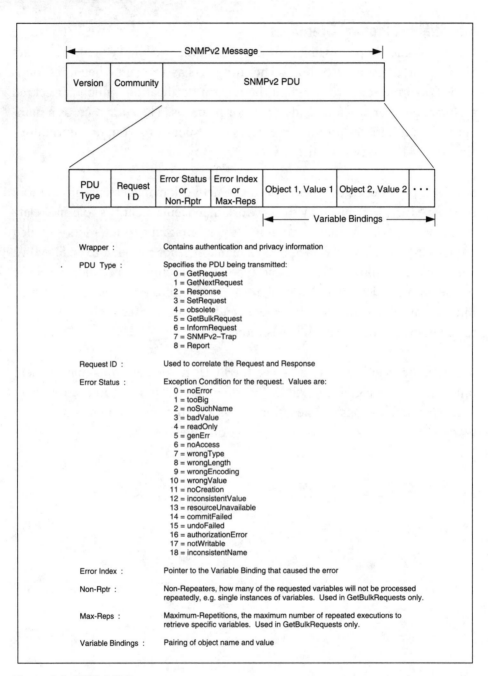

Figure 5-2 SNMPv2 PDU structure

5.5.1 SNMPv2 PDUs

SNMPv2 defines eight PDU types, of which three are new: the GetBulkRequest, the InformRequest, and the Report. In addition, the SNMPv2-Trap PDU format has been revised from the SNMPv1 Trap to conform to the format and structure of the other PDUs (recall that in SNMPv1, the Trap PDU had a unique format).

The following is a list of all the SNMPv2 PDUs, along with their assigned tag numbers:

PDU/Tag Number	Description
GetRequest [0]	Retrieves values of objects listed within the variable bindings field.
GetNextRequest [1]	Retrieves values of objects that are the lexicographical successors of the variables, up to the end of the MIB view of this request.
Response [2]	Generated in response to a GetRequest, GetNextRequest, GetBulkRequest, SetRequest, or InformRequest PDU.
SetRequest [3]	Establishes the value of a variable.
GetBulkRequest [5]	Retrieves a large amount of data, such as the contents of a large table.
InformRequest [6]	Allows one manager to communicate information in its MIB view to another manager.
SNMPv2-Trap [7]	Used by an SNMPv2 agent to provide information regarding an exceptional condition. The Trap PDU, defined for SNMPv1 with tag [4], is now considered obsolete. The Coexistence document, RFC 1908, discusses conversion from the Trap PDU to the SNMPv2-Trap PDU.
Report [8]	Included in SNMPv2, but its usage is not defined in RFC 1905. It is expected that any Administrative Framework that makes use of this PDU would define its usage and semantics (see RFC 1905, page 6).

The PDUs that the SNMPv2 entity generates or receives depend on the entity's role as an agent or manager:

SNMPv2 PDU	Agent Generate	Agent Receive	Manager Generate	Manager Receive
GetRequest		X	X	
GetNextRequest		X	X	
Response	X		X	X
SetRequest		X	X	
GetBulkRequest		X	X	
InformRequest			X	X
SNMPv2-Trap	X			X

5.5.2 SNMPv2 PDU syntax

The SNMPv2 message consists of the wrapper that encapsulates an SNMPv2 PDU. The wrapper is determined by the administrative framework and may contain the authentication and privacy information. The syntax of the SNMPv2 PDUs is similar to the structures defined in SNMPv1. Significant enhancements include error status codes that detail why protocol operations were unsuccessful.

The PDU consists of four fields—the PDU Type field, the Request ID field, the Error Status field, and the Error Index field (see Figure 5-2)—plus the variable bindings. The PDU Type field specifies which one of the eight PDUs is being transmitted. The Request ID correlates the request and response PDUs.

The Error Status field includes new exception conditions. When errors occur in the processing of the GetRequest, GetNextRequest, GetBulkRequest, SetRequest, or InformRequest PDUs, the SNMPv2 entity prepares a Response PDU with the Error Status field set to help the manager identify and correct the problem. The following table shows how the PDUs use these error codes:

SNMPv2 Error	Get	GetNext	GetBulk	Set	Inform
noError	x	x	x	x	x
tooBig	x	x		x	x
noSuchName[1]					
badValue[1]					
readOnly[1]					
genErr	x	x	x	x	
noAccess				x	
wrongType				x	
wrongLength				x	
wrongEncoding				x	
wrongValue				x	
noCreation				x	
inconsistentValue				x	
resourceUnavailable				x	
commitFailed				x	
undoFailed				x	
authorizationError	x^2	x^2	x^2	x^2	x^2
notWritable				x	
inconsistentName				x	

Notes:

(1) Never generated by an SNMPv2 entity (proxy capability only), per RFC 1905, pages 6 and 18, and RFC 1908, page 7.

(2) Unused with SNMPv2, per RFC 1901, page 5.

The Error Index field is used with the Error Status code. When errors occur in the processing of the variable bindings, the Error Index field identifies the binding that caused the error. An error in the first binding would have Index = 1, an error in the second binding would have Index = 2, and so on.

5.5.2.1 The GetBulkRequest PDU

The GetBulkRequest (which some literature calls the "awesome GetBulkRequest") retrieves large amounts of data. The GetBulkRequest PDU enhances the GetNext PDU; it essentially executes multiple GetNext requests (lexicographically ordered) with a single PDU. The structure of the GetBulkRequest PDU resembles that of the other PDUs, but changes the syntax of two fields. It replaces Error Status with Non-Repeaters, and Error Index with Max-Repetitions.

The values of the Non-Repeaters and Max-Repetitions fields indicate the processing requested. The Non-Repeaters field defines the number of requested variables that will not be processed repeatedly; it is used when some of the variables are scalar objects with only one variable. The Max-Repetitions field defines the maximum number of repeated executions that retrieve specific variables.

The retrieved variables return in the Response PDU that corresponds to the request. One variable binding in the Response PDU is requested for the first N variable bindings in the GetBulkRequest. M variable bindings are requested for each of the R remaining variable bindings in the GetBulkRequest. The following expression gives the total number of requested variable bindings:

Total Variable Bindings = N + (M * R), where

N = the minimum of:

    (a)   the value of the Non-Repeaters field

    and

    (b)   the number of variable bindings in the GetBulkRequest

M = the value of the Max-Repetitions field in the GetBulkRequest

R = the minimum of

  (a)   the number of variable bindings in the GetBulkRequest less N

and

  (b)   zero

Processing continues until all of the requested variables have been retrieved or the maximum size of the Response PDU is reached. The maximum size is determined by the smallest maximum message size that the source can generate or by the maximum message size that the destination can accept. The Response PDU then returns with the variables that the GetBulk requested.

5.5.2.2 InformRequest PDU

The InformRequest PDU performs manager-to-manager, not agent-to-manager, communication. The requesting application specifies the destination(s) to which an InformRequest PDU will be sent. The first two variable bindings that the PDU transmits are the sysUpTime.0 (from MIB-II) and the snmpTrapOID.i (from the SNMP Trap group in the SNMPv2 MIB—RFC 1907). Subsequent variable bindings contain information in the MIB view of a party, which is local to the manager that transmitted the InformRequest.

5.5.2.3 SNMPv2-Trap PDU

In SNMP version 1, the syntax of the Trap PDU differed from the other PDUs. With SNMPv2, the SNMPv1 Trap is now obsolete and has been replaced by the SNMPv2-Trap PDU, which maintains a structure consistent with the other SNMPv2 PDUs. Agents transmit SNMPv2 PDUs when an exceptional situation occurs. The destination(s) to which an SNMPv2-Trap PDU is sent is determined by the implementation of that SNMP application. The first variable in the SNMPv2-Trap is sysUpTime.0, from MIB-II. The second variable is snmpTrapOID.0, from the Traps group within the SNMPv2 MIB, which contains the administratively assigned name of the notification. Subsequent variables provide more information on the Trap.

5.5.3 SNMPv2 PDU Definitions

For your reference, the following is a list of definitions for the SNMP PDUs, taken from the SNMPv2 Protocol Operations document [5-6]:

```
SNMPv2-PDU DEFINITIONS ::= BEGIN

IMPORTS
  ObjectName, ObjectSyntax, Integer32
      FROM SNMPv2-SMI;

-- protocol data units
PDUs ::=
  CHOICE {
        get-request
            GetRequest-PDU,
        get-next-request
            GetNextRequest-PDU,
        get-bulk-request
            GetBulkRequest-PDU,
        response
            Response-PDU,
        set-request
            SetRequest-PDU,
        inform-request
            InformRequest-PDU,
        snmpV2-trap
            SNMPv2-Trap-PDU,
        report
            Report-PDU,
  }

-- PDUs

GetRequest-PDU ::=
  [0]
```

```
        IMPLICIT PDU
GetNextRequest-PDU ::=
 [1]
        IMPLICIT PDU
Response-PDU ::=
 [2]
        IMPLICIT PDU
SetRequest-PDU ::=
 [3]
        IMPLICIT PDU
-- [4] is obsolete
GetBulkRequest-PDU ::=
 [5]
        IMPLICIT BulkPDU
InformRequest-PDU ::=
 [6]
        IMPLICIT PDU
SNMPv2-Trap-PDU ::=
 [5]
        IMPLICIT PDU
-- Usage and precise semantics of Report-PDU are not presently
-- defined.  Any SNMP administrative framework making use of
-- this PDU must define its usage and semantics.
Report PDU ::=
 [8]
        IMPLICIT PDU
max-bindings
 INTEGER ::= 2147483647
PDU ::=
    SEQUENCE {
        request-id
            Integer32,
        error-status                            -- sometimes ignored
            INTEGER {
```

```
                    noError(0),
                    tooBig(1),
                    noSuchName(2),        -- for proxy compatibility
                    badValue(3),          -- for proxy compatibility
                    readOnly(4),          -- for proxy compatibility
                    genErr(5),
                    noAccess(6),
                    wrongType(7),
                    wrongLength(8),
                    wrongEncoding(9),
                    wrongValue(10),
                    noCreation(11),
                    inconsistentValue(12),
                    resourceUnavailable(13),
                    commitFailed(14),
                    undoFailed(15),
                    authorizationError(16),
                    notWritable(17),
                    inconsistentName(18)
                },
            error-index                   -- sometimes ignored
                INTEGER (0..max-bindings),
            variable-bindings             -- values are sometimes ignored
                VarBindList
        }
BulkPDU ::=                               -- MUST be identical in
    SEQUENCE {                            -- structure to PDU
        request-id
            Integer32,
        non-repeaters
            INTEGER (0..max-bindings),
        max-repetitions
            INTEGER (0..max-bindings),
        variable-bindings                 -- values are ignored
```

```
                VarBindList
        }
-- variable binding
VarBind ::=
    SEQUENCE {
        name
            ObjectName,
        CHOICE {
        value
            ObjectSyntax,
        unSpecified              -- in retrieval requests
            NULL,

                                 -- exceptions in responses

        noSuchObject[0]
            IMPLICIT NULL,
        noSuchInstance[1]
            IMPLICIT NULL,
        endOfMibView[2]
            IMPLICIT NULL
        }
    }
-- variable-binding list
VarBindList ::=
        SEQUENCE (SIZE (0..max-bindings)) OF
            VarBind
END
```

5.6 SNMPv2 Transport Mappings

SNMP version 1 was originally defined for transmission over UDP and IP. Subsequent research explored the use of SNMP with other transport protocols, including OSI transport (RFC 1418), AppleTalk's Datagram Delivery Protocol (DDP) (RFC 1419), and Novell's Internetwork Packet Exchange (IPX) (RFC 1420). SNMPv2 formally defines implementations over these other transports in the Transport Mapping document, RFC 1906 [5-7] (see

Figure 5-3). The Transport Mapping document also includes instructions to provide proxy to SNMPv1 and for the use of the Basic Encoding Rules (BER).

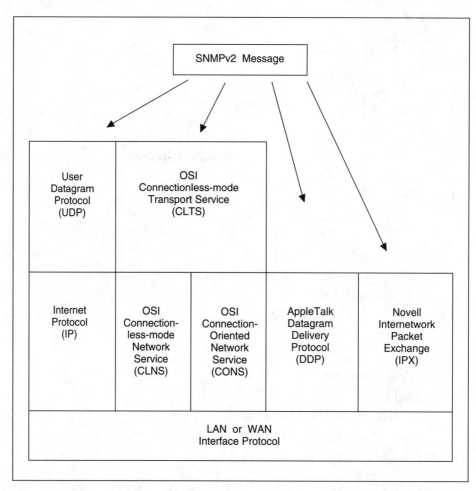

Figure 5-3 Transport mappings for SNMPv2

5.6.1 SNMPv2 over UDP

SNMPv2 over UDP is the preferred transport mapping. UDP provides compatibility with SNMPv1 at both the Transport and Network layers, although other higher-layer issues, such as SNMPv2 PDU structures, remain. RFC 1906 also suggests that SNMPv2 agents continue the practice of listening on UDP port 161, and that notifications listen on UDP port 162. (UDP port 162 was previously defined for SNMP traps.) Figure 5-4 illustrates the details of the UDP header, which precedes the SNMP message within the transmitted frame.

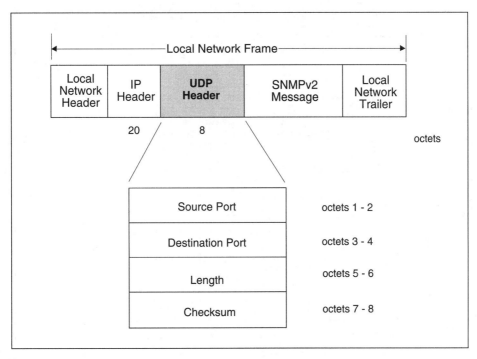

Figure 5-4 SNMPv2 over UDP

5.6.2 SNMPv2 over OSI

RFC 1449 defines two options for transmitting SNMPv2 messages over OSI protocols. Both send the SNMPv2 message in a single transport service data unit (TSDU) using the provisions of the OSI Connectionless-mode Transport Service (CLTS). Then at the Network layer, either a Connectionless-mode Network Service (CLNS) or a Connection-oriented Network Service (CONS) may be used.

When you use Connectionless-Mode Network Service, you would use the OSI Connectionless Network Protocol (CLNP) as the Network layer protocol. Figure 5-5 shows details of the CLNP header, the position of the CLTS header, and the SNMPv2 message within the transmission frame.

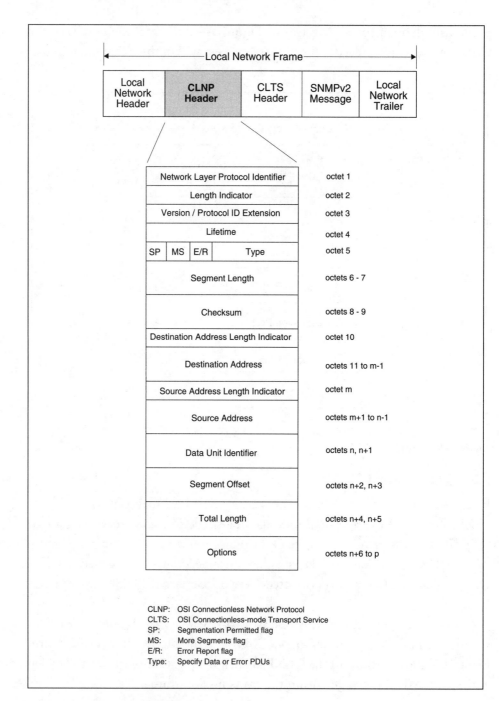

Figure 5-5 SNMPv2 over ISO CLNP

5.6.3 SNMPv2 over AppleTalk DDP

Apple Computer's AppleTalk protocol suite is another option available for SNMPv2 transport. The SNMPv2 message is sent in a single Datagram Delivery Protocol (DDP) datagram, which operates at the OSI Network layer. Figure 5-6 shows the details of the DDP header and the position of the SNMPv2 message within the transmission frame. The final octet of the DDP header specifies the DDP Type, indicating the protocol in use. SNMPv2 messages use DDP Type = 8, since Apple has previously defined types 1 through 7. Other DDP parameters, such as socket numbers, are also defined for SNMPv2 use. SNMPv2 entities acting in the agent role use DDP socket number 8; notification sinks, which are entities receiving a notification, use DDP socket number 9.

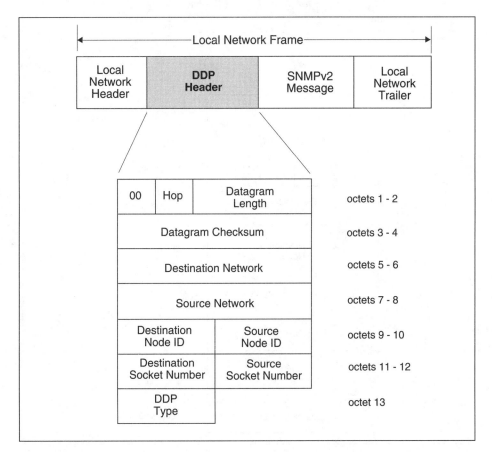

Figure 5-6 SNMPv2 over the AppleTalk DDP

5.6.4. SNMPv2 over Novell IPX

Novell Inc.'s NetWare protocol suite defines the Internetwork Packet Exchange (IPX) protocol at the Network layer. SNMPv2 messages are serialized into a single IPX datagram, as shown in Figure 5-7. Within the IPX header is a Packet Type parameter that specifies the protocol in use. SNMPv2 messages use Packet Type = 4, which is defined as a Packet Exchange Protocol packet. SNMPv2 entities acting in the agent role listen on IPX socket number 36879 (900FH), while notification sinks listen on socket 36880 (9010H).

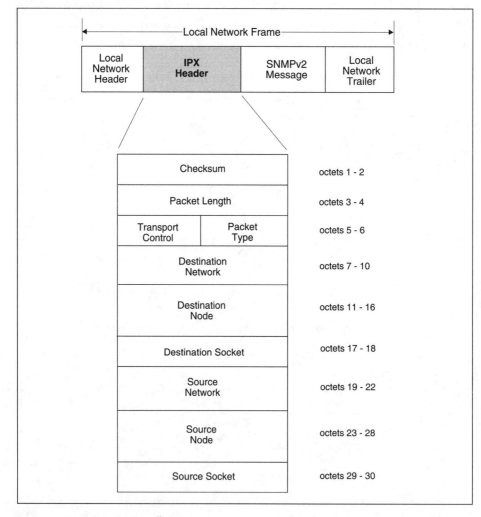

Figure 5-7 SNMPv2 over Novell IPX

5.6.5 SNMPv2 transport mapping definitions

For your reference, this section reproduces the following transport mapping definitions from RFC 1906 [5-7]. Note the use of the TEXTUAL-CONVENTIONS macro, and the DISPLAY-HINT within each type, which provides information about how the different types of addresses are to be displayed. Recall the following abbreviations:

Abbreviation	Meaning
x	hexadecimal
d	decimal
o	octal
b	binary

The transport mapping definitions are:

```
SNMPv2-TM DEFINITIONS ::= BEGIN
IMPORTS
    OBJECT-IDENTITY, snmpDomains, snmpProxys
        FROM SNMPv2-SMI
    TEXTUAL-CONVENTION
        FROM SNMPv2-TC;
-- SNMPv2 over UDP over IPv4
snmpUDPDomain  OBJECT-IDENTITY
    STATUS    current
    DESCRIPTION
        "The SNMPv2 over UDP transport domain.  The corresponding
        transport address is of type SnmpUDPAddress."
    ::= { snmpDomains 1 }
SnmpUDPAddress ::= TEXTUAL-CONVENTION
    DISPLAY-HINT "1d.1d.1d.1d/2d"
    STATUS    current
```

DESCRIPTION
    "Represents a UDP address:

octets	contents	encoding
1-4	IP-address	network-byte order
5-6	UDP-port	network-byte order

    "

SYNTAX   OCTET STRING (SIZE (6))

-- SNMPv2 over OSI
snmpCLNSDomain OBJECT-IDENTITY
    STATUS   current
    DESCRIPTION
        "The SNMPv2 over CLNS transport domain. The corresponding
        transport address is of type SnmpOSIAddress."
    ::= { snmpDomains 2 }
snmpCONSDomain OBJECT-IDENTITY
    STATUS   current
    DESCRIPTION
        "The SNMPv2 over CONS transport domain. The corresponding
        transport address is of type SnmpOSIAddress."
    ::= { snmpDomains 3 }
SnmpOSIAddress ::= TEXTUAL-CONVENTION
    DISPLAY-HINT "*1x:/1x:"
    STATUS   current
    DESCRIPTION
        "Represents an OSI transport-address:

octets	contents	encoding
1	length of NSAP	'n' as an unsigned-integer
		(either 0 or from 3 to 20)
2..(n+1)	NSAP	concrete binary representation
(n+2)..m	TSEL	string of (up to 64) octets

        "

SYNTAX   OCTET STRING (SIZE (1 | 4..85))

-- SNMPv2 over DDP
snmpDDPDomain OBJECT-IDENTITY
   STATUS   current
   DESCRIPTION
      "The SNMPv2 over DDP transport domain. The corresponding
      transport address is of type SnmpNBPAddress."
   ::= { snmpDomains 4 }
SnmpNBPAddress ::= TEXTUAL-CONVENTION
   STATUS   current
   DESCRIPTION
      "Represents an NBP name:

octets	contents	encoding
1	length of object	'n' as an unsigned integer
2..(n+1)	object	string of (up to 32) octets
n+2	length of type	'p' as an unsigned integer
(n+3)..(n+2+p)	type	string of (up to 32) octets
n+3+p	length of zone	'q' as an unsigned integer
(n+4+p)..(n+3+p+q)	zone	string of (up to 32) octets

      For comparison purposes, strings are case-insensitive All
      strings may contain any octet other than 255 (hex ff)."
   SYNTAX   OCTET STRING (SIZE (3..99))

-- SNMPv2 over IPX
snmpIPXDomain OBJECT-IDENTITY
   STATUS   current
   DESCRIPTION
      "The SNMPv2 over IPX transport domain. The corresponding
      transport address is of type SnmpIPXAddress."
   ::= { snmpDomains 5 }
SnmpIPXAddress ::= TEXTUAL-CONVENTION
   DISPLAY-HINT "4x.1x:1x:1x:1x:1x:1x.2d"
   STATUS   current
   DESCRIPTION
      "Represents an IPX address:

231

```
        octets    contents          encoding
        1-4       network-number    network-byte order
        5-10      physical-address  network-byte order
        11-12     socket-number     network-byte order
     "
SYNTAX      OCTET STRING (SIZE (12))


-- for proxy to SNMPv1 (RFC 1157)
rfc1157Proxy   OBJECT IDENTIFIER ::= { snmpProxys 1 }
rfc1157Domain OBJECT-IDENTITY
    STATUS     current
    DESCRIPTION
        "The transport domain for SNMPv1 over UDP.  The
        corresponding transport address is of type SnmpUDPAddress."
    ::= { rfc1157Proxy 1 }
-- ::= { rfc1157Proxy 2 }          this OID is obsolete
END
```

5.7 The SNMPv2 MIB

The April 1993 version of SNMPv2 (RFCs 1441–1452) provided three MIB documents. The first, RFC 1450, described a MIB module for SNMPv2 objects, which was identified by {snmpModules 1}. The second, RFC 1451, coordinated multiple management stations and was therefore called the Manager-to-Manager MIB, identified as {snmpModules 2}. The third module, RFC 1447, supported the SNMPv2 security protocols and was called the Party MIB {snmpModules 3}.

With the removal of the security-related aspects in the January 1996 version of SNMPv2 (RFCs 1901-1908), the MIB required revision as well. The fundamental structure is still the same, however (review Figure 5-1):

Branch	OID	RFC References
snmpV2	{ 1.3.6.1.6 }	1442, 1902
snmpDomains	{ 1.3.6.1.6.1 }	1442, 1902, 1906

snmpProxys	{ 1.3.6.1.6.2 }	1442, 1902, 1906
snmpModules	{ 1.3.6.1.6.3 }	1442, 1902
snmpMIB	{ 1.3.6.1.6.3.1 }	1450, 1907
snmpM2M	{ 1.3.6.1.6.3.2 }	1451
partyMIB	{ 1.3.6.1.6.3.3 }	1447

Note that the last two branches (the Manager to Manager MIB and the Party MIB) are placeholders (with no currently defined objects) pending completion of the work in these areas. When that work is complete, it is possible that entirely new MIBs, having new OIDs, will be developed as replacements for snmpM2M and partyMIB. Make sure to consult the final RFC documents when these issues are settled.)

In view of the work that is incomplete at the time of this writing, this section focuses on the structure of the snmpMIB branch, from RFC 1907 [5-8]. The changes include:

> The inclusion of the *system* group from MIB-II; the addition of object resource information, which describes the SNMPv2 entity's support for various MIB modules, is also added to the *system* group (see Figure 5-8a).

> The inclusion of the *snmp* group from MIB-II, making obsolete a number of objects and adding two new ones: snmpSilentDrops { snmp 31 } and snmpProxyDrops { snmp 32 } (see Figure 5-8a).

> Changes to the *snmpMIB* group, making obsolete a number of objects and adding others (see Figure 5-8b). The objects within snmpMIB now fall into several categories: information for notifications and well-known traps; a set group, which allows managers to coordinate set operations; conformance information; and compliance statements.

Further details on these revisions are available in RFC 1907; use the other references in the table above as supplementary resources.

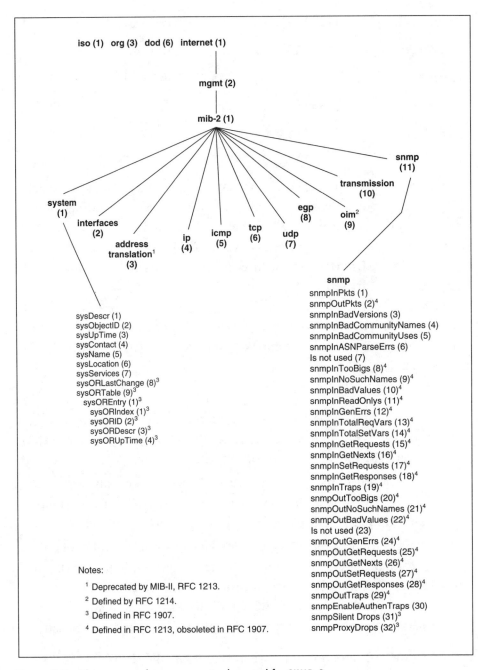

Figure 5-8a. The system and snmp groups implemented for SNMPv2

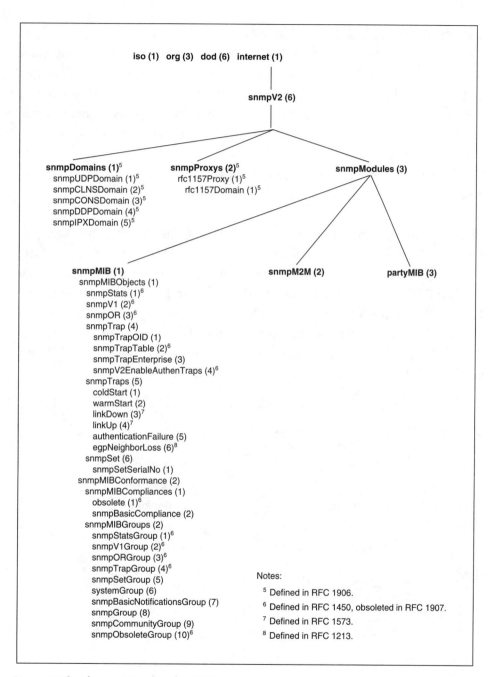

Figure 5-8b. The snmpMIB group for SNMPv2

5.8 Coexistence of SNMPv1 and SNMPv2

The Coexistence document, RFC 1908 [5-9], presents a number of guidelines that outline the modifications necessary for successful coexistence of SNMPv1 and SNMPv2. Some of the issues noted in RFC 1908 deal with MIB structures, such as object definitions, trap definitions, compliance statements. and capabilities statements, that must be updated to conform to the specifications in SNMPv2.

From a practical point of view, two methods are defined to achieve coexistence: a proxy agent and a bilingual manager.

The proxy agent translates between SNMPv1 to/from SNMPv2 messages (see Figure 5-9). When translating from SNMPv2 to SNMPv1, GetRequest, GetNextRequest, or SetRequest PDUs from the manager are passed directly to the SNMPv1 agent. GetBulkRequest PDUs are translated into GetNextPDUs. For translating from SNMPv1 to SNMPv2, the GetResponse PDU is passed unaltered to the manager. An SNMPv1 Trap PDU is mapped to an SNMPv2-Trap PDU, with the two new variable bindings, sysUpTime.0 and snmpTrapOID.0, prepended to the variable bindings field.

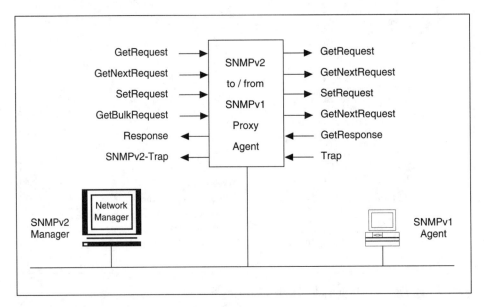

Figure 5-9. SNMPv1/SNMPv2 proxy agent operation

The second alternative is a bilingual manager, which incorporates both the SNMPv1 and SNMPv2 protocols. When the manager needs to communicate with an agent, it selects the protocol appropriate for the application.

5.9 SNMPv2 Security

When SNMPv1 was first published (circa 1988), the community name and the version number in the SNMP header provided the only message security capabilities. This provision, known as the *trivial* protocol, assured that both agent and manager recognized the same community name before proceeding with network management operations.

Additional research into security issues yielded three documents on the subject, all released in July 1992:

RFC	Title
1351	SNMP Administrative Model
1352	SNMP Security Protocols
1353	Definitions for Managed Objects for Administration of SNMP Parties

Further refinements of the above yielded three additional documents, all released in April 1993:

RFC	Title
1445	Administrative Model for SNMPv2
1446	Security Protocols for SNMPv2
1447	Party MIB for SNMPv2

These RFCs were designed to address the authentication and privacy of network management communication. *Authentication* assures the appropriate origin of the message, while *privacy* protects the messages from disclosure.

Unfortunately, implementing these enhancements proved to be more complex than either vendors or network managers anticipated; consequently, few products containing these improvements were developed. The result, SNMPv2C, with community-based security, has been the subject of this chapter.

Nevertheless, requirements for enhanced SNMP security exist. An administrative framework for SNMPv2, defined in the experimental RFC 1909 [5-10], describes how network management can be effective in a variety of configurations and environments, using various techniques such as authorization, authentication and privacy. In addition, two alternatives have been proposed to address the security aspects in particular. The first is called SNMPv2U, which stands for a User-based security model; it is described in the experimental RFC 1910 [5-11] and references [5-12] and [5-13]. The second is called SNMPv2* (pronounced SNMP vee-two-star), and is described in references [5-14] and [5-15]. As might be expected, both proposals have very vocal proponents. An IETF working group, called the SNMPv3 (formally called the SNMPng for next generation) working group is chartered with proposing a resolution; readers interested in following the discussion may wish to investigate Reference [5-16].

This chapter concludes our discussion of the three aspects of the Internet Network Management Framework. In Chapter 6, we will discuss the underlying transport protocols that are used in conjunction with SNMP for network management communication.

5.11 References

[5-1]   Case, J.D., K. McCloghrie, M.T. Rose, and S.L. Waldbusser, "Introduction to version 2 of the Network Management Framework." *RFC 1441*, April 1993.

[5-2]   Case, J., K. McCloghrie, M. Rose,and S. Waldbusser, "Introduction to Community-based SNMPv2." *RFC 1901*, January 1996.

[5-3]   Case, J., K. McCloghrie, M. Rose, and S. Waldbusser, "Structure of Management Information for version 2 of the Simple Network Management Protocol (SNMPv2)." *RFC 1902*, January 1996.

[5-4]   Case, J., K. McCloghrie, M. Rose, and S. Waldbusser, 'Textual Conventions for version 2 of the Simple Network Management Protocol (SNMPv2)." *RFC 1903,* January 1996.

[5-5]   Case, J., K. McCloghrie, M. Rose, and S. Waldbusser, "Conformance Statements for version 2 of the Simple Network Management Protocol (SNMPv2)." *RFC 1904,* January 1996.

[5-6]   Case, J., K. McCloghrie, M. Rose, and S. Waldbusser, "Protocol Operations for version 2 of the Simple Network Management Protocol (SNMPv2)." *RFC 1905,* January 1996.

[5-7]   Case, J., K. McCloghrie, M. Rose, and S. Waldbusser, "Transport Mappings for version 2 of the Simple Network Management Protocol (SNMPv2)." *RFC 1906,* January 1996.

[5-8]   Case, J., K. McCloghrie, M. Rose, and S. Waldbusser, "Management Information Base for version 2 of the Simple Network Management Protocol (SNMPv2)." *RFC 1907,* January 1996.

[5-9]   Case, J.D., K. McCloghrie, M.T. Rose, and S.L. Waldbusser. "Coexistence between version 1 and version 2 of the Internet-standard Network Management Framework." *RFC 1908,* January 1996.

[5-10]   McCloghrie, K., editor. "An Administrated Infrastructure for SNMPv2." RFC 1909, February 1996.

[5-11]   Waters, G., editor. "User-based Security Model for SNMPv2." *RFC 1910,* February 1996.

[5-12]   Waters, Glenn. "The User-based Security Model for SNMPv2." *ConneXions, the Interoperability Report* (May 1996): 12–21.

[5-13]   For further information on SNMPv2U, consult http://www.simple-times.orb/pub/simple-times/usec/, or subscribe to the SNMPv2U mailing list by sending an email to: usec-mib-request@fv.com.

[5-14]   Partain, David. "An Introduction to SNMPv2*." *ConneXions, the Interoperability Report* (May 1996): 22–33.

[5-15]   For further information on SNMPv2*, consult http: //www.
snmp.com/v2star.html, or subscribe to the SNMPv2* mailing list
by sending an email to: snmpv2star-request@snmp.com.

[5-16]   For further information on SNMPv3, consult http://www.
tis.com/docs/research/network/snmp-ng.html, or subscribe to the
SNMPv3 mailing list by sending an email to: snmpv3-
request@tis.com.

Lower Layer Support for SNMP

So far, this book has discussed network management applications and the languages and protocols, such as ASN.1 and SNMP, that manage complex internetworks. An underlying communication infrastructure is also necessary for the manager and agent to communicate network management information. This infrastructure exists at the OSI Transport, Network, and Data Link layers (review Figure 4-1a), or at the ARPA Host-to-Host, Internet, and Network Interface layers.

SNMP messages fit inside the OSI Data Link layer or ARPA Local Network layer frame. To send SNMP messages, the system requires the User Datagram Protocol (UDP) and the Internet Protocol (IP), as shown in Figure 6-1. Together, the SNMP message, plus UDP and IP headers, comprise an IP datagram. This chapter discusses these supporting protocols.

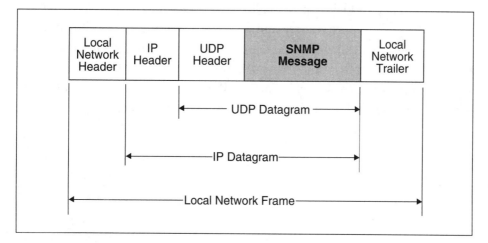

Figure 6-1. An SNMP message within a transmission frame

6.1 User Datagram Protocol (UDP)

UDP provides a connectionless host-to-host communication path for the SNMP message. A connectionless path is one in which the communication channel is not established prior to the transmission of data. Instead, the network transmits the data in a package called a datagram. The datagram contains all of the addressing information necessary for the SNMP message to reach its intended destination. UDP is described in RFC 768 [6-1] and is an ARPA Host-to-Host (or OSI Transport layer) protocol. UDP assumes that IP, which is also connectionless, is the underlying ARPA Internet (or OSI Network Layer) protocol.

The UDP service requires minimal overhead, and therefore uses the relatively small UDP header shown in Figure 6-2. Note in the figure that each horizontal group of bits, called a word, is 32 bits wide. The first two fields in the UDP header are the Source and Destination Port numbers (each 2 octets in length) that identify the higher-layer protocol process that the datagram carries. Port number 161 (decimal) identifies SNMP messages, and port number 162 identifies SNMP traps. (Note that the SNMP agent processes use these defined ports; the manager may use these ports or any other port. Thus, multiple managers can address the same agent process.) The Source Port field is optional, and when not used contains all zeros. The Length field (2 octets) is the length of the UDP datagram, which has a minimum value of 8 octets. The Checksum field (2 octets) is also optional, and is filled with all zeros if the upper layer protocol (ULP) process does not require a checksum. The checksum is calculated by using the Pseudo Header, which includes the source and destination IP addresses, the Protocol field obtained from the IP header, and the length of the UDP datagram. The use of the IP address to calculate the Pseudo Header assures that the UDP datagram is delivered to the correct destination network and host.

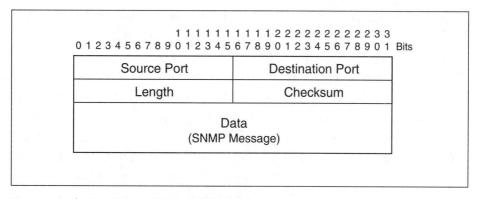

Figure 6-2. The User Datagram Protocol (UDP) header

Other host processes that use UDP as the Host-to-Host protocol include the Time protocol, port number 37; the Domain Name Server (DNS), port number 53; the Bootstrap Protocol (BOOTP) server and client, port numbers 67 and 68, respectively; the Trivial File Transfer Protocol (TFTP), port number 69; and the Sun Microsystems Remote Procedure Call (SunRPC), port number 111. All of these applications are designed with the assumption that if the Host-to-Host connection fails, some higher-layer process (such as the network management application itself) would recover. Other applications require more reliable end-to-end data transmissions, and therefore use the more rigorous Transmission Control Protocol (TCP), which is discussed in detail in the companion volume *Troubleshooting TCP/IP* [6-2].

6.2 Internet Protocol (IP)

IP, as defined in RFC 791 [6-3], works closely with UDP. IP handles datagram delivery. In other words, the IP destination address routes the datagram to the correct host on the specified network. The UDP port address then routes the datagram within the host to the correct host process.

To deliver datagrams, IP deals with two issues: addressing and fragmentation. The *address* assures that the datagram arrives at the correct destination. Datagram transmission is analogous to mailing a letter. When you mail a letter, you write a source and destination address on the envelope, place the information to be sent inside, and drop the resulting message in a mailbox. With the postal service, the mailbox is a blue (or red, depending on where you live) box. With the Internet, the mailbox service is the node where you enter the network.

Fragmentation is necessary because the sequence of LANs and WANs that any particular datagram may traverse can have differing frame sizes, and the IP datagram must fit within these varying frames (see Figure 6-1). For example, if the endpoint is attached to an IEEE 802.3 LAN with a maximum data field size of 1500 octets, IP must fragment the large IP datagram into smaller pieces (fragments) that will fit into the constraining frame. The distant node then reassembles the fragments back into a single IP datagram (sort of a reverse Humpty-Dumpty).

As you can see in Figure 6-3, the IP header contains at least 20 octets of control information. Version (4 bits) defines the current version of IP and should be equal to four. Internet Header Length (IHL, 4 bits) measures the length of the IP header in 32-bit words. (The minimum value would be five 32-bit words, or 20 octets.) The IHL also provides a measurement (or offset) for where the higher-layer information, such as the TCP header, begins within the datagram. The Type of Service (8 bits) tells the network the quality of service requested for this particular datagram. Values include:

Bits 0-2:	Precedence (or relative importance of this datagram)
111	Network Control
110	Internetwork Control
101	CRITIC/ECP
100	Flash Override
011	Flash
010	Immediate
001	Priority
000	Routine
Bit 3:	Delay, 0 = Normal, 1 = Low

Bit 4:   Throughput, 0 = Normal, 1 = High

Bit 5:   Reliability, 0 =Normal, 1 = High

Bits 6-7:   Reserved for future use (set to 0)

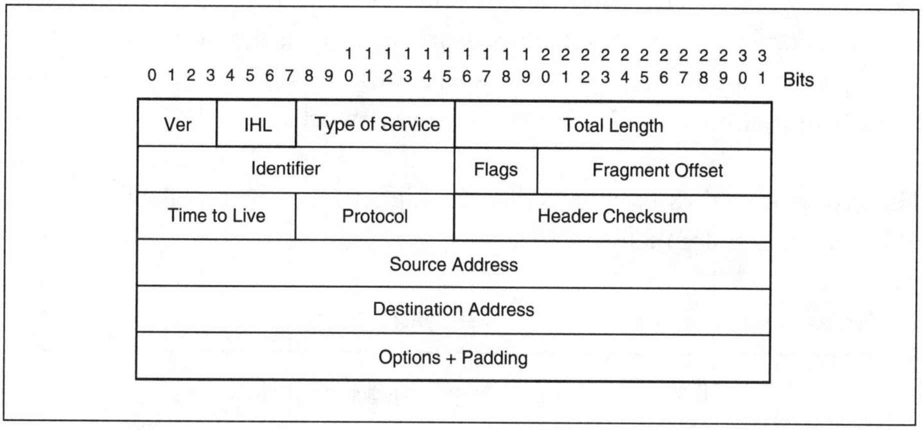

```
                              1 1 1 1 1 1 1 1 1 1 2 2 2 2 2 2 2 2 2 2 3 3
              0 1 2 3 4 5 6 7 8 9 0 1 2 3 4 5 6 7 8 9 0 1 2 3 4 5 6 7 8 9 0 1   Bits

              |  Ver  |  IHL  |  Type of Service  |          Total Length          |
              |        Identifier       |  Flags  |        Fragment Offset         |
              |   Time to Live  |    Protocol    |        Header Checksum          |
              |                        Source Address                             |
              |                      Destination Address                          |
              |                       Options + Padding                           |
```

Figure 6-3. Internet Protocol (IP) header

The Total Length field (16 bits) measures the length, in octets, of the IP datagram (the IP header plus higher-layer information). The 16-bit field allows
for a datagram of up to 65,535 octets in length, although at minimum all
hosts must be able to handle datagrams of 576 octets in length.

The next 32-bit word contains three fields that deal with datagram fragmen-
tation/reassembly. The sender assigns the Identification field (16 bits) to
reassemble the fragments into the datagram. Three flags indicate how the fragmentation process is to be handled:

Bit 0:   Reserved (set to 0)

Bit 1:   (DF) 0 = May fragment, 1 = Don't fragment

Bit 2:   (MF) 0 = Last fragment, 1 = More fragments

The last field within this word is a 13-bit Fragment Offset, which indicates
where in the complete message this fragment belongs. This offset is measured
in 64-bit units.

The next word in the IP header contains a time-to-live (TTL) measurement, which is the maximum amount of time that the datagram is allowed to live within the internet. When TTL = 0, the datagram is destroyed. This field is a fail-safe measure that prevents misaddressed datagrams from wandering around the internet forever. TTL may be measured in either router hops or seconds, with a maximum of 255 of either measurement. If the measurement is in seconds, the maximum of 255 seconds is equivalent to 4.25 minutes (a long time to be "lost" within today's high-speed internetworks).

The Protocol field (8 bits) identifies the higher-layer protocol following the IP header. Examples include:

Decimal	Keyword	Description
1	ICMP	Internet ControlMessage Protocol
6	TCP	Transmission Control Protocol
17	UDP	User Datagram Protocol

RFC 1700, "Assigned Numbers" [6-4], provides a more detailed listing of the protocols defined. A 16-bit Header Checksum completes the third 32-bit word.

The fourth and fifth words of the IP header contain the Source and Destination Addresses, respectively. Addressing may be implemented at several architectural layers. For example, hardware addresses are used at the ARPA Network Interface layer (or OSI Data Link layer) and are associated with a specific network interface card, usually burned into an address ROM on the card. The addresses within the IP header are the Internet layer (or OSI Network layer) addresses. The Internet address is a logical address that routes the IP datagram through the Internet to the correct host and network (LAN, MAN, or WAN).

6.3 Internet Addressing

Each 32-bit IP address is divided into Host ID and Network ID sections, and may take one of five formats, Class A through E addresses, as shown in Figure 6-4. The formats differ in the number of bits allocated to the Host and Network IDs and are identified by the first three bits. Class A addresses are designed for very large networks having many hosts; they are identified by Bit 0 = 0. Bits 1 through 7 identify the network, and Bits 8 through 31 identify the specific host on that network. With a seven-bit Network ID, only 128 class A addresses are available. Of these, addresses 0 and 127 are reserved.

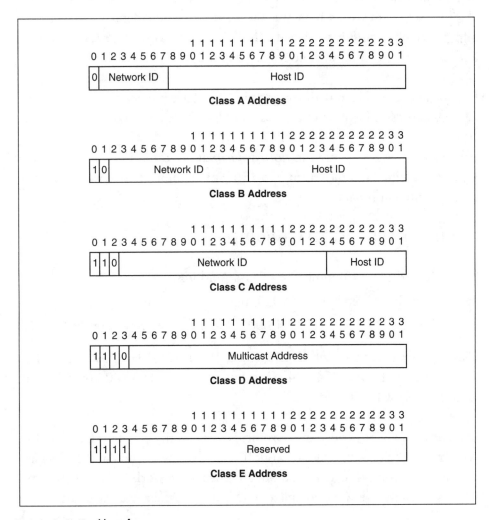

Figure 6-4. IP address formats

Class B addresses are designed for corporate internetworks having multiple LANs. Class B addresses are identified by the first two bits having a value of 10 (binary). The next 14 bits identify the Network and the remaining 16 bits identify the Host. As many as 16,384 Class B addresses are possible, with addresses 0 and 16,383 reserved.

Class C addresses are generally used for smaller networks such as LANs. Class C addresses begin with a binary 110. The next 21 bits identify the Network, and the remaining 8 bits identify the Host. A total of 2,097,152 Class C addresses are possible, with addresses 0 and 2,097,151 reserved.

Class D addresses begin with a binary 1110 and are intended for multicasting. Class E addresses begin with a binary 1111 and are reserved for future use.

All IP addresses are written in *dotted decimal notation*, in which each octet is given a decimal number from 0 to 256. For example, network 10.56.31.84 is represented in binary as

00001010 00110111 00011111 1010100

➤   The first bit (0) indicates a Class A address.

➤   The next seven bits (0001010) represent the Network ID (decimal 10).

➤   The last 24 bits (00110111 00011111 1010100) represent the Host ID.

Class A addresses begin with 1-127, Class B with 128-191, Class C with 192-223, and Class D with 224-254. Thus, an address of 150.100.200.5 is easily identified as a Class B address.

IP addresses may be divided into two fields that identify a Network and a Host. A central authority assigns the Network ID, and the network administrator assigns the Host ID. Routers send a packet to a particular network (using the Network ID), and then the Network completes the delivery to the particular Host.

If an organization had two networks, it could request two Network ID assignments from the central authority. Unfortunately, this would cause the routing tables within Hosts and Routers to greatly expand. As more Network IDs were assigned, the routing tables would continue to grow. The popularity of LANs in the mid-1980s inspired the Internet community to revise the IP address structure to allow for an additional field that would identify a subnetwork within an assigned Network ID. Thus the Network, Host address has been replaced with Network, Subnetwork, Host. The space required for the Subnetwork field comes from reducing the Host field. The central authority assigns the Network ID, and the individual organization assigns the Subnetwork IDs as well as the Host IDs on each subnetwork.

6.4 Internet Control Message Protocol (ICMP)

If internetworks were flawless, datagrams would always be routed to their intended destination with no errors, excessive delays, or retransmissions. Unfortunately, this is not the case. As discussed previously, IP provides a connectionless service to the attached hosts but requires an additional module, known as the Internet Control Message Protocol (ICMP), to report any errors that may occur in the processing of those datagrams. Examples of errors would be undeliverable datagrams or incorrect routes. The protocol is also used to test the path to a distant host (known as a PING) or to request an address mask for a particular subnet. ICMP is an integral part of IP and must be implemented in IP modules contained in hosts and routers. The standard for ICMP is RFC 792 [6-5].

IP datagrams contain ICMP messages. In other words, ICMP is a user (client) of IP, and the IP header precedes the ICMP message. The datagram would thus be IP header, ICMP header, and finally ICMP data. Protocol = 1 identifies ICMP within the IP header. A Type field within the ICMP header further identifies the purpose and format of the ICMP message. Any data required to complete the ICMP message follows the ICMP header.

Thirteen ICMP message formats have been defined, each with a specific ICMP header format. Two of these formats (Information Request/Reply) are considered obsolete, and several others share a common message structure. The result is six unique message formats, as shown in Figure 6-5.

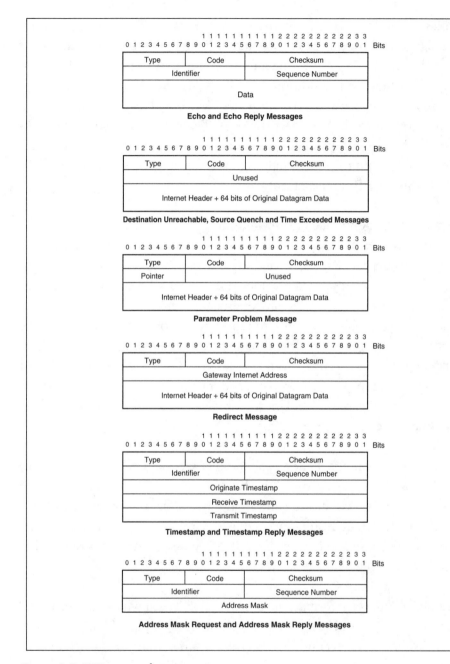

Figure 6-5. ICMP message formats

Network managers need to understand each of these ICMP messages because they contain valuable information about network status. All the headers share the first three fields. The Type field (1 octet) identifies one of the thirteen unique ICMP messages. These include:

Type Code	ICMP Message
0	Echo Reply
3	Destination Unreachable
4	Source Quench
5	Redirect
8	Echo
11	Time Exceeded
12	Parameter Problem
13	Timestamp
14	Timestamp Reply
15	Information Request (obsolete)
16	Information Reply (obsolete)
17	Address Mask Request
18	Address Mask Reply

The second field is labeled Code (1 octet) and elaborates on specific message types. For example, the Code field for the Destination Unreachable message indicates whether the network, host, protocol, or port was the unreachable entity. The third field is a Checksum (2 octets) on the ICMP message. The ICMP message formats diverge after the third field.

The Echo message (ICMP Type = 8) tests the communication path from a sender to a receiver via the Internet. On many hosts, this function is known as PING.

The sender transmits an Echo message, which may contain an Identifier (2 octets) and a Sequence Number (2 octets) as well as data. When the intended destination receives the message, it reverses the source and destination addresses, recomputes the checksum, and returns an Echo Reply (ICMP Type = 0). The contents of the Data field (if any) would also return to the sender.

The Destination Unreachable message (ICMP Type = 3) is used when the router or host is unable to deliver the datagram. This message is returned to the source host of the datagram in question, and its Code field includes the specific reason for the delivery problem:

Code	Meaning
0	Net Unreachable
1	Host Unreachable
2	Protocol Unreachable
3	Port Unreachable
4	Fragmentation Needed and DF Set
5	Source Route Failed

Routers use codes 0, 1, 4, or 6. Hosts use codes 2 or 3. For example, when a datagram arrives at a router, it does a table lookup to determine the outgoing path to use. If the router determines that the destination network is unreachable (that is, a distance of infinite hops away), it returns a Net Unreachable message. Similarly, if a host is unable to process a datagram because the requested protocol or port is inactive, it would return a Protocol Unreachable or Port Unreachable message, respectively. Included in the Destination Unreachable message is the IP header plus the first 64 bits (8 octets) of the datagram in question. This returned data helps the host diagnose the failure in the transmission process.

The advantage of the datagram's connectionless nature is its simplicity. The disadvantage is its inability to regulate the amount of traffic into the network.

As an analogy, consider the problem that your local post office faces. To handle the maximum possible number of letters, it needs enough boxes to handle the holiday rush. Building many boxes might be wasteful, however, because many of the boxes may not be used fully during the summer. If a router or host becomes congested with datagrams, it may send a Source Quench message (ICMP Type = 4) asking the source of those datagrams to reduce its output. This mechanism is similar to traffic signals that regulate the flow of cars onto a freeway. The Source Quench message does not use the second 32-bit word of the ICMP header, but fills it with zeros. The rest of the message contains the IP header and the first 8 octets of the datagram that triggered the request.

Hosts do not always choose the correct destination address for a particular datagram, and occasionally send one to the wrong router. This scenario can occur when the host is initialized and its routing tables are incomplete. When such a routing mistake occurs, the router receiving the datagram returns a Redirect message to the host specifying a better route. The Code field in the datagram would contain the following information:

Code	Message
0	Redirect datagrams for the network
1	Redirect datagrams for the host
2	Redirect datagrams for the type of service and network
3	Redirect datagrams for the type of service and host

The Redirect message (ICMP Type = 5) contains the router (gateway) address necessary for the datagram to reach the desired destination. In addition, the IP header plus the first 8 octets of the datagram in question return to the source host to aid the diagnostic processes.

Another potential problem of connectionless networks is that datagrams can get lost within the network. Alternatively, congestion could prevent all fragments of a datagram from being reassembled within the host's required time.

Either of these situations could trigger an ICMP Time Exceeded message (ICMP Type = 11). This message contains two codes: time-to-live exceeded in transmit (code = 0), and fragment reassembly time exceeded (code = 1). The rest of the message has the same format as the Source Quench message: the second word contains all Zeros and the rest of the message contains the IP header and first 8 octets of the offending datagram.

If a datagram cannot be processed because of errors, higher-layer processes recognize the errors and discard the datagram. Parameter problems within an IP datagram header (such as incorrect Type of Service field) would trigger the sending of an ICMP Parameter Problem message (ICMP Type = 12) to the source of that datagram, identifying the location of the problem. The message contains a pointer that identifies the octet with the error. The rest of the message contains the IP datagram header plus the first 8 octets of data, as before.

The Timestamp message (ICMP Type = 13) and Timestamp Reply message (ICMP Type = 14) either measure the round-trip transit time between two machines or synchronize the clocks of two different machines. The first two words of the Timestamp and Timestamp Reply messages are similar to the Echo and Echo Reply messages. The next five fields contain timestamps, measured in milliseconds since midnight, Universal Time (UT). The Timestamp requester fills in the Originate field when it transmits the request; the recipient fills in the Receive Timestamp upon its receipt. The recipient also fills in the Transmit Timestamp when it transmits the Timestamp Reply message. With this information, the requester can estimate the remote processing and round-trip transit times. (Note that these are only estimates, since network delay is a highly variable measurement.) The remote processing time is the Received Timestamp minus Transmit Timestamp. The round-trip transit time is the Timestamp Reply message arrival time minus the Originate Timestamp. With these two calculations, the two clocks can be synchronized.

The subnetting requirements (RFC 950) added the Address Mask Request (ICMP Type = 17) and Address Mask Reply (ICMP Type = 18) to the ICMP message set. It is assumed that the requesting host knows its own internet address. (If not, it uses RARP to discover its Internet address.) The host broadcasts the Address Mask Request message to destination address 256.256.256.255 and fills the Address Mask field of the ICMP message with zeros, and the IP router that knows the correct address mask responds. For example, the response for a Class B network (when subnet addresses are not used) would be 256.256.0.0. A Class B network using an 8-bit subnet field would be 256.256.256.0. Section 4.2 of *Troubleshooting TCP/IP* provides additional details on subnet addresses.

6.5 Network Interface Protocols

The lowest layer of the ARPA architectural model is the Network Interface layer, which encompasses the OSI Data Link and Physical layers. This layer is responsible for the network hardware and topology, such as Ethernet, token ring, FDDI, and so on. WAN protocols, such as dial-up or leased-line connections, X.25, or Frame Relay, can also be implemented at this layer. Because most SNMP implementations involve local, not remote manager/agent relationships, we will concentrate on the LAN protocols in this section. For more information on the WAN options, consult Chapter 3 of *Troubleshooting TCP/IP* [6-2].

6.5.1 Ethernet

DEC, Intel, and Xerox (known collectively as DIX) developed Ethernet in 1973. The first version, known as Experimental Ethernet, operated at 3 Mbps, and used 8-bit addresses. This later became Ethernet Version 1, and finally Ethernet Version 2, which we use today. Ethernet Version 2 transmits at 10 Mbps and uses 48-bit addresses. Ethernet was the first LAN to achieve wide acceptance, and much of its development coincided with research into the Internet protocols. As a result, many TCP/IP-based internetworks contain Ethernet segments.

One word of caution is in order, however. In the early 1980s, the DIX Ethernet Standard became the model for IEEE 802.3, the Carrier Sense Multiple Access with Collision Detection (CSMA/CD). The IEEE improved the DIX version and published IEEE 802.3 in 1983. The Ethernet and IEEE 802.3

standards are similar, but not identical. This section discusses Ethernet. Section 6.5.2 talks about IEEE 802.3.

The Ethernet frame format, shown in Figure 6-6, defines a length of between 64 and 1518 octets, including the header, data, and trailer. The header consists of Destination and Source addresses that are 6 octets (48 bits) each, plus a 2-octet field known as the Type (or Ethertype) field. The Ethernet-designated destination address for broadcast frames is all ONES (FFFFFFFFFFFFH). The type designates the higher-layer protocol in use within the Data field. A number of these Ethernet Protocol Types are defined, and can be found in RFC 1340.

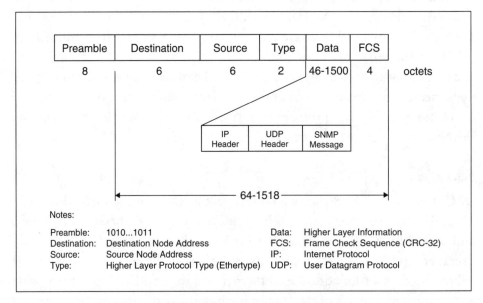

Figure 6-6. Ethernet frame with SNMP message (©1982 Digital Equipment Corp.)

The Data field must be between 46 and 1500 octets in length. If an extremely short IP datagram is transmitted (less than 46 octets), the data field is padded with zeros to reach the minimum 46 octet length. (This padding is not considered part of the IP datagram length and is not counted in the Total Length field within the IP header.) The Internet Standard for Ethernet networks (RFC 894 [6-6]) and Appendix B of the IP specification (RFC 791) provide further details on the specific data formats.

6.5.2 IEEE 802.3

As we studied previously, the IEEE 802.3 standard, which is covered by the RFC 1042 [6-7] Internet standard, is similar but not identical to the DIX Ethernet. Figure 6-7 shows the IEEE 802.3 format. IEEE 802.3's Destination and Source address fields may be 2 or 6 octets long, although the 6-octet length, which matches the Ethernet address lengths, is most common. The Address Resolution Protocol (ARP) maps the IP address (32 bits) to the IEEE 802 address (48 bits). The ARP hardware code for IEEE 802 networks is 6. However, broadcast addresses for both Ethernet and IEEE 802 networks are consistent with all Ones.

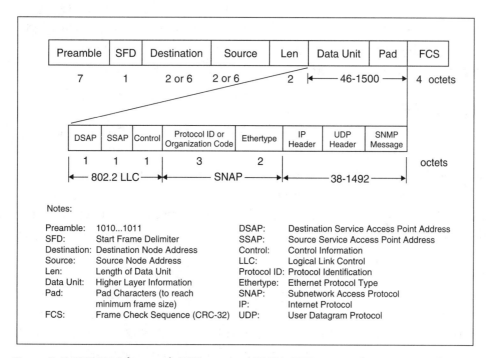

Figure 6-7. IEEE 802.3 frame with SNMP message (©1990, IEEE)

Next, the IEEE 802.3 frame defines a Length field, which specifies the length of the Data unit. Recall that in the Ethernet frame this was the Ethertype, indicating the higher-layer protocol in use. These two octets (the Ethertype or Length fields) distinguish whether the frame format is Ethernet or IEEE 802.3, respectively. If the Data Link layer driver mixes these up, confusion will result. For example, if the destination host expects an Ethernet frame (with an Ethertype field), it cannot respond to an IEEE 802.3 frame containing the Length field.

The Data field contains the information from the higher layers, plus two IEEE-defined headers. The first header is the Logical Link Control (LLC) header defined by IEEE 802.2. The LLC header includes destination and source service access point addresses (DSAP and SSAP, respectively) and a control field. The second header is known as the Sub-Network Access Protocol (SNAP), defined by IEEE Standard 802-1990. This header includes a Protocol ID or Organization Code field (3 octets) and an Ethertype field (2 octets). The combination of the LLC and SNAP headers allows the higher-layer protocol in use to have both an SAP and Ethertype designation. The rest of the Data field contains the higher-layer information, such as an IP datagram.

6.5.3 IEEE 802.5

The IEEE 802.5 token ring has enjoyed great success, partly because of strong support from major networking companies such as Apple, IBM, and Proteon, and partly because of the protocol's built-in provision for internetworking. This provision is known as *source routing* and uses the Routing Information (RI) field to connect rings via bridges. The RI field specifies the path the frame must take from its source to its destination. The mechanism for determining that path is called *route discovery*.

The IP Datagram occupies the Information field of the token ring frame, as shown in Figure 6-8. Any necessary Routing Information precedes the Information field. Inside the Information field is the IEEE 802.2 LLC header (3 octets), SNAP header (5 octets), and the IP datagram (variable length). Given a minimum IP datagram header of 20 octets, the protocol overhead (LLC + SNAP + IP) is 28 octets per IP datagram. The maximum length of the Information field (and thus the encapsulated IP datagram) varies, depending on the *token holding time* parameter. This parameter specifies the length of time a particular node may hold the token before it must pass the token to its downstream neighbor. RFC 1042 [6-7] discusses an example token holding time of

9 milliseconds, which results in a maximum length of the IP header plus datagram of 4464 octets.

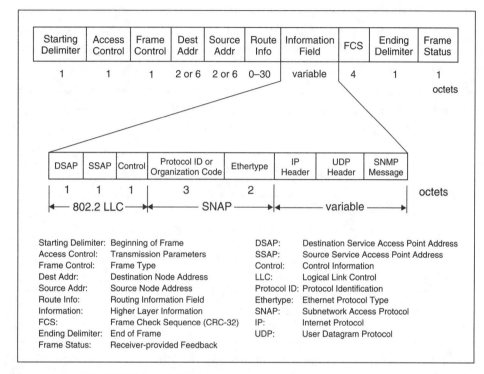

Figure 6-8. IEEE 802.5 frame with SNMP message

6.5.4 ARCNET

Datapoint Corporation developed the Attached Resource Computer Network (ARCNET) in 1977. ARCNET is a token-passing architecture that can have several Physical layer implementations, including a linear bus, a star, or a branching tree. The original version supported a transmission rate of 2.5 Mbps and up to 255 workstations, and is standardized as ANSI 878.1. In February 1992, Datapoint announced ARCNETPLUS, a 20 Mbps network which is downward-compatible with the original ARCNET.

The Internet standard for ARCNET, RFC 1201 [6-8], suggests methods for encapsulating both IP and ARP datagrams within the ARCNET frame. Three frame formats are available, as shown in Figures 6-9a, b, and c. Note that this RFC supersedes the older version (RFC 1051) and makes a number of protocol enhancements for improved TCP/IP support. The short frame format (Figure 6-9a) limits the transmitted client data to 249 octets. The long frame (Figure 6-9b) allows between 253 and 504 octets of client data. An exception frame (Figure 6-9c) is used with frames having 250 to 252 octets of client data. (Note that the frame formats shown in Figure 6-9 appear in the software buffers. The format transmitted by the hardware duplicates the Destination ID [DID], does not send the Unused and Protocol ID fields, and adds some hardware framing.)

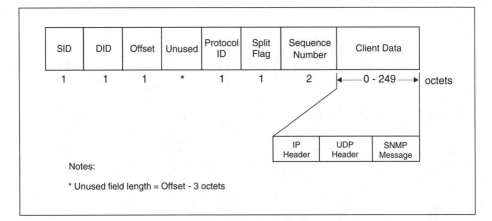

Figure 6-9a. ARCNET short frame format with SNMP message

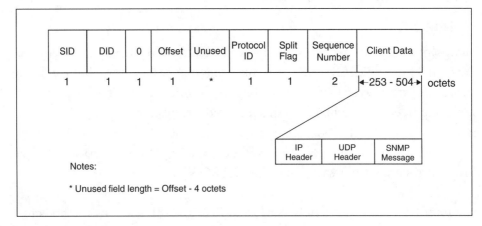

Figure 6-9b. ARCNET long frame format with SNMP message

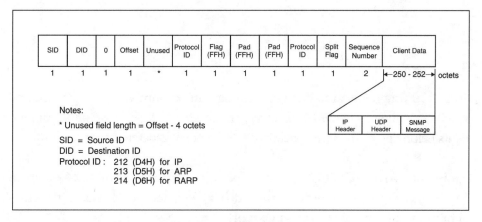

Figure 6-9c. ARCNET exception frame format with SNMP message

The ARCNET frame may contain up to 512 octets, of which 504 may be client data. The sender fragments larger packets, using the Split Flag and Sequence Number fields to identify the fragments. The Split Flag takes on one of three values depending on the fragmentation required. Unfragmented packets use Split Flag = 0. The first fragment of a fragmented packet uses Split Flag = ((T-2)*2)+1, where T = total number of expected fragments. Subsequent fragments use Split Flag = ((N-1)*2), where N is the number of this fragment.

For example, assume that a packet requires 8 fragments. The Split Flag values would be:

Fragment	Split Flag (decimal)
1	13
2	2
3	4
4	6
5	8
6	10

7	12
8	14

Up to 120 fragments are allowed, yielding a maximum value of 238 decimal (EEH). This allows up to 60,480 octets per packet (120 * 504 = 60,480). All fragments belonging to the same packet use an identical 2-octet Sequence Number.

Datapoint's ARCNETPLUS standard permits a Data field of 4224 octets in length. Currently, no Internet standard (RFC) exists that discusses the fragmentation requirements for this network.

Another unique characteristic of ARCNET and ARCNETPLUS is their addressing structures, which define an 8-bit address field and allow 255 unique hardware addresses as well as a broadcast designation (address = 0). (This address is implemented with an 8-position DIP switch, which you must set manually on each ARCNET or ARCNETPLUS card. A human error in duplicating these switch settings can cause ARCNET to fail; ARCNETPLUS offers an algorithm to detect duplicate addresses.)

6.5.5 FDDI

ANSI developed the Fiber Data Distributed Interface (FDDI) as a standard for fiber-optic data transmission. FDDI is a token-passing ring architecture that operates at 100 Mbps. (The actual data rate for FDDI is 125 Mbps, but 1 out of 5 bits handles overhead.) Because of its transmission rate, FDDI may emerge as a significant alternative to Ethernet or token ring for local data transport. The FDDI frame structure, shown in Figure 6-10, is similar to IEEE 802.6. The maximum frame size is 4500 octets (or 9000 symbols, with 4 bits/symbol). When 6-octet addressing (the most common) is used, the MAC-layer header (preamble through source address) uses 16 octets, and the MAC-layer trailer uses 6 octets. Subtracting the headers from the maximum frame size leaves 4478 octets for data. The IEEE 802.2 LLC header requires three octets, yielding a maximum IP datagram length of 4475 octets. (Because FDDI does not typically use SNAP, the figure does not show the SNAP header, but there is no technical constraint on the use of SNAP. If present, the SNAP header would immediately follow the IEEE 802.2 header.) RFC 1188 [6-9] defines support for FDDI within TCP/IP-based internetworks.

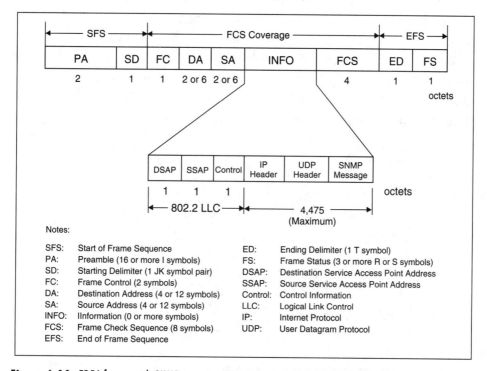

Figure 6.10. FDDI frame with SNMP message *(Courtesy American National Standards Institute)*

6.6 Address Translation

In the previous two sections, we discussed the differences between the Internet address, used by IP, and the local address, used by the LAN or WAN hardware. We also saw that the IP address is a 32-bit logical address, but the physical hardware address depends on the hardware. For example, ARCNET has an 8-bit hardware address and Ethernet has a 48-bit hardware address. Thus, translation between the physical and logical addresses is necessary. The Address Resolution Protocol (ARP) described in RFC 826 [6-10] translates from an IP address to a hardware address. The Reverse Address Resolution Protocol (RARP), detailed in RFC 903 [6-11], does the opposite, as its name implies.

6.6.1 Address Resolution Protocol (ARP)

Assume that a device on an Ethernet, Host X, wishes to deliver a datagram to another device on the same Ethernet, Host Y. Host X knows Host Y's destination protocol (IP) address, but does not know Host Y's hardware (Ethernet) address. Host X would therefore broadcast an ARP packet (shown in Figure 6-11) on the Ethernet to determine Host Y's hardware address. The packet consists of 28 octets, primarily addresses, contained within the Data field of a local network frame. A device that recognizes its own protocol address responds with the requested hardware address. The individual fields of the ARP message show how the protocol operates.

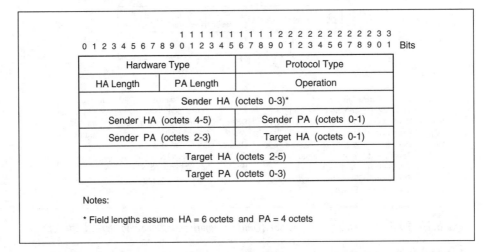

Figure 6-11. Address Resolution Protocol (ARP) and Reverse Address Resolution Protocol (RARP) packet formats

The first field, Hardware (2 octets), defines the type of hardware in use. Current values are listed in RFC 1700. Examples include Hardware = 1 (Ethernet), 6 (IEEE 802 Networks), 7 (ARCNET), and 11 (LocalTalk). The second field, Protocol (2 octets), identifies the protocol address in use. For example, Protocol = 0800H would identify IP addresses.

The next two fields allow the ARP packet to work with addressing schemes of different lengths (Figure 6-11 represents the most common scheme, where

6 octets are required for the Hardware Address and 4 octets are required for the Protocol Address). To make the protocol more adaptive, the HA Length (1 octet) and PA Length (1 octet) specify the lengths, in octets, of the addresses to be used. Figure 6-11 represents the most common scenario. Six octets (48 bits) are required for Hardware Address (HA Length = 6) and 4 octets (32 bits) for the Protocol Address (PA Length =4). The Operation field (2 octets) defines an ARP Request = 1 or ARP Reply =2.

The next fields contain the addresses themselves. With an ARP Request message, the Target Hardware Address (HA) field is unknown and is sent filled with zeros. The ARP Reply packet from the target host inserts the requested address in the field. When it receives the ARP Reply, the originating station records the information in a table (known as the ARP cache) so that it doesn't need to make the same request again and again. Routers have an ARP cache with a finite lifetime so the table won't grow too large.

6.6.2 Reverse Address Resolution Protocol (RARP)

Most network hosts are intelligent enough to remember their hardware and protocol addresses. Diskless workstations, however, depend on a server to provide much of their intelligence. The diskless workstation would know its hardware address (HA), which is coded into its ROM, but it may not know its protocol address (PA), which the server assigns. The RARP can discover the unknown PA given a known HA and a RARP server to supply the desired answer.

The process of determining an unknown protocol address is similar to that of finding an unknown hardware address. The same packet structure is used (review Figure 6-11), with only minor modifications to the field values required. The Operation field adds two new values, 3 (RARP Request) and 4 (RARP Reply). When the RARP Request is made, the Sender HA, Sender PA, and Target HA are transmitted. The RARP Reply contains the requested Target PA.

6.7 Using SNMP with UDP and IP

This section shows how the SNMP GetRequest and GetResponse PDUs fit within the structure of an Ethernet frame (review Figure 6-1). In this section we will examine the Ethernet frame format, the IP header, the UDP header, the SNMP PDUs, and the ASN.1 encoding of the variable bindings.

Trace 6.7a shows four layers of protocol operating in two Frames, 7 and 8. You can easily identify the Data Link Control (DLC) layer as Ethernet because of the Ethertype (or Type) field (review Figure 6-6). The next field, the IP Header, is 20 octets long, has routine service, and is not fragmented. The Protocol field identifies the next higher layer (UDP), while the source and destination addresses identify the origin and destination of this datagram.

The UDP header gives the source and destination port numbers. Note that the SunMgr assigns port number 3234 for SNMP, while the Retix bridge (GoldGate) uses the standard port number of 161 for SNMP.

The SNMP authentication header, containing the version number and community string, precede the SNMP PDU. We see the PDU identified (GetRequest) and the various error fields. Next comes the variable bindings, which consist of an object name and its value. The GetRequest PDU uses NULL for all the Value fields (Frame 7), while the GetResponse (Frame 8) contains the actual values retrieved. To review, you could return to Figure 3-2 and trace the subtree for the System group, verifying the accuracy of the OID designation {1.3.6.1.2.1....}.

Trace 6.7a. Using SNMP with Ethernet, IP, and UDP

Sniffer Network Analyzer data 10-Nov at 10:29:36 file GOLD_SYS.ENC Pg 1

```
------------------------------------- Frame 7 -------------------------------------
DLC: ----- DLC Header -----
DLC:
DLC: Frame 7 arrived at 10:29:37.30; frame size is 138 (008A hex) bytes
DLC: Destination = Station Retix 034CF1, GoldGate
DLC: Source     = Station Sun  0900C8, SunMgr
DLC: Ethertype  = 0800 (IP)
DLC:
```

```
IP:    ----- IP Header -----
IP:
IP:    Version = 4, header length = 20 bytes
IP:    Type of service = 00
IP:        000. .... = routine
IP:        ...0 .... = normal delay
IP:        .... 0... = normal throughput
IP:        .... .0.. = normal reliability
IP:    Total length = 124 bytes
IP:    Identification = 20055
IP:    Flags = 0X
IP:    .0.. .... = may fragment
IP:    ..0. .... = last fragment
IP:    Fragment offset = 0 bytes
IP:    Time to live = 60 seconds/hops
IP:    Protocol = 17 (UDP)
IP:    Header checksum = A5C5 (correct)
IP:    Source address = [XXX.YYY.128.4]
IP:    Destination address = [XXX.YYY.1.10]
IP:    No options
IP:
UDP:   ----- UDP Header -----
UDP:
UDP:   Source port = 3234 (SNMP)
UDP:   Destination port = 161
UDP:   Length = 104
UDP:   No checksum
UDP:
SNMP: ----- Simple Network Management Protocol (Version 1) -----
SNMP:
SNMP: Version = 0
SNMP: Community = public
SNMP: Command = Get request
SNMP: Request ID = 0
```

SNMP: Error status = 0 (No error)
SNMP: Error index = 0
SNMP:
SNMP: Object = {1.3.6.1.2.1.1.3.0} (sysUpTime.0)
SNMP: Value = NULL
SNMP:
SNMP: Object = {1.3.6.1.2.1.1.1.0} (sysDescr.0)
SNMP: Value = NULL
SNMP:
SNMP: Object = {1.3.6.1.2.1.1.2.0} (sysObjectID.0)
SNMP: Value = NULL
SNMP:
SNMP: Object = {1.3.6.1.2.1.1.3.0} (sysUpTime.0)
SNMP: Value = NULL
SNMP:
SNMP: Object = {1.3.6.1.2.1.1.6.0} (system.6.0)
SNMP: Value = NULL
SNMP:

-- Frame 8 --
DLC: ----- DLC Header -----
DLC:
DLC: Frame 8 arrived at 10:29:37.33; frame size is 195 (00C3 hex) bytes
DLC: Destination = Station Sun   0900C8, SunMgr
DLC: Source   = Station Retix 034CF1, GoldGate
DLC: Ethertype   = 0800 (IP)
DLC:
IP: ----- IP Header -----
IP:
IP: Version = 4, header length = 20 bytes
IP: Type of service = 00
IP: 000. .... = routine
IP: ...0 .... = normal delay
IP: .... 0... = normal throughput

IP: .... .0.. = normal reliability
IP: Total length = 181 bytes
IP: Identification = 0
IP: Flags = 0X
IP: .0.. .... = may fragment
IP: ..0. .... = last fragment
IP: Fragment offset = 0 bytes
IP: Time to live = 16 seconds/hops
IP: Protocol = 17 (UDP)
IP: Header checksum = 1FE4 (correct)
IP: Source address = [XXX.YYY.1.10]
IP: Destination address = [XXX.YYY.128.4]
IP: No options
IP:
UDP: ----- UDP Header -----
UDP:
UDP: Source port = 161 (SNMP)
UDP: Destination port = 3234
UDP: Length = 161
UDP: Checksum = 6417 (correct)
UDP:
SNMP: ----- Simple Network Management Protocol (Version 1) -----
SNMP:
SNMP: Version = 0
SNMP: Community = public
SNMP: Command = Get response
SNMP: Request ID = 0
SNMP: Error status = 0 (No error)
SNMP: Error index = 0
SNMP:
SNMP: Object = {1.3.6.1.2.1.1.3.0} (sysUpTime.0)
SNMP: Value = 240267300 hundredths of a second
SNMP:
SNMP: Object = {1.3.6.1.2.1.1.1.0} (sysDescr.0)

```
SNMP: Value  = Retix Local Ethernet Bridge Model 2265M
SNMP:
SNMP: Object = {1.3.6.1.2.1.1.2.0} (sysObjectID.0)
SNMP: Value  = {1.3.6.1.4.1.72.8.3}
SNMP:
SNMP: Object = {1.3.6.1.2.1.1.3.0} (sysUpTime.0)
SNMP: Value  = 240267300 hundredths of a second
SNMP:
SNMP: Object = {1.3.6.1.2.1.1.6.0} (system.6.0)
SNMP: Value  =
SNMP:
```

Trace 6.7b amplifies the first trace by looking at the actual ASN.1-encoded information included within the SNMP PDUs. Frame 7 begins with a SEQUENCE OF type, code 30H, followed by the length of the encoding (94 octets, or 5E). (These two octets are shown in bold within the hexadecimal display and are the 43rd and 44th octets transmitted.) The ASN.1 encoding continues within the SNMP PDU, using the TLV (Type-Length-Value) structure discussed in Chapter 2. You can identify the first OID Value requested (line 6.1) by looking for the preceding OID. That information is the 71st octet transmitted, with an OBJECT IDENTIFIER type (06H), a Length of 8 octets (08H), and a Value of 2B 06 01 02 01 01 03 00H. Recall that the 1.3 prefix is translated into a 43 decimal (or 2BH) through the expression we studied in Section 2.5.3.3. The rest of the PDU follows in a similar manner.

The final example (see Figure 6-12) shows how the SNMP GetRequest PDU is encapsulated within the Ethernet frame. Frame 7 illustrates this with the hexadecimal characters shown below their respective fields. The data capture begins with the destination address (08 00 90 03 4C F1), which identifies the Retix bridge. Likewise, the source address (08 00 20 09 00 C8) identifies the Sun Manager. The Ethertype field (08 00) indicates that IP will be the next protocol in the Data field. You can decode the IP header, UDP header, SNMP authentication header, and SNMP GetRequest PDU (including the Variable Bindings) in a similar manner.

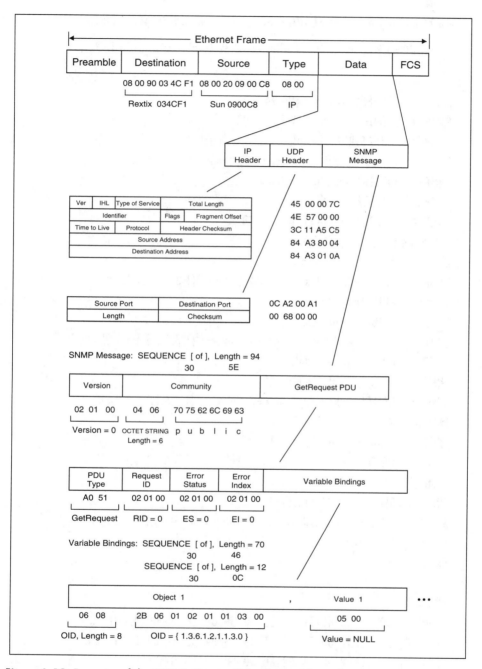

Figure 6-12. Expansion of the SNMP GetRequest PDU within an Ethernet frame

Trace 6.7b. ASN.1 encoding of SNMP GetRequest and GetResponse PDUs

Sniffer Network Analyzer data 10-Nov at 10:29:36 file GOLD_SYS.ENC Pg 1

```
------------------------------------------ Frame 7 ------------------------------------------
SNMP: 1.1 SEQUENCE [of], Length=94
SNMP: 2.1 INTEGER, Length=1, Value = "0"
SNMP: 2.2 OCTET STRING, Length=6, Value = "public"
SNMP: 2.3 Context-Specific Constructed [0], Length=81
SNMP: 3.1 INTEGER, Length=1, Value = "0"
SNMP: 3.2 INTEGER, Length=1, Value = "0"
SNMP: 3.3 INTEGER, Length=1, Value = "0"
SNMP: 3.4 SEQUENCE [of], Length=70
SNMP: 4.1 SEQUENCE [of], Length=12
SNMP: 6.1 OBJECT IDENTIFIER, Length=8, Value = "{1.3.6.1.2.1.1.3.0}"
SNMP: 6.2 NULL, Length=0, Value = ""
SNMP: 4.2 SEQUENCE [of], Length=12
SNMP: 6.1 OBJECT IDENTIFIER, Length=8, Value = "{1.3.6.1.2.1.1.1.0}"
SNMP: 6.2 NULL, Length=0, Value = ""
SNMP: 4.3 SEQUENCE [of], Length=12
SNMP: 6.1 OBJECT IDENTIFIER, Length=8, Value = "{1.3.6.1.2.1.1.2.0}"
SNMP: 6.2 NULL, Length=0, Value = ""
SNMP: 4.4 SEQUENCE [of], Length=12
SNMP: 6.1 OBJECT IDENTIFIER, Length=8, Value = "{1.3.6.1.2.1.1.3.0}"
SNMP: 6.2 NULL, Length=0, Value = ""
SNMP: 4.5 SEQUENCE [of], Length=12
SNMP: 6.1 OBJECT IDENTIFIER, Length=8, Value = "{1.3.6.1.2.1.1.6.0}"
SNMP: 6.2 NULL, Length=0, Value = ""
SNMP:

ADDR HEX                                                        ASCII
0000  08 00 90 03 4C F1 08 00 20 09 00 C8 08 00 4500     ....L... .....E.
0010  00 7C 4E 57 00 00 3C 11 A5 C5 84 A3 80 04 84A3     .|NW..<.........
0020  01 0A 0C A2 00 A1 00 68 00 00 30 5E 02 01 0004     .......h..0^....
```

```
0030   06 70 75 62 6C 69 63 A0 51 02 01 00 02 01 0002    .public.Q.......
0040   01 00 30 46 30 0C 06 08 2B 06 01 02 01 01 0300    ..0F0...+.......
0050   05 00 30 0C 06 08 2B 06 01 02 01 01 01 00 0500    ..0...+.........
0060   30 0C 06 08 2B 06 01 02 01 01 02 00 05 00 300C    0...+.........0.
0070   06 08 2B 06 01 02 01 01 03 00 05 00 30 0C 0608    ..+.........0...
0080   2B 06 01 02 01 01 06 00 05 00                     +.........
```

-- Frame 8 --

SNMP: 1.1 SEQUENCE [of], Length=150

SNMP: 2.1 INTEGER, Length=1, Value = "0"

SNMP: 2.2 OCTET STRING, Length=6, Value = "public"

SNMP: 2.3 Context-Specific Constructed [2], Length=136

SNMP: 3.1 INTEGER, Length=1, Value = "0"

SNMP: 3.2 INTEGER, Length=1, Value = "0"

SNMP: 3.3 INTEGER, Length=1, Value = "0"

SNMP: 3.4 SEQUENCE [of], Length=125

SNMP: 4.1 SEQUENCE [of], Length=16

SNMP: 6.1 OBJECT IDENTIFIER, Length=8, Value = "{1.3.6.1.2.1.1.3.0}"

SNMP: 6.2 Application Primitive [3], Length=4, Data = "<0E>R0$"

SNMP: 4.2 SEQUENCE [of], Length=51

SNMP: 6.1 OBJECT IDENTIFIER, Length=8, Value = "{1.3.6.1.2.1.1.1.0}"

SNMP: 6.2 OCTET STRING, Length=39, Value = "Retix Local Ethernet
                                        Bridge Model 2265M"

SNMP: 4.3 SEQUENCE [of], Length=20

SNMP: 6.1 OBJECT IDENTIFIER, Length=8, Value = "{1.3.6.1.2.1.1.2.0}"

SNMP: 6.2 OBJECT IDENTIFIER, Length=8, Value = "{1.3.6.1.4.1.72.8.3}"

SNMP: 4.4 SEQUENCE [of], Length=16

SNMP: 6.1 OBJECT IDENTIFIER, Length=8, Value = "{1.3.6.1.2.1.1.3.0}"

SNMP: 6.2 Application Primitive [3], Length=4, Data = "<0E>R0$"

SNMP: 4.5 SEQUENCE [of], Length=12

SNMP: 6.1 OBJECT IDENTIFIER, Length=8, Value = "{1.3.6.1.2.1.1.6.0}"

SNMP: 6.2 OCTET STRING, Length=0, Value = ""

SNMP:

```
ADDR HEX                                                                ASCII
0000  08 0020  09 00 C8 08 00 90 03 4C F1 08 00 4500   .. ........L...E.
0010  00 B500  00 00 00 10 11 1F E4 84 A3 01 0A 84A3   ................
0020  80 0400  A1 0C A2 00 A1 64 17 30 81 96 02 0100   ........d.0.....
0030  04 0670  75 62 6C 69 63 A2 81 88 02 01 00 0201   ..public........
0040  00 0201  00 30 7D 30 10 06 08 2B 06 01 02 0101   ....0}0...+.....
0050  03 0043  04 0E 52 30 24 30 33 06 08 2B 06 0102   ..C..RO$O3..+...
0060  01 0101  00 04 27 52 65 74 69 78 20 4C 6F 6361   .....'Retix Loca
0070  6C 2045  74 68 65 72 6E 65 74 20 42 72 69 6467   l Ethernet Bridg
0080  65 204D  6F 64 65 6C 20 32 32 36 35 4D 30 1406   e Model 2265M0..
0090  08 2B06  01 02 01 01 02 00 06 08 2B 06 01 0401   .+.........+....
00A0  48 0803  30 10 06 08 2B 06 01 02 01 01 03 0043   H..0...+.......C
00B0  04 0E52  30 24 30 0C 06 08 2B 06 01 02 01 0106   ..RO$O...+......
00C0  00 0400                                          ...
```

This chapter completes our tour of the Internet Network Management Framework. Chapter 7 discusses what happens when the systems (from Chapter 1) and the protocols (from Chapters 2 through 6) don't work together as designed.

6.8 References

[6-1]   Postel, J. "User Datagram Protocol." *RFC 768*, ISI, August 1980.

[6-2]   Miller, Mark A. *Troubleshooting TCP/IP*, Second edition. New York, NY: M&T Books, Inc. 1996.

[6-3]   Postel, J. "Internet Protocol." *RFC 791*, September 1981.

[6-4]   Reynolds, J., and J. Postel, "Assigned Numbers." *RFC 1700*, October 1994.

[6-5]   Postel, J. "Internet Control Message Protocol." *RFC 792*, September 1981.

[6-6]   Horning, Charles. "A Standard for the Transmission of IP Datagrams over Ethernet Networks." *RFC 894*, April 1984.

[6-7]   Postel, J., and J. Reynolds. "A Standard for the Transmission of IP Datagrams over IEEE 802 Networks." *RFC 1042*, February 1988.

[6-8]   Provan, D. "Transmitting IP Traffic over ARCNET Networks." *RFC 1201*, February 1991.

[6-9]   Katz, D. "A Proposed Standard for the Transmission of IP Datagrams over FDDI Networks." *RFC 1188*, October 1990.

[6-10]   Plummer, D. "An Ethernet Address Resolution Protocol, or Converting Network Protocol Addresses to 48-bit Ethernet Addresses for Transmission on Ethernet Hardware." *RFC 826*, November 1982.

[6-11]   Finlayson, R., et.= al. "A Reverse Address Resolution Protocol." *RFC 903*, June 1984.

7 Case Studies in Implementing SNMP

So far, this book has described the technical details of SNMP. This chapter provides case studies from live networks that show how these concepts apply to the real world. These studies demonstrate actual internetwork management challenges and solutions. For consistency, all of the case studies were captured with a Network General Corp. Sniffer protocol analyzer.

7.1 Verifying Access Control with the Community Name

To warm you up to the idea of protocol analysis, let's start with a problem that has a simple solution. As Section 4.3 discussed, the SNMP message consists of an authentication header and one of five SNMP PDUs. The authentication header contains the SNMP version number and the community name. The agent uses the community name as a password to validate the identity of the manager. If the community names of the manager and the agent are identical, message processing proceeds. If not, there is an authentication failure. Depending on the agent's SNMP implementation, it will either discard the offending message, generate a trap, or both.

In the topology shown in Figure 7-1, the network administrator has set the community name of both the manager and the agent to "public," a common default value. (Now is a good time to check the community name for your network devices and change this default value. Doing so will greatly increase the security on your internetwork!)

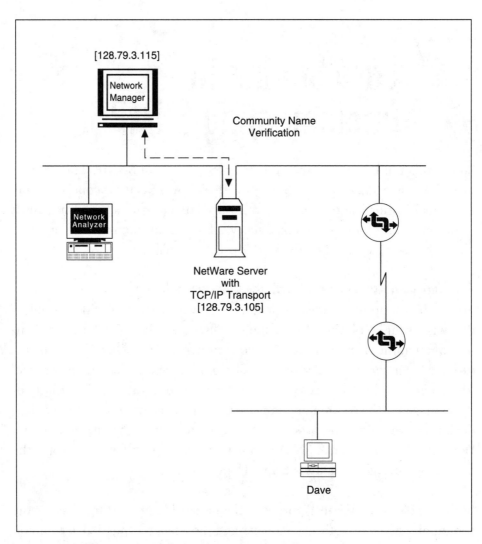

Figure 7-1. Verifying access with the community name

In frame 9 of Trace 7.1a, the manager requests the IP routing table {1.3.6.1.2.1.4.21} using a GetNextRequest. The manager requests values for the ipRouteDest, ipRouteNextHop, ipRouteType, and ipRouteIfIndex objects (Frame 9 of Trace 7.1b). The values of these objects are returned in Frames 10 through 54, and can be used to generate the following table:

IpRouteDest	ipRouteIfIndex	ipRouteNextHop	ipRouteType
0.0.0.0	2	128.79.3.200	4
128.79.0.0	2	128.79.3.200	3
128.79.2.0	2	128.79.3.202	4
128.79.3.0	2	128.79.3.105	3
128.79.4.0	2	128.79.3.200	4
128.79.5.0	2	128.79.3.201	4
128.79.6.0	2	128.79.3.200	4
128.79.7.0	2	128.79.3.201	4
128.79.8.0	2	128.79.3.201	4
128.79.9.0	2	128.79.3.202	4
128.79.12.0	2	128.79.3.200	4
128.79.14.0	2	128.79.3.200	4
128.79.15.0	2	128.79.3.201	4
128.79.16.0	2	128.79.3.201	4
128.79.18.0	2	128.79.3.201	4
128.79.20.0	2	128.79.3.201	4
128.79.40.0	2	128.79.3.200	4
128.79.120.0	2	128.79.3.200	4
128.79.180.0	2	128.79.3.201	4
128.79.200.0	2	128.79.3.201	4

The ipRouteDest object contains the destination IP address for this route. The first entry is 0.0.0.0, indicating a default route. The ipRouteIfIndex identifies the local interface through which the next hop of this route may be reached.

Each of these entries specifies interface number 2. The ipRouteNextHop is the IP address of the next hop of the route. The ipRouteType has one of four possible values: other (1), none of the following; invalid (2), an invalidated route; direct (3), a route to a directly connected subnetwork; and indirect (4), a route to a nonlocal (or remote) subnetwork. In the table, the second and fourth entries are direct; the remaining entries are destined for remote networks.

The GetNext operation stops in Frame 56 when the agent returns the lexicographical next object within the router's table (see Trace 7.1c): the ipRouteProto {1.3.6.1.2.1.4.21.1.9} and the ipRouteMetric1 {1.3.6.1.2.1.4.21.1.3}.

As an experiment, the network administrator changed the agent console's community name from "public" to "test." Frames 59 to 63 of Trace 7.1a show the results. In Frames 59 to 60, the manager and agent confirm their communication path by using ICMP Echo and Echo Reply messages (these messages are often called the "PING" commands). Satisfied that the communication path is working, the manager issues a GetNext request for values of three objects in the Interfaces group. The agent does not respond, so the manager retransmits the request at 5 second intervals in Frames 62 and 63. This is a fruitless exercise because the community name on the agent has been changed. The agent will not respond until the new community name is validated.

This case study illustrates several issues. First, the community name provides some access security for the agents. Second, SNMP is communicated via connectionless transport, which does not guarantee reliable delivery. Therefore, when the message did not seem to be getting across the LAN, the manager retransmitted the message in Frames 62 and 63. In fact, the message did get across the LAN, but it was not accepted because of the invalid community name.

This case study also presents a third, more subtle lesson. Recall from Section 3.3.4 that the IP routing table (MIB-II, RFC 1213) was replaced with the IP forwarding table in RFC 1354. This example shows that a manager does not conform to the current MIB standards. However, because the manager and agent MIBs were both out of date, the communication succeeds. If the manager MIB had been updated and no longer supported the IP routing table, an error would have been returned in response to the first GetNext request.

Trace 7.1a. IP routing table retrieval (summary)

Sniffer Network Analyzer data 5-Oct at 09:04:44, file NAME.ENC Pg 1

SUMMARY	Delta T	Destination	Source	Summary
9	0.0043	Agent	Manager	SNMP GetNext ipRouteDest .. ipRouteIfIndex (4 items)
10	0.0102	Manager	Agent	SNMP GetReply ipRouteDest .. ipRouteIfIndex (4 items)
11	0.0482	Agent	Manager	SNMP GetNext ipRouteDest .. ipRouteIfIndex (4 items)
53	0.0662	Agent	Manager	SNMP GetNext ipRouteDest .. ipRouteIfIndex (4 items)
54	0.0104	Manager	Agent	SNMP GetReply ipRouteDest .. ipRouteIfIndex (4 items)
55	0.0687	Agent	Manager	SNMP GetNext ipRouteDest .. ipRouteIfIndex (4 items)
56	0.0138	Manager	Agent	SNMP GetReply ipRouteIfIndex .. ipRouteMetric1 (4 items)
57	65.7201	HP133ADE	HP17B65F	ARP C PA=[128.79.3.105] PRO=IP
58	0.0005	HP17B65F	HP133ADE	ARP R PA=[128.79.3.105] HA=080009133ADE PRO=IP
59	82.5076	Agent	Manager	ICMP Echo
60	0.0008	Manager	Agent	ICMP Echo reply
61	50.1077	Agent	Manager	SNMP GetNext ifIndex .. ifPhysAddress (3 items)
62	4.9924	Agent	Manager	SNMP GetNext ifIndex .. ifPhysAddress (3 items)
63	5.0003	Agent	Manager	SNMP GetNext ifIndex .. ifPhysAddress (3 items)

Trace 7.1b. IP routing table retrieval details (GetNext Requests)

Sniffer Network Analyzer data 5-Oct at 09:04:44, file NAME.ENC Pg 1
-------------------------------------- Frame 9 --------------------------------------
SNMP: ----- Simple Network Management Protocol (Version 1) -----
SNMP:
SNMP: Version = 0
SNMP: Community = public
SNMP: Command = Get next request
SNMP: Request ID = 11386
SNMP: Error status = 0 (No error)
SNMP: Error index = 0
SNMP:
SNMP: Object = {1.3.6.1.2.1.4.21.1.1} (ipRouteDest)
SNMP: Value = NULL
SNMP:
SNMP: Object = {1.3.6.1.2.1.4.21.1.7} (ipRouteNextHop)
SNMP: Value = NULL
SNMP:
SNMP: Object = {1.3.6.1.2.1.4.21.1.8} (ipRouteType)
SNMP: Value = NULL
SNMP:
SNMP: Object = {1.3.6.1.2.1.4.21.1.2} (ipRouteIfIndex)
SNMP: Value = NULL
SNMP:

-------------------------------------- Frame 10 --------------------------------------
SNMP: ----- Simple Network Management Protocol (Version 1) -----
SNMP:
SNMP: Version = 0
SNMP: Community = public
SNMP: Command = Get response
SNMP: Request ID = 11386
SNMP: Error status = 0 (No error)
SNMP: Error index = 0

SNMP:
SNMP: Object = {1.3.6.1.2.1.4.21.1.1.0.0.0.0} (ipRouteDest.0.0.0.0)
SNMP: Value = [0.0.0.0]
SNMP:
SNMP: Object = {1.3.6.1.2.1.4.21.1.7.0.0.0.0} (ipRouteNextHop.0.0.0.0)
SNMP: Value = [128.79.3.200]
SNMP:
SNMP: Object = {1.3.6.1.2.1.4.21.1.8.0.0.0.0} (ipRouteType.0.0.0.0)
SNMP: Value = 4 (indirect)
SNMP:
SNMP: Object = {1.3.6.1.2.1.4.21.1.2.0.0.0.0} (ipRouteIfIndex.0.0.0.0)
SNMP: Value = 2
SNMP:

Trace 7.1c. IP routing table retrieval details (End of GetNext)

Sniffer Network Analyzer data 5-Oct at 09:04:44, file NAME.ENC Pg 1
-- Frame 55 --
SNMP: ----- Simple Network Management Protocol (Version 1) -----
SNMP:
SNMP: Version = 0
SNMP: Community = public
SNMP: Command = Get next request
SNMP: Request ID = 11409
SNMP: Error status = 0 (No error)
SNMP: Error index = 0
SNMP:
SNMP: Object = {1.3.6.1.2.1.4.21.1.1.128.79.200.0}
        (ipRouteDest.128.79.200.0)
SNMP: Value = NULL
SNMP:
SNMP: Object = {1.3.6.1.2.1.4.21.1.7.128.79.200.0}
        (ipRouteNextHop.128.79.200.0)

SNMP: Value = NULL
SNMP:
SNMP: Object = {1.3.6.1.2.1.4.21.1.8.128.79.200.0}
        (ipRouteType.128.79.200.0)
SNMP: Value = NULL
SNMP:
SNMP: Object = {1.3.6.1.2.1.4.21.1.2.128.79.200.0}
        (ipRouteIfIndex.128.79.200.0)
SNMP: Value = NULL
SNMP:

-- Frame 56 --
SNMP: ----- Simple Network Management Protocol (Version 1) -----
SNMP:
SNMP: Version = 0
SNMP: Community = public
SNMP: Command = Get response
SNMP: Request ID = 11409
SNMP: Error status = 0 (No error)
SNMP: Error index = 0
SNMP:
SNMP: Object = {1.3.6.1.2.1.4.21.1.2.0.0.0.0} (ipRouteIfIndex.0.0.0.0)
SNMP: Value = 2
SNMP:
SNMP: Object = {1.3.6.1.2.1.4.21.1.8.0.0.0.0} (ipRouteType.0.0.0.0)
SNMP: Value = 4 (indirect)
SNMP:
SNMP: Object = {1.3.6.1.2.1.4.21.1.9.0.0.0.0} (ipRouteProto.0.0.0.0)
SNMP: Value = 2 (local)
SNMP:
SNMP: Object = {1.3.6.1.2.1.4.21.1.3.0.0.0.0} (ipRouteMetric1.0.0.0.0)
SNMP: Value = 1
SNMP:

7.2 Verifying Access Control with the Community Name and IP Address

Many network devices, such as routers, allow the network administrator to configure multiple SNMP community names for remote access. In addition, the network device can have a filter that specifies the IP address of the remote manager. Thus, the combination of the community name and the IP address acts as a two–level method of remote access security.

In this example, a router was configured with two SNMP communities (see Figure 7-2). The first uses community name = abcsnmp and allows access with IP address [XXX.YYY.ZZZ.145]. The second uses community name = xyzs-nmp and allows access with IP address [XXX.YYY.ZZZ.146]. Let's see how the router reacts to an invalid request.

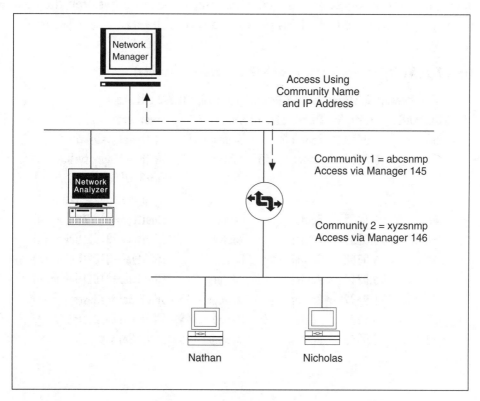

Figure 7-2 Agent access from multiple communities

In Frame 64 of Trace 7.2a, Manager 145 issues a GetRequest for the value of the sysDescr object. As you can see in Frame 64 of Trace 7.2b, that GetRequest includes the community name = abcsnmp. Since a match exists between the community name and the IP address, the router issues a GetResponse (Frame 65) containing the system description

Value = /usr3/wf/wf.rel/v5.75/wf.pj/proto.ss/ace_test.p/

In the second scenario, the manager attempts to access the router using the same IP address [XXX.YYY.ZZZ.145], but with a different community name (xyzsnmp). The GetRequest is transmitted in Frame 70 and then retransmitted in Frames 71 and 72. The router never responds. Recall that the IP address [XXX.YYY.ZZZ.145] and the community name (xyzsnmp) are valid on the agent, but not in this combination. Thus, the association between the community name and the IP address provides a second level of access security.

Trace 7.2a Verifying access control with IP addresses (summary)

Sniffer Network Analyzer data 16-Nov at 17:04:10, file 7-2.ENC, Pg 1

SUMMARY	Delta T	Destination	Source	Summary
64	0.0013	Router	Manager 145	SNMP Get sysDescr
65	0.0479	Manager 145	Router	SNMP GetReply sysDescr = /usr3/wf/wf.rel/v5.75/wf.pj/proto.ss/ace_test.p/
66	4.1358	Router	Router	Ethertype=8102(Unknown)
67	5.0239	Router	Router	Ethertype=8102(Unknown)
68	5.0388	Router	Router	Ethertype=8102(Unknown)
69	5.0314	Router	Router	Ethertype=8102(Unknown)
70	1.9592	Router	Manager 145	SNMP Get sysDescr
71	0.9971	Router	Manager 145	SNMP Get sysDescr
72	2.0045	Router	Manager 145	SNMP Get sysDescr

Trace 7.2b Verifying access control with IP addresses (details)

Sniffer Network Analyzer data 16-Nov at 17:04:10, file 7-2.ENC, Pg 1

-- Frame 64 --

SNMP: ----- Simple Network Management Protocol (Version 1) -----

SNMP:

SNMP: Version = 0

SNMP: Community = abcsnmp

SNMP: Command = Get request

SNMP: Request ID = 1888324335

SNMP: Error status = 0 (No error)

SNMP: Error index = 0

SNMP:

SNMP: Object = {1.3.6.1.2.1.1.1.0} (sysDescr.0)

SNMP: Value = NULL

SNMP:

-- Frame 65 --

SNMP: ----- Simple Network Management Protocol (Version 1) -----

SNMP:

SNMP: Version = 0

SNMP: Community = abcsnmp

SNMP: Command = Get response

SNMP: Request ID = 1888324335

SNMP: Error status = 0 (No error)

SNMP: Error index = 0

SNMP:

SNMP: Object = {1.3.6.1.2.1.1.1.0} (sysDescr.0)

SNMP: Value = /usr3/wf/wf.rel/v5.75/wf.pj/proto.ss/ace_test.p/

SNMP:

.

.

.

```
------------------------------------ Frame 70 ------------------------------------
SNMP: ----- Simple Network Management Protocol (Version 1) -----
SNMP:
SNMP: Version = 0
SNMP: Community = xyzsnmp
SNMP: Command = Get request
SNMP: Request ID = 586726387
SNMP: Error status = 0 (No error)
SNMP: Error index = 0
SNMP:
SNMP: Object = {1.3.6.1.2.1.1.1.0} (sysDescr.0)
SNMP: Value = NULL
SNMP:


------------------------------------ Frame 71 ------------------------------------
SNMP: ----- Simple Network Management Protocol (Version 1) -----
SNMP:
SNMP: Version = 0
SNMP: Community = xyzsnmp
SNMP: Command = Get request
SNMP: Request ID = 586726387
SNMP: Error status = 0 (No error)
SNMP: Error index = 0
SNMP:
SNMP: Object = {1.3.6.1.2.1.1.1.0} (sysDescr.0)
SNMP: Value = NULL
SNMP:


------------------------------------ Frame 72------------------------------------
SNMP: ----- Simple Network Management Protocol (Version 1) -----
SNMP:
SNMP: Version = 0
SNMP: Community = xyzsnmp
SNMP: Command = Get request
```

```
SNMP: Request ID = 586726387
SNMP: Error status = 0 (No error)
SNMP: Error index = 0
SNMP:
SNMP: Object = {1.3.6.1.2.1.1.1.0} (sysDescr.0)
SNMP: Value = NULL
SNMP:
```

7.3 Verifying that a Set Command has been Properly Received and Implemented

The connectionless nature of SNMP's UDP transport leaves some doubt as to whether the agent has actually acted on a Set command from the manager. Testing that the Set actually occurred requires a three-step process. In the first step, the network manager reads the current value of an object. In the second step, the network manager issues the Set command. In the third step, it rereads that value to confirm that it was changed. This example shows these three steps in detail.

The internetwork in this example contains several Ethernet segments and is managed by a DECmcc console (see Figure 7-3). The goal is to assign a value to an object on the SynOptics (now Bay Networks) hub, which contains an SNMP agent. The hub also contains a SynOptics private enterprise MIB with OID prefix {1.3.6.1.4.1.45}. To assign the value, the agent must be configured to allow access from a remote manager, as illustrated in Section 7.2. For the SynOptics hubs, the SNMP configuration parameters establish several communities, each with different access rights. The read-only community is typically named "public." The read-write community is typically named "administrator." A third community usually called "trap1" defines the devices that will receive traps.

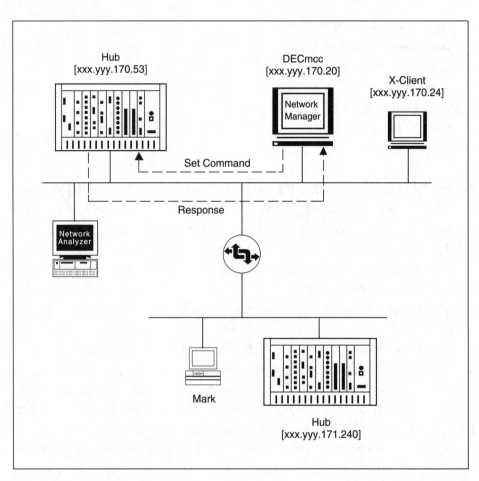

Figure 7-3 Verifying a Set command

As mentioned previously, the first step in testing the Set command, which occurs in Frames 5 to 8 (Trace 7.3a), is for the network manager to read the values of the SynOptics MIB. The SynOptics MIB is an extensive private MIB that contains objects such as the subnet mask [255.255.255.0], default gateway [XXX.YYY.170.250], boot file server address [XXX.YYY.170.20], and many others (see Frame 6 in Trace 7.3b). You should obtain documentation on private enterprise MIBs from the vendor when you initialize the network management system so that these details will be readily available. Note that the value we want to change is the Trap Receiver Community, OID {SynOptics 1.3.2.4.20.1.3.XXX.YYY.170.20}. From the detail of Frame 6, you can see that the fourteenth Objects Value = "public."

The second step begins in Frame 9 when the manager attempts to Set the Trap community to the value "test." Frame 10 returns an authentication failure trap, which indicates that the receiver of the trap (the Hub agent) did not permit the manager to set the object's value. This failure occurred because the Set command (Frame 9) specified a Community name = public, and that community was specified for a read-only (not read-write) operation.

When the network administrator realized his mistake, he issued another Set command in Frame 21, with the SNMP community name = administrator, and a value for the Trap Receiver Community = trap1. This time, the SNMP Set command was authenticated and the Response (Frame 22) indicated "no error." The third step occurs in Frames 23 and 24, where a GetNext for the SynOptics private MIB objects (Frame 24) verifies that the value has been written as specified.

Trace 7.3a Verifying a Set command (summary)

Sniffer Network Analyzer data 23-Sep at 08:40:52 file SNMP71_7.ENC Pg 1

SUMMARY	Delta T	Destination	Source	Summary
5	27.1787	[XXX.YYY.170...	Manager	SNMP GetNext
				SynOptics.1.3.2.4.1.0 ..
				SynOptics.1.3.2.4.21.0
				(16 items)
6	0.2388	Manager	Hub Agent	SNMP GetReply
				SynOptics.1.3.2.4.2.0 ..
				SynOptics.2.1.1.1.1.1
				(16 items)

7	0.0064	Hub Agent	Manager	SNMP GetNext
				SynOptics.1.3.2.4.3.0 ..
				SynOptics.1.3.2.4.9.0
				(7 items)
				SynOptics.1.3.2.4.1 ..
				SynOptics.1.3.2.4.21
				(16 items)
24	0.2185	Manager	Hub Agent	SNMP GetReply
				SynOptics.1.3.2.4.1.0 ..
				SynOptics.1.3.2.4.21.0
				(16 items)

Trace 7.3b Verifying a Set command (details)

Sniffer Network Analyzer data 23-Sep at 08:40:52, file SNMP71_7.ENC, Pg 1
-- Frame 6 --
SNMP: ----- Simple Network Management Protocol (Version 1) -----
SNMP:
SNMP: Version = 0
SNMP: Community = public
SNMP: Command = Get response
SNMP: Request ID = 717281288
SNMP: Error status = 0 (No error)
SNMP: Error index = 0
SNMP:
SNMP: Object = {1.3.6.1.4.1.45.1.3.2.4.2.0} (SynOptics.1.3.2.4.2.0)
SNMP: Value = 0
SNMP:
SNMP: Object = {1.3.6.1.4.1.45.1.3.2.4.11.0} (SynOptics.1.3.2.4.11.0)
SNMP: Value = [255.255.255.0]
SNMP:
SNMP: Object = {1.3.6.1.4.1.45.1.3.2.4.12.0} (SynOptics.1.3.2.4.12.0)
SNMP: Value = [XXX.YYY.170.250]
SNMP:

```
SNMP: Object = {1.3.6.1.4.1.45.1.3.2.4.13.0} (SynOptics.1.3.2.4.13.0)
SNMP: Value = [XXX.YYY.170.20], Manager
SNMP:
SNMP: Object = {1.3.6.1.4.1.45.1.3.2.4.14.0} (SynOptics.1.3.2.4.14.0)
SNMP: Value = /tftpboot/syn2.cfg
SNMP:
SNMP: Object = {1.3.6.1.4.1.45.1.3.2.4.15.0} (SynOptics.1.3.2.4.15.0)
SNMP: Value = 2
SNMP:
SNMP: Object = {1.3.6.1.4.1.45.1.3.2.4.16.0} (SynOptics.1.3.2.4.16.0)
SNMP: Value = 1
SNMP:
SNMP: Object = {1.3.6.1.4.1.45.1.3.2.4.17.0} (SynOptics.1.3.2.4.17.0)
SNMP: Value = 9600 (gauge)
SNMP:
SNMP: Object = {1.3.6.1.4.1.45.1.3.2.4.18.0} (SynOptics.1.3.2.4.18.0)
SNMP: Value =
SNMP:
SNMP: Object = {1.3.6.1.4.1.45.1.3.2.4.19.0} (SynOptics.1.3.2.4.19.0)
SNMP: Value =
SNMP:
SNMP: Object = {1.3.6.1.4.1.45.1.3.2.4.20.1.1.XXX.YYY.170.20}
              (SynOptics.1.3.2.4.20.1.1.XXX.YYY ...
SNMP: Value = 1
SNMP:
SNMP: Object = {1.3.6.1.4.1.45.1.3.2.4.3.0} (SynOptics.1.3.2.4.3.0)
SNMP: Value = 1
SNMP:
SNMP: Object = {1.3.6.1.4.1.45.1.3.2.4.20.1.2.XXX.YYY.170.20}
              (SynOptics.1.3.2.4.20.1.2.XXX.YYY ...
SNMP: Value = [XXX.YYY.170.20], Manager
SNMP:
SNMP: Object = {1.3.6.1.4.1.45.1.3.2.4.20.1.3.XXX.YYY.170.20}
              (SynOptics.1.3.2.4.20.1.3.XXX.YYY ...
```

SNMP: Value = public
SNMP:
SNMP: Object = {1.3.6.1.4.1.45.1.3.2.4.21.0} (SynOptics.1.3.2.4.21.0)
SNMP: Value = 2
SNMP:
SNMP: Object = {1.3.6.1.4.1.45.2.1.1.1.1.1} (SynOptics.2.1.1.1.1.1)
SNMP: Value = 1
SNMP:

.
.
.

-------------------------------------- Frame 9 --------------------------------------
SNMP: ----- Simple Network Management Protocol (Version 1) -----
SNMP:
SNMP: Version = 0
SNMP: Community = public
SNMP: Command = Set request
SNMP: Request ID = 717288552
SNMP: Error status = 0 (No error)
SNMP: Error index = 0
SNMP:
SNMP: Object = {1.3.6.1.4.1.45.1.3.2.4.20.1.3.XXX.YYY.170.20}
                    (SynOptics.1.3.2.4.20.1.3.XXX.YYY ...
SNMP: Value = test
SNMP:

-------------------------------------- Frame 10 --------------------------------------
SNMP: ----- Simple Network Management Protocol (Version 1) -----
SNMP:
SNMP: Version = 0
SNMP: Community = public
SNMP: Command = Trap
SNMP: Enterprise = {1.3.6.1.4.1.45.3.8.1}

SNMP: Network address = [XXX.YYY.170.53]
SNMP: Generic trap = 4 (Authentication failure)
SNMP: Specific trap = 0
SNMP: Time ticks = 57631330
SNMP:

   .

   .

   .

--------------------------------------- Frame 21 ---------------------------------------
SNMP: ----- Simple Network Management Protocol (Version 1) -----
SNMP:
SNMP: Version = 0
SNMP: Community = administrator
SNMP: Command = Set request
SNMP: Request ID = 717288651
SNMP: Error status = 0 (No error)
SNMP: Error index = 0
SNMP:
SNMP: Object = {1.3.6.1.4.1.45.1.3.2.4.20.1.3.XXX.YYY.170.20}
                (SynOptics.1.3.2.4.20.1.3.XXX.YYY ...
SNMP: Value = trap1
SNMP:

--------------------------------------- Frame 22 ---------------------------------------
SNMP: ----- Simple Network Management Protocol (Version 1) -----
SNMP:
SNMP: Version = 0
SNMP: Community = administrator
SNMP: Command = Get response
SNMP: Request ID = 717288651
SNMP: Error status = 0 (No error)
SNMP: Error index = 0
SNMP:

SNMP: Object = {1.3.6.1.4.1.45.1.3.2.4.20.1.3.XXX.YYY.170.20}
                (SynOptics.1.3.2.4.20.1.3.XXX.YYY ...
SNMP: Value = trap1
SNMP:

.

.

.

------------------------------------- Frame 24-------------------------------------
SNMP: ----- Simple Network Management Protocol (Version 1) -----
SNMP:
SNMP: Version = 0
SNMP: Community = public
SNMP: Command = Get response
SNMP: Request ID = 717281434
SNMP: Error status = 0 (No error)
SNMP: Error index = 0
SNMP:
SNMP: Object = {1.3.6.1.4.1.45.1.3.2.4.1.0} (SynOptics.1.3.2.4.1.0)
SNMP: Value = 2
SNMP:
SNMP: Object = {1.3.6.1.4.1.45.1.3.2.4.10.0} (SynOptics.1.3.2.4.10.0)
SNMP: Value = [XXX.YYY.170.53]
SNMP:
SNMP: Object = {1.3.6.1.4.1.45.1.3.2.4.11.0} (SynOptics.1.3.2.4.11.0)
SNMP: Value = [255.255.255.0]
SNMP:
SNMP: Object = {1.3.6.1.4.1.45.1.3.2.4.12.0} (SynOptics.1.3.2.4.12.0)
SNMP: Value = [XXX.YYY.170.250]
SNMP:
SNMP: Object = {1.3.6.1.4.1.45.1.3.2.4.13.0} (SynOptics.1.3.2.4.13.0)
SNMP: Value = [XXX.YYY.170.20], Manager
SNMP:
SNMP: Object = {1.3.6.1.4.1.45.1.3.2.4.14.0} (SynOptics.1.3.2.4.14.0)
SNMP: Value = /tftpboot/syn2.cfg

```
SNMP:
SNMP: Object = {1.3.6.1.4.1.45.1.3.2.4.15.0} (SynOptics.1.3.2.4.15.0)
SNMP: Value = 2
SNMP:
SNMP: Object = {1.3.6.1.4.1.45.1.3.2.4.16.0} (SynOptics.1.3.2.4.16.0)
SNMP: Value = 1
SNMP:
SNMP: Object = {1.3.6.1.4.1.45.1.3.2.4.17.0} (SynOptics.1.3.2.4.17.0)
SNMP: Value = 9600 (gauge)
SNMP:
SNMP: Object = {1.3.6.1.4.1.45.1.3.2.4.18.0} (SynOptics.1.3.2.4.18.0)
SNMP: Value =
SNMP:
SNMP: Object = {1.3.6.1.4.1.45.1.3.2.4.19.0} (SynOptics.1.3.2.4.19.0)
SNMP: Value =
SNMP:
SNMP: Object = {1.3.6.1.4.1.45.1.3.2.4.2.0} (SynOptics.1.3.2.4.2.0)
SNMP: Value = 0
SNMP:
SNMP: Object = {1.3.6.1.4.1.45.1.3.2.4.20.1.1.XXX.YYY.170.20}
                SynOptics.1.3.2.4.20.1.1.XXX.YYY ...
SNMP: Value = 1
SNMP:
SNMP: Object = {1.3.6.1.4.1.45.1.3.2.4.20.1.2.XXX.YYY.170.20}
                (SynOptics.1.3.2.4.20.1.2.XXX.YYY ...
SNMP: Value = [XXX.YYY.170.20], Manager
SNMP:
SNMP: Object = {1.3.6.1.4.1.45.1.3.2.4.20.1.3.XXX.YYY.170.20}
                (SynOptics.1.3.2.4.20.1.3.XXX.YYY ...
SNMP: Value = trap1
SNMP:
SNMP: Object = {1.3.6.1.4.1.45.1.3.2.4.21.0} (SynOptics.1.3.2.4.21.0)
SNMP: Value = 2
SNMP:
```

7.4 Verifying that the Agent Transmitted, and the Manager Received, a Trap PDU

The example in Section 7.3 showed how to verify that a Set command accomplished what it was meant to do despite UDP's connectionless transport. This case study builds on that example by verifying that another device received the agent-generated Trap message.

In this example (see Figure 7-4), the Trap transmitter is the SynOptics intelligent hub, and the manager receives the trap. An X-Windows client workstation acts as the manager's display console. A configuration table within the agent's SNMP parameters defines the IP address of the receiver. When a trap is generated, it is automatically displayed in one of the workstation's windows.

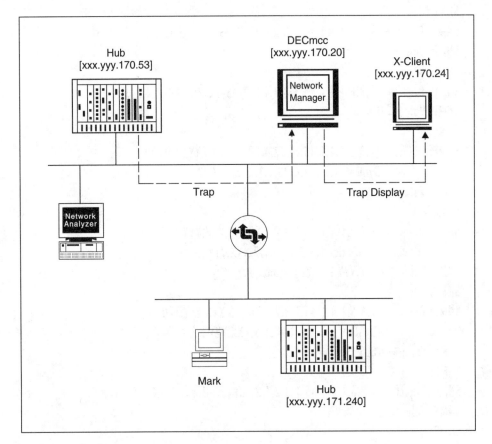

Figure 7-4. Verifying a trap

As noted previously, SNMP messages are transmitted using connectionless transport via UDP, which provides minimal error control. However, some applications, such as the X-Windows system, demand more rigorous error control and require guaranteed delivery of every octet of information, in sequence, at the proper time. The TCP Transport layer protocol addresses these requirements. Frames 1 and 2 of Trace 7.4a show the X Client and the manager exchanging information using TCP. Within the TCP header (and shown in the trace) are the destination and source port numbers (D and S, respectively), an acknowledgment number (ACK), a sequence number (SEQ), a length (LEN), and a window advertisement (WIN).

In Frame 3, the manager sends a Set command to the hub agent; the agent responds with a trap (Authentication failure) in Frame 6. The manager then sends the trap information to the X Client for display within the alarm window (Frame 8). Upon receiving the trap, the X Client sends a TCP acknowledgment in Frame 9 and displays the trap.

Trace 7.4a. Verifying trap reception (summary)

Sniffer Network Analyzer data 23-Sep at 08:50:38, file SNMP75.ENC, Pg 1

SUMMARY	Delta T	Destination	Source	Summary
1		Manager	X Client	TCP D=4255 S=6000
				ACK=584967877
				SEQ=1899543417
				LEN=32 WIN=2920
2	0.0903	X Client	Manager	TCP D=6000 S=4255
				ACK=1899543449
				WIN=16384
3	0.4468	Hub Agent	Manager	SNMP Set
				SynOptics.1.3.2.4.20.1.
				3.XXX.YYY.170.20 = trap1
6	0.0276	Manager	Hub Agent	SNMP Trap - v1
				Authentication failure

| 8 | 3.5293 | X Client | Manager | XWIN C (3) Poly Text8's at 27,20 "[23-Sep-1992 08:43:23] Alarm Type[nms_trapd] from Object[snmpmg.sim.XX.COM]"; at 27,38 "TRAP [authent ... |
| 9 | 0.0714 | Manager | X Client | TCP D=4255 S=6000 ACK=584968457 WIN=2920 |

Trace 7.4b. Verifying trap reception (details)

Sniffer Network Analyzer data 23-Sep at 08:50:38, file SNMP75.ENC, Pg 1

```
---------------------------------------- Frame 1 ----------------------------------------
TCP: ----- TCP header -----
TCP:
TCP: Source port = 6000 (X Windows)
TCP: Destination port = 4255
TCP: Sequence number = 1899543417
TCP: Acknowledgment number = 584967877
TCP: Data offset = 20 bytes
TCP: Flags = 18
TCP: ..0. .... = (No urgent pointer)
TCP: ...1 .... = Acknowledgment
TCP: .... 1... = Push
TCP: .... .0.. = (No reset)
TCP: .... ..0. = (No SYN)
TCP: .... ...0 = (No FIN)
TCP: Window = 2920
TCP: Checksum = 8A63 (correct)
TCP: No TCP options
TCP: [32 byte(s) of data]
TCP:
```

-------------------------------------- Frame 2 --------------------------------------
TCP: ----- TCP header -----
TCP:
TCP: Source port = 4255
TCP: Destination port = 6000 (X Windows)
TCP: Sequence number = 584967877
TCP: Acknowledgment number = 1899543449
TCP: Data offset = 20 bytes
TCP: Flags = 10
TCP: ..0. .... = (No urgent pointer)
TCP: ...1 .... = Acknowledgment
TCP: .... 0... = (No push)
TCP: .... .0.. = (No reset)
TCP: .... ..0. = (No SYN)
TCP: ....0 = (No FIN)
TCP: Window = 16384
TCP: Checksum = B7AC (correct)
TCP: No TCP options
TCP:

-------------------------------------- Frame 3 --------------------------------------
SNMP: ----- Simple Network Management Protocol (Version 1) -----
SNMP:
SNMP: Version = 0
SNMP: Community = public
SNMP: Command = Set request
SNMP: Request ID = 717289096
SNMP: Error status = 0 (No error)
SNMP: Error index = 0
SNMP:
SNMP: Object = {1.3.6.1.4.1.45.1.3.2.4.20.1.3.XXX.YYY.170.20}
                (SynOptics.1.3.2.4.20.1.3.XXX.YYY ...
SNMP: Value = trap1
SNMP:

----------------------------------- Frame 6 -----------------------------------

SNMP: ----- Simple Network Management Protocol (Version 1) -----

SNMP:

SNMP: Version = 0

SNMP: Community = trap1

SNMP: Command = Trap

SNMP: Enterprise = {1.3.6.1.4.1.45.3.8.1}

SNMP: Network address = [XXX.YYY.170.53]

SNMP: Generic trap = 4 (Authentication failure)

SNMP: Specific trap = 0

SNMP: Time ticks = 57685810

SNMP:

----------------------------------- Frame 8 -----------------------------------

XWIN: ----- X Windows -----

XWIN:

XWIN: Request opcode = 74 (Poly Text8)

XWIN: Drawable = 01D00034, Graphics context = 01D0001E

XWIN: X = 27, Y = 20

XWIN: Delta = 0

XWIN: String = "[23-Sep-1992 08:43:23] Alarm Type[nms_trapd]
                from Object[snmpmg.sim.XX.COM]"

XWIN:

XWIN: Request opcode = 74 (Poly Text8)

XWIN: Drawable = 01D00034, Graphics context = 01D0001E

XWIN: X = 27, Y = 38

XWIN: Delta = 0

XWIN: String = "TRAP [authentication failure] received, agent =
                XXX.YYY.170.53(syn2.sim.XX.COM) ...

XWIN:

XWIN: Request opcode = 74 (Poly Text8)

XWIN: Drawable = 01D00034, Graphics context = 01D0001E

XWIN: X = 27, Y = 56

XWIN: Delta = 0

XWIN: String = " specific-trap = 0."
XWIN:

------------------------------------ Frame 9 ------------------------------------
TCP: ----- TCP header -----
TCP:
TCP: Source port = 6000 (X Windows)
TCP: Destination port = 4255
TCP: Sequence number = 1899543609
TCP: Acknowledgment number = 584968457
TCP: Data offset = 20 bytes
TCP: Flags = 10
TCP: ..0. .... = (No urgent pointer)
TCP: ...1 .... = Acknowledgment
TCP: .... 0... = (No push)
TCP: .... .0.. = (No reset)
TCP: .... ..0. = (No SYN)
TCP: ....0 = (No FIN)
TCP: Window = 2920
TCP: Checksum = E960 (correct)
TCP: No TCP options
TCP:

7.5. Communicating Device and Link Status with Traps

One of the most useful aspects of SNMP traps is their ability to communicate significant events to a remote network manager. This example illustrates how vendors embellish traps to provide additional information for their customers. The internetwork for this case study consists of more than 20,000 workstations, over 500 servers, and over 350 bridges and routers. Without SNMP, managing such extensive systems would be extremely difficult. In the example shown in Figure 7-5, a remote Router D and another serial link are having difficulties. This example shows how SNMP alerts the network manager to the problems.

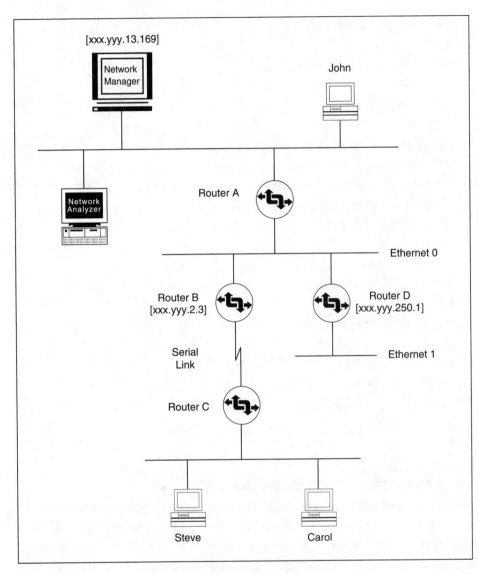

Figure 7-5. Communicating device and link status information

Router D with IP address [XXX.YYY.250.1] has a power failure and then returns to normal operation. In Frame 1 of Trace 7.5a, it signals to the manager by sending a LinkUp trap. The SNMP standard (RFC 1157) requires that the trap include the name and value of the ifIndex instance for the affected interface. The router's manufacturer, Cisco Systems, Inc., includes additional information to further identify the interface (see Trace 7.5b). For example, in Frame 1, the Enterprise = {1.3.6.1.4.1.9.1.1} identifies Cisco. The first three object values transmitted come from the ifTable under the Interfaces subtree {1.3.6.1.2.1.2}. These are the ifIndex (1 or 2); the ifDescription (Ethernet0 or Ethernet1); and the ifType (ethernet-csmacd). The last object value, taken from Cisco's private MIB, further identifies what happened (the link is now up).

In Frame 210, a second problem occurs on the serial link between Router B and Router C. This failure triggers the transmission of LinkDown traps from the router. As before, the Enterprise field identifies a Cisco device as the source of the traps and further identifies the failed router port by its IP address: [XXX.YYY.2.3]. The four object values transmitted to the manager communicate the link description (serial0); the type of link (proprietary point-to-point serial); and the reason for the trap (down).

Thus, if failures occur on other segments or communication links, which could even be across the country from each other, SNMP traps can alert the manager that a problem exists. Further troubleshooting by using software utilities such as ICMP Echo (PING) messages, SNMP queries (such as the IP or ICMP groups), or test equipment (such as network analyzers) can then proceed.

Trace 7.5a. Link up and link down traps (summary)

Sniffer Network Analyzer data 23-Mar at 13:08:58, file A:TRAP.ENC, Pg 1

SUMMARY	Delta T	Destination	Source	Summary
1		Manager	Router D	SNMP Trap -v1 Link up ifIndex .. cisco.2.2.1.1.20.1 (4 items)
2	0.4585	Manager	Router D	SNMP Trap -v1 Link up ifIndex .. cisco.2.2.1.1.20.2 (4 items)

.
.

| 210 | 27.6608 | Manager | Router B | SNMP Trap Link down ifIndex .. cisco.2.2.1.1.20.1 (4 items) |

Trace 7.5b. Link up and link down traps (details)

Sniffer Network Analyzer data 23-Mar at 13:08:58, file A:TRAP.ENC, Pg 1

```
------------------------------------- Frame 1 -------------------------------------
SNMP: ----- Simple Network Management Protocol (Version 1) -----
SNMP:
SNMP: Version = 0
SNMP: Community = public
SNMP: Command = Trap
SNMP: Enterprise = {1.3.6.1.4.1.9.1.1}
SNMP: Network address = [XXX.YYY.12.250]
SNMP: Generic trap = 3 (Link up)
SNMP: Specific trap = 0
SNMP: Time ticks = 797
SNMP:
SNMP: Object = {1.3.6.1.2.1.2.2.1.1.1} (ifIndex.1)
SNMP: Value = 1
SNMP:
SNMP: Object = {1.3.6.1.2.1.2.2.1.2.1} (ifDescr.1)
SNMP: Value = Ethernet0
SNMP:
SNMP: Object = {1.3.6.1.2.1.2.2.1.3.1} (ifType.1)
SNMP: Value = 6 (ethernet-csmacd)
SNMP:
SNMP: Object = {1.3.6.1.4.1.9.2.2.1.1.20.1} (cisco.2.2.1.1.20.1)
SNMP: Value = up
SNMP:
```

```
------------------------------------- Frame 2 -------------------------------------
SNMP: ----- Simple Network Management Protocol (Version 1) -----
SNMP:
SNMP: Version = 0
SNMP: Community = public
SNMP: Command = Trap
SNMP: Enterprise = {1.3.6.1.4.1.9.1.1}
SNMP: Network address = [XXX.YYY.12.250]
SNMP: Generic trap = 3 (Link up)
SNMP: Specific trap = 0
SNMP: Time ticks = 799
SNMP:
SNMP: Object = {1.3.6.1.2.1.2.2.1.1.2} (ifIndex.2)
SNMP: Value = 2
SNMP:
SNMP: Object = {1.3.6.1.2.1.2.2.1.2.2} (ifDescr.2)
SNMP: Value = Ethernet1
SNMP:
SNMP: Object = {1.3.6.1.2.1.2.2.1.3.2} (ifType.2)
SNMP: Value = 6 (ethernet-csmacd)
SNMP:
SNMP: Object = {1.3.6.1.4.1.9.2.2.1.1.20.2} (cisco.2.2.1.1.20.2)
SNMP: Value = up
SNMP:


------------------------------------- Frame 210-------------------------------------
SNMP: ----- Simple Network Management Protocol (Version 1) -----
SNMP:
SNMP: Version = 0
SNMP: Community = public
SNMP: Command = Trap
SNMP: Enterprise = {1.3.6.1.4.1.9.1.1}
SNMP: Network address = [XXX.YYY.2.3]
SNMP: Generic trap = 2 (Link down)
```

```
SNMP: Specific trap = 0
SNMP: Time ticks = 45039280
SNMP:
SNMP: Object = {1.3.6.1.2.1.2.2.1.1.1} (ifIndex.1)
SNMP: Value = 1
SNMP:
SNMP: Object = {1.3.6.1.2.1.2.2.1.2.1} (ifDescr.1)
SNMP: Value = Serial0
SNMP:
SNMP: Object = {1.3.6.1.2.1.2.2.1.3.1} (ifType.1)
SNMP: Value = 22 (propPointToPointSerial)
SNMP:
SNMP: Object = {1.3.6.1.4.1.9.2.2.1.1.20.1} (cisco.2.2.1.1.20.1)
SNMP: Value = down
SNMP:
```

7.6 Proper Interpretation of Private Enterprise Traps

Some vendors define traps that have meaning only within their systems. In this example, Network General Corp.'s Distributed Sniffer System is monitoring traffic on one segment of an internetwork (see Figure 7-6). The Sniffer allows the network administrator to set thresholds for various traffic parameters and to transmit a trap to the Network Management console if any of these thresholds are exceeded. You'll need a copy of the vendor's MIB, such as the one from Network General Corp. shown in Definition 7-1, to properly interpret these enterprise-specific traps. This case study looks at several examples (see Trace 7.6).

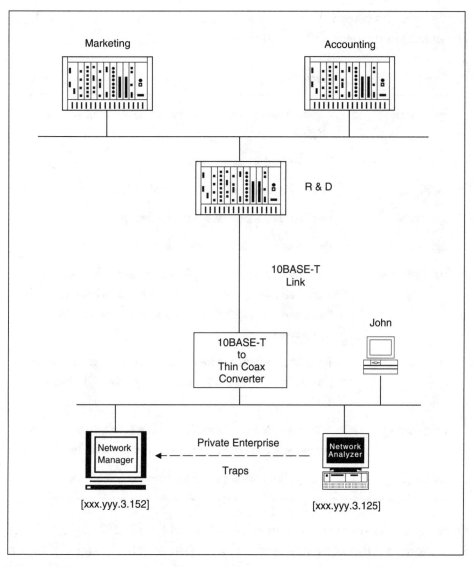

Figure 7-6. Using private enterprise traps

Each trap sent from the Distributed Sniffer System to the management console contains nine objects that are all contained within the ngcTrapTable. These objects are identified as belonging to the Network General private enterprises subtree {1.3.6.1.4.1.110}, then are further defined according to Network General's private MIB. For example, the sequence {1.3.6.1.4.1.110.1.1.1.1.1.1.3}

309

identifies the object ngcTrText, which is the third object within the ngcTrapTable. The objects in the ngcTrapTable are:

Object	Description
ngcTrSequence	A counter of the number of NGC alarm traps generated since the agent was last initialized.
ngcTrId	The application that generated this NGC alarm.
ngcTrText	An ASCII string describing the NGC alarm condition/cause.
ngcTrPriority	The priority level as set on the agent for this Class and Type of trap.
ngcTrClass	The Class number of the described NGC alarm.
ngcTrType	The Type number of the described NGC alarm. For each application, the alarm numbers will range from 1 to n, where n may increase as future versions of the alarm-generating applications (monitor or analyzer) detect additional network problems.
ngcTrTime	The time that the condition or event that caused the alarm occurred. This value is given in seconds since 00:00:00 Greenwich mean time (GMT) January 1, 1970.
ngcTrSuspect	An ASCII string describing the host that caused the NGC alarm. (Note: The current version of Expert Analyzer generates a null string for this field.)
ngcTrDiagId	An integer identifying the diagnosis that triggered this NGC alarm.

Trace 7.6 shows seven traps from Frames 106, 144, 237, 252, 267, 318, and 377. (Note that this trace has been filtered to show only the traps; thus, the frame numbers are not sequential.) The cause of each trap is defined by the third object, ngcTrText, which provides an ASCII text string describing the event that the Distributed Sniffer System (DSS) generated. This description starts with "<SegEN01>," which is the name of the segment, ring, or link on which the trace was taken. This trace was taken on Ethernet segment number 01. Following the segment name is a textual description of the diagnosis made by the DSS real-time expert system. This description may be followed

by one or more addresses and possibly by a current threshold setting that has been exceeded—the description contains as much information for the network manager as can be provided in a single line of text.

The agent sends each trap as an SNMP trap PDU. The PDU header contains the fields shown at the beginning of the trace (Version, Community, Command, Enterprise, and so on). The field labeled "Enterprise" contains the OID of the product transmitting the trap. The number {1.3.6.1.4.1} represents {iso.org.dod.internet.private.enterprises}. The next number, 110, which was assigned by a central registration authority, represents Network General Corporation. Companies pay for a subtree under "enterprises" and are granted the right to administer the numbers under this subtree. Network General assigns the rest of the object identifier beyond the 110 in its MIB. The network address of the device sending the trap (the DSS Server) follows the Enterprise number.

The SNMP header also indicates the Generic Trap type. All enterprise-specific traps, such as the seven in this trace, include a Specific Trap field. These are also defined in the MIB extensions. For example, the Specific Trap type in Frame 106 has a value of 1029, which is defined in the MIB as the ngcRouterStorm object, with a textual description.

Each trap then includes the nine values of the objects from the ngcTrapTable. Note that each OID begins with the Network General private enterprises code, plus a suffix that identifies the specific object within the ngcTrapTable. For example, the OID {1.3.6.1.4.1.110.1.1.1.1.1.4.1} identifies the first instance of the ngcTrPriority object. Also note that, according to the definition of the ngcTrapEntry object within the NGC MIB: "there is always one entry in the (ngcTrapTable), indexed by the integer value 1," meaning that this is a conceptual table that always has a single column (or just one instance).

Frame 106 (with Specific Trap = 1029) indicates a router storm, where the router identified by IP address [XXX.YYY.3.94] is broadcasting its routing tables too frequently, which wastes bandwidth unnecessarily. The Specific Trap ngcRouterStorm describes the problem: "the specified router has reconfirmed one or more of its routes more frequently than seems reasonable."

Frame 144 (with Specific Trap = 1004) shows excessive repeated requests from a station called "moon" that exceed a threshold set at 30%. Note that the Sniffer correlates that station's IP address with the station name "moon," and provides the network manager with the station name instead of the IP address for convenience. The Specific Trap ngcRequestLoops describes the problem: "a station is repeating the same application request after receiving an appropriate reply."

Frame 237 (with Specific Trap = 1027) shows route flapping, where one or more routes from the indicated router [XXX.YYY.3.94] are toggling rapidly between valid and invalid. The Specific Trap ngcRouteFlapping describes the problem: "the specified router has changed one or more routes from valid to invalid and back too frequently." A similar problem, but coming from other routers, is identified in Frames 267 and 318.

Frame 252 (with Specific Trap = 1028) shows that a router with IP address [XXX.YYY.3.94] has a routing table that is not stabilizing properly. In other words, several routes are rapidly exchanging position as they vie for the "best route" to a particular destination. The Specific Trap ngcRouteSuperceded describes the problem: "the specified router has changed the metrics on one or more routes too frequently. The analyzer makes this diagnosis if any route changes between being the best route to its destination and not being the best route more than three times in one minute."

Lastly, Frame 377 (with Specific Trap = 1010) indicates multiple routers (exceeding the threshold of three in this case) to the station [XXX.YYY.3.94]. The Specific Trap ngcMultipleRouters describes the problem: "the number of routers being used to gain access to a local or remote station has exceeded a threshold."

Enterprise-specific traps can be quite useful for network managers, but you'll need copies of the MIB and other vendor documentation to properly interpret these traps.

Trace 7.6. Interpreting enterprise-specific traps

Sniffer Network Analyzer data from 13-Feb at 17:42:54, File TRAPS.ENC, Pg 1

```
-------------------------------------- Frame 106 --------------------------------------
SNMP: ----- Simple Network Management Protocol (Version 1) -----
SNMP:
SNMP: Version = 0
SNMP: Community = PUBLIC
SNMP: Command = Trap
SNMP: Enterprise = {1.3.6.1.4.1.110}
SNMP: Network address = [XXX.YYY.3.125], DSS Server
SNMP: Generic trap = 6 (Enterprise specific)
SNMP: Specific trap = 1029
SNMP: Time ticks = 502900
SNMP:
SNMP: Object = {1.3.6.1.4.1.110.1.1.1.1.1.1.1.1.1} (Network General
Corp.1.1.1.1.1.1.1.1)
SNMP: Value  = 6 (counter)
SNMP:
SNMP: Object = {1.3.6.1.4.1.110.1.1.1.1.1.1.1.2.1} (Network General
Corp.1.1.1.1.1.1.2.1)
SNMP: Value  = 3
SNMP:
SNMP: Object = {1.3.6.1.4.1.110.1.1.1.1.1.1.1.3.1} (Network General
Corp.1.1.1.1.1.1.3.1)
SNMP: Value  = <SegEN01> Router storm from [XXX.YYY.3.94]
SNMP:
SNMP: Object = {1.3.6.1.4.1.110.1.1.1.1.1.1.1.4.1} (Network General
Corp.1.1.1.1.1.1.4.1)
SNMP: Value  = 1
```

SNMP:
SNMP: Object = {1.3.6.1.4.1.110.1.1.1.1.1.1.5.1} (Network General
Corp.1.1.1.1.1.1.5.1)
SNMP: Value = 3
SNMP:
SNMP: Object = {1.3.6.1.4.1.110.1.1.1.1.1.1.6.1} (Network General
Corp.1.1.1.1.1.1.6.1)
SNMP: Value = 29
SNMP:
SNMP: Object = {1.3.6.1.4.1.110.1.1.1.1.1.1.7.1} (Network General
Corp.1.1.1.1.1.1.7.1)
SNMP: Value = 855884389 (counter)
SNMP:
SNMP: Object = {1.3.6.1.4.1.110.1.1.1.1.1.1.8.1} (Network General
Corp.1.1.1.1.1.1.8.1)
SNMP: Value = NULL
SNMP:
SNMP: Object = {1.3.6.1.4.1.110.1.1.1.1.1.1.9.1} (Network General
Corp.1.1.1.1.1.1.9.1)
SNMP: Value = -2115947897
SNMP:

-------------------------------------- Frame 144 --------------------------------------
SNMP: ----- Simple Network Management Protocol (Version 1) -----
SNMP:
SNMP: Version = 0
SNMP: Community = PUBLIC
SNMP: Command = Trap
SNMP: Enterprise = {1.3.6.1.4.1.110}
SNMP: Network address = [XXX.YYY.3.125], DSS Server
SNMP: Generic trap = 6 (Enterprise specific)
SNMP: Specific trap = 1004
SNMP: Time ticks = 503700
SNMP:

SNMP: Object = {1.3.6.1.4.1.110.1.1.1.1.1.1.1.1} (Network General
Corp.1.1.1.1.1.1.1.1.1)
SNMP: Value = 7 (counter)
SNMP:
SNMP: Object = {1.3.6.1.4.1.110.1.1.1.1.1.1.2.1} (Network General
Corp.1.1.1.1.1.1.2.1)
SNMP: Value = 3
SNMP:
SNMP: Object = {1.3.6.1.4.1.110.1.1.1.1.1.1.3.1} (Network General
Corp.1.1.1.1.1.1.3.1)
SNMP: Value = <SegEN01> Excessive repeated requests: moon <threshold: 30 %>
SNMP:
SNMP: Object = {1.3.6.1.4.1.110.1.1.1.1.1.1.4.1} (Network General
Corp.1.1.1.1.1.1.4.1)
SNMP: Value = 1
SNMP:
SNMP: Object = {1.3.6.1.4.1.110.1.1.1.1.1.1.5.1} (Network General
Corp.1.1.1.1.1.1.5.1)
SNMP: Value = 3
SNMP:
SNMP: Object = {1.3.6.1.4.1.110.1.1.1.1.1.1.6.1} (Network General
Corp.1.1.1.1.1.1.6.1)
SNMP: Value = 4
SNMP:
SNMP: Object = {1.3.6.1.4.1.110.1.1.1.1.1.1.7.1} (Network General
Corp.1.1.1.1.1.1.7.1)
SNMP: Value = 855884397 (counter)
SNMP:
SNMP: Object = {1.3.6.1.4.1.110.1.1.1.1.1.1.8.1} (Network General
Corp.1.1.1.1.1.1.8.1)
SNMP: Value = NULL
SNMP:
SNMP: Object = {1.3.6.1.4.1.110.1.1.1.1.1.1.9.1} (Network General
Corp.1.1.1.1.1.1.9.1)

SNMP: Value = -2115946872
SNMP:

------------------------------------- Frame 237 -------------------------------------
SNMP: ----- Simple Network Management Protocol (Version 1) -----
SNMP:
SNMP: Version = 0
SNMP: Community = PUBLIC
SNMP: Command = Trap
SNMP: Enterprise = {1.3.6.1.4.1.110}
SNMP: Network address = [XXX.YYY.3.125], DSS Server
SNMP: Generic trap = 6 (Enterprise specific)
SNMP: Specific trap = 1027
SNMP: Time ticks = 505900
SNMP:
SNMP: Object = {1.3.6.1.4.1.110.1.1.1.1.1.1.1.1} (Network General
Corp.1.1.1.1.1.1.1.1)
SNMP: Value = 8 (counter)
SNMP:
SNMP: Object = {1.3.6.1.4.1.110.1.1.1.1.1.1.2.1} (Network General
Corp.1.1.1.1.1.1.2.1)
SNMP: Value = 3
SNMP:
SNMP: Object = {1.3.6.1.4.1.110.1.1.1.1.1.1.3.1} (Network General
Corp.1.1.1.1.1.1.3.1)
SNMP: Value = <SegEN01> Route flapping from [XXX.YYY.3.94]
SNMP:
SNMP: Object = {1.3.6.1.4.1.110.1.1.1.1.1.1.4.1} (Network General
Corp.1.1.1.1.1.1.4.1)
SNMP: Value = 2
SNMP:
SNMP: Object = {1.3.6.1.4.1.110.1.1.1.1.1.1.5.1} (Network General
Corp.1.1.1.1.1.1.5.1)
SNMP: Value = 3

SNMP:
SNMP: Object = {1.3.6.1.4.1.110.1.1.1.1.1.1.6.1} (Network General
Corp.1.1.1.1.1.1.6.1)
SNMP: Value = 27
SNMP:
SNMP: Object = {1.3.6.1.4.1.110.1.1.1.1.1.1.7.1} (Network General
Corp.1.1.1.1.1.1.7.1)
SNMP: Value = 855884419 (counter)
SNMP:
SNMP: Object = {1.3.6.1.4.1.110.1.1.1.1.1.1.8.1} (Network General
Corp.1.1.1.1.1.1.8.1)
SNMP: Value = NULL
SNMP:
SNMP: Object = {1.3.6.1.4.1.110.1.1.1.1.1.1.9.1} (Network General
Corp.1.1.1.1.1.1.9.1)
SNMP: Value = -2115944055
SNMP:

-- Frame 252 --
SNMP: ----- Simple Network Management Protocol (Version 1) -----
SNMP:
SNMP: Version = 0
SNMP: Community = PUBLIC
SNMP: Command = Trap
SNMP: Enterprise = {1.3.6.1.4.1.110}
SNMP: Network address = [XXX.YYY.3.125], DSS Server
SNMP: Generic trap = 6 (Enterprise specific)
SNMP: Specific trap = 1028
SNMP: Time ticks = 506200
SNMP:
SNMP: Object = {1.3.6.1.4.1.110.1.1.1.1.1.1.1.1} (Network General
Corp.1.1.1.1.1.1.1.1)
SNMP: Value = 9 (counter)
SNMP:

SNMP: Object = {1.3.6.1.4.1.110.1.1.1.1.1.1.2.1} (Network General
Corp.1.1.1.1.1.1.2.1)
SNMP: Value = 3
SNMP:
SNMP: Object = {1.3.6.1.4.1.110.1.1.1.1.1.1.3.1} (Network General
Corp.1.1.1.1.1.1.3.1)
SNMP: Value = <SegEN01> Route superseded too frequently from [XXX.YYY.3.94]
SNMP:
SNMP: Object = {1.3.6.1.4.1.110.1.1.1.1.1.1.4.1} (Network General
Corp.1.1.1.1.1.1.4.1)
SNMP: Value = 1
SNMP:
SNMP: Object = {1.3.6.1.4.1.110.1.1.1.1.1.1.5.1} (Network General
Corp.1.1.1.1.1.1.5.1)
SNMP: Value = 3
SNMP:
SNMP: Object = {1.3.6.1.4.1.110.1.1.1.1.1.1.6.1} (Network General
Corp.1.1.1.1.1.1.6.1)
SNMP: Value = 28
SNMP:
SNMP: Object = {1.3.6.1.4.1.110.1.1.1.1.1.1.7.1} (Network General
Corp.1.1.1.1.1.1.7.1)
SNMP: Value = 855884419 (counter)
SNMP:
SNMP: Object = {1.3.6.1.4.1.110.1.1.1.1.1.1.8.1} (Network General
Corp.1.1.1.1.1.1.8.1)
SNMP: Value = NULL
SNMP:
SNMP: Object = {1.3.6.1.4.1.110.1.1.1.1.1.1.9.1} (Network General
Corp.1.1.1.1.1.1.9.1)
SNMP: Value = -2115944054
SNMP:

```
------------------------------------- Frame 267 -------------------------------------
SNMP: ----- Simple Network Management Protocol (Version 1) -----
SNMP:
SNMP: Version = 0
SNMP: Community = PUBLIC
SNMP: Command = Trap
SNMP: Enterprise = {1.3.6.1.4.1.110}
SNMP: Network address = [XXX.YYY.3.125], DSS Server
SNMP: Generic trap = 6 (Enterprise specific)
SNMP: Specific trap = 1027
SNMP: Time ticks = 506500
SNMP:
SNMP: Object = {1.3.6.1.4.1.110.1.1.1.1.1.1.1.1} (Network General
Corp.1.1.1.1.1.1.1.1)
SNMP: Value  = 10 (counter)
SNMP:
SNMP: Object = {1.3.6.1.4.1.110.1.1.1.1.1.1.2.1} (Network General
Corp.1.1.1.1.1.1.2.1)
SNMP: Value  = 3
SNMP:
SNMP: Object = {1.3.6.1.4.1.110.1.1.1.1.1.1.3.1} (Network General
Corp.1.1.1.1.1.1.3.1)
SNMP: Value  = <SegEN01> Route flapping from [XXX.YYY.3.94]
SNMP:
SNMP: Object = {1.3.6.1.4.1.110.1.1.1.1.1.1.4.1} (Network General
Corp.1.1.1.1.1.1.4.1)
SNMP: Value  = 2
SNMP:
SNMP: Object = {1.3.6.1.4.1.110.1.1.1.1.1.1.5.1} (Network General
Corp.1.1.1.1.1.1.5.1)
SNMP: Value  = 3
SNMP:
SNMP: Object = {1.3.6.1.4.1.110.1.1.1.1.1.1.6.1} (Network General
Corp.1.1.1.1.1.1.6.1)
```

SNMP: Value = 27
SNMP:
SNMP: Object = {1.3.6.1.4.1.110.1.1.1.1.1.1.7.1} (Network General
Corp.1.1.1.1.1.1.7.1)
SNMP: Value = 855884419 (counter)
SNMP:
SNMP: Object = {1.3.6.1.4.1.110.1.1.1.1.1.1.8.1} (Network General
Corp.1.1.1.1.1.1.8.1)
SNMP: Value = NULL
SNMP:
SNMP: Object = {1.3.6.1.4.1.110.1.1.1.1.1.1.9.1} (Network General
Corp.1.1.1.1.1.1.9.1)
SNMP: Value = -2115944053
SNMP:

-------------------------------------- Frame 318 --------------------------------------
SNMP: ----- Simple Network Management Protocol (Version 1) -----
SNMP:
SNMP: Version = 0
SNMP: Community = PUBLIC
SNMP: Command = Trap
SNMP: Enterprise = {1.3.6.1.4.1.110}
SNMP: Network address = [XXX.YYY.3.125], DSS Server
SNMP: Generic trap = 6 (Enterprise specific)
SNMP: Specific trap = 1027
SNMP: Time ticks = 507600
SNMP:
SNMP: Object = {1.3.6.1.4.1.110.1.1.1.1.1.1.1.1} (Network General
Corp.1.1.1.1.1.1.1.1)
SNMP: Value = 11 (counter)
SNMP:
SNMP: Object = {1.3.6.1.4.1.110.1.1.1.1.1.1.2.1} (Network General
Corp.1.1.1.1.1.1.2.1)
SNMP: Value = 3

SNMP:
SNMP: Object = {1.3.6.1.4.1.110.1.1.1.1.1.1.3.1} (Network General
Corp.1.1.1.1.1.1.3.1)
SNMP: Value = <SegEN01> Route flapping from [XXX.YYY.3.80]
SNMP:
SNMP: Object = {1.3.6.1.4.1.110.1.1.1.1.1.1.4.1} (Network General
Corp.1.1.1.1.1.1.4.1)
SNMP: Value = 2
SNMP:
SNMP: Object = {1.3.6.1.4.1.110.1.1.1.1.1.1.5.1} (Network General
Corp.1.1.1.1.1.1.5.1)
SNMP: Value = 3
SNMP:
SNMP: Object = {1.3.6.1.4.1.110.1.1.1.1.1.1.6.1} (Network General
Corp.1.1.1.1.1.1.6.1)
SNMP: Value = 27
SNMP:
SNMP: Object = {1.3.6.1.4.1.110.1.1.1.1.1.1.7.1} (Network General
Corp.1.1.1.1.1.1.7.1)
SNMP: Value = 855884435 (counter)
SNMP:
SNMP: Object = {1.3.6.1.4.1.110.1.1.1.1.1.1.8.1} (Network General
Corp.1.1.1.1.1.1.8.1)
SNMP: Value = NULL
SNMP:
SNMP: Object = {1.3.6.1.4.1.110.1.1.1.1.1.1.9.1} (Network General
Corp.1.1.1.1.1.1.9.1)
SNMP: Value = -2115942004
SNMP:

-------------------------------------- Frame 377 --------------------------------------
SNMP: ----- Simple Network Management Protocol (Version 1) -----
SNMP:
SNMP: Version = 0

SNMP: Community = PUBLIC
SNMP: Command = Trap
SNMP: Enterprise = {1.3.6.1.4.1.110}
SNMP: Network address = [XXX.YYY.3.125], DSS Server
SNMP: Generic trap = 6 (Enterprise specific)
SNMP: Specific trap = 1010
SNMP: Time ticks = 509000
SNMP:
SNMP: Object = {1.3.6.1.4.1.110.1.1.1.1.1.1.1.1} (Network General
Corp.1.1.1.1.1.1.1.1)
SNMP: Value = 12 (counter)
SNMP:
SNMP: Object = {1.3.6.1.4.1.110.1.1.1.1.1.1.2.1} (Network General
Corp.1.1.1.1.1.1.2.1)
SNMP: Value = 3
SNMP:
SNMP: Object = {1.3.6.1.4.1.110.1.1.1.1.1.1.3.1} (Network General
Corp.1.1.1.1.1.1.3.1)
SNMP: Value = <SegEN01> Multiple routers to station [XXX.YYY.3.94] <threshold:
3 routers>
SNMP:
SNMP: Object = {1.3.6.1.4.1.110.1.1.1.1.1.1.4.1} (Network General
Corp.1.1.1.1.1.1.4.1)
SNMP: Value = 1
SNMP:
SNMP: Object = {1.3.6.1.4.1.110.1.1.1.1.1.1.5.1} (Network General
Corp.1.1.1.1.1.1.5.1)
SNMP: Value = 3
SNMP:
SNMP: Object = {1.3.6.1.4.1.110.1.1.1.1.1.1.6.1} (Network General
Corp.1.1.1.1.1.1.6.1)
SNMP: Value = 10
SNMP:

SNMP: Object = {1.3.6.1.4.1.110.1.1.1.1.1.1.1.7.1} (Network General
Corp.1.1.1.1.1.1.7.1)
SNMP: Value = 855884449 (counter)
SNMP:
SNMP: Object = {1.3.6.1.4.1.110.1.1.1.1.1.1.1.8.1} (Network General
Corp.1.1.1.1.1.1.8.1)
SNMP: Value = NULL
SNMP:
SNMP: Object = {1.3.6.1.4.1.110.1.1.1.1.1.1.1.9.1} (Network General
Corp.1.1.1.1.1.1.9.1)
SNMP: Value = -2115940211
SNMP:

Definition 7-1. Network General Corp. MIB

```
--

--        NGC.ASN: Network General Corporation MIB extensions.

--

--                Network General Corporation
--                   4200 Bohannon Drive
--                  Menlo Park, CA  94025
--                    (415) 473-2000

--

--                    June 18, 1996
--                       Rev 3.0

--


NGC-MIB DEFINITIONS ::= BEGIN

IMPORTS

enterprises, NetworkAddress, IpAddress,
       Counter                          FROM RFC1155-SMI

DisplayString                           FROM RFC1213-MIB
```

```
-- EntryStatus, OwnerString                    FROM RFC1271-MIB

OBJECT-TYPE                                     FROM RFC1212

TRAP-TYPE                                       FROM RFC1215-MIB;

-- This MIB module uses the extended OBJECT-TYPE macro as defined in
-- RFC 1212 and the TRAP-TYPE macro as defined in RFC 1215.  It also
-- uses the EntryStatus textual convention as defined in RFC 1271.


--  Network General Corporation enterpise

ngc             OBJECT IDENTIFIER ::= { enterprises 110 }

ngcSystems      OBJECT IDENTIFIER ::= { ngc 1 }
   ngcServers      OBJECT IDENTIFIER ::= { ngcSystems 1 }
   ngcMonitor      OBJECT IDENTIFIER ::= { ngcServers 1 }


-- The ngcTrap group.  This group contains objects describing the last
-- Network General 'alarm' resulting in transmission of a SNMP trap
-- message.


ngcTrap         OBJECT IDENTIFIER ::= { ngcMonitor 1 }

ngcTrapTable OBJECT-TYPE
     SYNTAX  SEQUENCE OF NgcTrapEntry
     ACCESS  not-accessible
     STATUS  mandatory
     DESCRIPTION
        "The agent's table of NGC alarm information."
     ::= { ngcTrap 1 }


ngcTrapEntry OBJECT-TYPE
     SYNTAX  NgcTrapEntry
     ACCESS  not-accessible
     STATUS  mandatory
```

DESCRIPTION
"Information about the last NGC alarm trap generated by the
agent. There is always one entry in this table, indexed by
integer value 1"
INDEX   { INTEGER (1) }
::= { ngcTrapTable 1 }

NgcTrapEntry ::=
    SEQUENCE {
        ngcTrSequence
            Counter,
        ngcTrId
            INTEGER,
        ngcTrText
            DisplayString (SIZE (0..80)),
        ngcTrPriority
            INTEGER,
        ngcTrClass
            INTEGER,
        ngcTrType
            INTEGER,
        ngcTrTime
            Counter,
        ngcTrSuspect
            DisplayString (SIZE (0..32)),
        ngcTrDiagId
            INTEGER
    }

ngcTrSequence OBJECT-TYPE
    SYNTAX Counter
    ACCESS read-only
    STATUS mandatory
    DESCRIPTION

"A counter of the number of NGC alarm traps generated since the
agent was last initialized."
::= { ngcTrapEntry 1 }

ngcTrId OBJECT-TYPE
        SYNTAX INTEGER {
                monitor(1),
                analyzer(3)
            }
        ACCESS read-only
        STATUS mandatory
        DESCRIPTION
          "The application which generated this NGC alarm."
        ::= { ngcTrapEntry 2 }

ngcTrText OBJECT-TYPE
        SYNTAX DisplayString (SIZE (0..80))
        ACCESS read-only
        STATUS mandatory
        DESCRIPTION
          "An ASCII string describing the NGC alarm condition/cause."
        ::= { ngcTrapEntry 3 }

ngcTrPriority OBJECT-TYPE
        SYNTAX INTEGER {
                inform(1),
                warning(2),
                minor(3),
                major(4),
                critical(5)
            }
        ACCESS read-only
        STATUS mandatory

DESCRIPTION
   "The priority level as set on the agent for this Class and Type of
   trap."
   ::= { ngcTrapEntry 4 }

ngcTrClass OBJECT-TYPE
   SYNTAX INTEGER
   ACCESS read-only
   STATUS mandatory
   DESCRIPTION
   "The Class number of the described NGC alarm."
   ::= { ngcTrapEntry 5 }

ngcTrType OBJECT-TYPE
   SYNTAX INTEGER
   ACCESS read-only
   STATUS mandatory
   DESCRIPTION
   "The Type number of the described NGC alarm. Each application may
   generate alarm types in a pre-defined range of values for that
   application. See TRAP-TYPE macro definitions later in this MIB,
   or product operations manual for a list of alarm types currently
   generated."
   ::= { ngcTrapEntry 6 }

ngcTrTime OBJECT-TYPE
   SYNTAX Counter
   ACCESS read-only
   STATUS mandatory
   DESCRIPTION
   "The time that the condition or event occurred which caused
   generation of this alarm. This value is given in seconds since
   00:00:00 Greenwich mean time (GMT) January 1, 1970."
   ::= { ngcTrapEntry 7 }

ngcTrSuspect OBJECT-TYPE
    SYNTAX DisplayString (SIZE (0..32))
    ACCESS read-only
    STATUS mandatory
    DESCRIPTION
      "An ASCII string describing the host which caused the NGC alarm.
      (Note: current version of Expert Analyzer generates a null
      string for this field.)"
    ::= { ngcTrapEntry 8 }

ngcTrDiagId OBJECT-TYPE
    SYNTAX INTEGER
    ACCESS read-only
    STATUS mandatory
    DESCRIPTION
      "An integer identifying the diagnosis which triggered this NGC
      alarm."
    ::= { ngcTrapEntry 9 }

-- The ngcMibs branch of the NGC mib. This group contains both generic
-- and product specific mib definitions for the NGC product line.

ngcMibs   OBJECT IDENTIFIER ::= { ngc 2 }

-- The ngcAdmin branch of the NGC mib. This group contains generic
-- objects that are used to administer the agents in NGC products.

ngcAdmin   OBJECT IDENTIFIER ::= { ngcMibs 1 }

-- The ngcAdminBoot branch of the NGC mib. This group contains objects
-- that are used to administer the boot features of NGC products.

ngcAdminBoot   OBJECT IDENTIFIER ::= { ngcAdmin 1 }

ngcRemBootEnable OBJECT-TYPE

SYNTAX INTEGER { enabled(1), disabled(2) }
ACCESS read-write
STATUS mandatory
DESCRIPTION
   "If enabled when the agent is rebooted then the agent will
    attempt to boot from one of the boot servers defined in the
    ngcRemoteBootServerTable."
::= { ngcAdminBoot 1 }

ngcRemBootServerTable OBJECT-TYPE
    SYNTAX SEQUENCE OF NgcRemBootServerEntry
    ACCESS not-accessible
    STATUS mandatory
    DESCRIPTION
       "The agent's table of remote boot servers."
    ::= { ngcAdminBoot 2 }

ngcRemBootServerEntry OBJECT-TYPE
    SYNTAX NgcRemBootServerEntry
    ACCESS not-accessible
    STATUS mandatory
    DESCRIPTION
       "Information about a remote boot server."
    INDEX { ngcRemBootServerIndex }
    ::= { ngcRemBootServerTable 1 }

NgcRemBootServerEntry ::=
    SEQUENCE {
       ngcRemBootServerIndex
          INTEGER,
       ngcRemBootServerIpAddr
          IpAddress,
       ngcRemBootServerFileName
          DisplayString

```
        }

ngcRemBootServerIndex OBJECT-TYPE
      SYNTAX  INTEGER
      ACCESS  read-only
      STATUS  mandatory
      DESCRIPTION
        "A unique value identifying the ngcRemBootServerEntry."
      ::= { ngcRemBootServerEntry 1 }


ngcRemBootServerIpAddr OBJECT-TYPE
      SYNTAX  IpAddress
      ACCESS  read-write
      STATUS  mandatory
      DESCRIPTION
        "The IP address of this remote boot server."
      ::= { ngcRemBootServerEntry 2 }


ngcRemBootServerFileName OBJECT-TYPE
      SYNTAX  DisplayString (SIZE (0..64))
      ACCESS  read-write
      STATUS  mandatory
      DESCRIPTION
        "The name of the binary file residing on the remote boot
         server.  This is the file that will be loaded, via TFTP,
         when the agent is rebooted."
      ::= { ngcRemBootServerEntry 3 }


-- The ngcAdminControl branch of the NGC mib.  This group contains
-- objects that are used to perform control operations on the NGC
-- products.

ngcAdminControl    OBJECT IDENTIFIER ::= { ngcAdmin 2 }

ngcCtrlAction OBJECT-TYPE
```

```
SYNTAX  INTEGER {
        other(1),
        reset(2)
    }
ACCESS  read-write
STATUS  mandatory
DESCRIPTION
    "A control to force the agent to perform a desired action.  The
    agent will always return the value 'other(1)' in response to a
    get or getnext request.  When set to 'reset(2)' the agent
    reinitializes."
::= { ngcAdminControl 1 }
```

-- The ngcProducts branch of the NGC MIB is used to identify specific
-- product types in the family of Network General Corporation products.
-- There are no actual objects that can be operated on in this branch of
-- the MIB. These object IDs are used in the sysObjectId object of each
-- NGC product's MIB.

```
ngcProducts        OBJECT IDENTIFIER ::= { ngc 3 }

ngcProdSystems      OBJECT IDENTIFIER ::= { ngcProducts 1 }
  ngcProdStandAlone  OBJECT IDENTIFIER ::= { ngcProducts 2 }
  ngcDSSSystems       OBJECT IDENTIFIER ::= { ngcProdSystems 1 }
  ngcDSSProbes        OBJECT IDENTIFIER ::= { ngcDSSSystems 1 }
  ngcDSSServers       OBJECT IDENTIFIER ::= { ngcDSSSystems 2 }
  ngcDSSConsoles      OBJECT IDENTIFIER ::= { ngcDSSSystems 3 }
```

-- The following object ID is used as the value for the sysObjectID
-- object of NGC's standalone RMON Probe system.

```
ngcRMONProbe       OBJECT IDENTIFIER ::= { ngcDSSProbes 1 }
```

-- The following object ID is used as the value for the sysObjectID
-- object of NGC's Distributed Sniffer Server.

ngcExpertServer   OBJECT IDENTIFIER ::= { ngcDSSServers 1 }

-- Network General Corporation Enterprise-Specific Traps

ngcExcessStationErrors TRAP-TYPE
    ENTERPRISE ngc
    VARIABLES { ngcTrSequence, ngcTrId, ngcTrText, ngcTrPriority,
          ngcTrClass, ngcTrType, ngcTrTime, ngcTrSuspect,
          ngcTrDiagId }
    DESCRIPTION
     "The monitor has detected that the number of error packets from
     a station has exceeded a threshold."
    ::= 1

ngcNoResponse TRAP-TYPE
    ENTERPRISE ngc
    VARIABLES { ngcTrSequence, ngcTrId, ngcTrText, ngcTrPriority,
          ngcTrClass, ngcTrType, ngcTrTime, ngcTrSuspect,
          ngcTrDiagId }
    DESCRIPTION
     "The monitor has determined that a station is not responding to
     incoming network traffic."
    ::= 2

ngcStationIdle TRAP-TYPE
    ENTERPRISE ngc
    VARIABLES { ngcTrSequence, ngcTrId, ngcTrText, ngcTrPriority,
          ngcTrClass, ngcTrType, ngcTrTime, ngcTrSuspect,
          ngcTrDiagId }
    DESCRIPTION
     "The monitor has detected that a station's idle time has exceeded
     a threshold."
    ::= 3

ngcRelativeUsageThresholdExceeded TRAP-TYPE

ENTERPRISE ngc
VARIABLES { ngcTrSequence, ngcTrId, ngcTrText, ngcTrPriority,
ngcTrClass, ngcTrType, ngcTrTime, ngcTrSuspect,
ngcTrDiagId }
DESCRIPTION
"The monitor has determined that the relative network usage of one
station has exceeded a threshold."
::= 4

ngcExcessNetworkErrors TRAP-TYPE
ENTERPRISE ngc
VARIABLES { ngcTrSequence, ngcTrId, ngcTrText, ngcTrPriority,
ngcTrClass, ngcTrType, ngcTrTime, ngcTrSuspect,
ngcTrDiagId }
DESCRIPTION
"The monitor has detected that the overall number of errors on the
network has exceeded a threshold."
::= 5

ngcNetworkIdle TRAP-TYPE
ENTERPRISE ngc
VARIABLES { ngcTrSequence, ngcTrId, ngcTrText, ngcTrPriority,
ngcTrClass, ngcTrType, ngcTrTime, ngcTrSuspect,
ngcTrDiagId }
DESCRIPTION
"The monitor has detected that the entire network has been idle
for a period of time exceeding a threshold."
::= 6

ngcAbsoluteUsageThresholdExceeded TRAP-TYPE
ENTERPRISE ngc
VARIABLES { ngcTrSequence, ngcTrId, ngcTrText, ngcTrPriority,
ngcTrClass, ngcTrType, ngcTrTime, ngcTrSuspect,
ngcTrDiagId }

DESCRIPTION
"The monitor has determined that the overall network usage has exceeded a threshold."
::= 7

ngcUnknownStation TRAP-TYPE
ENTERPRISE ngc
VARIABLES { ngcTrSequence, ngcTrId, ngcTrText, ngcTrPriority,
ngcTrClass, ngcTrType, ngcTrTime, ngcTrSuspect,
ngcTrDiagId }
DESCRIPTION
"The monitor has detected a station which has not been previously identified by the user."
::= 8

ngcIllegalSourceAddress TRAP-TYPE
ENTERPRISE ngc
VARIABLES { ngcTrSequence, ngcTrId, ngcTrText, ngcTrPriority,
ngcTrClass, ngcTrType, ngcTrTime, ngcTrSuspect,
ngcTrDiagId }
DESCRIPTION
"The monitor has detected a non-unicast DLC source address."
::= 9

ngcBroadcastThresholdExceeded TRAP-TYPE
ENTERPRISE ngc
VARIABLES { ngcTrSequence, ngcTrId, ngcTrText, ngcTrPriority,
ngcTrClass, ngcTrType, ngcTrTime, ngcTrSuspect,
ngcTrDiagId }
DESCRIPTION
"The monitor has determined that the broadcast rate threshold has been exceeded."
::= 10

ngcOversizedFrame TRAP-TYPE
    ENTERPRISE ngc
    VARIABLES { ngcTrSequence, ngcTrId, ngcTrText, ngcTrPriority,
            ngcTrClass, ngcTrType, ngcTrTime, ngcTrSuspect,
            ngcTrDiagId }
    DESCRIPTION
      "The monitor has detected an oversized frame."
    ::= 11

ngcBeacon TRAP-TYPE
    ENTERPRISE ngc
    VARIABLES { ngcTrSequence, ngcTrId, ngcTrText, ngcTrPriority,
            ngcTrClass, ngcTrType, ngcTrTime, ngcTrSuspect,
            ngcTrDiagId }
    DESCRIPTION
      "The monitor has detected a ring beacon (Token Ring)."
    ::= 12

ngcPollFail TRAP-TYPE
    ENTERPRISE ngc
    VARIABLES { ngcTrSequence, ngcTrId, ngcTrText, ngcTrPriority,
            ngcTrClass, ngcTrType, ngcTrTime, ngcTrSuspect,
            ngcTrDiagId }
    DESCRIPTION
      "The monitor has detected that a ring poll did not complete, or
      was missing one or more stations (Token Ring)."
    ::= 13

ngcCollisionThresholdExceeded TRAP-TYPE
    ENTERPRISE ngc
    VARIABLES { ngcTrSequence, ngcTrId, ngcTrText, ngcTrPriority,
            ngcTrClass, ngcTrType, ngcTrTime, ngcTrSuspect,
            ngcTrDiagId }
    DESCRIPTION

"The monitor has determined that the collision rate threshold has
been exceeded (Ethernet)."
::= 14

ngcExcessFileRetransmissions TRAP-TYPE
    ENTERPRISE ngc
    VARIABLES { ngcTrSequence, ngcTrId, ngcTrText, ngcTrPriority,
            ngcTrClass, ngcTrType, ngcTrTime, ngcTrSuspect,
            ngcTrDiagId }
    DESCRIPTION
        "The expert system has detected that the percent of file transfers
        that are retransmissions has exceeded a threshold and the number of
        requests has exceeded a threshold."
    ::= 1001

ngcSlowFileProcess TRAP-TYPE
    ENTERPRISE ngc
    VARIABLES { ngcTrSequence, ngcTrId, ngcTrText, ngcTrPriority,
            ngcTrClass, ngcTrType, ngcTrTime, ngcTrSuspect,
            ngcTrDiagId }
    DESCRIPTION
        "The expert system has determined that the ratio of slow file
        transfers to normal file transfers has exceeded a threshold."
    ::= 1002

ngcSlowServer TRAP-TYPE
    ENTERPRISE ngc
    VARIABLES { ngcTrSequence, ngcTrId, ngcTrText, ngcTrPriority,
            ngcTrClass, ngcTrType, ngcTrTime, ngcTrSuspect,
            ngcTrDiagId }
    DESCRIPTION
        "The expert system has determined that a server station is
        responding slowly to application requests."
    ::= 1003

ngcRequestLoops TRAP-TYPE
    ENTERPRISE ngc
    VARIABLES { ngcTrSequence, ngcTrId, ngcTrText, ngcTrPriority,
            ngcTrClass, ngcTrType, ngcTrTime, ngcTrSuspect,
            ngcTrDiagId }
    DESCRIPTION
        "The expert system has detected that a station is repeating the
        same application request after receiving an appropriate reply."
    ::= 1004

ngcFailingRequest TRAP-TYPE
    ENTERPRISE ngc
    VARIABLES { ngcTrSequence, ngcTrId, ngcTrText, ngcTrPriority,
            ngcTrClass, ngcTrType, ngcTrTime, ngcTrSuspect,
            ngcTrDiagId }
    DESCRIPTION
        "The expert system has detected that the number of application
        requests denied has exceeded a threshold."
    ::= 1005

ngcBrokenConnection TRAP-TYPE
    ENTERPRISE ngc
    VARIABLES { ngcTrSequence, ngcTrId, ngcTrText, ngcTrPriority,
            ngcTrClass, ngcTrType, ngcTrTime, ngcTrSuspect,
            ngcTrDiagId }
    DESCRIPTION
        "The expert system has detected a broken connection."
    ::= 1006

ngcRetransmission TRAP-TYPE
    ENTERPRISE ngc
    VARIABLES { ngcTrSequence, ngcTrId, ngcTrText, ngcTrPriority,
            ngcTrClass, ngcTrType, ngcTrTime, ngcTrSuspect,
            ngcTrDiagId }

DESCRIPTION
"The expert system has detected that the number of retransmissions
on this connection has exceeded a threshold."
::= 1007

ngcDuplicateAddress TRAP-TYPE
ENTERPRISE ngc
VARIABLES { ngcTrSequence, ngcTrId, ngcTrText, ngcTrPriority,
ngcTrClass, ngcTrType, ngcTrTime, ngcTrSuspect,
ngcTrDiagId }
DESCRIPTION
"The expert system has detected two or more DLC stations with the
same network address."
::= 1008

ngcLocalRouter TRAP-TYPE
ENTERPRISE ngc
VARIABLES { ngcTrSequence, ngcTrId, ngcTrText, ngcTrPriority,
ngcTrClass, ngcTrType, ngcTrTime, ngcTrSuspect,
ngcTrDiagId }
DESCRIPTION
"The expert system has detected a router which is routing traffic
between two or more local stations."
::= 1009

ngcMultipleRouters TRAP-TYPE
ENTERPRISE ngc
VARIABLES { ngcTrSequence, ngcTrId, ngcTrText, ngcTrPriority,
ngcTrClass, ngcTrType, ngcTrTime, ngcTrSuspect,
ngcTrDiagId }
DESCRIPTION
"The expert system has determined that the number of routers being
used to gain access to a local or remote station has exceeded a
threshold."

::= 1010

ngcATalkSubnetDown TRAP-TYPE
    ENTERPRISE ngc
    VARIABLES { ngcTrSequence, ngcTrId, ngcTrText, ngcTrPriority,
           ngcTrClass, ngcTrType, ngcTrTime, ngcTrSuspect,
           ngcTrDiagId }
    DESCRIPTION
      "The expert system has determined that the specified AppleTalk
      network, while previously advertised, has not been advertised by
      any local router in over a minute. This implies that communication
      between that network and the local one is now impossible."
    ::= 1011

ngcATalkBadRouteTable TRAP-TYPE
    ENTERPRISE ngc
    VARIABLES { ngcTrSequence, ngcTrId, ngcTrText, ngcTrPriority,
           ngcTrClass, ngcTrType, ngcTrTime, ngcTrSuspect,
           ngcTrDiagId }
    DESCRIPTION
      "The expert system has determined that some entries sent in the
      specified router's routing table had illegal or nonsensical values,
      indicating that its routing table is corrupt."
    ::= 1012

ngcATalkSubnetAddrClash TRAP-TYPE
    ENTERPRISE ngc
    VARIABLES { ngcTrSequence, ngcTrId, ngcTrText, ngcTrPriority,
           ngcTrClass, ngcTrType, ngcTrTime, ngcTrSuspect,
           ngcTrDiagId }
    DESCRIPTION
      "The expert system has determined that two AppleTalk networks have
      been observed with ranges that overlap each other."
    ::= 1013

ngcHighBurstRate TRAP-TYPE
    ENTERPRISE ngc
    VARIABLES { ngcTrSequence, ngcTrId, ngcTrText, ngcTrPriority,
           ngcTrClass, ngcTrType, ngcTrTime, ngcTrSuspect,
           ngcTrDiagId }
    DESCRIPTION
      "The expert system has determined that during a 1-minute interval,
      the percent of time the LAN was in LAN overload has exceeded a
      threshold."
    ::= 1014

ngcUnderloadedWAN TRAP-TYPE
    ENTERPRISE ngc
    VARIABLES { ngcTrSequence, ngcTrId, ngcTrText, ngcTrPriority,
           ngcTrClass, ngcTrType, ngcTrTime, ngcTrSuspect,
           ngcTrDiagId }
    DESCRIPTION
      "The expert system has detected that the data rate on the network
      dipped below a threshold. (WAN)"
    ::= 1015

ngcExcessBroadcasts TRAP-TYPE
    ENTERPRISE ngc
    VARIABLES { ngcTrSequence, ngcTrId, ngcTrText, ngcTrPriority,
           ngcTrClass, ngcTrType, ngcTrTime, ngcTrSuspect,
           ngcTrDiagId }
    DESCRIPTION
      "The expert system has determined that the broadcast/multicast
      rate has exceeded a threshold."
    ::= 1016

ngcExcessRingEntries TRAP-TYPE
    ENTERPRISE ngc
    VARIABLES { ngcTrSequence, ngcTrId, ngcTrText, ngcTrPriority,
           ngcTrClass, ngcTrType, ngcTrTime, ngcTrSuspect,

ngcTrDiagId }
DESCRIPTION
"The expert system has determined that the MAC level ring entries
for a station has exceeded a threshold (Token Ring)."
::= 1017

ngcExcessRingPurges TRAP-TYPE
ENTERPRISE ngc
VARIABLES { ngcTrSequence, ngcTrId, ngcTrText, ngcTrPriority,
ngcTrClass, ngcTrType, ngcTrTime, ngcTrSuspect,
ngcTrDiagId }
DESCRIPTION
"The expert system has detected that the number of ring purge
frames has exceeded a threshold (Token Ring)."
::= 1018

ngcLANOverutilized TRAP-TYPE
ENTERPRISE ngc
VARIABLES { ngcTrSequence, ngcTrId, ngcTrText, ngcTrPriority,
ngcTrClass, ngcTrType, ngcTrTime, ngcTrSuspect,
ngcTrDiagId }
DESCRIPTION
"The expert system has determined that the number of 'receiver
congestion' frames reported by the NIC has exceeded a threshold
(LAN)."
::= 1019

ngcStationRemoved TRAP-TYPE
ENTERPRISE ngc
VARIABLES { ngcTrSequence, ngcTrId, ngcTrText, ngcTrPriority,
ngcTrClass, ngcTrType, ngcTrTime, ngcTrSuspect,
ngcTrDiagId }
DESCRIPTION
"The expert system has detected that a station has removed itself
from the ring (Token Ring)."

```
      ::= 1020


ngcBeaconDetected TRAP-TYPE
      ENTERPRISE ngc
      VARIABLES { ngcTrSequence, ngcTrId, ngcTrText, ngcTrPriority,
             ngcTrClass, ngcTrType, ngcTrTime, ngcTrSuspect,
             ngcTrDiagId }
      DESCRIPTION
        "The expert system has detected a ring beacon (Token Ring)."
      ::= 1021


ngcExcessRingBursts TRAP-TYPE
      ENTERPRISE ngc
      VARIABLES { ngcTrSequence, ngcTrId, ngcTrText, ngcTrPriority,
             ngcTrClass, ngcTrType, ngcTrTime, ngcTrSuspect,
             ngcTrDiagId }
      DESCRIPTION
        "The expert system has determined that the number of line and/or
        burst errors from one station has exceeded a threshold (Token Ring)."
      ::= 1022


ngcExcessHDLCRetransmissions TRAP-TYPE
      ENTERPRISE ngc
      VARIABLES { ngcTrSequence, ngcTrId, ngcTrText, ngcTrPriority,
             ngcTrClass, ngcTrType, ngcTrTime, ngcTrSuspect,
             ngcTrDiagId }
      DESCRIPTION
        "The expert system has determined that the rate of HDLC
        retransmissions has exceeded a threshold (WAN)."
      ::= 1023


ngcWANCongested TRAP-TYPE
      ENTERPRISE ngc
      VARIABLES { ngcTrSequence, ngcTrId, ngcTrText, ngcTrPriority,
```

ngcTrClass, ngcTrType, ngcTrTime, ngcTrSuspect,
ngcTrDiagId }
DESCRIPTION
"The expert system has determined that the data rate on the
network exceeded a threshold (WAN)."
::= 1024

ngcUnderloadCongestion TRAP-TYPE
ENTERPRISE ngc
VARIABLES { ngcTrSequence, ngcTrId, ngcTrText, ngcTrPriority,
ngcTrClass, ngcTrType, ngcTrTime, ngcTrSuspect,
ngcTrDiagId }
DESCRIPTION
"The expert system has detected WAN congestion during WAN
underload (WAN)."
::= 1025

ngcPhysicalError TRAP-TYPE
ENTERPRISE ngc
VARIABLES { ngcTrSequence, ngcTrId, ngcTrText, ngcTrPriority,
ngcTrClass, ngcTrType, ngcTrTime, ngcTrSuspect,
ngcTrDiagId }
DESCRIPTION
"The expert system has detected that the rate of invalid frames
exceeded a threshold."
::= 1026

ngcRouteFlapping TRAP-TYPE
ENTERPRISE ngc
VARIABLES { ngcTrSequence, ngcTrId, ngcTrText, ngcTrPriority,
ngcTrClass, ngcTrType, ngcTrTime, ngcTrSuspect,
ngcTrDiagId }
DESCRIPTION
"The expert system has determined that the specified router has

changed one or more routes from valid to invalid and back too
frequently."
::= 1027

ngcRouteSuperseded TRAP-TYPE
    ENTERPRISE ngc
    VARIABLES { ngcTrSequence, ngcTrId, ngcTrText, ngcTrPriority,
         ngcTrClass, ngcTrType, ngcTrTime, ngcTrSuspect,
         ngcTrDiagId }
    DESCRIPTION
      "The expert system has determined that the specified router has
      changed the metrics on one or more routes too frequently. The
      analyzer makes this diagnosis if any route changes between being the
      best route to its destination and not being the best route more than
      three times in one minute."
    ::= 1028

ngcRouterStorm TRAP-TYPE
    ENTERPRISE ngc
    VARIABLES { ngcTrSequence, ngcTrId, ngcTrText, ngcTrPriority,
         ngcTrClass, ngcTrType, ngcTrTime, ngcTrSuspect,
         ngcTrDiagId }
    DESCRIPTION
      "The expert system has determined that the specified router has
      reconfirmed one or more of its routes more frequently than seems
      reasonable."
    ::= 1029

ngcNonsenseRoute TRAP-TYPE
    ENTERPRISE ngc
    VARIABLES { ngcTrSequence, ngcTrId, ngcTrText, ngcTrPriority,
         ngcTrClass, ngcTrType, ngcTrTime, ngcTrSuspect,
         ngcTrDiagId }
    DESCRIPTION

"The expert system has determined that the specified router has sent
frames suggesting that frames be sent to a next hop address that is
not on the local subnet."
::= 1030

ngcMisdirectedFrame TRAP-TYPE
    ENTERPRISE ngc
    VARIABLES { ngcTrSequence, ngcTrId, ngcTrText, ngcTrPriority,
          ngcTrClass, ngcTrType, ngcTrTime, ngcTrSuspect,
          ngcTrDiagId }
    DESCRIPTION
        "The expert system has determined that the specified station has
        sent one or more frames in which the IP destination address is not
        on the local subnet and the DLC destination address is not that of
        a router advertising a route to the IP destination."
    ::= 1031

ngcRouterCrash TRAP-TYPE
    ENTERPRISE ngc
    VARIABLES { ngcTrSequence, ngcTrId, ngcTrText, ngcTrPriority,
          ngcTrClass, ngcTrType, ngcTrTime, ngcTrSuspect,
          ngcTrDiagId }
    DESCRIPTION
        "The expert system has determined that the specified router has let
        more than half of its advertised routes expire."
    ::= 1032

ngcContinuedBeaconing TRAP-TYPE
    ENTERPRISE ngc
    VARIABLES { ngcTrSequence, ngcTrId, ngcTrText, ngcTrPriority,
          ngcTrClass, ngcTrType, ngcTrTime, ngcTrSuspect,
          ngcTrDiagId }
    DESCRIPTION
        "The expert system has determined that the specified station has

continously sent beacon frames for more than 5 seconds to attempt
to detect the location of the ring break (FDDI)."
::= 1033

ngcExcessErrorFrames TRAP-TYPE
    ENTERPRISE ngc
    VARIABLES { ngcTrSequence, ngcTrId, ngcTrText, ngcTrPriority,
            ngcTrClass, ngcTrType, ngcTrTime, ngcTrSuspect,
            ngcTrDiagId }
    DESCRIPTION
        "The expert system has determined that the number of error frames
        detected by the MAC during the last minute has exceeded a threshold
        (FDDI)."
    ::= 1034

ngcExcessLostFrames TRAP-TYPE
    ENTERPRISE ngc
    VARIABLES { ngcTrSequence, ngcTrId, ngcTrText, ngcTrPriority,
            ngcTrClass, ngcTrType, ngcTrTime, ngcTrSuspect,
            ngcTrDiagId }
    DESCRIPTION
        "The expert system has determined that the number of frames lost by
        the MAC has exceeded a threshold (FDDI)."
    ::= 1035

ngcExcessUncopiedFrames TRAP-TYPE
    ENTERPRISE ngc
    VARIABLES { ngcTrSequence, ngcTrId, ngcTrText, ngcTrPriority,
            ngcTrClass, ngcTrType, ngcTrTime, ngcTrSuspect,
            ngcTrDiagId }
    DESCRIPTION
        "The expert system has determined that the number of frames not
        copied by the MAC has exceeded a threshold (FDDI)."
    ::= 1036

ngcExcessLinkRejects TRAP-TYPE
    ENTERPRISE ngc
    VARIABLES { ngcTrSequence, ngcTrId, ngcTrText, ngcTrPriority,
          ngcTrClass, ngcTrType, ngcTrTime, ngcTrSuspect,
          ngcTrDiagId }
    DESCRIPTION
      "The expert system has determined that the number of links rejected
      by the port has exceeded a threshold (FDDI)."
    ::= 1037

ngcExcessLinkErrors TRAP-TYPE
    ENTERPRISE ngc
    VARIABLES { ngcTrSequence, ngcTrId, ngcTrText, ngcTrPriority,
          ngcTrClass, ngcTrType, ngcTrTime, ngcTrSuspect,
          ngcTrDiagId }
    DESCRIPTION
      "The expert system has determined that the number of link errors
      monitored by the port has exceeded a threshold (FDDI)."
    ::= 1038

ngcRingWrapped TRAP-TYPE
    ENTERPRISE ngc
    VARIABLES { ngcTrSequence, ngcTrId, ngcTrText, ngcTrPriority,
          ngcTrClass, ngcTrType, ngcTrTime, ngcTrSuspect,
          ngcTrDiagId }
    DESCRIPTION
      "The expert system has determined that the trunk ring wrapped at
      this station (FDDI)."
    ::= 1039

ngcRingOpStorm TRAP-TYPE
    ENTERPRISE ngc
    VARIABLES { ngcTrSequence, ngcTrId, ngcTrText, ngcTrPriority,
          ngcTrClass, ngcTrType, ngcTrTime, ngcTrSuspect,

ngcTrDiagId }
DESCRIPTION
"The expert system has determined that the number of RingOps has exceeded a threshold (FDDI)."
::= 1040

ngcClaimBeaconOscillation TRAP-TYPE
ENTERPRISE ngc
VARIABLES { ngcTrSequence, ngcTrId, ngcTrText, ngcTrPriority,
ngcTrClass, ngcTrType, ngcTrTime, ngcTrSuspect,
ngcTrDiagId }
DESCRIPTION
"The expert system has determined that the ring oscillated between the claim process and the beacon process. The number of beacon and claim cycles has exceeded a threshold (FDDI)."
::= 1041

ngcClocksAbsent TRAP-TYPE
ENTERPRISE ngc
VARIABLES { ngcTrSequence, ngcTrId, ngcTrText, ngcTrPriority,
ngcTrClass, ngcTrType, ngcTrTime, ngcTrSuspect,
ngcTrDiagId }
DESCRIPTION
"The expert system has determined that the clock has disappeared (WAN)."
::= 1042

ngcDBSecurityBreach TRAP-TYPE
ENTERPRISE ngc
VARIABLES { ngcTrSequence, ngcTrId, ngcTrText, ngcTrPriority,
ngcTrClass, ngcTrType, ngcTrTime, ngcTrSuspect,
ngcTrDiagId }
DESCRIPTION
"The expert system has determined that an attempt to connect to an

SQL database server failed."
    ::= 1043

ngcDBSlowConnection TRAP-TYPE
    ENTERPRISE ngc
    VARIABLES { ngcTrSequence, ngcTrId, ngcTrText, ngcTrPriority,
           ngcTrClass, ngcTrType, ngcTrTime, ngcTrSuspect,
           ngcTrDiagId }
    DESCRIPTION
     "The expert system has determined that a slow connection to an SQL
     database server was detected."
    ::= 1044

ngcDBSlowResponse TRAP-TYPE
    ENTERPRISE ngc
    VARIABLES { ngcTrSequence, ngcTrId, ngcTrText, ngcTrPriority,
           ngcTrClass, ngcTrType, ngcTrTime, ngcTrSuspect,
           ngcTrDiagId }
    DESCRIPTION
     "The expert system has determined that a slow response to an SQL
     database server was detected."
    ::= 1045

ngcExcessSingleBufferPkts TRAP-TYPE
    ENTERPRISE ngc
    VARIABLES { ngcTrSequence, ngcTrId, ngcTrText, ngcTrPriority,
           ngcTrClass, ngcTrType, ngcTrTime, ngcTrSuspect,
           ngcTrDiagId }
    DESCRIPTION
     "The expert system has determined that there have been excessive
     Single Buffer Mode packets from a connection endpoint."
    ::= 1046

ngcExcessProbePackets TRAP-TYPE

ENTERPRISE ngc
VARIABLES { ngcTrSequence, ngcTrId, ngcTrText, ngcTrPriority,
        ngcTrClass, ngcTrType, ngcTrTime, ngcTrSuspect,
        ngcTrDiagId }
DESCRIPTION
    "The expert system has determined that the connection endpoint
    received too many probe packets as a percentage of total packets.
    There is a definite packet loss between the communicating endpoints."
    ::= 1047

ngcExcessIPC157Errs TRAP-TYPE
    ENTERPRISE ngc
    VARIABLES { ngcTrSequence, ngcTrId, ngcTrText, ngcTrPriority,
            ngcTrClass, ngcTrType, ngcTrTime, ngcTrSuspect,
            ngcTrDiagId }
    DESCRIPTION
        "The expert system has determined that the connection has received
        too many IPC 157 packets as a percentage of total packets."
        ::= 1048

ngcExcessIPC162Errs TRAP-TYPE
    ENTERPRISE ngc
    VARIABLES { ngcTrSequence, ngcTrId, ngcTrText, ngcTrPriority,
            ngcTrClass, ngcTrType, ngcTrTime, ngcTrSuspect,
            ngcTrDiagId }
    DESCRIPTION
        "The expert system has determined that the connection has received
        too many IPC 162 packets as a percentage of total packets."
        ::= 1049

ngcExcessNETRPCAborts TRAP-TYPE
    ENTERPRISE ngc
    VARIABLES { ngcTrSequence, ngcTrId, ngcTrText, ngcTrPriority,
            ngcTrClass, ngcTrType, ngcTrTime, ngcTrSuspect,

ngcTrDiagId }
DESCRIPTION
"The expert system has determined that the connection has received
too many NETRPC Abort packets as a percentage of total packets."
::= 1050

ngcExcessNETRPCRejects TRAP-TYPE
ENTERPRISE ngc
VARIABLES { ngcTrSequence, ngcTrId, ngcTrText, ngcTrPriority,
ngcTrClass, ngcTrType, ngcTrTime, ngcTrSuspect,
ngcTrDiagId }
DESCRIPTION
"The expert system has determined that the connection has received
too many NETRPC Reject packets as a percentage of total packets."
::= 1051

ngcExcessFailedLogins TRAP-TYPE
ENTERPRISE ngc
VARIABLES { ngcTrSequence, ngcTrId, ngcTrText, ngcTrPriority,
ngcTrClass, ngcTrType, ngcTrTime, ngcTrSuspect,
ngcTrDiagId }
DESCRIPTION
"The expert system has determined that the connection has received
too many failed logins."
::= 1052

END

7.7 Incompatible Private Enterprise MIBs

SNMP's popularity has encouraged numerous vendors to incorporate the protocol and its functions into their products. Unfortunately, any time more than one vendor gets involved in a system, incompatibilities can arise, as illustrated in this example (see Figure 7-7).

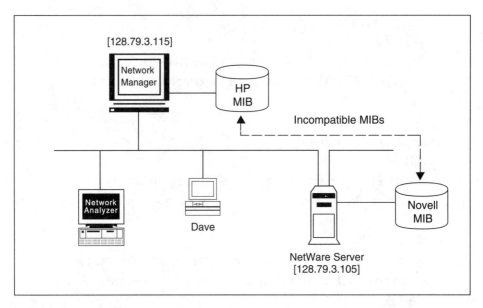

Figure 7-7. Incompatible private enterprise MIBs

The manager in this case is a Hewlett-Packard OpenView console, and the agent is a Novell file server running NetWare v3.11 with the TCP/IP and SNMP options. The manager requests the value of a specific object from the agent in Frame 1; the response is "no such name." The details of the captured frames identify what happened (see Trace 7.7).

In the first IP datagram (Frame 1), the manager's SNMP process includes Identification = 29913 to identify the message. Note that the HP manager assigned Source port = 4837 on its host and used the Destination port = 161, the standard SNMP port, for the agent's host. Also note that the Community name = public. The SNMP GetRequest PDU has a Request ID = 1840, which is used to correlate this request with the agent's response. The object in question is from the private enterprise tree {1.3.6.1.4.1} and is further identified as belonging to the Hewlett-Packard enterprise {1.3.6.1.4.1.11}. The specific object is {1.3.6.1.4.1.11.2.3.1.1.3.0} or {HP 2.3.1.1.3.0}, which identifies the CPU utilization. (Note that the network analyzer is programmed to identify the HP subtree {1.3.6.1.4.1.11}, but not the exact object. We know that this object is CPU utilization from looking into the details of HP's private MIB.)

The agent responds in Frame 2. Note that the agent uses a different Identification (22662) for the IP datagram. This is not a problem, since IP processes of the manager and agent are independent. The agent correctly designates the Destination port (4837) within its UDP header, which sends the SNMP reply to the manager's SNMP process. The agent's message contains the community name (public) and the Request ID (1840) that correlate with the manager's request. The last two fields provide a clue to the problem: the Error Status = 2 (no such name) and the Error Index = 1. These specify that the object name given in the GetRequest was unknown to the agent, and that the first object specified contained the error. When you consider that the HP manager was asking a Novell server for its CPU utilization, the confusion isn't surprising. Thus, while both manager and agent support MIB-II, their private enterprise MIBs are incompatible. This is another example of systems that are standards based, yet incompatible.

Trace 7.7. Inconsistent private enterprise MIBs

Sniffer Network Analyzer data 5-Oct at 09:42:54, file PRVMIB2.ENC Pg 1

```
--------------------------------------- Frame 1 ---------------------------------------
DLC: ----- DLC Header -----
DLC:
DLC: Frame 1 arrived at 09:43:20.8073; Frame size is 87 (0057 hex) bytes.
DLC: Destination = Station H-P  133ADE
DLC: Source   = Station H-P  17B65F
DLC: Ethertype = 0800 (IP)
DLC:
IP:  ----- IP Header -----
IP:
IP:  Version = 4, header length = 20 bytes
IP:  Type of service = 00
IP:     000. .... = routine
IP:     ...0 .... = normal delay
IP:     .... 0... = normal throughput
IP:     .... .0.. = normal reliability
IP:  Total length = 73 bytes
```

```
IP:  Identification = 29913
IP:  Flags = 0X
IP:  .0.. .... = may fragment
IP:  ..0. .... = last fragment
IP:  Fragment offset = 0 bytes
IP:  Time to live = 30 seconds/hops
IP:  Protocol = 17 (UDP)
IP:  Header checksum = 2051 (correct)
IP:  Source address = [128.79.3.115], Manager
IP:  Destination address = [128.79.3.105], Agent
IP:  No options
IP:
UDP: ----- UDP Header -----
UDP:
UDP: Source port = 4837 (SNMP)
UDP: Destination port = 161
UDP: Length = 53
UDP: Checksum = CBCC (correct)
UDP:
SNMP: ----- Simple Network Management Protocol (Version 1) -----
SNMP:
SNMP: Version = 0
SNMP: Community = public
SNMP: Command = Get request
SNMP: Request ID = 1840
SNMP: Error status = 0 (No error)
SNMP: Error index = 0
SNMP:
SNMP: Object = {1.3.6.1.4.1.11.2.3.1.1.3.0} (HP.2.3.1.1.3.0)
SNMP: Value = NULL
SNMP:
```

```
------------------------------------- Frame 2 -------------------------------------
DLC: ----- DLC Header -----
DLC:
DLC: Frame 2 arrived at 09:43:20.8093; Frame size is 88 (0058 hex) bytes.
DLC: Destination = Station H-P  17B65F
DLC: Source   = Station H-P  133ADE
DLC: Ethertype = 0800 (IP)
DLC:
IP:  ----- IP Header -----
IP:
IP:  Version = 4, header length = 20 bytes
IP:  Type of service = 00
IP:    000. .... = routine
IP:    ...0 .... = normal delay
IP:    .... 0... = normal throughput
IP:    .... .0.. = normal reliability
IP:  Total length = 73 bytes
IP:  Identification = 22662
IP:  Flags = 0X
IP:  .0.. .... = may fragment
IP:  ..0. .... = last fragment
IP:  Fragment offset = 0 bytes
IP:  Time to live = 128 seconds/hops
IP:  Protocol = 17 (UDP)
IP:  Header checksum = DAA3 (correct)
IP:  Source address = [128.79.3.105], Agent
IP:  Destination address = [128.79.3.115], Manager
IP:  No options
IP:
UDP: ----- UDP Header -----
UDP:
```

```
UDP: Source port = 161 (SNMP)
UDP: Destination port = 4837
UDP: Length = 53
UDP: No checksum
UDP:
SNMP: ----- Simple Network Management Protocol (Version 1) -----
SNMP:
SNMP: Version = 0
SNMP: Community = public
SNMP: Command = Get response
SNMP: Request ID = 1840
SNMP: Error status = 2 (No such name)
SNMP: Error index = 1
SNMP:
SNMP: Object = {1.3.6.1.4.1.11.2.3.1.1.3.0} (HP.2.3.1.1.3.0)
SNMP: Value = NULL
SNMP:
```

7.8 Proper Handling of an Invalid Object Identifier (OID)

Chapters 2 and 3 discussed the ASN.1 encodings for objects within the SNMP MIBs. These encodings are based on a tree structure, and specific object identifiers (OIDs) locate the positions of objects on the tree. Since these OIDs are sequences of numbers, a mistake of just one digit renders the sequence invalid. This example shows how an agent responds to a manager's mistake.

In this example, the manager wishes to obtain the value of the system description (see Figure 7-8 and Trace 7.8a). The first time the request is made (Frame 1), a correct response is returned (Frame 3). The second request (Frame 4) is unsuccessful (Frame 5). The details of the SNMP messages (Trace 7.8b) reveal that an invalid OID caused the problem.

In the first GetRequest (Frame 1 of Trace 7.8b), the OID given for sysDescr is {1.3.6.1.2.1.1.1.0}. This OID consists of the prefix {1.3.6.1.2.1.1.1} and an instance (.0). Recall that an instance of .0 indicates a scalar object, that is, one that occurs only once. (Columnar objects may have multiple instances, requiring a suffix of .2, .3, .4, and so on. In these cases, the suffix identifies the specific instance of interest.) In Frame 3, you can see that the GetResponse returns:

Value = /usr3/wf/wf.rel/v5.75/wf.pj/proto.ss/ace_test.p/.

So far, so good.

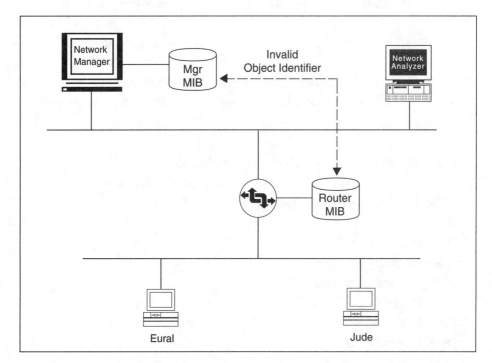

Figure 7-8. Invalid Object Identifier (OID)

Now, as an experiment, the network administrator issues another GetRequest (Frame 4), which returns an error (Frame 5). The details show why this problem occurred. The GetRequest contains an invalid OID {1.3.6.1.3.1.1.1.1}, otherwise known as sysDescr.1. Since this is a scalar, not a tabular, object the ASN.1 syntax is invalid. The response returned in Frame 5 indicates this error: No such name. Thus, the agent provided a proper response for an OID that was not within its MIB.

Trace 7.8a. Handling an invalid object identifier (summary)

Sniffer Network Analyzer data 16-Nov at 17:43:32, file 7-15.ENC, Pg 1

SUMMARY	Delta T	Destination	Source	Summary
1		Router	Manager 146	SNMP Get sysDescr
2	0.0488	Router	SGI 020C5D	ARP R PA=[XXX.YYY.3.146] HA=080069020C5D PRO=IP
3	0.0031	Manager 146	Router	SNMP GetReply sysDescr = /usr3/wf/wf.rel/v5.75 /wf.pj/proto.ss /ace_test.p/
4	7.2153	Router	Manager 146	SNMP Get sysDescr
5	0.0421	Manager 146	Router	SNMP GetReply No such name sysDescr

Trace 7.8b. Handling an invalid object identifier (details)
--------------------------------------- Frame 1 ---------------------------------------
SNMP: ----- Simple Network Management Protocol (Version 1) -----
SNMP:
SNMP: Version = 0
SNMP: Community = xyzsnmp
SNMP: Command = Get request
SNMP: Request ID = 13227000
SNMP: Error status = 0 (No error)
SNMP: Error index = 0
SNMP:
SNMP: Object = {1.3.6.1.2.1.1.1.0} (sysDescr.0)
SNMP: Value = NULL
SNMP:

--------------------------------------- Frame 3 ---------------------------------------
SNMP: ----- Simple Network Management Protocol (Version 1) -----
SNMP:
SNMP: Version = 0

SNMP: Community = xyzsnmp
SNMP: Command = Get response
SNMP: Request ID = 13227000
SNMP: Error status = 0 (No error)
SNMP: Error index = 0
SNMP:
SNMP: Object = {1.3.6.1.2.1.1.1.0} (sysDescr.0)
SNMP: Value = /usr3/wf/wf.rel/v5.75/wf.pj/proto.ss/ace_test.p/
SNMP:

-------------------------------------- Frame 4 --------------------------------------
SNMP: ----- Simple Network Management Protocol (Version 1) -----
SNMP:
SNMP: Version = 0
SNMP: Community = xyzsnmp
SNMP: Command = Get request
SNMP: Request ID = 1094416166
SNMP: Error status = 0 (No error)
SNMP: Error index = 0
SNMP:
SNMP: Object = {1.3.6.1.2.1.1.1.1} (sysDescr.1)
SNMP: Value = NULL
SNMP:

-------------------------------------- Frame 5 --------------------------------------
SNMP: ----- Simple Network Management Protocol (Version 1) -----
SNMP:
SNMP: Version = 0
SNMP: Community = xyzsnmp
SNMP: Command = Get response
SNMP: Request ID = 1094416166
SNMP: Error status = 2 (No such name)
SNMP: Error index = 1

```
SNMP:
SNMP: Object = {1.3.6.1.2.1.1.1.1} (sysDescr.1)
SNMP: Value = NULL
SNMP:
```

7.9 Supporting the RMON MIB with a Network Monitor

One of the significant enhancements to distributed network management has been the Remote Monitoring MIB (RMON). Both Ethernet and token ring versions of RMON are available (as discussed in Sections 3.4 and 3.5). RMON extends the reach of the network manager to remote LAN segments located anywhere on that internetwork. The RMON agent can be a simple device that connects to a local LAN segment and gathers statistics on that segment's performance. RMON agents can also be built into internetworking devices such as bridges, routers, and intelligent hubs. The RMON manager could be a software application running on the network management console. This example shows sample statistics that this Ethernet RMON agent can tabulate for the manager (see Figure 7-9).

The Ethernet RMON MIB contains nine groups (review Figure 3-12). The first group maintains a table of statistics, measured on the agent's segment. The second group contains historical information about significant network events. In Trace 7.9a, the manager wishes to retrieve the statistics table and check its values. Frames 86 and 88 transmit the Manager's GetNextRequests, and Frames 87 and 89 contain the RMON agent's responses. Note that only one instance of the etherStatsTable exists, as all of the OIDs in the GetResponse messages (Frames 87 and 89) end with the suffix .1.

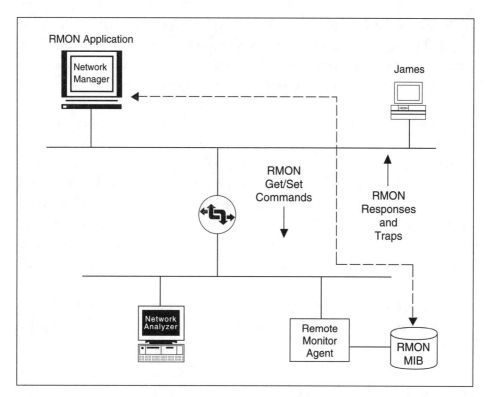

Figure 7-9. Retrieving remote information using the RMON MIB

The details of the agent's response show the statistics that are maintained (see Trace 7.9b). Of particular interest are the number of errored frames (fragments, jabbers, and collisions), which are counted by objects {1.3.6.1.2.1.16.1.1.1.11}, 12, and 13, respectively. Both Frames 87 and 89 reveal values of 21,389 fragments, 4 jabbers, and 163 collisions, respectively, for those objects. (Review the Statistics group of Figure 3-12, the RMON Ethernet MIB.)

Next, the manager issues a Set command followed by a Get for confirmation to store configuration entries in the History Control table {1.3.6.1.2.1.16.2.1}. This table contains various parameters that control the periodic sampling of statistics. The sampled values are stored in the Ether History table {1.3.6.1.2.1.16.2.2}. A two-step process stores the configuration entries. In the first step (Frames 90 and 91), the manager picks a random instance number between 1 and 65535 (52021 in this case), and issues a Set to the historyControlStatus object

{1.3.6.1.2.1.16.2.1.1.7.52021} with Value = 2 (createRequest). The instance number (52021) identifies the table and prevents another manager from creating the same table with the same instance. This SetRequest succeeded, as the GetResponse (Frame 91) was returned with Error Status = 0 (No error).

The second step (Frame 92) stores the configuration entries. Among the values set are the buckets requested (100), the control interval (five seconds), and the control owner (Armon). The RMON agent confirms these values in Frame 93 and indicates a value of 1 (valid) for the historyControlStatus object {1.3.6.1.2.1.16.2.1.1.7.52021}. To confirm the creation of the table, the manager issues a GetRequest for the table objects in Frame 94, which are returned with their values in Frame 95. All objects were created as indicated in the SetRequest command.

In summary, the RMON MIB provides a way to manage remote and directly connected network devices. The next two case studies will explore the capabilities of RMON in greater detail.

Trace 7.9a. RMON MIB objects (summary)

Sniffer Network Analyzer data 30-Mar at 15:01:14, RMON3.ENC, Pg 1

SUMMARY	Delta T	Destination	Source	Summary
86	3.1904	RMON Agent	Manager	SNMP GetNext sysUpTime .. rmon.1.1.1.21 (22 items)
87	0.0079	Manager	RMON Agent	SNMP GetReply sysUpTime .. rmon.1.1.1.21.1 (22 items)
88	0.0813	RMON Agent	Manager	SNMP GetNext sysUpTime .. rmon.1.1.1.21.1 (22 items)
89	0.0301	Manager	RMON Agent	SNMP GetReply sysUpTime .. rmon.2.1.1.1.1 (22 items)
90	0.2267	RMON Agent	Manager	SNMP Set rmon.2.1.1.7.52021 = 2
91	0.0019	Manager	RMON Agent	SNMP GetReply rmon.2.1.1.7.52021 = 2

92	0.3165	RMON Agent	Manager	SNMP Set
				rmon.2.1.1.2.52021
				.. rmon.2.1.1.7.52021
				(5 items)
93	0.0025	Manager	RMON Agent	SNMP GetReply
				rmon.2.1.1.2.52021
				.. rmon.2.1.1.7.52021
				(5 items)
94	0.4172	RMON Agent	Manager	SNMP Get sysUpTime ..
				rmon.2.1.1.7.52021
				(8 items)
95	0.0025	Manager	RMON Agent	SNMP GetReply sysUpTime ..
				rmon.2.1.1.7.52021
				(8 items)

Trace 7.9b. RMON MIB objects (details)

Sniffer Network Analyzer data 30-Mar at 15:01:14, RMON3.ENC, Pg 1

```
------------------------------------ Frame 86 ------------------------------------
NMP: ----- Simple Network Management Protocol (Version 1) -----
SNMP:
SNMP: Version = 0
SNMP: Community = armon
SNMP: Command = Get next request
SNMP: Request ID = 0
SNMP: Error status = 0 (No error)
SNMP: Error index = 0
SNMP:
SNMP: Object = {1.3.6.1.2.1.1.3} (sysUpTime)
SNMP: Value = NULL
SNMP:
SNMP: Object = {1.3.6.1.2.1.16.1.1.1.1} (rmon.1.1.1.1)
SNMP: Value = NULL
SNMP:
```

SNMP: Object = {1.3.6.1.2.1.16.1.1.1.2} (rmon.1.1.1.2)
SNMP: Value = NULL
SNMP:
SNMP: Object = {1.3.6.1.2.1.16.1.1.1.3} (rmon.1.1.1.3)
SNMP: Value = NULL
SNMP:
SNMP: Object = {1.3.6.1.2.1.16.1.1.1.4} (rmon.1.1.1.4)
SNMP: Value = NULL
SNMP:
SNMP: Object = {1.3.6.1.2.1.16.1.1.1.5} (rmon.1.1.1.5)
SNMP: Value = NULL
SNMP:
SNMP: Object = {1.3.6.1.2.1.16.1.1.1.6} (rmon.1.1.1.6)
SNMP: Value = NULL
SNMP:
SNMP: Object = {1.3.6.1.2.1.16.1.1.1.7} (rmon.1.1.1.7)
SNMP: Value = NULL
SNMP:
SNMP: Object = {1.3.6.1.2.1.16.1.1.1.8} (rmon.1.1.1.8)
SNMP: Value = NULL
SNMP:
SNMP: Object = {1.3.6.1.2.1.16.1.1.1.9} (rmon.1.1.1.9)
SNMP: Value = NULL
SNMP:
SNMP: Object = {1.3.6.1.2.1.16.1.1.1.10} (rmon.1.1.1.10)
SNMP: Value = NULL
SNMP:
SNMP: Object = {1.3.6.1.2.1.16.1.1.1.11} (rmon.1.1.1.11)
SNMP: Value = NULL
SNMP:
SNMP: Object = {1.3.6.1.2.1.16.1.1.1.12} (rmon.1.1.1.12)
SNMP: Value = NULL
SNMP:
SNMP: Object = {1.3.6.1.2.1.16.1.1.1.13} (rmon.1.1.1.13)
SNMP: Value = NULL

SNMP:
SNMP: Object = {1.3.6.1.2.1.16.1.1.1.14} (rmon.1.1.1.14)
SNMP: Value = NULL
SNMP:
SNMP: Object = {1.3.6.1.2.1.16.1.1.1.15} (rmon.1.1.1.15)
SNMP: Value = NULL
SNMP:
SNMP: Object = {1.3.6.1.2.1.16.1.1.1.16} (rmon.1.1.1.16)
SNMP: Value = NULL
SNMP:
SNMP: Object = {1.3.6.1.2.1.16.1.1.1.17} (rmon.1.1.1.17)
SNMP: Value = NULL
SNMP:
SNMP: Object = {1.3.6.1.2.1.16.1.1.1.18} (rmon.1.1.1.18)
SNMP: Value = NULL
SNMP:
SNMP: Object = {1.3.6.1.2.1.16.1.1.1.19} (rmon.1.1.1.19)
SNMP: Value = NULL
SNMP:
SNMP: Object = {1.3.6.1.2.1.16.1.1.1.20} (rmon.1.1.1.20)
SNMP: Value = NULL
SNMP:
SNMP: Object = {1.3.6.1.2.1.16.1.1.1.21} (rmon.1.1.1.21)
SNMP: Value = NULL
SNMP:

-- Frame 87 --
SNMP: ----- Simple Network Management Protocol (Version 1) -----
SNMP:
SNMP: Version = 0
SNMP: Community = armon
SNMP: Command = Get response
SNMP: Request ID = 0
SNMP: Error status = 0 (No error)
SNMP: Error index = 0

365

SNMP:
SNMP: Object = {1.3.6.1.2.1.1.3.0} (sysUpTime.0)
SNMP: Value = 10132171 hundredths of a second
SNMP:
SNMP: Object = {1.3.6.1.2.1.16.1.1.1.1.1} (rmon.1.1.1.1.1)
SNMP: Value = 1
SNMP:
SNMP: Object = {1.3.6.1.2.1.16.1.1.1.2.1} (rmon.1.1.1.2.1)
SNMP: Value = {1.3.6.1.2.1.2.2.1.1.1}
SNMP:
SNMP: Object = {1.3.6.1.2.1.16.1.1.1.3.1} (rmon.1.1.1.3.1)
SNMP: Value = 0 (counter)
SNMP:
SNMP: Object = {1.3.6.1.2.1.16.1.1.1.4.1} (rmon.1.1.1.4.1)
SNMP: Value = 1557016926 (counter)
SNMP:
SNMP: Object = {1.3.6.1.2.1.16.1.1.1.5.1} (rmon.1.1.1.5.1)
SNMP: Value = 7705082 (counter)
SNMP:
SNMP: Object = {1.3.6.1.2.1.16.1.1.1.6.1} (rmon.1.1.1.6.1)
SNMP: Value = 272349 (counter)
SNMP:
SNMP: Object = {1.3.6.1.2.1.16.1.1.1.7.1} (rmon.1.1.1.7.1)
SNMP: Value = 20682 (counter)
SNMP:
SNMP: Object = {1.3.6.1.2.1.16.1.1.1.8.1} (rmon.1.1.1.8.1)
SNMP: Value = 2082 (counter)
SNMP:
SNMP: Object = {1.3.6.1.2.1.16.1.1.1.9.1} (rmon.1.1.1.9.1)
SNMP: Value = 0 (counter)
SNMP:
SNMP: Object = {1.3.6.1.2.1.16.1.1.1.10.1} (rmon.1.1.1.10.1)
SNMP: Value = 0 (counter)
SNMP:

SNMP: Object = {1.3.6.1.2.1.16.1.1.1.11.1} (rmon.1.1.1.11.1)
SNMP: Value = 21389 (counter)
SNMP:
SNMP: Object = {1.3.6.1.2.1.16.1.1.1.12.1} (rmon.1.1.1.12.1)
SNMP: Value = 4 (counter)
SNMP:
SNMP: Object = {1.3.6.1.2.1.16.1.1.1.13.1} (rmon.1.1.1.13.1)
SNMP: Value = 163 (counter)
SNMP:
SNMP: Object = {1.3.6.1.2.1.16.1.1.1.14.1} (rmon.1.1.1.14.1)
SNMP: Value = 2425300 (counter)
SNMP:
SNMP: Object = {1.3.6.1.2.1.16.1.1.1.15.1} (rmon.1.1.1.15.1)
SNMP: Value = 3309942 (counter)
SNMP:
SNMP: Object = {1.3.6.1.2.1.16.1.1.1.16.1} (rmon.1.1.1.16.1)
SNMP: Value = 448315 (counter)
SNMP:
SNMP: Object = {1.3.6.1.2.1.16.1.1.1.17.1} (rmon.1.1.1.17.1)
SNMP: Value = 94386 (counter)
SNMP:
SNMP: Object = {1.3.6.1.2.1.16.1.1.1.18.1} (rmon.1.1.1.18.1)
SNMP: Value = 1019509 (counter)
SNMP:
SNMP: Object = {1.3.6.1.2.1.16.1.1.1.19.1} (rmon.1.1.1.19.1)
SNMP: Value = 386237 (counter)
SNMP:
SNMP: Object = {1.3.6.1.2.1.16.1.1.1.20.1} (rmon.1.1.1.20.1)
SNMP: Value = monitor
SNMP:
SNMP: Object = {1.3.6.1.2.1.16.1.1.1.21.1} (rmon.1.1.1.21.1)
SNMP: Value = 1
SNMP:

```
-------------------------------------- Frame 88 --------------------------------------
SNMP: ----- Simple Network Management Protocol (Version 1) -----
SNMP:
SNMP: Version = 0
SNMP: Community = armon
SNMP: Command = Get next request
SNMP: Request ID = 0
SNMP: Error status = 0 (No error)
SNMP: Error index = 0
SNMP:
SNMP: Object = {1.3.6.1.2.1.1.3} (sysUpTime)
SNMP: Value = NULL
SNMP:
SNMP: Object = {1.3.6.1.2.1.16.1.1.1.1.1} (rmon.1.1.1.1.1)
SNMP: Value = NULL
SNMP:
SNMP: Object = {1.3.6.1.2.1.16.1.1.1.2.1} (rmon.1.1.1.2.1)
SNMP: Value = NULL
SNMP:
SNMP: Object = {1.3.6.1.2.1.16.1.1.1.3.1} (rmon.1.1.1.3.1)
SNMP: Value = NULL
SNMP:
SNMP: Object = {1.3.6.1.2.1.16.1.1.1.4.1} (rmon.1.1.1.4.1)
SNMP: Value = NULL
SNMP:
SNMP: Object = {1.3.6.1.2.1.16.1.1.1.5.1} (rmon.1.1.1.5.1)
SNMP: Value = NULL
SNMP:
SNMP: Object = {1.3.6.1.2.1.16.1.1.1.6.1} (rmon.1.1.1.6.1)
SNMP: Value = NULL
SNMP:
SNMP: Object = {1.3.6.1.2.1.16.1.1.1.7.1} (rmon.1.1.1.7.1)
SNMP: Value = NULL
SNMP:
```

SNMP: Object = {1.3.6.1.2.1.16.1.1.1.8.1} (rmon.1.1.1.8.1)
SNMP: Value = NULL
SNMP:
SNMP: Object = {1.3.6.1.2.1.16.1.1.1.9.1} (rmon.1.1.1.9.1)
SNMP: Value = NULL
SNMP:
SNMP: Object = {1.3.6.1.2.1.16.1.1.1.10.1} (rmon.1.1.1.10.1)
SNMP: Value = NULL
SNMP:
SNMP: Object = {1.3.6.1.2.1.16.1.1.1.11.1} (rmon.1.1.1.11.1)
SNMP: Value = NULL
SNMP:
SNMP: Object = {1.3.6.1.2.1.16.1.1.1.12.1} (rmon.1.1.1.12.1)
SNMP: Value = NULL
SNMP:
SNMP: Object = {1.3.6.1.2.1.16.1.1.1.13.1} (rmon.1.1.1.13.1)
SNMP: Value = NULL
SNMP:
SNMP: Object = {1.3.6.1.2.1.16.1.1.1.14.1} (rmon.1.1.1.14.1)
SNMP: Value = NULL
SNMP:
SNMP: Object = {1.3.6.1.2.1.16.1.1.1.15.1} (rmon.1.1.1.15.1)
SNMP: Value = NULL
SNMP:
SNMP: Object = {1.3.6.1.2.1.16.1.1.1.16.1} (rmon.1.1.1.16.1)
SNMP: Value = NULL
SNMP:
SNMP: Object = {1.3.6.1.2.1.16.1.1.1.17.1} (rmon.1.1.1.17.1)
SNMP: Value = NULL
SNMP:
SNMP: Object = {1.3.6.1.2.1.16.1.1.1.18.1} (rmon.1.1.1.18.1)
SNMP: Value = NULL
SNMP:
SNMP: Object = {1.3.6.1.2.1.16.1.1.1.19.1} (rmon.1.1.1.19.1)

SNMP: Value = NULL
SNMP:
SNMP: Object = {1.3.6.1.2.1.16.1.1.1.20.1} (rmon.1.1.1.20.1)
SNMP: Value = NULL
SNMP:
SNMP: Object = {1.3.6.1.2.1.16.1.1.1.21.1} (rmon.1.1.1.21.1)
SNMP: Value = NULL
SNMP:

------------------------------------- Frame 89 -------------------------------------
SNMP: ----- Simple Network Management Protocol (Version 1) -----
SNMP:
SNMP: Version = 0
SNMP: Community = armon
SNMP: Command = Get response
SNMP: Request ID = 0
SNMP: Error status = 0 (No error)
SNMP: Error index = 0
SNMP:
SNMP: Object = {1.3.6.1.2.1.1.3.0} (sysUpTime.0)
SNMP: Value = 10132180 hundredths of a second
SNMP:
SNMP: Object = {1.3.6.1.2.1.16.1.1.1.2.1} (rmon.1.1.1.2.1)
SNMP: Value = {1.3.6.1.2.1.2.2.1.1.1}
SNMP:
SNMP: Object = {1.3.6.1.2.1.16.1.1.1.3.1} (rmon.1.1.1.3.1)
SNMP: Value = 0 (counter)
SNMP:
SNMP: Object = {1.3.6.1.2.1.16.1.1.1.4.1} (rmon.1.1.1.4.1)
SNMP: Value = 1557018586 (counter)
SNMP:
SNMP: Object = {1.3.6.1.2.1.16.1.1.1.5.1} (rmon.1.1.1.5.1)
SNMP: Value = 7705087 (counter)
SNMP:
SNMP: Object = {1.3.6.1.2.1.16.1.1.1.6.1} (rmon.1.1.1.6.1)

SNMP: Value = 272349 (counter)
SNMP:
SNMP: Object = {1.3.6.1.2.1.16.1.1.1.7.1} (rmon.1.1.1.7.1)
SNMP: Value = 20682 (counter)
SNMP:
SNMP: Object = {1.3.6.1.2.1.16.1.1.1.8.1} (rmon.1.1.1.8.1)
SNMP: Value = 2082 (counter)
SNMP:
SNMP: Object = {1.3.6.1.2.1.16.1.1.1.9.1} (rmon.1.1.1.9.1)
SNMP: Value = 0 (counter)
SNMP:
SNMP: Object = {1.3.6.1.2.1.16.1.1.1.10.1} (rmon.1.1.1.10.1)
SNMP: Value = 0 (counter)
SNMP:
SNMP: Object = {1.3.6.1.2.1.16.1.1.1.11.1} (rmon.1.1.1.11.1)
SNMP: Value = 21389 (counter)
SNMP:
SNMP: Object = {1.3.6.1.2.1.16.1.1.1.12.1} (rmon.1.1.1.12.1)
SNMP: Value = 4 (counter)
SNMP:
SNMP: Object = {1.3.6.1.2.1.16.1.1.1.13.1} (rmon.1.1.1.13.1)
SNMP: Value = 163 (counter)
SNMP:
SNMP: Object = {1.3.6.1.2.1.16.1.1.1.14.1} (rmon.1.1.1.14.1)
SNMP: Value = 2425301 (counter)
SNMP:
SNMP: Object = {1.3.6.1.2.1.16.1.1.1.15.1} (rmon.1.1.1.15.1)
SNMP: Value = 3309943 (counter)
SNMP:
SNMP: Object = {1.3.6.1.2.1.16.1.1.1.16.1} (rmon.1.1.1.16.1)
SNMP: Value = 448315 (counter)
SNMP:
SNMP: Object = {1.3.6.1.2.1.16.1.1.1.17.1} (rmon.1.1.1.17.1)
SNMP: Value = 94388 (counter)
SNMP:

SNMP: Object = {1.3.6.1.2.1.16.1.1.1.18.1} (rmon.1.1.1.18.1)
SNMP: Value = 1019510 (counter)
SNMP:
SNMP: Object = {1.3.6.1.2.1.16.1.1.1.19.1} (rmon.1.1.1.19.1)
SNMP: Value = 386237 (counter)
SNMP:
SNMP: Object = {1.3.6.1.2.1.16.1.1.1.20.1} (rmon.1.1.1.20.1)
SNMP: Value = monitor
SNMP:
SNMP: Object = {1.3.6.1.2.1.16.1.1.1.21.1} (rmon.1.1.1.21.1)
SNMP: Value = 1
SNMP:
SNMP: Object = {1.3.6.1.2.1.16.2.1.1.1.1} (rmon.2.1.1.1.1)
SNMP: Value = 1
SNMP:

-------------------------------------- Frame 90 --------------------------------------
SNMP: ----- Simple Network Management Protocol (Version 1) -----
SNMP:
SNMP: Version = 0
SNMP: Community = armon
SNMP: Command = Set request
SNMP: Request ID = 0
SNMP: Error status = 0 (No error)
SNMP: Error index = 0
SNMP:
SNMP: Object = {1.3.6.1.2.1.16.2.1.1.7.52021} (rmon.2.1.1.7.52021)
SNMP: Value = 2
SNMP:

-------------------------------------- Frame 91 --------------------------------------
SNMP: ----- Simple Network Management Protocol (Version 1) -----
SNMP:
SNMP: Version = 0
SNMP: Community = armon

SNMP: Command = Get response
SNMP: Request ID = 0
SNMP: Error status = 0 (No error)
SNMP: Error index = 0
SNMP:
SNMP: Object = {1.3.6.1.2.1.16.2.1.1.7.52021} (rmon.2.1.1.7.52021)
SNMP: Value = 2
SNMP:

------------------------------------- Frame 92 -------------------------------------
SNMP: ----- Simple Network Management Protocol (Version 1) -----
SNMP:
SNMP: Version = 0
SNMP: Community = armon
SNMP: Command = Set request
SNMP: Request ID = 0
SNMP: Error status = 0 (No error)
SNMP: Error index = 0
SNMP:
SNMP: Object = {1.3.6.1.2.1.16.2.1.1.2.52021} (rmon.2.1.1.2.52021)
SNMP: Value = {1.3.6.1.2.1.2.2.1.1.1}
SNMP:
SNMP: Object = {1.3.6.1.2.1.16.2.1.1.3.52021} (rmon.2.1.1.3.52021)
SNMP: Value = 100
SNMP:
SNMP: Object = {1.3.6.1.2.1.16.2.1.1.5.52021} (rmon.2.1.1.5.52021)
SNMP: Value = 5
SNMP:
SNMP: Object = {1.3.6.1.2.1.16.2.1.1.6.52021} (rmon.2.1.1.6.52021)
SNMP: Value = Armon
SNMP:
SNMP: Object = {1.3.6.1.2.1.16.2.1.1.7.52021} (rmon.2.1.1.7.52021)
SNMP: Value = 1
SNMP:

```
------------------------------------ Frame 93 --------------------------------------
SNMP: ----- Simple Network Management Protocol (Version 1) -----
SNMP:
SNMP: Version = 0
SNMP: Community = armon
SNMP: Command = Get response
SNMP: Request ID = 0
SNMP: Error status = 0 (No error)
SNMP: Error index = 0
SNMP:
SNMP: Object = {1.3.6.1.2.1.16.2.1.1.2.52021} (rmon.2.1.1.2.52021)
SNMP: Value = {1.3.6.1.2.1.2.2.1.1.1}
SNMP:
SNMP: Object = {1.3.6.1.2.1.16.2.1.1.3.52021} (rmon.2.1.1.3.52021)
SNMP: Value = 100
SNMP:
SNMP: Object = {1.3.6.1.2.1.16.2.1.1.5.52021} (rmon.2.1.1.5.52021)
SNMP: Value = 5
SNMP:
SNMP: Object = {1.3.6.1.2.1.16.2.1.1.6.52021} (rmon.2.1.1.6.52021)
SNMP: Value = Armon
SNMP:
SNMP: Object = {1.3.6.1.2.1.16.2.1.1.7.52021} (rmon.2.1.1.7.52021)
SNMP: Value = 1
SNMP:


------------------------------------ Frame 94 --------------------------------------
SNMP: ----- Simple Network Management Protocol (Version 1) -----
SNMP:
SNMP: Version = 0
SNMP: Community = armon
SNMP: Command = Get request
SNMP: Request ID = 0
SNMP: Error status = 0 (No error)
```

SNMP: Error index = 0
SNMP:
SNMP: Object = {1.3.6.1.2.1.1.3.0} (sysUpTime.0)
SNMP: Value = NULL
SNMP:
SNMP: Object = {1.3.6.1.2.1.16.2.1.1.1.52021} (rmon.2.1.1.1.52021)
SNMP: Value = NULL
SNMP:
SNMP: Object = {1.3.6.1.2.1.16.2.1.1.2.52021} (rmon.2.1.1.2.52021)
SNMP: Value = NULL
SNMP:
SNMP: Object = {1.3.6.1.2.1.16.2.1.1.3.52021} (rmon.2.1.1.3.52021)
SNMP: Value = NULL
SNMP:
SNMP: Object = {1.3.6.1.2.1.16.2.1.1.4.52021} (rmon.2.1.1.4.52021)
SNMP: Value = NULL
SNMP:
SNMP: Object = {1.3.6.1.2.1.16.2.1.1.5.52021} (rmon.2.1.1.5.52021)
SNMP: Value = NULL
SNMP:
SNMP: Object = {1.3.6.1.2.1.16.2.1.1.6.52021} (rmon.2.1.1.6.52021)
SNMP: Value = NULL
SNMP:
SNMP: Object = {1.3.6.1.2.1.16.2.1.1.7.52021} (rmon.2.1.1.7.52021)
SNMP: Value = NULL
SNMP:

------------------------------------- Frame 95 -------------------------------------
SNMP: ----- Simple Network Management Protocol (Version 1) -----
SNMP:
SNMP: Version = 0
SNMP: Community = armon
SNMP: Command = Get response
SNMP: Request ID = 0

```
SNMP: Error status = 0 (No error)
SNMP: Error index = 0
SNMP:
SNMP: Object = {1.3.6.1.2.1.1.3.0} (sysUpTime.0)
SNMP: Value = 10132279 hundredths of a second
SNMP:
SNMP: Object = {1.3.6.1.2.1.16.2.1.1.1.52021} (rmon.2.1.1.1.52021)
SNMP: Value = 52021
SNMP:
SNMP: Object = {1.3.6.1.2.1.16.2.1.1.2.52021} (rmon.2.1.1.2.52021)
SNMP: Value = {1.3.6.1.2.1.2.2.1.1.1}
SNMP:
SNMP: Object = {1.3.6.1.2.1.16.2.1.1.3.52021} (rmon.2.1.1.3.52021)
SNMP: Value = 100
SNMP:
SNMP: Object = {1.3.6.1.2.1.16.2.1.1.4.52021} (rmon.2.1.1.4.52021)
SNMP: Value = 100
SNMP:
SNMP: Object = {1.3.6.1.2.1.16.2.1.1.5.52021} (rmon.2.1.1.5.52021)
SNMP: Value = 5
SNMP:
SNMP: Object = {1.3.6.1.2.1.16.2.1.1.6.52021} (rmon.2.1.1.6.52021)
SNMP: Value = Armon
SNMP:
SNMP: Object = {1.3.6.1.2.1.16.2.1.1.7.52021} (rmon.2.1.1.7.52021)
SNMP: Value = 1
SNMP:
```

7.10 Measuring Host Statistics with RMON

To diagnose many network problems, it is necessary to look beyond the overall health of the network and focus on the operation of individual devices. The RMON hosts, hostTopN, and matrix groups are designed for those purposes: they look at host operation, hosts whose operation tops a list of particular statistics, and a matrix of host-to-host communication, respectively. In this example, we will use the capabilities of RMON to look at some host-specific characteristics, and then we'll zoom in on one particular host to discover its communications characteristics (see Figure 7-10).

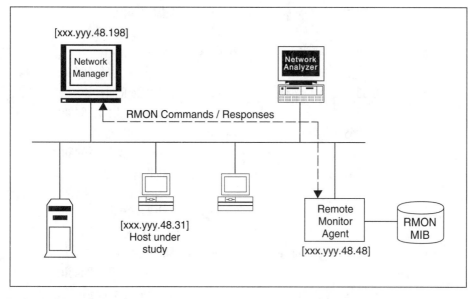

Figure 7-10. Gathering host statistics

A summary of the network operation shows a variety of RMON activities (Trace 7.10a). Note that Frames 1–2 are accessing information from the host-Table, {1.3.6.1.2.1.16.4.2} or {rmon 4.2}; Frames 3–32 are accessing information from the matrixSDTable {1.3.6.1.2.1.16.6.2} or {rmon 6.2}; and Frame 33–52 are accessing information from the matrixDSTable, {1.3.6.1.2.16.6.3 } or {rmon 6.3}. (As a review, the hostTable contains statistical data about a particular host; the matrixSDTable contains statistics for a particular conversation between two addresses, indexed by source and destination MAC addresses; and the matrixDSTable contains statistics for a particular conversation between two addresses, but this time, indexed by destination and source MAC addresses.)

Trace 7.10a. RMON host information (summary)

Sniffer Network Analyzer data from 25-Feb at 17:24:44, file TOPNIPCN.ENC, Page 1

SUMMARY	Delta T	Destination	Source	Summary
M 1		Probe	Manager	SNMP Get
				rmon.4.2.1.1.20480...
2	0.0032	Manager	Probe	SNMP GetReply
				rmon.4.2.1.1.20480...
3	0.0052	Probe	Manager	SNMP GetNext
				rmon.6.2.1.1.20480...
4	0.0032	Manager	Probe	SNMP GetReply
				rmon.6.2.1.1.20480...
5	0.0049	Probe	Manager	SNMP GetNext
				rmon.6.2.1.1.20480...
6	0.0031	Manager	Probe	SNMP GetReply
				rmon.6.2.1.1.20480...
7	0.0047	Probe	Manager	SNMP GetNext
				rmon.6.2.1.1.20480...
8	0.0031	Manager	Probe	SNMP GetReply
				rmon.6.2.1.1.20480...
9	0.0046	Probe	Manager	SNMP GetNext
				rmon.6.2.1.1.20480...
10	0.0032	Manager	Probe	SNMP GetReply
				rmon.6.2.1.1.20480...
11	0.0047	Probe	Manager	SNMP GetNext
				rmon.6.2.1.1.20480...
12	0.0031	Manager	Probe	SNMP GetReply
				rmon.6.2.1.1.20480...
13	0.0048	Probe	Manager	SNMP GetNext
				rmon.6.2.1.1.20480...
14	0.0030	Manager	Probe	SNMP GetReply
				rmon.6.2.1.1.20480...
15	0.0047	Probe	Manager	SNMP GetNext
				rmon.6.2.1.1.20480...

16	0.0031	Manager	Probe	SNMP GetReply
				rmon.6.2.1.1.20480...
17	0.0046	Probe	Manager	SNMP GetNext
				rmon.6.2.1.1.20480...
18	0.0032	Manager	Probe	SNMP GetReply
				rmon.6.2.1.1.20480...
19	0.0048	Probe	Manager	SNMP GetNext
				rmon.6.2.1.1.20480...
20	0.0031	Manager	Probe	SNMP GetReply
				rmon.6.2.1.1.20480...
21	0.0047	Probe	Manager	SNMP GetNext
				rmon.6.2.1.1.20480...
22	0.0031	Manager	Probe	SNMP GetReply
				rmon.6.2.1.1.20480...
23	0.0049	Probe	Manager	SNMP GetNext
				rmon.6.2.1.1.20480...
24	0.0030	Manager	Probe	SNMP GetReply
				rmon.6.2.1.1.20480...
25	0.0047	Probe	Manager	SNMP GetNext
				rmon.6.2.1.1.20480...
26	0.0031	Manager	Probe	SNMP GetReply
				rmon.6.2.1.1.20480...
27	0.0047	Probe	Manager	SNMP GetNext
				rmon.6.2.1.1.20480...
28	0.0031	Manager	Probe	SNMP GetReply
				rmon.6.2.1.1.20480.
29	0.0048	Probe	Manager	SNMP GetNext
				rmon.6.2.1.1.20480...
30	0.0030	Manager	Probe	SNMP GetReply
				rmon.6.2.1.1.20480...
31	0.0048	Probe	Manager	SNMP GetNext
				rmon.6.2.1.1.20480.
32	0.0030	Manager	Probe	SNMP GetReply
				rmon.6.2.1.1.20480...

33	0.0048	Probe	Manager	SNMP GetNext rmon.6.3.1.1.20480...
34	0.0030	Manager	Probe	SNMP GetReply rmon.6.3.1.1.20480...
35	0.0047	Probe	Manager	SNMP GetNext rmon.6.3.1.1.20480...
36	0.0031	Manager	Probe	SNMP GetReply rmon.6.3.1.1.20480...
37	0.0046	Probe	Manager	SNMP GetNext rmon.6.3.1.1.20480...
38	0.0032	Manager	Probe	SNMP GetReply rmon.6.3.1.1.20480...
39	0.0047	Probe	Manager	SNMP GetNext rmon.6.3.1.1.20480...
40	0.0031	Manager	Probe	SNMP GetReply rmon.6.3.1.1.20480...
41	0.0047	Probe	Manager	SNMP GetNext rmon.6.3.1.1.20480...
42	0.0031	Manager	Probe	SNMP GetReply rmon.6.3.1.1.20480...
43	0.0046	Probe	Manager	SNMP GetNext rmon.6.3.1.1.20480...
44	0.0032	Manager	Probe	SNMP GetReply rmon.6.3.1.1.20480...
45	0.0047	Probe	Manager	SNMP GetNext rmon.6.3.1.1.20480...
46	0.0031	Manager	Probe	SNMP GetReply rmon.6.3.1.1.20480...
47	0.0047	Probe	Manager	SNMP GetNext rmon.6.3.1.1.20480...
48	0.0031	Manager	Probe	SNMP GetReply rmon.6.3.1.1.20480..
49	0.0049	Probe	Manager	SNMP GetNext mon.6.3.1.1.20480...

50	0.0032	Manager	Probe	SNMP GetReply
				rmon.6.3.1.1.20480...
51	0.0048	Probe	Manager	SNMP GetNext
				rmon.6.3.1.1.20480...
52	0.0031	Manager	Probe	SNMP GetReply
				rmon.6.3.1.1.20480...

Details of the hostTable are shown in Trace 7.10b. Note that the GetRequest (Frame 1), which was issued by the network management application, asks for the values of all objects within the hostTable, plus the value of the sysUpTime object {1.3.6.1.2.1.1.3.0}. The GetNext response (Frame 2) returns the values of these objects (note that in the first ten object names in the following table, the prefix "host" has been deleted for brevity):

Address	CreationOrder	Index	InPkt	OutPkts	InOctets	OutOctets	OutErrors	OutBroadcastPkt	OutMulticastPkts	sysUpTime
F1A1E01F	12	20480	493	710	192789	67601	0	40	0	798171

Note from Trace 7.10b that the index given for each object (20480.6.126.241.XXX.YYY.48.31) is selected by the Console and includes the IP address of the workstation that initiated the request (XXX.YYY.48.31). Also note that the value of the sysUpTime object provides a timestamp for the data in this entry.

Trace 7.10b. RMON hostTable Retrieval

Sniffer Network Analyzer data from 25-Feb at 17:24:44, file TOPNIPCN.ENC, Page 1

```
-------------------------------------- Frame 1 --------------------------------------
SNMP: ----- Simple Network Management Protocol (Version 1) -----
SNMP:
SNMP: Version = 0
SNMP: Community = public
SNMP: Command = Get request
SNMP: Request ID = 1133668601
SNMP: Error status = 0 (No error)
```

SNMP: Error index = 0
SNMP:
SNMP: Object = {1.3.6.1.2.1.16.4.2.1.1.20480.6.126.241.XXX.YYY.48.31}
(rmon.4.2.1.1.20480.6.126. ...
SNMP: Value = NULL
SNMP:
SNMP: Object = {1.3.6.1.2.1.16.4.2.1.2.20480.6.126.241.XXX.YYY.48.31}
(rmon.4.2.1.2.20480.6.126. ...
SNMP: Value = NULL
SNMP:
SNMP: Object = {1.3.6.1.2.1.16.4.2.1.3.20480.6.126.241.XXX.YYY.48.31}
(rmon.4.2.1.3.20480.6.126. ...
SNMP: Value = NULL
SNMP:
SNMP: Object = {1.3.6.1.2.1.16.4.2.1.4.20480.6.126.241.XXX.YYY.48.31}
(rmon.4.2.1.4.20480.6.126. ...
SNMP: Value = NULL
SNMP:
SNMP: Object = {1.3.6.1.2.1.16.4.2.1.5.20480.6.126.241.XXX.YYY.48.31}
(rmon.4.2.1.5.20480.6.126. ...
SNMP: Value = NULL
SNMP:
SNMP: Object = {1.3.6.1.2.1.16.4.2.1.6.20480.6.126.241.XXX.YYY.48.31}
(rmon.4.2.1.6.20480.6.126. ...
SNMP: Value = NULL
SNMP:
SNMP: Object = {1.3.6.1.2.1.16.4.2.1.7.20480.6.126.241.XXX.YYY.48.31}
(rmon.4.2.1.7.20480.6.126. ...
SNMP: Value = NULL
SNMP:
SNMP: Object = {1.3.6.1.2.1.16.4.2.1.8.20480.6.126.241.XXX.YYY.48.31}
(rmon.4.2.1.8.20480.6.126. ...
SNMP: Value = NULL

SNMP:
SNMP: Object = {1.3.6.1.2.1.16.4.2.1.9.20480.6.126.241.XXX.YYY.48.31}
(rmon.4.2.1.9.20480.6.126. ...
SNMP: Value = NULL
SNMP:
SNMP: Object = {1.3.6.1.2.1.16.4.2.1.10.20480.6.126.241.XXX.YYY.48.31}
(rmon.4.2.1.10.20480.6.12 ...
SNMP: Value = NULL
SNMP:
SNMP: Object = {1.3.6.1.2.1.1.3.0} (sysUpTime.0)
SNMP: Value = NULL
SNMP:

----------------------------------- Frame 2 -----------------------------------
SNMP: ----- Simple Network Management Protocol (Version 1) -----
SNMP:
SNMP: Version = 0
SNMP: Community = public
SNMP: Command = Get response
SNMP: Request ID = 1133668601
SNMP: Error status = 0 (No error)
SNMP: Error index = 0
SNMP:
SNMP: Object = {1.3.6.1.2.1.16.4.2.1.1.20480.6.126.241.XXX.YYY.48.31}
(rmon.4.2.1.1.20480.6.126. ...
SNMP: Value = ~<F1A1>E0<1F>
SNMP:
SNMP: Object = {1.3.6.1.2.1.16.4.2.1.2.20480.6.126.241.XXX.YYY.48.31}
(rmon.4.2.1.2.20480.6.126. ...
SNMP: Value = 12
SNMP:
SNMP: Object = {1.3.6.1.2.1.16.4.2.1.3.20480.6.126.241.XXX.YYY.48.31}
(rmon.4.2.1.3.20480.6.126. ...

SNMP: Value = 20480
SNMP:
SNMP: Object = {1.3.6.1.2.1.16.4.2.1.4.20480.6.126.241.XXX.YYY.48.31}
(rmon.4.2.1.4.20480.6.126. ...
SNMP: Value = 493 (counter)
SNMP:
SNMP: Object = {1.3.6.1.2.1.16.4.2.1.5.20480.6.126.241.XXX.YYY.48.31}
(rmon.4.2.1.5.20480.6.126. ...
SNMP: Value = 710 (counter)
SNMP:
SNMP: Object = {1.3.6.1.2.1.16.4.2.1.6.20480.6.126.241.XXX.YYY.48.31}
(rmon.4.2.1.6.20480.6.126. ...
SNMP: Value = 192789 (counter)
SNMP:
SNMP: Object = {1.3.6.1.2.1.16.4.2.1.7.20480.6.126.241.XXX.YYY.48.31}
(rmon.4.2.1.7.20480.6.126. ...
SNMP: Value = 67601 (counter)
SNMP:
SNMP: Object = {1.3.6.1.2.1.16.4.2.1.8.20480.6.126.241.XXX.YYY.48.31}
(rmon.4.2.1.8.20480.6.126. ...
SNMP: Value = 0 (counter)
SNMP:
SNMP: Object = {1.3.6.1.2.1.16.4.2.1.9.20480.6.126.241.XXX.YYY.48.31}
(rmon.4.2.1.9.20480.6.126. ...
SNMP: Value = 40 (counter)
SNMP:
SNMP: Object = {1.3.6.1.2.1.16.4.2.1.10.20480.6.126.241.XXX.YYY.48.31}
(rmon.4.2.1.10.20480.6.12 ...
SNMP: Value = 0 (counter)
SNMP:
SNMP: Object = {1.3.6.1.2.1.1.3.0} (sysUpTime.0)
SNMP: Value = 798171 hundredths of a second
SNMP:

Frames 3–32 retrieve the values of the matrixSDTable, with the retrieval of the first row illustrated in Frames 3–4, the second row in Frames 5–6, the third row in Frames 7–8, and so on, as shown in Trace 7.10c. (As in the previous example, the term "matrix" is deleted from each of the first six object names shown in the column headings for brevity). Notice the change in the values of the sysUpTime object at each table entry:

SDSourceAddress	SDDestAddress	SDIndex	SDPkts	SDOctets	SDErrors	sysUpTime
F1A1E01F	F1A1E0201	20480	27	2361	0	798172
F1A1E01F	F1A1E0202	20480	24	2112	0	798173
F1A1E01F	F1A1E06	20480	1	94	0	798174

Trace 7.10c. RMON matrixSDTable retrieval

Sniffer Network Analyzer data from 25-Feb at 17:24:44, file TOPNIPCN.ENC, Page 1

```
-------------------------------------- Frame 3 --------------------------------------
SNMP: ----- Simple Network Management Protocol (Version 1) -----
SNMP:
SNMP: Version = 0
SNMP: Community = public
SNMP: Command = Get next request
SNMP: Request ID = 1133668602
SNMP: Error status = 0 (No error)
SNMP: Error index = 0
SNMP:
SNMP: Object =
{1.3.6.1.2.1.16.6.2.1.1.20480.6.126.241.XXX.YYY.48.31.6.0.0.0.0.0.0}
(rmon.6.2.1. ...
SNMP: Value  = NULL
SNMP:
```

SNMP: Object =
{1.3.6.1.2.1.16.6.2.1.2.20480.6.126.241.XXX.YYY.48.31.6.0.0.0.0.0.0}
(rmon.6.2.1. ...
SNMP: Value = NULL
SNMP:
SNMP: Object =
{1.3.6.1.2.1.16.6.2.1.3.20480.6.126.241.XXX.YYY.48.31.6.0.0.0.0.0.0}
(rmon.6.2.1. ...
SNMP: Value = NULL
SNMP:
SNMP: Object =
{1.3.6.1.2.1.16.6.2.1.4.20480.6.126.241.XXX.YYY.48.31.6.0.0.0.0.0.0}
(rmon.6.2.1. ...
SNMP: Value = NULL
SNMP:
SNMP: Object =
{1.3.6.1.2.1.16.6.2.1.5.20480.6.126.241.XXX.YYY.48.31.6.0.0.0.0.0.0}
(rmon.6.2.1. ...
SNMP: Value = NULL
SNMP:
SNMP: Object =
{1.3.6.1.2.1.16.6.2.1.6.20480.6.126.241.XXX.YYY.48.31.6.0.0.0.0.0.0}
(rmon.6.2.1. ...
SNMP: Value = NULL
SNMP:
SNMP: Object = {1.3.6.1.2.1.1.3} (sysUpTime)
SNMP: Value = NULL
SNMP:

-------------------------------------- Frame 4 --------------------------------------
SNMP: ----- Simple Network Management Protocol (Version 1) -----
SNMP:
SNMP: Version = 0
SNMP: Community = public

SNMP: Command = Get response
SNMP: Request ID = 1133668602
SNMP: Error status = 0 (No error)
SNMP: Error index = 0
SNMP:
SNMP: Object =
{1.3.6.1.2.1.16.6.2.1.1.20480.6.126.241.XXX.YYY.48.31.6.126.241.XXX.YYY.2.1}
(rmon ...
SNMP: Value = ~<F1A1>E0<1F>
SNMP:
SNMP: Object =
{1.3.6.1.2.1.16.6.2.1.2.20480.6.126.241.XXX.YYY.48.31.6.0.0.0.0.0.0}
(rmon.6.2.1. ...
SNMP: Value = ~<F1A1>E<0201>
SNMP:
SNMP: Object =
{1.3.6.1.2.1.16.6.2.1.3.20480.6.126.241.XXX.YYY.48.31.6.0.0.0.0.0.0}
(rmon.6.2.1. ...
SNMP: Value = 20480
SNMP:
SNMP: Object =
{1.3.6.1.2.1.16.6.2.1.4.20480.6.126.241.XXX.YYY.48.31.6.0.0.0.0.0.0}
(rmon.6.2.1. ...
SNMP: Value = 27 (counter)
SNMP:
SNMP: Object =
{1.3.6.1.2.1.16.6.2.1.5.20480.6.126.241.XXX.YYY.48.31.6.0.0.0.0.0.0}
(rmon.6.2.1. ...
SNMP: Value = 2361 (counter)
SNMP:
SNMP: Object =
{1.3.6.1.2.1.16.6.2.1.6.20480.6.126.241.XXX.YYY.48.31.6.0.0.0.0.0.0}
(rmon.6.2.1. ...
SNMP: Value = 0 (counter)

SNMP:
SNMP: Object = {1.3.6.1.2.1.1.3.0} (sysUpTime.0)
SNMP: Value = 798172 hundredths of a second
SNMP:

-------------------------------------- Frame 5 --------------------------------------
SNMP: ----- Simple Network Management Protocol (Version 1) -----
SNMP:
SNMP: Version = 0
SNMP: Community = public
SNMP: Command = Get next request
SNMP: Request ID = 1133668603
SNMP: Error status = 0 (No error)
SNMP: Error index = 0
SNMP:
SNMP: Object =
{1.3.6.1.2.1.16.6.2.1.1.20480.6.126.241.XXX.YYY.48.31.6.126.241.XXX.YYY.2.1}
(rmon ...
SNMP: Value = NULL
SNMP:
SNMP: Object =
{1.3.6.1.2.1.16.6.2.1.2.20480.6.126.241.XXX.YYY.48.31.6.126.241.XXX.YYY.2.1}
(rmon ...
SNMP: Value = NULL
SNMP:
SNMP: Object =
{1.3.6.1.2.1.16.6.2.1.3.20480.6.126.241.XXX.YYY.48.31.6.126.241.XXX.YYY.2.1}
(rmon ...
SNMP: Value = NULL
SNMP:
SNMP: Object =
{1.3.6.1.2.1.16.6.2.1.4.20480.6.126.241.XXX.YYY.48.31.6.126.241.XXX.YYY.2.1}
(rmon ...
SNMP: Value = NULL

SNMP:
SNMP: Object =
{1.3.6.1.2.1.16.6.2.1.5.20480.6.126.241.XXX.YYY.48.31.6.126.241.XXX.YYY.2.1}
(rmon ...
SNMP: Value = NULL
SNMP:
SNMP: Object =
{1.3.6.1.2.1.16.6.2.1.6.20480.6.126.241.XXX.YYY.48.31.6.126.241.XXX.YYY.2.1}
(rmon ...
SNMP: Value = NULL
SNMP:
SNMP: Object = {1.3.6.1.2.1.1.3} (sysUpTime)
SNMP: Value = NULL
SNMP:

-------------------------------------- Frame 6 --------------------------------------
SNMP: ----- Simple Network Management Protocol (Version 1) -----
SNMP:
SNMP: Version = 0
SNMP: Community = public
SNMP: Command = Get response
SNMP: Request ID = 1133668603
SNMP: Error status = 0 (No error)
SNMP: Error index = 0
SNMP:
SNMP: Object =
{1.3.6.1.2.1.16.6.2.1.1.20480.6.126.241.XXX.YYY.48.31.6.126.241.XXX.YYY.2.2}
(rmon ...
SNMP: Value = ~<F1A1>E0<1F>
SNMP:
SNMP: Object =
{1.3.6.1.2.1.16.6.2.1.2.20480.6.126.241.XXX.YYY.48.31.6.126.241.XXX.YYY.2.1}
(rmon ...
SNMP: Value = ~<F1A1>E<0202>

SNMP:
SNMP: Object =
{1.3.6.1.2.1.16.6.2.1.3.20480.6.126.241.XXX.YYY.48.31.6.126.241.XXX.YYY.2.1}
(rmon ...
SNMP: Value = 20480
SNMP:
SNMP: Object =
{1.3.6.1.2.1.16.6.2.1.4.20480.6.126.241.XXX.YYY.48.31.6.126.241.XXX.YYY.2.1}
(rmon ...
SNMP: Value = 24 (counter)
SNMP:
SNMP: Object =
{1.3.6.1.2.1.16.6.2.1.5.20480.6.126.241.XXX.YYY.48.31.6.126.241.XXX.YYY.2.1}
(rmon ...
SNMP: Value = 2112 (counter)
SNMP:
SNMP: Object =
{1.3.6.1.2.1.16.6.2.1.6.20480.6.126.241.XXX.YYY.48.31.6.126.241.XXX.YYY.2.1}
(rmon ...
SNMP: Value = 0 (counter)
SNMP:
SNMP: Object = {1.3.6.1.2.1.1.3.0} (sysUpTime.0)
SNMP: Value = 798173 hundredths of a second
SNMP:

-- Frame 7 --
SNMP: ----- Simple Network Management Protocol (Version 1) -----
SNMP:
SNMP: Version = 0
SNMP: Community = public
SNMP: Command = Get next request
SNMP: Request ID = 1133668604
SNMP: Error status = 0 (No error)
SNMP: Error index = 0

SNMP:
SNMP: Object =
{1.3.6.1.2.1.16.6.2.1.1.20480.6.126.241.XXX.YYY.48.31.6.126.241.XXX.YYY.2.2}
(rmon ...
SNMP: Value = NULL
SNMP:
SNMP: Object =
{1.3.6.1.2.1.16.6.2.1.2.20480.6.126.241.XXX.YYY.48.31.6.126.241.XXX.YYY.2.2}
(rmon ...
SNMP: Value = NULL
SNMP:
SNMP: Object =
{1.3.6.1.2.1.16.6.2.1.3.20480.6.126.241.XXX.YYY.48.31.6.126.241.XXX.YYY.2.2}
(rmon ...
SNMP: Value = NULL
SNMP:
SNMP: Object =
{1.3.6.1.2.1.16.6.2.1.4.20480.6.126.241.XXX.YYY.48.31.6.126.241.XXX.YYY.2.2}
(rmon ...
SNMP: Value = NULL
SNMP:
SNMP: Object =
{1.3.6.1.2.1.16.6.2.1.5.20480.6.126.241.XXX.YYY.48.31.6.126.241.XXX.YYY.2.2}
(rmon ...
SNMP: Value = NULL
SNMP:
SNMP: Object =
{1.3.6.1.2.1.16.6.2.1.6.20480.6.126.241.XXX.YYY.48.31.6.126.241.XXX.YYY.2.2}
(rmon ...
SNMP: Value = NULL
SNMP:
SNMP: Object = {1.3.6.1.2.1.1.3} (sysUpTime)
SNMP: Value = NULL
SNMP:

```
-------------------------------------- Frame 8 ----------------------------------------
SNMP: ----- Simple Network Management Protocol (Version 1) -----
SNMP:
SNMP: Version = 0
SNMP: Community = public
SNMP: Command = Get response
SNMP: Request ID = 1133668604
SNMP: Error status = 0 (No error)
SNMP: Error index = 0
SNMP:
SNMP: Object =
{1.3.6.1.2.1.16.6.2.1.1.20480.6.126.241.XXX.YYY.48.31.6.126.241.XXX.YYY.6.83}
(rmo ...
SNMP: Value  = ~<F1A1>E0<1F>
SNMP:
SNMP: Object =
{1.3.6.1.2.1.16.6.2.1.2.20480.6.126.241.XXX.YYY.48.31.6.126.241.XXX.YYY.2.2}
(rmon ...
SNMP: Value  = ~<F1A1>E<06>S
SNMP:
SNMP: Object =
{1.3.6.1.2.1.16.6.2.1.3.20480.6.126.241.XXX.YYY.48.31.6.126.241.XXX.YYY.2.2}
(rmon ...
SNMP: Value  = 20480
SNMP:
SNMP: Object =
{1.3.6.1.2.1.16.6.2.1.4.20480.6.126.241.XXX.YYY.48.31.6.126.241.XXX.YYY.2.2}
(rmon ...
SNMP: Value  = 1 (counter)
SNMP:
SNMP: Object =
{1.3.6.1.2.1.16.6.2.1.5.20480.6.126.241.XXX.YYY.48.31.6.126.241.XXX.YYY.2.2}
(rmon ...
SNMP: Value  = 94 (counter)
```

SNMP:
SNMP: Object =
{1.3.6.1.2.1.16.6.2.1.6.20480.6.126.241.XXX.YYY.48.31.6.126.241.XXX.YYY.2.2}
(rmon ...
SNMP: Value = 0 (counter)
SNMP:
SNMP: Object = {1.3.6.1.2.1.1.3.0} (sysUpTime.0)
SNMP: Value = 798174 hundredths of a second
SNMP:

Similar information is obtained from the matrixDSTable, but this time it is indexed by the destination and then source address, as shown in Frames 33–52 (see Trace 7.10d). The first row entry is given in Frame 34, the second in Frame 36, the third in Frame 38, and so on. As before, note the small differences in the sysUpTime values:

DSSourceAddress	DSDestAddress	DSIndex	DSPkts	DSOctets	DSErrors	sysUpTime
F1A1E0201	F1A1E01F	20480	27	3614	0	798184
F1A1E0202	F1A1E01F	20480	15	1110	0	798185
F1A1E06	F1A1E01F	20480	1	94	0	798186

Trace 7.10d. RMON matrixDSTable retrieval

Sniffer Network Analyzer data from 25-Feb at 17:24:44, file TOPNIPCN.ENC, Page 1

------------------------------------- Frame 33 -------------------------------------
SNMP: ----- Simple Network Management Protocol (Version 1) -----
SNMP:
SNMP: Version = 0
SNMP: Community = public
SNMP: Command = Get next request
SNMP: Request ID = 1133668617
SNMP: Error status = 0 (No error)

SNMP: Error index = 0
SNMP:
SNMP: Object =
{1.3.6.1.2.1.16.6.3.1.1.20480.6.126.241.XXX.YYY.48.31.6.0.0.0.0.0.0}
(rmon.6.3.1. ...
SNMP: Value = NULL
SNMP:
SNMP: Object =
{1.3.6.1.2.1.16.6.3.1.2.20480.6.126.241.XXX.YYY.48.31.6.0.0.0.0.0.0}
(rmon.6.3.1. ...
SNMP: Value = NULL
SNMP:
SNMP: Object =
{1.3.6.1.2.1.16.6.3.1.3.20480.6.126.241.XXX.YYY.48.31.6.0.0.0.0.0.0}
(rmon.6.3.1. ...
SNMP: Value = NULL
SNMP:
SNMP: Object =
{1.3.6.1.2.1.16.6.3.1.4.20480.6.126.241.XXX.YYY.48.31.6.0.0.0.0.0.0}
(rmon.6.3.1. ...
SNMP: Value = NULL
SNMP:
SNMP: Object =
{1.3.6.1.2.1.16.6.3.1.5.20480.6.126.241.XXX.YYY.48.31.6.0.0.0.0.0.0}
(rmon.6.3.1. ...
SNMP: Value = NULL
SNMP:
SNMP: Object =
{1.3.6.1.2.1.16.6.3.1.6.20480.6.126.241.XXX.YYY.48.31.6.0.0.0.0.0.0}
(rmon.6.3.1. ...
SNMP: Value = NULL
SNMP:
SNMP: Object = {1.3.6.1.2.1.1.3} (sysUpTime)
SNMP: Value = NULL
SNMP:

-------------------------------------- Frame 34 --------------------------------------
SNMP: ----- Simple Network Management Protocol (Version 1) -----
SNMP:
SNMP: Version = 0
SNMP: Community = public
SNMP: Command = Get response
SNMP: Request ID = 1133668617
SNMP: Error status = 0 (No error)
SNMP: Error index = 0
SNMP:
SNMP: Object =
{1.3.6.1.2.1.16.6.3.1.1.20480.6.126.241.XXX.YYY.48.31.6.126.241.XXX.YYY.2.1}
(rmon ...
SNMP: Value = ~<F1A1>E<0201>
SNMP:
SNMP: Object =
{1.3.6.1.2.1.16.6.3.1.2.20480.6.126.241.XXX.YYY.48.31.6.0.0.0.0.0.0}
(rmon.6.3.1. ...
SNMP: Value = ~<F1A1>E0<1F>
SNMP:
SNMP: Object =
{1.3.6.1.2.1.16.6.3.1.3.20480.6.126.241.XXX.YYY.48.31.6.0.0.0.0.0.0}
(rmon.6.3.1. ...
SNMP: Value = 20480
SNMP:
SNMP: Object =
{1.3.6.1.2.1.16.6.3.1.4.20480.6.126.241.XXX.YYY.48.31.6.0.0.0.0.0.0}
(rmon.6.3.1. ...
SNMP: Value = 27 (counter)
SNMP:
SNMP: Object =
{1.3.6.1.2.1.16.6.3.1.5.20480.6.126.241.XXX.YYY.48.31.6.0.0.0.0.0.0}
(rmon.6.3.1. ...
SNMP: Value = 3614 (counter)

SNMP:
SNMP: Object =
{1.3.6.1.2.1.16.6.3.1.6.20480.6.126.241.XXX.YYY.48.31.6.0.0.0.0.0.0}
(rmon.6.3.1. ...
SNMP: Value = 0 (counter)
SNMP:
SNMP: Object = {1.3.6.1.2.1.1.3.0} (sysUpTime.0)
SNMP: Value = 798184 hundredths of a second
SNMP:

-------------------------------------- Frame 35 --------------------------------------
SNMP: ----- Simple Network Management Protocol (Version 1) -----
SNMP:
SNMP: Version = 0
SNMP: Community = public
SNMP: Command = Get next request
SNMP: Request ID = 1133668618
SNMP: Error status = 0 (No error)
SNMP: Error index = 0
SNMP:
SNMP: Object =
{1.3.6.1.2.1.16.6.3.1.1.20480.6.126.241.XXX.YYY.48.31.6.126.241.XXX.YYY.2.1}
(rmon ...
SNMP: Value = NULL
SNMP:
SNMP: Object =
{1.3.6.1.2.1.16.6.3.1.2.20480.6.126.241.XXX.YYY.48.31.6.126.241.XXX.YYY.2.1}
(rmon ...
SNMP: Value = NULL
SNMP:
SNMP: Object =
{1.3.6.1.2.1.16.6.3.1.3.20480.6.126.241.XXX.YYY.48.31.6.126.241.XXX.YYY.2.1}
(rmon ...
SNMP: Value = NULL

SNMP:
SNMP: Object =
{1.3.6.1.2.1.16.6.3.1.4.20480.6.126.241.XXX.YYY.48.31.6.126.241.XXX.YYY.2.1}
(rmon ...
SNMP: Value = NULL
SNMP:
SNMP: Object =
{1.3.6.1.2.1.16.6.3.1.5.20480.6.126.241.XXX.YYY.48.31.6.126.241.XXX.YYY.2.1}
(rmon ...
SNMP: Value = NULL
SNMP:
SNMP: Object =
{1.3.6.1.2.1.16.6.3.1.6.20480.6.126.241.XXX.YYY.48.31.6.126.241.XXX.YYY.2.1}
(rmon ...
SNMP: Value = NULL
SNMP:
SNMP: Object = {1.3.6.1.2.1.1.3} (sysUpTime)
SNMP: Value = NULL
SNMP:

-------------------------------------- Frame 36 --------------------------------------
SNMP: ----- Simple Network Management Protocol (Version 1) -----
SNMP:
SNMP: Version = 0
SNMP: Community = public
SNMP: Command = Get response
SNMP: Request ID = 1133668618
SNMP: Error status = 0 (No error)
SNMP: Error index = 0
SNMP:
SNMP: Object =
{1.3.6.1.2.1.16.6.3.1.1.20480.6.126.241.XXX.YYY.48.31.6.126.241.XXX.YYY.2.2}
(rmon ...
SNMP: Value = ~<F1A1>E<0202>

SNMP:
SNMP: Object =
{1.3.6.1.2.1.16.6.3.1.2.20480.6.126.241.XXX.YYY.48.31.6.126.241.XXX.YYY.2.1}
(rmon ...
SNMP: Value = ~<F1A1>E0<1F>
SNMP:
SNMP: Object =
{1.3.6.1.2.1.16.6.3.1.3.20480.6.126.241.XXX.YYY.48.31.6.126.241.XXX.YYY.2.1}
(rmon ...
SNMP: Value = 20480
SNMP:
SNMP: Object =
{1.3.6.1.2.1.16.6.3.1.4.20480.6.126.241.XXX.YYY.48.31.6.126.241.XXX.YYY.2.1}
(rmon ...
SNMP: Value = 15 (counter)
SNMP:
SNMP: Object =
{1.3.6.1.2.1.16.6.3.1.5.20480.6.126.241.XXX.YYY.48.31.6.126.241.XXX.YYY.2.1}
(rmon ...
SNMP: Value = 1110 (counter)
SNMP:
SNMP: Object =
{1.3.6.1.2.1.16.6.3.1.6.20480.6.126.241.XXX.YYY.48.31.6.126.241.XXX.YYY.2.1}
(rmon ...
SNMP: Value = 0 (counter)
SNMP:
SNMP: Object = {1.3.6.1.2.1.1.3.0} (sysUpTime.0)
SNMP: Value = 798185 hundredths of a second
SNMP:

-------------------------------------- Frame 37 --------------------------------------
SNMP: ----- Simple Network Management Protocol (Version 1) -----
SNMP:
SNMP: Version = 0

SNMP: Community = public
SNMP: Command = Get next request
SNMP: Request ID = 1133668619
SNMP: Error status = 0 (No error)
SNMP: Error index = 0
SNMP:
SNMP: Object =
{1.3.6.1.2.1.16.6.3.1.1.20480.6.126.241.XXX.YYY.48.31.6.126.241.XXX.YYY.2.2}
(rmon ...
SNMP: Value = NULL
SNMP:
SNMP: Object =
{1.3.6.1.2.1.16.6.3.1.2.20480.6.126.241.XXX.YYY.48.31.6.126.241.XXX.YYY.2.2}
(rmon ...
SNMP: Value = NULL
SNMP:
SNMP: Object =
{1.3.6.1.2.1.16.6.3.1.3.20480.6.126.241.XXX.YYY.48.31.6.126.241.XXX.YYY.2.2}
(rmon ...
SNMP: Value = NULL
SNMP:
SNMP: Object =
{1.3.6.1.2.1.16.6.3.1.4.20480.6.126.241.XXX.YYY.48.31.6.126.241.XXX.YYY.2.2}
(rmon ...
SNMP: Value = NULL
SNMP:
SNMP: Object =
{1.3.6.1.2.1.16.6.3.1.5.20480.6.126.241.XXX.YYY.48.31.6.126.241.XXX.YYY.2.2}
(rmon ...
SNMP: Value = NULL
SNMP:
SNMP: Object =
{1.3.6.1.2.1.16.6.3.1.6.20480.6.126.241.XXX.YYY.48.31.6.126.241.XXX.YYY.2.2}
(rmon ...

SNMP: Value = NULL
SNMP:
SNMP: Object = {1.3.6.1.2.1.1.3} (sysUpTime)
SNMP: Value = NULL
SNMP:

-------------------------------------- Frame 38 --------------------------------------
SNMP: ----- Simple Network Management Protocol (Version 1) -----
SNMP:
SNMP: Version = 0
SNMP: Community = public
SNMP: Command = Get response
SNMP: Request ID = 1133668619
SNMP: Error status = 0 (No error)
SNMP: Error index = 0
SNMP:
SNMP: Object =
{1.3.6.1.2.1.16.6.3.1.1.20480.6.126.241.XXX.YYY.48.31.6.126.241.XXX.YYY.6.83}
(rmo ...
SNMP: Value = ~<F1A1>E<06>S
SNMP:
SNMP: Object =
{1.3.6.1.2.1.16.6.3.1.2.20480.6.126.241.XXX.YYY.48.31.6.126.241.XXX.YYY.2.2}
(rmon ...
SNMP: Value = ~<F1A1>E0<1F>
SNMP:
SNMP: Object =
{1.3.6.1.2.1.16.6.3.1.3.20480.6.126.241.XXX.YYY.48.31.6.126.241.XXX.YYY.2.2}
(rmon ...
SNMP: Value = 20480
SNMP:
SNMP: Object =
{1.3.6.1.2.1.16.6.3.1.4.20480.6.126.241.XXX.YYY.48.31.6.126.241.XXX.YYY.2.2}
(rmon ...

```
SNMP: Value  = 1 (counter)
SNMP:
SNMP: Object =
{1.3.6.1.2.1.16.6.3.1.5.20480.6.126.241.XXX.YYY.48.31.6.126.241.XXX.YYY.2.2}
(rmon ...
SNMP: Value  = 94 (counter)
SNMP:
SNMP: Object =
{1.3.6.1.2.1.16.6.3.1.6.20480.6.126.241.XXX.YYY.48.31.6.126.241.XXX.YYY.2.2}
(rmon ...
SNMP: Value  = 0 (counter)
SNMP:
SNMP: Object = {1.3.6.1.2.1.1.3.0} (sysUpTime.0)
SNMP: Value  = 798186 hundredths of a second
SNMP:
```

In summary, RMON can provide a number of host-derived statistics; and stores these statistics in several different ways for the convenience of the end user.

7.11 Event Notification Using RMON

In the previous example, we studied how RMON maintains statistics of a network's operation. In this case study, we will show how RMON can extend that capability to send a notification if a particular network parameter has exceeded the range of acceptable operation. The network consists of a single Ethernet segment with an attached RMON network management console and remote monitoring agent, or probe (Figure 7-11). In order for the probe to monitor and respond to a particular network statistic, it must first be programmed by the manager (see Trace 7.11a).

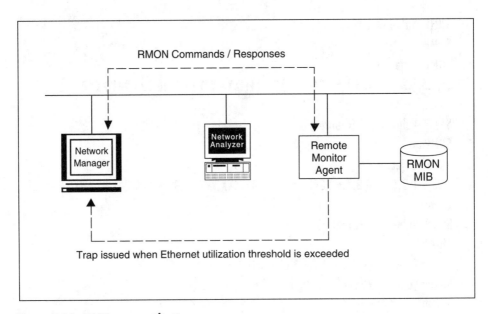

RMON Commands / Responses

Trap issued when Ethernet utilization threshold is exceeded

Figure 7-11. RMON event notification

Trace 7.11a. RMON threshold analysis summary

Sniffer Network Analyzer data from 21-Feb at 16:47:08, file TRAP.ENC, Page 1

SUMMARY	Delta T	Destination	Source	Summary
M 1		Probe	Manager	SNMP Get sysUpTime .. ifSpeed (3 items)
2	0.0020	Manager	Probe	SNMP GetReply sysUpTime .. ifSpeed (3 items)
3	0.0396	Probe	Manager	SNMP Get sysUpTime
4	0.0007	Probe	Manager	SNMP Set Protools.2.1.2.XXX.YYY.135.195, Protools.2.1.3.XXX.YYY.135.195
5	0.0006	Manager	Probe	SNMP GetReply sysUpTime = 69284 ticks
6	0.0008	Manager	Probe	SNMP GetReply Protools.2.1.2.XXX.YYY.135.195, Protools.2.1.3.XXX.YYY.135.195

7	0.0041	Probe	Manage	SNMP GetNext rmon.4.1.1.5.0, rmon.4.1.1.2.0
8	0.0008	Probe	Manager	SNMP GetNext rmon.1.1.1.20.0, rmon.1.1.1.2.0
9	0.0008	Manager	Probe	SNMP GetReply rmon.4.1.1.5.1, rmon.4.1.1.2.1
10	0.0008	Manager	Probe	SNMP GetReply rmon.1.1.1.20.1, rmon.1.1.1.2.1
11	0.0155	Probe	Manager	SNMP Set rmon.9.1.1.7.31860 = 2
12	0.0006	Probe	Manager	SNMP Get rmon.1.1.1.5.1
13	0.0008	Manager	Probe	SNMP GetReply rmon.9.1.1.7.31860 = 2
14	0.0007	Manager	Probe	SNMP GetReply rmon.1.1.1.5.1 = 74126
15	0.0012	Probe	Manager	SNMP Set rmon.9.1.1.2.31860 .. rmon.9.1.1.6.31860 (4 items)
16	0.0014	Manager	Probe	SNMP GetReply rmon.9.1.1.2.31860 .. rmon.9.1.1.6.31860 (4 items)
17	0.0012	Probe	Manager	SNMP Set rmon.9.1.1.7.31860 = 1
18	0.0010	Manager	Probe	SNMP GetReply rmon.9.1.1.7.31860 = 1
19	0.0011	Probe	Manager	SNMP Set rmon.3.1.1.12.29148 = 2

20	0.0010	Manager	Probe	SNMP GetReply rmon.3.1.1.12.29148 = 2
21	0.0025	Probe	Manager	SNMP Set rmon.3.1.1.2.29148 .. rmon.3.1.1.11.29148 (9 items)
22	0.0019	Manager	Probe	SNMP GetReply rmon.3.1.1.2.29148 .. rmon.3.1.1.11.29148 (9 items)
23	0.0016	Probe	Manager	SNMP Set rmon.3.1.1.12.29148 = 1
24	0.0010	Manager	Probe	SNMP GetReply rmon.3.1.1.12.29148 = 1
25	0.0011	Probe	Manager	SNMP GetNext rmon.9.2.1.3.31860, rmon.9.2.1.4.31860
26	0.0014	Manager	Probe	SNMP GetReply rmon.11.1.0, rmon.11.1.0
27	0.0011	Probe	Manager	SNMP Get rmon.9.1.1.7.31860, rmon.3.1.1.12.29148
28	0.0010	Manager	Probe	SNMP GetReply rmon.9.1.1.7.31860, rmon.3.1.1.12.29148
29	4.9868	Probe	Manager	SNMP Get sysUpTime = 69284 ticks
30	0.0003	Probe	Manager	SNMP Get rmon.1.1.1.5.1 = 74126
31	0.0009	Manager	Probe	SNMP GetReply sysUpTime = 69787 ticks
32	0.0007	Manager	Probe	SNMP GetReply rmon.1.1.1.5.1 = 74582

33	0.0087	Manager	Probe	SNMP Trap-v1 Enterprise specific
				rmon.3.1.1.1.29148 ..
				rmon.3.1.1.7.29148 (5 items)
34	0.0003	Probe	Manager	ICMP Destination unreachable
				(Port unreachable)
35	0.0091	Probe	Manager	SNMP GetNext
				rmon.9.2.1.3.31860,
				rmon.9.2.1.4.31860
36	0.0012	Manager	Probe	SNMP GetReply
				rmon.9.2.1.3.31860.1,
				rmon.9.2.1.4.31860.1
37	0.1371	Probe	Manager	SNMP GetNext
				rmon.9.2.1.3.31860.1,
				rmon.9.2.1.4.31860.1
38	0.0013	Manager	Probe	SNMP GetReply
				rmon.9.2.1.4.31860.1,
				rmon.11.1.0
39	0.0039	Probe	Manager	SNMP Get
				rmon.9.1.1.7.31860,
				rmon.3.1.1.12.29148
40	0.0010	Manager	Probe	SNMP GetReply
				rmon.9.1.1.7.31860,
				rmon.3.1.1.12.29148
41	1.8471	Probe	Manager	SNMP Set
				rmon.3.1.1.12.29148 = 4
42	0.0004	Probe	Manager	SNMP Set
				rmon.9.1.1.7.31860 = 4
43	0.0008	Manager	Probe	SNMP GetReply
				rmon.3.1.1.12.29148 = 4
44	0.0003	Probe	Manager	ICMP Destination unreachable
				(Port unreachable)
45	0.0011	Manager	Probe	SNMP GetReply
				rmon.9.1.1.7.31860 = 4

In Frame 4, the Manager sets the value of a Protools private MIB object, called etherUtilization, to a threshold that is acceptable for the current network conditions. The Probe issues a confirmation in Frame 6. In Frames 11–18, the Manager initializes values in the eventTable, which creates a row entry that is indexed by a random number chosen by the Manager (31860). Note that in Frame 15 (Trace 7.11b), values of four of the objects from the eventTable {1.3.6.1.2.1.16.9.1} are specified:

Object	OID	Value
eventDescription	{rmon 9.1.1.2 }	% Network usage
eventType	{rmon 9.1.1.3 }	4
eventCommunity	{rmon 9.1.1.4 }	public
eventOwner	{rmon 9.1.1.6 }	FM/X (XXX.YYY.135.195) : PID 3632 ID 0x008a0310

The eventDescription object provides a textual description that describes the event (% Network usage). The eventType object defines the type of notification that the probe will make as a result of this event. The RMON MIB, RFC 1757, defines Type = 4 as a "log-and-trap" notification. The eventCommunity object defines the community where the SNMP trap will be sent. The eventOwner object defines the entity that configured this entry. In this case, it is Network General's Foundation Manager for UNIX product, an RMON console, with the IP address specified above. The PID value is a process identification assigned by the Manager.

Frame 16 is a GetResponse from the Probe to the Manager to confirm the parameters that were set. In Frame 17, the Manager issues another SetRequest, this time for the eventStatus object {1.3.6.1.2.1.16.9.1.1.7} with Value = 1, which validates this table entry. The Probe sends a confirming GetResponse in Frame 18.

Trace 7.11b. RMON eventTable initialization

Sniffer Network Analyzer data from 21-Feb at 16:47:08, file TRAP.ENC, Page 1

```
----------------------------------- Frame 15 --------------------------------------
SNMP: ----- Simple Network Management Protocol (Version 1) -----
SNMP:
SNMP: Version = 0
SNMP: Community = public
SNMP: Command = Set request
SNMP: Request ID = 918004690
SNMP: Error status = 0 (No error)
SNMP: Error index = 0
SNMP:
SNMP: Object = {1.3.6.1.2.1.16.9.1.1.2.31860} (rmon.9.1.1.2.31860)
SNMP: Value  = % Network usage
SNMP:
SNMP: Object = {1.3.6.1.2.1.16.9.1.1.3.31860} (rmon.9.1.1.3.31860)
SNMP: Value  = 4
SNMP:
SNMP: Object = {1.3.6.1.2.1.16.9.1.1.4.31860} (rmon.9.1.1.4.31860)
SNMP: Value  = public
SNMP:
SNMP: Object = {1.3.6.1.2.1.16.9.1.1.6.31860} (rmon.9.1.1.6.31860)
SNMP: Value  = FM/X (XXX.YYY.135.195) : PID 3632 ID 0x008a0310
SNMP:


----------------------------------- Frame 16 --------------------------------------
SNMP: ----- Simple Network Management Protocol (Version 1) -----
SNMP:
SNMP: Version = 0
SNMP: Community = public
SNMP: Command = Get response
SNMP: Request ID = 918004690
SNMP: Error status = 0 (No error)
```

SNMP: Error index = 0
SNMP:
SNMP: Object = {1.3.6.1.2.1.16.9.1.1.2.31860} (rmon.9.1.1.2.31860)
SNMP: Value = % Network usage
SNMP:
SNMP: Object = {1.3.6.1.2.1.16.9.1.1.3.31860} (rmon.9.1.1.3.31860)
SNMP: Value = 4
SNMP:
SNMP: Object = {1.3.6.1.2.1.16.9.1.1.4.31860} (rmon.9.1.1.4.31860)
SNMP: Value = public
SNMP:
SNMP: Object = {1.3.6.1.2.1.16.9.1.1.6.31860} (rmon.9.1.1.6.31860)
SNMP: Value = FM/X (XXX.YYY.135.195) : PID 3632 ID 0x008a0310
SNMP:

-------------------------------------- Frame 17 --------------------------------------
SNMP: ----- Simple Network Management Protocol (Version 1) -----
SNMP:
SNMP: Version = 0
SNMP: Community = public
SNMP: Command = Set request
SNMP: Request ID = 918004691
SNMP: Error status = 0 (No error)
SNMP: Error index = 0
SNMP:
SNMP: Object = {1.3.6.1.2.1.16.9.1.1.7.31860} (rmon.9.1.1.7.31860)
SNMP: Value = 1
SNMP:

-------------------------------------- Frame 18 --------------------------------------
SNMP: ----- Simple Network Management Protocol (Version 1) -----
SNMP:
SNMP: Version = 0
SNMP: Community = public

SNMP: Command = Get response
SNMP: Request ID = 918004691
SNMP: Error status = 0 (No error)
SNMP: Error index = 0
SNMP:
SNMP: Object = {1.3.6.1.2.1.16.9.1.1.7.31860} (rmon.9.1.1.7.31860)
SNMP: Value = 1
SNMP:

Reviewing Frames 19–24 in Trace 7.11a, the Manager initializes the alarmTable {1.3.6.1.2.1.16.3.1}. Note that in Frame 19, the Manager sets the alarmStatus object to a Value = 2 (createRequest, per RFC 1757), and selects a random number for an index for this table entry (29148). Other values of the alarmStatus table are set in Frame 21 (Trace 7.11c), including:

Object	OID	Value
alarmInterval	{rmon 3.1.1.2}	5
alarmVariable	{rmon 3.1.1.3}	{1.3.6.1.4.1.209.2.2.1.2.1}
alarmSampleType	{rmon 3.1.1.4}	1
alarmRisingThreshold	{rmon 3.1.1.7}	1
alarmFallingThreshold	{rmon 3.1.1.8}	1
alarmFallingEventIndex	{rmon 3.1.1.10}	0
alarmRisingEventIndex	{rmon 3.1.1.9}	31860
alarmOwner	{rmon 3.1.1.11}	FM/X (XXX.YYY.135.195) : PID 3632 ID 0x008a0310

Trace 7.11c. RMON alarmTable initialization

Sniffer Network Analyzer data from 21-Feb at 16:47:08, file TRAP.ENC, Page 1

------------------------------------- Frame 21 -------------------------------------
SNMP: ----- Simple Network Management Protocol (Version 1) -----
SNMP:
SNMP: Version = 0
SNMP: Community = public
SNMP: Command = Set request
SNMP: Request ID = 918004693
SNMP: Error status = 0 (No error)
SNMP: Error index = 0
SNMP:
SNMP: Object = {1.3.6.1.2.1.16.3.1.1.2.29148} (rmon.3.1.1.2.29148)
SNMP: Value = 5
SNMP:
SNMP: Object = {1.3.6.1.2.1.16.3.1.1.3.29148} (rmon.3.1.1.3.29148)
SNMP: Value = {1.3.6.1.4.1.209.2.2.1.2.1}
SNMP:
SNMP: Object = {1.3.6.1.2.1.16.3.1.1.4.29148} (rmon.3.1.1.4.29148)
SNMP: Value = 1
SNMP:
SNMP: Object = {1.3.6.1.2.1.16.3.1.1.4.29148} (rmon.3.1.1.4.29148)
SNMP: Value = 1
SNMP:
SNMP: Object = {1.3.6.1.2.1.16.3.1.1.7.29148} (rmon.3.1.1.7.29148)
SNMP: Value = 1
SNMP:
SNMP: Object = {1.3.6.1.2.1.16.3.1.1.8.29148} (rmon.3.1.1.8.29148)
SNMP: Value = 1
SNMP:
SNMP: Object = {1.3.6.1.2.1.16.3.1.1.10.29148} (rmon.3.1.1.10.29148)
SNMP: Value = 0
SNMP:

```
SNMP: Object = {1.3.6.1.2.1.16.3.1.1.9.29148} (rmon.3.1.1.9.29148)
SNMP: Value  = 31860
SNMP:
SNMP: Object = {1.3.6.1.2.1.16.3.1.1.11.29148} (rmon.3.1.1.11.29148)
SNMP: Value  = FM/X (XXX.YYY.135.195) : PID 3632 ID 0x008a0310
SNMP:
```

In Frame 23, the Manager sets the alarmStatus object to a value of 1 (valid, per RFC 1757), which is confirmed in Frame 24.

The network does exceed the threshold of network utilization that was specified; as a result, the Probe issues a trap in Frame 33 (Trace 7.11d). Note that this is an enterprise-specific trap, and that the trap reports the values of some objects from the alarmTable {1.3.6.1.2.1.16.3.1}. These objects are:

Object	OID	Value
alarmIndex	{rmon.3.1.1.1}	29148
alarmVariable	{rmon.3.1.1.3}	{ 1.3.6.1.4.1.209.2.2.1.2.1 }
alarmSampleType	{rmon.3.1.1.4}	1
alarmValue	{rmon.3.1.1.5}	3
alarmRisingThreshold	{rmon.3.1.1.7}	1

The alarmIndex object uniquely identifies an entry in the alarm table; its value is a random value that was originally determined by the Manager (review Frame 19). The alarmVariable object identifies the OID of the variable to be sampled. In this case, the variable is derived from a Private MIB (enterprise 209 is assigned to ProTools, now part of Network General Corp.). The alarmSampleType specifies the method of sampling the selected variable and calculating the value to be compared against the thresholds. The value of 1 specifies an absolute value, meaning that the value of the selected variable will be compared directly with the thresholds at the end of the sampling interval. The alarmValue object is the value of the statistic during the last sampling period. Finally, the alarmRisingThreshold is a threshold for the sampled statistic. According to RFC 1757, when the current sampled value is greater than or equal to this threshold, and the value at the last sampling interval was less than this threshold, a single event will be generated.

Trace 7.11d. Trap sent in response to an excessive network condition.

Sniffer Network Analyzer data from 21-Feb at 16:47:08, file TRAP.ENC, Page 1

```
------------------------------------ Frame 33 ------------------------------------
SNMP: ----- Simple Network Management Protocol (Version 1) -----
SNMP:
SNMP: Version = 0
SNMP: Community = public
SNMP: Command = Trap
SNMP: Enterprise = {1.3.6.1.2.1.16}
SNMP: Network address = [XXX.YYY.135.11], Probe
SNMP: Generic trap = 6 (Enterprise specific)
SNMP: Specific trap = 1
SNMP: Time ticks = 69788
SNMP:
SNMP: Object = {1.3.6.1.2.1.16.3.1.1.1.29148} (rmon.3.1.1.1.29148)
SNMP: Value  = 29148
SNMP:
SNMP: Object = {1.3.6.1.2.1.16.3.1.1.3.29148} (rmon.3.1.1.3.29148)
SNMP: Value  = {1.3.6.1.4.1.209.2.2.1.2.1}
SNMP:
SNMP: Object = {1.3.6.1.2.1.16.3.1.1.4.29148} (rmon.3.1.1.4.29148)
SNMP: Value  = 1
SNMP:
SNMP: Object = {1.3.6.1.2.1.16.3.1.1.5.29148} (rmon.3.1.1.5.29148)
SNMP: Value  = 3
SNMP:
SNMP: Object = {1.3.6.1.2.1.16.3.1.1.7.29148} (rmon.3.1.1.7.29148)
SNMP: Value  = 1
SNMP:
```

The next step is for the Manager to retrieve the values from the logTable (recall that the eventType object set in Frame 11 specified a "log-and-trap" event, event type = 4). Frames 35–36 read the values from this logTable, and Frames 37–38 (which are not shown in the trace) merely confirm that all entries in that table have been read (see Trace 7.11e). Frame 36 contains the entries of the logTable, indexed by the random number initially selected by the Manager (31860):

Object	OID	Value
logTime	{rmon.9.2.1.3}	69788
logDescription	{rmon.9.2.1.4}	% Network usage 3. Over threshold of (1)

Trace 7.11e. Reading the logTable

Sniffer Network Analyzer data from 21-Feb at 16:47:08, file: TRAP.ENC, Page 1

```
---------------------------------------- Frame 35 ----------------------------------------
SNMP: ----- Simple Network Management Protocol (Version 1) -----
SNMP:
SNMP: Version = 0
SNMP: Community = public
SNMP: Command = Get next request
SNMP: Request ID = 918004699
SNMP: Error status = 0 (No error)
SNMP: Error index = 0
SNMP:
SNMP: Object = {1.3.6.1.2.1.16.9.2.1.3.31860} (rmon.9.2.1.3.31860)
SNMP: Value  = NULL
SNMP:
SNMP: Object = {1.3.6.1.2.1.16.9.2.1.4.31860} (rmon.9.2.1.4.31860)
SNMP: Value  = NULL
SNMP:
```

```
------------------------------------- Frame 36 -------------------------------------
SNMP: ----- Simple Network Management Protocol (Version 1) -----
SNMP:
SNMP: Version = 0
SNMP: Community = public
SNMP: Command = Get response
SNMP: Request ID = 918004699
SNMP: Error status = 0 (No error)
SNMP: Error index = 0
SNMP:
SNMP: Object = {1.3.6.1.2.1.16.9.2.1.3.31860.1} (rmon.9.2.1.3.31860.1)
SNMP: Value  = 69788 (time ticks)
SNMP:
SNMP: Object = {1.3.6.1.2.1.16.9.2.1.4.31860.1} (rmon.9.2.1.4.31860.1)
SNMP: Value  = % Network usage   3. Over threshold of (1)
SNMP:
```

The balance of the events (review Trace 7.11a) read and invalidate the alarmTable and eventTable by setting the values of the alarmStatus {rmon 3.1.1.12} and eventStatus {rmon 9.1.1.7} to a value of 4 (invalid).

In summary, this trace has illustrated how the RMON alarm and event groups interact to provide both monitoring and notification of significant network conditions.

7.12 Comparing Network Management Alternatives: Accessing Remote Bridge Parameters with TELNET and SNMP

To summarize the examples discussed in this chapter, this section looks at two alternatives for accessing the configuration parameters and operational statistics of a remote bridge. One alternative is to access the bridge with a workstation and to access the bridge's configuration menus using the Telecommunication Network Protocol (TELNET). TELNET allows a remote user to access a host or device as if it were a local terminal. The second alternative is to access the bridge with the management console using SNMP and retrieve the appropriate MIB information. Let's compare these two methods.

In the first method, a Sun Workstation initiates a TELNET session with the 3Com bridge (see Figure 7-12). The network administrator uses commands defined by 3Com to retrieve the system parameters and statistics. Each of these commands is then sent from the workstation to the bridge in a TEL-NET message, and the bridge returns a corresponding response. For example, in Frame 1 (see Trace 7.12a), the system version is requested using the 3Com show -sys ver command. The bridge responds with:

"SW/NBII-BR-5.0.1, booted on Mon Mar 22 12:05 from local floppy" (see Trace 7.12b).

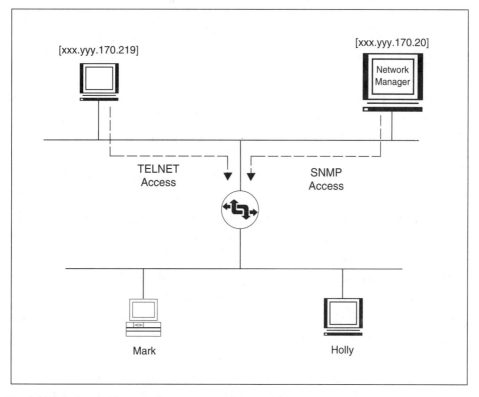

Figure 7-12. Remote device configuration using TELNET and SNMP

Subsequent requests obtain the system contact (Frames 7 through 10), the system location (Frames 11 through 14), and the system name (Frames 15 through 18). The network administrator next accesses the IP Address Translation (ARP) table (Frames 19 through 53) and the IP table (Frames 54 through 65). The final operation retrieves the Path Statistics, such as the number of packets transmitted and received, collisions, and network utilization (Frames 66 through 99). The TELNET method requires the transmission of a total of 99 frames, including 8,599 octets of information.

The second method uses the network management console to access the bridge's MIB using SNMP (see Trace 7.12c). The administrator queries the System group (Frames 1 through 4), the Address Translation group (Frames 5 through 18), the IP group (Frames 19 through 22), and the Interfaces group (Frames 23 through 42). The details of these transactions reveal almost identical information as that discovered earlier (see Trace 7.12d). The SNMP method requires the transmission of a total of 42 frames and 8,910 octets of information.

The question, then, is which of these two methods is best? From a network traffic point of view, the results are almost identical: 8,599 octets are transmitted using TELNET, and 8,910 octets using SNMP.

From a practical angle, however, SNMP has an advantage. TELNET requires the network manager to have a workstation available, to understand TELNET commands, and to understand the product-specific parameters, menus, configuration screens, and so on, that are part of that managed system. SNMP does not require these details. The administrator simply goes to the management console, accesses the device in question (the 3Com bridge), and enters well-known SNMP commands. Few details of that bridge's internal configuration are necessary. What's more, SNMP may also use vendor-specific traps to alert the administrator to significant events.

In summary, great synergies can come from using an open network management platform instead of a multitude of vendor-specific solutions. Perhaps this is one reason that SNMP has achieved its great popularity!

Trace 7.12a. Accessing bridge parameters with a TELNET session (summary)

Sniffer Network Analyzer data 26-Mar at 13:52:54, file DIG1.ENC, Pg 1

SUMMARY	Delta T	Destination	Source	Summary
1		3Com Bridge	Sun Station	Telnet C PORT=2200 show -sys ver<0D0A>
2	0.0031	Sun Station	3Com Bridge	Telnet R PORT=2200 SW/NBII-BR-5.0.1, booted on Mon Mar 22
3	0.0005	Sun Station	3Com Bridge	Telnet R PORT=2200 nb2 REM: 1.0.2 <0D0A>
4	0.0007	Sun Station	3Com Bridge	Telnet R PORT=2200 Copyright 1985-1992 3Com Corporation<0D0A>
5	0.0015	Sun Station	3Com Bridge	Telnet R PORT=2200 [24]nbii650b#
6	0.1308	3Com Bridge	Sun Station	TCP D=23 S=2200 ACK=344321989 WIN=4096
7	9.9600	3Com Bridge	Sun Station	Telnet C PORT=2200 show -sys scon<0D0A>
8	0.0029	Sun Station	3Com Bridge	Telnet R PORT=2200 SysCONtact = "John Doe"<0D0A>
9	0.0014	Sun Station	3Com Bridge	Telnet R PORT=2200 [25]nbii650b#
10	0.0357	3Com Bridge	Sun Station	TCP D=23 S=2200 ACK=344322028 WIN=4096
11	4.8660	3Com Bridge	Sun Station	Telnet C PORT=2200 show -sys sloc<0D0A>
12	0.0030	Sun Station	3Com Bridge	Telnet R PORT=2200 SysLOCation = "650 Computer Room"<0D0A>

13	0.0015	Sun Station	3Com Bridge	Telnet R PORT=2200
				[26]nbii650b#
14	0.1295	3Com Bridge	Sun Station	TCP D=23 S=2200
				ACK=344322077
				WIN=4096
15	4.8946	3Com Bridge	Sun Station	Telnet C PORT=2200
				show -sys snam<0D0A>
16	0.0029	Sun Station	3Com Bridge	Telnet R PORT=2200
				SysNAMe =
				"nbii650b"<0D0A>
17	0.0015	Sun Station	3Com Bridge	Telnet R PORT=2200
				[27]nbii650b#
18	0.1011	3Com Bridge	Sun Station	TCP D=23 S=2200
				ACK=344322113
				WIN=4096
19	4.4364	3Com Bridge	Sun Station	Telnet C PORT=2200
				show -ip addr<0D0A>
20	0.0029	Sun Station	3Com Bridge	Telnet R PORT=2200
				---IP Address Trans...
				XXX.YYY.170.214
.				
.				
.				
54	5.2126	3Com Bridge	Sun Station	Telnet C PORT=2200
				show -ip netaddr<0D0A>
55	0.0030	Sun Station	3Com Bridge	Telnet R PORT=2200
				---IP Directly Conn..
56	0.0010	Sun Station	3Com Bridge	Telnet R PORT=2200 IP
				Address Port
				Subnet Mask Status...
.				
.				
.				
66	15.9375	3Com Bridge	Sun Station	Telnet C PORT=2200
				show stat -path<0D0A>

67	0.0046	Sun Station	3Com Bridge	Telnet R PORT=2200 ACCUMULATED VALUES<0D0A>
68	0.0006	Sun Station	3Com Bridge	Telnet R PORT=2200 <0D0A>
69	0.0010	Sun Station	3Com Bridge	Telnet R PORT=2200 == PATH statistic...
70	0.0007	Sun Station	3Com Bridge	Telnet R PORT=2200
71	0.0010	Sun Station	3Com Bridge	Telnet R PORT=2200
.				
.				
.				
96	0.0010	Sun Station	3Com Bridge	Telnet R PORT=2200 Byte/Sec Rcv Good: Packets 29885492 2732272...
97	0.0009	Sun Station	3Com Bridge	Telnet R PORT=2200 Xmit Bad: Pkt/Sec
98	0.0014	Sun Station	3Com Bridge	Telnet R PORT=2200 [30]nbii650b#
99	0.1944	3Com Bridge	Sun Station	TCP D=23 S=2200 ACK=344324928 WIN=4096

Trace 7.12b. Accessing bridge parameters with a TELNET session (details)

Sniffer Network Analyzer data 26-Mar at 13:52:54, file DIG1.ENC, Pg 1

-------------------------------------- Frame 1 --------------------------------------
Telnet:----- Telnet data -----
Telnet:
Telnet:show -sys ver<0D0A>
Telnet:

```
----------------------------------- Frame 2 ---------------------------------------
Telnet:----- Telnet data -----
Telnet:
Telnet:SW/NBII-BR-5.0.1, booted on Mon Mar 22 12:05 from local floppy<0D0A>
Telnet:


----------------------------------- Frame 3 ---------------------------------------
Telnet:----- Telnet data -----
Telnet:
Telnet:nb2 REM: 1.0.2 <0D0A>
Telnet:


----------------------------------- Frame 4 ---------------------------------------
Telnet:----- Telnet data -----
Telnet:
Telnet:Copyright 1985-1992, 3Com Corporation<0D0A>
Telnet:


----------------------------------- Frame 5 ---------------------------------------
Telnet:----- Telnet data -----
Telnet:
Telnet:[24]nbii650b#
Telnet:


----------------------------------- Frame 7 ---------------------------------------
Telnet:----- Telnet data -----
Telnet:
Telnet:show -sys scon<0D0A>
Telnet:


----------------------------------- Frame 8 ---------------------------------------
Telnet:----- Telnet data -----
Telnet:
Telnet:SysCONtact = "John Doe"<0D0A>
Telnet:
```

```
------------------------------------ Frame 9 ------------------------------------
Telnet:----- Telnet data -----
Telnet:
Telnet:[25]nbii650b#
Telnet:
```

Trace 7.12c. Accessing remote bridge parameters with SNMP (summary)

Sniffer Network Analyzer data 26-Mar at 13:55:46, file DIG2.ENC, Pg 1

SUMMARY	Delta T	Destination	Source	Summary
1		3Com Bridge	Manager	SNMP GetNext sysDescr .. sysServices (7 items)
2	0.0035	Manager	3Com Bridge	SNMP GetReply sysDescr .. sysServices (7 items)
.				
.				
.				
5	1.2927	3Com Bridge	Manager	SNMP GetNext atIfIndex .. atNetAddress (3 items)
6	0.0038	Manager	3Com Bridge	SNMP GetReply atIfIndex .. atNetAddress (3 items)
.				
.				
.				
19	2.6261	3Com Bridge	Manager	SNMP GetNext ipAdEntAddr .. ipAdEntReasmMaxSize (5 items)
20	0.0034	Manager	3Com Bridge	SNMP GetReply ipAdEntAddr .. ipAdEntReasmMaxSize (5 items)
.				
.				
.				

23	2.3142	3Com Bridge	Manager	SNMP GetNext ifIndex .. ifOutOctets (16 items)
24	0.0106	Manager	3Com Bridge	SNMP GetReply ifIndex .. ifOutOctets (16 items)
.				
.				
.				
41	0.0045	3Com Bridge	Manager	SNMP GetNext ifOutUcastPkts .. ifSpecific (6 items)
42	0.0058	Manager	3Com Bridge	SNMP GetReply ifOutNUcastPkts .. atIfIndex (6 items)

Trace 7.12d. Accessing remote bridge parameters with SNMP (summary)

Sniffer Network Analyzer data 26-Mar at 13:55:46, file DIG2.ENC, Pg 1

```
--------------------------------------- Frame 1 ---------------------------------------
SNMP: ----- Simple Network Management Protocol (Version 1) -----
SNMP:
SNMP: Version = 0
SNMP: Community = public
SNMP: Command = Get next request
SNMP: Request ID = 733178616
SNMP: Error status = 0 (No error)
SNMP: Error index = 0
SNMP:
SNMP: Object = {1.3.6.1.2.1.1.1} (sysDescr)
SNMP: Value = NULL
SNMP:
SNMP: Object = {1.3.6.1.2.1.1.2} (sysObjectID)
```

SNMP: Value = NULL
SNMP:
SNMP: Object = {1.3.6.1.2.1.1.3} (sysUpTime)
SNMP: Value = NULL
SNMP:
SNMP: Object = {1.3.6.1.2.1.1.4} (sysContact)
SNMP: Value = NULL
SNMP:
SNMP: Object = {1.3.6.1.2.1.1.5} (sysName)
SNMP: Value = NULL
SNMP:
SNMP: Object = {1.3.6.1.2.1.1.6} (sysLocation)
SNMP: Value = NULL
SNMP:
SNMP: Object = {1.3.6.1.2.1.1.7} (sysServices)
SNMP: Value = NULL
SNMP:

-------------------------------------- Frame 2 --------------------------------------
SNMP: ----- Simple Network Management Protocol (Version 1) -----
SNMP:
SNMP: Version = 0
SNMP: Community = public
SNMP: Command = Get response
SNMP: Request ID = 733178616
SNMP: Error status = 0 (No error)
SNMP: Error index = 0
SNMP:
SNMP: Object = {1.3.6.1.2.1.1.1.0} (sysDescr.0)
SNMP: Value = SW/NBII-BR-5.0.1
SNMP:
SNMP: Object = {1.3.6.1.2.1.1.2.0} (sysObjectID.0)
SNMP: Value = {1.3.6.1.4.1.43.1.4}
SNMP:

SNMP: Object = {1.3.6.1.2.1.1.3.0} (sysUpTime.0)
SNMP: Value = 35594870 hundredths of a second
SNMP:
SNMP: Object = {1.3.6.1.2.1.1.4.0} (sysContact.0)
SNMP: Value = John Doe
SNMP:
SNMP: Object = {1.3.6.1.2.1.1.5.0} (sysName.0)
SNMP: Value = nbii650b
SNMP:
SNMP: Object = {1.3.6.1.2.1.1.6.0} (sysLocation.0)
SNMP: Value = 650 Computer Room
SNMP:
SNMP: Object = {1.3.6.1.2.1.1.7.0} (sysServices.0)
SNMP: Value = 74
SNMP:

.
.
.

-------------------------------------- Frame 5 --------------------------------------
SNMP: ----- Simple Network Management Protocol (Version 1) -----
SNMP:
SNMP: Version = 0
SNMP: Community = public
SNMP: Command = Get next request
SNMP: Request ID = 733178619
SNMP: Error status = 0 (No error)
SNMP: Error index = 0
SNMP:
SNMP: Object = {1.3.6.1.2.1.3.1.1.1} (atIfIndex)
SNMP: Value = NULL
SNMP:
SNMP: Object = {1.3.6.1.2.1.3.1.1.2} (atPhysAddress)
SNMP: Value = NULL
SNMP:

SNMP: Object = {1.3.6.1.2.1.3.1.1.3} (atNetAddress)
SNMP: Value = NULL
SNMP:

-- Frame 6 --
SNMP: ----- Simple Network Management Protocol (Version 1) -----
SNMP:
SNMP: Version = 0
SNMP: Community = public
SNMP: Command = Get response
SNMP: Request ID = 733178619
SNMP: Error status = 0 (No error)
SNMP: Error index = 0
SNMP:
SNMP: Object = {1.3.6.1.2.1.3.1.1.1.0.1.XXX.YYY.170.0}
(atIfIndex.0.1.XXX.YYY.170.0)
SNMP: Value = 0
SNMP:
SNMP: Object = {1.3.6.1.2.1.3.1.1.2.0.1.XXX.YYY.170.0}
 (atPhysAddress.0.1.XXX.YYY.170.0)
SNMP: Value = FFFFFFFFFFFF, Broadcast
SNMP:
SNMP: Object = {1.3.6.1.2.1.3.1.1.3.0.1.XXX.YYY.170.0}
(atNetAddress.0.1.XXX.YYY.170.0)
SNMP: Value = [XXX.YYY.170.0]
SNMP:

.

.

.

-- Frame 19 --
SNMP: ----- Simple Network Management Protocol (Version 1) -----
SNMP:
SNMP: Version = 0
SNMP: Community = public

425

SNMP: Command = Get next request
SNMP: Request ID = 733178620
SNMP: Error status = 0 (No error)
SNMP: Error index = 0
SNMP:
SNMP: Object = {1.3.6.1.2.1.4.20.1.1} (ipAdEntAddr)
SNMP: Value = NULL
SNMP:
SNMP: Object = {1.3.6.1.2.1.4.20.1.2} (ipAdEntIfIndex)
SNMP: Value = NULL
SNMP:
SNMP: Object = {1.3.6.1.2.1.4.20.1.3} (ipAdEntNetMask)
SNMP: Value = NULL
SNMP:
SNMP: Object = {1.3.6.1.2.1.4.20.1.4} (ipAdEntBcastAddr)
SNMP: Value = NULL
SNMP:
SNMP: Object = {1.3.6.1.2.1.4.20.1.5} (ipAdEntReasmMaxSize)
SNMP: Value = NULL
SNMP:

-- Frame 20 --
SNMP: ----- Simple Network Management Protocol (Version 1) -----
SNMP:
SNMP: Version = 0
SNMP: Community = public
SNMP: Command = Get response
SNMP: Request ID = 733178620
SNMP: Error status = 0 (No error)
SNMP: Error index = 0
SNMP:
SNMP: Object = {1.3.6.1.2.1.4.20.1.1.XXX.YYY.170.214}
        (ipAdEntAddr.XXX.YYY.170.214)
SNMP: Value = [XXX.YYY.170.214], 3Com Bridge
SNMP:

SNMP: Object = {1.3.6.1.2.1.4.20.1.2.XXX.YYY.170.214}
      (ipAdEntIfIndex.XXX.YYY.170.214)
SNMP: Value = 0
SNMP:
SNMP: Object = {1.3.6.1.2.1.4.20.1.3.XXX.YYY.170.214}
      (ipAdEntNetMask.XXX.YYY.170.214)
SNMP: Value = [255.255.255.0]
SNMP:
SNMP: Object = {1.3.6.1.2.1.4.20.1.4.XXX.YYY.170.214}
      (ipAdEntBcastAddr.XXX.YYY.170.214)
SNMP: Value = 0
SNMP:
SNMP: Object = {1.3.6.1.2.1.4.20.1.5.XXX.YYY.170.214}
      (ipAdEntReasmMaxSize.XXX.YYY.170.214)
SNMP: Value = 65535
SNMP:

   .

   .

   .

-------------------------------------- Frame 23 --------------------------------------
SNMP: ----- Simple Network Management Protocol (Version 1) -----
SNMP:
SNMP: Version = 0
SNMP: Community = public
SNMP: Command = Get next request
SNMP: Request ID = 733178622
SNMP: Error status = 0 (No error)
SNMP: Error index = 0
SNMP:
SNMP: Object = {1.3.6.1.2.1.2.2.1.1} (ifIndex)
SNMP: Value = NULL
SNMP:
SNMP: Object = {1.3.6.1.2.1.2.2.1.2} (ifDescr)
SNMP: Value = NULL

SNMP:
SNMP: Object = {1.3.6.1.2.1.2.2.1.3} (ifType)
SNMP: Value = NULL
SNMP:
SNMP: Object = {1.3.6.1.2.1.2.2.1.4} (ifMtu)
SNMP: Value = NULL
SNMP:
SNMP: Object = {1.3.6.1.2.1.2.2.1.5} (ifSpeed)
SNMP: Value = NULL
SNMP:
SNMP: Object = {1.3.6.1.2.1.2.2.1.6} (ifPhysAddress)
SNMP: Value = NULL
SNMP:
SNMP: Object = {1.3.6.1.2.1.2.2.1.7} (ifAdminStatus)
SNMP: Value = NULL
SNMP:
SNMP: Object = {1.3.6.1.2.1.2.2.1.8} (ifOperStatus)
SNMP: Value = NULL
SNMP:
SNMP: Object = {1.3.6.1.2.1.2.2.1.9} (ifLastChange)
SNMP: Value = NULL
SNMP:
SNMP: Object = {1.3.6.1.2.1.2.2.1.10} (ifInOctets)
SNMP: Value = NULL
SNMP:
SNMP: Object = {1.3.6.1.2.1.2.2.1.11} (ifInUcastPkts)
SNMP: Value = NULL
SNMP:
SNMP: Object = {1.3.6.1.2.1.2.2.1.12} (ifInNUcastPkts)
SNMP: Value = NULL
SNMP:
SNMP: Object = {1.3.6.1.2.1.2.2.1.13} (ifInDiscards)
SNMP: Value = NULL
SNMP:
SNMP: Object = {1.3.6.1.2.1.2.2.1.14} (ifInErrors)

SNMP: Value = NULL
SNMP:
SNMP: Object = {1.3.6.1.2.1.2.2.1.15} (ifInUnknownProtos)
SNMP: Value = NULL
SNMP:
SNMP: Object = {1.3.6.1.2.1.2.2.1.16} (ifOutOctets)
SNMP: Value = NULL
SNMP:

--------------------------------------- Frame 24 ---------------------------------------
SNMP: ----- Simple Network Management Protocol (Version 1) -----
SNMP:
SNMP: Version = 0
SNMP: Community = public
SNMP: Command = Get response
SNMP: Request ID = 733178622
SNMP: Error status = 0 (No error)
SNMP: Error index = 0
SNMP:
SNMP: Object = {1.3.6.1.2.1.2.2.1.1.1} (ifIndex.1)
SNMP: Value = 1
SNMP:
SNMP: Object = {1.3.6.1.2.1.2.2.1.2.1} (ifDescr.1)
SNMP: Value = 3Com NETBuilderETH/1-1
SNMP:
SNMP: Object = {1.3.6.1.2.1.2.2.1.3.1} (ifType.1)
SNMP: Value = 6 (ethernet-csmacd)
SNMP:
SNMP: Object = {1.3.6.1.2.1.2.2.1.4.1} (ifMtu.1)
SNMP: Value = 1500 octets
SNMP:
SNMP: Object = {1.3.6.1.2.1.2.2.1.5.1} (ifSpeed.1)
SNMP: Value = 10000000 bits per second
SNMP:
SNMP: Object = {1.3.6.1.2.1.2.2.1.6.1} (ifPhysAddress.1)

429

SNMP: Value = Bridge034ACD
SNMP:
SNMP: Object = {1.3.6.1.2.1.2.2.1.7.1} (ifAdminStatus.1)
SNMP: Value = 1 (up)
SNMP:
SNMP: Object = {1.3.6.1.2.1.2.2.1.8.1} (ifOperStatus.1)
SNMP: Value = 1 (up)
SNMP:
SNMP: Object = {1.3.6.1.2.1.2.2.1.9.1} (ifLastChange.1)
SNMP: Value = 1995 hundredths of a second
SNMP:
SNMP: Object = {1.3.6.1.2.1.2.2.1.10.1} (ifInOctets.1)
SNMP: Value = 1611173470 octets
SNMP:
SNMP: Object = {1.3.6.1.2.1.2.2.1.11.1} (ifInUcastPkts.1)
SNMP: Value = 13162801 packets
SNMP:
SNMP: Object = {1.3.6.1.2.1.2.2.1.12.1} (ifInNUcastPkts.1)
SNMP: Value = 8368939 packets
SNMP:
SNMP: Object = {1.3.6.1.2.1.2.2.1.13.1} (ifInDiscards.1)
SNMP: Value = 0 packets
SNMP:
SNMP: Object = {1.3.6.1.2.1.2.2.1.14.1} (ifInErrors.1)
SNMP: Value = 579 packets
SNMP:
SNMP: Object = {1.3.6.1.2.1.2.2.1.15.1} (ifInUnknownProtos.1)
SNMP: Value = 6620842 packets
SNMP:
SNMP: Object = {1.3.6.1.2.1.2.2.1.16.1} (ifOutOctets.1)
SNMP: Value = -1258921820 octets
SNMP:

.

.

.

```
------------------------------------ Frame 41 ------------------------------------
SNMP: ----- Simple Network Management Protocol (Version 1) -----
SNMP:
SNMP: Version = 0
SNMP: Community = public
SNMP: Command = Get next request
SNMP: Request ID = 733178609
SNMP: Error status = 0 (No error)
SNMP: Error index = 0
SNMP:
SNMP: Object = {1.3.6.1.2.1.2.2.1.17.4} (ifOutUcastPkts.4)
SNMP: Value = NULL
SNMP:
SNMP: Object = {1.3.6.1.2.1.2.2.1.18.4} (ifOutNUcastPkts.4)
SNMP: Value = NULL
SNMP:
SNMP: Object = {1.3.6.1.2.1.2.2.1.19.4} (ifOutDiscards.4)
SNMP: Value = NULL
SNMP:
SNMP: Object = {1.3.6.1.2.1.2.2.1.20.4} (ifOutErrors.4)
SNMP: Value = NULL
SNMP:
SNMP: Object = {1.3.6.1.2.1.2.2.1.21.4} (ifOutQLen.4)
SNMP: Value = NULL
SNMP:
SNMP: Object = {1.3.6.1.2.1.2.2.1.22.4} (ifSpecific.4)
SNMP: Value = NULL
SNMP:


------------------------------------ Frame 42 ------------------------------------

SNMP: ----- Simple Network Management Protocol (Version 1) -----
SNMP:
SNMP: Version = 0
SNMP: Community = public
```

431

```
SNMP: Command = Get response
SNMP: Request ID = 733178609
SNMP: Error status = 0 (No error)
SNMP: Error index = 0
SNMP:
SNMP: Object = {1.3.6.1.2.1.2.2.1.18.1} (ifOutNUcastPkts.1)
SNMP: Value = 10078921 packets
SNMP:
SNMP: Object = {1.3.6.1.2.1.2.2.1.19.1} (ifOutDiscards.1)
SNMP: Value = 0 packets
SNMP:
SNMP: Object = {1.3.6.1.2.1.2.2.1.20.1} (ifOutErrors.1)
SNMP: Value = 409 packets
SNMP:
SNMP: Object = {1.3.6.1.2.1.2.2.1.21.1} (ifOutQLen.1)
SNMP: Value = 0 packets
SNMP:
SNMP: Object = {1.3.6.1.2.1.2.2.1.22.1} (ifSpecific.1)
SNMP: Value = {0}
SNMP:
SNMP: Object = {1.3.6.1.2.1.3.1.1.1.0.1.XXX.YYY.170.0}
        (atIfIndex.0.1.XXX.YYY.170.0)
SNMP: Value = 0
SNMP:
```

This chapter has looked at various issues that network administrators may encounter when implementing SNMP. Many of these problems arise as the result of vendor-specific implementations that may be incompatible with each other. The wise network manager will be alert for these incompatibilities so that the challenge of managing complex internetworks can be simplified.

 # Addresses of Standards Organizations

ANSI STANDARDS

American National Standards
   Institute
11 West 42nd Street
New York, NY 10036
Tel: (212) 642-4900
Fax: (212) 398-0023
URL: http://www.ansi.org

ATIS PUBLICATIONS

Alliance for Telecommunications
   Industry Solutions (formerly the
   Exchange Carriers Standards
   Association)
1200 G St. N.W., Suite 500
Washington, DC 20005
Tel: (202) 628-6380
Fax: (202) 393-5453
URL: http://www.atis.org

AT&T PUBLICATIONS

Lucent Technologies
P.O. Box 19901
Indianapolis, IN 46219
Tel: (317) 322-6557 or
   (888) 582-3688
Fax: (800) 566-9568
URL: http://ciccatii.attdocs.com

BELLCORE STANDARDS

Bell Communications Research
Information Management Services
8 Corporate Place, Suite 3A-184
Piscataway, NJ 08854-4196
Tel: (908) 699-5800 or
   (800) 521-2673
Fax: (908) 336-2559
URL: http://www.bellcore.com

CSA STANDARDS

Canadian Standards Association
178 Rexdale Boulevard
Etobicoke, ONT M9W 1R9
Canada
Tel: (416) 747-4363
Fax: (416) 747-2473

DDN STANDARDS

DDN Network Information Center
Government Systems, Inc.
7990 Boeing Court, M/S CV-50
Vienna, VA 22183
Tel: (703) 821-6266 or
   (800) 365-3642

DISA STANDARDS
Defense Information Systems Agency
URL: http://www.itsi.disa.mil

ECMA STANDARDS
European Computer Manufacturers
    Association
114 Rue de Rhone
CH-1204 Geneva
Switzerland
Tel: 41 22 849 60 00
Fax: 41 22 849 60 01
Email: helpdesk@ecma.ch
URL: http://www.ecma.ch

EIA STANDARDS
Electronic Industries Association
2500 Wilson Blvd.
Arlington, VA 22201
Tel: (703) 907-7500
Fax: (703) 907-7501
URL: http://www.eia.org

ETSI STANDARDS
European Telecommunications
    Standards Institute
Route des Lucioles
F-06921
Sophia Antipolis
Cedex
France
Tel: 33 492 94 42 00
Fax: 33 493 65 47 16
Email: webmaster@etsi.fr
URL: http://www.etsi.fr

FEDERAL INFORMATION PROCESSING STANDARDS (FIPS)
U.S. Department of Commerce
National Technical Information Service
5285 Port Royal Road
Springfield, VA 22161
Tel: (703) 487-4650 or
    (800) 553-6847
Fax: (703) 321-8547

IEC STANDARDS
International Electrotechnical
    Commission
3, Rue de Varembé
P.O. Box 131
1211 Geneva 20
Switzerland
Tel: 41 22 919 02 11
Fax: 41 22 919 03 00
URL: http://www.iec.ch

IEEE STANDARDS
Institute of Electrical and Electronics
    Engineers
445 Hoes Lane
Piscataway, NJ 08855-1331
Tel: (908) 981-1393 or (800) 678-IEEE
Fax: (908) 562-1571
URL: http://www.ieee.org

INTERNET STANDARDS
Internet Society International
12020 Sunrise Valley Drive
Suite 210
Reston, VA 22191-3429
Tel: (703) 648-9888
Fax: (703) 648-9887
Email: isoc@isoc.org
URL: http://www.isoc.org

(See Appendix D for further
information)

ISO STANDARDS

International Organization for
  Standardization
1, Rue de Varembé
Case postale 56
CH-1211 Geneva 20
Switzerland
Tel: 41 22 749-0111
Fax: 41 22 733-3430
Email: central@iso.ch
URL: http://www.iso.ch

ITU STANDARDS

International Telecommunications
  Union
Information Services Department
Place des Nations
CH-1211 Geneva 20
Switzerland
Tel: 41 22 730 6141
Fax: 41 22 730 5194
Email: sales@itu.ch
URL: http://www.itu.ch

NATIONAL INSTITUTE OF STANDARDS AND TECHNOLOGY STANDARDS

Technology Building 820, NIST N,
  Room B-562
Gaithersburg, MD 20899
Tel: (301) 975-2816
Fax: (301) 948 6213
URL: http://www.ncsl.nist.gov

WWW STANDARDS

World Wide Web Consortium
Massachusetts Institute of Technology
Laboratory for Computer Science
545 Technology Square
Cambridge, MA 02139
Tel: (617) 253-2613
Fax: (617) 258-8682
E-Mail: www-request@w3.org
URL: http://www.w3.org

Many of the above standards may be
  purchased from:

Global Engineering Documents
15 Inverness Way East
Englewood, CO 80112
Tel: (303) 397-2715 or
  (800) 854-7179
Fax: (303) 397-2740
URL: http://www.ihs.com

Phillips Business Information, Inc.
1201 Seven Locks Road
Potomac, MD 20854
Tel: (301) 424 3338 or
  (800) 777-5006
Fax: (301) 309-3847
E-mail: clientservices.pbi@phillips.com

Acronyms and Abbreviations

A	ampere
AARP	AppleTalk Address Resolution Protocol
ABP	alternate bipolar
ACK	acknowledgement
ACS	asynchronous communication server
ACSE	Association Control Service Element
ACTLU	activate logical unit
ACTPU	activate physical unit
ADSP	AppleTalk Data Stream Protocol
AEP	AppleTalk Echo Protocol
AFP	AppleTalk Filing Protocol
AFRP	ARCNET Fragmentation Protocol
AGS	asynchronous gateway server
AI	artificial intelligence
AMI	alternate mark inversion
AMT	address mapping table
ANSI	American National Standards Institute
API	applications program interface
APPC	Advanced Program-to-Program Communication
ARE	all routes explorer
ARI	address recognized indicator bit

ARM	administrative runtime module
ARP	Address Resolution Program
ARPA	Advanced Research Projects Agency
ARPANET	Advanced Research Projects Agency Network
ASCII	American Standard Code for Information Interchange
ASN.1	Abstract Syntax Notation One
ASP	AppleTalk Session Protocol
ATM	Asynchronous Transfer Mode
ATP	AppleTalk Transaction Protocol
AVM	administrative view module
B8ZS	bipolar with 8 ZERO substitution
BC	block check
BER	Basic Encoding Rules
BIOS	Basic Input/Output System
BITNET	Because It's Time NETwork
BIU	basic information unit
BOC	Bell Operating Company
BOOTP	Bootstrap Protocol
BPDU	bridge protocol data unit
bps	bits per second
BPV	bipolar violations
BRI	basic rate interface
BSC	binary synchronous communication
BSD	Berkeley Software Distribution
BTU	basic transmission unit
BUI	browser user interface
CCIS	common channel interoffice signaling
CCITT	International Telegraph and Telephone Consultative Committee

CCR	commitment, concurrency, and recovery
CICS	customer information communication system
CLNP	Connectionless Network Protocol
CLNS	Connectionless-mode Network Services
CLTP	Connectionless Transport Protocol
CMIP	Common Management Information Protocol
CMIS	Common Management Information Service
CMISE	Common Management Information Service Element
CMOL	CMIP on IEEE 802.2 Logical Link Control
CMOT	Common Management Information Protocol over TCP/IP
CONS	Connection-mode Network Services
CORBA	Common Object Request Broker Architecture
COS	Corporation for Open Systems
CPE	customer premises equipment
CPE	convergence protocol entity
CRC	cyclic redundancy check
CREN	The Corporation for Research and Educational Networking
CRS	configuration report server
CSMA/CD	Carrier Sense Multiple Access with Collision Detection
CSNET	computer+science network
CSU	channel service unit
CTERM	Command Terminal Protocol
DAP	Data Access Protocol
DARPA	Defense Advanced Research Projects Agency
DAT	duplicate address test
DCA	Defense Communications Agency
DCC	Data Country Code

DCE	data circuit-terminating equipment
DDCMP	Digital Data Communications Message Protocol
DDN	Defense Data Network
DDP	Datagram Delivery Protocol
DECmcc	DEC Management Control Center
DEMPR	DEC multiport repeater
DIX	DEC, Intel, and Xerox
DL	data link
DLC	data link control
DMA	direct memory access
DMI	Desktop Management Interface
DMTF	Desktop Management Task Force
DNIC	Data Network Identification Code
DNS	Domain Name System
DOD	Department of Defense
DPA	demand protocol architecture
DRP	DECnet Routing Protocol
DSAP	destination service access point
DSU	data service unit
DSU/CSU	data service unit/channel service unit
DTE	data terminal equipment
DTR	data terminal ready
EBCDIC	Extended Binary Coded Decimal Interchange Code
ECL	End Communication layer
ECSA	Exchange Carriers Standards Association
EDI	electronic data interchange
EGA	enhanced graphics array
EGP	Exterior Gateway Protocol
EIA	Electronic Industries Association

ELAP	EtherTalk Link Access Protocol
EOT	end of transmission
ESF	extended superframe format
ES-IS	End System to Intermediate System Protocol
FAL	file access listener
FAT	file access table
FCC	Federal Communications Commission
FCI	frame copied indicator bit
FCS	frame check sequence
FDDI	fiber data distributed interface
FDM	frequency division multiplexing
FID	format identifier
FIPS	Federal Information Processing Standard
FM	function management
FMD	function management data
FT1	fractional T1
FTAM	File Transfer Access and Management
FTP	File Transfer Protocol
G	giga-
GB	gigabyte
GHz	gigahertz
GOSIP	Government OSI profile
GUI	graphical user interface
HA	hardware address
HDLC	high-level data link control
HEMS	high-level entity management system
HLLAPI	High-level language API
HMMO	Hypermedia Managed Object
HMOM	Hypermedia Object Manager

HMMP	Hypermedia Management Protocol
HMMS	Hypermedia Management Schema
HTML	Hypertext Markup Language
HTTP	Hypertext Transfer Protocol
Hz	hertz
IAB	Internet Activities Board
IANA	Internet Assigned Numbers Authority
ICD	international code designator
ICMP	Internet Control Message Protocol
ICP	Internet Control Protocol
IDP	Internetwork Datagram Protocol
IEEE	Institute of Electrical and Electronics Engineers
IETF	Internet Engineering Task Force
I/G	individual/group
IGP	Interior Gateway Protocol
IGRP	Internet Gateway Routing Protocol
IMPS	interface message processors
I/O	input/output
IOC	inter-office channel
IP	Internet Protocol
IPC	Interprocess Communications Protocol
IPX	Internetwork Packet Exchange Protocol
IR	Internet router
IRTF	Internet Research Task Force
ISDN	Integrated Services Digital Network
IS-IS	Intermediate System to Intermediate System Protocol
ISO	International Organization for Standardization
ISODE	ISO Development Environment
ITU	International Telecommunication Union

IXC	inter-exchange carrier
JDBC	Java Database Connectivity
JMAPI	Java Management Application Programming Interface
Kbps	kilobits per second
KHz	kilohertz
LAA	locally administered address
LAN	local area network
LAP	link access procedure
LAPB	Link Access Procedure Balanced
LAPD	Link Access Procedure D Channel
LAT	Local Area Transport
LATA	local access transport area
LAVC	local area VAX cluster
LDAP	Lightweight Directory Access Protocol
LEC	local exchange carrier
LEN	length
LF	largest frame
LLAP	LocalTalk Link Access Protocol
LLC	Logical Link Control
LME	layer management entity
LMI	layer management interface
LMMP	LAN/MAN Management Protocol
LMMPE	LAN/MAN Management Protocol Entity
LMMS	LAN/MAN Management Service
LMMU	LAN/MAN Management User
LPP	Lightweight Presentation Protocol
LSB	least significant bit
LSL	Link Support layer
MAC	medium access control

MAN	metropolitan area network
Mbps	megabits per second
MHS	message handling service
MHz	megahertz
MIB	management information base
MILNET	MILitary NETwork
MIOX	Multiprotocol Interconnect over X.25
MIPS	millions instructions per second
MIS	management information systems
MLID	multiple link interface driver
MNP	Microcom Networking Protocol
MOP	Maintenance Operations Protocol
MSAU	multistation access unit
MSB	most significant bit
MTA	message transfer agent
MTBF	mean time between failures
MTTR	mean time to repair
MTU	maximum transmission unit
MUX	multiplex, multiplexor
NACS	NetWare Asynchronous Communications Server
NAK	negative acknowledgement
NASI	NetWare Asynchronous Service Interface
NAU	network addressable unit
NAUN	nearest active upstream neighbor
NBP	Name Binding Protocol
NCP	Network Control Program
NCP	NetWare Core Protocol
NCSI	network communications services interface
NDIS	Network Driver Interface Standard

NetBEUI	NetBIOS Extended User Interface
NetBIOS	Network Basic Input/Output System
NFS	Network File System
NIC	network information center
NIC	network interface card
NICE	network information and control exchange
NIS	names information socket
NIST	National Institute of Standards and Technology
NLM	netware loadable module
NMS	network management station
NOC	network operations center
NOS	network operating system
NSF	National Science Foundation
NSP	Network Services Protocol
NT	network termination
OC1	optical carrier, level 1
ODI	Open Data Link Interface
OID	object identifier
OIM	OSI Internet management
OSF	Open Software Foundation
OSI	Open Systems Interconnection
OSI-RM	Open Systems Interconnection Reference Model
OSPF	Open Shortest Path First
PA	protocol address
PABX	private automatic branch exchange
PAD	packet assembler and disassembler
PAP	Printer Access Protocol
PBX	private branch exchange
PCI	protocol control information

PCM	pulse code modulation
PDN	public data network
PDU	protocol data unit
PEP	Packet Exchange Protocol
PLEN	protocol length
POP	point of presence
POSIX	Portable Operating System Interface-UNIX
POTS	plain old telephone service
PPP	Point-to-Point Protocol
PSN	packet switch node
PSP	presentation services process
PSPDN	packet switched public data network
PTP	point-to-point
PUC	Public Utility Commission
RARP	Reverse Address Resolution Protocol
RBOC	Regional Bell Operating Company
RC	routing control
RD	route descriptor
RFC	request for comments
RFS	remote file system
RH	request/response header
RI	routing information
RII	route information indicator
RIP	Routing Information Protocol
RJE	remote job entry
ROSE	Remote Operations Service Element
RMI	Remote Method Invocation
RMON	remote monitoring
RPC	remote procedure call

RPS	ring parameter server
RSX	Realtime Resource-Sharing eXecutive
RT	routing type
RU	request/response unit
SABME	set asynchronous balanced mode extended
SAP	service access point
SAP	Service Advertising Protocol
SCS	system communication services
SDLC	Synchronous Data Link Control
SDN	software defined network
SEQ	sequence
SGMP	Simple Gateway Management Protocol
SLIP	Serial Line IP
SMB	server message block
SMDS	Switched Multimegabit Data Service
SMI	structure of management information
SMI	system management interface
SMTP	Simple Mail Transfer Protocol
SNA	System Network Architecture
SNADS	Systems Network Architecture Distribution Services
SNAP	sub-network access protocol
SNMP	Simple Network Management Protocol
SOH	start of header
SONET	Synchronous Optical Network
SPP	Sequenced Packet Protocol
SPX	Sequenced Packet Exchange protocol
SR	source routing
SRF	specifically routed frame
SRI	Stanford Research Institute

SRT	source routing transparent
SSAP	source service access point
STE	spanning tree explorer
SUA	stored upstream address
SVC	switched virtual circuit
TB	terabyte
TCP	Transmission Control Protocol
TCP/IP	Transmission Control Protocol/Internet Protocol
TDM	time division multiplexing
TELNET	Telecommunications Network Protocol
TFTP	Trivial File Transfer Protocol
TH	transmission header
TLAP	TokenTalk Link Access Protocol
TLI	Transport Layer Interface
TLV	Type-Length-Value encoding
TP	Transport Protocol
TSR	terminate-and-stay resident
UA	unnumbered acknowledgement
UA	user agent
UDP	User Datagram Protocol
U/L	universal/local
ULP	Upper Layer Protocols
UNMA	unified network management architecture
UT	universal time
UTP	unshielded twisted pair
UUCP	UNIX to UNIX copy program
V	volt
VAN	value-added network
VAP	value-added process

VARP	VINES Address Resolution Protocol
VFRP	VINES Fragmentation Protocol
VGA	video graphics array
VICP	VINES Internet Control Protocol
VINES	Virtual Networking System
VIP	VINES Internet Protocol
VIPC	VINES Interprocess Communications
VLSI	very large-scale integration
VMS	virtual memory system
VRTP	VINES Routing Update Protocol
VSPP	VINES Sequenced Packet Protocol
VT	virtual terminal
WAN	wide area network
WBEM	Web-based Enterprise Management
WIN	window
XDR	External data representation
XID	exchange identification
XMP	X/Open Management Protocol
XNS	Xerox Network System
ZIP	Zone Information Protocol
ZIS	Zone Information Socket
ZIT	Zone Information Table

 # Selected Manufacturers of SNMP-related Internetworking Products

Access Beyond
One Palmer Terrace
Carlstadt, NJ 07072
(201) 438-2400
(800) 456-7844
Fax: (201) 438-7767

Acer America
2641 Orchard Parkway
San Jose, CA 95135
(408) 433-6200
(800) 733-2237
Fax: (408) 922-2953

ADC Kentrox
14375 NW Science Park Drive
Portland, OR 97229
(503) 643-1681
(800) 733-5511
Fax: (503) 626-3628

ADI Systems
2115 Ringwood Avenue
San Jose, CA 95131
(408) 944-0100
(800) 228-0530
Fax: (408) 944-0300

Advanced Logic Research
9401 Jeronimo
Irvine, CA 92718
(714) 581-6770
(800) 444-4257
Fax: (714) 581-9240

AG Group Inc.
2540 Camino Diablo Suite #200
Walnut Creek, CA 94956
(510) 937-7900
(800) 466-2447
Fax: (510) 937-2479

Agranat Systems Inc.
1345 Main Street
Waltham, MA 02154
(617) 893-7868
Fax: (617) 893-5740

Alcatel Network Systems
2912 Wake Forest Road
Raleigh, NC 27609
(919) 850-6000
(Fax) (919) 850-6171

Allen Systems Group
750 11th Street South
Naples, FL 34102
(941) 263-8447
Fax: (941) 263-1952

Allied Telesis, Inc.
950 Kifer Road
Sunnyvale, CA 94086
(408) 730-0950
(800) 424-4282
Fax: (408) 736-0100

Alpha Technologies
3767 Alpha Way
Bellingham, WA 90226
(360) 647-2360
(800) 322-5742
Fax: (360) 671-4936

Alta Group of Cadence Systems
555 N. Matilda
Sunnyvale, Ca 94086
(408) 733-1595
Fax: (408) 523-4601

American Hytech Corporation
565 William Pitt Way
Pittsburgh, PA 15238
(412) 826-3333
Fax: (412) 826-3335

American Power Conversion Corporation
132 Fairgrounds Road
West Kingston, RI 02892
(401) 789-5735
(800) 800-4272
Fax: (401) 789-3710

AMP
2800 Fulling Mill Road
P.O. Box 3068
Harrisburg, PA 17105
(717) 564-0100
(800) 522-6752
Fax: (717) 986-7575

Andrew Corporation
23610 Telo Avenue
Torrance, CA 90505
(310) 784-8000
(800) 328-2696
Fax: (310) 784-8090

Anixter Brothers, Inc.
6602 Owens Drive, Suite #300
Pleasanton, CA 94588
(510) 463-1223
(800) 278-2802
Fax: (510) 463-1255

Ansel Communications
8711 148th Avenue NE
Redmond, WA 98052
(206) 869-4928
(800) 341-7978
Fax: (206) 869-5015

Apertus
7275 Fly Cloud Drive
Eden Prairie, MN 55344
(612) 828-0300
(800) 826-0313
Fax: (612) 828-0299

Apple Computer, Inc.
20525 Mariani Avenue
Cupertino, CA 95014
(408) 996-1010
(800) 776-2333
Fax: (408) 974-6726

Applied Digital Access
9855 Scanton Road
San Diego, CA 92121
(619) 623-2200
Fax: (619) 623-2208

APT Communications, Inc.
9607 Dr. Perry Road
Ijamsville, MD 21754
(301) 874-3305
(800) 842-0626
Fax: (301) 874-3308

Asante Technologies
821 Fox Lane
San Jose, CA 95131
(408) 435-8388
(800) 662-9686
Fax: (408) 432-1117

Ascend
1701 Harbor Bay Parkway
Alameda, CA 94502
(510) 769-6001
Fax: (510) 814-2300

Ascom Timeplex Inc.
400 Chestnut Ridge Road
Woodcliff Lake, NJ 07675
(201) 391-1111
Fax: (201) 391-0852

AST Computer
16215 Altone Parkway
Irvine, CA 92619
(714) 727-4141
(800) 876-4278

Astrocom
2700 Sumner Street NE
Minneapolis, MN 55413
(612) 378-7800
(800) 669-6242
(612) 378-1070

Attachmate Corporation
3617 131st Avenue SE
Bellevue, WA 98006
(206) 644-4010
(800) 426-6283
Fax: (206) 747-9924

Auspex Systems Inc.
5200 Great American Parkway
Santa Clara, CA 95054
(408) 492-0900
Fax: (408) 986-2020

Autotrol Technology
12500 N. Washington Street
Denver, CO 80241
(303) 452-4919
(800) 233 2882
Fax: (303) 252-2249

Avanti Technology
13492 Reasearch Blvd. #120
Austin, TX 78750
(512) 335-12168
(800) 638-1168
Fax: (512) 335-7838

Aydin Computer & Monitor Systems

700 Dresher Road
Horsham, PA 19044
(215) 657-8600
Fax: (215) 657-5470

Banyan Systems, Inc.

120 Flanders Road
Westboro, MA 01581
(508) 898-1000
(800) 222-6926
Fax: (800) 932-9226

Bay Networks

200 Bulfinch Drive
Andover, MA 01810
(508) 682-1600
(800) 526-2489
Fax: (508) 682-3200

BBN Communications Corporation

150 Cambridge Park Drive
Cambridge, MA 02140
(617) 873-2000
Fax: (617) 873-6846

BGS Systems

1 First Avenue
Waltham, MA 02254
(617) 891-0000
Fax: (617) 890-0000

Bear Computer Systems Inc.

9584 Topanga Canyon Blvd.
Chatsworth CA 91311
(818) 341-0403
(800) 255-0662
Fax: (818) 341-1831

Bellcore

331 Newman Springs Road
Red Bank, NJ 07701-7030
(908) 758-2000
(800) 521-2673

Best Power Technology

N9246 Highway 80
Necedah, WI 54646
(608) 565-7200
(800) 365-5794
Fax: (608) 565-2929

BGS Systems, Incorporated

One First Avenue
Waltham, MA 02254
(617) 891-0000
Fax: (617) 890-0000

Black Box Corporation

P.O. Box 12800
Pittsburgh, PA 15241
(412) 746-5500
(800) 552-6816
Fax: (412) 746-0746

BMC

1190 Saratoga Avenue Suite #130
San Jose, CA 95129
(408) 556-0720
Fax: (408) 556-0735

BMC Software, Inc.

2101 City West Blvd.
Houston, TX 77042
(713) 918-8800

Boole & Babbage
3131 Zanker Road
San Jose, CA 95134
(408) 525-3000
(800) 544-2152
Fax: (408) 526-3055

Brideway
P.O. Box 229
Redmond, WA 98073-0229
(206) 881-4270
(800) 275-6849
Fax: (206) 861-1774

BRIO Technology, Inc.
3950 Fabian Way Suite #200
Palo Alto, CA 94303
(415) 856-8000
(800) 874-2746
Fax: (415) 856-8020

Brixton Systems
185 Alewise Parkway
Cambridge, MA 02138
(617) 876-5359

Bytex
4 Technology Drive
Westborough MA 01581
(508) 366-8000
(800) 227-1145
Fax: (508) 366-7977

Cabletron Systems, Inc.
35 Industrial Way
Rochester, NH 03866-0505
(603) 332-9400
Fax: (603) 335-4658

CACI Products
3333 N. Torey Pines Ct. #3333
La Jolla, CA 92037
(619) 457-9681
Fax: (619) 457-1184

Candle Corporation
2425 Olympic Blvd.
Santa Monica, CA 90404
(310) 829-5800
Fax: (310) 582-4287

Castle Rock Computing
20863 Stevens Creek Boulevard
Suite 530
Cupertino, CA 95014
(408) 366-6540
Fax: (408) 252-2379

Cayman Systems, Inc.
100 Maple Street
Stoneham, MA 02180
(617) 279-1101
(800) 473-4776
Fax: (617) 438-5560

CD Connections
P.O. Box 1798
Norcross, GA 30071
(770) 446-1332
(800) 344-8426
Fax: (770) 446-9164

Centura Software
1060 Marsh Road
Menlo Park, CA 94025
(415) 321-8500
(800) 444-8782
Fax: (415) 617-4772

Cheyenne Software Inc.
3 Express Way Plaza
Roslyn Heights, NY 11577
(516) 465-4000
(800) 243-9462
Fax: (516) 484-3446

Cisco Systems, Inc.
1525 O'Brien Drive
Menlo Park, CA 94025
(408) 526-4000
(800) 553-6387
Fax: (408) 526-4100

Citrix Systems
6400 NW 6th Way
Ft. Lauderdale, FL 33309
(800) 437-7503
Fax: (934) 267-9319

Clarify, Incorporated
2125 O'Nel Drive
San Jose, CA 95131
(408) 573-3000
Fax: (408) 573-3001

Clary
1960 S. Walker Avenue
Monrovia, CA 91016
(818) 359-4486
(800) 442-5279
Fax: (818) 305-0254

Clearpoint Research Corporation
25 Birch Street Unit #B41
Milford, MA 01757
(508) 473-6111
(800) 253-2778
Fax: (508) 473-0112

CNet Technology
1455 McCandless Drive
Milpidas, CA 95034
(408) 934-0800
(800) 486-2638
Fax: (408) 934-0900

Codenoll Technology
200 Corporate Blvd. South
Yonkers, NY 10701
(914) 965-6300
(800) 966-1512
Fax: (914) 965-9811

Codex/Motorola
20 Cabot Blvd.
Mansfield, MA 02048
(508) 261-4000

Compatible Systems Corporation
P.O. Drawer 17220
Boulder, CO 80308
(303) 444-9532
(800) 356-0283
Fax: (303) 444-9595

COMPAQ Computer Corporation
20555 State Highway 249
MS 040505/RM 4519
Houston, TX 77070
(713) 514-4711
(800) 345-1518
Fax: (713) 518-7379

Computer Associates International, Inc.
1 Computer Associates Plaza
Islandia, NY 11788
(516) 342-6952

Computer Network Technology

6500 Wedgwood Road
Maple Grove, MN 55369
(612) 550-8000
Fax: (612) 550-8800

Compuware Corporation

31440 Northwestern Highway
Farmington Hills, MI 48334-2564
(810) 737-7300
(800) 535-8707

Concord Communications, Inc.

33 Boston Post Road West
Marlborough, MA 01752
(508) 460-4646
Fax: (508) 481-9772

Concurrent Computer Corporation

2101 W. Cypress Creek Road
Fort Lauderdale, FL 33309
(954) 974-1700
(800) 666-4544
Fax: (954) 977-5580

Connectware

1301 E. Arapaho Road
Richardson, TX 75081
(415) 578-6457
(800) 357-0852

Control Data Systems

4201 N. Lexington Avenue
Arden Hills, MN 55126
(612) 415-2999
(800) 345-6628
Fax: (612) 415-3000

CrossComm Corporation

450 Donald Lynch Blvd.
Marlborough, MA 01752
(508) 481-4060
(800) 388-1200
Fax: (508) 490-5535

Crystal Point, Inc.

22232 17th Avenue S.E. Suite #307
Bothell, WA 98021
(206) 487-3656
(800) 982-0628
Fax: (206) 487-3773

Dalcon Computer Services

1321 Murfreesboro Road
Nashville, TN 37217
(615) 366-4300
Fax: (615) 361-3800

Danpex

1342 Ridder Park Drive
San Jose, CA 95131
(408) 437-7557
(800) 452-1551
Fax: (408) 437-7559

Data General Corporation

4400 Computer Drive
Westboro, MA 01580
(508) 898-5000
(800) 328-2436
Fax: (508) 366-1319

Data Interface Systems Corporation

11824 Jollyville Road Suite #500
Austin, TX 78759
(512) 335-8200
(800) 351-4244
Fax: (512) 335-9110

Datapoint Corporation
8410 Datapoint Drive
San Antonio, TX 78229-8410
(210) 593-7000
(800) 733-1500
Fax: (210) 593-7920

DataTech Systems
20 C Commerce Way
Totow, NJ 07512
(201) 890-4800
Fax: (201) 890-2880

Daystar Digital, Inc.
5556 Atlanta Highway
Flowery Branch, GA 30542
(770) 967-2077
Fax: (800) 438-0370

Dell Computer Corporation
1 Dell Way
Round Rock, TX 78682
(512) 338-4400
(800) 426-5150
Fax: (512) 728-0568

Denmac Systems, Inc.
1945 Technology Road Unit #4
Northbrook, IL 60062
(847) 291-7760
(800) 315-0952
Fax: (847) 291-7763

Desktalk Systems, Inc.
19401 S. Vermont Avenue Suite #F100
Torrance, CA 90502
(310) 323-5998
(800) 337-5825
Fax: (310) 323-6197

Dickens Data Systems
1175 Northmeadow Parkway Suite #150
Roswell, GA 30076
(770) 625-7500
(800) 448-6177
Fax: (770) 625-7525

Digilog
2360 Maryland Road
Willow Grove, PA 19090
(215) 830-9400
(800) 344-4564
Fax: (215) 830-9444

Digital Equipment Corporation
111 Powder Mill Road
Maynard, MA 01754
(508) 493-5111
(800) 344-4825
Fax: (508) 493-7374

Digital Link
217 Humboldt Court
Sunnyvale, CA 94089
(408) 745-6200
(800) 441-1142
Fax: (408) 745-6250

Digitech Industries
55 Kenosha Avenue
Danbury, CT 06813
(203) 797-2676
Fax: (203) 797-2682

D-Link Systems
5 Musick
Irvine, CA 92718
(714) 455-1688
Fax: (714) 455-2521

E-Comms
5720 144th Street NW
Gig Harbor, WA 98332
(206) 857-3399
(800) 247-1431
Fax: (206) 857-3444

Eicon Technology Corporation
14755 Preston Road Suite #620
Dallas, TX 75240
(214) 239-3270
(800) 803-4266
Fax: (972) 239-3304

Emulex Corporation
14711 N.E. 29th Place
Bellevue, WA 98007
(206) 881-5773
(800) 950-5774
Fax: (206) 867-5022

Encore Computer Systems Division
6901 W. Sunrise Blvd.
Plantation, FL 33313
(954) 587-2900
Fax: (954) 797-5793

Epilogue Technology Corporation
201 Moffett Park Drive
Sunnyvale, CA 94089
(408) 542-1500
Fax: (408) 542-1961

Equinox Systems
One Equinox Way
Sunrise, FL 33351-6709
(954) 746-9000
(800) 275-3500
Fax: (954) 746-9101

Essex Systems, Inc.
P.O. Box 68
Middleton MA 01949
(508) 750-6200
(800) 672-8272
Fax: (508) 750-4699

Farallon Computing, Inc.
2470 Mariner Sq. Loop
Alameda, CA 94501
(510) 814-5100
Fax: (510) 814-5020

Fastland Technologies, Inc.
5151 George Street, 11th Floor
Halifax, Nova Scotia B3J3M3
Canada
(902) 421-5353
(800) 947-6752
Fax: (902) 421-5356

Fast Net
13800 Senlac
Dallas, TX 75234
(214) 654-5000
(800) 327-8638
Fax: (214) 654-5500

FEL Computing
10 Main Street
P.O. Box 72
Williamsville, VT 05362
(802) 348-7171
(800) 639-4110
Fax: (802) 348-7124

FiberCom Inc.
3353 Orange Avenue N.E.
Roanoke, VA 24012
(540) 342-6700
(800) 423-1183
Fax: (540) 342-5961

Fore Systems
174 Thorn Hill Road
Warrendale, PA 15086
(412) 772-6600
Fax: (412) 772-6500

Franz Inc.
1995 University Avenue
Berkeley, CA 94704
(510) 548-3600
(800) 325-6766

Frederick Engineering Inc.
10200 Old Columbia Road
Columbia, MD 21046
(410) 290-9000
(888) 866-9001
Fax: (410) 381-7180

Frontier Software Development, Inc.
321 Billerica Road
Chelmsford, MA 01824
(508) 244-4000
Fax: (508) 244-4004

Frontier Technologies Inc.
10201 N. Port Washington Road 13 West
Mequon, WI 53092
(414) 241-4555
(800) 929-3054
Fax: (414) 241-7084

FTP Software, Inc.
2 High Street
No. Andover, MA 01845
(508) 685-4000
(800) 382-4387
Fax: (508) 794-4477

Fujitsu America, Inc.
3055 Orchard Drive
San Jose, CA 95134-2022
(408) 432-1300
(800) 626-4686
Fax: (408) 432-1318

Fulcrum Technologies, Inc.
785 Carling Avenue
Ottawa, Ontario K1S5H4
(613) 238-1761
Fax: (613) 238-7695

Gandalf Data Inc.
501 Delran Parkway
Delran, NJ 08075
(609) 461-8100
(800) 426-3253
Fax: (609) 461-5186

Garrett Technologies
48531 Warm Springs Blvd. Suite #401
Freemont, CA 94539
(510) 438-9071
Fax: (510) 438-9072

General DataCom, Inc.
1579 Straits Turnpike
Middlebury, CT 06762-1299
(203) 574-1118
Fax: (203) 758-1460

General Signal
13000 Midlantic Drive
Mt. Laurel, NJ 08054
(609) 234-7900
(800) 222-0187
Fax: (609) 778-8700

GN Net Test
63 S. Street
Hopkinton, MA 01748
(508) 435-3800
(800) 233-3800
Fax: (508) 435-0448

Hadax Electronics
310 Phillips Avenue
South Hackensack, NJ 07606
(201) 807-1155
Fax: (201) 807-1782

Hayes Microcomputer Products, Inc.
P.O. Box 105203
Atlanta, GA 30348
(770) 840-9200
Fax: (770) 447-0178

Helios Systems
1996 Lundy Avenue
San Jose, CA 95131
(408) 432-0292
(800) 366-2983
Fax: (408) 943-1309

Hewlett-Packard Company
3000 Hanover Street
Palo Alto, CA 94304
(415) 857-1501
(800) 752-0900

Hewlett-Packard
Colorado Telecommunications Division
5070 Centennial Blvd.
Colorado Springs, CO 80919
(719) 531-4000
Fax: (719) 531-4505

Hewlett-Packard Business Computing Systems
19091 Pruneridge Avenue
Cupertino, CA 95014
(800) 752-0900

Honeywell Information Systems
Federal Systems Divisions
7900 West Park Drive
McLean, VA 22102
(703) 827-3894
Fax: (703) 827-3729

Humming Bird Communications
706 St. Hillsborough Street
Raleigh, NC 27603
(919) 831-8989
(800) 463-6637
Fax: (919) 831-8990

IBM
Old Orchard Road
Armonk, NY 10504
(914) 765-1900
(800) 426-2468
Fax: (800) 232-9426

IDEAssociates, Inc.
7 Oak Park
Bedford, MA 01301
(617) 275-2800
(800) 257-5027
Fax: (617) 533-0500

Imagenet
70 Walnut Street
Welsely, MA 02181
(617) 239-8197
Fax: (617) 239-8198

IMC Networks
16931 Milliken Avenue
Irvine, CA 92606
(714) 724-1070
(800) 624-1070
Fax: (714) 724-1020

Information Presentation Technologies
994 Mill Street Suite #200
San Luis Obispo, CA 93401
(805) 541-3000
Fax: (805) 541-3037

Informix Software, Inc.
16011 College Blvd.
Lenexa, KS 66219
(913) 599-7100
(800) 331-1763
Fax: (913) 599-8590

Inotech
11240 Waples Mill Suite #200
Fairfax, VA 22030
(800) 466-8324

Intel Corporation
2402 W. Beardsley Road
Phoenix, AZ 85027
(503) 696-8080
(800) 538-3373
Fax: (800) 525-3019

Intergraph Corporation
1 Madison Industrial Park
Huntsville, AL 35894-0001
(205) 730-2000
(800) 345-4856
Fax: (205) 730-9441

Interlink Computer Sciences, Inc.
47370 Fremont Blvd.
Fremont, CA 94538
(510) 657-9800
(800) 422-3711
Fax: (510) 659-6381

International Data Sciences
475 Jefferson Blvd.
Warwick, RI 02886
(401) 737-9900
(800) 437-3282
Fax: (401) 737-9911

International Network Services
1213 Innsbruck Drive
Sunnyvale, CA 94088
(408) 542-0100
(888) 467-8100
Fax: (408) 542-0101

J & L Information Systems
9600 Topanag Canyon Blvd.
Chatsworth, CA 91311
(818) 709-1778
(800) 456-1333
Fax: (818) 882-1424

Kaspia Systems, Inc.
8625 SW Cascade Suite #602
Beaverton, OR 97008
(503) 644-1800
Fax: (503) 520-0600

LANart

145 Rosemary Street
Needham, MA 02194
(617) 444-1994
(800) 292-1994
Fax: (617) 444-3692

LANCast

12 Murphy Drive
Nashua, NH 03062
(603) 880-1833
(800) 952-6227
Fax: (603) 881-9888

LAN City

200 Bulfinch Drive
Andover, MA 01810
(508) 682-1600
(800) 526-2489
Fax: (508) 682-1300

LAND-5

9747 Business Park Avenue Suite #100
San Diego, CA 92131
(619) 566-2514
(800) 526-3885
Fax: (619) 566-3611

LANOptics

2445 Midway Road Bldg. #2
Carlton, TX 75006
(972) 738-6900
(800) 533-8439
Fax: (972) 738-6999

Lantronix

15353 Barranca Parkway
Irvine, CA 92618
(714) 453-3990
(800) 422-7055
Fax: (714) 453-3995

Lanwan Technologies

1566 La Pradera Drive
Campbell, CA 95008
(408) 374-8190
Fax: (408) 741-0152

LarseCom Incorporated

4600 Patrick Henry Drive
Santa Clara, CA 95052
(408) 988-6600
Fax: (408) 986-8690

Lebert Corporation

9650 Jeronimo Road
Irvine, CA 92618
(714) 457-3600
Fax: (714) 457-3719

Legato Systems

3210 Porter Drive
Palo Alto, Ca 94304
(415) 812-6000
Fax: (415) 812-6032

Liebert

1050 Deerborn Drive
Columbus, OH 43229
(614) 841-5747
(800) 877-9222
Fax: (614) 841-6901

Link Age Software
11 Church Street Suite #400
Toronto, Ontario MSE1W1
Canada
(416) 862-7148
Fax: (416) 862-2569

Livingston Enterprises, Inc.
4464 Willow Road
Pleasanton, CA 94588
(510) 426-0770
(800) 458-9966
Fax: (510) 426-8951

Lockhead Martin
9970 Federal Drive
Colorado Springs, CO 80921
(719) 594-1000
Fax: (719) 594-1305

Luxcom Inc.
3249 Laurelview Court
Fremont, CA 94538
(510) 770-3300
(888) 458-9266
Fax: (510) 770-3399

Madge Networks, Inc.
2310 North 1st Street
San Jose, CA 95131
(408) 955-0700
(800) 876-2343
Fax: (408) 955-0970

Make Systems Inc.
San Antonio Circle Suite #225
Mountain View, CA 94040
(415) 941-9800
(800) 545-6253
Fax: (415) 941-5856

Maximum Computer Technologies Inc.
1000 Cobb Place Blvd. Suite #210
Kennesaw, GA 30144
(770) 428-5000
(800) 582-9337
Fax: (770) 428-5009

MCI Communications Corporation
8003 W. Park Drive
McLean, VA 22102
(800) 888-0800
Fax: (703) 260-7099

Meridian
11 McBride Corporation Center Dr.
   Suite #250
Chesterfield, MO 63005
(314) 532-7708
Fax: (314) 532-3242

MGE-UPS Systems
1660 Civic Avenue
Costa Mesa, CA 92626
(514) 435-1445
(800) 344-0570

Micom Systems, Inc.
4100 Los Angeles Avenue
Simi Valley, CA 93063
(805) 583-8600
(800) 642-6687
Fax: (805) 583-1997

Microcom, Inc.
500 River Ridge Drive
Norwood, MA 02062-5028
(617) 551-1000
(800) 822-8224
Fax: (617) 551-1006

Micro Dyne
3601 Eisenhaurer Avenue Suite #300
Alexandria, VA 22304
(703) 329-3700
(800) 255-3967
Fax: (703) 329-3722

Micro Integration
1 Science Park
Frostburg, MA 215322
(301) 689-0800
(800) 832-4526
Fax: (301) 689-0808

Micromuse
780 3rd Avenue 8th Floor
New York, NY 10017
(212) 758-1222
Fax: (212) 753-5252

Microsoft Corporation
One Microsoft Way
Redmond, WA 98052-6399
(206) 882-8080
Fax: (206) 936-7329

Micro Technology
4905 E. La Palma Avenue
Anaheim, CA 92807
(714) 970-0300
(800) 999-9684
Fax: (714) 970-5743

Microtest, Inc.
4747 No. 22nd Street
Phoenix, AZ 85016
(602) 952-6400
(800) 526-9675
Fax: (602) 952-6401

Midnight Networks Inc.
200 5th Avenue
Waltham, MA 02154
(617) 890-1001
(888) 809-8378
Fax: (617) 890-0028

Mil 3 Incorporated
3007 Tilden Street NW
Washington, DC 20008
(202) 364-6182
Fax: (202) 364-6182

Miramar Systems
121 Gray Avenue Suite #200
Santa Barbara, CA 93101
(805) 966-2432
(800) 862-2526
Fax: (805) 965-1824

Mitsubishi Electronics America
5665 Plaza Drive
Cypress, CA 90630
(800) 843-2515
Fax: (800) 937-2094

Momentum Software Corporation
777 Terrace Avenue
Hasbrouck Heights, NJ 07604
(201) 288-5373
(800) 767-1462
Fax: (201) 288-5474

Motorola Codex
20 Cabot Blvd.
Mansfield, MA 02048
(508) 261-4000
(800) 544-0062
Fax: (508) 261-7118

Mt. Xinu, Inc.
2560 9th Street, Suite #312
Berkeley, CA 94710
(510) 644-0146
Fax: (510) 644-2680

Multi-Tech Systems
2205 Woodale Drive
Mounds View, MN 55112
(612) 785-3500
(800) 328-9717
Fax: (612) 785-9874

Mux Lab
5540 Cote De Liesse
Mt. Royal, Quebec H4P 1A5
Canada
(514) 735-2741
(800) 361-1965
Fax: (514) 735-8057

National Information Bureau
14 Washington Road Suite #202
Princeton Junction, NJ 08550
(609) 936-2900
(800) 553-3776
Fax: (609) 936-2859

National Semiconductor
2900 Semiconductor Dr. 16-195 M/S
Santa Clara, CA 95052
(800) 721-5000
Fax: (408) 721-6526

NBase Communications
12401 Middlebrook Road Suite #160
Germantown, MD 20874
(301) 601-2800
(800) 966-4444
Fax: (301) 601-2902

NCR Corporation
1700 S. Patterson Blvd.
Dayton, OH 45479
(937) 445-5000
(800) 225-5627

NEC America
1525 Walnut Hill Lane
Irving, TX 75038
(214) 518-5000
(800) 222-4632
Fax: (214) 518-5572

Neon Software, Inc.
3685 Mt. Diablo Blvd. Suite #203
Lafayette, CA 94549
(510) 283-9771
(800) 334-6366
Fax: (510) 283-6507

Netcom Systems, Inc.
20500 Nordhoff
Chatsworth, CA 91311
(818) 700-5100
Fax: (818) 709-0827

NetFrame Systems
1545 Barber Lane
Milpitas, CA 95035
(408) 474-1000
Fax: (408) 474-4100

NetIQ
275 Saratoga Avenue Suite #260
Santa Clara, CA 95050
(408) 556-0888
Fax: (408) 248-9118

Netlink

1881 Worcester Road
Framingham, MA 01701
(508) 879-6306
(800) 638-5465
Fax: (508) 872-8136

NetManage, Inc.

10725 N. Deanza Blvd.
Cupertino, CA 95014
(408) 973-7171
Fax: (408) 257-6405

NetPhone

313 Boston Post Road West
Marlbough, MA 01752
(508) 787-1000
Fax: (508) 787-1030

Netscape Communications Corporation

501 E. Middlefield Road
Mountain View, CA 94043
(415) 937-2555
(800) 638-7483
Fax: (415) 528-4140

Netsolve, Inc.

9130 Jollyville Road Suite #200
Austin, TX 78759
(512) 795-3000
(800) 638-7658

Netsys Technologies, Inc.

100 Hamlter Avenue Suite #100
Palo Alto, CA 94301
(415) 833-7500
(800) 638-5065
Fax: (415) 833-7597

Network Appliance

319 Bernardo Avenue
Mountain View, CA 94043
(415) 428-5100
(800) 220-4622
Fax: (415) 428-5151

Network Communications Corporation

5501 Green Valley Drive
Bloomington, MN 55437
(612) 844-0584
(800) 451-1984
Fax: (612) 844-0487

Network Design and Analysis

60 Gough Road 2nd Floor
Markem, Ontario L3R87
Canada
(905) 477-9534
(800) 387-4234
Fax: (905) 477-9572

Network Equipment Technologies, Inc.

800 Saginaw Drive
Redwood City, CA 94063
(415) 366-4400
(800) 234-4638
Fax: (415) 366-5675

Network General Corporation

4200 Bohannon Drive
Menlo Park, CA 94025
(415) 473-2000
(800) 764-3337
Fax: (415) 321-0855

467

Network Performance Institute
P.O. Box 41-4295
Miami, FL 33141
(305) 864-2744
Fax: (305) 868-0530

Network Peripherals, Inc.
1371 McCarthy Blvd.
Milpitas, CA 95035
(408) 321-7300
(800) 674-8855
Fax: (408) 321-9218

Network Systems Corporation
7600 Boone Avenue North
Minneapolis, MN 55428
(612) 424-8777
(800) 248-8777
Fax: (612) 424-1661

Newbridge Networks
593 Herndon Parkway
Herndon, VA 22070-5241
(703) 834-3600
(800) 343-3600
Fax: (703) 471-7080

NewWay Internet Services
P.O. Box 957
Milton, WA 98354
(800) 782-1010
Fax: (206) 838-8489

Novadigm, Incorporated
One International Blvd. Suite #200
Mahwah, NJ 07495
(201) 512-1000
(800) 526-6682
Fax: (201) 512-1001

Novell, Inc.
122 East 1700 South
Provo, UT 84606
(801) 429-7000
(888) 321-4272
Fax: (801) 228-9516

Novell, Inc.
2180 Fortune Drive
San Jose, CA 95131
(408) 434-2300
(800) 453-1267

Ollicom USA
900 E. Park Blvd. Suite #250
Plano, TX 75074
(214) 423-7560
(800) 265-4266
Fax: (214) 423-7261

Onion Peel Software LLC
4208 Six Forks Road Suite #246
Raleigh, N.C. 27609
(919) 571-7910

OpenConnect Systems Inc.
2711 LBJ Freeway Suite #800
Dallas, TX 75234
(214) 484-5200
Fax: (214) 551-5881

Open Route Networks
9 Technology Drive
Westborough, MA 01581
(508) 879-6994
(800) 545-7464
Fax: (508) 366-8901

468

Openvision Technologies, Inc.
7133 Koll Center Parkway, Suite #200
Pleasanton, CA 94566
(510) 426-6400
(800) 223-6736
Fax: (510) 426-6486

Optical Data Systems
1101 E. Arapaho Road
Richardson, TX 75081
(214) 234-6400
Fax: (214) 234-4059

Oracle Corporation
500 Oracle Parkway
Redwood Shores, CA 94065
(415) 506-7000
(800) 392-2999
Fax: (415) 506-7200

Osi Com
7402 Hollister Avenue
Santa Barbara, CA 93117
(805) 968-4262
(888) 767-4767
Fax: (805) 968-6478

Packard Bell
5701 Lindero Canyon Road
West Lake Village, CA 91362
(801) 579-0090
(800) 733-5858
Fax: (801) 579-0093

PairGain Technologies
14402 Franklin Avenue
Tuston, CA 92680-7013
(714) 832-9922
Fax: (714) 832-9924

Pacific Softworks
4000 Via Pescador
Camarillo, CA 93012
(805) 484-2128
Fax: (805) 484-3929

PeopleSoft
4440 Rosewood Drive
Pleasanton, CA 94588-3031
(510) 225-3000
(800) 947-7753
Fax: (510) 225-3100

Peregrine Systems Inc.
12670 Highbluff Drive
San Diego, CA 92130
(619) 481-500
(800) 638-5231
Fax: (619) 481-1751

Persoft Inc.
465 Science Drive
Madison, WI 53711
(608) 273-6000
(800) 368-5283
Fax: (608) 273-8227

Platinum Technology Inc.
8045 Leesburg Pike, 3rd Floor
Vienna, VA 22182
(703) 620-6500
(800) 442-6861
Fax: (800) 442-4230

Plexcom
2255 Agate Court
Simi Valley, CA 93065
(805) 522-3333
(800) 753-9526
Fax: (805) 583-4764

Process Software Corporation

959 Concord Street
Framingham, MA 01701
(508) 879-6994
(800) 722-7770
Fax: (508) 879-0042

Proginet Corporation

200 Garden City Plaza
Garden City, NY 11530
(516) 248-2000
Fax: (516) 248-3360

Proteon, Inc.

9 Technology Drive
Westborough, MA 01581
(508) 898-2800
(800) 545-7464
Fax: (508) 366-8901

PSI

250 Jordan Road
Troy, NY 12180
(518) 283-8860
Fax: (518) 283-8904

Pyramid Technology Corporation

3860 No. 1st Street
San Jose, CA 95134
(408) 428-9000
Fax: (408) 428-7480

Quarterdeck

13160 Mindanao Way
Marina Del Rey, CA 90292-9705
(310)309-3700
(800) 683-6696
Fax: (310) 309-3217

Racal Data Communications

1601 N. Harrison Parkway
Sunrise, FL 33323-2899
(305) 846-1601
(800) 333-4143
Fax: (305) 846-5510

Racore Computer Products

170 Knowles Drive #204
Los Gatos, CA 95030
(408) 374-8290
(800) 635-1274
Fax: (408) 374-6653

RAD Data Communications, Inc.

900 Corporate Drive
Mahwah, NJ 07430
(201) 529-1100
(800) 444-7234
Fax: (201) 529-5777

Relational Technology Systems, Inc.

1601 Trapelo Road
Waltham, MA 02154
(617) 890-2888
(800) 661-7096
Fax: (617) 890-2953

Remedy Corporation

1505 Salado Drive
Mountain View, CA 94043
(415) 903-5200
Fax: (415) 903-9001

Retix

4640 Admiralty Way N. Tower
6th Floor
Marina Del Ray, CA 90292
(310) 828-3400
(800) 255-2333
Fax: (310) 828-2255

RFI Communications & Security

360 Turtle Creek Court
San Jose, CA 95125-1389
(408) 298-5400
Fax: (408) 275-0156

SAS Institute

SAS Campus Drive
Cary, NC 27513
(919) 677-8000

SBE, Inc.

4550 No. Canyon Road
San Ramon, CA 94583
(510) 355-2000
(800) 925—2666
Fax: (510) 355-2020

Scopus Technology Inc.

1900 Powell Street Suite #700
Emeryville, CA 94608
(510) 597-5800
(800) 972-6787
Fax: (510) 497-5994

SEA Gate

19925 Stevens Creek Blvd. #150
Cupertino, CA 95014
(408) 342-4500
(800) 447-9300
Fax: (408) 342-4600

Shiva Corporation

28 Crosby Drive
Bedford, MA 01730
(617) 270-8300
(800) 458-3550
Fax: (617) 270-8599

Silicon Graphics—Cray Research

655 Lone Oak Drive
Egan, MN 55121
(612) 452-6650
(800) 284-2729
Fax: (612) 683-7199

Silicon Graphics, Inc.

2011 N. Shoreline Blvd.
Mountain View, CA 94043-1389
(415) 960-1980
(800) 326-1020
Fax: (415) 961-0595

Simpact Associates, Inc.

9210 Sky Park Court
San Diego, CA 92123
(619) 565-1865
(800) 697-1865
Fax: (619) 565-4112

Simware, Inc.

2 Gurdwara Road
Ottawa, Ontario K2E 1A2
Canada
(613) 727-1779
(800) 267-9991
Fax: (613) 727-8797

Sirius Systems, Inc.
Box 2202
Petersburg, VA 23804
(804) 733-7944
Fax: (804) 861-0358

Smith Micro Software
51 Columbia
Eliso Viejo, CA 92656
(714) 362-5800
(714) 362-2300

SNMP Research
3001 Kimberlin Heights Road
Knoxville, TN 37920
(423) 573-1434
Fax: (423) 573-9197

Softronics
5085 List Drive
Colorado Springs, CO 80919
(719) 593-9540
(800) 225-8590
Fax: (719) 548-1878

SoftSwitch, Inc.
640 Lee Road #200
Wayne, PA 19087
(610) 640-9600
Fax: (610) 251-3550

Software AG of North America, Inc.
11190 Sunrise Valley Drive
Reston, VA 20191-5424
(703) 860-5050
(800) 423-2227
Fax: (703) 391-6975

Software Kinetics Ltd.
65 Iber Road
Stittsville, Ontario, K2S 1E7
Canada
(613) 831-0888
Fax: (613) 831-1836

Solcom Systems Inc.
1801 Robert Fulton Dr. Suite #400
Reston, VA 20191
(703) 758-6722
Fax: (703) 758-3568

SONY Corporation
3300 Zanker Road
San Jose, CA 95134
(408) 432-1600

Standard Microsystems Corporation
80 Arkay Drive
Hauppauge, NY 11788
(516) 273-3100
(800) 553-7731
Fax: (516) 273-5550

StarNine Technologies
2550 9th St. Suite 112
Berkeley, CA 94710
(510) 548-0391
Fax: (510) 548-0393

Star Tek, Inc.
80 Central Street
Boxborough, MA 01719
(508) 264-1400
(800) 225-8528
Fax: (508) 264-1418

Sterling Software
504 N. 4th Street
Fairfield, IA 52556
(515) 472-7077
(800) 331-8575
Fax: (515) 472-7198

Stratus Computer, Inc.
55 Fairbanks Blvd.
Marlboro, MA 01752
(508) 460-2000

Sun Microsystems Inc.
2550 Garcia Avenue
Mountain View, CA 94043-1100
(415) 960-1300
(800) 872-4786
Fax: (415) 856-2114

Sunsoft Incorporated
2550 Garcia Avenue
Moutain View, CA 94043
(415) 960-1300
(800) 786-0404
Fax: (415) 961-6070

Sybase Inc.
3665 Discovery Drive
Boulder, CO 80303
(303) 443-2706
(800) 423-8737
Fax: (303) 413-4167

Symantec
4445 Broad Hollow Road Suite #200
Melville, NY 11747
(516) 465-2400
Fax: (516) 465-2401

Sync Research
40 Parker
Irvine, CA 92618
(714) 588-2070
(800) 275-7962
Fax: (714) 457-6282

SystemSoft Corporation
2 Vision Drive
Natick, MA 01760-2059
(508) 651-0088
(800) 449-7973
Fax: (508) 651-8188

Systran
4126 Linden Avenue
Dayton, OH 45432
(937) 252-5601
Fax: (937) 258-2729

3Com Corporation
5400 Bayfront Drive
Santa Clara, CA 95052
(408) 764-5000
Fax: (408) 764-5001

T3plus Networking, Inc.
2840 San Tomas Expressway
Santa Clara, CA 95051
(408) 727-4545
(800) 477-7050
Fax: (408) 727-4545

Tangram Enterprise Solutions Inc.
7 Great Valley Parkway E. Suite #300
East Malvern, PA 19355
(610) 647-0440
(800) 722-2482
Fax: (610) 640-1379

Tangent Computer Inc.
197 Airport Blvd.
Burlingame, CA 94010
(415) 342-9388
(800) 800-6060
Fax: (415) 342-9380

Technically Elite
6330 Ignacio
San Jose, CA 95119-1209
(408) 574-2300
(800) 474-7888
Fax: (408) 629-8300

Tekelec
26580 W. Agoura Road
Calabasas, CA 91302
(818) 880-5656
(800) 835-3532
Fax: (818) 880-6993

Tektronix, Inc.
625 SE Salmon Avenue
Redmond, OR 97756
(503) 923-0333
(800) 833-9200
Fax: (503) 923-4440

Telco Systems Inc.
63 Nahatan Street
Norwood, MA 02062
(617) 255-9400
Fax: (617) 551-0535

Telebit Corporation
1 Executive Drive
Chelmsford, MA 01824
(508) 441-2181
(800) 835-3248
Fax: (508) 441-9060

Telecommunications Techniques Corporation
20400 Observation Drive
Germantown, MD 20874
(301) 353-1550
(800) 638-2049
Fax: (301) 353-0731

Telematics International, Inc.
1201 West Cypress Creek Road
Ft. Lauderdale, FL 33309
(954) 772-3070
(800) 833-4580
Fax: (954) 351-4405

Tenon Intersystems
1123 Chapala Street Suite #200
Santa Barbara, CA 93101
(805) 963-6983
(800) 662-2410
Fax: (805) 962-8202

The Santa Cruz Operation
400 Encinal Street
P.O. Box 1900
Santa Cruz, CA 95061-1900
(408) 425-7222
(800) 726-8649
Fax: (408) 458-4227

Toshiba International
13131 W. Little York
Houston, TX 77041
(713) 466-0277
(800) 231-1412
Fax: (713) 937-9533

Transition Networks

6475 City W. Parkway
Eden Prairie, MN 55344
(612) 941-7600
(800) 526-9267
Fax: (612) 941-2322

Trellis Network Services, Inc.

225 Turnpike Road
South Borough, MA 01772
(508) 485-7200
(800) 793-3390
Fax) (508) 485-3370

Tripp Lite

500 N. Oruans
Chicago, IL 60610
(312) 755-5400
Fax: (312) 644-6505

Triticom

9971 Valley View Road Suite #150
Eden Prairie, MN 55344
(612) 937-0772
Fax: (612) 937-1998

TxPort

127 JetPlex Circle
Madison, AL 35758
(205) 772-3770
(800) 285-2755
Fax: (205) 772-3388

UB Networks

3990 Freedom Circle
Santa Clara, Ca 95054
(408) 496-0111
(800) 777-4526
Fax: (408) 970-7337

UDS Motorola, Inc.

5000 Bradford Drive
Huntsville, AL 35805-1993
(205) 430-8000
(800) 451-2369
Fax: (205) 830-5657

Ungermann-Bass, Inc.

3990 Freedom Circle
Santa Clara, CA 95052-8030
(408) 987-6687
(800) 873-6381

Unify Corporation

181 Metro Drive
San Jose, CA 95110
(408) 467-4511
Fax: (408) 467-4511

Unimax Systems Corporation

430 First Avenue North
Minneapolis, MN 55401
(612) 341-0946
(800) 886-0390
Fax: (612) 338-5436

Unisys

5151 Camino Ruiz
Camarillo, CA 93011
(805) 987-6811
Fax: (805) 388-7790

U.S. Robotics Software

8100 N. McCormick Blvd.
Skokie, IL 60076-2920
(847) 982-5010
(800) 877-2677
Fax: (847) 933-5800

Utopia Technology Partners, Inc.
125 E. Sir Francis Drake Blvd. Suite
   #300
Larkspur, CA 94939
(415) 464-4500
(800) 956-1301
Fax: (415) 464-4510

UNET Technologies/AlterNet
3060 Williams Drive
Fairfax, VA 22031
(703) 204-8000
(800) 488-6384
Fax: (703) 206-5601

Verilink Corporation
145 Baytech Drive
San Jose, CA 95134
(408) 945-1199
(800) 543-1008
Fax: (408) 262-6260

Versant Object Technology
1380 Willow Road
Menlo Park, CA 94025
(415) 329-7500
(800) 837-7268
Fax: (415) 325-2380

Visteon Corporation
2250 Lucieu Way Suite #250
Maitland, FL 32751
(407) 667-4100
(800) 847-8366
Fax: (407) 667-4105

Visual Networks
2092 Gaither Road
Rockville, MD 20850
(301) 208-6784
(800) 708-4784
Fax: (301) 258-5137

Walker Richer and Quinn, Inc.
1500 Dexter Avenue North
Seattle, WA 98109
(800) 872-2829
Fax: (206) 271-0293

Wall Data, Inc.
2300 Geng Road Suite #200
Palo Alto, CA 94303
(415) 812-1600
(800) 487-8622
Fax: (415) 821-1656

Wandel and Goltermann
1030 Swabia Court
Research Triangle Park, NC 27709
(919) 941-5730
(800) 346-6332
Fax: (919) 941-5751

Wang Laboratories
600 Technical Park Drive
Belricka, MA 01821
(508) 967-5000
(800) 639-9264
Fax: (508) 967-0829

Weblogic Inc.
417 Montgomery Street 7th Floor
San Francisco, CA 94104
(415) 394-8616
Fax: (415) 394-8619

Webster Computer Corporation
16040 Redwood Lodge Road
Los Gatos, CA 95030
(408) 353-5252
(800) 457-0903
Fax: (408) 357-2550

Western Digital Corporation
8105 Irvine Center Drive
Irvine, CA 92718
(714) 932-5000
(800) 832-4778
Fax: (714) 932-6098

White Pine Software, Inc.
542 Amhurst Street
Nashua, NH 03063
(603) 886-9050
(800) 241-7463
Fax: (603) 886-9051

Whittaker Communications
2200 Lawson Lane
Santa Clara, CA 95054
(408) 565-6000
(800) 395-5267

Wilcom Products
Rt. 3 Daniel Webster Highway
Laconia, NH 03246
(603) 524-2622
(800) 222-1898
Fax: (603) 524-3735

Wild Card Technologies
180 W. Beaver Creek Road
Richmond Hill, Ontario L4B 1B4
Canada
(905) 731-6444
(800) 661-8210
Fax: (905) 731-7017

Wingra Software Inc.
450 Science Drive 1 West
Madison, WI 53711
(608) 238-8637
(800) 544-5465
Fax: (608) 238-8986

Xerox Corporation
100 Clinton Avenue South Suite #05B
Rochester, NY 14644
(716) 423-5090
Fax: (716) 423-5479

Xinetron Inc.
3022 Acott Blvd.
Santa Clara, CA 95054
(408) 727-5509
(800) 345-4415
Fax: (408) 727-6499

Xircom
23 Corporate Center Drive
Thousand Oaks, CA 91320
(805) 376-9300
Fax: (805) 376-9220

Xylan
26707 W Agora Road
Calabasa, CA 91302
(818) 880-3500
(800) 999-9526
Fax: (818) 880-3505

Xyplex Networks

295 Foster Street
Littleton, MA 01460-2016
(508) 952-4700
Fax: (508) 952-4702

Zenith Electronics Corporation

Communication Products Division
1000 Milwaukee Avenue
Glenview, IL 60025
(847) 391-7000
(800) 788-7244
Fax: (847) 391-8919

 # Sources of Internet Information

Much of the adminstration functions for the Internet are handled by the Inter-NIC. Directory and Database services are handled by AT&T, while Registration Services are handled by Network Solutions, Inc. Addresses for these organizations are listed below.

Internet Directory and Database Services

AT&T
Tel: (908) 668-6587 or (800) 862-0677
Email: admin@ds.internic.net
URL: ftp://ds.internic.net

Registration Services

Network Solutions, Inc.
Attn.: InterNIC Registration Services
505 Huntmar Park Drive
Herndon, VA 22070
Tel: (703) 742-4777
Email: admin@rs.internic.net

Internet Organizations

A number of groups contribute to the management, operation and proliferation of the Internet. These include (in alphabetical order):

CommerceNet
URL: http://www.commerce.net
Email: info@commerce.net

Commercial Internet Exchange Association
Tel: (703) 824-9249
URL: http://www.cix.org
Email: helpdesk@cix.org

Internet Architecture Board
URL: http://www.iab.org
Email: iab-contact@isi.edu

Internet Assigned Numbers Authority
URL: http://www.iana.org
Email: iana@isi.edu

Internet Engineering Task Force
URL: http://www.ietf.cnri.reston.va.us
Email: ietf-web@ietf.org

Internet Society
URL: http://www.isoc.org
Email: isoc@isoc.org

World Wide Web Consortium
URL: http://www.w3.org
Email: admin@w3.org

Obtaining RFCs

The following is an excerpt from the file *rfc-retrieval.txt,* which is available from many of the RFC repositories listed below. This information is subject to change; obtain the current version of the rfc-retrieval file if problems occur. Also note that each RFC site may have instructions for file retrieval (such as a particular subdirectory) that are unique to that location.

RFCs may be obtained via e-mail or FTP from many RFC repositories. The Primary Repositories will have the RFC available when it is first announced, as will many Secondary Repositories. Some Secondary Repositories may take a few days to make available the most recent RFCs.

Many of these repositories now also have World Wide Web servers. Try the following URL as a starting point:

http://www.isi.edu/rfc-editor/

Primary Repositories

RFCs can be obtained via FTP from DS.INTERNIC.NET, NIS.NSF.NET, NISC.JVNC.NET, FTP.ISI.EDU, WUARCHIVE.WUSTL.EDU, SRC.DOC.IC. AC.UK, FTP.NCREN.NET, FTP.SESQUI.NET, or NIS.GARR.IT.

1. DS.INTERNIC.NET—InterNIC Directory and Database Services

    RFCs may be obtained from DS.INTERNIC.NET via FTP, WAIS, and electronic mail. Through FTP, RFCs are stored as rfc/rfcnnnn.txt or rfc/rfcnnnn.ps where "nnnn" is the RFC number. Log in as "anonymous" and provide your e-mail address as the password. Through WAIS, you may either use your local WAIS client or telnet to DS.INTERNIC.NET and log in as "wais" (no password required) to access a WAIS client. Help information and a tutorial for using WAIS are available online. The WAIS database to search is "rfcs."

    Directory and Database Services also provides a mail server interface. Send a mail message to mailserv@ds.internic.net and include any of the following commands in the message body:

document-by-name rfcnnnn	where "nnnn" is the RFC number. The text version is sent.
file /ftp/rfc/rfcnnnn.yyy	where "nnnn" is the RFC number and "yyy" is "txt" or "ps."
help	to get information on how to use the mailserver.

    The InterNIC Directory and Database Services Collection of Resource Listings, Internet Documents such as RFCs, FYIs, STDs, and Internet Drafts, and Publicly Accessible Databases are also now available via

Gopher. All our collections are waisindexed and can be searched from the Gopher menu.

To access the InterNIC Gopher Servers, please connect to "internic.net" port 70.

Contact: admin@ds.internic.net

2.   NIS.NSF.NET

To obtain RFCs from NIS.NSF.NET via FTP, log in with username "anonymous" and password "guest"; then connect to the directory of RFCs with cd /internet/documents/rfc. The file name is of the form rfcnnnn.txt (where "nnnn" refers to the RFC number).

For sites without FTP capability, electronic mail query is available from NIS.NSF.NET. Address the request to NIS-INFO@NIS.NSF.NET and leave the subject field of the message blank. The first text line of the message must be "send rfcnnnn.txt" with nnnn the RFC number.

Contact: rfc-mgr@merit.edu

3.   NISC.JVNC.NET

RFCs can also be obtained via FTP from NISC.JVNC.NET, with the pathname rfc/rfcNNNN.txt (where "NNNN" refers to the number of the RFC). An index can be obtained with the pathname rfc/rfc-index.txt.

JvNCnet also provides a mail service for those sites which cannot use FTP. Address the request to "SENDRFC@NISC.JVNC.NET" and in the "Subject:" field of the message indicate the RFC number, as in "Subject: rfcNNNN" (where NNNN is the RFC number). Please note that RFCs whose numbers are less than 1000 need not place a leading "0". (For example, RFC932 is fine.) For a complete index to the RFC library, enter "rfc-index" in the "Subject:" field, as in "Subject: rfc-index". No text in the body of the message is needed.

Contact: rfc-admin@nisc.jvnc.net

4.   FTP.ISI.EDU

RFCs can be obtained via FTP from FTP.ISI.EDU, with the pathname in-notes/rfcnnnn.txt (where "nnnn" refers to the number of the RFC). Log in with FTP username "anonymous" and password "guest."

RFCs can also be obtained via electronic mail from ISI.EDU by using the RFC-INFO service. Address the request to "rfc-info@isi.edu" with a message body of:

> Retrieve: RFC
> Doc-ID: RFCnnnn

(Where "nnnn" refers to the number of the RFC (always use 4 digits—the DOC-ID of RFC 822 is "RFC0822")). The RFC-INFO@ISI.EDU server provides other ways of selecting RFCs based on keywords and such; for more information send a message to "rfc-info@isi.edu" with the message body "help: help".

Contact: RFC-Manager@ISI.EDU

5. WUARCHIVE.WUSTL.EDU

RFCs can also be obtained via FTP from WUARCHIVE.WUSTL.EDU, with the pathname info/rfc/rfcnnnn.txt.Z (where "nnnn" refers to the number of the RFC and "Z" indicates that the document is in compressed form).

At WUARCHIVE.WUSTL.EDU the RFCs are in an "archive" file system and various archives can be mounted as part of an NFS file system. Please contact Chris Myers (chris@wugate.wustl.edu) if you want to mount this file system in your NFS.

Contact: chris@wugate.wustl.edu

6. SRC.DOC.IC.AC.UK

RFCs can be obtained via FTP from SRC.DOC.IC.AC.UK with the pathname rfc/rfcnnnn.txt.Z or rfc/rfcnnnn.ps.Z (where "nnnn" refers to the number of the RFC). Log in with FTP username "anonymous" and password "your-email-address". To obtain the RFC Index, use the pathname rfc/rfc-index.txt.gz. (The trailing .gz indicates that the document is in compressed form.)

SRC.DOC.IC.AC.UK also provides an automatic mail service for those sites in the UK which cannot use FTP. Address the request to info-server@doc.ic.ac.uk with a Subject: line of "wanted" and a message body of:

```
request sources
topic path rfc/rfcnnnn.txt.gz
request end
```

(Where "nnnn" refers to the number of the RFC.) Multiple requests may be included in the same message by giving multiple "topic path" commands on separate lines. To request the RFC Index, the command should read: topic path rfc/rfc-index.txt.gz.

The archive is also available using NIFTP and the ISO FTAM system.

Contact: ukuug-soft@doc.ic.ac.uk

7. FTP.NCREN.NET

To obtain RFCs from FTP.NCREN.NET via FTP, log in with username "anonymous" and your internet e-mail address as password. The RFCs can be found in the directory /rfc, with file names of the form rfcNNNN.txt or rfcNNNN.ps, where NNNN refers to the RFC number.

This repository is also accessible via WAIS and the Internet Gopher.

Contact: rfc-mgr@ncren.net

8. FTP.SESQUI.NET

RFCs can be obtained via FTP from FTP.SESQUI.NET, with the pathname pub/rfc/rfcnnnn.xxx (where "nnnn" refers to the number of the RFC and "xxx" indicates the document form: txt for ASCII and ps for Postscript).

At FTP.SESQUI.NET the RFCs are in an "archive" file system and various archives can be mounted as part of an NFS file system. Please contact RFC-maintainer (rfc-maint@sesqui.net) if you want to mount this file system in your NFS.

Contact: rfc-maint@sesqui.net

9. NIS.GARR.IT

RFCs can be obtained from NIS.GARR.IT FTP archive with the pathname mirrors/RFC/rfcnnnn.txt (where "nnnn" refers to the number of the RFC). Log in with FTP, username "anonymous" and password "guest".

Summary of the ways to get an RFC from GARR-NIS FTP archive:

Via ftp:	ftp.nis.garr.it directory mirrors/RFC
Via gopher:	gopher.nis.garr.it folders
	GARR-NIS anonymous FTP
	"ftp.nis.garr.it"
	mirrors
	RFC
Via WWW:	ftp://ftp.nis.garr.it/mirrors/RFC
Via e-mail:	send a mail to dbserv@nis.garr.it whose body contains "get
	mirrors/RFC/rfc<number>.[txt,ps]."

To get a file in the FTP archive via electronic mail, put the get <fullpathname> command either in the subject or as a mail body line of a mail message sent to dbserv@nis.garr.it. <fullpathname> must be the concatenation of two strings, the directory path and the filename.

Remember: use uppercase and lowercase exactly! The directory path is listed at the beginning of each block of files.

Example: to get RFC1004...the command should be:

get mirrors/RFC/rfc1004.txt.

Secondary Repositories:

Sweden

Host:	sunic.sunet.se
Directory:	rfc
Host:	chalmers.se

Directory: rfc

Germany

Site: EUnet Germany

Host: ftp.Germany.EU.net

Directory: pub/documents/rfc

France

Site: Institut National de la Recherche en Informatique et
                  Automatique (INRIA)

Address: info-server@inria.fr

Notes: RFCs are available via email to the above address.Info
                  Server manager is Mireille Yamajako (yamajako@inria.fr).

Site: Centre d'Informatique Scientifique et Medicale (CISM)

Contact: ftpmaint@univ-lyon1.fr

Host   ftp.univ-lyon1.fr

Directories: pub/rfc/* Classified by hundreds pub/mirrors/rfc Mir-
                  ror of Internic

Notes: Files compressed with gzip. Online decompression done
                  by the FTP server.

Netherlands

Site: EUnet

Host: mcsun.eu.net

Directory: rfc

Notes: RFCs in compressed format.

Finland

Site: FUNET

Host: nic.funet.fi

Directory: index/RFC

Directory:	/pub/doc/networking/documents/rfc
Notes:	RFCs in compressed format. Also provides e-mail access by sending mail to archive-server@nic.funet.fi.

Norway

Host:	ugle.unit.no
Directory:	pub/rfc

Denmark

Site:	University of Copenhagen
Host:	ftp.denet.dk
Directory:	rfc

Australia and Pacific Rim

Site:	munnari
Contact:	Robert Elz <kre@cs.mu.OZ.AU>
Host:	munnari.oz.au
Directory:	rfc
Notes:	RFCs in compressed format rfcNNNN.Z post-script RFCs rfcNNNN.ps.Z

Site:	The Programmers' Society University of Technology, Sydney
Contact:	ftp@progsoc.uts.edu.au
Host:	ftp.progsoc.uts.edu.au
Directory:	rfc (or std).

Both are stored uncompressed.

South Africa

Site:	The Internet Solution
Contact:	ftp-admin@is.co.za

Host:	ftp.is.co.za
Directory:	internet/in-notes/rfc

United States

Site:	cerfnet
Contact:	help@cerf.net
Host:	nic.cerf.net
Directory:	netinfo/rfc

Site:	NASA NAIC
Contact:	rfc-updates@naic.nasa.gov
Host:	naic.nasa.gov
Directory:	files/rfc

Site:	NIC.DDN.MIL (DOD users only)
Contact:	NIC@nic.ddn.mil
Host:	NIC.DDN.MIL
Directory:	rfc/rfcnnnn.txt
Note:	Only DOD users may obtain RFCs via FTP from NIC.DDN.MIL. Internet users should NOT use this source due to inadequate connectivity.

Site:	uunet
Contact:	James Revell <revell@uunet.uu.net>
Host:	ftp.uu.net
Directory:	inet/rfc

The RFC-Info Service

The following describes the RFC-Info Service, which is an Internet document and information retrieval service. The text that follows describesthe service in detail; it was obtained by using "Help:Help" as discussed below.

RFC-Info is an e-mail based service to help in locating and retrieving RFCs, FYIs, STDs, and IMRs. Users can ask for "lists" of all RFCs, FYIs, STDs, and IMRs having certain attributes such as their ID number, keywords, title, author, issuing organization, and date.

To use the service send e-mail to RFC-INFO@ISI.EDU with your requests in the body of the message. Feel free to put anything in the SUBJECT; the system ignores it. The body of the message is processed with case independence.

To get started you may send a message to RFC-INFO@ISI.EDU with requests such as in the following examples (without the explanation between [ ]):

Help: Help	[to get this information page]
List: FYI	[list the FYI notes]
List: RFC	[list RFCs with window as keyword or in title]
	Keywords: window
List: FYI	[list FYIs about windows]
	Keywords: window
List: *	[list all documents by Cooper]
	Author: Cooper
List: RFC	[list RFCs about ARPANET, ARPA NETWORK, etc.]
	title: ARPA*NET
List: RFC	[list RFCs issued by MITRE, dated 7+8/1991]
	Organization: MITRE
	Dated-after: Jul-01-1991
	Dated-before: Aug-31-1991
List: RFC	[list RFCs obsoleting a given RFC]
	Obsoletes: RFC0010

List: RFC	[list RFCs by authors starting with "Bracken"] Author: Bracken* [* is a wild card matching all endings]
List: IMR	[list the IMRs for the first 6 months of 92] Dated-after: Dec-31-1991 Dated-before: Jul-01-1992
Retrieve: RFC	[retrieve RFC 822] Doc-ID: RFC0822 [note, always 4 digits in RFC#]
Retrieve: FYI	[retrieve FYI 4] Doc-ID: FYI0004 [note, always 4 digits in FYI#]
Retrieve: STD	[retrieve STD 1] Doc-ID: STD0001 [note, always 4 digits in STD#]
Retrieve: IMR	[retrieve May 1992 Internet Monthly Report] Doc-ID: IMR9205 [note, always 4 digits = YYMM]
	Help: Manual [to retrieve the long user manual, 30+ pages] Help: List [how to use the LIST request] Help: Retrieve [how to use the RETRIEVE request] Help: Topics [list topics for which help is available] Help: Dates ["Dates" is such a topic]

List: keywords   [list the keywords in use]

List: organizations   [list the organizations known to the system]

A useful way to test this service is to retrieve the file "Where and how to get new RFCs" (which is also the file rfc-retrieval.txt noted above in the section Obtaining RFCs). Place the following in the message body:

```
Help: ways_to_get_rfcs
```

Internet Mailing Lists

A number of mailing lists are maintained on the Internet for the purpose of soliciting information and discussions on specific subjects. In addition, a number of the Internet Engineering Task Force (IETF) working groups maintain a list for the exchange of information that is specific to that group.

For example, the IETF maintains two lists: the IETF General Discussion list and the IETF Announcement list. To join the IETF Announcement list, send a request to:

```
ietf-announce-request@ietf.org
```

To join the IETF General Discussion, send a request to:

```
ietf-request@ietf.org
```

A number of other mailing lists are available. To join a mailing list, send a message to the associated request list:

```
listname-request@listhost (for example, snmp-request@psi.com)
```

with the following as the message body:

```
subscribe listname (for example, subscribe snmp)
```

A complete listing of the current IETF working groups and their respective mailing lists is available at:

http://www.ietf.cnri.reston.va.us/mailinglists.html

SNMP-related mailing lists of interest include:

- ➤ SNMP general discussion: snmp@psi.com
- ➤ SNMPv2 working group: snmpv2@tis.com
- ➤ SNMPv3 working group: snmpv3@tis.com
- ➤ RMON MIB working group: rmonmib@cisco.com

The Simple Times Newsletter

The Simple Times is a periodically published newsletter that details various topics relevant to SNMP. It is freely distributed via electronic form on the Internet. *The Simple Times* is available in three editions: HTML, ASCII, and PostScript. For further information, send a message to:

st-subscriptions@simple-times.org

with a Subject: line of:

help

Back issues are available from:

http://www.simple-times.org
ftp://ftp.simple-times.org

 # Network Management RFCs

This appendix contains a listing of network management Request for Comments (RFC) documents, available via the Internet. This information was retrieved using the RFC Info Service, as described in Appendix D, using several applicable keywords. For each entry, there are notations for author(s), publication date, and so on; most importantly, there are other RFCs that may either update or make obsolete a particular listing. In the event that the RFC you are researching has been updated or made obsolete, go to the new RFC for more current information.

TYPE: RFC
DOC-ID: **RFC1052**
TITLE: IAB recommendations for the development of Internet network management standards
AUTHORS: V.G. Cerf
DATE: Apr-01-1988
FORMAT: ASCII
CHAR-COUNT: 30569

TYPE: RFC
DOC-ID: **RFC1065**
TITLE: Structure and identification of management information for TCP/IP-based internets
AUTHORS: K. McCloghrie, M.T. Rose
DATE: Aug-01-1988
FORMAT: ASCII
CHAR-COUNT: 38858
OBSOLETES: RFC1034
OBSOLETED-BY: RFC1155

TYPE: RFC
DOC-ID: **RFC1066**
TITLE: Management Information Base for network management of TCP/IP-based internets
AUTHORS: K. McCloghrie, M.T. Rose
DATE: Aug-01-1988
FORMAT: ASCII
CHAR-COUNT: 135177
OBSOLETED-BY: RFC1156

TYPE: RFC
DOC-ID: **RFC1067**
TITLE: Simple Network Management Protocol
AUTHORS: J.D. Case, M. Fedor, M.L. Schoffstall, J. Davin
DATE: Aug-01-1988
FORMAT: ASCII
CHAR-COUNT: 69592
OBSOLETED-BY: RFC1098

TYPE: RFC
DOC-ID: **RFC1095**
TITLE: Common Management
  Information Services and Protocol
  over TCP/IP (CMOT)
AUTHORS: U.S. Warrier, L. Besaw
DATE: Apr-01-1989
FORMAT: ASCII
CHAR-COUNT: 157506
OBSOLETED-BY: RFC1189

TYPE: RFC
DOC-ID: **RFC1098**
TITLE: Simple Network Management
  Protocol (SNMP)
AUTHORS: J.D. Case, M. Fedor, M.L.
  Schoffstall, C. Davin
DATE: Apr-01-1989
FORMAT: ASCII
CHAR-COUNT: 71563
OBSOLETES: RFC1067
OBSOLETED-BY: RFC1157

TYPE: RFC
DOC-ID: **RFC1109**
TITLE: Report of the second Ad Hoc
  Network Management Review Group
AUTHORS: V.G. Cerf
DATE: Aug-01-1989
FORMAT: ASCII
CHAR-COUNT: 20642

TYPE: RFC
DOC-ID: **RFC1147**
TITLE: FYI on a network management
  tool catalog: Tools for monitoring
  and debugging TCP/IP internets and
  interconnected devices
AUTHORS: R.H. Stine
DATE: Apr-01-1990

FORMAT: ASCII, PS
CHAR-COUNT: 336906, 555225
OBSOLETED-BY: RFC1470
UPDATED-BY: FYI0002
SEE-ALSO: FYI0002

TYPE: RFC
DOC-ID: **RFC1155**
TITLE: Structure and identification of
  management information for
  TCP/IP-based internets
AUTHORS: M.T. Rose, K.
  McCloghrie
DATE: May-01-1990
FORMAT: ASCII
CHAR-COUNT: 40927
OBSOLETES: RFC1065

TYPE: RFC
DOC-ID: **RFC1156**
TITLE: Management Information Base
  for network management of TCP/IP-
  based internets
AUTHORS: K. McCloghrie, M.T.
  Rose
DATE: May-01-1990
FORMAT: ASCII
CHAR-COUNT: 138781
OBSOLETES: RFC1066

TYPE: RFC
DOC-ID: **RFC1157**
TITLE: Simple Network Management
  Protocol (SNMP)
AUTHORS: J.D. Case, M. Fedor, M.L.
  Schoffstall, C. Davin
DATE: May-01-1990
FORMAT: ASCII
CHAR-COUNT: 74894
OBSOLETES: RFC1098

TYPE: RFC
DOC-ID: **RFC1158**
TITLE: Management Information Base
for network management of TCP/IP-
based internets: MIB-II
AUTHORS: M.T. Rose
DATE: May-01-1990
FORMAT: ASCII
CHAR-COUNT: 212152
OBSOLETED-BY: RFC1213

TYPE: RFC
DOC-ID: **RFC1161**
TITLE: SNMP over OSI
AUTHORS: M.T. Rose
DATE: Jun-01-1990
FORMAT: ASCII
CHAR-COUNT: 16036
OBSOLETED-BY: RFC1418

TYPE: RFC
DOC-ID: **RFC1162**
TITLE: Connectionless Network
Protocol (ISO 8473) and End System
to Intermediate System (ISO 9542)
Management Information Base
AUTHORS: G. Satz
DATE: Jun-01-1990
FORMAT: ASCII
CHAR-COUNT: 109893
OBSOLETED-BY: RFC1238

TYPE: RFC
DOC-ID: **RFC1187**
TITLE: Bulk table retrieval with the
SNMP
AUTHORS: M.T. Rose, K.
McCloghrie, J.R. Davin
DATE: Oct-01-1990
FORMAT: ASCII
CHAR-COUNT: 27220

TYPE: RFC
DOC-ID: **RFC1189**
TITLE: Common Management
Information Services and Protocols
for the Internet (CMOT and CMIP)
AUTHORS: U.S. Warrier, L. Besaw, L.
LaBarre, B.D. Handspicker
DATE: Oct-01-1990
FORMAT: ASCII
CHAR-COUNT: 32928
OBSOLETES: RFC1095

TYPE: RFC
DOC-ID: **RFC1212**
TITLE: Concise MIB definitions
AUTHORS: M.T. Rose, K. McCloghrie
DATE: Mar-01-1991
FORMAT: ASCII
CHAR-COUNT: 43579

TYPE: RFC
DOC-ID: **RFC1213**
TITLE: Management Information Base
for network management of TCP/IP-
based internets: MIB-II
AUTHORS: K. McCloghrie, M.T. Rose
DATE: Mar-01-1991
FORMAT: ASCII
CHAR-COUNT: 146080
OBSOLETES: RFC1158
OBSOLETED-BY: RFC2011, RFC2012,
RFC2013

TYPE: RFC
DOC-ID: **RFC1214**
TITLE: OSI internet management:
Management Information Base
AUTHORS: L. LaBarre
DATE: Apr-01-1991
FORMAT: ASCII
CHAR-COUNT: 172564

TYPE: RFC
DOC-ID: **RFC1215**
TITLE: Convention for defining traps for
  use with the SNMP
AUTHORS: M.T. Rose
DATE: Mar-01-1991
FORMAT: ASCII
CHAR-COUNT: 19336

TYPE: RFC
DOC-ID: **RFC1224**
TITLE: Techniques for managing
  asynchronously generated alerts
AUTHORS: L. Steinberg
DATE: May-01-1991
FORMAT: ASCII
CHAR-COUNT: 54303

TYPE: RFC
DOC-ID: **RFC1227**
TITLE: SNMP MUX protocol and MIB
AUTHORS: M.T. Rose
DATE: May-01-1991
FORMAT: ASCII
CHAR-COUNT: 25868

TYPE: RFC
DOC-ID: **RFC1228**
TITLE: SNMP-DPI: Simple Network
  Management Protocol Distributed
  Program Interface
AUTHORS: G. Carpenter, B. Wijnen
DATE: May-01-1991
FORMAT: ASCII
CHAR-COUNT: 96972
OBSOLETED-BY: RFC1592

TYPE: RFC
DOC-ID: **RFC1229**
TITLE: Extensions to the generic-
  interface MIB
AUTHORS: K. McCloghrie
DATE: May-01-1991
FORMAT: ASCII
CHAR-COUNT: 36022
UPDATED-BY: RFC1239

TYPE: RFC
DOC-ID: **RFC1230**
TITLE: IEEE 802.4 Token Bus MIB
AUTHORS: K. McCloghrie, R. Fox
DATE: May-01-1991
FORMAT: ASCII
CHAR-COUNT: 53100
UPDATED-BY: RFC1239

TYPE: RFC
DOC-ID: **RFC1231**
TITLE: IEEE 802.5 Token Ring MIB
AUTHORS: K. McCloghrie, R. Fox, E.
  Decker
DATE: May-01-1991
FORMAT: ASCII
CHAR-COUNT: 53542
OBSOLETED-BY: RFC1743, RFC1748
UPDATED-BY: RFC1239

TYPE: RFC
DOC-ID: **RFC1232**
TITLE: Definitions of managed objects
  for the DS1 Interface type
AUTHORS: F. Baker, C.P. Kolb
DATE: May-01-1991
FORMAT: ASCII
CHAR-COUNT: 60757
OBSOLETED-BY: RFC1406
UPDATED-BY: RFC1239

TYPE: RFC
DOC-ID: **RFC1233**
TITLE: Definitions of managed objects
for the DS3 Interface type
AUTHORS: T.A. Cox, K. Tesink
DATE: May-01-1991
FORMAT: ASCII
CHAR-COUNT: 49559
OBSOLETED-BY: RFC1407
UPDATED-BY: RFC1239

TYPE: RFC
DOC-ID: **RFC1238**
TITLE: CLNS MIB for use with
Connectionless Network Protocol
(ISO 8473) and End System to
Intermediate System (ISO 9542)
AUTHORS: G. Satz
DATE: Jun-01-1991
FORMAT: ASCII
CHAR-COUNT: 65159
OBSOLETES: RFC1162

TYPE: RFC
DOC-ID: **RFC1239**
TITLE: Reassignment of experimental
MIBs to standard MIBs
AUTHORS: J.K. Reynolds
DATE: Jun-01-1991
FORMAT: ASCII
CHAR-COUNT: 3656
UPDATES: RFC1229, RFC1230,
RFC1231, RFC1232, RFC1233

TYPE: RFC
DOC-ID: **RFC1243**
TITLE: AppleTalk Management
Information Base
AUTHORS: S. Waldbusser
DATE: Jul-01-1991

FORMAT: ASCII
CHAR-COUNT: 61985
OBSOLETED-BY: RFC1742

TYPE: RFC
DOC-ID: **RFC1248**
TITLE: OSPF Version 2 Management
Information Base
AUTHORS: F. Baker, R. Coltun
DATE: Jul-01-1991
KEYWORDS: OSPF, SPF, MIB, routing,
network management
ORGANIZATION: ACC, Computer
Science Center, Network Working
Group
FORMAT: ASCII
CHAR-COUNT: 74347
OBSOLETED-BY: RFC1252

TYPE: RFC
DOC-ID: **RFC1252**
TITLE: OSPF Version 2 Management
Information Base
AUTHORS: F. Baker, R. Coltun
DATE: Aug-01-1991
KEYWORDS: OSPF, SPF, MIB,
routing, network management
ORGANIZATION: ACC, Computer
Science Center, Network Working
Group
FORMAT: ASCII
CHAR-COUNT: 74471
OBSOLETES: RFC1248
OBSOLETED-BY: RFC1253
SEE-ALSO: RFC1247, RFC1245

TYPE: RFC
DOC-ID: **RFC1253**
TITLE: OSPF Version 2 Management
Information Base
AUTHORS: F. Baker, R. Coltun
DATE: Aug-01-1991
ORGANIZATION: ACC, Computer
Science Center, Network Working
Group
FORMAT: ASCII
CHAR-COUNT: 74453
OBSOLETES: RFC1252
OBSOLETED-BY: RFC1850
SEE-ALSO: RFC1247, RFC1245,
RFC1246

TYPE: RFC
DOC-ID: **RFC1270**
TITLE: SNMP communications services
AUTHORS: F. Kastenholz
DATE: Oct-01-1991
FORMAT: ASCII
CHAR-COUNT: 26167

TYPE: RFC
DOC-ID: **RFC1271**
TITLE: Remote network monitoring
Management Information Base
AUTHORS: S. Waldbusser
DATE: Nov-01-1991
FORMAT: ASCII
CHAR-COUNT: 184111
OBSOLETED-BY: RFC1757

TYPE: RFC
DOC-ID: **RFC1283**
TITLE: SNMP over OSI
AUTHORS: M. Rose
DATE: December 1991

KEYWORDS: ISO, Management, MIB
ORGANIZATION: Dover Beach
Consulting, Inc.
FORMAT: ASCII
CHAR-COUNT: 16857
OBSOLETED-BY: RFC1418

TYPE: RFC
DOC-ID: **RFC1284**
TITLE: Definitions of Managed Objects
for the Ethernet-like Interface Types
AUTHORS: J. Cook
DATE: December 1991
KEYWORDS: SNMP, MIB,
Management
ORGANIZATION: Chipcom
Corporation
FORMAT: ASCII
CHAR-COUNT: 43225
OBSOLETED-BY: RFC1398

TYPE: RFC
DOC-ID: **RFC1285**
TITLE: FDDI Management Information
Base
AUTHORS: J. Case
DATE: January 1992
KEYWORDS: standard, standards, MIB,
SNMP
ORGANIZATION: SNMP Research,
Incorporated
FORMAT: ASCII
CHAR-COUNT: 99747
UPDATED-BY: RFC1512

TYPE: RFC
DOC-ID: **RFC1286**
TITLE: Definitions of Managed Objects
for Bridges
AUTHORS: E. Decker, P. Langille, A.
Rijsinghani, K. McCloghrie
DATE: December, 1991
KEYWORDS: SNMP, MIB, standard,
standards
ORGANIZATION: Cisco Systems, Inc.,
Digital Equipment Corporation,
Hughes LAN Systems, Inc.
FORMAT: ASCII
CHAR-COUNT: 79104
OBSOLETED-BY: RFC1493, RFC1525

TYPE: RFC
DOC-ID: **RFC1289**
TITLE: DECnet Phase IV MIB Extensions
AUTHORS: J. Saperia
DATE: December 1991
KEYWORDS: SNMP, Management,
protocol, standard, standards
ORGANIZATION: Digital Equipment
Corporation
FORMAT: ASCII
CHAR-COUNT: 122272
OBSOLETED-BY: RFC1559

TYPE: RFC
DOC-ID: **RFC1298**
TITLE: SNMP over IPX
AUTHORS: R. Wormley, S. Bostock
DATE: February 1992
ORGANIZATION: Novell, Inc.
FORMAT: ASCII
CHAR-COUNT: 7878
OBSOLETED-BY: RFC1420

TYPE: RFC
DOC-ID: **RFC1303**
TITLE: A Convention for Describing
SNMP-based Agents
AUTHORS: K. McCloghrie, M. Rose
DATE: February 1992
KEYWORDS: SNMP, MIB, Network
Management
ORGANIZATION: Hughes LAN
Systems, Dover Beach Consulting
FORMAT: ASCII
CHAR-COUNT: 22915
SEE-ALSO: RFC1155, RFC1212,
RFC1213, RFC1157

TYPE: RFC
DOC-ID: **RFC1304**
TITLE: Definitions of Managed Objects
for the SIP Interface Type
AUTHORS: T. Cox, K. Tesink, Editors
DATE: February 1992
KEYWORDS: Standard, MIB, Network
Management, SMDS
ORGANIZATION: Bell
Communications Research
FORMAT: ASCII
CHAR-COUNT: 52491
OBSOLETED-BY: RFC1694

TYPE: RFC
DOC-ID: **RFC1315**
TITLE: Management Information Base
for Frame Relay DTEs
AUTHORS: C. Brown, F. Baker, C.
Carvalho
DATE: April 1992
KEYWORDS: MIB
FORMAT: ASCII
CHAR-COUNT: 33825

TYPE: RFC
DOC-ID: **RFC1316**
TITLE: Definitions of Managed Objects
for Character Stream Devices
AUTHORS: B. Stewart
DATE: April 1992
KEYWORDS: MIB
ORGANIZATION: Xyplex
FORMAT: ASCII
CHAR-COUNT: 35143
OBSOLETED-BY: RFC1658

TYPE: RFC
DOC-ID: **RFC1317**
TITLE: Definitions of Managed Objects
for RS-232-like Hardware Devices
AUTHORS: B. Stewart
DATE: April 1992
KEYWORDS: MIB
ORGANIZATION: Xyplex
FORMAT: ASCII
CHAR-COUNT: 30442
OBSOLETED-BY: RFC1659

TYPE: RFC
DOC-ID: **RFC1318**
TITLE: Definitions of Managed Objects
for Parallel-printer-like Hardware
Devices
AUTHORS: B. Stewart
DATE: April 1992
KEYWORDS: MIB
ORGANIZATION: Xyplex
FORMAT: ASCII
CHAR-COUNT: 19570
OBSOLETED-BY: RFC1660

TYPE: RFC
DOC-ID: **RFC1321**
TITLE: The MD5 Message-Digest
Algorithm
AUTHORS: R. Rivest
DATE: April 1992
KEYWORDS: security, signature,
encryption
ORGANIZATION: MIT Laboratory
for Computer Science
FORMAT: ASCII
CHAR-COUNT: 35222

TYPE: RFC
DOC-ID: **RFC1351**
TITLE: SNMP Administrative Model
AUTHORS: J. Davin, J. Galvin, K.
McCloghrie
DATE: July 1992
KEYWORDS: network management,
authentication
ORGANIZATION: MIT Laboratory
for Computer Science, Trusted
Information
FORMAT: ASCII
CHAR-COUNT: 80721

TYPE: RFC
DOC-ID: **RFC1352**
TITLE: SNMP Security Protocols
AUTHORS: J. Galvin, K. McCloghrie,
J. Davin
DATE: July 1992
KEYWORDS: network management,
authentication
ORGANIZATION: Trusted Information
Systems, Hughes LAN Systems, MIT
FORMAT: ASCII
CHAR-COUNT: 95732

TYPE: RFC
DOC-ID: **RFC1353**
TITLE: Definitions of Managed Objects
AUTHORS: K. McCloghrie, J. Davin,
   J. Galvin
DATE: July 1992
KEYWORDS: network management,
   authentication
ORGANIZATION: Hughes LAN
   Systems, MIT Laboratory for
   Computer Science
FORMAT: ASCII
CHAR-COUNT: 59556

TYPE: RFC
DOC-ID: **RFC1354**
TITLE: IP Forwarding Table MIB
AUTHORS: F. Baker
DATE: July 1992
KEYWORDS: Network Management,
   Route Table
ORGANIZATION: ACC
FORMAT: ASCII
CHAR-COUNT: 24905

TYPE: RFC
DOC-ID: **RFC1368**
TITLE: Definition of Managed Objects
   for IEEE 802.3 Repeater Devices
AUTHORS: D. McMaster, K.
   McCloghrie
DATE: October 1992
KEYWORDS: MIB, hub, management
ORGANIZATION: SynOptics Comm-
   unications, Hughes LAN Systems
FORMAT: ASCII
CHAR-COUNT: 83905
OBSOLETED-BY: RFC1516

TYPE: RFC
DOC-ID: **RFC1369**
TITLE: Implementation Notes and Exper-
   ience for the Internet Ethernet MIB
AUTHORS: F. Kastenholz
DATE: October 1992
KEYWORDS: management
ORGANIZATION: Clearpoint Research
FORMAT: ASCII
CHAR-COUNT: 13961

TYPE: RFC
DOC-ID: **RFC1381**
TITLE: SNMP MIB Extension for X.25
   LAPB
AUTHORS: D. Throop, F. Baker
DATE: November 1992
KEYWORDS: management
ORGANIZATION: Data General Cor-
   poration, Advanced Computer
   Communications
FORMAT: ASCII
CHAR-COUNT: 71253

TYPE: RFC
DOC-ID: **RFC1382**
TITLE: SNMP MIB Extension for the
   X.25 Packet Layer
AUTHORS: D. Throop
DATE: November 1992
KEYWORDS: management
ORGANIZATION: Data General
   Corporation
FORMAT: ASCII
CHAR-COUNT: 153877

TYPE: RFC
DOC-ID: **RFC1389**
TITLE: RIP Version 2 MIB Extensions
AUTHORS: G. Malkin, F. Baker
DATE: January 1993
KEYWORDS: RIP-2, Management,
  Information, Base
ORGANIZATION: Xylogics, ACC
FORMAT: ASCII
CHAR-COUNT: 23569
OBSOLETED-BY: RFC1724

TYPE: RFC
DOC-ID: **RFC1398**
TITLE: Definitions of Managed Objects
  for the Ethernet-Like Interface Types
AUTHORS: F. Kastenholz
DATE: January 1993
KEYWORDS: MIB, Management
ORGANIZATION: FTP Software, Inc.
FORMAT: ASCII
CHAR-COUNT: 36684
OBSOLETES: RFC1284
OBSOLETED-BY: RFC1643, STD0050,
  RFC1623

TYPE: RFC
DOC-ID: **RFC1406**
TITLE: Definitions of Managed Objects
  for the DS1 and E1 Interface Types
AUTHORS: F. Baker, J. Watt, Editors
DATE: January 1993
KEYWORDS: T1, MIB, Management,
  SNMP
ORGANIZATION: Advanced
  Computer Communications,
  Newbridge Networks Corporation
FORMAT: ASCII
CHAR-COUNT: 97559
OBSOLETES: RFC1232

TYPE: RFC
DOC-ID: **RFC1407**
TITLE: Definitions of Managed Objects
  for the DS3/E3 Interface Type
AUTHORS: Tracy A. Cox, Kaj Tesink
DATE: January 1993
KEYWORDS: T3, MIB, Management,
  SNMP
ORGANIZATION: Bell Communica-
  tions Research
FORMAT: ASCII
CHAR-COUNT: 90682
OBSOLETES: RFC1233

TYPE: RFC
DOC-ID: **RFC1414**
TITLE: Identification MIB
AUTHORS: M. StJohns, M. Rose
DATE: January 1993
KEYWORDS: Management, SNMP
ORGANIZATION: DARPA/CSTO,
  Dover Beach Consulting, Inc.
FORMAT: ASCII
CHAR-COUNT: 14165

TYPE: RFC
DOC-ID: **RFC1418**
TITLE: SNMP over OSI
AUTHORS: M. Rose
DATE: March 1993
KEYWORDS: Management
ORGANIZATION: Dover Beach
  Consulting, Inc.
FORMAT: ASCII
CHAR-COUNT: 7721
OBSOLETES: RFC1161, RFC1283

TYPE: RFC
DOC-ID: **RFC1419**
TITLE: SNMP over AppleTalk
AUTHORS: G. Minshall, M. Ritter
DATE: March 1993
KEYWORDS: Management
ORGANIZATION: Novell, Inc., Apple
 Computer, Inc.
FORMAT: ASCII
CHAR-COUNT: 16470

TYPE: RFC
DOC-ID: **RFC1420**
TITLE: SNMP over IPX
AUTHORS: S. Bostock
DATE: March 1993
KEYWORDS: Management
ORGANIZATION: Novell, Inc.
FORMAT: ASCII
CHAR-COUNT: 6762
OBSOLETES: RFC1298

TYPE: RFC
DOC-ID: **RFC1441**
TITLE: Introduction to version 2 of the
 Internet-standard Network
 Management Framework
AUTHORS: J. Case, K. McCloghrie,
 M. Rose, S. Waldbusser
DATE: April 1993
KEYWORDS: SNMP, Management,
 Framework
ORGANIZATION: Research, Inc.,
 Hughes LAN Systems, Dover Beach
 Consulting, Inc., Carnegie Mellon
 University
FORMAT: ASCII
CHAR-COUNT: 25386

TYPE: RFC
DOC-ID: **RFC1442**
TITLE: Structure of Management Infor-
 mation for version 2 of the Simple Net-
 work Management Protocol (SNMPv2)
AUTHORS: J. Case, K. McCloghrie,
 M. Rose, S. Waldbusser
DATE: April 1993
KEYWORDS: SNMP, Management,
 Framework, SMI
ORGANIZATION: SNMP Research,
 Inc., Hughes LAN Systems, Dover
 Beach Consulting, Inc., Carnegie
 Mellon University
FORMAT: ASCII
CHAR-COUNT: 95779
OBSOLETED-BY: RFC1902

TYPE: RFC
DOC-ID: **RFC1443**
TITLE: Textual Conventions for version
 2 of the Simple Network Management
 Protocol (SNMPv2)
AUTHORS: J. Case, K. McCloghrie,
 M. Rose, S. Waldbusser
DATE: April 1993
KEYWORDS: SNMP, Management,
 Framework
ORGANIZATION: SNMP Research,
 Inc., Hughes LAN Systems, Dover
 Beach Consulting, Inc., Carnegie
 Mellon University
FORMAT: ASCII
CHAR-COUNT: 60947
OBSOLETED-BY: RFC1903

TYPE: RFC
DOC-ID: **RFC1444**
TITLE: Conformance Statements for version 2 of the Simple Network Management Protocol (SNMPv2)
AUTHORS: J. Case, K. McCloghrie, M. Rose, S. Waldbusser
DATE: April 1993
KEYWORDS: SNMP, Management, Framework
ORGANIZATION: SNMP Research, Inc., Hughes LAN Systems, Dover Beach Consulting, Inc., Carnegie Mellon University
FORMAT: ASCII
CHAR-COUNT: 57744
OBSOLETED-BY: RFC1904

TYPE: RFC
DOC-ID: **RFC1445**
TITLE: Administrative Model for version 2 of the Simple Network Management Protocol (SNMPv2)
AUTHORS: J. Galvin, K. McCloghrie
DATE: April 1993
KEYWORDS: SNMP, Management, Framework
ORGANIZATION: Trusted Information Systems, Inc., Hughes LAN Systems
FORMAT: ASCII
CHAR-COUNT: 99443

TYPE: RFC
DOC-ID: **RFC1446**
TITLE: Security Protocols for version 2 of the Simple Network Management Protocol (SNMPv2)
AUTHORS: J. Galvin, K. McCloghrie
DATE: April 1993

KEYWORDS: SNMP, Management, Framework
ORGANIZATION: Trusted Information Systems, Inc., Hughes LAN Systems
FORMAT: ASCII
CHAR-COUNT: 108733

TYPE: RFC
DOC-ID: **RFC1447**
TITLE: Party MIB for version 2 of the Simple Network Management Protocol (SNMPv2)
AUTHORS: K. McCloghrie, J. Galvin
DATE: April 1993
KEYWORDS: SNMP, Management, Framework
ORGANIZATION: Hughes LAN Systems, Trusted Information Systems, Inc.
FORMAT: ASCII
CHAR-COUNT: 80762

TYPE: RFC
DOC-ID: **RFC1448**
TITLE: Protocol Operations for version 2 of the Simple Network Management Protocol (SNMPv2)
AUTHORS: J. Case, K. McCloghrie, M. Rose, S. Waldbusser
DATE: April 1993
KEYWORDS: SNMP, Management, Framework
ORGANIZATION: SNMP Research, Inc., Hughes LAN Systems, Dover Beach Consulting, Inc., Carnegie Mellon University
FORMAT: ASCII
CHAR-COUNT: 74224
OBSOLETED-BY: RFC1905

TYPE: RFC
DOC-ID: **RFC1449**
TITLE: Transport Mappings for version 2 of the Simple Network Management Protocol (SNMPv2)
AUTHORS: J. Case, K. McCloghrie, M. Rose, S. Waldbusser
DATE: April 1993
KEYWORDS: SNMP, Management, Framework
ORGANIZATION: SNMP Research, Inc., Hughes LAN Systems, Dover Beach Consulting, Inc., Carnegie Mellon University
FORMAT: ASCII
CHAR-COUNT: 41161
OBSOLETED-BY: RFC1906

TYPE: RFC
DOC-ID: **RFC1450**
TITLE: Management Information Base for version 2 of the Simple Network Management Protocol (SNMPv2)
AUTHORS: J. Case, K. McCloghrie, M. Rose, S. Waldbusser
DATE: April 1993
KEYWORDS: SNMP, Management, Framework
ORGANIZATION: SNMP Research, Inc., Hughes LAN Systems, Dover Beach Consulting, Inc., Carnegie Mellon University
FORMAT: ASCII
CHAR-COUNT: 42172
OBSOLETED-BY: RFC1907

TYPE: RFC
DOC-ID: **RFC1451**
TITLE: Manager-to-Manager Management Information Base

AUTHORS: J. Case, K. McCloghrie, M. Rose, S. Waldbusser
DATE: April 1993
KEYWORDS: SNMP, Management, Framework
ORGANIZATION: SNMP Research, Inc., Hughes LAN Systems, Dover Beach Consulting, Inc., Carnegie Mellon University
FORMAT: ASCII
CHAR-COUNT: 62935

TYPE: RFC
DOC-ID: **RFC1452**
TITLE: Coexistence between version 1 and version 2 of the Internet-standard Network Management Framework
AUTHORS: J. Case, K. McCloghrie, M. Rose, S. Waldbusser
DATE: April 1993
KEYWORDS: SNMP, Management, Framework
ORGANIZATION: SNMP Research, Inc., Hughes LAN Systems, Dover Beach Consulting, Inc., Carnegie Mellon University
FORMAT: ASCII
CHAR-COUNT: 32176
OBSOLETED-BY: RFC1908

TYPE: RFC
DOC-ID: **RFC1461**
TITLE: SNMP MIB extension for Multiprotocol Interconnect over X.25
AUTHORS: D. Throop
DATE: May 1993
ORGANIZATION: Data General Corporation
FORMAT: ASCII
CHAR-COUNT: 47945

TYPE: RFC
DOC-ID: **RFC1470**
TITLE: FYI on a Network Management
Tool Catalog: Tools for Monitoring
and Debugging TCP/IP Internets and
Interconnected Devices
AUTHORS: R. Enger, J. Reynolds
DATE: June 1993
KEYWORDS: NOCTOOLS
ORGANIZATION: ANS, ISI
FORMAT: ASCII
CHAR-COUNT: 308528
OBSOLETES: RFC1147
SEE-ALSO: FYI0002

TYPE: RFC
DOC-ID: **RFC1471**
TITLE: The Definitions of Managed
Objects for the Link Control Protocol
of the Point-to-Point Protocol
AUTHORS: F. Kastenholz
DATE: June 1993
KEYWORDS: Management,
Framework, PPP
ORGANIZATION: FTP Software, Inc.
FORMAT: ASCII
CHAR-COUNT: 53558

TYPE: RFC
DOC-ID: **RFC1472**
TITLE: The Definitions of Managed
Objects for the Security Protocols of
the Point-to-Point Protocol
AUTHORS: F. Kastenholz
DATE: June 1993
KEYWORDS: Management,
Framework, PPP
ORGANIZATION: FTP Software, Inc.
FORMAT: ASCII
CHAR-COUNT: 27152

TYPE: RFC
DOC-ID: **RFC1473**
TITLE: The Definitions of Managed
Objects for the IP Network Control
Protocol of the Point-to-Point Protocol
AUTHORS: F. Kastenholz
DATE: June 1993
KEYWORDS: Management,
Framework, PPP
ORGANIZATION: FTP Software, Inc.
FORMAT: ASCII
CHAR-COUNT: 20484

TYPE: RFC
DOC-ID: **RFC1474**
TITLE: The Definitions of Managed
Objects for the Bridge Network
Control Protocol of the Point-to-
Point Protocol
AUTHORS: F. Kastenholz
DATE: June 1993
KEYWORDS: Management,
Framework, PPP
ORGANIZATION: FTP Software, Inc.
FORMAT: ASCII
CHAR-COUNT: 31846

TYPE: RFC
DOC-ID: **RFC1493**
TITLE: Definitions of Managed Objects
for Bridges
AUTHORS: E. Decker, P. Langille, A.
Rijsinghani, K. McCloghrie
DATE: July 1993
KEYWORDS: SNMP, MIB, standard,
standards
ORGANIZATION: Cisco Systems,
Inc., Digital Equipment Corporation,
Hughes LAN Systems, Inc.
FORMAT: ASCII

CHAR-COUNT: 74493
OBSOLETES: RFC1286

TYPE: RFC
DOC-ID: **RFC1503**
TITLE: Algorithms for Automating
  Administration in SNMPv2 Managers
AUTHORS: K. McCloghrie, M. Rose
DATE: August 1993
KEYWORDS: Management, SNMP
ORGANIZATION: Hughes LAN
  Systems, Dover Beach Consulting, Inc.
FORMAT: ASCII
CHAR-COUNT: 33542

TYPE: RFC
DOC-ID: **RFC1512**
TITLE: FDDI Management
  Information Base
AUTHORS: J. Case, A. Rijsinghani
DATE: September 1993
KEYWORDS: MIB, SNMP
ORGANIZATION: University of
  Tennessee, SNMP Research,
  Incorporated
FORMAT: ASCII
CHAR-COUNT: 108589
UPDATES: RFC1285

TYPE: RFC
DOC-ID: **RFC1513**
TITLE: Token Ring Extensions to the
  Remote Network Monitoring MIB
AUTHORS: S. Waldbusser
DATE: September 1993
KEYWORDS: Monitoring, SNMP
ORGANIZATION: Carnegie Mellon
  University
FORMAT: ASCII
CHAR-COUNT: 121974
UPDATES: 1271

TYPE: RFC
DOC-ID: **RFC1514**
TITLE: Host Resources MIB
AUTHORS: P. Grillo, S. Waldbusser
DATE: September 1993
KEYWORDS: Management, SNMP
ORGANIZATION: Carnegie Mellon
  University
FORMAT: ASCII
CHAR-COUNT: 63775

TYPE: RFC
DOC-ID: **RFC1515**
TITLE: Definitions of Managed Objects
  for IEEE 802.3 Medium Attachment
  Units (MAUs)
AUTHORS: D. McMaster, K.
  McCloghrie, S. Roberts
DATE: September 1993
KEYWORDS: MIB, Management, SNMP
ORGANIZATION: SynOptics
  Communications, Inc., Hughes LAN
  Systems, Inc., Farallon Computing, Inc.
FORMAT: ASCII
CHAR-COUNT: 52828

TYPE: RFC
DOC-ID: **RFC1516**
TITLE: 802.3 Repeater MIB
AUTHORS: D. McMaster, K.
  McCloghrie
DATE: September 1993
KEYWORDS: Management, SNMP
ORGANIZATION: SynOptics
  Communications, Inc., Hughes LAN
  Systems, Inc.
FORMAT: ASCII
CHAR-COUNT: 82918
OBSOLETES: RFC1368
OBSOLETED-BY: RFC2108

TYPE: RFC
DOC-ID: **RFC1525**
TITLE: Definitions of Managed Objects
for Source Routing Bridges
AUTHORS: E. Decker, K. McCloghrie,
P. Langille, A. Rijsinghani
DATE: September 1993
KEYWORDS: MIB, Management, SNMP
ORGANIZATION: Cisco Systems, Inc.,
Hughes LAN Systems, Inc., Digital
Equipment Corporation
FORMAT: ASCII
CHAR-COUNT: 38100
OBSOLETES: RFC1286

TYPE: RFC
DOC-ID: **RFC1559**
TITLE: DECnet Phase IV MIB Extensions
AUTHORS: J. Saperia
DATE: December 1993
KEYWORDS: Management, SNMP
ORGANIZATION: Digital Equipment
Corporation
FORMAT: ASCII
CHAR-COUNT: 125427
OBSOLETES: RFC1289

TYPE: RFC
DOC-ID: **RFC1565**
TITLE: Network Services Monitoring
MIB
AUTHORS: S. Kille, N. Freed
DATE: January 1994
KEYWORDS: Management,
Information, Base
ORGANIZATION: ISODE Consortium,
Innosoft International, Inc.
FORMAT: ASCII
CHAR-COUNT: 29761

TYPE: RFC
DOC-ID: **RFC1566**
TITLE: Mail Monitoring MIB
AUTHORS: S. Kille, N. Freed
DATE: January 1994
KEYWORDS: Management,
Information, Base
ORGANIZATION: ISODE Consortium,
Innosoft International, Inc.
FORMAT: ASCII
CHAR-COUNT: 33136

TYPE: RFC
DOC-ID: **RFC1567**
TITLE: X.500 Directory Monitoring MIB
AUTHORS: G. Mansfield, S. Kille
DATE: January 1994
KEYWORDS: Management,
Information, Base
ORGANIZATION: AIC Systems
Laboratories, ISODE Consortium
FORMAT: ASCII
CHAR-COUNT: 33527

TYPE: RFC
DOC-ID: **RFC1573**
TITLE: Evolution of the Interfaces
Group of MIB-II
AUTHORS: K. McCloghrie, F.
Kastenholz
DATE: January 1994
KEYWORDS: Management,
Information, Base
ORGANIZATION: Hughes LAN
Systems, FTP Software
FORMAT: ASCII
CHAR-COUNT: 123057
OBSOLETES: 1229

TYPE: RFC
DOC-ID: **RFC1592**
TITLE: Simple Network Management
  Protocol Distributed Protocol
  Interface Version 2.0
AUTHORS: B. Wijnen, G. Carpenter,
  K. Curran, A. Sehgal, G. Waters
DATE: March 1994
KEYWORDS: SNMP, DPT, IBM
ORGANIZATION: IBM International
  Operations, IBM T.J. Watson Research
  Center, Bell Northern Research Ltd.
FORMAT: ASCII
CHAR-COUNT: 135259
OBSOLETES: RFC1228

TYPE: RFC
DOC-ID: **RFC1593**
TITLE: SNA APPN Node MIB
AUTHORS: W. McKenzie, J. Cheng
DATE: March 1994
KEYWORDS: IBM, Management
ORGANIZATION: IBM Networking
  Systems
FORMAT: ASCII
CHAR-COUNT: 207882

TYPE: RFC
DOC-ID: **RFC1595**
TITLE: Definitions of Managed Objects
  for the SONET/SDH Interface Type
AUTHORS: T. Brown, K. Tesink
DATE: March 1994
KEYWORDS: MIB, Management, SNMP
ORGANIZATION: Bell
  Communications Research
FORMAT: ASCII
CHAR-COUNT: 121937

TYPE: RFC
DOC-ID: **RFC1596**
TITLE: Definitions of Managed Objects
  for Frame Relay Service
AUTHORS: T. Brown, Editor
DATE: March 1994
KEYWORDS: FR, MIB, Management,
  SNMP
ORGANIZATION: Bell Communica-
  tions Research
FORMAT: ASCII
CHAR-COUNT: 88795
OBSOLETED-BY: RFC1604

TYPE: RFC
DOC-ID: **RFC1604**
TITLE: Definitions of Managed Objects
  for Frame Relay Service
AUTHORS: T. Brown, Editor
DATE: March 1994
KEYWORDS: MIB, Management,
  SNMP, Network
ORGANIZATION: Bell Communi-
  cations Research
FORMAT: ASCII
CHAR-COUNT: 88770
OBSOLETES: RFC1596

TYPE: RFC
DOC-ID: **RFC1611**
TITLE: DNS Server MIB Extensions
AUTHORS: R. Austein, J. Saperia
DATE: May 1994
KEYWORDS: Domain, Name, System,
  Management, Information, Base
ORGANIZATION: Epilogue Technol-
  ogy Corporation, Digital Equipment
  Corporation
FORMAT: ASCII
CHAR-COUNT: 58700

TYPE: RFC
DOC-ID: **RFC1612**
TITLE: DNS Resolver MIB Extensions
AUTHORS: R. Austein, J. Saperia
DATE: May 1994
KEYWORDS: Domain, Name, System,
Management, Information, Base
ORGANIZATION: Epilogue Technol-
ogy Corporation, Digital Equipment
Corporation
FORMAT: ASCII
CHAR-COUNT: 61382

TYPE: RFC
DOC-ID: **RFC1623**
TITLE: Definitions of Managed Objects
for the Ethernet-like Interface Types
AUTHORS: F. Kastenholz
DATE: May 1994
KEYWORDS: MIB, Management,
Information, Base
ORGANIZATION: FTP Software, Inc.
FORMAT: ASCII
CHAR-COUNT: 38745
OBSOLETES: RFC1398
OBSOLETED-BY: RFC1643,
STD0050
SEE-ALSO: STD0050

TYPE: RFC
DOC-ID: **RFC1628**
TITLE: UPS Management Information
Base
AUTHORS: J. Case
DATE: May 1994
KEYWORDS: Uninterruptible, Power,
Supply, MIB
ORGANIZATION: SNMP Research,
Incorporated

FORMAT: ASCII
CHAR-COUNT: 83439

TYPE: RFC
DOC-ID: **RFC1643**
TITLE: Definitions of Managed Objects
for the Ethernet-like Interface Types
AUTHORS: F. Kastenholz
DATE: July 1994
KEYWORDS: MIB, Network,
Management, SNMP, Ethernet
ORGANIZATION: FTP Software, Inc.
FORMAT: ASCII
CHAR-COUNT: 39008
OBSOLETES: RFC1623, RFC1398
SEE-ALSO: STD0050

TYPE: RFC
DOC-ID: **RFC1650**
TITLE: Definitions of Managed Objects
for the Ethernet-like Interface Types
using SMIv2
AUTHORS: F. Kastenholz
DATE: August 1994
KEYWORDS: MIB, Management,
Information, Base, 802.3
ORGANIZATION: FTP Software, Inc.
FORMAT: ASCII
CHAR-COUNT: 40484

TYPE: RFC
DOC-ID: **RFC1657**
TITLE: Definitions of Managed Objects
for the Fourth Version of the Border
Gateway Protocol (BGP-4) using
SMIv2
AUTHORS: S. Willis, J. Burruss, J.
Chu, Editors
DATE: July 1994
KEYWORDS: MIB, Management,
Information, Base

ORGANIZATION: Wellfleet
Communications Inc., IBM Corp.
FORMAT: ASCII
CHAR-COUNT: 45505

TYPE: RFC
DOC-ID: **RFC1658**
TITLE: Definitions of Managed Objects
for Character Stream Devices using
SMIv2
AUTHORS: B. Stewart
DATE: July 1994
KEYWORDS: MIB, Network,
Management, Base
ORGANIZATION: Xyplex, Inc.
FORMAT: ASCII
CHAR-COUNT: 32579
OBSOLETES: RFC1316

TYPE: RFC
DOC-ID: **RFC1659**
TITLE: Definitions of Managed Objects
for RS-232-like Hardware Devices
using SMIv2
AUTHORS: B. Stewart
DATE: July 1994
KEYWORDS: MIB, Network,
Management, Base
ORGANIZATION: Xyplex, Inc.
FORMAT: ASCII
CHAR-COUNT: 36479
OBSOLETES: RFC1317

TYPE: RFC
DOC-ID: **RFC1660**
TITLE: Definitions of Managed Objects
for Parallel-printer-like Hardware
Devices using SMIv2
AUTHORS: B. Stewart
DATE: July 1994

KEYWORDS: MIB, Network,
Management, Base
ORGANIZATION: Xyplex, Inc.
FORMAT: ASCII
CHAR-COUNT: 16784
OBSOLETES: RFC1318

TYPE: RFC
DOC-ID: **RFC1665**
TITLE: Definitions of Managed Objects
for SNA NAUs using SMIv2
AUTHORS: Z. Kielczewski, D.
Kostick, K. Shih, Editors
DATE: July 1994
KEYWORDS: MIB, Management,
Information, Base, System, Network,
Architecture, Addressable, Units
ORGANIZATION: Eicon Technology
Corporation, Bell Communications
FORMAT: ASCII
CHAR-COUNT: 133381
OBSOLETED-BY: RFC1666

TYPE: RFC
DOC-ID: **RFC1666**
TITLE: Definitions of Managed Objects
for SNA NAUs using SMIv2
AUTHORS: Z. Kielczewski, D.
Kostick, K. Shih, Editors
DATE: August 1994
KEYWORDS: Network, Management,
SNMP, MIB, Protocol, Units, Archi-
tecture, Addressable, Information,
System
ORGANIZATION: Eicon Technology
Corporation, Bellcore, Novell
FORMAT: ASCII
CHAR-COUNT: 134385
OBSOLETES: RFC1665

511

TYPE: RFC
DOC-ID: **RFC1694**
TITLE: Definitions of Managed Objects
for SMDS Interfaces using SMIv2
AUTHORS: T. Brown, K. Tesink, Editors
DATE: August 1994
KEYWORDS: Standard, MIB,
Network, Management, Switched,
Multimegabit, Data, Service,
Informatiom, Base, SMDS
ORGANIZATION: Bell
Communications Research
FORMAT: ASCII
CHAR-COUNT: 70856
OBSOLETES: RFC1304

TYPE: RFC
DOC-ID: **RFC1695**
TITLE: Definitions of Managed Objects
for ATM Management Version 8.0
using SMIv2
AUTHORS: M. Ahmed, K. Tesink,
Editors
DATE: August 1994
KEYWORDS: MIB, Management,
Information, Base, Asychronous,
Transmission, Mode
ORGANIZATION: Bell Communica-
tions Research
FORMAT: ASCII
CHAR-COUNT: 175461

TYPE: RFC
DOC-ID: **RFC1696**
TITLE: Modem Management
Information Base (MIB) using SMIv2
AUTHORS: J. Barnes, L. Brown, R.
Royston, S. Waldbusser
DATE: August 1994

ORGANIZATION: Xylogics, Inc.,
Motorola, US Robotics, Inc.,
Carnegie Mellon University
FORMAT: ASCII
CHAR-COUNT: 54054

TYPE: RFC
DOC-ID: **RFC1697**
TITLE: Relational Database
Management System (RDBMS)
Management Information Base
(MIB) using SMIv2
AUTHORS: D. Brower, Editor; B.
Purvy, RDBMSMIB Working Group
Chair; A. Daniel, M. Sinykin, J. Smith
DATE: August 1994
ORGANIZATION: The ASK Group,
INGRES DBMS Development, Oracle
Corporation, Informix Software, Inc.,
FORMAT: ASCII
CHAR-COUNT: 76202

TYPE: RFC
DOC-ID: **RFC1724**
TITLE: RIP Version 2 MIB Extension
AUTHORS: G. Malkin, F. Baker
DATE: November 1994
KEYWORDS: RIP-2, Management,
Information, Base
ORGANIZATION: Xylogics, Inc.,
Cisco Systems
FORMAT: ASCII
CHAR-COUNT: 29645
OBSOLETES: RFC1389

TYPE: RFC
DOC-ID: **RFC1742**
TITLE: AppleTalk Management
Information Base II
AUTHORS: S. Waldbusser, K. Frisa
DATE: January 1995
ORGANIZATION: Carnegie Mellon
University, FORE Systems, Inc.
FORMAT: ASCII
CHAR-COUNT: 168306
OBSOLETES: RFC1243

TYPE: RFC
DOC-ID: **RFC1743**
TITLE: IEEE 802.5 MIB using SMIv2
AUTHORS: K. McCloghrie, E. Decker
DATE: December 1994
KEYWORDS: Management, Informa-
tion, Base, SNMP
ORGANIZATION: Cisco Systems, Inc.
FORMAT: ASCII
CHAR-COUNT: 43224
OBSOLETES: RFC1231
OBSOLETED-BY: RFC1748

TYPE: RFC
DOC-ID: **RFC1747**
TITLE: Definitions of Managed Objects
for SNA Data Link Control (SDLC)
using SMIv2
AUTHORS: J. Hilgeman, Chair; S. Nix,
A. Bartky, W. Clark, Editors
DATE: January 1995
ORGANIZATION: Apertus Technol-
ogies, Inc., Metaplex, Inc., Sync
Research, Inc.
FORMAT: ASCII
CHAR-COUNT: 147388

TYPE: RFC
DOC-ID: **RFC1748**
TITLE: IEEE 802.5 MIB using SMIv2
AUTHORS: K. McCloghrie, E. Decker
DATE: December 1994
KEYWORDS: Management,
Information, Base, SNMP
ORGANIZATION: Cisco Systems, Inc.
FORMAT: ASCII
CHAR-COUNT: 43224
OBSOLETES: RFC1743, RFC1231
UPDATED-BY: RFC1749

TYPE: RFC
DOC-ID: **RFC1749**
TITLE: IEEE 802.5 Station Source
Routing MIB using SMIv2
AUTHORS: K. McCloghrie, F. Baker,
E. Decker
DATE: December 1994
KEYWORDS: Management,
Information, Base, SNMP
ORGANIZATION: Cisco Systems, Inc.
FORMAT: ASCII
CHAR-COUNT: 17563
UPDATES: RFC1748

TYPE: RFC
DOC-ID: **RFC1757**
TITLE: Remote Network Monitoring
Management Information Base
AUTHORS: S. Waldbusser
DATE: February 1995
KEYWORDS: MIB, RMON
ORGANIZATION: Carnegie Mellon
University
FORMAT: ASCII
CHAR-COUNT: 208117
OBSOLETES: RFC1271

TYPE: RFC
DOC-ID: **RFC1759**
TITLE: Printer MIB
AUTHORS: R. Smith, F. Wright, T.
Hastings, S. Zilles, J. Gyllenskog
DATE: March 1995
KEYWORDS: Management,
Information, Base
ORGANIZATION: Texas Instruments,
Lexmark International, Xerox
FORMAT: ASCII
CHAR-COUNT: 239228

TYPE: RFC
DOC-ID: **RFC1792**
TITLE: TCP/IPX Connection MIB
Specification
AUTHORS: T. Sung
DATE: April 1995
KEYWORDS: Transmission, Control,
Protocol, Management,
Information, Base
ORGANIZATION: Novell, Inc.
FORMAT: ASCII
CHAR-COUNT: 16389

TYPE: RFC
DOC-ID: **RFC1850**
TITLE: OSPF Version 2 Management
Information Base
AUTHORS: F. Baker, R. Coltun
DATE: November1995
KEYWORDS: Open, Shortest, Path,
First, SPF, MIB, routing, network
management
ORGANIZATION: Cisco Systems, Inc.,
RainbowBridge Communications

FORMAT: ASCII
CHAR-COUNT: 140255
OBSOLETES: RFC1253

TYPE: RFC
DOC-ID: **RFC1901**
TITLE: Introduction to Community-
based SNMPv2
AUTHORS: SNMPv2 Working Group,
J. Case, K. McCloghrie, M. Rose, S.
Waldbusser
DATE: January 1996
KEYWORDS: Simple, Network,
Management, Protocol, Version, 2
ORGANIZATION: SNMP Research,
Cisco Systems, Dover Beach Consul-
ting, International Network Services
FORMAT: ASCII
CHAR-COUNT: 15903

TYPE: RFC
DOC-ID: **RFC1902**
TITLE: Structure of Management Infor-
mation for Version 2 of the Simple
Management Protocol (SNMPv2)
AUTHORS: SNMPv2 Working Group,
J. Case, K. McCloghrie, M. Rose, S.
Waldbusser
DATE: January 1996
KEYWORDS: Simple, Network,
Management, Protocol, Version, 2
ORGANIZATION: SNMP Research,
Cisco Systems, Dover Beach Consul-
ting, International Network Services
FORMAT: ASCII
CHAR-COUNT: 77453
OBSOLETES: RFC1442

TYPE: RFC
DOC-ID: **RFC1903**
TITLE: Textual Conventions for
Version 2 of the Simple Network
Management Protocol (SNMPv2)
AUTHORS: SNMPv2 Working Group,
J. Case, K. McCloghrie, M. Rose, S.
Waldbusser
DATE: January 1996
KEYWORDS: Simple, Network,
Management, Protocol, Version, 2
ORGANIZATION: SNMP Research,
Cisco Systems, Dover Beach Consul-
ting, InternationalNetwork Services
FORMAT: ASCII
CHAR-COUNT: 52652
OBSOLETES: RFC1443

TYPE: RFC
DOC-ID: **RFC1904**
TITLE: Conformance Statements for
Version 2 of the Simple Network
Management Protocol (SNMPv2)
AUTHORS: SNMPv2 Working Group,
J. Case, K. McCloghrie, M. Rose, S.
Waldbusser
DATE: January 1996
KEYWORDS: Simple, Network,
Management, Protocol, Version, 2
ORGANIZATION: SNMP Research,
Cisco Systems, Dover Beach Consul-
ting, InternationalNetwork Services
FORMAT: ASCII
CHAR-COUNT: 47083
OBSOLETES: RFC1444

TYPE: RFC
DOC-ID: **RFC1905**
TITLE: Protocol Operations for
Version 2 of the Simple Network
Management Protocol (SNMPv2)
AUTHORS: SNMPv2 Working Group,
J. Case, K. McCloghrie, M. Rose, S.
Waldbusser
DATE: January 1996
KEYWORDS: Simple, Network,
Management, Protocol, Version, 2
ORGANIZATION: SNMP Research,
Cisco Systems, Dover Beach Consul-
ting, International Network Services
FORMAT: ASCII
CHAR-COUNT: 55526
OBSOLETES: RFC1448

TYPE: RFC
DOC-ID: **RFC1906**
TITLE: Transport Mappings for
Version 2 of the Simple Network
Management Protocol (SNMPv2)
AUTHORS: SNMPv2 Working Group,
J. Case, K. McCloghrie, M. Rose, S.
Waldbusser
DATE: January 1996
KEYWORDS: Simple, Network,
Management, Protocol, Version, 2
ORGANIZATION: SNMP Research,
Cisco Systems, Dover Beach Consul-
ting, International Network Services
FORMAT: ASCII
CHAR-COUNT: 27465
OBSOLETES: RFC1449

TYPE: RFC
DOC-ID: **RFC1907**
TITLE: Management Information Base
for Version 2 of the Simple Network
Management Protocol (SNMPv2)
AUTHORS: SNMPv2 Working Group,
J. Case, K. McCloghrie, M. Rose, S.
Waldbusser
DATE: January 1996
KEYWORDS: Simple, Network,
Management, Protocol, Version, 2
ORGANIZATION: SNMP Research,
Cisco Systems, Dover Beach Consul-
ting, International Network Services
FORMAT: ASCII
CHAR-COUNT: 34881
OBSOLETES: RFC1450

TYPE: RFC
DOC-ID: **RFC1908**
TITLE: Coexistence between Version 1
and Version 2 of the Internet-standard
Network Management Framework
AUTHORS: SNMPv2 Working Group,
J. Case, K. McCloghrie, M. Rose, S.
Waldbusser
DATE: January 1996
KEYWORDS: Simple, Network,
Management, Protocol, Version, 2
ORGANIZATION: SNMP Research,
Cisco Systems, Dover Beach Consul-
ting, International Network Services
FORMAT: ASCII
CHAR-COUNT: 21463
OBSOLETES: RFC1452

TYPE: RFC
DOC-ID: **RFC1909**
TITLE: An Administrative
Infrastructure for SNMPv2
AUTHORS: K. McCloghrie
DATE: February 1996
KEYWORDS: Simple, Network,
Management, Protocol, Version, 2
ORGANIZATION: Cisco Systems, Inc.
FORMAT: ASCII
CHAR-COUNT: 45773

TYPE: RFC
DOC-ID: **RFC1910**
TITLE: User-based Security Model for
SNMPv2
AUTHORS: G. Waters
DATE: February 1996
KEYWORDS: Simple, Network,
Management, Protocol, Version, 2
ORGANIZATION: Bell-Northern
Research Ltd.
FORMAT: ASCII
CHAR-COUNT: 98252

TYPE: RFC
DOC-ID: **RFC1988**
TITLE: Conditional Grant of Rights to
Specific Hewlett-Packard Patents in
Conjunction With the Internet Engin-
eering Task Force's Internet-Standard
Network Management Framework
AUTHORS: G. McAnally, D. Gilbert,
J. Flick
DATE: August 1996
KEYWORDS: HP
ORGANIZATION: Hewlett-Packard
Company
FORMAT: ASCII
CHAR-COUNT: 3821

TYPE: RFC
DOC-ID: **RFC2006**
TITLE: The Definitions of Managed
  Objects for IP Mobility Support
  using SMIv2
AUTHORS: D. Cong, M. Hamlen, C.
  Perkins
DATE: October 1996
KEYWORDS: Internet, Protocol, MIB,
  Managed, Information, Base
ORGANIZATION: Motorola, Inc., IBM
  Corporation
FORMAT: ASCII
CHAR-COUNT: 95030

TYPE: RFC
DOC-ID: **RFC2011**
TITLE: SNMPv2 Management Infor-
  mation Base for the Internet Protocol
  using SMIv2
AUTHORS: K. McCloghrie
DATE: November 1996
KEYWORDS: IP, Simple, Network,
  Management, Protocol, MIB
ORGANIZATION: Cisco Systems, Inc.
FORMAT: ASCII
CHAR-COUNT: 31168
OBSOLETES: RFC1213

TYPE: RFC
DOC-ID: **RFC2012**
TITLE: SNMPv2 Management Infor-
  mation Base for the Transmission
  Control Protocol using SMIv2
AUTHORS: K. McCloghrie
DATE: November 1996
KEYWORDS: TCP, Simple, Network,
  Management, Protocol, MIB
ORGANIZATION: Cisco Systems, Inc.
FORMAT: ASCII

CHAR-COUNT: 16792
OBSOLETES: RFC1213

TYPE: RFC
DOC-ID: **RFC2013**
TITLE: SNMPv2 Management
  Information Base for the User
  Datagram Protocol using SMIv2
AUTHORS: K. McCloghrie
DATE: November 1996
KEYWORDS: Simple, Network,
  Management, Protocol, MIB, UDP
ORGANIZATION: Cisco Systems, Inc.
FORMAT: ASCII
CHAR-COUNT: 9333
OBSOLETES: RFC1213

TYPE: RFC
DOC-ID: **RFC2020**
TITLE: IEEE 802.12 Interface MIB
AUTHORS: J. Flick
DATE: October 1996
KEYWORDS: Management,
  Information, Base
ORGANIZATION: Hewlett Packard
  Company
FORMAT: ASCII
CHAR-COUNT: 72135

TYPE: RFC
DOC-ID: **RFC2021**
TITLE: Remote Network Monitoring
  Management Information Base
  Version 2 using SMIv2
AUTHORS: S. Waldbusser
DATE: January 1997
KEYWORDS: RMON, MIB
FORMAT: ASCII
CHAR-COUNT: 262223

517

TYPE: RFC
DOC-ID: **RFC2024**
TITLE: Definitions of Managed Objects
for Data Link Switching using SMIv2
AUTHORS: D. Chen, P. Gayek, S. Nix
DATE: October 1996
KEYWORDS: MIB, DLSW,
Management, Information, Base
ORGANIZATION: IBM Networking
Systems, Metaplex, Inc.
FORMAT: ASCII
CHAR-COUNT: 173952

TYPE: RFC
DOC-ID: **RFC2037**
TITLE: Entity MIB using SMIv2
AUTHORS: K. McCloghrie, A.
Bierman
DATE: October 1996
KEYWORDS: Management, Information, Base, SNMP
ORGANIZATION: Cisco Systems, Inc.
FORMAT: ASCII
CHAR-COUNT: 74362

TYPE: RFC
DOC-ID: **RFC2039**
TITLE: Applicability of Standards Track
MIBs to Management of World Wide
Web Servers
AUTHORS: C. Kalbfleisch
DATE: November 1996
KEYWORDS: Management,
Information, Base, HTTP
ORGANIZATION: OnRamp
Technologies, Inc.
FORMAT: ASCII
CHAR-COUNT: 31966

TYPE: RFC
DOC-ID: **RFC2051**
TITLE: Definitions of Managed
Objects for APPC using SMIv2
AUTHORS: M. Allen, B. Clouston, Z.
Kielczewski, W. Kwan, B. Moore
DATE: October 1996
ORGANIZATION: Wall Data, Cisco
Systems, Jupiter Technology Inc.,
IBM Corporation
FORMAT: ASCII
CHAR-COUNT: 239359

TYPE: RFC
DOC-ID: **RFC2064**
TITLE: Traffic Flow Measurement:
Meter MIB
AUTHORS: N. Brownlee
DATE: January 1997
KEYWORDS: Management,
Information, Base, Network, Data
ORGANIZATION: The University of
Auckland
FORMAT: ASCII
CHAR-COUNT: 67520

TYPE: RFC
DOC-ID: **RFC2074**
TITLE: Remote Network Monitoring
MIB Protocol Identifiers
AUTHORS: A. Bierman, R. Iddon
DATE: January 1997
KEYWORDS: RMON, Management,
Information, Base
ORGANIZATION: Cisco Systems,
Inc., 3Com/AXON
FORMAT: ASCII
CHAR-COUNT: 81262

TYPE: RFC
DOC-ID: **RFC2096**
TITLE: IP Forwarding Table MIB
AUTHORS: F. Baker
DATE: January 1997
KEYWORDS: Management, Information, Base, Internet, Protocol
ORGANIZATION: Cisco Systems
FORMAT: ASCII
CHAR-COUNT: 1354

TYPE: RFC
DOC-ID: **RFC2108**
TITLE: Definitions of Managed Objects for IEEE 802.3 Repeater Devices using SMIv2
AUTHORS: K. de Graaf, D. Romascanu, D. McMaster, K. McCloghrie
DATE: February 1997
KEYWORDS: MIB, Management, Information, Base
ORGANIZATION: 3Com Corporation, Madge Networks (Israel) Ltd., Cisco Systems Inc.
FORMAT: ASCII
CHAR-COUNT: 166336
OBSOLETES: RFC1516

F Network Management Parameters from RFC 1700

The "Assigned Numbers" document, currently RFC 1700, contains a number of network management parameters. The parameters are updated frequently, and the current file names are listed at the end of each section. This appendix is an excerpt from those files.

For the management of hosts and gateways on the Internet, a data structure for the information has been defined. This data structure should be used with any of several possible management protocols, such as the "Simple Network Management Protocol" (SNMP), RFC1157, or the "Common Management Information Protocol over TCP" (CMOT), RFC1095.

The data structure is the "Structure and Identification of Management Information for TCP/IP-based Internets" (SMI), RFC1155, and the "Management Information Base for Network Management of TCP/IP-based Internets" (MIB-II), RFC1213. The SMI includes the provision for parameters or codes to indicate experimental or private data structures. These parameter assignments are listed here.

Object Identifiers

The network management object identifiers are under the iso (1), org (3), dod (6), internet (1), or 1.3.6.1, branch of the name space. The major branches are:

1	iso
1.3	org
1.3.6	dod
1.3.6.1	internet

1.3.6.1.1	directory
1.3.6.1.2	mgmt
1.3.6.1.2.1	mib-2
1.3.6.1.2.1.2.2.1.3	ifType
1.3.6.1.2.1.10	transmission
1.3.6.1.2.1.10.23	transmission.ppp
1.3.6.1.2.1.27	application
1.3.6.1.2.1.28	mta
1.3.6.1.3	experimental
1.3.6.1.4	private
1.3.6.1.4.1	enterprise
1.3.6.1.5	security
1.3.6.1.6	SNMPv2
1.3.6.1.7	mail

SMI Directory Codes

Prefix: iso.org.dod.internet.directory (1.3.6.1.1)

Decimal	Name	Description
0	Reserved	Reserved for future use

SMI mgmt Codes

Prefix: iso.org.dod.internet.mgmt (1.3.6.1.2)

Decimal	Name	Description
0	Reserved	
1	MIB	

SMI mib-2 Codes

Prefix: iso.org.dod.internet.mgmt.mib-2 (1.3.6.1.2.1)

Decimal	Name	Description	Reference
0	Reserved	Reserved	
1	system	System	RFC1213
2	interfaces	Interfaces	RFC1213
3	at	Address Translation	RFC1213
4	ip	Internet Protocol	RFC1213
5	icmp	Internet Control Message	RFC1213
6	tcp	Transmission Control Protocol	RFC1213]
7	udp	User Datagram Protocol	RFC1213
8	egp	Exterior Gateway Protocol	RFC1213
9	cmot	CMIP over TCP	RFC1213
10	transmission	Transmission	RFC1213
11	snmp	Simple Network Management	RFC1213
12	GenericIF	Generic Interface Extensions	RFC1229, RFC1239
13	Appletalk	Appletalk Networking	RFC1742
14	ospf	Open Shortest Path First	RFC1253
15	bgp	Border Gateway Protocol	RFC1657
16	rmon	Remote Network Monitoring	RFC1271
17	bridge	Bridge Objects	RFC1286
18	DecnetP4	Decnet Phase 4	RFC1559
19	Character	Character Streams	RFC1658
20	snmpParties	SNMP Parties	RFC1353
21	snmpSecrets	SNMP Secrets	RFC1353
22	snmpDot3RptrMgt	Repeaters	RFC2108
23	rip-2	Routing Information Protocol	RFC1389

24	ident	Identification Protocol	RFC1414
25	host	Host Resources	RFC1514
26	snmpDot3MauMgt 802.3	Medium Attachment Units	RFC1515
27	application	Network Services Monitoring	RFC1565
28	mta	Mail Monitoring	RFC1566
29	dsa	X.500 Directory Monitoring	RFC1567
30	IANAifType	Interface Types	RFC1573
31	ifMIB	Interface Types	RFC1573
32	dns	Domain Name System	RFC1611
33	upsMIB	Uninterruptible Power Supplies	RFC1628
34	snanauMIB	SNA NAU MIB	RFC1666
35	etherMIB	Ethernet-like generic objects	RFC1650
36	sipMIB	SMDS interface objects	RFC1694
37	atmMIB	ATM objects	RFC1695
38	mdmMIB	Dial-up modem objects	RFC1696
39	rdbmsMIB	Relational database objects	RFC1697
40	flowMIB	Traffic flow objects	RFC2064
41	snaDLC	SNA SDLC	RFC1747
42	dot5SrMIB	Token Ring Station Source Route	RFC1748
43	printMIB	Printer	RFC1759
44	mipMIB	Mobile IP	RFC2006
45	dot12MIB	IEEE 802.12	RFC2020
46	dlswMIB	Data Link Switch	RFC2024
47	entityMIB	Entity	RFC2037
48	ipMIB	Internet Protocol MIB Module	RFC2011
49	tcpMIB	TCP MIB Module	RFC2012
50	udpMIB	UDP MIB Module	RFC2013

SMI mib-2.interface Codes

Prefix: iso.org.dod.internet.mgmt.mib-2.interface (1.3.6.1.2.1.2)

...mib-2.interface.ifTable.ifEntry.ifType

(1.3.6.1.2.1.2.2.1.3)

For a functional mib language definition please see the file *mib/ianaiftype.mib* on ftp.isi.edu.

Rules for real mib names:

➤ the first letter is a lowercase letter

➤ if it's made of several words, the second and later word's first letter is uppercase

➤ digits are ok, but not as the first letter

➤ no hyphens in the word

➤ no periods in the word

Thus by way of example we have:

traif	kosher
ddn-x25	ddnX25,
FDDI	fddi,
smds-dxi	smdsDxi,
IEEE802.11	ieee80211,

➤ Finally, the last item in the list has no comma, while all previous items have a comma

SMI ifType Definitions

Decimal	Name	Description	Reference
1	other	none of the following	RFC1213
2	regular1822	BBN Report 1822	RFC1213
3	hdh1822	BBN Report 1822	RFC1213
4	ddn-x25	BBN Report 1822	RFC1213
5	x25	X.25	RFC1382
6	ethernet-csmacd		RFC1213
7	IEEE802.3	CSMACD-like Objects	RFC1284
8	IEEE802.4	Token Bus-like Objects	RFC1230
9	IEEE802.5	Token Ring-like Objects	RFC1231
10	iso88026-man		RFC1213
11	starLan		RFC1213
12	proteon-10Mbit		RFC1213
13	proteon-80Mbit		RFC1213
14	hyperchannel		RFC1213
15	FDDI	FDDI Objects	RFC1285
16	lapb	LAP B	RFC1381
17	sdlc		RFC1213
18	ds1	T1/E1 Carrier Objects	RFC1406
19	e1	obsolete	
20	basicISDN		RFC1213
21	primaryISDN		RFC1213
22	propPointToPointSerial		RFC1213
23	ppp	Point-to-Point Protocol	RFC1471
24	softwareLoopback		RFC1213
25	eon		RFC1213

26	ethernet-3Mbit		RFC1213
27	nsip		RFC1213
28	slip		RFC1213
29	ultra		RFC1213
30	ds3	DS3/E3 Interface Objects	RFC1407
31	sip	SMDS Interface Objects	RFC1304
32	frame-relay	Frame Relay Objects for	RFC1315
33	RS-232	RS-232 Objects	RFC1659
34	Parallel	Parallel Printer Objects	RFC1660
35	arcnet	ARC network	
36	arcnet-plus	ARC network plus	
37	atm	ATM	
38	MIOX25	MIOX25	RFC1461
39	SONET	SONET or SDH	
40	x25ple	X.25 packet level	RFC1382
41	iso88022llc	802.2 LLC	
42	localTalk		
43	smds-dxi	SMDS DXI	
44	frameRelayService	Frame Relay DCE	RFC1604
45	v35	V.35	
46	hssi	HSSI	
47	hippi	HIPPI	
48	modem	Generic modem	
49	aal5	AAL5 over ATM	
50	sonetPath		
51	sonetVT		
52	smds-icip	SMDS Inter-Carrier Interface Protocol	
53	propVirtual	Proprietary virtual/internal interface	
54	propMultiLink	Proprietary multi-link multiplexing	

55	ieee80212	100BaseVG	
56	fibre-channel	Fibre Channel	
57	hippiInterfaces	HIPPI interfaces	
58	FrameRelayInterconnect	Interconnet over FR <suspect>	
59	aflane8023	ATM Emulated LAN for 802.3	
60	aflane8025	ATM Emulated LAN for 802.5	
61	cctEmul	ATM Emulated circuit	
62	fastEther	Fast Ethernet (100BaseT)	
63	isdn	ISDN and X.25	RFC1356
64	v11	CCITT V.11/X.21	
65	v36	CCITT V.36	
66	g703-64k	CCITT G703 at 64Kbps	
67	g703-2mb	CCITT G703 at 2Mbps	
68	qllc	SNA QLLC	
69	fastEtherFX	Fast Ethernet (100BaseFX)	
70	channel	Channel	
71	IEEE802.11	Radio spread spectrum	
72	ibm370parChan	IBM System 360/370 OEMI Channel	
73	ESCON	IBM Enterprise Systems Connection	
74	DLSw	Data Link Switching	
75	ISDNs	ISDN S/T interface	
76	ISDNu	ISDN U interface	
77	lapd	Link Access Protocol D	
78	ip-switch	IP Switching Objects	
79	rsrb	Remote Source Route Bridging	
80	atm-logical	ATM Logical Port	
81	ds0	Digital Signal Level 0	
82	ds0Bundle	Group of DS0s on the same ds1	
83	bsc	Bisynchronous Protocol	

84	async	Asynchronous Protocol
85	cnr	Combat Net Radio
86	iso88025Dtr	ISO 802.5r DTR
87	eplrs	Enhanced Pos Loc Report Sys
88	arap	Appletalk Remote Access Protocol
89	propCnls	Proprietary Connectionless Proto.
90	hostPad	CCITT-ITU X.29 PAD Protocol
91	termPad	CCITT-ITU X.3 PAD Facility
92	frameRelayMPI	Multiproto Interconnect over FR
93	x213	CCITT-ITU X213
94	adsl	Asymmetric Digital Subscriber Loop
95	radsl	Rate-Adapt. Digital Subscriber Loop
96	sdsl	Symmetric Digital Subscriber Loop
97	vdsl	Very H-Speed Digital Subscriber Loop
98	iso88025CRFPInt	ISO 802.5 CRFP
99	myrinet	Myricom Myrinet
100	voiceEM	Voice recEive and transMit (E&M)
101	voiceFXO	Voice Foreign Exchange Office
102	voiceFXS	Voice Foreign Exchange Station
103	voiceEncap	Voice encapsulation
104	voiceOverIp	Voice over IP encapsulation
105	atmDxi	ATM DXI
106	atmFuni	ATM FUNI
107	atmIma	ATM IMA
108	pppMultilinkBundle	PPP Multilink Bundle

SMI mib-2.transmission Codes

Prefix: iso.org.dod.internet.mgmt.mib-2.transmission (1.3.6.1.2.1.10)

Decimal	Name	Description	Reference
5	x25	X.25	RFC1382
7	IEEE802.3	CSMACD-like Objects	RFC1650
8	IEEE802.4	Token Bus-like Objects	RFC1230
9	dot5	Token Ring-like Objects	RFC1743
15	FDDI	FDDI Objects	RFC1285
16	lapb	LAP B	RFC1381
18	ds1	T1 Carrier Objects	RFC1406
19	e1	E1 Carrier Objects	RFC1406
23	ppp	Point-to-Point Protocol	RFC1471
30	ds3	DS3/E3 Interface Objects	RFC1407
31	sip	SMDS Interface Objects	RFC1694
32	frame-relay	Frame Relay Objects	RFC1315
33	RS-232	RS-232 Objects	RFC1659
34	Parallel	Parallel Printer Objects	RFC1660
35	arcnet	ARC network	
36	arcnet-plus	ARC network plus	
37	atm	ATM	
38	MIOX25	MIOX25	RFC1461
39	sonetMIB	SONET MIB	RFC1595
44	frnetservMIB	Frame Relay Service MIB for DCE	RFC1604

SMI mib-2.transmission.ppp Codes

Prefix: iso.org.dod.internet.mgmt.mib-2.transmission.ppp (1.3.6.1.2.1.10.23)

Decimal	Name	Description	Reference
1	pppLcp	ppp link control	RFC1471
2	pppSecurity	ppp security	RFC1472
3	ppplp	ppp IP network control	RFC1473
4	pppBridge	ppp bridge network control	RFC1474

SMI mib-2.application Codes

Prefix: iso.org.dod.internet.mgmt.mib-2.application (1.3.6.1.2.1.27)

...mib-2.application.assocTable.assocEntry.assocApplicationProtocol

(1.3.6.1.2.1.27.2.1.3)

assocApplicationProtocol OBJECT-TYPE

SYNTAX OBJECT IDENTIFIER

MAX-ACCESS read-only

STATUS current

DESCRIPTION

> "An identification of the protocol being used for the application. For an OSI Application, this will be the Application Context. For Internet applications, the IANA maintains a registry of the OIDs which correspond to well-known applications. If the application protocol is not listed in the registry, an OID value of the form {applTCPProtoID port} or {applUDProtoID port} are used for TCP-based and UDP-based protocols, respectively. In either case 'port' corresponds to the primary port number being used by the protocol."

::= {assocEntry 3}

Decimal	Name
0	Reserved

...mib-2.application.applTCPProtoID

(1.3.6.1.2.1.27.3)

...mib-2.application.applUDPProtoID

(1.3.6.1.2.1.27.4)

-- OIDs of the form {applTCPProtoID port} are intended to be used

-- for TCP-based protocols that don't have OIDs assigned by other

-- means. {applUDPProtoID port} serves the same purpose for

-- UDP-based protocols. In either case 'port' corresponds to

-- the primary port number being used by the protocol. For example,

-- assuming no other OID is assigned for SMTP, an OID of

-- {applTCPProtoID 25} could be used, since SMTP is a TCP-based

-- protocol that uses port 25 as its primary port.

Prefix: iso.org.dod.internet.mgmt.mib-2.mta (1.3.6.1.2.1.28)

...mib-2.mta.MailGroupTable.MailGroupEntry.mtaGroupMailProtocol

(1.3.6.1.2.1.28.2.1.24)

mtaGroupMailProtocol OBJECT-TYPE

SYNTAX OBJECT IDENTIFIER

MAX-ACCESS read-only

STATUS current

DESCRIPTION

> "An identification of the protocol being used by this group. For a group employing OSI protocols, this will be the Application

Context. For Internet applications, the IANA maintains a registry of the OIDs which correspond to well-known message transfer protocols. If the application protocol is not listed in the registry, an OID value of the form {applTCPProtoID port} or {applUDPProtoID port} is used for TCP-based and UDP-based protocols, respectively. In either case 'port' corresponds to the primary port number being used by the group. applTCPProtoID and applUDPProtoID are defined in [5]."

::= {mtaGroupEntry 24}

Decimal	Name
0	Reserved

SMI Experimental Codes
Prefix: iso.org.dod.internet.experimental (1.3.6.1.3)

Decimal	Name	Description
0	Reserved	
1	CLNS	ISO CLNS Objects
*2	T1-Carrier	T1 Carrier Objects
*3	IEEE802.3	Ethernet-like Objects
*4	IEEE802.5	Token Ring-like Objects
*5	DECNet-PHIV	DECNet Phase IV
*6	Interface	Generic Interface Objects
*7	IEEE802.4	Token Bus-like Objects
*8	FDDI	FDDI Objects
9	LANMGR-1	LAN Manager V1 Objects
10	LANMGR-TRAPS	LAN Manager Trap Objects
11	Views	SNMP View Objects
12	SNMP-AUTH	SNMP Authentication Objects

*13	BGP	Border Gateway Protocol
*14	Bridge	Bridge MIB
*15	DS3	DS3 Interface Type
*16	SIP	SMDS Interface Protocol
*17	Appletalk	Appletalk Networking
*18	PPP	PPP Objects
*19	Character MIB	Character MIB
*20	RS-232 MIB	RS-232 MIB
*21	Parallel MIB	Parallel MIB
22	atsign-proxy	Proxy via Community
*23	OSPF	OSPF MIB
24	Alert-Man	Alert-Man
25	FDDI-Synoptics	FDDI-Synoptics
*26	Frame Relay	Frame Relay MIB
*27	rmon	Remote Network Management MIB
28	IDPR	IDPR MIB
29	HUBMIB	IEEE 802.3 Hub MIB
30	IPFWDTBLMIB	IP Forwarding Table MIB
31	LATM MIB	
32	SONET MIB	
33	IDENT	
*34	MIME-MHS	
35	MAUMIB	IEEE 802.3 Mau MIB
36	Host Resources	Host Resources MIB
37	ISIS-MIB	Integrated ISIS protocol MIB
38	Chassis	Chassis MIB
39	ups ups	
40	App-Mon	Application Monitoring MIB
41	ATM UNI	ATM

42	FC Fibre Channel	
*43	DNS	Domain Name Service
44	X.25	X.25 MIB
45	Frame Relay Service	Frame Relay Service MIB
46	Madman-Applications	
47	Madman-MTA	
48	Madman-DSA	
49	Modem	
50	SNA NAU	
51	SDLC	SDLC
52	DNS	Domain Name Service
53	network-objects	IP info ix X.500
54	printmib	
55	rdbmsmib	
56	sipMIB	
57	stIlmib	ST-II protocol MIB
58	802.5 SSR MIB	802.5 Stn Source Routing MIB
59	igmpMIB	
60	ipRouteMIB	
61	pimMIB	
62	dvmrpMIB	
63	dot12MIB	IEEE 802.12 Interface MIB
64	vgRptrMIB	IEEE 802.12 Repeater MIB
65	schema	Schema Publishing
66	hippi-ep	HIPPI End Point
67	hippi-sd	HIPPI Switch Device
68	dlsw	Data Link SWitch
69	mipMobile IP	
70	secModelMIB	Security Model

71	rsvp	Resource Reservation Protocol
72	intSrv	Integrated Services Protocol
73	Madman-Alarm-Generation	
74	IPv6 MIB	MIB for IPv6
75	rdrrn	Rapidly Deploy Radio Resh Net
76	aris ARIS Protocol	

* = obsoleted

SMI Private Codes

Prefix: iso.org.dod.internet.private (1.3.6.1.4)

Decimal	Name	Description
0	Reserved	
1	enterprise	private enterprises

SMI Private Enterprise Codes

Prefix: iso.org.dod.internet.private.enterprise (1.3.6.1.4.1)

See the file "enterprise-numbers".

SMI Security Codes

Prefix: iso.org.dod.internet.security (1.3.6.1.5)

Decimal	Name	Description
0	Reserved	
1	kerberosV4	Kerberos version 4 objects
2	kerberosV5	Kerberos version 5 objects
3	integrity	integrity algorithms
4	confide	confidentiality algorithms

5	mechanisms	security mechanisms
6	nametypes	name system designators
7	services	security services

SMI Security for Integrity Codes

Prefix: iso.org.dod.internet.security (1.3.6.1.5.3)

Decimal	Name	Description
0	Reserved	
1	md5-DES-CBC	md5-DES-CBC
2	sum64-DES-CBC	sum64-DES-CBC

SMI Security for Confidentiality Codes

Prefix: iso.org.dod.internet.security (1.3.6.1.5.4)

Decimal	Name
0	Reserved

SMI Security for Mechanism Codes

Prefix: iso.org.dod.internet.security.mechanisms (1.3.6.1.5.5)

Decimal	Name	Description
0	Reserved	
1	SPKM	Simple Public Key Mechanism
2	SNEGO	Simple GSS-API Negotiation
3	PIMP	EM-Based IDUP Mechanism
4	MIM	MSP-Based IDUP Mechanism
5	p7im	PKCS #7-Based IDUP Mechanism

| 6 | meim | MOSS-Enabling IDUP Mechanism |
| 7 | pkix | Public Key Infrastructure |

SMI Security for Mechanism SPKM Codes

Prefix: iso.org.dod.internet.security (1.3.6.1.5.5.1)

Decimal	Name
1	spkm-1
2	spkm-2
10	spkmGssTokens

SMI Security for Name System Designators Codes (nametypes)

Prefix: iso.org.dod.internet.security (1.3.6.1.5.6)

Decimal	Name
0	Reserved
1	Domain Name System names
2	gss-host-based-services
3	gss-anonymous-name
4	gss-api-exported-name

SMI Security Services Codes

Prefix: iso.org.dod.internet.security.services (1.3.6.1.5.7)

Decimal	Name	Description
0	Reserved	
1	conf	confidentiality services
2	integrity	data integrity services
3	doa	data origin authen. services

4	non-rep	non-repudiation services
5	acc	access control services
6	dflow	data flow services
7	time	time services

SMI Security Services Codes (conf)

Prefix: iso.org.dod.internet.security.services.conf (1.3.6.1.5.7.1)

Decimal	Name	Description
0	Reserved	
1	per-conf	perform conf. (encrypt)
2	rec-conf	receive conf. (decrypt)

SMI Security Services Codes (integrity)

Prefix: iso.org.dod.internet.security.services.integrity (1.3.6.1.5.7.2)

Decimal	Name	Description
0	Reserved	
1	per-int	perform integrity (e.g. MAC)
2	rec-int	receive integrity (verify MAC)

SMI Security Services Codes (doa)

Prefix: iso.org.dod.internet.security.services.doa (1.3.6.1.5.7.3)

Decimal	Name	Description
0	Reserved	
1	per-doa	perform DOA (e.g., sign)
2	rec-doa	receive DOA (verify sig)

SMI Security Services Codes (non-rep)

Prefix: iso.org.dod.internet.security.services.non-rep (1.3.6.1.5.7.4)

Decimal	Name	Description
0	Reserved	
1	per-poo	create proof-of-origin
2	rec-poo	verify proof-of-origin
3	per-pod	create proof-of-delivery
4	rec-pod	verify proof-of-delivery

SMI Security Services Codes (acc)

Prefix: iso.org.dod.internet.security.services.acc (1.3.6.1.5.7.5)

Decimal	Name	Description
0	Reserved	
1	per-acc	apply access control
2	rec-acc	verify access control

SMI Security Services Codes (dflow)

Prefix: iso.org.dod.internet.security.services.dflow (1.3.6.1.5.7.6)

Decimal	Name	Description
0	Reserved	
1	per-dflow	perform data flow
2	rec-dflow	receive data flow

SMI Security Services Codes (time)

Prefix: iso.org.dod.internet.security.services.time (1.3.6.1.5.7.7)

Decimal	Name	Description
0	Reserved	
1	ttime	use trusted time
2	utime	use untrusted time

SMI SNMPv2 Codes

Prefix: iso.org.dod.internet.snmpv2 (1.3.6.1.6)

Decimal	Name	Description	Reference
1	smmpDomains		RFC1902
2	smnpProxys		RFC1902
3	smnpModules		RFC1902

SMI mail Codes

Prefix: iso.org.dod.internet.mail (1.3.6.1.7)

Decimal	Name	Description	Reference
1	mime-mhs	MIME MHS Mappings	RFC1495

The preceding information was derived from the following file:

ftp://ftp.isi.edu/in-notes/iana/assignments/smi-numbers

SMI Network Management Private Enterprise Codes

Prefix: iso.org.dod.internet.private.enterprise (1.3.6.1.4.1)

Decimal	Name
0	Reserved
1	Proteon
2	IBM
3	CMU
4	Unix
5	ACC
6	TWG
7	CAYMAN
8	PSI
9	Cisco
10	NSC
11	Hewlett Packard
12	Epilogue
13	U of Tennessee
14	BBN
15	Xylogics, Inc.
16	Timeplex
17	Canstar
18	Wellfleet
19	TRW
20	MIT
21	EON
22	Fibronics
23	Novell
24	Spider Systems
25	NSFNET
26	Hughes LAN Systems
27	Intergraph
28	Interlan
29	Vitalink Communications
30	Ulana

31	NSWC
32	Santa Cruz Operation
33	Xyplex
34	Cray
35	Bell Northern Research
36	DEC
37	Touch
38	Network Research Corp.
39	Baylor College of Medicine
40	NMFECC-LLNL
41	SRI
42	Sun Microsystems
43	3Com
44	CMC
45	SynOptics
46	Cheyenne Software
47	Prime Computer
48	MCNC/North Carolina
49	Chipcom
50	Optical Data Systems
51	gated
52	Cabletron Systems
53	Apollo Computers
54	DeskTalk Systems, Inc.
55	SSDS
56	Castle Rock Computing
57	MIPS Computer Systems
58	TGV, Inc.
59	Silicon Graphics, Inc.
60	University of British Columbia
61	Merit
62	NetEdge
63	Apple Computer, Inc.
64	Gandalf
65	Dartmouth
66	David Systems
67	Reuter

68	Cornell
69	LMS
70	Locus Computing Corp.
71	NASA
72	Retix
73	Boeing
74	AT&T
75	Ungermann-Bass
76	Digital Analysis Corporation
77	LAN Manager
78	Netlabs
79	ICL
80	Auspex Systems
81	Lannet Company
82	Network Computing Devices
83	Raycom Systems
84	Pirelli Focom, Ltd.
85	Datability Software Systems
86	Network Application Technology
87	LINK (Lokales Informatik-Netz Karlsruhe)
88	NYU
89	RND
90	InterCon Systems Corporation
91	Coral Network Corporation
92	Webster Computer Corporation
93	Frontier Technologies Corporation
94	Nokia Data Communications
95	Allen-Bradely Company
96	CERN
97	Sigma Network Systems
98	Emerging Technologies, Inc.
99	SNMP Research
100	Ohio State University
101	Ultra Network Technologies
102	Microcom
103	Lockheed Martin
104	Micro Technology

105	Process Software Corporation
106	Data General Corporation
107	Bull Company
108	Emulex Corporation
109	Warwick University Computing Services
110	Network General Corporation
111	Oracle
112	Control Data Corporation
113	Hughes Aircraft Company
114	Synernetics, Inc.
115	Mitre
116	Hitachi, Ltd.
117	Telebit
118	Salomon Technology Services
119	NEC Corporation
120	Fibermux
121	FTP Software, Inc.
122	Sony
123	Newbridge Networks Corporation
124	Racal-Datacom
125	CR SYSTEMS
126	DSET Corporation
127	Computone
128	Tektronix, Inc.
129	Interactive Systems Corporation
130	Banyan Systems, Inc.
131	Sintrom Datanet Limited
132	Bell Canada
133	Crosscomm Corporation
134	Rice University
135	OnStream Networks
136	Concurrent Computer Corporation
137	Basser
138	Luxcom
139	Artel
140	Independence Technologies, Inc. (ITI)
141	Frontier Software Development

142	Digital Computer Limited
143	Eyring, Inc.
144	Case Communications
145	Penril DataComm, Inc.
146	American Airlines
147	Sequent Computer Systems
148	Bellcore
149	Konkord Communications
150	University of Washington
151	Develcon
152	Solarix Systems
153	Unifi Communications Corp.
154	Roadnet
155	Network Systems Corp.
156	ENE (European Network Engineering)
157	Dansk Data Elektronik A/S
158	Morning Star Technologies
159	Dupont EOP
160	Legato Systems, Inc.
161	Motorola
162	European Space Agency (ESA)
163	BIM
164	Rad Data Communications, Ltd.
165	Intellicom
166	Shiva Corporation
167	Fujikura America
168	Xlnt Designs INC (XDI)
169	Tandem Computers
170	BICC
171	D-Link Systems, Inc.
172	AMP, Inc.
173	Netlink
174	C. Itoh Electronics
175	Sumitomo Electric Industries (SEI)
176	DHL Systems, Inc.
177	Network Equipment Technologies
178	APTEC Computer Systems

179	Schneider & Koch & Co.
180	Hill Air Force Base
181	ADC Kentrox
182	Japan Radio Co.
183	Versitron
184	Telecommunication Systems
185	Interphase
186	Toshiba Corporation
187	Clearpoint Research Corp.
188	Ascom
189	Fujitsu America
190	NetCom Solutions, Inc.
191	NCR
192	Dr. Materna GmbH
193	Ericsson Business Communications
194	Metaphor Computer Systems
195	Patriot Partners
196	The Software Group Limited (TSG)
197	Kalpana, Inc.
198	University of Waterloo
199	CCL/ITRI
200	Coeur Postel
201	Mitsubish Cable Industries, Ltd.
202	SMC
203	Crescendo Communication, Inc.
204	Goodall Software Engineering
205	Intecom
206	Victoria University of Wellington
207	Allied Telesis, Inc.
208	Cray Communications A/S
209	Protools
210	Nippon Telegraph and Telephone Corp.
211	Fujitsu Limited
212	Network Peripherals, Inc.
213	Netronix, Inc.
214	University of Wisconsin
215	NetWorth, Inc.

216	Tandberg Data A/S
217	Technically Elite Concepts, Inc.
218	Labtam Australia Pty., Ltd.
219	Republic Telcom Systems, Inc.
220	ADI Systems, Inc.
221	Microwave Bypass Systems, Inc.
222	Pyramid Technology Corp.
223	Unisys Corp
224	LANOPTICS LTD., Israel
225	NKK Corporation
226	MTrade UK, Ltd.
227	Acals
228	ASTEC, Inc.
229	Delmarva Power
230	Telematics International, Inc.
231	Siemens Nixdorf Informations Systems
232	Compaq
233	NetManage, Inc.
234	NCSU Computing Center
235	Empirical Tools and Technologies
236	Samsung Group
237	Takaoka Electric Mfg. Co., Ltd.
238	Netrix Systems Corporation
239	WINDATA
240	RC International A/S
241	Netexp Research
242	Internode Systems Pty., Ltd.
243	netCS Informationstechnik GmbH
244	Lantronix
245	Avatar Consultants
246	Furukawa Electric Co., Ltd.
247	Nortel Data Network Systems GmbH & Co.
248	Richard Hirschmann GmbH & Co.
249	G2R, Inc.
250	University of Michigan
251	Netcomm, Ltd.
252	Sable Technology Corporation

253	Xerox
254	Conware Computer Consulting GmbH
255	Compatible Systems Corp.
256	Scitec Communications Systems, Ltd.
257	Transarc Corporation
258	Matsushita Electric Industrial Co., Ltd.
259	ACCTON Technology
260	Star-Tek, Inc.
261	Codenoll Tech. Corp.
262	Formation, Inc.
263	Seiko Instruments, Inc. (SII)
264	RCE (Reseaux de Communication d'Entreprise S.A.)
265	Xenocom, Inc.
266	KABELRHEYDT
267	Systech Computer Corporation
268	Visual
269	SDD (Scandinavian Airlines Data Denmark A/S)
270	Zenith Electronics Corporation
271	TELECOM FINLAND
272	BinTec Computersystems
273	EUnet Germany
274	PictureTel Corporation
275	Michigan State University
276	GTE Government Systems
277	Cascade Communications Corp.
278	Hitachi Cable, Ltd.
279	Olivetti
280	Vitacom Corporation
281	INMOS
282	AIC Systems Laboratories, Ltd.
283	Cameo Communications, Inc.
284	Diab Data AB
285	Olicom A/S
286	Digital-Kienzle Computersystems
287	CSELT(Centro Studi E Laboratori Telecomunicazioni)
288	Electronic Data Systems
289	McData Corporation

290	Harris Corporation
291	Technology Dynamics, Inc.
292	DATAHOUSE Information Systems, Ltd.
293	Securicor 3net (NDL), Ltd.
294	Texas Instruments
295	PlainTree Systems, Inc.
296	Hedemann Software Development
297	Fuji Xerox Co., Ltd.
298	Asante Technology
299	Stanford University
300	Digital Link
301	Raylan Corporation
302	Datacraft
303	Hughes
304	Farallon Computing, Inc.
305	GE Information Services
306	Gambit Computer Communications
307	Livingston Enterprises, Inc.
308	Star Technologies
309	Micronics Computers, Inc.
310	Basis, Inc.
311	Microsoft
312	US West Advance Technologies
313	University College London
314	Eastman Kodak Company
315	Network Resources Corporation
316	Atlas Telecom
317	Bridgeway
318	American Power Conversion Corp.
319	DOE Atmospheric Radiation Measurement Project
320	VerSteeg CodeWorks
321	Verilink Corp
322	Sybus Corporation
323	Tekelec
324	NASA Ames Research Center
325	Simon Fraser University
326	Fore Systems, Inc.

327	Centrum Communications, Inc.
328	NeXT Computer, Inc.
329	Netcore, Inc.
330	Northwest Digital Systems
331	Andrew Corporation
332	DigiBoard
333	Computer Network Technology Corp.
334	Lotus Development Corp.
335	MICOM Communication Corporation
336	ASCII Corporation
337	PUREDATA Research
338	NTT DATA
339	Empros Systems International
340	Kendall Square Research (KSR)
341	ORNL
342	Network Innovations
343	Intel Corporation
344	Compuware Corporation
345	Epson Research Center
346	Fibernet
347	Box Hill Systems Corporation
348	American Express Travel Related Services
349	Compu-Shack
350	Parallan Computer, Inc.
351	Stratacom
352	Open Networks Engineering, Inc.
353	ATM Forum
354	SSD Management, Inc.
355	Automated Network Management, Inc.
356	Magnalink Communications Corporation
357	Kasten Chase Applied Research
358	Skyline Technology, Inc.
359	Nu-Mega Technologies, Inc.
360	Morgan Stanley & Co., Inc.
361	Integrated Business Network
362	L & N Technologies, Ltd.
363	Cincinnati Bell Information Systems, Inc.

364	OSCOM International
365	MICROGNOSIS
366	Datapoint Corporation
367	RICOH Co., Ltd.
368	Axis Communications AB
369	Pacer Software
370	3COM/Axon Robin Iddon
371	Brixton Systems, Inc.
372	GSI
373	Tatung Co., Ltd.
374	DIS Research, Ltd.
375	Quotron Systems, Inc.
376	Dassault Electronique
377	Corollary, Inc.
378	SEEL, Ltd.
379	Lexcel
380	Sophisticated Technologies, Inc.
381	OST
382	Megadata Pty., Ltd.
383	LLNL Livermore Computer Center
384	Dynatech Communications
385	Symplex Communications Corp.
386	Tribe Computer Works
387	Taligent, Inc.
388	Symbol Technologies, Inc.
389	Lancert
390	Alantec
391	Ridgeback Solutions
392	Metrix, Inc.
393	Symantec Corporation
394	NRL Communication Systems Branch
395	I.D.E. Corporation
396	Matsushita Electric Works, Ltd.
397	MegaPAC
398	Pinacl Communication Systems, Ltd.
399	Hitachi Computer Products (America), Inc.
400	METEO FRANCE

401	PRC Inc.
402	Wal*Mart Stores, Inc.
403	Nissin Electric Company, Ltd.
404	Distributed Support Information Standard
405	SMDS Interest Group (SIG)
406	SolCom Systems, Ltd.
407	Bell Atlantic
408	Advanced Multiuser Technologies Corporation
409	Mitsubishi Electric Corporation
410	C.O.L. Systems, Inc.
411	University of Auckland
412	Desktop Management Task Force (DMTF)
413	Klever Computers, Inc.
414	Amdahl Corporation
415	JTEC Pty, Ltd.
416	Matra Communcation
417	HAL Computer Systems
418	Lawrence Berkeley Laboratory
419	Dale Computer Corporation
420	IPTC, Universitaet of Tuebingen
421	Bytex Corporation
422	Cogwheel, Inc.
423	Lanwan Technologies
424	Thomas-Conrad Corporation
425	TxPort
426	Compex, Inc.
427	Evergreen Systems, Inc.
428	HNV, Inc.
429	U.S. Robotics, Inc.
430	Canada Post Corporation
431	Open Systems Solutions, Inc.
432	Toronto Stock Exchange
433	Mamakos\TransSys Consulting
434	EICON
435	Jupiter Systems
436	SSTI
437	Grand Junction Networks

438	Anasazi, Inc.
439	Edward D. Jones and Company
440	Amnet, Inc.
441	Chase Research
442	PEER Networks
443	Gateway Communications, Inc.
444	Peregrine Systems
445	Daewoo Telecom
446	Norwegian Telecom Research
447	WilTel
448	Ericsson-Camtec
449	Codex
450	Basis
451	AGE Logic
452	INDE Electronics
453	ISODE Consortium
454	J.I. Case
455	Trillium
456	Bacchus Inc.
457	MCC
458	Stratus Computer
459	Quotron
460	Beame & Whiteside
461	Cellular Technical Services
462	Shore Microsystems, Inc.
463	Telecommunications Techniques Corp.
464	DNPAP (Technical University Delft)
465	Plexcom, Inc.
466	Tylink
467	Brookhaven National Laboratory
468	Computer Communication Systems
469	Norand Corp.
470	MUX-LAP
471	Premisys Communications, Inc
472	Bell South Telecommunications
473	J. Stainsbury PLC
474	Ki Research, Inc.

475	Wandel and Goltermann Technologies
476	Emerson Computer Power
477	Network Software Associates
478	Procter and Gamble
479	Meridian Technology Corporation
480	QMS, Inc.
481	Network Express
482	LANcity Corporation
483	Dayna Communications, Inc.
484	kn-X, Ltd.
485	Sync Research, Inc.
486	PremNet
487	SIAC
488	New York Stock Exchange
489	American Stock Exchange
490	FCR Software, Inc.
491	National Medical Care, Inc.
492	Dialog Communication Systems AG
493	NorTele
494	Madge Networks, Inc.
495	Memotec Communications
496	CTON Nick Hennenfent
497	Leap Technology, Inc.
498	General DataComm, Inc.
499	ACE Communications, Ltd.
500	Automatic Data Processing (ADP)
501	Programa SPRITEL
502	Adacom
503	Metrodata, Ltd.
504	Ellemtel Telecommunication Systems Laboratories
505	Arizona Public Service
506	NETWIZ, Ltd.
507	Science and Engineering Research Council
508	The First Boston Corporation
509	Hadax Electronics, Inc.
510	VTKK
511	North Hills Israel, Ltd.

512	TECSIEL
513	Bayerische Motoren Werke (BMW) AG
514	CNET Technologies
515	MCI
516	Human Engineering AG (HEAG)
517	FileNet Corporation
518	NFT-Ericsson
519	Dun & Bradstreet
520	Intercomputer Communications
521	Defense Intelligence Agency
522	Telesystems SLW, Inc.
523	APT Communications
524	Delta Airlines
525	California Microwave
526	Avid Technology, Inc.
527	Integro Advanced Computer Systems
528	RPTI
529	Ascend Communications, Inc.
530	Eden Computer Systems, Inc.
531	Kawasaki-Steel Corp
532	Barclays
533	B.U.G., Inc.
534	Exide Electronics
535	Superconducting Supercollider Lab.
536	Triticom
537	Universal Instruments Corp.
538	Information Resources, Inc.
539	Applied Innovation, Inc.
540	Crypto AG
541	Infinite Networks, Ltd.
542	Rabbit Software
543	Apertus Technologies
544	Equinox Systems, Inc.
545	Hayes Microcomputer Products
546	Empire Technologies, Inc.
547	Glaxochem, Ltd.
548	Software Professionals, Inc

549	Agent Technology, Inc.
550	Dornier GMBH
551	Telxon Corporation
552	Entergy Corporation
553	Garrett Communications, Inc.
554	Agile Networks, Inc.
555	Larscom
556	Stock Equipment
557	ITT Corporation
558	Universal Data Systems, Inc.
559	Sonix Communications, Ltd.
560	Paul Freeman Associates, Inc.
561	John S. Barnes, Corp.
562	Northern Telecom, Ltd.
563	CAP Debris
564	Telco Systems NAC
565	Tosco Refining Co.
566	Russell Info Sys
567	University of Salford
568	NetQuest Corp.
569	Armon Networking Ltd.
570	IA Corporation
571	AU-System Communicaton AB
572	GoldStar Information & Communications, Ltd.
573	SECTRA AB
574	ONEAC Corporation
575	Tree Technologies
576	GTE Government Systems
577	Denmac Systems, Inc.
578	Interlink Computer Sciences, Inc.
579	Bridge Information Systems, Inc.
580	Leeds and Northrup Australia (LNA)
581	BHA Computer
582	Newport Systems Solutions, Inc.
583	azel Corporation
584	ROBOTIKER
585	PeerLogic, Inc.

586	Digital Transmission Systems
587	Far Point Communications
588	Xircom
589	Mead Data Central
590	Royal Bank of Canada
591	Advantis, Inc.
592	Chemical Banking Corp.
593	Eagle Technology
594	British Telecom
595	Radix BV
596	TAINET Communication System Corp.
597	Comtek Services, Inc.
598	Fair Issac
599	AST Research, Inc.
600	Soft*Star s.r.l. Ing.
601	Bancomm
602	Trusted Information Systems, Inc.
603	Harris & Jeffries, Inc.
604	Axel Technology Corp.
605	GN Navtel, Inc.
606	CAP debis
607	Lachman Technology, Inc.
608	Galcom Networking, Ltd.
609	BAZIS
610	SYNAPTEL
611	Investment Management Services, Inc.
612	Taiwan Telecommunication Lab
613	Anagram Corporation
614	Univel
615	University of California, San Diego
616	CompuServe
617	Telstra—OTC Australia
618	Westinghouse Electric Corp.
619	DGA Ltd.
620	Elegant Communications, Inc.
621	Experdata
622	Unisource Business Networks Sweden AB

623	Molex, Inc.
624	Quay Financial Software
625	VMX, Inc.
626	Hypercom, Inc.
627	University of Guelph
628	DIaLOGIKa
629	NBASE Switch Communication
630	Anchor Datacomm B.V.
631	PACDATA
632	University of Colorado
633	Tricom Communications Limited
634	Santix Software GmbH
635	FastComm Communications Corp.
636	The Georgia Institute of Technology
637	Alcatel Data Networks
638	GTECH
639	UNOCAL Corporation
640	First Pacific Network
641	Lexmark International
642	Qnix Computer
643	Jigsaw Software Concepts (Pty), Ltd.
644	VIR, Inc.
645	SFA Datacomm,, Inc.
646	SEIKO Communication Systems, Inc.
647	Unified Management
648	RADLINX, Ltd.
649	Microplex Systems, Ltd.
650	Objecta Elektronik & Data AB
651	Phoenix Microsystems
652	Distributed Systems International, Inc.
653	Evolving Systems, Inc.
654	SAT GmbH
655	CeLAN Technology, Inc.
656	Landmark Systems Corp.
657	Netone Systems Co., Ltd.
658	Loral Data Systems
659	Cellware Broadband Technology

660	Mu-Systems
661	IMC Networks Corp.
662	Octel Communications Corp.
663	RIT Technologies, Ltd.
664	Adtran
665	PowerPlay Technologies, Inc.
666	Oki Electric Industry Co., Ltd.
667	Specialix International
668	INESC (Instituto de Engenharia de Sistemas e Computadores)
669	Globalnet Communications
670	Product Line Engineer SVEC Computer Corp.
671	Printer Systems Corp.
672	Contec Micro Electronics USA
673	Unix Integration Services
674	Dell Computer Corporation
675	Whittaker Electronic Systems
676	QPSX Communications
677	Loral WDI
678	Federal Express Corp.
679	E-COMMS, Inc.
680	Software Clearing House
681	Antlow Computers, Ltd.
682	Emcom Corp.
683	Extended Systems, Inc.
684	Sola Electric
685	Esix Systems, Inc.
686	3M/MMM
687	Cylink Corp.
688	Znyx Advanced Systems Division, Inc.
689	Texaco, Inc.
690	McCaw Cellular Communication Corp.
691	ASP Computer Product, Inc.
692	HiPerformance Systems
693	Regionales Rechenzentrum
694	SAP AG
695	ElectroSpace System, Inc.
696	(Unassigned)

697	MultiPort Corporation
698	Combinet, Inc.
699	TSCC
700	Teleos Communications, Inc.
701	Alta Research
702	Independence Blue Cross
703	ADACOM Station Interconnectivity, Ltd.
704	MIROR Systems
705	Merlin Gerin
706	Owen-Corning Fiberglas
707	Talking Networks, Inc.
708	Cubix Corporation
709	Formation, Inc.
710	Lannair, Ltd.
711	LightStream Corp.
712	LANart Corp.
713	University of Stellenbosch
714	Wyse Technology
715	DSC Communications Corp.
716	NetEc
717	Breltenbach Software Engineering GmbH
718	Victor Company of Japan, Limited
719	Japan Direx Corporation
720	NECSY Network Control Systems
721	ISDN Systems Corp.
722	Zero-One Technologies, Ltd.
723	Radix Technologies, Inc.
724	National Institute of Standards and Technology
725	Digital Technology, Inc.
726	Castelle Corp.
727	Presticom, Inc.
728	Showa Electric Wire & Cable Co., Ltd.
729	SpectraGraphics
730	Connectware, Inc.
731	Wind River Systems
732	RADWAY International, Ltd.
733	System Management ARTS, Inc.

734	Persoft, Inc.
735	Xnet Technology Inc.
736	Unison-Tymlabs
737	Micro-Matic Research
738	B.A.T.M. Advance Technologies
739	University of Copenhagen
740	Network Security Systems, Inc.
741	JNA Telecommunications
742	Encore Computer Corporation
743	Central Intelligent Agency
744	ISC (GB) Limited
745	Digital Communication Associates
746	CyberMedia, Inc.
747	Distributed Systems International, Inc.
748	Peter Radig EDP-Consulting
749	Vicorp Interactive Systems
750	Inet, Inc.
751	Argonne National Laboratory
752	Tek Logix
753	North Western University
754	Astarte Fiber Networks
755	Diederich & Associates, Inc.
756	Florida Power Corporation
757	ASK/INGRES
758	Open Network Enterprise
759	The Home Depot
760	Pan Dacom Telekommunikations
761	NetTek
762	Karlnet Corp.
763	Efficient Networks, Inc.
764	Fiberdata
765	Lanser
766	Telebit Communications A/S
767	HILAN GmbH
768	Network Computing, Inc.
769	Walgreens Company
770	Internet Initiative Japan, Inc.

771	GP van Niekerk Ondernemings
772	Queen's University Belfast
773	Securities Industry Automation Corporation
774	SYNaPTICS
775	Data Switch Corporation
776	Telindus Distribution
777	MAXM Systems Corporation
778	Fraunhofer Gesellschaft
779	EQS Business Services
780	CNet Technology, Inc.
781	Datentechnik GmbH
782	Network Solutions, Inc.
783	Viaman Software
784	Schweizerische Bankgesellschaft Zuerich
785	University of Twente—TIOS
786	Simplesoft, Inc.
787	Stony Brook, Inc.
788	Unified Systems Solutions, Inc.
789	Network Appliance Corporation
790	Ornet Data Communication Technologies, Ltd.
791	Computer Associates International
792	Multipoint Network, Inc.
793	NYNEX Science & Technology
794	Commercial Link Systems
795	Adaptec, Inc.
796	Softswitch
797	Link Technologies, Inc.
798	IIS
799	Mobile Solutions, Inc.
800	Xylan Corp.
801	Airtech Software Forge Limited
802	National Semiconductor
803	Video Lottery Technologies
804	National Semiconductor Corp
805	Applications Management Corp
806	Travelers Insurance Company
807	Taiwan International Standard Electronics Ltd.

808	US Patent and Trademark Office
809	Hynet, LTD.
810	Aydin, Corp.
811	ADDTRON Technology Co., LTD.
812	Fannie Mae
813	MultiNET Services
814	GECKO mbH
815	Memorex Telex
816	Advanced Communications Networks (ACN) SA
817	Telekurs AG
818	Victron bv
819	CF6 Company
820	Walker Richer and Quinn, Inc.
821	Saturn Systems
822	Mitsui Marine and Fire Insurance Co.
823	Loop Telecommunication International, Inc.
824	Telenex Corporation
825	Bus-Tech, Inc.
826	ATRIE
827	Gallagher & Robertson A/S
828	Networks Northwest, Inc.
829	Conner Peripherials
830	Elf Antar France
831	Lloyd Internetworking
832	Datatec Industries, Inc.
833	TAICOM
834	Brown's Operating System Services, Ltd.
835	MiLAN Technology Corp.
836	NetEdge Systems, Inc.
837	NetFrame Systems
838	Xedia Corporation
839	Pepsi
840	Tricord Systems, Inc.
841	Proxim, Inc.
842	Applications Plus, Inc.
843	Pacific Bell
844	Scorpio Communications

845	TPS-Teleprocessing Systems
846	Technology Solutions Company
847	Computer Site Technologies
848	NetPort Software
849	Alon Systems
850	Tripp Lite
851	NetComm Limited
852	Precision Systems, Inc. (PSI)
853	Objective Systems Integrators
854	Simpact, Inc.
855	Systems Enhancement Corporation
856	Information Integration, Inc.
857	CETREL S.C.
858	Platinum Technology, Inc.
859	Olivetti North America
860	WILMA
861	ILX Systems, Inc.
862	Total Peripherals, Inc.
863	SunNetworks Consultant
864	Arkhon Technologies, Inc.
865	Computer Sciences Corporation
866	Philips Communication d'Entreprise
867	Katron Technologies, Inc.
868	Transition Engineering, Inc.
869	Altos Engineering Applications, Inc.
870	Nicecom, Ltd.
871	Fiskars/Deltec
872	AVM GmbH
873	Comm Vision
874	Institute for Information Industry
875	Legent Corporation
876	Network Automation
877	NetTech
878	Coman Data Communications, Ltd.
879	Skattedirektoratet
880	Client-Server Technologies
881	Societe Internationale de Telecommunications Aeronautiques

882	Maximum Strategy, Inc.
883	Integrated Systems, Inc.
884	E-Systems
885	Reliance Comm/Tec
886	Summa Four, Inc.
887	J & L Information Systems
888	Forest Computer, Inc.
889	Palindrome Corp.
890	ZyXEL Communications Corp.
891	Network Managers (UK), Ltd.
892	Sensible Office Systems, Inc.
893	Informix Software
894	Dynatek Communications
895	Versalynx Corp.
896	Potomac Scheduling Communications Company
897	Sybase, Inc.
898	DiviCom, Inc.
899	Datus elektronische Informationssysteme GmbH
900	Matrox Electronic Systems Limited
901	Digital Products, Inc.
902	Scitex Corp., Ltd.
903	RAD Vision
904	Tran Network Systems
905	Scorpion Logic
906	Inotech, Inc.
907	Controlled Power Co.
908	Elsag Bailey, Incorporate
909	J.P. Morgan
910	Clear Communications Corp.
911	General Technology, Inc.
912	Adax, Inc.
913	Mtel Technologies, Inc.
914	Underscore, Inc.
915	SerComm Corp.
916	Allegiance Corporation
917	Tellus Technology
918	Continuous Electron Beam Accelerator Facility

919	Canoga Perkins
920	R.I.S. Technologies
921	INFONEX Corp.
922	WordPerfect Corp.
923	NRaD
924	Hong Kong Telecommunications, Ltd.
925	Signature Systems
926	Alpha Technologies, Ltd.
927	PairGain Technologies, Inc.
928	Sonic Systems
929	Steinbrecher Corp.
930	Centillion Networks, Inc.
931	Network Communication Corp.
932	Sysnet A.S.
933	Telecommunication Systems Lab
934	QMI
935	Phoenixtec Power Co., Ltd.
936	Hirakawa Hewtech Corp.
937	No Wires Needed B.V.
938	Primary Access
939	FD Software AS
940	g.a.m.s. edv-dienstleistungen
941	Nemesys Research, Ltd.
942	Pacific Communication Sciences, Inc. (PSCI)
943	Level One Communications, Inc.
944	Fast Track, Inc.
945	Andersen Consulting, OM/NI Practice
946	Bay Technologies Pty, Ltd.
947	Integrated Network Corp.
948	CyberPro International
949	Wang Laboratories, Inc.
950	Polaroid Corp.
951	Sunrise Sierra
952	Silcon Group
953	Coastcom
954	4th DIMENSION SOFTWARE, Ltd.
955	SEIKO SYSTEMS, Inc.

956	PERFORM
957	TV/COM International
958	Network Integration, Inc.
959	Sola Electric, A Unit of General Signal
960	Gradient Technologies, Inc.
961	Tokyo Electric Co., Ltd.
962	Codonics, Inc.
963	Delft Technical University
964	Carrier Access Corp.
965	eoncorp
966	Naval Undersea Warfare Center
967	AWA Limited
968	Distinct Corp.
969	National Technical University of Athens
970	BGS Systems, Inc.
971	McCaw Wireless Data, Inc.
972	Bekaert
973	Epic Data, Inc.
974	Prodigy Services Co.
975	First Pacific Networks (FPN)
976	Xylink, Ltd.
977	Relia Technologies Corp.
978	Legacy Storage Systems, Inc.
979	Digicom, SPA
980	Ark Telecom
981	National Security Agency (NSA)
982	Southwestern Bell Corporation
983	Virtual Design Group, Inc.
984	Rhone Poulenc
985	Swiss Bank Corporation
986	ATEA N.V.
987	Computer Communications Specialists, Inc.
988	Object Quest, Inc.
989	DCL System International, Ltd.
990	SOLITON SYSTEMS K.K.
991	U S Software
992	Systems Research and Applications Corporation

993	University of Florida
994	Dantel, Inc.
995	Multi-Tech Systems, Inc.
996	Softlink, Ltd.
997	ProSum
998	March Systems Consultancy, Ltd.
999	Hong Technology, Inc.
1000	Internet Assigned Number Authority
1001	PECO Energy Co.
1002	United Parcel Service
1003	Storage Dimensions, Inc.
1004	ITV Technologies, Inc.
1005	TCPSI
1006	Promptus Communications, Inc.
1007	Norman Data Defense Systems
1008	Pilot Network Services, Inc.
1009	Integrated Systems Solutions Corporation
1010	SISRO
1011	NetVantage
1012	Marconi S.P.A.
1013	SURECOM
1014	Royal Hong Kong Jockey Club
1015	Gupta
1016	Tone Software Corporation
1017	Opus Telecom
1018	Cogsys, Ltd.
1019	Komatsu, Ltd.
1020	ROI Systems, Inc.
1021	Lightning Instrumentation SA
1022	TimeStep Corp.
1023	INTELSAT
1024	Network Research Corporation Japan, Ltd.
1025	Relational Development, Inc.
1026	Emerald Systems, Corp.
1027	Mitel, Corp.
1028	Software AG
1029	MillenNet, Inc.

1030	NK-EXA Corp.
1031	BMC Software
1032	StarFire Enterprises, Inc.
1033	Hybrid Networks, Inc.
1034	Quantum Software GmbH
1035	Openvision Technologies Limited
1036	Healthcare Communications, Inc. (HCI)
1037	SAIT Systems
1038	SAT
1039	CompuSci, Inc.
1040	Aim Technology
1041	CIESIN
1042	Systems & Technologies International
1043	Israeli Electric Company (IEC)
1044	Phoenix Wireless Group, Inc.
1045	SWL
1046	nCUBE
1047	Cerner, Corp.
1048	Andersen Consulting
1049	Lincoln Telephone Company
1050	Acer
1051	Cedros
1052	AirAccess
1053	Expersoft Corporation
1054	Eskom
1055	SBE, Inc.
1056	EBS, Inc.
1057	American Computer and Electronics, Corp.
1058	Syndesis Limited
1059	Isis Distributed Systems, Inc.
1060	Priority Call Management
1061	Koelsch & Altmann GmbH
1062	WIPRO INFOTECH, Ltd.
1063	Controlware
1064	Mosaic Software
1065	Canon Information Systems
1066	AmericaOnline

1067	Whitetree Network Technologies, Inc.
1068	Xetron Corp.
1069	Target Concepts, Inc.
1070	DMH Software
1071	Innosoft International, Inc.
1072	Controlware GmbH
1073	Telecommunications Industry Association (TIA)
1074	Boole & Babbage
1075	System Engineering Support, Ltd.
1076	SURFnet
1077	OpenConnect Systems, Inc.
1078	PDTS (Process Data Technology and Systems)
1079	Cornet, Inc.
1080	NetStar, Inc.
1081	Semaphore Communications, Corp.
1082	Casio Computer Co., Ltd.
1083	CSIR
1084	APOGEE Communications
1085	Information Management Company
1086	Wordlink, Inc.
1087	PEER
1088	Telstra Corp.
1089	Net X, Inc.
1090	PNC PLC
1091	DanaSoft, Inc.
1092	Yokogawa-Hewlett-Packard
1093	Universities of Austria/Europe
1094	Link Telecom, Ltd.
1095	Xirion bv
1096	Centigram Communications, Corp.
1097	Gensym Corp.
1098	Apricot Computers, Ltd.
1099	CANAL+
1100	Cambridge Technology Partners
1101	MoNet Systems, Inc.
1102	Metricom, Inc.
1103	Xact, Inc.

1104	First Virtual Holdings, Incorporated
1105	NetCell Systems, Inc.
1106	Uni-Q
1107	DISA Space System Development Division
1108	INTERSOLV
1109	Vela Research, Inc.
1110	Tetherless Access, Inc.
1111	Magistrat Wien
1112	Franklin Telecom, Inc.
1113	EDA Instruments, Inc.
1114	EFI Electronics, Corporation
1115	GMD
1116	Voicetek, Corp.
1117	Avanti Technology, Inc.
1118	ATLan LTD
1119	Lehman Brothers
1120	LAN-hopper Systems, Inc.
1121	Web-Systems
1122	Piller GmbH
1123	Symbios Logic, Inc.
1124	NetSpan, Corp.
1125	Nielsen Media Research
1126	Sterling Software
1127	Applied Network Technology, Inc.
1128	Union Pacific Railroad
1129	Tec Corporation
1130	Datametrics Systems Corporation
1131	Intersection Development Corporation
1132	BACS Limited, GB
1133	Engage Communication
1134	Fastware, S.A.
1135	LONGSHINE Electronics Corp.
1136	BOW Software, Inc.
1137	emotion, Inc.
1138	Rautaruukki steel factory, Information systems
1139	EMC Corp
1140	University of West England

1141	Com21
1142	Compression Tehnologies, Inc.
1143	Buslogic, Inc.
1144	Firefox Corporation
1145	Mercury Communications, Ltd.
1146	COMPUTER PROTOCOL MALAYSIA SDN. BHD.
1147	Institute for Information Industry
1148	Pacific Electric Wire & Cable Co., Ltd.
1149	MPR Teltech, Ltd.
1150	P-COM, Inc.
1151	Anritsu Corporation
1152	SPYRUS
1153	NeTpower, Inc.
1154	Diehl ISDN GmbH
1155	CARNet
1156	AS-TECH
1157	SG2 Innovation et Produits
1158	CellAccess Technology, Inc.
1159	Bureau of Meteorology
1160	Hi-TECH Connections, Inc.
1161	Thames Water Utilities Limited
1162	Micropolis, Corp.
1163	Integrated Systems Technology
1164	Brite Voice Systems, Inc.
1165	Associated Grocer
1166	General Instrument
1167	Stanford Telecom
1168	ICOM Informatique
1169	MPX Data Systems, Inc.
1170	Syntellect
1171	Perihelion Technology, Ltd.
1172	Shoppers Drug Mart
1173	Apollo Travel Services
1174	Time Warner Cable, Inc.
1175	American Technology Labs, Inc.
1176	Dow Jones & Company, Inc.
1177	FRA

1178	Equitable Life Assurance Society
1179	Smith Barney, Inc.
1180	Compact Data, Ltd.
1181	I.Net Communications
1182	YAMAHA Corporation
1183	Illinois State University
1184	RADGuard, Ltd.
1185	Calypso Software Systems, Inc.
1186	ACT Networks, Inc.
1187	Kingston Communications
1188	Incite
1189	VVNET, Inc.
1190	Ontario Hydro
1191	CS-Telecom
1192	ICTV, Inc.
1193	CORE International, Inc.
1194	Mibs4You
1195	ITK
1196	Network Integrity, Inc.
1197	BlueLine Software, Inc.
1198	Migrant Computing Services, Inc.
1199	Linklaters & Paines
1200	EJV Partners, L.P.
1201	Software and Systems Engineering, Ltd.
1202	VARCOM Corporation
1203	Equitel
1204	The Southern Company
1205	Dataproducts Corporation
1206	National Electrical Manufacturers Association
1207	RISCmanagement, Inc.
1208	GVC Corporation
1209	timonWare, Inc.
1210	Capital Resources Computer Corporation
1211	Storage Technology Corporation
1212	Tadiran Telecomunications, Ltd.
1213	NCP
1214	Operations Control Systems (OCS)

1215	The NASDAQ Stock Market, Inc.
1216	Tiernan Communications, Inc.
1217	Goldman, Sachs Company
1218	Advanced Telecommunications Modules, Ltd.
1219	Phoenix Data Communications
1220	Quality Consulting Services
1221	MILAN
1222	Instrumental, Inc.
1223	Yellow Technology Services, Inc.
1224	Mier Communications, Inc.
1225	Cable Services Group, Inc.
1226	Forte Networks, Inc.
1227	American Management Systems, Inc.
1228	Choice Hotels Intl.
1229	SEH Computertechnik
1230	McAFee Associates, Inc.
1231	Network Intelligent, Inc.
1232	Luxcom Technologies, Inc.
1233	ITRON, Inc.
1234	Linkage Software, Inc.
1235	Spardat AG
1236	VeriFone, Inc.
1237	Revco D.S., Inc.
1238	HRB Systems, Inc.
1239	Litton Fibercom
1240	XCD, Incorporated
1241	ProsjektLeveranser AS
1242	Halcyon, Inc.
1243	SBB
1244	LeuTek
1245	Zeitnet, Inc.
1246	Visual Networks, Inc.
1247	Coronet Systems
1248	SEIKO EPSON CORPORATION
1249	DnH Technologies
1250	Deluxe Data
1251	Michael A. Okulski, Inc.

1252	Saber Software Corporation
1253	Mission Systems, Inc.
1254	Siemens Plessey Electronics Systems
1255	Applied Communications, Inc.
1256	Transaction Technology, Inc.
1257	HST, Ltd.
1258	Michigan Technological University
1259	Next Level Communications
1260	Instinet Corp.
1261	Analog & Digital Systems, Ltd.
1262	Ansaldo Trasporti SpA
1263	ECCI
1264	Imatek Corporation
1265	PTT Telecom bv
1266	Data Race, Inc.
1267	Network Safety Corporation
1268	Application des Techniques Nouvelles en Electronique
1269	MFS Communications Company
1270	Information Services Division
1271	Ciena Corporation
1272	Ascom Nexion
1273	Standard Networks, Inc.
1274	Scientific Research Corporation
1275	micado SoftwareConsult GmbH
1276	Concert Management Services, Inc.
1277	University of Delaware
1278	Bias Consultancy, Ltd.
1279	Micromuse PLC.
1280	Translink Systems
1281	PI-NET
1282	Amber Wave Systems
1283	Superior Electronics Group, Inc.
1284	Network Telemetrics, Inc.
1285	BSW-Data
1286	ECI Telecom, Ltd.
1287	BroadVision
1288	ALFA, Inc.

1289	TELEFONICA SISTEMAS, S.A.
1290	Image Sciences, Inc.
1291	MITSUBISHI ELECTRIC INFORMATION NETWORK CORPORATION (MIND)
1292	Central Flow Management Unit
1293	Woods Hole Oceanographic Institution
1294	Raptor Systems, Inc.
1295	TeleLink Technologies, Inc.
1296	First Virtual Corporation
1297	Network Services Group
1298	SilCom Manufacturing Technology, Inc.
1299	NETSOFT, Inc.
1300	Fidelity Investments
1301	Telrad Telecommunications
1302	Seagate Software, Inc.
1303	LeeMah DataCom Security Corporation
1304	SecureWare, Inc.
1305	USAir, Inc.
1306	Jet Propulsion Laboratory
1307	ABIT Co
1308	Dataplex Pty., Ltd.
1309	Creative Interaction Technologies, Inc.
1310	Network Defenders, Inc.
1311	Optus Communications
1312	Klos Technologies, Inc.
1313	ACOTEC
1314	Datacomm Management Sciences, Inc.
1315	MG SOFT Co.
1316	Plessey Tellumat SA
1317	PaineWebber, Inc.
1318	DATASYS, Ltd.
1319	QVC, Inc.
1320	IPL Systems
1321	Pacific Micro Data, Inc.
1322	DeskNet Systems, Inc.
1323	TC Technologies
1324	Racotek, Inc.
1325	CelsiusTech AB

1326	Xing Technology Corp.
1327	dZine n.v.
1328	Electronic merchant Services, Inc.
1329	Linmor Information Systems Management, Inc.
1330	ABL Canada, Inc.
1331	University of Coimbra
1332	Iskratel, Ltd., Telecommunications Systems
1333	ISA Co., Ltd.
1334	CONNECT, Inc.
1335	Digital Video
1336	InterVoice, Inc.
1337	Liveware Tecnologia a Servico a, Ltd.a
1338	Precept Software, Inc.
1339	Heroix Corporation
1340	Holland House B.V.
1341	Dedalus Engenharia S/C, Ltd.a
1342	GEC ALSTHOM I.T.
1343	Deutsches Elektronen-Synchrotron (DESY) Hamburg
1344	Switchview, Inc.
1345	Dacoll, Ltd.
1346	NetCorp, Inc.
1347	KYOCERA Corporation
1348	The Longaberger Company
1349	ILEX
1350	Conservation Through Innovation, Limited
1351	Software Technologies Corporation
1352	Multex Systems, Inc.
1353	Gambit Communications, Inc.
1354	Central Data Corporation
1355	CompuCom Systems, Inc.
1356	Generex Systems GMBH
1357	Periphonics Corporation
1358	Freddie Mac
1359	Digital Equipment bv
1360	PhoneLink plc
1361	Voice-Tel Enterprises, Inc.
1362	AUDILOG

1363	SanRex Corporation
1364	Chloride
1365	GA Systems, Ltd.
1366	Microdyne Corporation
1367	Boston College
1368	France Telecom
1369	Stonesoft Corp
1370	A. G. Edwards & Sons, Inc.
1371	Attachmate Corp.
1372	LSI Logic
1373	interWAVE Communications, Inc.
1374	mdl-Consult
1375	Bunyip Information Systems, Inc.
1376	Nashoba Networks, Inc.
1377	Comedia Information AB
1378	Harvey Mudd College
1379	First National Bank of Chicago
1380	Department of National Defence (Canada)
1381	CBM Technologies, Inc.
1382	InterProc, Inc.
1383	Glenayre R&D, Inc.
1384	Telenet GmbH
1385	Softlab GmbH
1386	Storage Computer Corporation
1387	Nine Tiles Computer Systems, Ltd.
1388	Network People International
1389	Simple Network Magic Corporation
1390	Stallion Technologies Pty, Ltd.
1391	Loan System
1392	DLR—Deutsche Forschungsanstalt fuer Luft-und
1393	ICRA, Inc.
1394	Probita
1395	NEXOR, Ltd.
1396	American Internation Facsimile Products
1397	Tellabs
1398	DATAX
1399	IntelliSys Corporation

1400	Sandia National Laboratories
1401	Synerdyne Corp.
1402	UNICOM Electric, Inc.
1403	Central Design Systems, Inc.
1404	The Silk Road Group, Ltd.
1405	Positive Computing Concepts
1406	First Data Resources
1407	INETCO Systems Limited
1408	NTT Mobile Communications Network, Inc.
1409	Target Stores
1410	Advanced Peripherals Technologies, Inc.
1411	Funk Software, Inc.
1412	DunsGate, a Dun and Bradstreet Company
1413	AFP
1414	Comsat RSI Precision Controls Division
1415	Williams Energy Services Company
1416	ASP Technologies, Inc.
1417	Philips Communication Systems
1418	Dataprobe, Inc.
1419	ASTROCOM CORP.
1420	CSTI (Communication Systems Technology, Inc.)
1421	Sprint
1422	Syntax
1423	LIGHT-INFOCON
1424	Performance Technology, Inc.
1425	CXR Telecom
1426	Amir Technology Labs
1427	ISOCOR
1428	Array Technology Corportion
1429	Scientific-Atlanta, Inc.
1430	GammaTech, Inc.
1431	Telkom SA
1432	CIREL SYSTEMES
1433	Redflex Limited Australia
1434	Hermes—Enterprise Messaging, Ltd.
1435	Acacia Networks, Inc.
1436	NATIONAL AUSTRALIA BANK, Ltd.

1437	SineTec Technology Co., Ltd.
1438	Badger Technology, Inc.
1439	Arizona State University
1440	Xionics Document Technologies, Inc.
1441	Southern Information System, Inc.
1442	Nebula Consultants, Inc.
1443	SITRE, SA
1444	Paradigm Technology, Ltd.
1445	Telub AB
1446	Communications Network Services
1447	Martis Oy
1448	ISKRA TRANSMISSION
1449	QUALCOMM, Incorporated
1450	Netscape Communications Corp.
1451	BellSouth Wireless, Inc.
1452	NUKO Information Systems, Inc.
1453	IPC Information Systems, Inc.
1454	Estudios y Proyectos de Telecomunicacion, S.A.
1456	Terayon Corp.
1457	CyberGuard Corporation
1458	Silicon Systems, Inc.
1459	Jupiter Technology, Inc.
1460	Delphi Internet Services
1461	Kesmai Corporation
1462	Compact Devices, Inc.
1463	OPTIQUEST
1464	Loral Defense Systems-Eagan
1465	OnRamp Technologies
1466	Mark Wahl
1467	Loran International Technologies, Inc.
1468	S & S International PLC
1469	Atlantech Technologies, Ltd.
1470	IN-SNEC
1471	Melita International Corporation
1472	Sharp Laboratories of America
1473	Groupe Decan
1474	Spectronics Micro Systems Limited

1475	pc-plus COMPUTING GmbH
1476	Microframe, Inc.
1477	Telegate Global Access Technology, Ltd.
1478	Merrill Lynch & Co., Inc.
1479	JCPenney Co., Inc.
1480	The Torrington Company
1481	GS-ProActive
1482	BARCO Communication Systems
1483	vortex Computersysteme GmbH
1484	DataFusion Systems (Pty.), Ltd.
1485	Allen & Overy
1486	Atlantic Systems Group
1487	Kongsberg Informasjonskontroll AS
1488	ELTECO a.s.
1489	Schlumberger Limited
1490	CNI Communications Network International GmbH
1491	M&C Systems, Inc.
1492	OM Systems International (OMSI)
1493	DAVIC (Digital Audio-Visual Council)
1494	ISM GmbH
1495	E.F. Johnson Co.
1496	Baranof Software, Inc.
1497	University of Texas Houston
1498	Ukiah Software Solutions/EDS/HDS
1499	STERIA
1500	ATI Australia Pty Limited
1501	The Aerospace Corporation
1502	Orckit Communications, Ltd.
1503	Tertio Limited
1504	COMSOFT GmbH
1505	Innovative Software
1506	Technologic, Inc.
1507	Vertex Data Science Limited
1508	ESIGETEL
1509	Illinois Business Training Center
1510	Arris Networks, Inc.
1511	TeamQuest Corporation

1512	Sentient Networks
1513	Skyrr
1514	Tecnologia y Gestion de la Innovacion
1515	Connector GmbH
1516	Kaspia Systems, Inc.
1517	SmithKline Beecham
1518	NetCentric Corp.
1519	ATecoM GmbH
1520	Citibank Canada
1521	MMS (Matra Marconi Space)
1522	Intermedia Communications of Florida, Inc.
1523	School of Computer Science, University Science of Malaysia
1524	University of Limerick
1525	ACTANE
1526	Collaborative Information Technology Research Institute (CITRI)
1527	Intermedium A/S
1528	ANS CO+RE Systems, Inc.
1529	UUNET Technologies, Inc.
1530	Securicor Telesciences
1531	QSC Audio Products
1532	Australian Department of Employment, Education and Training
1533	Network Media Communications, Ltd.
1534	Sodalia
1535	Innovative Concepts, Inc.
1536	Japan Computer Industry, Inc.
1537	Telogy Networks, Inc.
1538	Merck & Company, Inc.
1539	GeoTel Communications Corporation
1540	Sun Alliance (UK)
1541	AG Communication Systems
1542	Pivotal Networking, Inc.
1543	TSI TelSys, Inc.
1544	Harmonic Systems, Incorporated
1545	ASTRONET Corporation
1546	Frontec Erik Steinholtz
1547	NetVision
1548	FlowPoint Corporation

1549	TRON B.V. Datacommunication
1550	Nuera Communication, Inc.
1551	Radnet, Ltd.
1552	Oce Nederland BV
1553	Air France
1554	Communications & Power Engineering, Inc.
1555	Charter Systems
1556	Performance Technologies, Inc.
1557	Paragon Networks International
1558	Skog-Data AS
1559	mitec a/s
1560	THOMSON-CSF/Departement Reseaux d'Entreprise
1561	Ipsilon Networks, Inc.
1562	Kingston Technology Corporation
1563	Harmonic Lightwaves
1564	InterActive Digital Solutions
1565	Coactive Aesthetics, Inc.
1566	Tech Data Corporation
1567	Z-Com
1568	COTEP
1569	Raytheon Company
1570	Telesend, Inc.
1571	NCC
1572	Forte Software, Inc.
1573	Secure Computing Corporation
1574	BEZEQ
1575	Technical University of Braunschweig
1576	Stac, Inc.
1577	StarNet Communications
1578	Universidade do Minho
1579	Department of Computer Science, University of Liverpool
1580	Tekram Technology, Ltd.
1581	RATP
1582	Rainbow Diamond Limited
1583	Magellan Communications, Inc.
1584	Bay Networks, Incorporated
1585	Quantitative Data Systems (QDS)

1586	ESYS Limited
1587	Switched Network Technologies (SNT)
1588	Brocade Communications Systems, Inc.
1589	Computer Resources International A/S (CRI)
1590	LuchtVerkeersBeveiliging
1591	GTIL
1592	XactLabs Corporation
1593	NetPro Computing, Inc.
1594	TELESYNC
1595	BOSCH Telecom
1596	INS GmbH
1597	Distributed Processing Technology
1598	Tivoli Systems, Inc.
1599	Network Management Technologies
1600	SIRTI
1601	TASKE Technology, Inc.
1602	CANON, Inc.
1603	Systems and Synchronous, Inc.
1604	XFER International
1605	Scandpower A/S
1606	Consultancy & Projects Group srl
1607	STS Technologies, Inc.
1608	Mylex Corporation
1609	CRYPTOCard Corporation
1610	LXE, Inc.
1611	BDM International, Inc.
1612	GE Spacenet Services, Inc.
1613	Datanet GmbH
1614	Opcom, Inc.
1615	Mlink Internet, Inc.
1616	Netro Corporation
1617	Net Partners, Inc.
1618	Peek Traffic—Transyt Corp.
1619	Comverse Information Systems
1620	Data Comm for Business, Inc.
1621	CYBEC Pty., Ltd.
1622	Mitsui Knowledge Industry Co., Ltd.

1623	NORDX/CDT, Inc.
1624	Blockade Systems Corp.
1625	Nixu Oy
1626	Australian Software Innovations (Services) Pty., Ltd.
1627	Omicron Telesystems, Inc.
1628	DEMON Internet, Ltd.
1629	PB Farradyne, Inc.
1630	Telos Corporation
1631	Manage Information Technologies
1632	Harlow Butler Broking Services, Ltd.
1633	Eurologic Systems, Ltd.
1634	Telco Research Corporation
1635	Mercedes-Benz AG
1636	HOB electronic GmbH
1637	NOAA
1638	Cornerstone Software
1639	Wink Communications
1640	Thomson Electronic Information Resources (TEIR)
1641	HITT Holland Institute of Traffic Technology B.V.
1642	KPMG
1643	Loral Federal Systems
1644	S.I.A.—Societa Interbancaria per l'Automazione
1645	United States Cellular Corp.
1646	AMPER DATOS S.A.
1647	Carelcomp Forest Oy
1648	Open Environment Australia
1649	Integrated Telecom Technology, Inc.
1650	Langner Gesellschaft fuer Datentechnik mbH
1651	Wayne State University
1652	SICC (SsangYong Information & Communications Corp.)
1653	THOMSON—CSF
1654	Teleconnect Dresden GmbH
1655	Panorama Software, Inc.
1656	CompuNet Systemhaus GmbH
1657	JAPAN TELECOM CO., Ltd.
1658	TechForce Corporation
1659	Granite Systems, Inc.

1660	Bit, Incorporated
1661	Companhia de Informatica do Parana—Celepar
1662	Rockwell International Corporation
1663	Ancor Communications
1664	Royal Institute of Technology
1665	SUNET, Swedish University Network
1666	Sage Instruments, Inc.
1667	Candle Corporation
1668	CSO GmbH
1669	M3i Systems, Inc.
1670	CREDINTRANS
1671	BIT Communications
1672	Pierce & Associates
1673	Real Time Strategies, Inc.
1674	R.I.C. Electronics
1675	Amoco Corporation
1676	Qualix Group, Inc.
1677	Sahara Networks, Inc.
1678	Hyundai Electronics Industries Co., Ltd.
1679	RICH, Inc.
1680	Amati Communications Corp.
1681	P.H.U. RysTECH
1682	Data Labs, Inc.
1683	Occidental Petroleum Services, Inc.
1684	Rijnhaave Internet Services
1685	Lynx Real-Time Systems, Inc.
1686	Pontis Consulting
1687	SofTouch Systems, Inc.
1689	McCormick Nunes Company
1690	Ume E5 Universitet
1691	NetiQ Corporation
1692	Starlight Networks
1693	Informacion Selectiva S.A. de C.V. (Infosel)
1694	HCL Technologies Limited
1695	Maryville Data Systems, Inc.
1696	EtherCom Corp
1697	MultiCom Software

1698	BEA Systems, Ltd.
1699	Advanced Technology, Ltd.
1700	Mobil Oil
1701	Arena Consulting Limited
1702	Netsys International (Pty), Ltd.
1703	Titan Information Systems Corp.
1704	Cogent Data Technologies
1705	Reliasoft Corporation
1706	Midland Business Systems, Inc.
1707	Optimal Networks
1708	Gresham Computing
1709	Science Applications International Corporation (SAIC)
1710	Acclaim Communications
1711	BISS Limited
1712	Caravelle, Inc.
1713	Diamond Lane Communications Corporation
1714	Infortrend Technology, Inc.
1715	Orda-B N.V.
1716	Ariel Corporation
1717	Datalex Communications, Ltd.
1718	Server Technology, Inc.
1719	Unimax Systems Corporation
1720	DeTeMobil GmbH
1721	INFONOVA GmbH
1722	Kudelski SA
1723	Pronet GmbH
1724	Westell, Inc.
1725	Nupon Computing, Inc.
1726	CIANET Ind e Com, Ltd.a (CIANET, Inc.)
1727	Aumtech of Virginia (amteva)
1728	CheongJo data communication, Inc.
1729	Genesys Telecommunications Laboratories, Inc.
1730	Progress Software
1731	ERICSSON FIBER ACCESS
1732	Open Access Pty, Ltd.
1733	Sterling Commerce
1734	Predictive Systems, Inc.

1735	Architel Systems Corporation
1736	US West !nterAct
1737	Eclipse Technologies, Inc.
1738	Navy
1739	Bindi Technologies, Pty, Ltd.
1740	Hallmark Cards, Inc.
1741	Object Design, Inc.
1742	Vision Systems
1743	Zenith Data Systems (ZDS)
1744	Gobi Corp.
1745	Universitat de Barcelona
1746	Institute for Simulation and Training (IST)
1747	US Agency for International Development
1748	Tut Systems, Inc.
1749	AnswerZ Pty., Ltd. (Australia)
1750	H.Bollmann Manufacturers, Ltd. (HBM)
1751	Lucent Technologies
1752	phase2 networks, Inc.
1753	Unify Corporation
1754	Gadzoox Microsystems, Inc.
1755	Network One, Inc.
1756	MuLogic b.v.
1757	Optical Microwave Networks, Inc.
1758	SITEL, Ltd.
1759	Cerg Finance
1760	American Internet Corporation
1761	PLUSKOM GmbH
1762	Dept. of Communications
1763	MindSpring Enterprises, Inc.
1764	Db-Tech, Inc.
1765	Apex Voice Communications, Inc.
1766	National DataComm Corporation
1767	Telenor Conax AS
1768	Patton Electronics Company
1769	The Fulgent Group, Ltd.
1770	BroadBand Technologies, Inc.
1771	Myricom, Inc.

1772	DecisionOne
1773	Tandberg Television
1774	AUDITEC SA
1775	PC Magic
1776	Philips Electronics NV
1777	ORIGIN
1778	CSG Systems
1779	Alphameric Technologies, Ltd.
1780	NCR Austria
1781	ChuckK, Inc.
1782	PowerTV, Inc.
1783	Active Software, Inc.
1784	Enron Capitol & Trade Resources
1785	ORBCOMM
1786	Jw direct shop
1787	B.E.T.A.
1788	Healtheon
1789	Integralis, Ltd.
1790	Folio Corporation
1791	ECTF
1792	WebPlanet
1793	nStor Corporation
1794	Deutsche Bahn AG
1795	Paradyne
1796	Nastel Technologies
1797	Metaphase Technology, Inc.
1798	Zweigart & Sawitzki
1799	PIXEL
1800	WaveAccess, Inc.
1801	The SABRE Group
1802	Far Point Systems
1803	PBS
1804	Consensus Development Corporation
1805	SAGEM SA
1806	I-Cube, Inc.
1807	INTRACOM S.A. (HELLENIC TELECOMMUNICATION AND ELECTRONICS INDUSTRY)
1808	Aetna, Inc.

1809	Dow Jones Telerate Systems, Inc.
1810	Czech Railways s.o. CIT
1811	Scan-Matic A/S
1812	DECISION Europe
1813	VTEL Corporation
1814	Bloomberg, L.P.
1815	Eyretel, Ltd.
1816	Rose-Hulman Institute of Technology
1817	Aether Technologies
1818	Infonet Software Solutions
1819	CSTI (Compagnie des Signaux/Technologies Informatiques)
1820	LEROY MERLIN
1821	Total Entertainment Network
1822	Open Port Technology
1823	Mikroelektronik Anwendungszentrum Hamburg GmbH
1824	International Management Consulting, Inc.
1825	Scalable Networks, Inc.
1826	MTech Systems
1827	RxSoft, Ltd.
1828	Dept. Computer Studies, Loughborough University
1829	Beta80 S.p.A.
1830	Galiso, Incorporated
1831	S2 Systems, Inc.
1832	Optivision, Inc.
1833	Countrywide Home Loans
1834	OA Laboratory Co., Ltd.
1835	SDX Business Systems, Ltd.
1836	West End Systems Corp.
1837	DK Digital Media
1838	Westel
1839	Fujitsu Telecommuncations Europe Limited
1840	Inmarsat
1841	TIMS Technology, Ltd.
1842	CallWare Technologies
1843	NextLink, L.L.C.
1844	TurnQuay Solutions Limited
1845	Accusort Systems, Inc.

1846	DEUTSCHER BUNDESTAG
1847	Joint Research Centre
1848	FaxSav
1849	Chevy Chase Applications Design
1850	Bank Brussel Lambert (BBL)
1851	OutBack Resource Group, Inc.
1852	Screen Subtitling Systems, Ltd.
1853	Cambridge Parallel Processing, Ltd.
1854	Boston University
1855	News Datacom, Ltd.
1856	NuTek 2000, Inc.
1857	Overland Mobile Communication AB
1858	Axon IT AB
1859	Gradient Medical Systems
1860	WaveSpan Corporation
1861	Net Research, Inc.
1862	Browncroft Community Church
1863	Net2Net Corporation
1864	US Internet
1865	Absolute Time
1866	VPNet
1867	NTech
1868	Nippon Unisoft Corporation
1869	Optical Transmission Labs, Inc.
1870	CyberCash, Inc.
1871	NetSpeed, Inc.
1873	Internet Middleware Corporation
1874	ISOnova GmbH
1875	Amiga IOPS Project
1876	Softbank Services Group
1877	Sourcecom Corporation
1878	Telia Promotor AB
1879	HeliOss Communications, Inc.
1880	Optical Access International, Inc.
1881	MMC Networks, Inc.
1882	Lanyon, Ltd.
1883	Rubico

1884	Quantum Telecom Solutions, Inc.
1885	Archinet
1886	i-cubed, Ltd.
1887	Siemens Switzerland, Ltd.
1888	GigaLabs, Inc.
1889	MET Matra-Ericsson
1890	JBM Electronics
1891	OPTIM Systems, Inc.
1892	Software Brewery
1893	WaveLinQ
1894	Siemens Stromberg-Carlson
1895	IEX Corporation
1896	TrueTime
1897	HT Communications, Inc.
1898	Avantcomp Oy
1899	InfoVista
1900	Unwired Planet
1901	Sea Wonders
1902	HeadStart Enterprise
1903	B-SMART, Inc.
1904	ISMA, Ltd.
1905	3DV Technology, Inc.
1906	StarCom Technologies, Inc.
1907	L.L. Bean
1908	NetIcs, Inc.
1909	Infratec plus GmbH
1910	The 3e Group
1911	GISE mbH
1912	lan & pc services
1913	RedPoint Software Corporation
1914	QUADRATEC
1915	I-95-CC
1916	Extreme Networks
1917	Village of Rockville Centre
1918	Swichtec Power Systems
1919	Deutscher Wetterdienst
1920	Bluebird Software

1921	Svaha Interactive Media, Inc.
1922	Sully Solutions
1923	Blue Line
1924	Castleton Network Systems Corp.
1925	Visual Edge Software, Ltd.
1926	NetGuard Technologies, Inc.
1927	SoftSell, Inc.
1928	MARNE SOFTWARE
1929	Cadia Networks, Inc.
1930	Milton
1931	Del Mar Solutions, Inc.
1932	KUMARAN SYSTEMS
1933	Equivalence
1934	Homewatch International, Inc.
1935	John Rivers
1936	Remark Services, Inc.
1937	Deloitte & Touche Consulting Group
1938	Flying Penguin Productions
1939	The Matrix
1940	Eastern Computers, Inc.
1941	Princeton BioMedica, Inc.
1942	SanCom Technology, Inc.
1943	National Computing Centre, Ltd.
1944	Aval Communications
1945	WORTEC SearchNet Co.
1946	Dogwood Media
1947	Allied Domecq
1948	Telesoft Russia
1949	UTStarcom, Inc.
1950	comunit
1951	Traffic Sofware, Ltd.
1952	Qualop Systems Corp
1953	Vinca Corporation
1954	AMTEC spa
1955	GRETACODER Data Systems AG
1956	KMSystems, Inc.
1957	GEVA

1958	Red Creek Communications, Inc.
1959	BORG Technology, Inc.
1960	Concord Electronics
1961	Richard Ricci DDS
1962	Link International Corp.
1963	Intermec Corp.
1964	OPTIMUM Data AG
1965	Innova Corporation
1966	Perle Systems Limited
1967	inktomi corporation
1968	TELE-TV Systems, L.P.
1969	Fritz-Haber-Institut
1970	mediaone.net
1971	SeaChange International
1972	CASTON Corporation
1973	Local Net
1974	JapanNet
1975	Nabisco
1976	micrologica GmbH
1977	NDG Software
1978	Northrop Grumman-Canada, Ltd.
1979	Global MAINTECH, Inc.
1980	Tele2 AB
1981	CLARiiON Advanced Storage Solutions
1982	ITS Corporation
1983	CleverSoft, Inc.
1984	The Perseus Group, Inc.
1985	Joe's WWW Pages
1986	Everything Internet Store
1987	LANology, Inc.
1988	Lycoming County PA
1989	Statens Institutions styrelse SiS
1990	INware Solutions, Inc.
1991	StarRidge Networks, Inc.
1992	Deutsche Bank
1993	Xyratex
1994	Bausch Datacom B.V.

1995	Advanced Radio Telecom (ART)
1996	Copper Mountain Communications, Inc.
1997	PlaNet Software
1998	Carltan Computer Corporation
1999	Littva Mitchell, Inc.
2000	TIBCO, Inc.
2001	Oki Data Corporation
2002	GoTel
2003	Adobe Systems, Incorporated
2004	Sentricity
2005	Aeroports De Paris
2006	ECONZ, Ltd.
2007	TELDAT, S.A.
2008	Offset Info Service srl
2009	A. J. Boggs & Company
2010	Stale Odegaard AS
2011	HUAWEI Technology Co., Ltd.
2012	Schroff GmbH
2013	Rehabilitation Institute of Chicago
2014	ADC Telecommunications, Inc.
2015	SYSTOR AG
2016	GralyMage, Inc.
2017	Symicron Computer Communications, Ltd.
2018	Scandorama AB
2019	I-NET
2020	Xland, Ltd.
2021	U.C. Davis, ECE Dept.
2022	CANARY COMMUNICATIONS, Inc.
2023	NetGain
2024	West Information Publishing Group
2025	Deutsche Bundesbank
2026	Digicom System, Inc.
2027	GAUSS GmbH
2028	Aldiscon
2029	Vivid Image
2030	AfriQ*Access, Inc.
2031	Reliant Networks Corporation

2031	ENVOY Corporation
2032	SEMA Group Telecoms
2033	McKinney Lighting & Sound
2034	Whole Systems Design, Inc.
2035	O'Reilly & Associates
2036	ATL Products
2037	Ernst and Young LLP
2038	Teleware Oy
2039	Fiducia Informationszentrale AG
2040	Kinetics, Inc.
2041	EMCEE Broadcast Products
2042	Clariant Corporation
2043	IEEE 802.5
2044	Open Development Corporation
2045	RFG Systems
2046	Aspect Telecommunications
2047	Leo & Associates
2048	SoftLinx, Inc.
2049	Generale Bank
2050	Windward Technologies, Inc.
2051	NetSolve, Incorporated
2052	Xantel
2053	arago, Institut fuer komplexes Datenmanagement GmbH
2054	Kokusai Denshin Denwa Co., Ltd.
2055	GILLAM-SATEL
2056	MOEBIUS SYSTEMS
2057	Financial Internet Technology
2058	MARC Systems
2059	Bova Gallery
2060	OSx Telecomunicacoes
2061	Telecom Solutions
2062	HolonTech Corporation
2063	Ardent Communications Corporation
2064	Aware, Inc.
2065	Racal Radio Limited
2066	Control Resources Corporation
2067	Advanced Fibre Communications (AFC)

2068	Elproma Electronica B.V.
2069	MTA SZTAKI
2070	Consensys Computers, Inc.
2071	Jade Digital Research Co.
2072	Byte This Interactive Pty., Ltd.
2073	Financial Network Technologies, Inc.
2074	BROKAT Informationssysteme GmbH
2075	MediaWise Networks
2076	Future Software
2077	Commit Information Systems
2078	Virtual Access, Ltd.
2079	JDS FITEL, Inc.
2080	IPM DATACOM
2081	StarBurst Communications Corporation
2082	Tollgrade Communications, Inc.
2083	Wildfire Communications, Inc.
2084	Sanken Electric Co., Ltd.
2085	Isolation Systems Limited
2086	AVIDIA Systems, Inc.
2087	WavePhore Networks, Inc.
2088	Radstone Technology Plc
2089	Philips Business Communications
2090	FMS Services
2091	Supernova Communications
2092	Murphy & Murphy Real Estate
2093	Multi-Platform Information Systems
2094	Allegro Consultants, Inc.
2095	AIAB
2096	Preview Multimedia Services
2097	Access Beyond
2098	SunBurst Technology, Inc.
2099	sotas
2100	CyberSouls Eternal Life Systems, Inc.
2101	HANWHA CORP./TELECOM
2102	COMET TELECOMMUNICATIONS, Inc.
2103	CARY SYSTEMS, Inc.
2105	Adicom Wireless, Inc.

2106	High Technology Software Corp.
2107	Lynk
2108	Robin's Limousine
2109	Secant Network Tech
2110	Orion Pictures Corporation
2111	Global Village Communication, Inc.
2112	ioWave, Inc.
2113	Signals and Semaphores
2114	Mayo Foundation
2115	KRONE AG
2116	Computer Networking Resources, Inc.
2117	Telenetworks
2118	Staffordshire University
2119	Broadband Networks, Inc.
2120	Federal Aviation Administration
2121	Technical Communications Corporation
2122	REZO+
2123	GrafxLab, Inc.
2124	Savant Corp
2125	COMTEC SYSTEMS CO., Ltd.
2126	Satcom Media
2127	UconX Corporation
2128	TPG Network
2129	CNJ, Incorporated
2130	Greenbrier & Russel
2131	mainnet
2132	Comnet Datensysteme
2133	Novadigm, Inc.
2134	Alfatech, Inc.
2135	Financial Sciences Corporation
2136	Electronics For Imaging, Inc.
2137	Casabyte
2138	AssureNet Pathways, Inc.
2139	Alexander LAN, Inc.
2140	Gill-Simpson
2141	MCNS, L.P.
2142	Future Systems, Inc.

2143	IMGIS
2144	Skywire Corporation
2145	Irdeto Consultants B.V.
2146	Peasantworks
2147	Onion Peel Software
2148	PS Partnership
2149	IRdg, Inc.
2150	SDS, Ltd.
2151	Promus Hotel Corporation
2152	Cavid Lawrence Center
2153	Insider Technologies, Ltd.
2154	Berkeley Networks
2155	Infonautics Corporation
2156	Easy Software
2157	CESG
2158	SALIX Technologies, Inc.
2159	Essential Communications
2160	University of Hawaii
2161	Foxtel Management Pty
2162	Advent Network Management
2163	Vayris, S.A.
2164	Telecom Multimedia Systems, Inc.
2165	Guardall, Ltd.
2166	WKK SYSTEMS, Inc.
2167	Prominet Corporation
2168	LMC Lan Management Consulting
2169	Lewis Enterprise
2170	Teles AG
2171	PCSI (Phoenix Control)
2172	Fourth Wave Designs, Inc.
2173	MediaGate, Inc.
2174	Interactive Online Services, Inc.
2175	Mutek Transcom, Ltd.
2176	University of Dortmund, IRB
2177	Network Diagnostic Clinic
2178	TSI—Telecom Systems, Ltd.
2179	Rheyn Techologies, Inc.

2180	Versanet Communications, Inc.
2181	EUnet Communications Services BV
2182	pow communications
2183	AM Communications, Inc.
2184	Open Architecture Systems Integration Solutions (OASIS), Inc.
2185	NetPartner s.r.o.
2186	Vina Technologies
2189	Deutsches Klimarechenzentrum GmbH
2190	ABSYSS
2191	Quadrophonics, Inc.
2192	Hypercore Technology, Inc.
2193	OBTK, Inc., dba Network Designs Corporation
2194	VOIS Corporation
2195	IXO S.A.
2196	Macro4 Open Systems, Ltd.
2197	Security Dynamics Technologies, Inc.
2198	NextWave Wireless, Inc.
2199	Pisces Consultancy
2200	TPS Call Sciences, Inc. (TPS)
2201	ICONSULT
2202	Third Point Systems
2203	MAS Technology, Ltd.
2204	Advanced Logic Research, Inc. (ALR)
2205	Documentum, Inc.
2206	Siemens Business Communication Systems, Inc.
2207	Telmax Communications Corp.
2208	Zypcom, Inc.
2209	Remote Sense
2210	OOTek Corporation
2211	eSoft, Inc.
2212	anydata limited
2213	Data Fellows, Ltd.
2214	Productions Medialog, Inc.
2215	Inovamerci, Lda
2216	OKITEC
2217	Vertex Networks, Inc.
2218	Pulse Communications

2219	CXA Communications, Ltd.
2220	IDD Information Service
2221	Atlas Computer Equipment, Inc.
2222	Syntegra Steve Barrow
2223	CCC Information Services
2224	W. Quinn Associates
2225	Broadcom Eireann Research, Ltd.
2226	Risk Management Services llc
2227	Watkins-Johnson Company
2228	Eric E. Westbrook
2229	Martinho-Davis Systems, Inc.
2230	XYPOINT Corporation
2231	Innovat Communications, Inc.
2232	Charleswood & Co.
2233	ID Software AS
2234	Telia AB
2235	Exploration Enterprises, Inc.
2236	Daimler-Benz Aerospace AG
2237	Xara Networks, Ltd.
2238	The FreeBSD Project
2239	World Merchandise Exchange (WOMEX), Ltd.
3000	IDB Systems, a Division of WorldCom, Inc.
3001	BAILO
3002	ADAXIS Group
3003	Packet Engines, Inc.
3004	Softwire Corporation
3005	TDS (Telecoms Data Systems)
3006	HCI Technologies
3007	TOPCALL International
3008	Open Service, Inc.
3009	Aichi Electronics Co., Ltd.
3010	University of Aizu
3011	VideoServer, Inc.
3012	Space & Telecommunications Systems Pte., Ltd.
3013	Bicol Infonet System, Inc.
3014	MediaSoft Telecom

3015	Synaxis Corporation
3016	OzEmail, Ltd.
3017	Arcxel Technologies, Inc.
3018	EnterNet Corporation
3019	Jones Waldo Holbrook McDonough
3020	University Access
3021	Sendit AB
3022	Telecom Sciences Corporation Limited
3023	Quality Quorm, Inc.
3024	Grapevine Systems, Inc.
3025	The Panda Project, Inc.
3026	Mission Control Development
3027	IONA Technologies, Ltd.
3028	Dialogic Corporation
3029	Digital Data Security
3030	ISCNI
3031	daoCon
3032	Beaufort Memorial Hospital
3033	Informationstechnik
3034	URMET SUD s.p.a.
3035	Avesta Technologies, Inc.
3036	Hyundai Electronics America
3037	DMV, Ltd.
3038	Fax International, Inc.
3039	MidAmerican Energy Company (MEC)
3040	Bellsouth.net
3041	Assured Access Technology, Inc.
3042	Logicon—Eagle Technology
3043	FREQUENTIS Nachrichtentechnik Ges.m.b.H
3044	ISIS 2000
3045	james e. gray, atty
3046	Jamaica Cable T.V. & Internet Services
3047	Information Technology Consultants Pty., Ltd.
3048	LinickGrp.com
3049	Yankee Know-How
3050	SeAH group

3051	Cinco Networks, Inc.
3052	Omnitronix, Inc.
3053	Genie Telecommunication, Inc.

The preceding information was derived from the following file:

ftp://ftp.isi.edu/in-notes/iana/assignments/enterprise-numbers

MIB Objects

This appendix provides a summary of the objects contained in various management information bases (MIBs), including the Internet-standard MIB (MIB-II) (see RFC 1213), the Remote Network Monitoring MIB for Ethernet (see RFC 1757), token ring (see RFC 1513), and RMON2 (see RFC 2021). Within each MIB, the object identifier (OID) of each major group is also noted.

Groups in MIB II

MIB-II is the Internet-standard MIB. That MIB contains the following groups (see Figure 3.1):

➤ System provides demographic information about the managed node's configuration, location, etc.

➤ Interfaces is a table containing information about the managed node's interfaces.

➤ Address Translation is used to convert IP to Physical addresses (now deprecated).

➤ IP contains Internet Protocol–related statistics and tables.

➤ ICMP contains Internet Control Message Protocol–related input/output statistics.

➤ TCP contains Transmission Control Protocol–related connection information and statistics.

➤ UDP contains User Datagram Protocol–related information and datagram statistics.

➤ EGP contains Exterior Gateway Protocol–related message statistics and a table of neighbor information.

> OIM contains OSI Internet Management–related information (defined in RFC 1214 as an arc within MIB-II, but not used with SNMP).

> Transmission contains information about the physical transmission medium.

> SNMP contains Simple Network Management Protocol–related information and statistics.

The System Group {1.3.6.1.2.1.1}

The System group provides a textual description of the entity in printable ASCII characters. Descriptions include a system description, OID, the length of time since its network management entity was reinitialized, and other administrative details. Implementation of the System group is mandatory. Objects within this group (see Figure 3-2) include:

> sysDescr is a textual description of the entity in printable ASCII characters.

> sysObjectID is the vendor's identification of the object.

> sysUpTime is the amount of time (measured in hundredths of seconds) since the network management portion of the system was last reinitialized.

> sysContact is the textual identification of the contact person for this managed node.

> sysName is an administratively assigned name for this node, i.e., the domain name.

> sysLocation is the physical location of the node.

> sysServices is the set of services that the entity primarily provides.

The Interfaces Group {1.3.6.1.2.1.2}

Information about the various hardware interfaces on a managed device is provided by the Interfaces group and presented in a table format (see Figure 3-3) . The first object (ifNumber) indicates the number of interfaces on that device. For each interface, a row is made in the table, with 22 column entries per row. The column entries provide information regarding those interfaces:

> ifNumber is the number of network interfaces present on this system.

➤ ifTable is a list of interface entries, with the number of entries given by the value of ifNumber.

  ➤ ifEntry is an interface entry containing objects at the subnetwork layer and below for a particular interface.

    ➤ ifIndex is a unique value, between 1 and the value of ifNumber, for each interface.

    ➤ ifDescr is a text string containing information about the interface.

    ➤ ifType is the specific type of interface, such as Ethernet, token ring, FDDI, frame relay, etc. (RFC 1213 lists the values for this object.)

    ➤ ifMTU is the largest IP datagram, measured in octets, that can be sent/received on this interface.

    ➤ ifSpeed is an estimate of the interface's current bandwidth measured in bits per second.

    ➤ ifPhysAddress is the interface's address at the protocol layer immediately below IP.

    ➤ ifAdminStatus is the desired state of the interface.

    ➤ ifOperStatus is the current operational state of the interface.

    ➤ ifLastChange is the value of sysUpTime at the time that the interface entered its current operational state.

    ➤ ifInOctets is the total number of octets received on the interface.

    ➤ ifInUcastPkts is the number of subnetwork-unicast packets delivered to a higher-layer protocol.

➤ ifInNUcastPkts is the number of subnetwork nonunicast packets delivered to a higher-layer protocol.

➤ ifInDiscards is the number of inbound packets that were discarded for reasons other than errors.

➤ ifInErrors is the number of inbound packets that contained errors, preventing their delivery to a higher-layer protocol.

➤ ifInUnknownProtos is the number of packets received but discarded because of an unknown or unsupported protocol.

➤ ifOutOctets is the total number of octets transmitted out of the interface.

➤ ifOutUcastPkts is the total number of packets that higher-level protocols requested be transmitted to a subnet-unicast address, including those that were discarded or not sent.

➤ ifOutNUcastPkts is the total number of packets that higher-level protocols requested be transmitted to a nonunicast (i.e., subnetwork broadcast or subnetwork multicast) address, including those that were discarded or not sent.

➤ ifOutDiscards is the number of outbound packets that were discarded for reasons other than errors.

➤ ifOutErrors is the number of outbound packets that could not be transmitted because of errors.

➤ ifOutQLen is the length, in packets, of the output packet queue.

➤ ifSpecific is a reference to MIB definitions specific to the particular media being used to realize the interface.

This value provides additional information on that interface.

The Address Translation Group {1.3.6.1.2.1.3}

The Address Translation group (see Figure 3-4) was included in MIB-I, but deprecated in MIB-II. The purpose of the Address Translation group was to provide a table that translated between IP addresses and physical (hardware) addresses. In MIB-II and future releases, each protocol group will contain its own translation tables. The Address Translation group contains the following objects:

➢ atTable is comprised of the Address Translation tables containing NetworkAddress to physical address equivalences.

    ➢ atEntry, where each entry contains one NetworkAddress to physical address equivalence.

        ➢ atIfIndex is an interface identifier that has the same value as ifIndex.

        ➢ atPhysAddress is the media-dependent physical address.

        ➢ atNetAddress is the NetworkAddress (IP address) that corresponds to the physical address.

The IP Group {1.3.6.1.2.1.4}

The IP (Internet Protocol) group (see Figure 3-5) provides specific information on the usage of that protocol by the various hosts and routers; it is mandatory for all managed nodes. Three tables are included in this group: an address table (ipAddrTable), an IP to physical address translation table (ipNetToMediaTable), and an IP forwarding table (ipForwardTable, which is defined in RFC 1354). The IP forwarding table replaces and obsoletes the IP route table that was included in MIB-II. The IP subtree contains the following objects:

➢ ipForwarding indicates whether or not this entity is acting as an IP router (a gateway, in Internet terminology).

➢ ipDefaultTTL is the default value inserted in the IP header's time-to-live field.

➤ ipInReceives is the total number of input datagrams received.

➤ ipInHdrErrors is the number of input datagrams discarded due to errors in their IP headers.

➤ ipInAddrErrors is the number of input datagrams discarded because the IP address in their IP header's destination field was not a valid address to be received at this entity.

➤ ipForwDatagrams is the number of IP datagrams for which this entity was not their final destination, and for which forwarding to another entity was required.

➤ ipInUnknownProtos is the number of datagrams received but discarded because of an unknown or unsupported protocol.

➤ ipInDiscards is the number of input datagrams received but discarded for reasons other than errors.

➤ ipInDelivers is the total number of input datagrams successfully delivered to IP user protocols, including ICMP.

➤ ipOutRequests is the total number of IP datagrams that local IP user-protocols (including ICMP) supplied to IP in request for transmission.

➤ ipOutDiscards is the number of output IP datagrams that were discarded for reasons other than errors.

➤ ipOutNoRoutes is the number of IP datagrams discarded because no route could be found to transmit them to their destination.

➤ ipReasmTimeout is the maximum number of seconds that received fragments are held while they are awaiting reassembly at this entity.

➤ ipReasmReqds is the number of IP fragments received that needed to be reassembled at this entity.

➤ ipReasmOKs is the number of IP datagrams successfully reassembled.

➤ ipReasmFails is the number of failures detected by the IP reassembly algorithm.

➤ ipFragOKs is the number of IP datagrams that have been successfully fragmented at this entity.

➤ ipFragFails is the number of IP datagrams that have been discarded at this entity because they could not be fragmented.

➤ ipFragCreates is the number of IP datagram fragments that have been created as a result of fragmentation at this entity.

➤ ipAddrTable is the table of addressing information relevant to this entry's IP addresses. There are five columns in this table.

  ➤ ipAddrEntry is the addressing information for one of this entity's IP addresses.

    ➤ ipAdEntAddr is the IP address to which this entry's addressing information pertains.

    ➤ ipAdEntIfIndex is the index value that identifies the interface to which this entry applies; it has the same value as ifIndex.

    ➤ ipAdEntNetMask is the subnet mask associated with the IP address of this entry.

    ➤ ipAdEntBcastAddr is the value of the least significant bit in the IP broadcast address.

    ➤ ipAdEntReasmMaxSize is the size of the largest IP datagram that this entity can reassemble.

➤ ipRoutingTable has been replaced and obsoleted by the ipForwardTable, {ip 24}, below.

➤ ipNetToMediaTable is the IP translation table used for mapping from IP addresses to physical addresses. This table contains the four columns below.

  ➤ ipNetToMediaEntry, where each entry contains one IPAddress to physical address equivalence.

    ➤ ipNetToMediaIfIndex is the interface on which this entry's equivalence is effective; it has the same value as ifIndex.

    ➤ ipNetToMediaPhysAddress is the media-dependent physical address.

> ➤ ipNetToMediaNetAddress is the IpAddress corresponding to the media-dependent physical address.

> ➤ ipNetToMediaType is the type of mapping.

➤ ipRoutingDiscards is the number of routing entries that were chosen to be discarded even though they are valid.

➤ ipForward is the IP forwarding table.

> ➤ ipForwardNumber is the number of current ipForwardTable entries that are not invalid.

> ➤ ipForwardTable is this entity's IP routing table, containing 15 columns.

>> ➤ ipForwardEntry is a particular route to a particular destination.

>>> ➤ ipForwardDest is the destination IP address of this route.

>>> ➤ ipForwardMask contains the subnet mask.

>>> ➤ ipForwardPolicy is the general set of conditions that would cause the selection of one multipath route.

>>> ➤ ipForwardNextHop, on remote routes, is the address of the next system en route.

>>> ➤ ipForwardIfIndex is the ifIndex value that identifies the local interface through which the next hop of this route should be reached.

>>> ➤ ipForwardType is the type of route.

>>> ➤ ipForwardProto is the routing mechanism by which this route was learned.

>>> ➤ ipForwardAge is the number of seconds since this route was last updated.

> ipForwardInfo is a reference to MIB definitions specific to the particular routing protocol which is responsible for this route.

> ipForwardNextHopAS is the Autonomous System number of the next hop.

> ipForwardMetric1 is the primary routing metric for this route.

> ipForwardMetric2 is an alternate routing metric for this route.

> ipForwardMetric3 is an alternate routing metric for this route.

> ipForwardMetric4 is an alternate routing metric for this route.

> ipForwardMetric5 is an alternate routing metric for this route.

The ICMP Group {1.3.6.1.2.1.5}

The ICMP (Internet Control Message Protocol) group (see Figure 3-6) is mandatory for all implementations. This group represents various operations of ICMP within the managed entity; it contains 26 scalar objects:

> icmpInMsgs is the total number of ICMP messages that the entity received.

> icmpInErrors is the number of ICMP messages that the entity received but determined as having ICMP-specific errors.

> icmpInDestUnreachs is the number of ICMP Destination Unreachable messages received.

> icmpInTimeExcds is the number of ICMP Time Exceeded messages received.

> icmpInParmProbs is the number of ICMP Parameter Problem messages received.

➤ icmpInSrcQuenchs is the number of ICMP Source Quench messages received.

➤ icmpInRedirects is the number of ICMP Redirect messages received.

➤ icmpInEchos is the number of ICMP Echo (request) messages received.

➤ icmpInEchoReps is the number of ICMP Echo Reply messages received.

➤ icmpInTimestamps is the number of ICMP Timestamp (request) messages received.

➤ icmpInTimestampReps is the number of ICMP Timestamp Reply messages received.

➤ icmpInAddrMasks is the number of ICMP Address Mask Request messages received.

➤ icmpInAddrMaskReps is the number of ICMP Address Mask Reply messages received.

➤ icmpOutMsgs is the total number of ICMP messages that this entity attempted to send.

➤ icmpOutErrors is the number of ICMP messages that this entity did not send because of ICMP–related problems.

➤ icmpOutDestUnreachs is the number of ICMP Destination Unreachable messages sent.

➤ icmpOutTimeExcds is the number of ICMP Time Exceeded messages sent.

➤ icmpOutParmProbs is the number of ICMP Parameter Problem messages sent.

➤ icmpOutSrcQuenchs is the number of ICMP Source Quence messages sent.

➤ icmpOutRedirects is the number of ICMP Redirect messages sent.

➤ icmpOutEchos is the number of ICMP Echo (request) messages sent.

➤ icmpOutEchoReps is the number of ICMP Echo Reply messages sent.

➤ icmpOutTimestamps is the number of ICMP Timestamp (request) messages sent.

➤ icmpOutTimestampReps is the number of ICMP Timestamp Reply messages sent.

➤ icmpOutAddrMasks is the number of ICMP Address Mask Request messages sent.

➤ icmpOutAddrMaskReps is the number of ICMP Address Mask Reply messages sent.

The TCP Group {1.3.6.1.2.1.6}

The TCP (Transmission Control Protocol) group (see Figure 3-7) is mandatory and provides information regarding TCP operation and connections. This group contains one table with the connection information (tcpConnTable) and 14 scalars:

➤ tcpRtoAlgorithm is the algorithm used to determine the timeout value used for retransmitting unacknowledged octets.

➤ tcpRtoMin is the minimum value (measured in milliseconds) permitted by a TCP implementation for the retransmission timeout.

➤ tcpRtoMax is the maximum value (measured in milliseconds) permitted by a TCP implementation for the retransmission timeout.

➤ tcpMaxConn is the limit on the total number of TCP connections the entity can support.

➤ tcpActiveOpens is the number of times TCP connections have made a transition to the SYN-SENT state from the CLOSED state.

➤ tcpPassiveOpens is the number of times TCP connections have made a direct transition to the SYN-REVD state from the LISTEN state.

➤ tcpAttemptFails is the number of failed connection attempts.

➤ tcpEstabResets is the number of resets that have occurred.

➤ tcpCurrEstab is the number of TCP connections having a current state of either ESTABLISHED or CLOSE-WAIT.

➤ tcpInSegs is the total number of segments received.

➤ tcpOutSegs is the total number of segments sent.

➤ tcpRetransSegs is the total number of segments retransmitted.

➤ tcpConnTable is a table containing information about this entity's existing TCP connections. There are five columns in this table (see below).

    ➤ tcpConnEntry has information about a particular current TCP connection.

        ➤ tcpConnState is the state of this TCP connection.

        ➤ tcpConnLocalAddress is the local IP address for this TCP connection.

        ➤ tcpConnLocalPort is the local port number for this TCP connection.

        ➤ tcpConnRemAddress is the remote IP address for this TCP connection.

        ➤ tcpConnRemPort is the remote port number for this TCP connection.

➤ tcpInErrs is the total number of segments received in error.

➤ tcpOutRsts is the number of TCP segments sent containing the RST flag.

The UDP Group {1.3.6.1.2.1.7}

The UDP (User Datagram Protocol) group (see Figure 3-8) is mandatory and provides information regarding UDP operation. This group is much smaller than the TCP group, given that UDP is a connectionless protocol unlike TCP's connection orientation. Therefore, no connection attempt, establishment, reset, or other such information needs to be compiled. The UDP group contains four scalars and one table (udpTable):

➤ udpInDatagrams is the total number of UDP datagrams delivered to UDP users.

➤ udpNoPorts is the total number of received UDP datagrams for which there was not an application at the destination port.

➤ udpInErrors is the number of received UDP datagrams that could not be delivered for reasons other than the lack of an application at the destination port.

➤ udpOutDatagrams is the total number of UDP datagrams sent from this entity.

➤ udpTable is a table containing UDP listener information, providing details about the UDP end points that are accepting datagrams.

➤ udpEntry contains information about a particular UDP listener. There are two columns in this table, as shown below.

➤ udpLocalAddress is the local IP address for this UDP listener.

➤ udpLocalPort is the local port number for this UPD listener.

The EGP Group {1.3.6.1.2.1.8}

The EGP (Exterior Gateway Protocol) group is mandatory for all systems that implement the EGP. This protocol is used for communication between autonomous (i.e., self-contained) systems, and is described in detail in RFC 904. This group (see Figure 3-9) includes five scalar objects and one table containing EGP neighbor information:

➤ egpInMsgs is the number of EGP messages received without error.

➤ egpInErrors is the number of EGP messages received that proved to be in error.

➤ egpOutMsgs is the total number of locally generated EGP messages.

➤ egpOutErrors is the number of locally generated EGP messages not sent due to resource limitations within an EGP entity.

➤ egpNeighTable is the EGP neighbor table.

➤ egpNeighEntry contains information about this entity's relationship with a particular EGP neighbor. This table contains 15 columns, listed below.

➤ egpNeighState is the EGP state of the local systems with respect to this entry's EGP neighbor.

➤ egpNeighAddr is the IP address of this entry's EGP neighbor.

➤ egpNeighAs is the autonomous system of this EGP peer.

➤ egpNeighInMsgs is the number of EGP messages received without error from this EGP peer.

➤ egpNeighInErrs is the number of EGP messages received from this EGP peer that contain errors.

➤ egpNeighOutMsgs is the number of locally generated EGP messages to this EGP peer.

➤ egpNeighOutErrs is the number of locally generated EGP messages not sent to this EGP peer due to resource limitations within an EGP entity.

➤ egpNeighInErrMsgs is the number of EGP-defined error messages received from this EGP peer.

➤ egpNeighOutErrMsgs is the number of EGP-defined error messages sent to this EGP peer.

➤ egpNeighStateUps is the number of EGP state transitions to the UP state with this EGP peer.

➤ egpNeighStateDowns is the number of EGP state transitions from the UP state to any other state with this EGP peer.

➤ egpNeighIntervalHello is the interval (measured in hundredths of a second) between EGP Hello command retransmissions.

➤ egpNeighIntervalPoll is the interval (measured in hundredths of a second) between EGP poll command retransmissions.

➤ egpNeighMode is the polling mode of this EGP entity.

➤ egpNeighEventTrigger is a control variable used to trigger operator-initiated Start and Stop events.

➤ egpAs is the autonomous system number of this EGP entity.

The CMOT (OIM) Group {1.3.6.1.2.1.9}

The CMOT (Common Management Information Protocol [CMIP] over TCP/IP) group is given a placeholder in MIB-II. At one time in the development of the Internet Network Management Framework, an effort was underway to use SNMP as an interim step, with CMOT as the long-term and OSI-compliant solution. As a result, this CMOT group was placed within MIB-II. The details of that subtree are given in RFC 1214, which specifies the OSI Internet Management (OIM) MIB. At the present time, it has a "historical" status.

The Transmission Group {1.3.6.1.2.1.10}

The Transmission group (see Figure 3-10) contains objects that relate to the transmission of the data. None of these objects are explicitly defined in RFC 1213. Mention is made in that document, however, of these transmission objects residing in the experimental subtree (1.3.6.1.3) until they are "proven." The "Assigned Numbers" document (currently RFC 1700) lists the following objects under the Transmission group:

➤ {1.3.6.1.2.1.10.5}, X.25 Packet Layer objects (RFC 1382)

➤ {1.3.6.1.2.1.10.7}, CSMA/CD-like objects (RFC 1643)

➤ {1.3.6.1.2.1.10.8}, Token Bus-like objects (RFC 1230)

➤ {1.3.6.1.2.1.10.9}, Token Ring-like objects (RFC 1748)

➤ {1.3.6.1.2.1.10.15}, FDDI objects (RFC 1512)

➤ {1.3.6.1.2.1.10.16}, X.25 LAPB objects (RFC 1381)

➤ {1.3.6.1.2.1.10.18}, DS1 Interface objects (RFC 1406)

➤ {1.3.6.1.2.1.10.19}, E1 Interface objects (RFC 1406)

➤ {1.3.6.1.2.1.10.23}, Point-to-Point Protocol objects (RFC 1471)

➤ {1.3.6.1.2.1.10.30}, DS3/E3 Interface objects (RFC 1407)

➤ {1.3.6.1.2.1.10.31}, SMDS Interface objects (RFC 1694)

- ➤ {1.3.6.1.2.1.10.32}, Frame Relay DTE objects (RFC 1315)
- ➤ {1.3.6.1.2.1.10.33}, RS-232 objects (RFC 1659)
- ➤ {1.3.6.1.2.1.10.34}, Parallel printer objects (RFC 1660)
- ➤ {1.3.6.1.2.1.10.35}, ARCNET objects)
- ➤ {1.3.6.1.2.1.10.36}, ARCNETPLUS objects
- ➤ {1.3.6.1.2.1.10.37}, ATM objects (RFC 1695)
- ➤ {1.3.6.1.2.1.10.38}, X.25 Interconnect objects (RFC 1461)
- ➤ {1.3.6.1.2.1.10.39}, SONET objects (RFC 1595)
- ➤ {1.3.6.1.2.1.10.44}, Frame Relay Service objects (RFC 1604)

The SNMP Group {1.3.6.1.2.1.11}

The SNMP group (see Figure 3-18) provides information on SNMP objects. There are a total of 30 scalar objects in this group:

- ➤ snmpInPkts is the total number of messages delivered to the SNMP entity from the transport service.
- ➤ snmpOutPkts is the total number of SNMP messages that were passed from the SNMP protocol entity to the transport service.
- ➤ snmpInBadVersions is the total number of SNMP messages that were for an unsupported SNMP version.
- ➤ snmpInBadCommunityNames is the total number of SNMP messages that used an SNMP community name not known to that entity.
- ➤ snmpInBadCommunityUses is the total number of SNMP messages that represented an SNMP operation that was not allowed by the SNMP community name in the message.
- ➤ snmpInASNParseErrs is the total number of ASN.1 or BER errors encountered.
- ➤ {snmp 7}. This is not used.
- ➤ snmpInTooBigs is the total number of SNMP PDUs received with the "tooBig" error-status field.

➤ snmpInNoSuchNames is the total number of SNMP PDUs received with the "noSuchName" error-status field.

➤ snmpInBadValues is the total number of SNMP PDUs received with the "badValue" error-status field.

➤ snmpInReadOnlys is the total number of SNMP PDUs received with the "readOnly" error-status field.

➤ snmpInGenErrs is the total number of SNMP PDUs received with the "genErr" error-status field.

➤ snmpInTotalReqVars is the total number of MIB objects that have been retrieved.

➤ snmpInTotalSetVars is the total number of MIB objects that have been altered.

➤ snmpInGetRequests is the total number of SNMP Get-Request PDUs accepted and processed.

➤ snmpInGetNexts is the total number of SNMP Get-Next PDUs received.

➤ snmpInSetRequests is the total number of SNMP Set-Request PDUs received.

➤ snmpInGetResponses is the total number of SNMP Get-Response PDUs received.

➤ snmpInTraps is the total number of SNMP Trap PDUs received.

➤ snmpOutTooBigs is the total number of SNMP PDUs sent with the "tooBig" error-status field.

➤ snmpOutNoSuchNames is the total number of SNMP PDUs sent with the "noSuchName" error-status field.

➤ snmpOutBadValues is the total number of SNMP PDUs sent with the "badValue" error-status field.

➤ {snmp 23}. This is not used.

➤ snmpOutGenErrs is the total number of SNMP PDUs sent with the "genErr" error-status field.

➤ snmpOutGetRequests is the total number of SNMP Get-Request PDUs sent.

➤ snmpOutGetNexts is the total number of SNMP Get-Next PDUs sent.

➤ snmpOutSetRequests is the total number of SNMP Set-Request PDUs sent.

➤ snmpOutGetResponses is the total number of SNMP Get-Response PDUs sent.

➤ snmpOutTraps is the total number of SNMP Trap PDUs sent.

➤ snmpEnableAuthenTraps indicates whether the SNMP agent process is permitted to generate authentication-failure traps.

The Ethernet RMON MIB {1.3.6.1.2.1.16}

The Remote Network Monitoring (RMON) MIB was developed for the purpose of standardizing the management information that is sent to and from remote network monitoring probes; it is presented in RFC 1757. SNMP agents supporting the RMON MIB can be located in a variety of distributed internetwork hardware, such as bridges or routers. The RMON MIB contains nine groups (see Figure 3-19). All of these groups are considered optional (not mandatory), but the implementation of certain groups also requires the use of other groups. For example, implementing the Filter group also requires the Packet Capture group. The nine Ethernet groups are summarized as follows:

➤ Statistics contains probe-measured statistics, such as the number and sizes of packets, broadcasts, collisions, etc.

➤ History records periodic statistical samples over time that can be used for trend analysis.

➤ Alarms compares statistical samples with preset thresholds, generating alarms when a particular threshold is crossed.

➤ Host maintains statistics of the hosts on the network, including the MAC addresses of the active hosts.

➤ HostTopN provides reports that are sorted by host table statistics, indicating which hosts are at the top of the list in a particular category.

➤ Matrix stores statistics in a traffic matrix regarding conversations between pairs of hosts.

➤ Filter allows packets to be matched according to a filter equation.

➤ Packet Capture allows packets to be captured after they pass through a logical channel.

➤ Event controls the generation and notification of events, which may also include the use of SNMP trap messages.

The Ethernet RMON Statistics Group {1.3.6.1.2.1.16.1}

The Statistics group is optional and contains a table of statistics that are measured by the probe. This information is available for each interface on the managed device. Each etherStatsEntry is a row in the table, containing the objects listed below:

➤ etherStatsTable is a list of Ethernet statistics entries.

   ➤ etherStatsEntry is a collection of statistics kept for a particular Ethernet interface.

      ➤ etherStatsIndex is an identifier of the etherStats entry.

      ➤ etherStatsDataSource is an identifier of the source of the data, i.e., the particular interface.

      ➤ etherStatsDropEvents is the total number of events that packets were dropped by the probe due to lack of resources.

      ➤ etherStatsOctets is the total number of octets of data received on the network.

      ➤ etherStatsPkts is the total number of packets received.

      ➤ etherStatsBroadcastPkts is the total number of good packets received that were directed to the broadcast address.

      ➤ etherStatsMulticastPkts is the total number of good packets received that were directed to a multicast address.

      ➤ etherStatsCRCAlignErrors is the total number of packets received that had alignment or Frame Check Sequence (FCS) errors.

➤ etherStatsUndersizePkts is the total number of packets received that were less than 64 octets long.

➤ etherStatsOversizePkts is the total number of packets received that were longer than 1518 octets.

➤ etherStatsFragments is the total number of packets received that had an alignment error or bad FCS and were less than 64 octets in length.

➤ etherStatsJabbers is the total number of packets received that had an alignment error or bad FCS and were longer than 1518 octets.

➤ etherStatsCollisions is the best estimate of the total number of collisions on this Ethernet segment.

➤ etherStatsPkts64Octets is the total number of packets received that were 64 octets in length.

➤ etherStatsPkts65to127Octets is the total number of packets received that were between 65 and 127 octets in length.

➤ etherStatsPkts128to255Octets is the total number of packets received that were between 128 and 255 octets in length.

➤ etherStatsPkts256to511Octets is the total number of packets received that were between 256 and 511 octets in length.

➤ etherStatsPkts512to1023Octets is the total number of packets received that were between 512 and 1023 octets in length.

➤ etherStatsPkts1024to1518Octets is the total number of packets received that were between 1024 and 1518 octets in length.

➤ etherStatsOwner is the entity that configured this entry and is therefore using the resources assigned to it.

➤ etherStatsStatus is the status of this etherStats entry.

The Ethernet RMON History Group {1.3.6.1.2.1.16.2}

The History group is optional and records periodic statistical sample information from a particular network, allowing this information to be subsequently retrieved. This group contains two tables, historyControlTable and etherHistoryTable. The historyControlTable is used to store configuration entries defining the interface, polling period, etc. RFC 1757 suggests two polling periods: 30 seconds for short-term polls and 30 minutes for long-term ones. The etherHistoryTable stores Ethernet-specific statistics. Objects in this group include the following:

➤ historyControlTable is a list of history control entries.

➤ historyControlEntry is a list of parameters that set up a periodic sampling of statistics.

➤ historyControlIndex is an index that identifies an entry in the historyControl table.

➤ historyControlDataSource is an identifier of the source of the data.

➤ historyControlBucketsRequested is the requested number of discrete time intervals over which data is to be saved.

➤ historyControlBucketsGranted is the number of discrete time intervals over which data shall be saved.

➤ historyControlInterval is the interval between 1 and 3600 seconds over which the data is sampled for each bucket.

➤ historyControlOwner is the entity that configured this entry and is therefore using the resources assigned to it.

> ➤ historyControlStatus is the status of this historyControl entry.

> ➤ etherHistoryTable is a list of Ethernet history entries.

> > ➤ etherHistoryEntry is a historical sample of Ethernet statistics on a particular Ethernet interface.

> > > ➤ etherHistoryIndex is the history of which this entry is a part; it is identified by the same value of historyControlIndex.

> > > ➤ etherHistorySampleIndex is an index that uniquely identifies the particular sample this entry represents.

> > > ➤ etherHistoryIntervalStart is the value of sysUpTime at the start of the interval over which this sample was measured.

> > > ➤ etherHistoryDropEvents is the total number of events in which packets were dropped by the probe due to lack of resources during this interval.

> > > ➤ etherHistoryOctets is the total number of octets of data received on the network.

> > > ➤ etherHistoryPkts is the number of packets received during this sampling interval.

> > > ➤ etherHistoryBroadcastPkts is the number of good packets received during this sampling interval that were directed to the broadcast address.

> > > ➤ etherHistoryMulticastPkts is the number of good packets received during this sampling interval that were directed to a multicast address.

> > > ➤ etherHistoryCRCAlignErrors is the number of packets received during this sampling interval that had alignment or FCS errors.

➤ etherHistoryUndersizePkts is the number of packets received during this interval that were less than 64 octets long.

➤ etherHistoryOversizePkts is the number of packets received during this sampling interval that were longer than 1518 octets.

➤ etherHistoryFragments is the number of packets received during this sampling interval that had an alignment error or bad FCS and were less than 64 octets in length.

➤ etherHistoryJabbers is the number of packets received during this interval that were longer than 1518 octets.

➤ etherHistoryCollisions is the best estimate of the total number of collisions on this Ethernet segment during this interval.

➤ etherHistoryUtilization is the best estimate, in hundredths of a percent, of the mean Physical layer network utilization on this interface during this interval.

The Ethernet RMON Alarm Group {1.3.6.1.2.1.16.3}

The Alarm group is optional, but it requires the implementation of the Events group. The Alarm group compares statistical samples from variables in the probe with preconfigured thresholds. The statistical information is stored in the alarmTable in twelve columns. When a particular sample crosses one of the preset thresholds, an event is generated. This group contains the following objects:

➤ alarmTable is a list of alarm entries.

   ➤ alarmEntry is a list of parameters that set up a periodic checking for alarm conditions.

      ➤ alarmIndex is an index that uniquely identifies an entry in the alarm table.

➤   alarmInterval is the interval, in seconds, over which data is sampled and compared with the rising and falling thresholds.

➤   alarmVariable is the object identifier of the particular variable to be sampled.

➤   alarmSampleType is the method of sampling the selected variable and calculating the value to be compared against the thresholds.

➤   alarmValue is the value of the statistic during the last sampling period.

➤   alarmStartupAlarm is the alarm that may be sent when this entry is first set to valid.

➤   alarmRisingThreshold is a threshold that generates a single event when the current sampled value is greater than or equal to this threshold, and the value at the last sampling interval was less than this threshold.

➤   alarmFallingThreshold is a threshold that generates a single event when the current sampled value is less than or equal to this threshold, and the value at the last sampling interval was greater than this threshold.

➤   alarmRisingEventIndex is the index of the eventEntry that is used when a rising threshold is crossed.

➤   alarmFallingEventIndex is the index of the eventEntry that is used when a falling threshold is crossed.

➤   alarmOwner is the entity that configured this entry and is using the resources assigned to it.

➤   alarmStatus is the status of this alarm entry.

The Ethernet RMON Host Group {1.3.6.1.2.1.16.4}

The Host group is an optional group that maintains information and statistics regarding the various hosts that are discovered to be active on the network. To do this, three tables are compiled. The first, hostControlTable, is six columns wide; it keeps information regarding the host discovery process and the interfaces that are being used. The second, hostTable, uses ten columns to maintain statistics on each host that is discovered and indexed by MAC address. The third table, hostTimeTable, contains the same information, but is indexed by the hostTimeCreationOrder. The Host group contains the following objects:

> hostControlTable is a list of host table control entries.

> > hostControlEntry is a list of parameters that set up the discovery and collection of statistics of hosts on a particular interface.

> > > hostControlIndex is an index that uniquely identifies an entry in the hostControl table, placing those statistics in the hostTable and the hostTimeTable.

> > > hostControlDataSource is an identifier of the source of the data for this instance of the host function.

> > > hostControlTableSize is the number of hostEntries in the hostTable and the hostTimetable.

> > > hostControlLastDeleteTime is the value of sysUpTime when the last entry was deleted.

> > > hostControlOwner is the entity that configured this entry and is using the resources assigned to it.

> > > hostControlStatus is the status of this hostControl entry.

> hostTable is a list of host entries.

> > hostEntry is a collection of statistics for a particular host that has been discovered on an interface of this device.

> > > hostAddress is the physical address of this host.

➤ hostCreationOrder is an index that defines the relative ordering of the creation time of hosts captured for a particular hostControlEntry.

➤ hostIndex is the set of collected host statistics of which this entry is a part.

➤ hostInPkts is the number of error-free packets transmitted to this address since it was added to the hostTable.

➤ hostOutPkts is the number of packets including errors transmitted by this address since it was added to the hostTable.

➤ hostInOctets is the number of error-free octets transmitted to this address since it was added to the hostTable.

➤ hostOutOctets is the number of octets transmitted by this address since it was added to the hostTable.

➤ hostOutErrors is the number of error packets transmitted by this address since it was added to the hostTable.

➤ hostOutBroadcastPkts is the number of good packets transmitted by this address to the broadcast address since this host was added to the hostTable.

➤ hostOutMulticastPkts is the number of good packets transmitted by this address to a multicast address since this host was added to the hostTable.

➤ hostTimeTable is a list of time-ordered host table entries.

➤ hostTimeEntry is a collection of statistics, in relative ordering of creation time, for a particular host that has been discovered on an interface of this device.

➤ hostTimeAddress is the physical address of this host.

➤ hostTimeCreationOrder is an index that uniquely defines an entry in the hostTime table. The ordering of the indexes is based on the order of each entry's insertion into the table.

➤ hostTimeIndex is the set of collected host statistics of which this entry is a part.

➤ hostTimeInPkts is the number of error-free packets transmitted to this address since it was added to the hostTimeTable.

➤ hostTimeOutPkts is the number of packets including errors transmitted by this address since it was added to the hostTimeTable.

➤ hostTimeInOctets is the number of error-free octets transmitted to this address since it was added to the hostTimeTable.

➤ hostTimeOutOctets is the number of octets transmitted by this address since it was added to the host-TimeTable.

➤ hostTimeOutErrors is the number of error packets transmitted by this address since it was added to the hostTimeTable.

➤ hostTimeOutBroadcastPkts is the number of good packets transmitted by this address to the broadcast address since this host was added to the hostTimeTable.

➤ hostTimeOutMulticastPkts is the number of good packets transmitted by this address to a multicast address since this host was added to the hostTimeTable.

The Ethernet RMON HostTopN Group {1.3.6.1.2.1.16.5}

The HostTopN group is an optional group that requires the implementation of the Host group. The HostTopN group is used to prepare reports describing hosts at the top of a list that is ordered by a particular statistic. Two tables are contained in this group. The hostTopNControlTable contains ten columns and initiates the generation of a particular report. The prepared report creates four columns in the hostTopNTable. This group has the following objects:

➤ hostTopNControlTable is a list of top N host control entries.

    ➤ hostTopNControlEntry is a set of parameters that control the creation of a report of the top N hosts according to several metrics. There are 10 columns in this table.

        ➤ hostTopNControlIndex is an index that uniquely identifies an entry in the hostTopNControl table, with each entry defining one report per interface.

        ➤ hostTopNHostIndex is the host table for which a top N report will be prepared on behalf of this entry; it is associated with the host table identified by the same value of hostIndex.

        ➤ hostTopNRateBase is the variable for each host that the hostTopNRate variable is based on.

        ➤ hostTopNTimeRemaining is the number of seconds left in the report currently being collected.

        ➤ hostTopNDuration is the number of seconds that this report has collected during the last sampling interval.

        ➤ hostTopNRequestSize is the maximum number of hosts requested for the top N table.

        ➤ hostTopNGrantedSize is the maximum number of hosts in the top N table.

        ➤ hostTopNStartTime is the value of sysUpTime when this top N report was last started.

        ➤ hostTopNOwner is the entity that configured this entry and is therefore using the resources assigned to it.

➤   hostTopNStatus is the status of this hostTopNControl entry.

➤   hostTopNTable is a list of top N host entries.

➤   hostTopNEntry is a set of statistics for a host that is part of a top N report. There are four columns in this table, listed below.

➤   hostTopNReport identifies the top N report of which this entry is a part.

➤   hostTopNIndex is an index that uniquely identifies an entry in the hostTopN table among those in the same report.

➤   hostTopNAddress is the physical address of this host.

➤   hostTopNRate is the amount of change in the selected variable during this sampling interval. The selected variable is this host's instance of the object selected by hostTopNRateBase.

The Ethernet RMON Matrix Group {1.3.6.1.2.1.16.6}

The Matrix group is an optional group that records statistics regarding conversations between pairs of addresses. In other words, this group compiles a traffic matrix of inter-node communication. To do this, three tables are generated, each having six columns. The matrixControlTable contains matrix parameters, the matrixSDTable is indexed by source and destination MAC addresses, and the matrixDSTable is indexed by the destination and source MAC addresses. This group contains the following objects:

➤   matrixControlTable is a list of information entries for the traffic matrix on each interface.

➤   matrixControlEntry contains information about a traffic matrix on a particular interface.

➤   matrixControlIndex is an index that uniquely identifies an entry in the matrixControl table. Each of these entries places statistical information in the matrixSD-Table and the matrixDSTable.

➢ matrixControlDataSource identifies the source of the data from which this entry creates a traffic matrix.

➢ matrixControlTableSize is the number of entries in the matrixSDTable and the matrixDSTable for this interface.

➢ matrixControlLastDeleteTime is the value of sysUpTime when the last entry was deleted from the portion of the matrixSDTable or matrixDSTable associated with this matrixControlEntry.

➢ matrixControlOwner is the entity that configured this entry and is therefore using the resources assigned to it.

➢ matrixControlStatus is the status of this matrixControl entry.

➢ matrixSDTable is a list of traffic matrix entities indexed by source and destination MAC addresses.

➢ matrixSDEntry is a collection of statistics for communications between two addresses on a particular interface.

➢ matrixSDSourceAddress is the source physical address.

➢ matrixSDDestAddress is the destination physical address.

➢ matrixSDIndex is the set of collected matrix statistics of which this entry is a part; it has the same value as matrixControlIndex.

➢ matrixSDPkts is the number of packets transmitted from the source address to the destination address.

➢ matrixSDOctets is the number of octets contained in all packets transmitted from the source address to the destination address.

➤ matrixSDErrors is the number of error packets trans-mitted from the source address to the destination address.

➤ matrixDSTable is a list of traffic matrix entities indexed by the destination and source MAC addresses.

➤ matrixDSEntry is a collection of statistics for communications between two addresses on a particular interface.

➤ matrixDSSourceAddress is the source physical address.

➤ matrixDSDestAddress is the destination physical address.

➤ matrixDSIndex is the set of collected matrix statistics of which this entry is a part; it has the same value as matrixControlIndex.

➤ matrixDSPkts is the number of packets transmitted from the source address to the destination address.

➤ matrixDSOctets is the number of octets contained in all packets transmitted from the source address to the destination address.

➤ matrixSDErrors is the number of error packets trans-mitted from the source address to the destination address.

The Ethernet RMON Filter Group {1.3.6.1.2.1.16.7}

The Filter group is an optional group that allows packets to be captured based on a filter. This is similar to a filter that can be set by a protocol analyzer that selectively captures packets containing data of a certain protocol, bit pattern, or length. The net effect of these filters is to create logical channels that match that particular filter pattern. This group contains two tables. The filterTable, with eleven columns, stores filter parameters. The channelTable, with twelve columns, is a list of packet channel entries. The Filter group contains the following objects:

➤ filterTable is a list of packet filter entries.

➤ filterEntry is a set of parameters for a packet filter applied on a particular interface.

    ➤ filterIndex is an index that uniquely identifies an entry in the filter table. Each entry defines one filter that is to be applied to every packet received on an interface.

    ➤ filterChannelIndex identifies the channel of which this filter is a part; it has the same value as the value of the channelIndex object.

    ➤ filterPktDataOffset is the offset from the beginning of each packet where a match of packet data will be attempted.

    ➤ filterPktData is the data that is to be matched with the input packet.

    ➤ filterPktDataMask is the mask that is applied to the match process.

    ➤ filterPktDataNotMask is the inversion mask that is applied to the match process.

    ➤ filterPktStatus is the status that is to be matched with the input packet.

    ➤ filterPktStatusMask is the mask that is applied to the status match process.

    ➤ filterPktStatusNotMask is the inversion mask that is applied to the status match process.

    ➤ filterOwner is the entity that configured this entry and is therefore using the resources assigned to it.

    ➤ filterStatus is the status of this filter entry.

➤ channelTable is a list of packet channel entries.

    ➤ channelEntry is a set of parameters for a packet channel applied on a particular interface.

➤ channelIndex is an index that uniquely identifies an entry in the channel table. Each entry defines one channel, which is a logical data and event stream.

➤ channelIfIndex uniquely identifies the interface on this remote network monitoring device to which the associated filters are applied.

➤ channelAcceptType controls the action of the filters associated with this channel.

➤ channelDataControl controls the flow of data through this channel.

➤ channelTurnOnEventIndex identifies the event that is configured to turn the associated channelDataControl from off to on when the event is generated.

➤ channelTurnOffEventIndex identifies the event that is configured to turn the associated channelDataControl from on to off when the event is generated.

➤ channelEventIndex identifies the event that is configured to be generated when the associated channelDataControl is on and a packet is matched.

➤ channelEventStatus is the event status of this channel.

➤ channelMatches is the number of times this channel has matched a packet.

➤ channelDescription is a comment describing this channel.

➤ channelOwner is the entity that configured this entry and is using the resources assigned to it.

➤ channelStatus is the status of this channel entry.

The Ethernet RMON Packet Capture Group {1.3.6.1.2.1.16.8}

The Packet Capture group is optional, but it requires the implementation of the Filter group. The Packet Capture group allows packets to be captured when a particular filter is matched. Two tables are defined in this group. The bufferControlTable, with thirteen columns, controls the captured packets output from a particular channel. The captured packets are then contained in the captureBufferTable, which contains seven columns. The Packet Capture group contains the following objects:

➤ bufferControlTable is a list of buffer control entries.

　➤ bufferControlEntry is a set of parameters that control the collection of a stream of packets that have matched filters.

　　➤ bufferControlIndex is an index that uniquely describes an entry in the bufferControl table. Each entry defines one set of packets that is captured and controlled by one or more filters.

　　➤ bufferControlChannelIndex is an index that identifies the channel that is the source of packets for this buffer-Control table; it has the same value as the channelIndex object.

　　➤ bufferControlFullStatus shows whether the buffer has room to accept new packets or whether it is full.

　　➤ bufferControlFullAction controls the action of the buffer when it reaches the full status.

　　➤ bufferControlCaptureSliceSize is the maximum number of octets of each packet that will be saved in this capture buffer.

　　➤ bufferControlDownloadSliceSize is the maximum number of octets of each packet in this capture buffer that will be returned in an SNMP retrieval of that packet.

➤ bufferControlDownloadOffset is the offset of the first octet of each packet in this capture buffer that will be returned in an SNMP retrieval of that packet.

➤ bufferControlMaxOctetsRequested is the requested maximum number of octets to be saved in this captureBuffer, including any implementation-specific overhead.

➤ bufferControlMaxOctetsGranted is the maximum number of octets that can be saved in this captureBuffer, including overhead.

➤ bufferControlCapturedPackets is the number of packets currently in this captureBuffer.

➤ bufferControlTurnOnTime is the value of sysUpTime when this capture buffer was first turned on.

➤ bufferControlOwner is the entity that configured this entry and is using the resources assigned to it.

➤ bufferControlStatus is the status of this buffer Control Entry.

➤ captureBufferTable is a list of packets captured off of a channel.

➤ captureBufferEntry is a packet captured off of an attached network.

➤ captureBufferControlIndex is the index of the bufferControlEntry with which this packet is associated.

➤ captureBufferIndex is an index that uniquely identifies an entry in the captureBuffer table associated with a particular bufferControlEntry.

➤ captureBufferPacketID is an index that describes the order of packets that are received on a particular interface.

➤ capturebufferPacketData is the data inside the packet.

➤ captureBufferPacketLength is the actual length (off the wire) of the packet stored in this entry.

➤ captureBufferPacketTime is the number of milliseconds that have passed since this capture buffer was first turned on when this packet was captured.

➤ captureBufferPacketStatus is a value that indicates the error status of this packet.

The Ethernet RMON Event Group {1.3.6.1.2.1.16.9}

The Event group is optional and controls the generation and notification of events on a particular device. A particular event may cause a log entry to be made and/or an SNMP Trap message to be sent. Two tables are included in this group: the eventTable, with seven columns, and the logTable, with four columns. This group contains the following objects:

➤ eventTable is a list of events to be generated.

➤ eventEntry is a set of parameters that describe an event to be generated when certain conditions are met.

➤ eventIndex is an index that uniquely identifies an entry in the event table. Each entry defines one event that is to be generated when the appropriate conditions occur.

➤ eventDescription is a comment describing this event entry.

➤ eventType is the type of notification that the probe will make about this event.

➤ eventCommunity. If an SNMP trap is to be sent, it will be sent to the SNMP community specified by this octet string.

➤ eventLastTimeSent is the value of sysUpTime at the time this event entry last generated an event.

➤ eventOwner is the entity that configured this entry and is using the resources assigned to it.

➤ eventStatus is the status of this event entry.

➤ logTable is a list of events that have been logged.

➤ logEntry is a set of data describing an event that has been logged.

➤ logEventIndex is the event entry that generated this log entry and has the same value of eventIndex.

➤ logIndex is an index that uniquely identifies an entry in the log table among those generated by the same eventEntries.

➤ logTime is the value of sysUpTime when this log entry was created.

➤ logDescription is an implementation-dependent description of the event that activated this log entry.

The Token Ring RMON MIB {1.3.6.1.2.1.16}

The token ring RMON MIB was developed as an extension to the Ethernet RMON MIB discussed in the previous section. Recall that the Ethernet RMON MIB defines nine groups, Statistics through Events. The token ring RMON MIB extends two of these groups, Statistics and History, and adds one group (see Figure 3-20) that is unique. This new group is known as tokenRing, with object identifier {rmon 10}.

The Statistics extensions allow for the collection of both token ring MAC-Layer errors and promiscuous errors. The MAC-Layer errors are specific to the token ring protocol, while the promiscuous errors are more general in nature. In a similar manner, the History information is divided into MAC-Layer and promiscuous details. The Token Ring group is used to record token ring–specific statistics, such as source routing information.

Token Ring RMON MAC-Layer Statistics Group {1.3.6.1.2.1.16.1.2}

The token ring MAC-Layer Statistics group contains one table, token-RingMLStatsTable, which records token ring network–specific errors. This group is optional and contains the following objects:

> tokenRingMLStatsTable is a list of MAC-Layer token ring statistics entries.

> > tokenRingMLStatsEntry is a collection of MAC-Layer statistics kept for a particular token ring interface.

> > > tokenRingMLStatsIndex uniquely identifies this token-RingMLStats entry.

> > > tokenRingMLStatsDataSource identifies the source of the data that this tokenRingMLStats entry is configured to analyze.

> > > tokenRingMLStatsDropEvents is the total number of events in which packets were dropped by the probe due to lack of resources.

> > > tokenRingMLStatsMacOctets is the total number of error-free octets of data in MAC packets received on the network.

> > > tokenRingMLStatsMacPkts is the total number of error-free MAC packets received.

> > > tokenRingMLStatsRingPurgeEvents is the total number of times that the ring enters the ring purge state from the normal ring state.

> > > tokenRingMLStatsRingPurgePkts is the total number of Ring Purge MAC packets detected by the probe.

> > > tokenRingMLStatsBeaconEvents is the total number of times that the ring enters the beaconing state.

➤ tokenRingMLStatsBeaconTime is the total number of times that the ring has been in the beaconing state.

➤ tokenRingMLStatsBeaconPkts is the total number of Beacon MAC packets detected by the probe.

➤ tokenRingMLStatsClaimTokenEvents is the total number of times the ring enters the monitor contention state.

➤ tokenRingMLStatsClaimTokenPkts is the total number of Claim Token MAC packets detected by the probe.

➤ tokenRingMLStatsNAUNChanges is the total number of NAUN changes detected by the probe.

➤ tokenRingMLStatsLineErrors is the total number of line errors reported in error-reporting packets detected by the probe.

➤ tokenRingMLStatsInternalErrors is the total number of adapter internal errors reported in error-reporting packets detected by the probe.

➤ tokenRingMLStatsBurstErrors is the total number of burst errors reported in error-reporting packets detected by the probe.

➤ tokenRingMLStatsACErrors is the total number of AC (address copied) errors reported in error-reporting packets detected by the probe.

➤ tokenRingMLStatsAbortErrors is the total number of abort delimiters reported in error-reporting packets detected by the probe.

➤ tokenRingMLStatsLostFrameErrors is the total number of lost frame errors reported in error-reporting packets detected by the probe.

> tokenRingMLStatsCongestionErrors is the total number of receive-congestion errors reported in error-reporting packets detected by the probe.

> tokenRingMLStatsFrameCopiedErrors is the total number of frame-copied errors reported in error-reporting packets detected by the probe.

> tokenRingMLStatsFrequencyErrors is the total number of frequency errors reported in error-reporting packets detected by the probe.

> tokenRingMLStatsTokenErrors is the total number of token errors reported in error-reporting packets detected by the probe.

> tokenRingMLStatsSoftErrorReports is the total number of soft error-report frames detected by the probe.

> tokenRingMLStatsRingPollEvents is the total number of ring poll events detected by the probe.

> tokenRingMLStatsOwner is the entity that configured this entry and is therefore using the resources assigned to it.

> tokenRingMLStatsStatus is the status of this token-RingMLStats entry.

Token Ring RMON Promiscuous Statistics Group {1.3.6.1.2.1.16.1.3}

The Token Ring Promiscuous Statistics group is used to collect promiscuous statistics, i.e., those that are token ring–specific but that may not be collected by all management systems. The information is compiled in a single table, the tokenRingPStatsTable. This group is optional and contains the following objects:

> tokenRingPStatsTable is a list of promiscuous token ring statistics entries.

> tokenRingPStatsEntry is a collection of promiscuous statistics kept for a particular token ring interface.

➤ tokenRingPStatsIndex is the value of this object, which uniquely identifies this tokenRingPStats entry.

➤ tokenRingPStatsDataSource represents the source of the data that this tokenRingPStats entry is configured to analyze.

➤ tokenRingPStatsDropEvents is the total number of events in which packets were dropped due to lack of resources.

➤ tokenRingPStatsDataOctets is the total number of error-free octets of data received on the network.

➤ tokenRingPStatsDataPkts is the total number of error-free packets received.

➤ tokenRingPStatsDataBroadcastPkts is the total number of good non-MAC packets received that were directed to an LLC broadcast address.

➤ tokenRingPStatsDataMulticastPkts is the total number of good non-MAC packets received that were directed to a local or global multicast or functional address.

➤ tokenRingPStatsDataPkts18to63Octets is the total number of error-free non-MAC packets received that were between 18 and 63 octets in length.

➤ tokenRingPStatsDataPkts64to127Octets is the total number of error-free non-MAC packets received that were between 64 and 127 octets in length.

➤ tokenRingPStatsDataPkts128to255Octets is the total number of error-free non-MAC packets received that were between 128 and 255 octets in length.

➤ tokenRingPStatsDataPkts256to511Octets is the total number of error-free non-MAC packets received that were between 256 and 511 octets in length.

➤ tokenRingPStatsDataPkts512to1023Octets is the total number of error-free non-MAC packets received that were between 512 and 1023 octets in length.

➤ tokenRingPStatsDataPkts1024to2047Octets is the total number of error-free non-MAC packets received that were between 1024 and 2047 octets in length.

➤ tokenRingPStatsDataPkts2048to4095Octets is the total number of error-free non-MAC packets received that were between 2048 and 4095 octets in length.

➤ tokenRingPStatsDataPkts4096to8191Octets is the total number of error-free non-MAC packets received that were between 4096 and 8191 octets in length.

➤ tokenRingPStatsDataPkts8192to18000Octets is the total number of error-free non-MAC packets received that were between 8192 and 18,000 octets in length.

➤ tokenRingPStatsDataPktsGreaterThan18000Octets is the total number of error-free non-MAC packets received that were greater than 18,000 octets in length.

➤ tokenRingPStatsOwner is the entity that configured this entry and is therefore using the resources assigned to it.

➤ tokenRingPStatsStatus is the status of this tokenRing-PStats entry.

Token Ring RMON MAC-Layer History Group {1.3.6.1.2.1.16.2.3}

The Token Ring Nonpromiscuous History group is similar to its counterpart in the Statistics group, but is measured over a particular sampling interval. It contains one table, tokenRingMLHistoryTable, with 27 columns. This group is optional and contains the following objects:

➤ tokenRingMLHistoryTable is a list of MAC-Layer token ring statistics entries.

➤ tokenRingMLHistoryEntry is a collection of MAC-Layer statistics kept for a particular token ring interface.

➤ tokenRingMLHistoryIndex is the history of which this entry is a part; it has the same value as that of historyControlIndex.

➤ tokenRingMLHistorySampleIndex is an index that uniquely identifies the particular MAC-Layer sample.

➤ tokenRingMLHistoryIntervalStart is the value of sysUpTime at the start of the interval over which this sample was measured.

➤ tokenRingMLHistoryDropEvents is the total number of events in which packets were dropped by the probe due to lack of resources during this sampling interval.

➤ tokenRingMLHistoryMacOctets is the total number of error-free octets of data in MAC packets received on the network during this sampling interval.

➤ tokenRingMLHistoryMacPkts is the total number of error-free MAC packets received during this sampling interval.

➤ tokenRingMLHistoryRingPurgeEvents is the total number of times that the ring entered the ring purge state from the normal ring state during the sampling interval.

➤ tokenRingMLHistoryRingPurgePkts is the total number of Ring Purge MAC packets detected by the probe during this sampling interval.

➤ tokenRingMLHistoryBeaconEvents is the total number of times that the ring entered the beaconing state during this sampling interval.

> tokenRingMLHistoryBeaconTime is the amount of time that the ring has been in the beaconing state during this sampling interval.

> tokenRingMLHistoryBeaconPkts is the total number of Beacon MAC packets detected by the probe during this sampling interval.

> tokenRingMLHistoryClaimTokenEvents is the total number of times that the ring entered the monitor contention state from normal ring state or ring purge state during this sampling interval.

> tokenRingMLHistoryClaimTokenPkts is the total number of Claim Token MAC packets detected by the probe during this sampling interval.

> tokenRingMLHistoryNAUNChanges is the total number of NAUN changes detected by the probe during this sampling interval.

> tokenRingMLHistoryLineErrors is the total number of line errors reported in error-reporting packets detected by the probe during this sampling interval.

> tokenRingMLHistoryInternalErrors is the total number of adapter internal errors reported in error-reporting packets detected by the probe during this sampling interval.

> tokenRingMLHistoryBurstErrors is the total number of burst errors reported in error-reporting packets detected by the probe during this sampling interval.

> tokenRingMLHistoryACErrors is the total number of AC (address copied) errors reported in error-reporting packets detected by the probe during this sampling interval.

> tokenRingMLHistoryAbortErrors is the total number of abort delimiters reported in error-reporting packets detected by the probe during this sampling interval.

➤ tokenRingMLHistoryLostFrameErrors is the total number of lost-frame errors reported in error-reporting packets detected by the probe during this sampling interval.

➤ tokenRingMLHistoryCongestionErrors is the total number of receive congestion errors reported in error-reporting packets detected by the probe during this sampling interval.

➤ tokenRingMLHistoryFrameCopiedErrors is the total number of frame-copied errors reported in error-reporting packets detected by the probe during this sampling interval.

➤ tokenRingMLHistoryFrequencyErrors is the total number of frequency errors reported in error-reporting packets detected by the probe during this sampling interval.

➤ tokenRingMLHistoryTokenErrors is the total number of token errors reported in error-reporting packets detected by the probe during this sampling interval.

➤ tokenRingMLHistorySoftErrorReports is the total number of soft error report frames detected by the probe during this sampling interval.

➤ tokenRingMLHistoryRingPollEvents is the total number of ring poll events detected by the probe during this sampling interval.

➤ tokenRingMLHistoryActiveStations is the maximum number of active stations on the ring detected by the probe during this sampling interval.

Token Ring RMON Promiscuous History Group {1.3.6.1.2.1.16.2.4}

The Token Ring Promiscuous History group is similar to its counterpart in the Statistics group, but is measured over a particular sampling interval. It contains one table, tokenRingPHistoryTable, with 18 columns. This group is optional and contains the following objects:

➤ tokenRingPHistoryTable is a list of promiscuous token ring statistics entries.

➤ tokenRingPHistoryEntry is a collection of promiscuous statistics kept for a particular token ring interface.

➤ tokenRingPHistoryIndex is a history of which this entry is a part; it has the same value as that of historyControlIndex.

➤ tokenRingPHistorySampleIndex is an index that uniquely identifies the particular sample this entry represents.

➤ tokenRingPHistoryIntervalStart is the value of sysUpTime at the start of the interval over which this sample was measured.

➤ tokenRingPHistoryDropEvents is the total number of events in which packets were dropped by the probe due to lack of resources during this sampling period.

➤ tokenRingPHistoryDataOctets is the total number of error-free octets of data received in non-MAC packets on the network.

➤ tokenRingPHistoryDataPkts is the total number of error-free non-MAC packets received during this sampling interval.

➤ tokenRingPHistoryDataBroadcastPkts is the total number of good non-MAC packets received during this sampling interval that were directed to an LLC broadcast address.

➤ tokenRingPHistoryDataMulticastPkts is the total number of good non-MAC packets received during this sampling interval that were directed to a local or global multicast or functional address.

➤ tokenRingPHistoryDataPkts18to63Octets is the total number of error-free non-MAC packets received during this sampling interval that were between 18 and 63 octets in length.

➤ tokenRingPHistoryDataPkts64to127Octets is the total number of error-free non-MAC packets received during this sampling interval that were between 64 and 127 octets in length.

➤ tokenRingPHistoryDataPkts128to255Octets is the total number of error-free non-MAC packets received during this sampling interval that were between 128 and 255 octets in length.

➤ tokenRingPHistoryDataPkts256to511Octets is the total number of error-free non-MAC packets received during this sampling interval that were between 256 and 511 octets in length.

➤ tokenRingPHistoryDataPkts512to1023Octets is the total number of error-free non-MAC packets received during this sampling interval that were between 512 and 1023 octets in length.

➤ tokenRingPHistoryDataPkts1024to2047Octets is the total number of error-free non-MAC packets received during this sampling interval that were between 1024 and 2047 octets in length.

➤ tokenRingPHistoryDataPkts2048to4095Octets is the total number of error-free non-MAC packets received during this sampling interval that were between 2048 and 4095 octets in length.

➤ tokenRingPHistoryDataPkts4096to8191Octets is the total number of error-free non-MAC packets received during this sampling interval that were between 4096 and 8191 octets in length.

> tokenRingPHistoryDataPkts8192to18000Octets is the total number of error-free non-MAC packets received during this sampling interval that were between 8192 and 18,000 octets in length.

> tokenRingPHistoryDataPktsGreaterThan18000Octets is the total number of error-free non-MAC packets received during this sampling interval that were greater than 18,000 octets in length.

Token Ring RMON Ring Station Group {1.3.6.1.2.1.16.10}

The Ring Station group is unique to the token ring RMON MIB and is optional. It consists of tables with token ring and source routing information. The tables include the ringStationControlTable {tokenRing 1}; the ringStationTable {token-Ring 2}; the ringStationOrderTable {tokenRing 3}; the ringStationConfigControlTable {tokenRing 4}; the ringStationConfigTable {tokenRing 5}; and the sourceRoutingStatsTable {tokenRing 6}. The Ring Station group is assigned OID {rmon 10}. Following is a description of the individual tables and their objects.

The ringStationControlTable {1.3.6.1.2.1.16.10.1} contains information relating to the discovery of—and statistics regarding—the various stations on the ring:

> ringStationControlTable is a list of ringStation table control entries.

> ringStationControlEntry is a list of parameters that set up the discovery of stations on a particular interface and the collection of statistics about these stations.

> ringStationControlIfIndex uniquely identifies the interface on this remote network monitoring device from which ringStation data is collected; it has the same value as ifIndex.

➤ ringStationControlTableSize is the number of ringStationEntries in the ringStationTable associated with this ringStationControlEntry.

➤ ringStationControlActiveStations is the number of active ringStationEntries in the ringStationTable associated with this ringControlEntry.

➤ ringStationControlRingState is the current status of this ring.

➤ ringStationControlBeaconSender is the address of the sender of the last Beacon frame received on this ring.

➤ ringStationControlBeaconNAUN is the address of the NAUN in the last Beacon frame received on this ring.

➤ ringStationControlActiveMonitor is the address of the Active Monitor on this segment.

➤ ringStationControlOrderChanges is the address of add and delete events in the ringStationControlTable associated with this ringStationControlEntry.

➤ ringStationControlOwner is the entity that configured this entry and is therefore using the resources assigned to it.

➤ ringStationControlStatus is the status of this ringStationControl entry.

The ringStationTable {1.3.6.1.2.1.16.10.2} contains entries for each station that has been or is currently on the ring. The objects include:

➤ ringStationTable is a list of ring station entries.

➤ ringStationEntry is a collection of statistics for a particular station that has been discovered on a ring monitored by this device.

> ➤ ringStationIfIndex uniquely identifies the interface on this remote network monitoring device on which this station was detected; it has the same value as ifIndex.

> ➤ ringStationMacAddress is the physical address of this station.

> ➤ ringStationLastNAUN is the physical address of the last known NAUN of this station.

> ➤ ringStationStationStatus is the status of this station on the ring.

> ➤ ringStationLastEnterTime is the value of sysUpTime at the time this station last entered the ring.

> ➤ ringStationLastExitTime is the value of sysUpTime at the time this station last exited the ring.

> ➤ ringStationDuplicateAddresses is the number of times this station experienced a duplicate address error.

> ➤ ringStationInLineErrors is the total number of line errors reported by this station in error-reporting packets detected by the probe.

> ➤ ringStationOutLineErrors is the total number of line errors reported in error-reporting packets sent by the nearest active downstream neighbor of this station and detected by the probe.

> ➤ ringStationInternalErrors is the total number of adapter internal errors reported by this station in error-reporting packets detected by the probe.

> ➤ ringStationInBurstErrors is the total number of burst errors reported by this station in error-reporting packets detected by the probe.

> ➤ ringStationOutBurstErrors is the total number of burst errors reported in error-reporting packets sent by the

nearest active downstream neighbor of this station and detected by the probe.

➤ ringStationACErrors is the total number of AC (address copied) errors pertaining to this station reported in error-reporting packets detected by the probe.

➤ ringStationAbortErrors is the total number of abort delimiters pertaining to this station reported in error-reporting packets detected by the probe.

➤ ringStationLostFrameErrors is the total number of lost-frame errors pertaining to this station reported in error-reporting packets detected by the probe.

➤ ringStationCongestionErrors is the total number of receive congestion errors pertaining to this station reported in error-reporting packets detected by the probe.

➤ ringStationFrameCopiedErrors is the total number of frame-copied errors pertaining to this station reported in error-reporting packets detected by the probe.

➤ ringStationFrequencyErrors is the total number of frequency errors pertaining to this station reported in error-reporting packets detected by the probe.

➤ ringStationTokenErrors is the total number of token errors pertaining to this station reported in error-reporting packets detected by the probe.

➤ ringStationInBeaconErrors is the total number of beacon frames sent by this station and detected by the probe.

➤ ringStationOutBeaconErrors is the total number of beacon frames detected by the probe that name this station as the NAUN.

➤ ringStationInsertions is the number of times the probe detected this station inserting onto the ring.

The ringStationOrder table {1.3.6.1.2.1.16.10.3} provides a list of ring station entries in ring-order sequence:

➤ ringStationOrderTable is a list of ring station entries for active stations, ordered by their ring-order.

➤ ringStationOrderEntry is a collection of statistics for a particular station that has been discovered on a ring monitored by this device.

➤ ringStationOrderIfIndex uniquely identifies the interface on this remote network monitoring device on which this station was detected; it has the same value as ifIndex.

➤ ringStationOrderOrderIndex denotes the location of this station with respect to other stations on the ring; it is equal to the number of hops downstream that this station is from the rmon probe.

➤ ringStationOrderMacAddress is the physical address of this station.

The ringStationConfig group {1.3.6.1.2.1.16.10.4} manages token ring nodes through active means, removing a station or updating that station's information as required:

➤ ringStationConfigControlTable is a list of token ring station configuration control entries.

➤ ringStationConfigControlEntry controls active management of stations by the probe. One entry exists in this table for each entry in the ringStationOrderTable.

➤ ringStationConfigControlIfIndex uniquely identifies the interface on this remote network monitoring device on which this station is detected; it has the same value as the ifIndex object.

> ringStationConfigControlMacAddress is the physical address of this station.

> ringStationConfigControlRemove: setting this object to "removing" causes a Remove Station MAC frame to be sent.

> ringStationConfigControlUpdateStats: setting this object to "updating" causes the configuration information associated with this entry to be updated.

The ringStationConfig table {1.3.6.1.2.1.16.10.5} is used to record entries that are obtained with the ringStationConfigControlUpdateStats variable (listed immediately above):

> ringStationConfigTable is a list of configuration entries for stations on a ring monitored by this probe.

> ringStationConfigEntry is a collection of statistics for a particular station that has been discovered on a ring monitored by this probe.

> ringStationConfigIfIndex uniquely identifies the interface on this remote network monitoring device on which this station is detected; it has the same value as the ifIndex object.

> ringStationConfigMacAddress is the physical address of this station.

> ringStationConfigUpdateTime is the value of sysUpTime at the time this configuration information was last updated (completely).

> ringStationConfigLocation is the assigned physical location of this station.

> ringStationConfigMicrocode is the microcode EC level of this station.

> ringStationConfigGroupAddress is the low-order 4 octets of the group address recognized by this station.

> ringStationConfigFunctionalAddress is the functional address recognized by this station.

The sourceRoutingStatsTable {1.3.6.1.2.1.16.10.6} collects data from the source routing information that may be contained within token ring packets:

> sourceRoutingStatsTable is a list of source routing statistics entries.

> sourceRoutingStatsEntry is a collection of source routing statistics kept for a particular token ring interface.

> sourceRoutingStatsIfIndex uniquely identifies the interface on this remote network monitoring device on which source routing statistics will be detected; it has the same value as the ifIndex object.

> sourceRoutingStatsRingNumber is the ring number of the ring monitored by this entry.

> sourceRoutingStatsInFrames is the count of frames sent into this ring from another ring.

> sourceRoutingStatsOutFrames is the count of frames sent from this ring to another ring.

> sourceRoutingStatsThroughFrames is the count of frames sent through this ring to another ring.

> sourceRoutingStatsAllRoutesBroadcastFrames is the total number of good frames received that were All Routes Broadcast.

> sourceRoutingStatsSingleRouteBroadcastFrames is the total number of good frames received that were Single Route Broadcast.

> sourceRoutingStatsInOctets is the count of octets in good frames sent into this ring from another ring.

➤ sourceRoutingStatsOutOctets is the count of octets in good frames sent from this ring to another ring.

➤ sourceRoutingStatsThroughOctets is the count of octets in good frames sent through this ring to another ring.

➤ sourceRoutingStatsAllRoutesBroadcastOctets is the total number of octets in good frames received that were All Routes Broadcast.

➤ sourceRoutingStatsSingleRoutesBroadcastOctets is the total number of octets in good frames received that were Single Route Broadcast.

➤ sourceRoutingStatsLocalLLCFrames is the total number of frames received that had no routing information.

➤ sourceRoutingStats1HopFrames is the total number of frames received whose route had 1 hop.

➤ sourceRoutingStats2HopsFrames is the total number of frames received whose route had 2 hops.

➤ sourceRoutingStats3HopsFrames is the total number of frames received whose route had 3 hops.

➤ sourceRoutingStats4HopsFrames is the total number of frames received whose route had 4 hops.

➤ sourceRoutingStats5HopsFrames is the total number of frames received whose route had 5 hops.

➤ sourceRoutingStats6HopsFrames is the total number of frames received whose route had 6 hops.

➤ sourceRoutingStats7HopsFrames is the total number of frames received whose route had 7 hops.

➤ sourceRoutingStats8HopsFrames is the total number of frames received whose route had 8 hops.

> ➤ sourceRoutingStatsMoreThan8HopsFrames is the total number of frames received whose route had more than 8 hops.

> ➤ sourceRoutingStatsOwner is the entity that configured this entry and is therefore using the resources assigned to it.

> ➤ sourceRoutingStatsStatus is the status of this sourceRoutingStats entry.

The RMON2 MIB {1.3.6.1.2.1.16}

The Remote Network Monitoring version 2 (RMON2) MIB upgrades the capabilities of the original RMON Ethernet and token ring MIBs (RFCs 1757 and 1513, respectively) by providing analysis up to the Application layer. RMON2 is defined in RFC 2021. RMON2 enhances the existing RMON groups, {1.3.6.1.2.1.16.1} through {1.3.6.1.2.1.16.10}; for example, the Dropped-Frames and LastCreateTime conventions are added to each of the existing tables within RMON. RMON2 also adds new groups, {1.3.6.1.2.1.16.11} through {1.3.6.1.2.1.16.20} (see Figures 3-21 and 3-22), as follows:

> ➤ Protocol Directory lists the inventory of protocols the probe has the capability of monitoring.

> ➤ Protocol Distribution collects the relative amounts of octets and packets for the different protocols detected.

> ➤ Address Map lists MAC address to network address bindings discovered by the probe.

> ➤ Network Layer Host counts the amount of traffic sent from and to each network address discovered by the probe.

> ➤ Network Layer Matrix counts the amount of traffic sent between each pair of network addresses discovered by the probe.

> ➤ Application Layer Host counts the amount of traffic, by protocol, sent from and to each network address discovered by the probe.

> ➤ Application Layer Matrix counts the amount of traffic, by protocol, sent between each pair of network addresses discovered by the probe.

➤ User History Collection combines mechanisms seen in the *Alarm* and *History* groups to provide user-specified history collections.

➤ Probe Configuration controls the configuration of various operating parameters of the probe.

➤ RMON Conformance describes the requirements for conformance to the RMON2 MIB.

Extensions to the RMON 1 MIB for RMON 2 Devices

RFC 2021 adds some objects and tables that extend both the Ethernet and token ring RMON MIBs. These extensions are shown below, illustrated with a summary of objects from the Ethernet and token ring MIBs for completeness. For clarity, the original objects are shown as placeholders only, without descriptions (the descriptions were provided in the sections above). The extension objects are shown with descriptions, as follows:

➤ statistics

    ➤ etherStatsTable

    ➤ tokenRingMLStatsTable

    ➤ tokenRingPStatsTable

    ➤ etherStats2Table contains the RMON-2 augmentations to RMON-1.

        ➤ etherStats2Entry contains the RMON-2 augmentations to RMON-1.

            ➤ etherStatsDroppedFrames is the total number of frames that were received by the probe and not counted otherwise.

            ➤ etherStatsCreateTime is the value of sysUpTime when this control entry was last activated.

    ➤ tokenRingMLStats2Table contains the RMON-2 augmentations to RMON-1.

        ➤ tokenRingMLStats2Entry contains the RMON-2 augmentations to RMON-1.

> ➤ tokenRingMLStatsDroppedFrames is the total number of frames that were received by the probe and not counted otherwise.

> ➤ tokenRingMLStatsCreateTime is the value of sysUpTime when this control entry was last activated.

➤ tokenRingPStats2Table contains the RMON-2 augmentations to RMON-1.

> ➤ tokenRingPStats2Entry contains the RMON-2 augmentations to RMON-1.

> > ➤ tokenRingPStatsDroppedFrames is the total number of frames that were received by the probe and not counted otherwise.

> > ➤ tokenRingPStatsCreateTime is the value of sysUpTime when this control entry was last activated.

➤ history

> ➤ historyControlTable

> ➤ etherHistoryTable

> ➤ tokenRingMLHistoryTable

> ➤ tokenRingPHistoryTable

> ➤ historyControl2Table contains the RMON-2 augmentations to RMON-1.

> > ➤ historyControl2Entry contains the RMON-2 augmentations to RMON-1.

> > > ➤ historyControlDroppedFrames is the total number of frames that were received by the probe and not counted otherwise.

➤ alarm

➤ hosts

- hostControlTable
- hostTable
- hostTimeTable
- hostControl2Table contains the RMON-2 augmentations to RMON-1.
    - hostControl2Entry contains the RMON-2 augmentations to RMON-1.
        - hostControlDroppedFrames is the total number of frames which were received by the probe and not counted otherwise.
        - hostControlCreateTime is the value of sysUpTime when this control entry was last activated.
- hostTopN
- matrix
    - matrixControlTable
    - matrixSDTable
    - matrixDSTable
    - matrixControl2Table contains the RMON-2 augmentations to RMON-1.
        - matrixControl2Entry contains the RMON-2 augmentations to RMON-1.
            - matrixControlDroppedFrames is the total number of frames which were received by the probe and not counted otherwise.
            - matrixControlCreateTime is the value of sysUpTime when this control entry was last activated.
- filter
    - filterTable

➤ channelTable

➤ channel2Table contains the RMON-2 augmentations to RMON-1.

  ➤ channel2Entry contains the RMON-2 augmentations to RMON-1.

    ➤ channelDroppedFrames is the total number of frames that were received by the probe and not counted otherwise.

    ➤ channelCreateTime is the value of sysUpTime when this control entry was last activated.

➤ filter2Table provides a variable-length packet filter feature to the RMON-2 filter table.

  ➤ filter2Entry provides a variable-length packet filter feature to the RMON-2 filter table.

    ➤ filterProtocolDirDataLocalIndex defines the packet filtering operations.

    ➤ filterProtocolDirLocalIndex defines the packet filtering operations.

➤ capture

➤ event

➤ tokenRing

  ➤ ringStationControlTable

  ➤ ringStationTable

  ➤ ringStationOrderTable

  ➤ ringStationConfigControlTable

  ➤ ringStationConfigTable

  ➤ sourceRouteStatsTable

  ➤ ringStationControl2Table contains the RMON-2 augmentations to RMON-1.

➤ ringStationControl2Entry contains the RMON-2 augmentations to RMON-1.

 ➤ ringStationControlDroppedFrames is the total number of frames that were received by the probe and not counted otherwise.

 ➤ ringStationControlCreateTime is the value of sysUpTime when this control entry was last activated.

➤ sourceRouteStats2Table contains the RMON-2 augmentations to RMON-1.

 ➤ sourceRouteStats2Entry contains the RMON-2 augmentations to RMON-1.

 ➤ sourceRouteStatsDroppedFrames is the total number of frames that were received by the probe and not counted otherwise.

 ➤ sourceRouteStatsCreateTime is the value of sysUpTime when this control entry was last activated.

The RMON2 Protocol Directory Group {1.3.6.1.2.1.16.11}

The Protocol Directory group lists the protocols the probe has the capability of monitoring; it allows the modification of entries in this list. This group consists of one scalar and one table, protocolDirTable. The objects in this group are:

➤ protocolDirLastChange is the value of sysUpTime at the time the protocol directory was last modified.

➤ protocolDirTable is a list of the protocols that this agent has the capability to decode and count.

 ➤ protocolDirEntry is a conceptual row in the protocolDirTable.

 ➤ protocolDirID is a unique identifier for a particular protocol.

> ➤ protocolDirParameters is a set of parameters for the associated protocolDirID.

> ➤ protocolDirLocalIndex is a unique identifier associated with this protocolDir entry.

> ➤ protocolDirDescr is a textual description of the protocol encapsulation.

> ➤ protocolDirType describes two attributes of this protocol directory entry.

> ➤ protocolDirAddressMapConfig describes and configures the probe's support for address mapping for this protocol.

> ➤ protocolDirHostConfig describes and configures the probe's support for the host tables for this protocol.

> ➤ protocolDirMatrixConfig describes and configures the probe's support for the matrix tables for this protocol.

> ➤ protocolDirOwner is the entity that configured this entry and is using the resources assigned to it.

> ➤ protocolDirStatus is the status of this protocol directory entry.

The RMON2 Protocol Distribution Group {1.3.6.1.2.1.16.12}

The Protocol Distribution group collects the relative amounts of octets and packets for the different protocols detected on a network segment. This group consists of two tables, the protocolDistControlTable and the protocolDistStatsTable:

> ➤ protocolDistControlTable controls the setup of protocol type distribution statistics tables.

> > ➤ protocolDistControlEntry is a conceptual row in the protocolDistControlTable.

➤ protocolDistControlIndex is a unique index for this protocolDistControlEntry.

➤ protocolDistControlDataSource is the source of data for this protocol distribution.

➤ protocolDistControlDroppedFrames is the total number of frames which were received by the probe and not counted otherwise.

➤ protocolDistControlCreateTime is the value of sysUpTime when this control entry was last activated.

➤ protocolDistControlOwner is the entity that configured this entry and is using the resources assigned to it.

➤ protocolDistControlStatus is the status of this protocol directory entry.

➤ protocolDistStatsTable is a table that contains one entry for every protocol in the protocolDirTable which has seen at least one packet.

➤ protocolDistStatsEntry is a conceptual row in the protocolDistStatsTable.

➤ protocolDistStatsPkts is the number of packets of this protocol type received without errors.

➤ protocolDistStatsOctets is the number of octets in packets received of this protocol type since it was added to the protocolDistStatsTable.

The RMON2 Address Map Group {1.3.6.1.2.1.16.13}

The Address Map group lists MAC address to network address bindings discovered by the probe, as well as what interface they were last seen on. This group contains scalar objects and two tables, the addressMapControlTable and the addressMapTable, as follows:

➤ addressMapInserts is the number of times an address mapping entry has been inserted into the addressMapTable.

➤ addressMapDeletes is the number of times an address mapping entry has been deleted from the addressMapTable (for any reason).

➤ addressMapMaxDesiredEntries is the maximum number of entries that are desired in the addressMapTable.

➤ addressMapControlTable is a table to control the collection of network layer address to physical address to interface mappings.

> ➤ addressMapControlEntry is a conceptual row in the addressMapControlTable.

> > ➤ addressMapControlIndex is a unique index for this entry in the addressMapControlTable.

> > ➤ addressMapControlDataSource is the source of the data for this addressMapControlEntry.

> > ➤ addressMapControlDroppedFrames is the total number of frames that were received by the probe and not counted otherwise.

> > ➤ addressMapControlOwner is the entity that configured this entry and is using the resources assigned to it.

> > ➤ addressMapControlStatus is the status of this addressMap control entry.

➤ addressMapTable is a table of network layer address to physical address to interface mappings.

> ➤ addressMapEntry is a conceptual row in the addressMapTable.

> > ➤ addressMapTimeMark is a TimeFilter for this entry.

> > ➤ addressMapNetworkAddress is the network address for this relation.

> > ➤ addressMapSource is the interface or port on which the associated network address was most recently seen.

> ➤ addressMapPhysicalAddress is the last source physical address on which the associated network address was seen.

> ➤ addressMapLastChange is the value of sysUpTime at the time this entry was last created or the values of the physical address were changed.

The RMON2 Network Layer Host group {1.3.6.1.2.1.16.14}

The Network Layer Host group counts the amount of traffic sent from and to each network address discovered by the probe:

> ➤ hlHostControlTable is a list of higher layer (non-MAC) host table control entries.

> > ➤ hlHostControlEntry is a conceptual row in the hlHostControlTable.

> > > ➤ hlHostControlIndex is an index that uniquely identifies an entry in the hlHostControlTable.

> > > ➤ hlHostControlDataSource is the source of data for the associated host tables.

> > > ➤ hlHostControlNlDroppedFrames is the total number of frames that were received by the probe and not counted otherwise.

> > > ➤ hlHostControlNlInserts is the number of times an nlHost entry has been inserted into the nlHost table.

> > > ➤ hlHostControlNlDeletes is the number of times an nlHost entry has been deleted from the nlHost table.

> > > ➤ hlHostControlNlMaxDesiredEntries is the maximum number of entries that are desired in the nlHostTable on behalf of this control entry.

➢ hlHostControlAlDroppedFrames is the total number of frames that were received by the probe and not counted otherwise.

➢ hlHostControlAlInserts is the number of times an alHost entry has been inserted into the alHost table.

➢ hlHostControlAlDeletes is the number of times an alHost entry has been deleted from the alHost table.

➢ hlHostControlAlMaxDesiredEntries is the maximum number of entries that are desired in the alHostTable on behalf of this control entry.

➢ hlHostControlOwner is the entity that configured this entry and is using the resources assigned to it.

➢ hlHostControlStatus is the status of this hlHostControlEntry.

➢ nlHostTable is a collection of statistics for a particular network layer address that has been discovered on an interface of this device.

➢ nlHostEntry is a conceptual row in the nlHostTable.

➢ nlHostTimeMark is a TimeFilter for this entry.

➢ nlHostAddress is the network address for this nlHostEntry.

➢ nlHostInPkts is the number of packets without errors transmitted to this address since it was added to the nlHostTable.

➢ nlHostOutPkts is the number of packets without errors transmitted by this address since it was added to the nlHostTable.

➢ nlHostInOctets is the number of octets transmitted to this address since it was added to the nlHostTable.

➤ nlHostOutOctets is the number of octets transmitted by this address since it was added to the nlHostTable.

➤ nlHostOutMacNonUnicastPkts is the number of packets without errors transmitted by this address that were directed to any MAC broadcast addresses or to any MAC multicast addresses since this host was added to the nlHostTable.

➤ nlHostCreateTime is the value of sysUpTime when this entry was last activated.

The RMON2 Network Layer Matrix Group {1.3.6.1.2.1.16.15}

The Network Layer Matrix group counts the amount of traffic sent between each pair of network addresses discovered by the probe. This group consists of five tables: hlMatrixControlTable, nlMatrixSDTable, nlMatrixDSTable, nlMatrixTopNControlTable, and the nlMatrixTopNTable:

➤ hlMatrixControlTable is a list of higher layer (non-MAC) matrix control entries.

➤ hlMatrixControlEntry is a conceptual row in the hlMatrixControlTable.

➤ hlMatrixControlIndex is an index that uniquely identifies an entry in the hlMatrixControlTable.

➤ hlMatrixControlDataSource is the source of the data for the associated matrix tables.

➤ hlMatrixControlNlDroppedFrames is the total number of frames that were received by the probe and not counted otherwise.

➤ hlMatrixControlNlInserts is the number of times an nlMatrix entry has been inserted into the nlMatrix tables.

➤ hlMatrixControlNlDeletes is the number of times an nlMatrix entry has been deleted from the nlMatrix tables.

➤ hlMatrixControlNlMaxDesiredEntries is the maximum number of entries that are desired in the nlMatrix tables on behalf of this control entry.

➤ hlMatrixControlAlDroppedFrames is the total number of frames that were received by the probe and not counted otherwise.

➤ hlMatrixControlAlInserts is the number of times an alMatrix entry has been inserted into the alMatrix tables.

➤ hlMatrixControlAlDeletes is the number of times an alMatrix entry has been deleted from the alMatrix tables.

➤ hlMatrixControlAlMaxDesiredEntries is the maximum number of entries that are desired in the alMatrix tables on behalf of this control entry.

➤ hlMatrixControlOwner is the entity that configured this entry and is using the resources assigned to it.

➤ hlMatrixControlStatus is the status of this hlMatrixControlEntry.

➤ nlMatrixSDTable is a list of traffic matrix entries that collect statistics for conversations between two network-level addresses, indexed by the source and destination addresses.

➤ nlMatrixSDEntry is a conceptual row in the nlMatrixSDTable.

➤ nlMatrixSDTimeMark is a TimeFilter for this entry.

➤ nlMatrixSDSourceAddress is the network source address for this nlMatrixSDEntry.

➤ nlMatrixSDDestAddress is the network destination address for this nlMatrixSDEntry.

➤ nlMatrixSDPkts is the number of packets transmitted without errors from the source address to the destination address since this entry was added to the nlMatrixSDTable.

➤ nlMatrixSDOctets is the number of octets transmitted from the source address to the destination address since this entry was added to the nlMatrixSDTable.

➤ nlMatrixSDCreateTime is the value of sysUpTime when this entry was last activated.

➤ nlMatrixDSTable is a list of traffic matrix entries that collect statistics for conversations between two network-level addresses, indexed by the destination and source addresses.

➤ nlMatrixDSEntry is a conceptual row in the nlMatrixDSTable.

➤ nlMatrixDSTimeMark is a TimeFilter for this entry.

➤ nlMatrixDSSourceAddress is the network source address for this nlMatrixDSEntry.

➤ nlMatrixDSDestAddress is the network destination address for this nlMatrixDSEntry.

➤ nlMatrixDSPkts is the number of packets transmitted without errors from the source address to the destination address since this entry was added to the nlMatrixDSTable.

➤ nlMatrixDSOctets is the number of octets transmitted from the source address to the destination address since this entry was added to the nlMatrixDSTable.

➤ nlMatrixDSCreateTime is the value of sysUpTime when this entry was last activated.

➤ nlMatrixTopNControlTable is a set of parameters that control the creation of a report of the top N matrix entries according to a selected metric.

➤ nMatrixTopNControlEntry is a conceptual row in the nlMatrixTopNControlTable.

　➤ nlMatrixTopNControlIndex is an index that uniquely identifies an entry in the nlMatrixTopNControlTable.

　➤ nlMatrixTopNControlMatrixIndex is the nlMatrix [SD/DS] table for which a top N report will be prepared on behalf of this entry.

　➤ nlMatrixTopNControlRateBase is the variable for each nlMatrix [SD/DS] entry that the nlMatrixTopNEntries are sorted by.

　➤ nlMatrixTopNControlTimeRemaining is the number of seconds left in the report currently being collected.

　➤ nlMatrixTopNControlGeneratedReports is the number of reports that have been generated by this entry.

　➤ nlMatrixTopNControlDuration is the number of seconds that this report has collected during the last sampling interval.

　➤ nlMatrixTopNControlRequestedSize is the maximum number of matrix entries requested for this report.

　➤ nlMatrixTopNControlGrantedSize is the maximum number of matrix entries in this report.

　➤ nlMatrixTopNControlStartTime is the value of sysUpTime when this top N report was last started.

　➤ nlMatrixTopNControlOwner is the entity that configured this entry and is therefore using the resources assigned to it.

　➤ nlMatrixTopNControlStatus is the status of this nMatrixTopNControlEntry.

➤ nlMatrixTopNTable is a set of statistics for those network layer matrix entries that have counted the highest number of octets or packets.

➤ nlMatrixTopNEntry is a conceptual row in the nlMatrixTopNTable.

  ➤ nlMatrixTopNIndex is an index that uniquely identifies an entry in the nlMatrixTopNTable.

  ➤ nlMatrixTopNProtocolDirLocalIndex is the protocolDirLocalIndex of the network layer protocol of this entry's network address.

  ➤ nlMatrixTopNSourceAddress is the network layer address of the source host in this conversation.

  ➤ nlMatrixTopNDestAddress is the network layer address of the destination host in this conversation.

  ➤ nlMatrixTopNPktRate is the number of packets seen from the source host to the destination host during this sampling interval.

  ➤ nlMatrixTopNReversePktRate is the number of packets seen from the destination host to the source host during this sampling interval.

  ➤ nlMatrixTopNOctetRate is the number of octets seen from the source host to the destination host during this sampling interval.

  ➤ nlMatrixTopNReverseOctetRate is the number of octets seen from the destination host to the source host during this sampling interval.

The RMON2 Application Layer Host Group {1.3.6.1.2.1.16.16}

The Application Layer Host group counts the amount of traffic, by protocol, sent from and to each network address discovered by the probe. Implementation of this group requires implementation of the Network Layer Host group. This group consists of one table, the alHostTable, with the following objects:

➤ alHostTable is a collection of statistics for a protocol from a particular network address that has been discovered on an interface of this device.

➤ alHostEntry is a conceptual row in the alHostTable.

➤ alHostTimeMark is a TimeFilter for this entry.

➤ alHostInPkts is the number of packets of this protocol type transmitted without errors to this address since it was added to the alHostTable.

➤ alHostOutPkts is the number of packets of this protocol type transmitted without errors by this address since it was added to the alHostTable.

➤ alHostInOctets is the number of octets of this protocol type transmitted to this address since it was added to the alHostTable.

➤ alHostOutOctets is the number of octets of this protocol type transmitted by this address since it was added to the alHostTable.

➤ alHostCreateTime is the value of sysUpTime when this entry was last activated.

The RMON2 Application Layer Matrix Group {1.3.6.1.2.1.16.17}

The Application Layer Matrix group counts the amount of traffic, by protocol, sent between each pair of network addresses discovered by the probe. Implementation of this group requires implementation of the Network Layer Matrix group. This group consists of four tables: the alMatrixSDTable, the alMatrixDSTable, the alMatrixTopNControlTable, and the alMatrixTopNTable, as follows:

➤ alMatrixSDTable is a list of application traffic matrix entries that collect statistics for conversations of a particular protocol between two network-level addresses, indexed by the source and destination addresses.

➤ alMatrixSDEntry is a conceptual row in the alMatrixSDTable.

- ➤ alMatrixSDTimeMark is a TimeFilter for this entry.

- ➤ alMatrixSDPkts is the number of packets of this protocol type transmitted without errors from the source address to the destination address since this entry was added to the alMatrixSDTable.

- ➤ alMatrixSDOctets is the number of octets in packets of this protocol type transmitted from the source address to the destination address since this entry was added to the alMatrixSDTable.

- ➤ alMatrixSDCreateTime is the value of sysUpTime when this entry was last activated.

➤ alMatrixDSTable is a list of traffic matrix entries that collect statistics for conversations of a particular protocol type between two network-level addresses, indexed by the destination and source addresses.

- ➤ alMatrixDSEntry is a conceptual row in the alMatrixDSTable.

  - ➤ alMatrixDSTimeMark is a TimeFilter for this entry.

  - ➤ alMatrixDSPkts is the number of packets of this protocol type transmitted without errors from the source address to the destination address since this entry was added to the alMatrixDSTable.

  - ➤ alMatrixDSOctets is the number of octets in packets of this protocol type transmitted from the source address to the destination address since this entry was added to the alMatrixDSTable.

  - ➤ alMatrixDSCreateTime is the value of sysUpTime when this entry was last activated.

➤ alMatrixTopNControlTable is a set of parameters that control the creation of a report of the top N matrix entries according to a selected metric.

➤ aMatrixTopNControlEntry is a conceptual row in the alMa-trixTopNControlTable.

➤ alMatrixTopNControlIndex is an index that uniquely identifies an entry in the alMatrixTopNControlTable.

➤ alMatrixTopNControlMatrixIndex is the alMatrix [SD/DS] table for which a top N report will be prepared on behalf of this entry.

➤ alMatrixTopNControlRateBase is the variable for each alMatrix [SD/DS] entry that the alMatrixTopNEntries are sorted by.

➤ alMatrixTopNControlTimeRemaining is the number of seconds left in the report currently being collected.

➤ alMatrixTopNControlGeneratedReports is the number of reports that have been generated by this entry.

➤ alMatrixTopNControlDuration is the number of seconds that this report has collected during the last sampling interval.

➤ alMatrixTopNControlRequestedSize is the maximum number of matrix entries requested for this report.

➤ alMatrixTopNControlGrantedSize is the maximum number of matrix entries in this report.

➤ alMatrixTopNControlStartTime is the value of sysUpTime when this top N report was last started.

➤ alMatrixTopNControlOwner is the entity that configured this entry and is therefore using the resources assigned to it.

➤ alMatrixTopNControlStatus is the status of this aMatrixTopNControlEntry.

➤ alMatrixTopNTable is a set of statistics for those application layer matrix entries that have counted the highest number of octets or packets.

➤ alMatrixTopNEntry is a conceptual row in the alMatrixTopNTable.

 ➤ alMatrixTopNIndex is an index that uniquely identifies an entry in the alMatrixTopNTable.

 ➤ alMatrixTopNProtocolDirLocalIndex is the protocolDirLocalIndex of the network layer protocol of this entry's network address.

 ➤ alMatrixTopNSourceAddress is the network layer address of the source host in this conversation.

 ➤ alMatrixTopNDestAddress is the network layer address of the destination host in this conversation.

 ➤ alMatrixTopNAppProtocolDirLocalIndex is the type of protocol counted by this matrix entry.

 ➤ alMatrixTopNPktRate is the number of packets seen of this protocol from the source host to the destination host during this sampling interval.

 ➤ alMatrixTopNReversePktRate is the number of packets seen of this protocol from the destination host to the source host during this sampling interval.

 ➤ alMatrixTopNOctetRate is the number of octets seen of this protocol from the source host to the destination host during this sampling interval.

 ➤ alMatrixTopNReverseOctetRate is the number of octets seen of this protocol from the destination host to the source host during this sampling interval.

The RMON2 User History Collection Group {1.3.6.1.2.1.16.18}

The User History Collection group combines mechanisms seen in the Alarm and History groups to provide user-specified history collection. It uses two additional control tables, usrHistoryControlTable and usrHistoryObjectTable, and one additional data table, usrHistoryTable. This function has traditionally been performed by the network management applications, but may now be off-loaded to the probe. The objects are:

➤ usrHistoryControlTable is a list of data-collection configuration entries.

 ➤ usrHistoryControlEntry is a list of parameters that set up a group of user-defined MIB objects to be sampled periodically (called a bucket group).

  ➤ usrHistoryControlIndex is an index that uniquely identifies an entry in the usrHistoryControlTable.

  ➤ usrHistoryControlObjects is the number of MIB objects to be collected in the portion of usrHistoryTable associated with this usrHistoryControlEntry.

  ➤ usrHistoryControlBucketsRequested is the requested number of discrete time intervals over which data is to be saved.

  ➤ usrHistoryControlBucketsGranted is the number of discrete time intervals over which data will be saved.

  ➤ usrHistoryControlInterval is the interval in seconds over which the data is sampled for each bucket.

  ➤ usrHistoryControlOwner is the entity that configured this entry and is therefore using the resources assigned to it.

  ➤ usrHistoryControlStatus is the status of this variable history control entry.

➤ usrHistoryObjectTable is a list of data-collection configuration entries.

 ➤ usrHistoryObjectEntry is list of MIB instances to be sampled periodically.

  ➤ usrHistoryObjectIndex is an index used to uniquely identify an entry in the usrHistoryObjectTable.

  ➤ usrHistoryObjectVariable is the object identifier of the particular variable to be sampled.

➤ usrHistoryObjectSampleType is the method of sampling the selected variable for storage in the usrHistoryTable.

➤ usrHistoryTable is a list of user-defined history entries.

➤ usrHistoryEntry is a historical sample of user-defined variables.

➤ usrHistorySampleIndex is an index that uniquely identifies the particular sample this entry represents.

➤ usrHistoryIntervalStart is the value of sysUpTime at the start of the interval over which this sample was measured.

➤ usrHistoryIntervalEnd is the value of j at the end of the interval over which this sample was measured.

➤ usrHistoryAbsValue is the absolute value of the user-specified statistic during the last sampling period.

➤ usrHistoryValStatus indicates the validity and sign of the data in the associated instance of userHistoryAbsValue.

The RMON2 Probe Configuration Group {1.3.6.1.2.1.16.19}

The Probe Configuration group controls the configuration of various operating parameters of the probe. This group contains a number of scalars, plus four tables: serialConfigTable, netConfigTable, trapDestTable, and serialConnectionTable. The objects are:

➤ probeCapabilities is an indication of the RMON MIB groups supported on at least one interface by this probe.

➤ probeSoftwareRev is the software revision of the device.

➤ probeHardwareRev is the hardware revision of the device.

➤ probeDateTime is the probe's current date and time.

➤ probeResetControl defines the probe's actions during boot or run times.

➤ probeDownloadFile is the file name to be downloaded from the TFTP server hen a download is next requested via this MIB.

➤ probeDownloadTFTPServer is the IP address of the TFTP server that contains the boot image.

➤ probeDownloadAction defines the probe's actions when downloading the boot image.

➤ probeDownloadStatus defines the status of the last download procedure.

➤ serialConfigTable is a table of serial interface configuration entries.

> ➤ serialConfigEntry is a set of configuration parameters for a particular serial interface on this device.

> > ➤ serialMode is the type of incoming connection to expect on this serial interface.

> > ➤ serialProtocol is the type of data link encapsulation to be used on this serial interface.

> > ➤ serialTimeout is the timeout value used when the management station has initiated the conversation over the serial link.

> > ➤ serialModemInitString is a control string that controls how a modem attached to this serial interface should be initialized.

> > ➤ serialModemHangupString is a control string that specifies how to disconnect a modem connection on this serial interface.

> > ➤ serialModemConnectResp is an ASCII string that describes the expected modem connection response code and associated bit rate.

> > ➤ serialModemNoConnectResp is an ASCII string that reports why a connection attempt failed.

> > ➤ serialDialoutTimeout is the number of seconds of inactivity allowed before terminating the connection on this serial interface.

> > ➤ serialStatus is the status of this serialConfigEntry.

➤ netConfigTable is a table of netConfigEntries.

➤ netConfigEntry is a set of configuration parameters for a particular network interface on this device.

   ➤ netConfigIPAddress is the IP address of this Net interface.

   ➤ netConfigSubnetMask is the subnet mask of this Net interface.

   ➤ netConfigStatus is the status of this netConfigEntry.

➤ netDefaultGateway is the IP address of the default gateway.

➤ trapDestTable defines the destination addresses for traps generated from the device.

   ➤ trapDestEntry includes a destination IP address to which to send traps for this community.

      ➤ trapDestIndex is a value that uniquely identifies this trapDestEntry.

      ➤ trapDestCommunity is a community to which this destination address belongs.

      ➤ trapDestProtocol is the protocol with which to send this trap.

      ➤ trapDestAddress is the address to send traps to on behalf of this entry.

      ➤ trapDestOwner is the entity that configured this entry and is using the resources assigned to it.

      ➤ trapDestStatus is the status of this trap destination entry.

➤ serialConnectionTable stores the parameters for a SLIP connection between the management station and the device.

   ➤ serialConnectionEntry is a configuration for a SLIP link over a serial line.

      ➤ serialConnectIndex is a value that uniquely identifies this serialConnectionEntry.

> ➤ serialConnectDestIPAddress is the IP address that can be reached at the other end of this serial connection.

> ➤ serialConnectType is the type of outgoing connection to make.

> ➤ serialConnectDialString is a control string that specifies how to dial the phone number in order to establish a modem connection.

> ➤ serialConnectSwitchConnectSeq is a control string that specifies how to establish a data switch connection.

> ➤ serialConnectSwitchDisconnectSeq is a control string that specifies how to terminate a data switch connection.

> ➤ serialConnectSwitchResetSeq is a control string that specifies how to reset a data switch in the event of a timeout.

> ➤ serialConnectOwner is the entity that configured this entry and is using the resources assigned to it.

> ➤ serialConnectStatus is the status of this serialConnectionEntry.

The RMON2 RMON Conformance Group {1.3.6.1.2.1.16.20}

The RMON Conformance group specifies the requirements for conformance to the RMON2 MIB. This group consists of two groups of scalar objects: rmon2MIBCompliances and rmon2MIBGroups:

> ➤ rmon2MIBCompliances describes various conformance requirements.

>> ➤ rmon2MIBCompliance describes the requirements for conformance to the RMON2 MIB.

>> ➤ rmon2MIBApplicationLayerCompliance describes the requirements for conformance to the RMON2 MIB with Application Layer enhancements.

> ➤ rmon2MIBGroup describes various object groups.

➤ protocolDirectoryGroup lists the inventory of protocols the probe has the capability of monitoring and allows the addition, deletion, and configuration of entries in this list.

➤ protocolDistributionGroup collects the relative amount of octets and packets for the different protocols detected on a network segment.

➤ addressMapGroup lists MAC address to network address bindings discovered by the probe, as well as what interface they were last seen on.

➤ nlHostGroup counts the amount of traffic sent from and to each network address discovered by the probe.

➤ nlMatrixGroup counts the amount of traffic sent between each pair of network addresses discovered by the probe.

➤ alHostGroup counts the amount of traffic, by protocol, sent from and to each network address discovered by the probe.

➤ alMatrixGroup counts the amount of traffic, by protocol, sent between each pair of network addresses discovered by the probe.

➤ usrHistoryGroup provides user-defined connection of historical information from MIB objects on the probe.

➤ probeInformationGroup describes the various operating parameters of the probe as well as controlling the local time of the probe.

➤ probeConfigurationGroup controls the configuration of the various operating parameters of the probe.

➤ rmon1EnhancementGroup adds some enhancements to RMON-1 that help management stations.

➤ rmon1EthernetEnhancementGroup adds some enhancements to RMON-1 that help management stations.

➤ rmon1TokenRingEnhancementGroup adds some enhancements to RMON-1 that help management stations.

Trademarks

PostScript is a trademark of Adobe Systems

Apple, the Apple logo, AppleTalk, EtherTalk, LocalTalk, Macintosh, and TokenTalk are registered trademarks of Apple Computer, Inc.

IntraSpection is a trademark of Asanté Technologies, Inc.

Banyan, the Banyan logo, and VINES are registered trademarks of Banyan Systems Inc., and StreetTalk, VANGuard and NetRPC are trademarks of Banyan Systems, Inc.

SPECTRUM is a registered trademark of Cabletron Systems, Inc.

DEC, DECmcc, DECnet, LAT, LAVC, Micro-VAX, MOP, POLYCENTER, ThinWire, Ultrix, VAX, and VAX Cluster are trademarks, and Ethernet is a registered trademark of Digital Equipment Corporation.

PC/TCP and LANWatch are registered trademarks of FTP Software, Inc.

HP is a trademark, and HP OpenView is a registered trademark of Hewlett-Packard Company.

Intel and Ethernet are registered trademarks of Intel Corporation.

IBM PC LAN, PC/AT, PC/XT, SNA, System/370, MicroChannel, NetBIOS, SAA, and System View are trademarks of International Business Machines Corporation; and AIX, AT, IBM, NetView, and PS/2 are registered trademarks of International Business Machines Corporation.

X and X Window System are trademarks of the Massachusetts Institute of Technology.

Microsoft, MS-DOS, LAN Manager and Windows are registered trademarks of Microsoft Corporation.

Network General and Sniffer Analyzer are trademarks of Network General Corporation.

IPX, ManageWise, NetWare, NetWare 386, Novell, and SPX are trademarks, and Novell is a registered trademark of Novell, Inc.

Proteon is a registered trademark of Proteon, Inc.

BSD is a trademark of the Regents of the University of California.

Java, Network File System, NFS, Sun, Sun Microsystems Inc., Sun Microsystems, SunNet, SunOS and SunSoft are trademarks or registered trademarks of Sun Microsystems, Inc. SPARC is a registered trademark of SPARC International, Inc., licensed to Sun Microsystems, Inc.

OSF, OSF/1, Motif and the OSF logo are trademarks, and OSF/Motif is a registered trademark of the Open Software Foundation, Inc.

Lattisnet is a trademark of SynOptics Communications.

TME 10 is a trademark, and Tivoli is a registered trademark of Tivoli Systems, Inc.

3COM is a registered trademark of 3Com Corporation.

UNIX is a registered trademark of X/Open Company Ltd.

Xerox, and XNS are trademarks, and Ethernet and Xerox are registered trademarks of Xerox Corporation.

All other trademarks are the property of their respective owners.

Index

A

Abstract syntax, defined, 55

Abstract Syntax Notation One (ASN.1)
- basic encoding rules, 68–84
- constructor/structured types, 56, 63–65
- conventions, summary of, 59–60
- defined types, 56, 65–67
- definition of SNMP, 195–99
- keywords, 56, 59
- macros, 57
- modules, 58–59
- objects, defining, 60–61
- primitive/simple types, 56, 61–63
- role of, 55–56
- rules, 59
- tagged, 67–68

types and values, 56–57

Access control, verifying
- with comunity name, 277–84
- with comunity name and IP address, 285–89

ACCESS field for OBJECT-TYPE macro, 100

Accessing bridge parameters, with TELNET and SNMP, 414–32

Accounting management, 16–17

Addressing
- Internet, 246–49
- Reverse Address Resolution Protocol, 263, 265
- translation, 263

Address Resolution Protocol (ARP), 257, 263, 264–65

Address Translation group, MIB managed object, 108–9, 609

D

E

J

Java Management Application
    Programming Interface
    (JMAPI), 29, 32–35

K

Keywords, ASN.1, 56, 59

L

LAN/MAN Management
    Protocol (LMMP), 19
LAN/MAN Management
    Protocol Entity (LMMPE),
    18–19
LAN/MAN Management
    Service (LMMS), 18, 19
LAN/MAN Management User
    (LMMU), 18
LANs, proliferation of, 2
Latched value, 66
Layer Management Entity
    (LME), 15

Layer Management Interface
    (LMI), 14
Length field
    encoding, 74–75
    indefinite form, 74
    long definite form, 74, 75
    short definite form, 74
Lexicographical order, 171, 218
Lightweight Presentation
    Protocol (LPP), 25
Logical Link Control (LLC),
    19, 258

M

MacAddress type, 211
McCloghrie, Keith, 201
Macros, ASN.1, 57
    AGENT-CAPABILITIES,
        209, 212
    MODULE-COMPLIANCE,
        209, 212
    NOTIFICATION-GROUP,
        212
    NOTIFICATION-TYPE, 209
    OBJECT-GROUP, 209, 212
    OBJECT-TYPE, 60–61,
        100–101, 206–9

R

W

X

Contents of CD

This CD contains a number of Request For Comments (RFC) public domain documents, published by various Working Groups of the Internet Engineering Task Force (IETF), that relate to SNMP, the SMI, MIBs and lower layer protocols, such as IP and UDP. In addition, there are three key documents on the CD:

➤ RFC-RETR.TXT, the file rfc-retrieval.txt, which provides instructions on ways to retrieve RFCs from the Internet

➤ RFC-INDX.TXT, the file rfc-index.txt, which is an index to the currently-available RFCs. This file is updated periodically, and available from the RFC repository sites.

➤ RFC1700.TXT, the Assigned Numbers document, which lists Internet-related Parameters

Files on this CD are either in ASCII text (.txt) or PostScript (.ps) formats.